EYEWITNESS *TRAVEL GUIDES*

THE GREEK ISLANDS

Main Consultant: MARC DUBIN

DK PUBLISHING, INC.
www.dk.com

ΙΕΡΩΝΥΜΟΣ ΝΜ 53

A DK Publishing Book

www.dk.com

Project Editor Jane Simmonds
Art Editor Stephen Bere
Editors Isabel Carlisle, Michael Ellis, Simon Farbrother, Claire Folkard, Marianne Petrou, Andrew Szudek
Designers Jo Doran, Paul Jackson, Elly King, Marisa Renzullo
Map Co-ordinators Emily Green, David Pugh
Researchers Garifalia Boussiopoulou, Veronica Wood
Picture Research Ellen Root
DTP Designer Adam Moore
Visualizer Joy Fitzsimmons
Language Consultant Georgia Gotsi
Production David Proffit

Managing Editor Georgina Matthews
Managing Art Editor Annette Jacobs
US Editors Michael Wise, Mary Sutherland
Deputy Editorial Director Douglas Amrine
Deputy Art Director Gillian Allan

Contributors and Consultants
Rosemary Barron, Marc Dubin, Stephanie Ferguson, Mike Gerrard, Andy Harris, Lynette Mitchell, Colin Nicholson, Robin Osborne, Barnaby Rogerson, Paul Sterry, Tanya Tsikas

Maps
Gary Bowes, Fiona Casey, Christine Purcell (ERA-Maptec Ltd)

Photographers
Max Alexander, Joe Cornish, Paul Harris, Rupert Horrox, Rob Reichenfeld, Linda Whitwam, Francesca Yorke

Illustrators
Stephen Conlin, Steve Gyapay, Maltings Partnership, Chris Orr & Associates, Mel Pickering, Paul Weston, John Woodcock

Text film output by Graphical Innovations (London)
Reproduced by Colourscan (Singapore)
Printed and bound by L. Rex Printing Company Limited, China
First American Edition, 1997
6 8 10 9 7 5

Published in the United States by
DK Publishing, Inc.,
95 Madison Avenue, New York, New York 10016
Reprinted with revisions 1998, 1999

Library of Congress Cataloging-in-Publication Data
Greek Islands. -- 1st American ed.
p. cm. -- (Eyewitness travel guides)
Includes index.
ISBN 0-7894-1453-8
1. Islands -- Greece -- Guidebooks. I Series.
DF716.G758 1996b 96-44380
914.9504'76 -- dc21 CIP

Every effort has been made to ensure that the information in this book is as up-to-date as possible at the time of going to press. However, details such as telephone numbers, opening hours, prices, gallery exhibitions, and travel information are liable to change. The publishers cannot accept responsibility for any consequences arising from the use of this book.

We would be delighted to receive any corrections and suggestions for incorporation in the next edition. Please write to the Managing Editor, Eyewitness Travel Guides, Dorling Kindersley, 9 Henrietta Street, London WC2E 8PS.

Throughout this book, floors are referred to in accordance with European usage. i.e, "first floor" is one flight up.

◁ **Fishermen unloading their catch at Mýkonos harbor in the Cyclades**

The harbor at Réthymno, Crete

Contents

The Turkish Prince Cem arriving in Rhodes (15th century)

Introducing the Greek Islands

Ancient Greece

Family on a scooter

The Greek Islands Area by Area

Gorgon's head from Evvoia

Garídes giouvétsi, shrimp with feta in a tomato sauce

Travelers' Needs

Survival Guide

Kámpos beach on Ikaría in the Northeast Aegean Islands

Néa Moní on Chíos, Northeast Aegean Islands

How to Use this Guide

This guide helps you to get the most from your visit to the Greek Islands. It provides both expert recommendations and detailed practical information. *Introducing the Greek Islands* maps the country in its historical and cultural context. *Ancient Greece* gives a background to the many remains and artifacts to be seen. The seven regional chapters, plus *A Short Stay in Athens,* describe important sights, with maps and illustrations. Restaurant and hotel recommendations can be found in *Travelers' Needs.* The *Survival Guide* has tips on everything from the Greek telephone system to transportation.

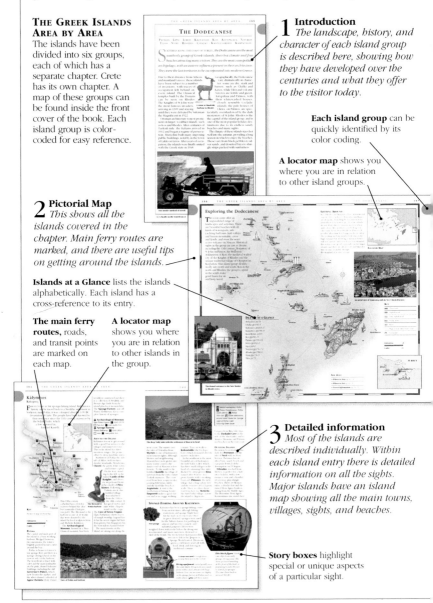

The Greek Islands Area by Area

The islands have been divided into six groups, each of which has a separate chapter. Crete has its own chapter. A map of these groups can be found inside the front cover of the book. Each island group is color-coded for easy reference.

1 Introduction
The landscape, history, and character of each island group is described here, showing how they have developed over the centuries and what they offer to the visitor today.

Each island group can be quickly identified by its color coding.

A locator map shows you where you are in relation to other island groups.

2 Pictorial Map
This shows all the islands covered in the chapter. Main ferry routes are marked, and there are useful tips on getting around the islands.

Islands at a Glance lists the islands alphabetically. Each island has a cross-reference to its entry.

The main ferry routes, roads, and transit points are marked on each map.

A locator map shows you where you are in relation to other islands in the group.

3 Detailed information
Most of the islands are described individually. Within each island entry there is detailed information on all the sights. Major islands have an island map showing all the main towns, villages, sights, and beaches.

Story boxes highlight special or unique aspects of a particular sight.

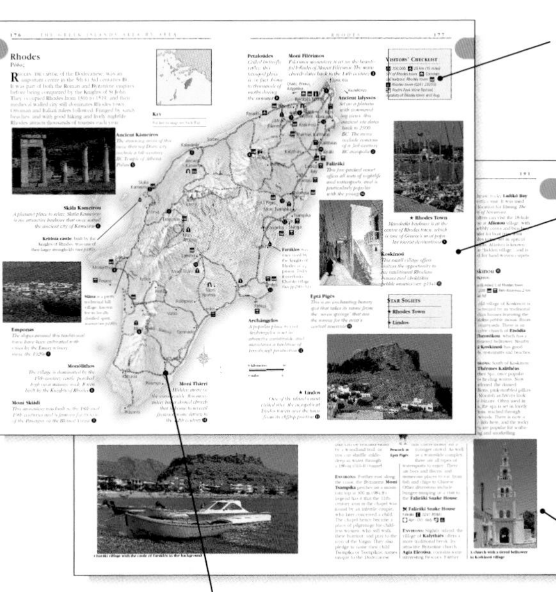

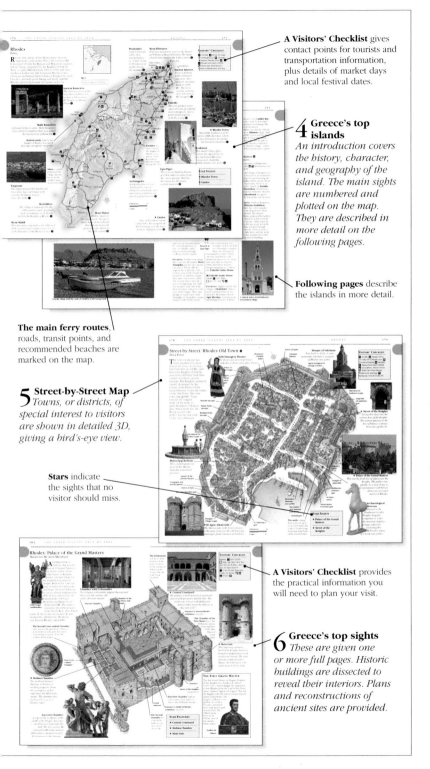

A Visitors' Checklist gives contact points for tourists and transportation information, plus details of market days and local festival dates.

4 Greece's top islands

An introduction covers the history, character, and geography of the island. The main sights are numbered and plotted on the map. They are described in more detail on the following pages.

Following pages describe the islands in more detail.

The main ferry routes, roads, transit points, and recommended beaches are marked on the map.

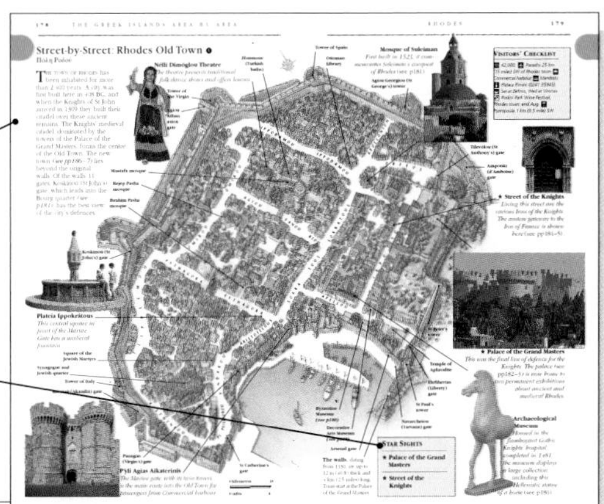

5 Street-by-Street Map

Towns, or districts, of special interest to visitors are shown in detailed 3D, giving a bird's-eye view.

Stars indicate the sights that no visitor should miss.

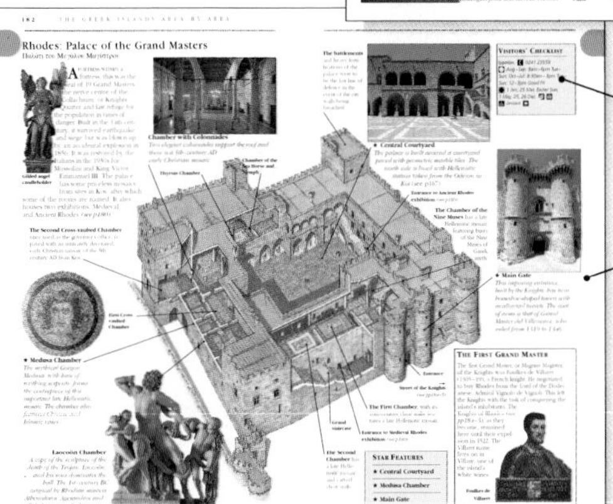

A Visitors' Checklist provides the practical information you will need to plan your visit.

6 Greece's top sights

These are given one or more full pages. Historic buildings are dissected to reveal their interiors. Plans and reconstructions of ancient sites are provided.

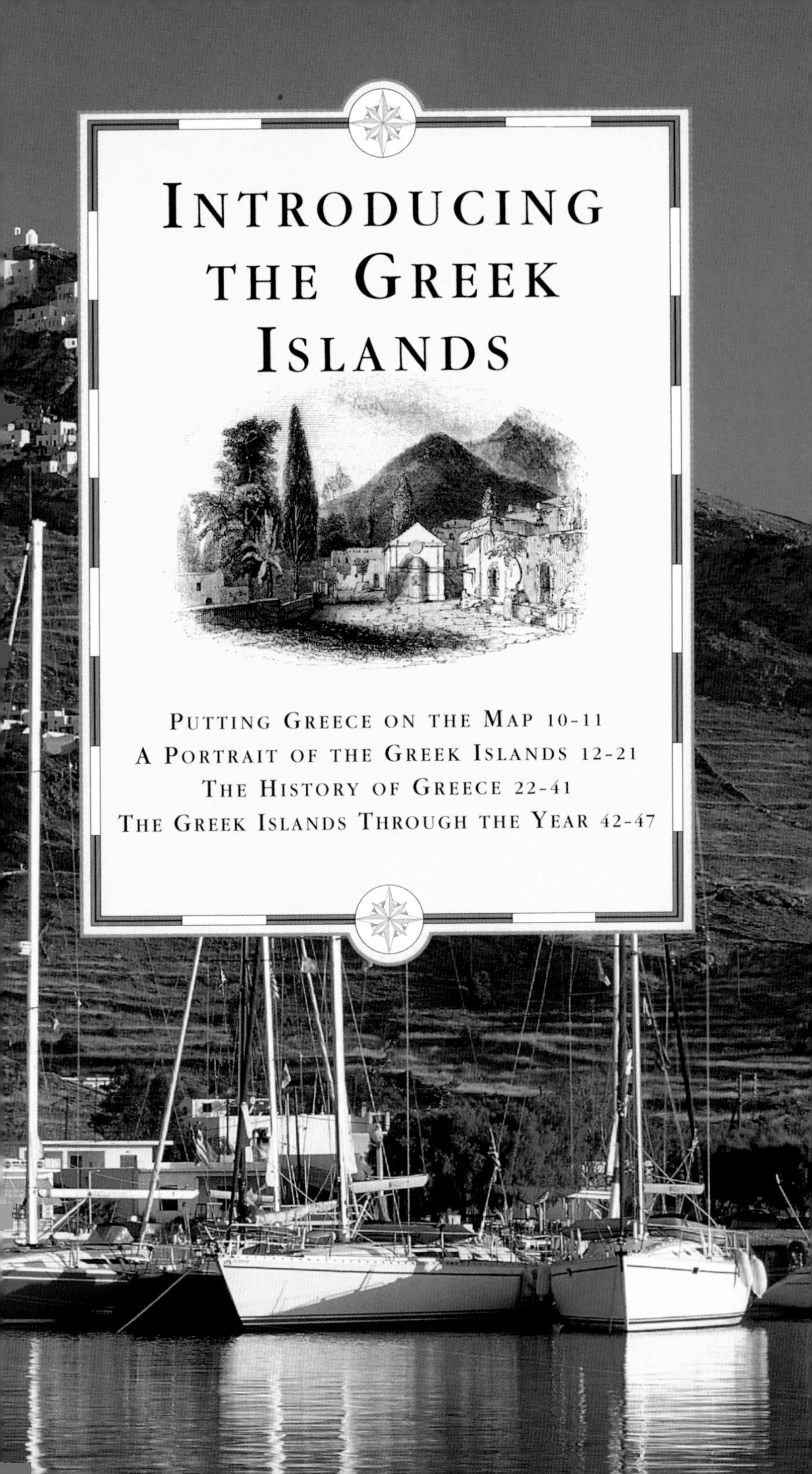

Introducing the Greek Islands

Putting Greece on the Map

Occupying the southernmost tip of the Balkan peninsula, Greece divides into over 2,000 islands stretching from the Ionian Sea in the west to the Aegean Sea and Turkey in the east. The mainland has borders with Albania, Bulgaria, Turkey, and Macedonia. Of the country's 10.2 million people, over ten percent live on the islands, while a third live in Athens.

◁ **View of Livádi harbor, overlooked by Chóra, on Sérifos**

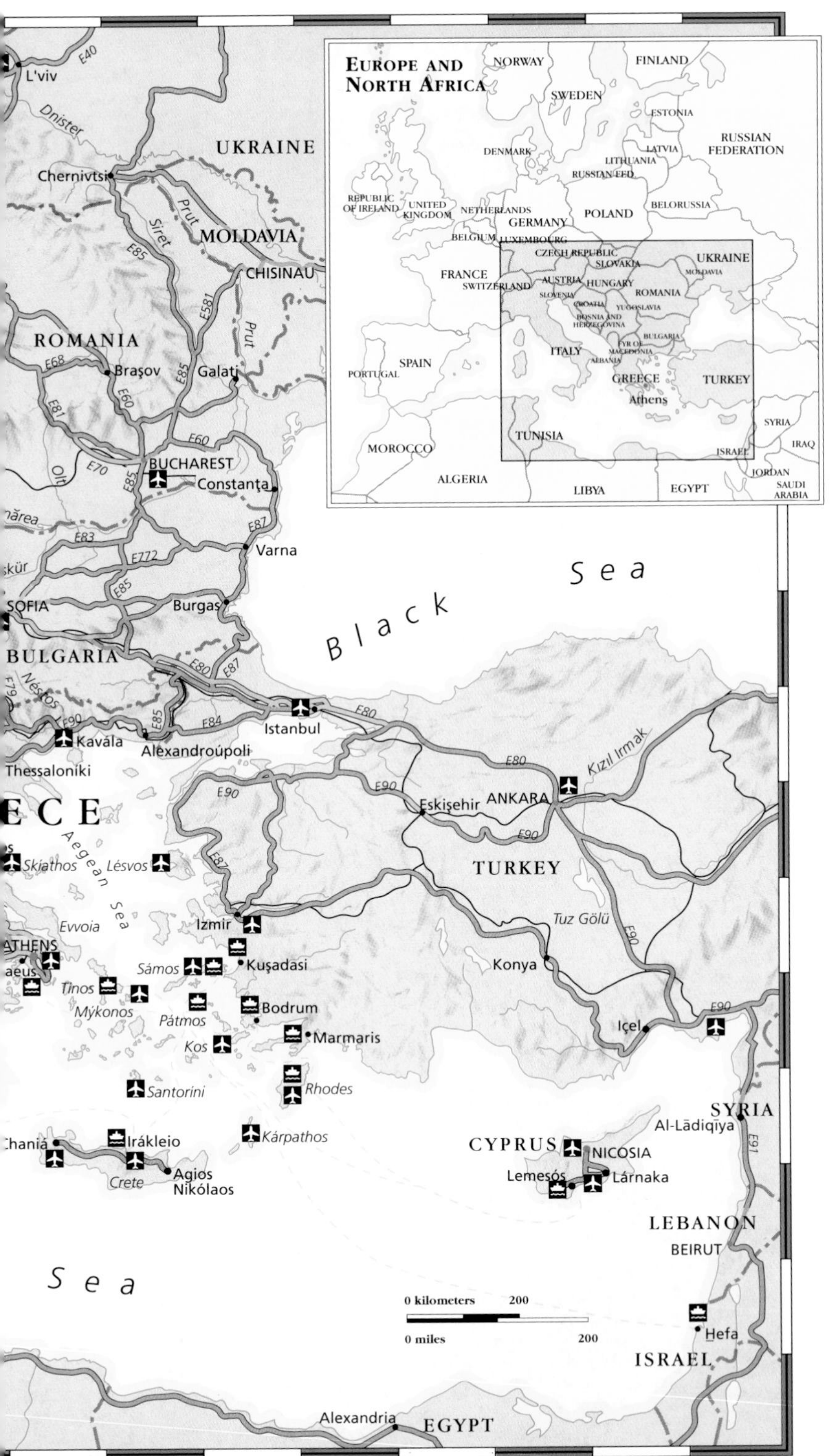

EUROPE AND NORTH AFRICA
NORWAY
FINLAND
SWEDEN
ESTONIA
RUSSIAN FEDERATION
DENMARK
LATVIA
LITHUANIA
RUSSIAN FED
REPUBLIC OF IRELAND
UNITED KINGDOM
NETHERLANDS
GERMANY
POLAND
BELORUSSIA
BELGIUM
LUXEMBOURG
CZECH REPUBLIC
SLOVAKIA
UKRAINE
FRANCE
SWITZERLAND
AUSTRIA
HUNGARY
MOLDAVIA
ROMANIA
SLOVENIA
CROATIA
YUGOSLAVIA
BOSNIA AND HERZEGOVINA
BULGARIA
FYR OF MACEDONIA
ALBANIA
ITALY
SPAIN
PORTUGAL
GREECE
Athens
TURKEY
SYRIA
IRAQ
TUNISIA
MOROCCO
ISRAEL
JORDAN
ALGERIA
LIBYA
EGYPT
SAUDI ARABIA
L'viv
E40
Dnister
UKRAINE
Chernivtsi
Prut
Siret
MOLDAVIA
E85
CHISINAU
E581
Prut
ROMANIA
E68
Braşov
E85
Galati
E60
E81
E60
BUCHAREST
E70
Olt
E85
Constanța
E87
E83
E772
Varna
E85
SOFIA
Burgas
BULGARIA
E80
E87
Néstos
E79
E90
E85
E84
Kavála
Alexandroúpoli
Istanbul
E80
Thessaloniki
Black Sea
E80
Kizil Irmak
E90
ANKARA
Eskişehir
E90
E90
Aegean Sea
Skiathos
Lésvos
E87
TURKEY
Evvoia
Izmir
Tuz Gölü
E90
ATHENS
Sámos
Kuşadasi
Konya
Tinos
Mýkonos
Pátmos
Bodrum
Kos
Marmaris
Içel
E90
Santoríni
Rhodes
SYRIA
Al-Lādiqīya
E91
Chaniá
Irákleio
Kárpathos
CYPRUS
NICOSIA
Crete
Agios Nikólaos
Lemesós
Lárnaka
LEBANON
BEIRUT
Sea
0 kilometers 200
0 miles 200
Hefa
ISRAEL
Alexandria
EGYPT

A Portrait of the Greek Islands

GREECE IS ONE OF THE MOST VISITED *European countries, but also one of the least known. At a geographical crossroads, the modern Greek state dates only from 1830, and combines elements of the Balkans, Middle East, and Mediterranean.*

Of the thousands of Greek islands, large and small, only about a hundred are today permanently inhabited. Barely ten percent of the country's population of just over ten million lives on the islands, and for centuries a large number of Greek islanders have lived abroad: currently there are over half as many Greeks outside the country as in. The proportion of their income sent back to relatives significantly bolsters island economies. Recently there has been a trend for reverse immigration, with expatriate Greeks returning home to influence the architecture and cuisine on many islands.

Greek Priest

Islands lying within sight of each other can have vastly different histories. Most of the archipelagos along sea lanes to the Middle East played a crucial role between the decline of Byzantium and the rise of modern Greece. Crete, the Ionian group, and the Cyclades were occupied by the Venetians and exposed to the influence of Italian culture. The Northeast Aegean and Dodecanese islands were ruled by Genoese and Crusader overlords in medieval times, while the Argo-Saronic isles were completely resettled by Albanian Christians.

Island and urban life in contemporary Greece have been transformed this century despite years of occupation and war, including a civil war, that ended

Fishermen mending their nets on Páros in the Cyclades

◁ A backstreet in Anógeia on Crete

A village café on Crete's Lasíthi Plateau

only after the 1967–74 colonels' Junta. Recently, based on the revenues from tourism, there has been a rapid transformation of many of the islands from backwater status to prosperity. Until the 1960s most of the Aegean islands lacked paved roads and basic utilities. Even larger islands boasted just a single bus and only a few taxis as transport and emigration either to Athens or overseas increased.

Frescoed saint from monastery of St. John, Pátmos

RELIGION, LANGUAGE, AND CULTURE

During the centuries of domination by Venetians and Ottomans *(see pp36–7)* the Greek Orthodox church preserved the Greek language, and with it Greek identity, through its liturgy and schools. The query *Eísai Orthódoxos* (Are you Orthodox?) is virtually synonymous with *Ellinas eísai* (Are you Greek?). Today, the Orthodox Church is still a powerful force, despite the secularizing reforms of the first democratically elected PASOK government of 1981–5. While no self-respecting couple would dispense with church baptisms for their children, civil marriages are now as valid in law as the religious service. Sunday mass is popular, particularly with women, who often socialize there as men do at *kafeneía* (cafés).

Many parish priests, recognizable by their tall stovepipe hats and long beards, marry and have a second trade (a custom that helps keep up the numbers of entrants to the church). However, there has also been a recent renaissance in celibate monastic life, perhaps as a reaction to post-war materialism.

The beautiful and subtle Greek language, that other hallmark of national identity, was for a long time

Traditional houses by the sea on Kefalloniá, the Ionian Islands

Stepped streets and whitewashed walls on Santoríni in the Cyclades

a field of conflict between the written *katharévousa*, an artificial form hastily devised around the time of Independence, and the slowly evolved everyday speech, or *dimotikí* (demotic Greek).

Today's prevalence of the more supple *dimotikí* was perhaps a foregone conclusion in an oral culture. Storytelling is still as prized in Greece as in Homer's time, with conversation pursued for its own sake in *kafeneía*. The bardic tradition is alive with poet-lyricists such as Mános Eleftheríou, Níkos Gátsos and Apóstolos Kaldarás. Collaborations such as theirs have produced accessible works that have played an important role keeping *dimotikí* alive from the 19th century until today.

During recent times of censorship under dictatorship or foreign rule, writers and singers have been a vital source of news and information.

A beach at Plakiás on Crete

Development and Diplomacy

While compared to most of its Balkan neighbors, Greece is a wealthy and stable country, by Western economic indicators Greece languishes at the bottom of the European Union and will be a net EU beneficiary for several years to come. The country's persistent negative trade deficit is aggravated by the large number of luxury goods imported on the basis of *xenomanía* – the belief that goods from abroad are of a superior quality to those made at home. Cars are the most conspicuous of these imports, since Greece is one of the very few European countries not to manufacture any of its own.

A family in Kos on their scooter

Greece still bears the hallmarks of a developing economy, with profits from the service sector and agriculture accounting for two-thirds of its GNP. With EU membership since 1981, and an economy that is more capitalist than not, Greece has lost its economic similarity to Eastern Europe before the fall of the Iron Curtain. Recent years have seen many improvements: loss-making enterprises

Windmills at Olympos on the island of Kárpathos, in the Dodecanese

have been sold off by the state, inflation has dipped to single figures for the first time since 1973, and interest rates are falling; the drachma has suffered entry to the ERM, however, and the unemployment figures, remain stubbornly high.

Children dressed for a festival in Koskinoú village, Rhodes

Tourism ranks as the largest hard currency earner, compensating for the depression in world shipping and the fact that Mediterranean agricultural products are duplicated within the EU. Now the life-blood of many islands, tourism has only been crucial since the late 1960s. The unprepossessing appearance of many island tourist facilities owes much to a mega-development ethos and permit-granting policy formulated under the Junta. More recent developments have an appearance that is more in harmony with their natural surroundings. Planners hope that traditional high-volume and low-spending package tourism will defer to the new rich of central Europe, pan-Orthodox pilgrimages, and special-interest tourism. To attract higher spenders the infrastructure of the islands is being upgraded, with plans for spas, yacht marinas, new airports, and telecommunications links.

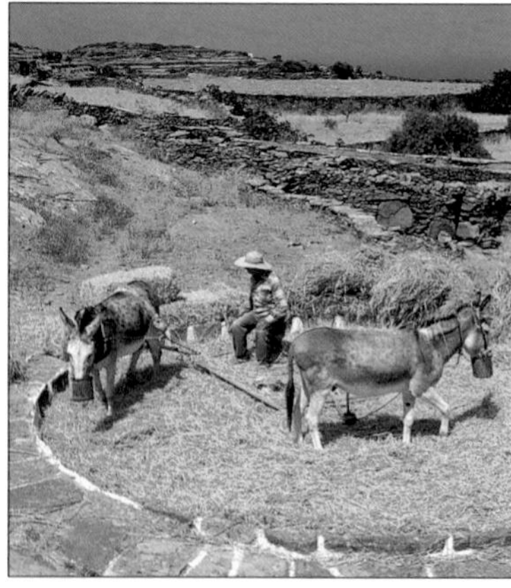

Threshing with donkeys in the Cyclades

The fact that the Greek state is less than 200 years old and that this century has been marked by political instability means that Greeks have very little faith in government institutions. Everyday life operates on networks

Festival bread from Chaniá's covered market on Crete

of personal friendships and official contacts. The classic political designations of Right and Left have only acquired their conventional meanings in Greece since the 1930s. Among politicians, the dominant figure of the first half of this century was the antiroyalist Liberal Elefthérios Venizélos, who came from Crete. The years since World War II have been overshadowed by two politicians: the late Andréas Papandréou, three times premier as head of the Panhellenic Socialist Movement (PASOK), and the late conservative premier Konstantínos Karamanlís, who died in 1998.

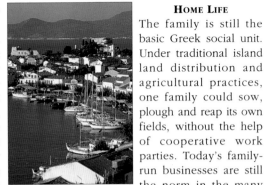

Thriving Pythagóreio harbor on the island of Sámos

With the Cold War over, Greece looks more than likely to assert its underlying Balkan identity. Relations with its nearest neighbors, and particularly with Albania, have improved considerably since the fall of the Communist regime there in 1990. Greece is already the number-one investor in neighboring Bulgaria, and after a recent rapprochement with Skopje (formerly Yugoslavian Macedonia), it seems as if Greece is now poised to become a significant regional power.

A man with his donkey in Mýkonos town in the Cyclades

Home Life

The family is still the basic Greek social unit. Under traditional island land distribution and agricultural practices, one family could sow, plough and reap its own fields, without the help of cooperative work parties. Today's family-run businesses are still the norm in the many port towns. Arranged marriages and granting of dowries, though officially banned, persist; most single young people live with their parents or another relative until marriage; and outside the largest university towns, such as Rhodes town, Irákleio, or Mytilíni, few couples dare to cohabit "in sin." Children from the smaller islets board with a relative while attending secondary school on the larger islands. Despite the renowned Greek love of children, Greece has a very low birth rate – in Europe, only Italy's is lower. Currently, the Greek birth rate is less than half of pre-World War II levels.

Fish at Crete's Réthymno market

Macho attitudes persist on the islands, and women often forgo any hope of a career in order to look after the house and children. Urban Greek women are seeing a rise in status as new imported attitudes have started to creep in. However, no amount of outside influence is likely to jeopardize the essentially Greek way of life, which remains vehemently traditional.

Vernacular Architecture on the Greek Islands

GREEK ISLAND ARCHITECTURE varies greatly, even between neighboring islands. Yet despite the fact that the generic island house does not exist, there are shared characteristics within and between island groups. The Venetians in the Cyclades and Ionian islands, and the Ottomans in the Northeast Aegean and Dodecanese strongly influenced the indigenous building styles developed by vernacular builders.

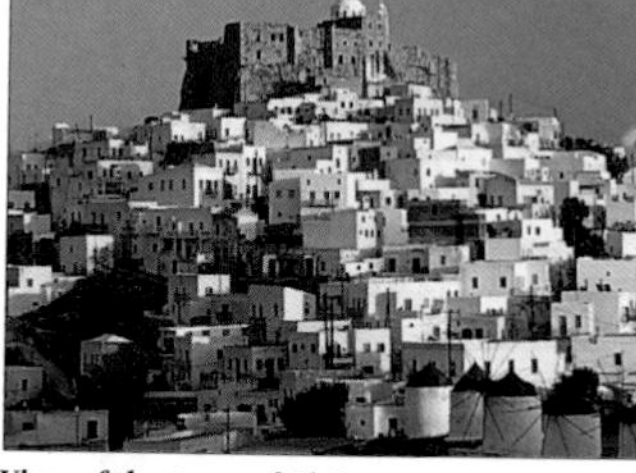

View of the town of Chóra on Astypálaia in the Dodecanese, with the kástro above

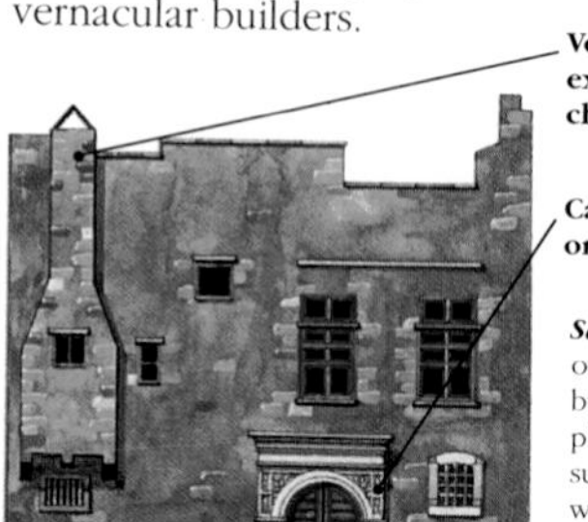

***Venetian-style town houses** on Crete date from Venice's 15th- to 17th-century occupation. Often built around a courtyard, the ground floor was used for storage.*

***Lesvian* pýrgoi** *are fortified tower dwellings at the center of a farming estate. First built in the 18th century, most surviving examples are 19th century and found near Mytilíni town.*

Rainwater gutter

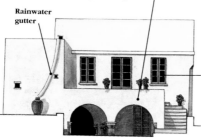

Arcade on ground floor supporting veranda

Double "French" windows of the parlor

***Sífnos* archontiká** *or town houses are found typically in Kástro, Artemónas, and Katavatí. They are two floored, as opposed to the one-story rural cottage.*

Kastro Architecture

The kástro or fortress dwelling of Antíparos dates from the 15th century. It is the purest form of a Venetian pirate-safe town plan in the Cyclades.

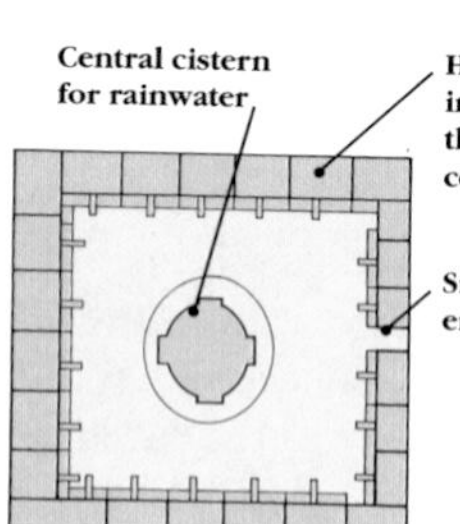

Plan of a courtyard kástro

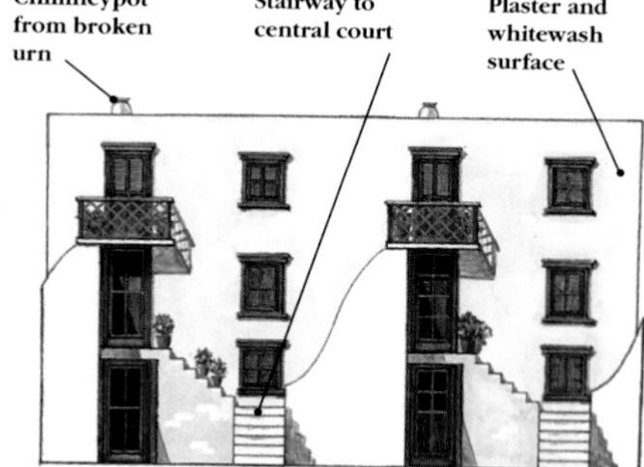

***Kástro housefronts,** with their right-angled staircases, face either onto a central courtyard or a grid of narrow lanes with limited access from outside. The seaward walls have tiny windows. Kástra are found on Síkinos, Kímolos, Sífnos, Antíparos, and Folégandros.*

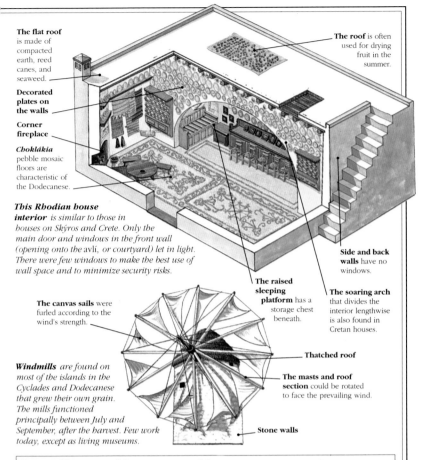

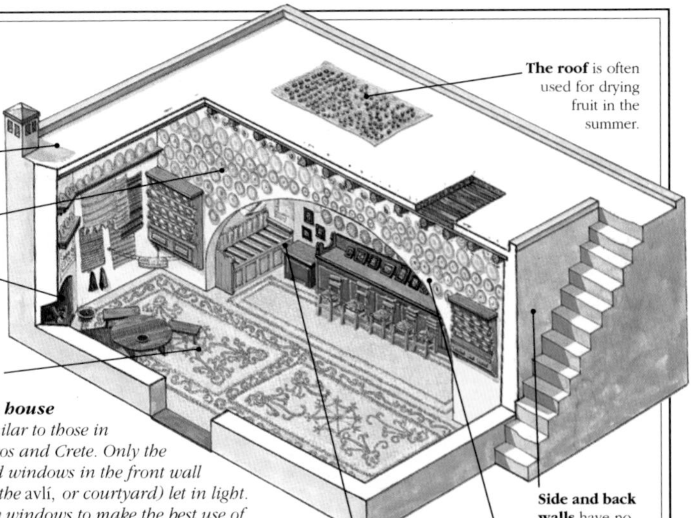

The flat roof is made of compacted earth, reed canes, and seaweed.

Decorated plates on the walls

Corner fireplace

Choklákia pebble mosaic floors are characteristic of the Dodecanese.

The roof is often used for drying fruit in the summer.

This Rhodian house interior *is similar to those in houses on Skýros and Crete. Only the main door and windows in the front wall (opening onto the* avlí, *or courtyard) let in light. There were few windows to make the best use of wall space and to minimize security risks.*

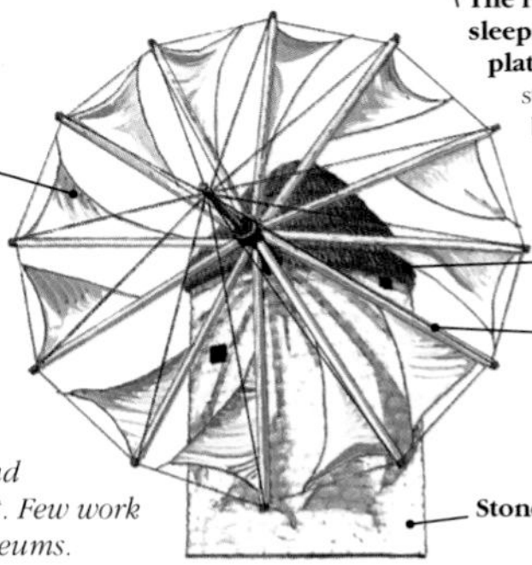

Side and back walls have no windows.

The raised sleeping platform has a storage chest beneath.

The soaring arch that divides the interior lengthwise is also found in Cretan houses.

The canvas sails were furled according to the wind's strength.

Thatched roof

The masts and roof section could be rotated to face the prevailing wind.

Stone walls

Windmills *are found on most of the islands in the Cyclades and Dodecanese that grew their own grain. The mills functioned principally between July and September, after the harvest. Few work today, except as living museums.*

Local Building Methods and Materials

Lava masonry is found on the volcanic islands of Lésvos, Límnos, Nísyros, and Mílos. The versatile and easily split schist is used in the Cyclades, while lightweight lath and plaster indicates Ottoman influence and is prevalent on Sámos, Lésvos, the Sporades, and other northern islands. Mud-and-rubble construction is common on all the islands for modest dwellings, as is the *dóma* or flat roof of tree trunks supporting packed reed canes overlaid with seaweed and earth.

Unmortared wall of schist slabs

Masoned volcanic boulders

Slate (or fish-scale) roof

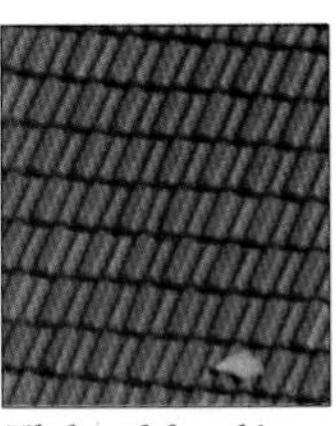

Tiled roof, found in the Dodecanese

Flat earthen roof or *dóma*

Arched buttresses for earthquake protection

Marine Life

Triton shell

By oceanic standards, the Mediterranean and Aegean are small, virtually land-locked seas with a narrow tidal range. This means that relatively little marine life is exposed at low tide, although coastal plants and shoreline birds are often abundant. However, if you snorkel close to the shore or dive below the surface of the azure coastal waters, a wealth of plant and animal life can be found. The creatures range in size from myriad shoals of tiny fish and dainty sea slugs to giant marine turtles, huge fish, and imposing spider crabs.

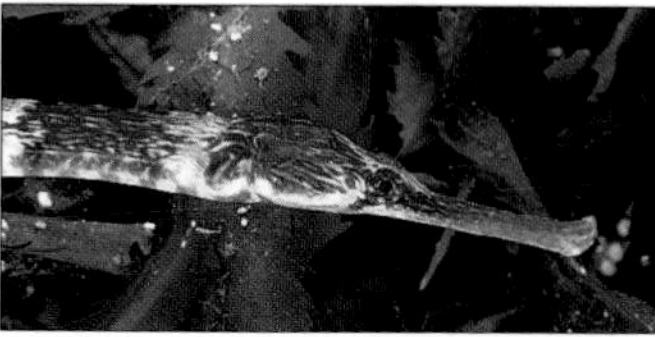

The great pipefish's *elongated body is easily mistaken for a piece of drifting seaweed. It lives among rocks, pebbles, and weed, often in rather shallow water, and can be spotted when snorkeling.*

The spiny spider crab *is ungainly when removed from water but agile and surprisingly fast-moving in its element. The long legs allow it to negotiate broken, stony ground easily.*

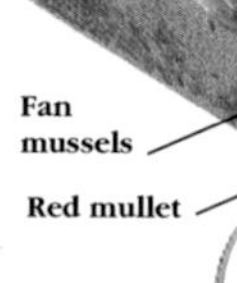

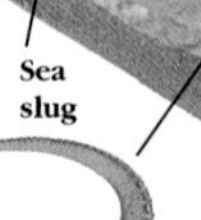

Top Snorkeling Areas

Snorkeling can be enjoyed almost anywhere around the Greek coast, although remoter areas are generally more rewarding.

- Kefalloniá and Zákynthos: you may find a rare loggerhead turtle *(see p87)* off the east coast.
- Rhodes: wide variety of fish near Líndos on the sheltered east coast.
- Evvoia: the sheltered waters of the west coast harbor sponges.
- Santoríni: the volcanic rock of the caldera has sharp drop-offs to explore.

The octopus *catches its prey of crabs and small fish with the rows of powerful suckers along each of its eight legs. It can also change its color and squeeze through the tiniest of crevices.*

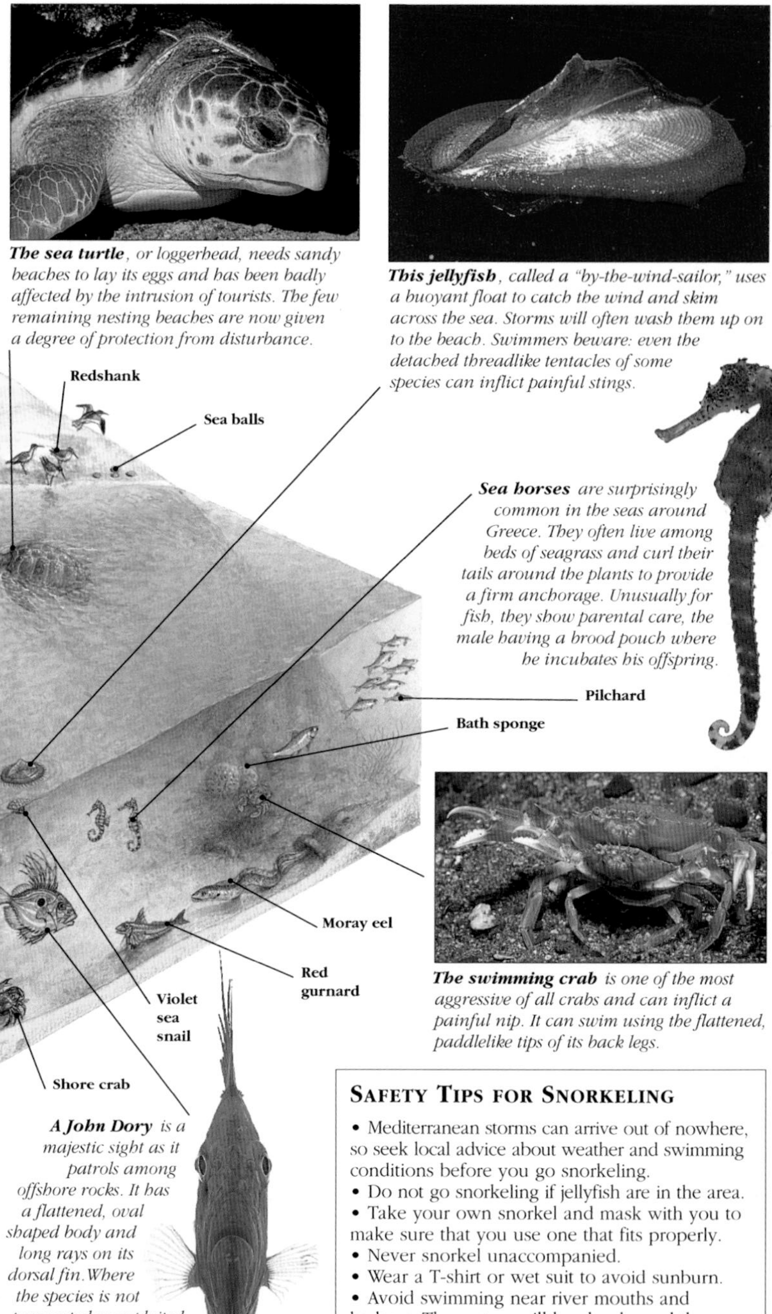

The sea turtle, *or loggerhead, needs sandy beaches to lay its eggs and has been badly affected by the intrusion of tourists. The few remaining nesting beaches are now given a degree of protection from disturbance.*

This jellyfish, *called a "by-the-wind-sailor," uses a buoyant float to catch the wind and skim across the sea. Storms will often wash them up on to the beach. Swimmers beware: even the detached threadlike tentacles of some species can inflict painful stings.*

Sea horses *are surprisingly common in the seas around Greece. They often live among beds of seagrass and curl their tails around the plants to provide a firm anchorage. Unusually for fish, they show parental care, the male having a brood pouch where he incubates his offspring.*

The swimming crab *is one of the most aggressive of all crabs and can inflict a painful nip. It can swim using the flattened, paddlelike tips of its back legs.*

A John Dory *is a majestic sight as it patrols among offshore rocks. It has a flattened, oval shaped body and long rays on its dorsal fin. Where the species is not persecuted or exploited, some individuals can become remarkably confident and even inquisitive.*

Safety Tips for Snorkeling

- Mediterranean storms can arrive out of nowhere, so seek local advice about weather and swimming conditions before you go snorkeling.
- Do not go snorkeling if jellyfish are in the area.
- Take your own snorkel and mask with you to make sure that you use one that fits properly.
- Never snorkel unaccompanied.
- Wear a T-shirt or wet suit to avoid sunburn.
- Avoid swimming near river mouths and harbors. The waters will be cloudy, and there may be risks from boats and pollution.
- Always stick close to the shore and check your position from time to time.

The History of Greece

The history of Greece is that of a nation, not of a land: the Greek idea of nationality is governed by language, religion, descent, and customs, not so much by location. Early Greek history is the story of internal struggles, from the Mycenaean and Minoan cultures of the Bronze Age to the competing city-states that emerged in the 1st millenium BC.

Alexander the Great, by the folk artist Theófilos

After the defeat of the Greek army by Philip of Macedon at Chaironeia in 338 BC, Greece became absorbed into Alexander the Great's Asian empire. With the defeat of the Macedonians by the Romans in 168 BC, Greece became a province of Rome. As part of the Eastern Empire she was ruled from Constantinople and in the 11th century became a powerful element within the new Byzantine world.

In 1453, when Constantinople fell to the Ottomans, Greece disappeared as a political entity. The Venetian republic quickly established fortresses on the coast and islands in order to compete with the Ottomans for control of the important trade routes in the Ionian and Aegean seas. Eventually, the realization that it was the democracy of Classical Athens that had inspired so many revolutions abroad gave the Greeks themselves the courage to rebel and, in 1821, to fight the Greek War of Independence. In 1830 the Great Powers that dominated Europe established a protectorate over Greece marking the end of Ottoman rule.

After almost a century of border disputes, Turkey defeated Greece in 1922. This was followed by the dictatorship of Metaxás, and then by the War years of 1940–8, during which half a million people were killed. The present borders of the Greek state have only existed since 1948, when Italy returned the Dodecanese. Now an established democracy and member of the European Union, Greece's fortunes seem to have come full circle after 2,000 years of foreign rule.

A map of Greece from the 1595 Atlas of Abraham Ortelius called *Theatrum Orbis Terrarum*

◁ **The Knights of the Order of St. John from a 15th-century history of the siege of Rhodes**

Prehistoric Greece

Mycenaean gold brooch

DURING THE BRONZE AGE three separate civilizations flourished in Greece: the Cycladic, during the third millennium; the Minoan, based on Crete but with an influence that spread throughout the Aegean islands; and the Mycenaean, which was based on the mainland but spread to Crete in about 1450 BC when the Minoans went into decline. Both the Minoan and Mycenaean cultures found their peak in the Palace periods of the second millennium when they were dominated by a centralized religion and bureaucracy.

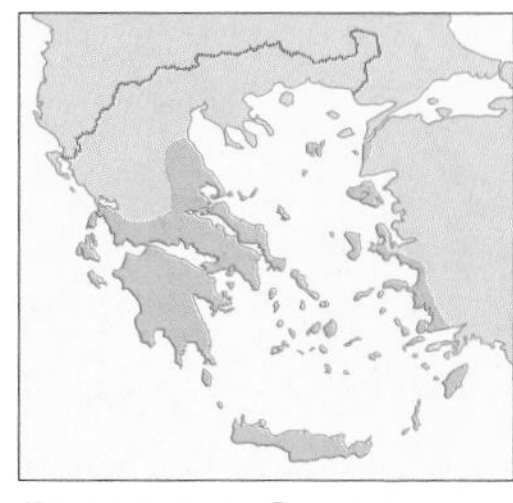

PREHISTORIC GREECE

Areas settled in the Bronze Age

Neolithic Head *(3000 BC)*
This figure was found on Alónnisos in the Sporades. It probably represents a fertility goddess who was worshiped by farmers to ensure a good harvest. These figures indicate a certain stability in early communities.

The town is unwalled, showing that inhabitants did not fear attack.

Multistory houses

Cycladic Figurine
Marble statues such as this, produced in the Bronze Age from about 2800 to 2300 BC, have been found in a number of tombs in the Cyclades.

Minoan Bathtub Sarcophagus
This type of coffin, dating to 1400 BC, is found only in Minoan art. It was probably used for a high-status burial.

TIMELINE

7000 Neolithic farmers in northern Greece

3200 Beginnings of Bronze Age cultures in Cyclades and Crete

2000 Arrival of first Greek-speakers on mainland Greece

200,000 BC | 5000 BC | 4000 BC | 3000 BC | 20

200,000 Evidence of Paleolithic civilization in northern Greece and Thessaly

"Frying Pan," vessel from Sýros (2500–2000 BC)

2800–2300 Kéros-Sýros culture flourishes in Cyclades

2000 Building of palaces begins in Crete, initiating First Palace Period

Mycenaean Death Mask
Large amounts of worked gold were discovered in the Peloponnese at Mycenae, the ancient city of Agamemnon. Masks like this were laid over the faces of the dead.

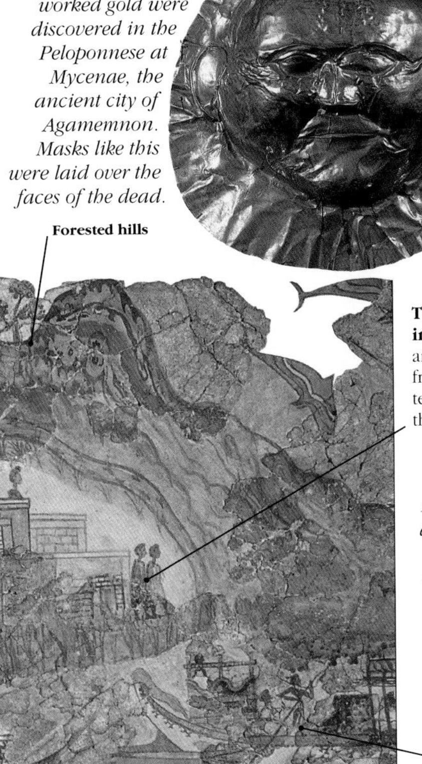

Forested hills

The inhabitants are on friendly terms with the visitors.

Oared sailing ships

Minoan Sea Scene

The wall paintings on Santoríni *(see pp234–7)* were preserved by the volcanic eruption at the end of the 16th century BC. This section shows ships departing from a coastal town. In contrast to the warlike Mycenaeans, Minoan art reflects a more stable community that dominated the Aegean through trade, not conquest.

Where to See Prehistoric Greece

The Museum of Cycladic Art in Athens *(see p287)* has the leading collection of Cycladic figurines in Greece. In the National Archaeological Museum *(p282)* Mycenaean gold and other prehistoric artifacts are on display. Akrotíri *(p237)* on Santoríni in the Cyclades has Minoan buildings surviving up to the third story. The city of Philakopi on Mílos *(p233)* also has Mycenaean walls dating to 1500 BC. Crete, the center of Minoan civilization, has the palaces of Knossos *(pp268–71)*, Phaestos *(pp262–3)*, and Agía Triáda *(p259)*.

Cyclopean Walls
Mycenaean citadels, such as this one at Tiryns in the Peloponnese, were encircled by walls of stone so large that later civilizations believed they had been built by giants. It is unclear whether the walls were used for defense or just to impress.

Mycenaean Octopus Jar
This 14th-century BC vase's decoration follows the shape of the pot. Restrained and symmetrical, it contrasts with relaxed Minoan prototypes.

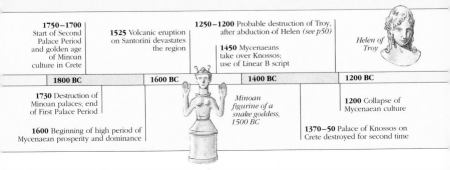

1750–1700 Start of Second Palace Period and golden age of Minoan culture in Crete

1525 Volcanic eruption on Santoríni devastates the region

1250–1200 Probable destruction of Troy, after abduction of Helen *(see p50)*

1450 Mycenaeans take over Knossos; use of Linear B script

Helen of Troy

1800 BC | 1600 BC | 1400 BC | 1200 BC

1730 Destruction of Minoan palaces; end of First Palace Period

1600 Beginning of high period of Mycenaean prosperity and dominance

Minoan figurine of a snake goddess, 1500 BC

1370–50 Palace of Knossos on Crete destroyed for second time

1200 Collapse of Mycenaean culture

The Dark Ages and Archaic Period

Silver coin from Athens

In about 1200 BC, Greece entered a period of darkness. There was widespread poverty, the population decreased, and many skills were lost. A cultural revival in about 800 BC accompanied the emergence of the city-states across Greece and inspired new styles of warfare, art, and politics. Greek colonies were established as far away as the Black Sea, present-day Syria, North Africa, and the western Mediterranean. Greece was defined by where Greeks lived.

Kouros *(530 BC)*
Kouroi *were early monumental male nude statues. Idealized representations rather than portraits, they were inspired by Egyptian statues, from which they take their frontal, forward-stepping pose.*

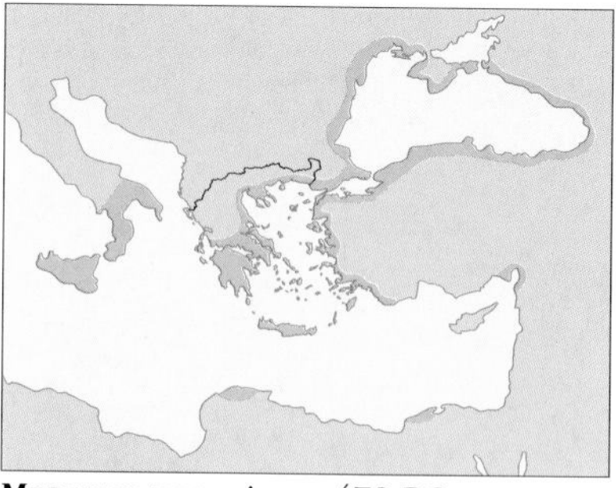

Mediterranean Area, 479 BC

Areas of Greek influence

Bronze breastplate

The double flute player kept the men marching in time.

Bronze greaves protected the legs.

Hoplite Warriors

The "Chigi" vase from Corinth, dating to about 750 BC, is one of the earliest clear depictions of the new style of warfare that evolved at that period. This required rigorously trained and heavily armed infantrymen called hoplites to fight in a massed formation or phalanx. The rise of the city-state may be linked to the spirit of equality felt by citizen hoplites fighting for their own community.

Solon *(640–558 BC)*
Solon was appointed to the highest magisterial position in Athens. His legal, economic, and political reforms heralded democracy.

Timeline

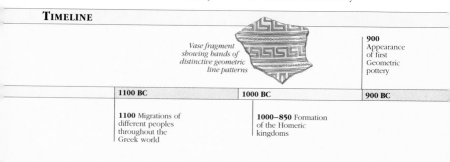

Vase fragment showing bands of distinctive geometric line patterns

1100 BC	1000 BC	900 BC
1100 Migrations of different peoples throughout the Greek world	**1000–850** Formation of the Homeric kingdoms	**900** Appearance of first Geometric pottery

6th-Century Vase *This bowl* (krater) *for mixing wine and water at elegant feasts is an early example of the art of vase painting. It depicts mythological and heroic scenes.*

Bronze helmets for protection

Spears were used for thrusting.

The phalanxes shoved and pushed, aiming to maintain an unbroken shield wall, a successful new technique.

Gorgon's head decoration

Characteristic round shields

Where to See Archaic Greece

Examples of *koúroi* can be found in the National Archaeological Museum *(see p282)* and in the Acropolis Museum *(p286)*, both in Athens. The National Archaeological Museum also houses the national collection of Greek Geometric, red-figure and black-figure vases. Old *koúroi* lie in the old marble quarry on Náxos *(pp226–9)*. Sámos boasts the impressive Efpalíneio tunnel *(p151)* and a collection of *koúroi (p150)*. Délos has a terrace of Archaic lions *(pp214–15)*, and the Doric temple of Aphaia on Aígina is well preserved *(pp94–5)*. Palaiókastro on Nísyros has huge fortifications *(p171)*.

Hunter Returning Home *(500 BC)* *Hunting for hares, deer, or wild boar was an aristocratic sport pursued by Greek nobles on foot with dogs, as depicted on this cup.*

Darius I *(ruled 521–486 BC)* *This relief from Persepolis shows the Persian king who tried to conquer the Greek mainland but was defeated at the battle of Marathon in 490.*

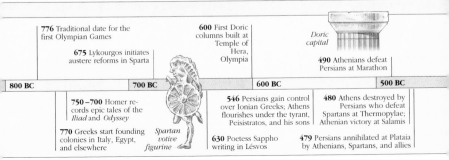

776 Traditional date for the first Olympian Games

675 Lykourgos initiates austere reforms in Sparta

600 First Doric columns built at Temple of Hera, Olympia

Doric capital

490 Athenians defeat Persians at Marathon

800 BC | 700 BC | 600 BC | 500 BC

750–700 Homer records epic tales of the *Iliad* and *Odyssey*

770 Greeks start founding colonies in Italy, Egypt, and elsewhere

Spartan votive figurine

546 Persians gain control over Ionian Greeks; Athens flourishes under the tyrant, Peisistratos, and his sons

630 Poetess Sappho writing in Lésvos

480 Athens destroyed by Persians who defeat Spartans at Thermopylae; Athenian victory at Salamis

479 Persians annihilated at Plataia by Athenians, Spartans, and allies

Classical Greece

Trading amphora

THE CLASSICAL PERIOD has always been considered the high point of Greek civilization. Around 150 years of exceptional creativity in thinking, writing, theater, and the arts produced the great tragedians Aeschylus, Sophocles, and Euripides as well as the great philosophical thinkers Socrates, Plato, and Aristotle. This was also a time of warfare and bloodshed however. The Peloponnesian Wars, which pitted the city-state of Athens and her allies against the city-state of Sparta, dominated the later 5th century BC. In the 4th century Sparta, Athens, and Thebes struggled for power only to be ultimately defeated by Philip of Macedon in 338 BC.

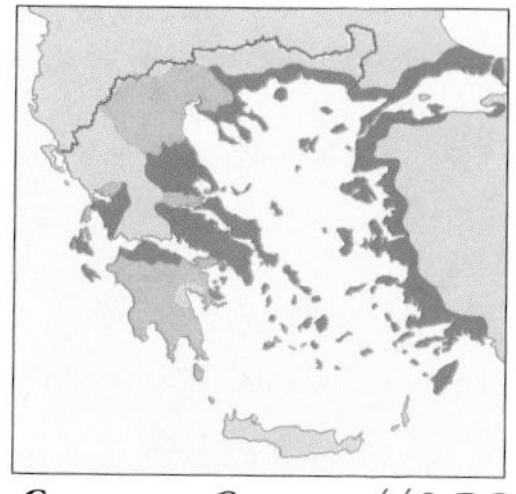

CLASSICAL GREECE, 440 BC

Athens and her allies

Sparta and her allies

Fish Shop
This 4th-century BC Greek painted vase comes from Cefalù in Sicily. Large parts of the island were inhabited by Greeks who were bound by a common culture, religion, and language.

THE SANCTUARY OF DELPHI
The sanctuary in central Greece, shown in this 1894 reconstruction, reached the peak of its political influence in the 5th and 4th centuries BC. Of central importance was the Oracle of Apollo, whose utterances influenced the decisions of city-states such as Athens and Sparta. Rich gifts dedicated to the god were placed by the states in treasuries that lined the Sacred Way.

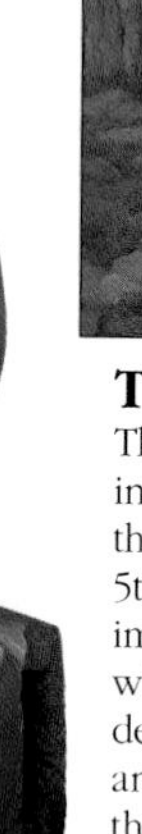

Perikles
This great democratic leader built up the Greek navy and masterminded the extensive building program in Athens between the 440s and 420s, including the Acropolis temples.

TIMELINE

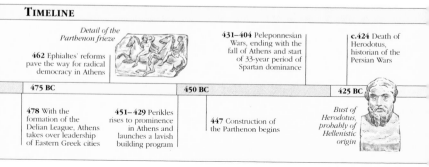

Detail of the Parthenon frieze

462 Ephialtes' reforms pave the way for radical democracy in Athens

431–404 Peleponnesian Wars, ending with the fall of Athens and start of 33-year period of Spartan dominance

c.424 Death of Herodotus, historian of the Persian Wars

475 BC | 450 BC | 425 BC

478 With the formation of the Delian League, Athens takes over leadership of Eastern Greek cities

451–429 Perikles rises to prominence in Athens and launches a lavish building program

447 Construction of the Parthenon begins

Bust of Herodotus, probably of Hellenistic origin

Gold Oak Wreath from Vergína
By the mid-4th century BC, Philip II of Macedon dominated the Greek world through diplomacy and warfare. This wreath comes from his tomb.

WHERE TO SEE CLASSICAL GREECE

Athens is dominated by the Acropolis and its religious buildings, including the Parthenon, erected as part of Perikles' mid-5th-century BC building program *(see pp284–6)*. The island of Delos, the mythological birthplace of Artemis and Apollo, was the center for the Delian league, the first Athenian naval league. The site contains examples of 5th-century BC sculpture *(pp214–5)*. On Rhodes, the 4th-century Temple of Athena at Líndos *(pp192–3)* is well preserved.

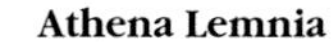

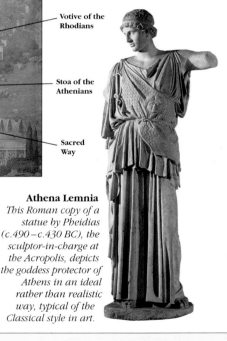

Athena Lemnia
This Roman copy of a statue by Pheidias (c.490–c.430 BC), the sculptor-in-charge at the Acropolis, depicts the goddess protector of Athens in an ideal rather than realistic way, typical of the Classical style in art.

Slave Boy *(400 BC)*
Slaves were fundamental to the Greek economy and used for all types of work. Many slaves were foreign; this boot boy came from as far as Africa.

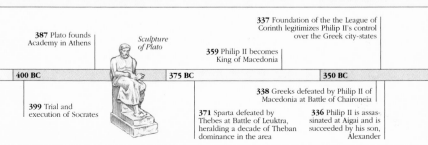

400 BC — 375 BC — 350 BC

387 Plato founds Academy in Athens

399 Trial and execution of Socrates

Sculpture of Plato

371 Sparta defeated by Thebes at Battle of Leuktra, heralding a decade of Theban dominance in the area

359 Philip II becomes King of Macedonia

338 Greeks defeated by Philip II of Macedonia at Battle of Chaironeia

337 Foundation of the the League of Corinth legitimizes Philip II's control over the Greek city-states

336 Philip II is assassinated at Aigai and is succeeded by his son, Alexander

Hellenistic Greece

Alexander the Great

ALEXANDER THE GREAT of Macedon fulfilled his father Philip's plans for the conquest of the Persians. He went on to create a vast empire that extended to India in the east and Egypt in the south. The Hellenistic period was extraordinary for the dispersal of Greek language, religion, and culture throughout the territories conquered by Alexander. It lasted from after Alexander's death in 323 BC until the Romans began to dismantle his empire in the mid-2nd century BC. For Greece, Macedonian domination was replaced by that of Rome in AD 168.

Relief of Hero Worship *(c.200 BC)*
Hero worship was part of Greek religion. Alexander, however, was worshiped as a god in his lifetime.

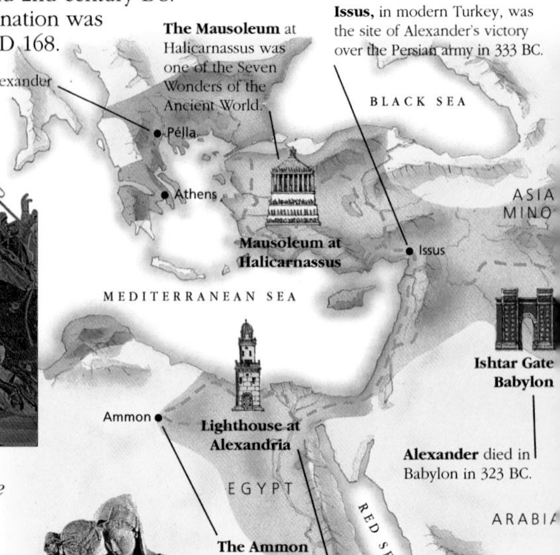

Péla was the birthplace of Alexander and capital of Macedonia.

The Mausoleum at Halicarnassus was one of the Seven Wonders of the Ancient World.

Issus, in modern Turkey, was the site of Alexander's victory over the Persian army in 333 BC.

BLACK SEA

Péla

Athens

ASIA MINO

Mausoleum at Halicarnassus

Issus

MEDITERRANEAN SEA

Ishtar Gate Babylon

Ammon

Lighthouse at Alexandria

EGYPT

RED SEA

ARABI

Alexander died in Babylon in 323 BC.

The Ammon oracle declared Alexander to be divine.

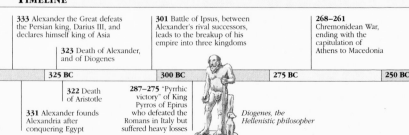

Alexandria, founded by Alexander, replaced Athens as the center of Greek culture.

KEY

— — — Alexander's route

Alexander's empire

Dependent regions

Alexander Defeats Darius III
This Pompeian mosaic shows the Persian leader overwhelmed at Issus in 333 BC. Macedonian troops are shown carrying their highly effective long pikes.

Terra-cotta Statue
This 2nd-century BC statue of two women gossiping is typical of a Hellenistic interest in private rather than public individuals.

TIMELINE

333 Alexander the Great defeats the Persian king, Darius III, and declares himself king of Asia

323 Death of Alexander, and of Diogenes

301 Battle of Ipsus, between Alexander's rival successors, leads to the breakup of his empire into three kingdoms

268–261 Chremonidean War, ending with the capitulation of Athens to Macedonia

325 BC | 300 BC | 275 BC | 250 BC

331 Alexander founds Alexandria after conquering Egypt

322 Death of Aristotle

287–275 "Pyrrhic victory" of King Pyrros of Epirus who defeated the Romans in Italy but suffered heavy losses

Diogenes, the Hellenistic philosopher

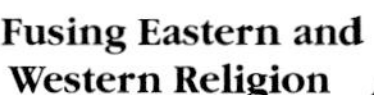

Fusing Eastern and Western Religion

This plaque from Afghanistan shows the Greek goddess Nike and the Asian goddess Cybele in a chariot pulled by lions.

Susa, capital of the Persian Empire, was captured in 331 BC. A mass wedding of Alexander's captains to Asian brides was held in 324 BC.

Alexander chose his wife, Roxane, from among Sogdian captives in 327 BC.

CASPIAN SEA

SOGDIANA

Roxane

Alexandropolis

Taxil

BACTRIA

PERSIA

Susa

War elephant

Sculpture from Persepolis

Beas

INDIA

GEDROSIA

PERSIAN GULF

ARABIAN SEA

Battle elephants were used against the Indian King Poros in 326 BC.

Alexander's army turned back at the River Beas.

The Persian religious center of Persepolis, in modern Iran, fell to Alexander in 330 BC.

Alexander's army suffered heavy losses in the Gedrosia desert.

Alexander the Great's Empire

In forming his empire Alexander covered huge distances. After defeating the Persians in Asia he moved to Egypt, then returned to Asia to pursue Darius, and then his murderers, into Bactria. In 326 his troops revolted in India and refused to go on. Alexander died in 323 in Babylon.

Where to See Hellenistic Greece

The Aegean was ruled by the Ptolemies in the 3rd and 2nd centuries BC from ancient Thíra on Santoríni, where there are Hellenistic remains: the Sanctuary of Artemídoros of Perge, the Royal Portico, and the Temple of Ptolemy III *(see p236)*. In Rhodes town, the Hospital of the Knights, now the Archaeological Museum *(p180)* houses a collection of Hellenistic sculpture. The Asklepieion on Kos *(p168)* was the seat of an order of medical priests. The Tower of the Winds *(p283)*, in Athens, was built by the Macedonian astronomer Andronikos Kyrrestes.

The Death of Archimedes
Archimedes was the leading Hellenistic scientist and mathematician. This mosaic from Renaissance Italy shows his murder in 212 BC by a Roman.

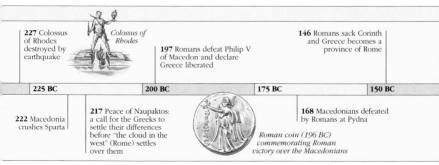

227 Colossus of Rhodes destroyed by earthquake

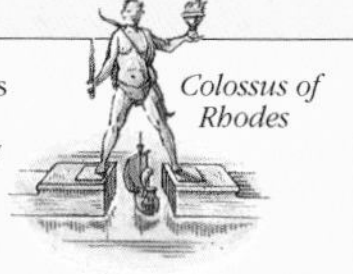

Colossus of Rhodes

197 Romans defeat Philip V of Macedon and declare Greece liberated

146 Romans sack Corinth and Greece becomes a province of Rome

225 BC | 200 BC | 175 BC | 150 BC

222 Macedonia crushes Sparta

217 Peace of Naupaktos: a call for the Greeks to settle their differences before "the cloud in the west" (Rome) settles over them

Roman coin (196 BC) commemorating Roman victory over the Macedonians

168 Macedonians defeated by Romans at Pydna

Roman Greece

Mark Antony

AFTER THE ROMANS GAINED CONTROL of Greece with the sack of Corinth in 146 BC, Greece became the cultural center of the Roman Empire. The Roman nobility sent their sons to be educated in the schools of philosophy in Athens. The end of the Roman civil wars between leading Roman statesmen was played out on Greek soil, finishing in the Battle of Actium in Thessaly in 31 BC. In AD 323 the Emperor Constantine founded the new eastern capital of Constantinople; the empire was later divided into the Greek-speaking East and the Latin-speaking West.

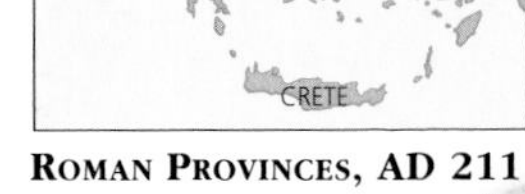

ROMAN PROVINCES, AD 211

Mithridates
In a bid to extend his territory, this ruler of Pontus, on the Black Sea, led the resistance to Roman rule in 88 BC. He was forced to make peace three years later.

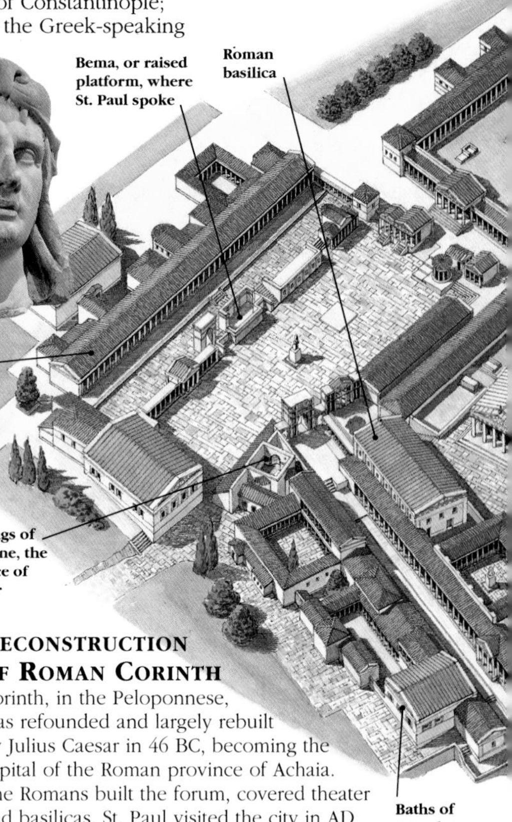

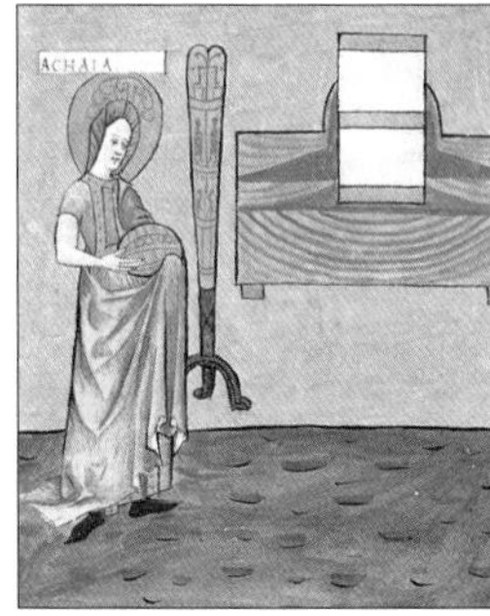

Notitia Dignitatum *(AD 395)*
As part of the Roman Empire, Greece was split into several provinces. The proconsul of the province of Achaia used this insignia.

RECONSTRUCTION OF ROMAN CORINTH

Corinth, in the Peloponnese, was refounded and largely rebuilt by Julius Caesar in 46 BC, becoming the capital of the Roman province of Achaia. The Romans built the forum, covered theater and basilicas. St. Paul visited the city in AD 50–51, working as a tent maker.

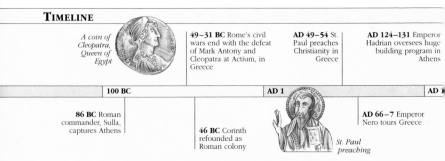

TIMELINE

A coin of Cleopatra, Queen of Egypt

49–31 BC Rome's civil wars end with the defeat of Mark Antony and Cleopatra at Actium, in Greece

AD 49–54 St. Paul preaches Christianity in Greece

AD 124–131 Emperor Hadrian oversees huge building program in Athens

100 BC | AD 1 | AD 1

86 BC Roman commander, Sulla, captures Athens

46 BC Corinth refounded as Roman colony

St. Paul preaching

AD 66–7 Emperor Nero tours Greece

Mosaic *(AD 180)* *This highly sophisticated Roman mosaic of Dionysos riding on a leopard comes from the House of Masks on Delos.*

Temple of Octavia

Odeion or Roman covered theater

Greek open-air theater

Archaic Greek Temple of Apollo

Where to See Roman Greece

In Athens the Theater of Herodes Atticus *(see p284)* at the foot of the Acropolis is an example of Roman architecture. To the southwest of the Acropolis, Hadrian's Arch, which leads from the Roman into the old Greek city, is still standing next to the Temple of Olympian Zeus *(p281)*. On Sámos *(p151)* and Santoríni *(p256)* there are remains of Roman baths. On Delos, Roman houses with mosaics survive *(pp214–15)*. Among them, the House of the Dolphins and the House of Masks are particularly well-preserved examples.

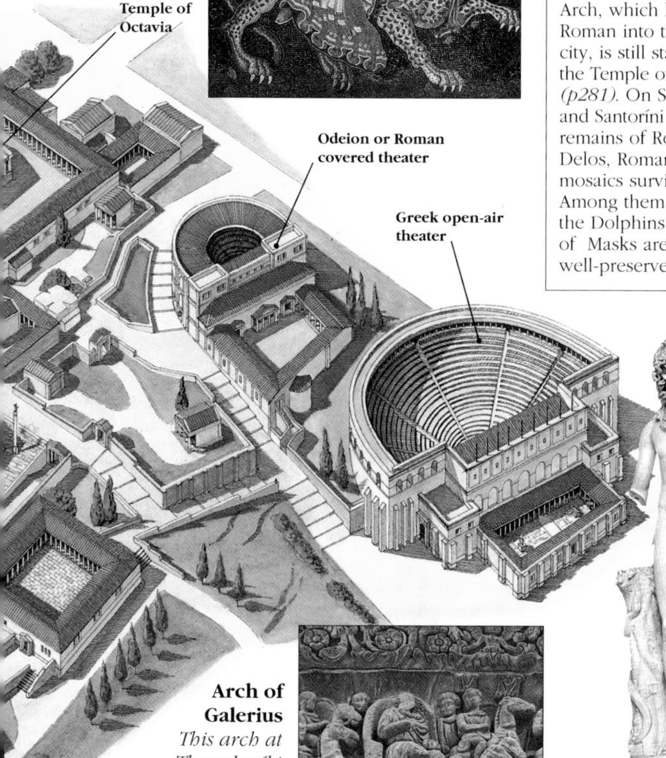

Arch of Galerius *This arch at Thessaloníki commemorates the Emperor Galerius's victory over the Persians. The carved panel shows Galerius in his chariot.*

Apollo Belevedere *Much Greek sculpture is known to us only through Roman copies of Greek originals, like this statue of Apollo.*

170 Pausanias completes guide to Greece for Roman travelers

267 Goths pillage Athens

323 Constantine becomes sole emperor of Roman Empire and establishes his capital in Constantinople

395 Goths devastate Athens and Peloponnese

381 Emperor Theodosius I makes Christianity state religion

AD 200

AD 300

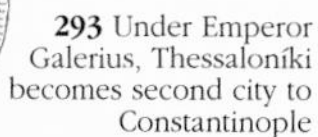

Coin of the Roman Emperor Galerius

293 Under Emperor Galerius, Thessaloníki becomes second city to Constantinople

393 Olympian games banned

395 Death of Theodosius I; formal division of Roman Empire into Latin west and Byzantine east

Byzantine and Crusader Greece

Byzantine court dress arm band

UNDER THE BYZANTINE EMPIRE, which at the end of the 4th century succeeded the old Eastern Roman Empire, Greece became Orthodox in religion and was split into administrative *themes*. When the capital, Constantinople, fell to the Crusaders in 1204, Greece was again divided, mostly between the Venetians and the Franks. Constantinople and Mystrás were recovered by the Byzantine Greeks in 1261, but the Turks' capture of Constantinople in 1453 marked the final demise of the Byzantine Empire. It left a legacy of hundreds of churches and a wealth of religious art.

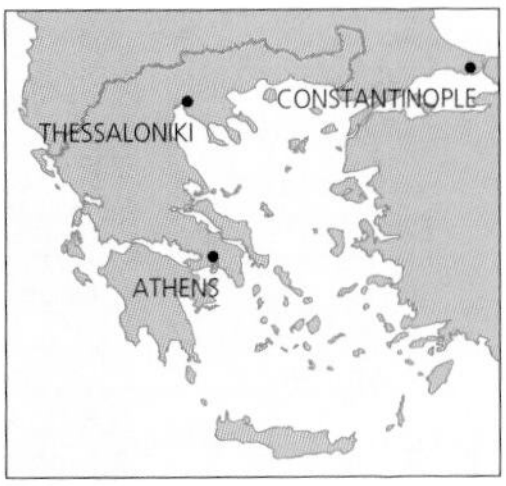

THESSALONIKI
CONSTANTINOPLE
ATHENS

BYZANTINE GREECE IN THE 10TH CENTURY

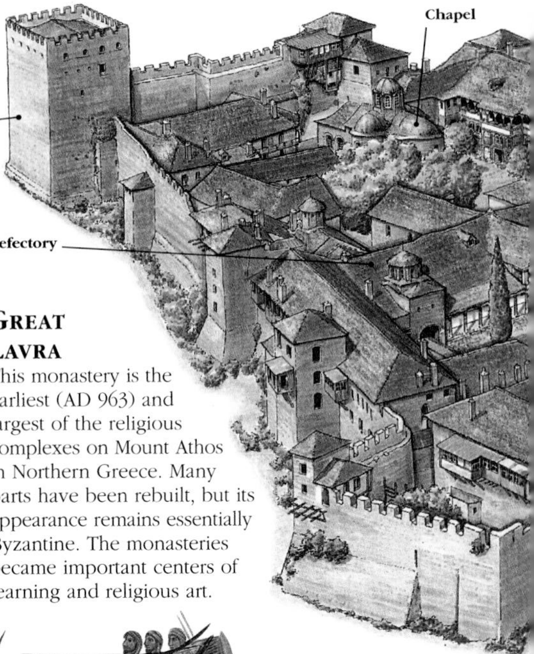

Two-Headed Eagle

In the Byzantine world, the emperor was also patriarch of the church, a dual role represented in this pendant of a two-headed eagle.

Chapel

Watch-tower of Tsimiskís

Refectory

GREAT LAVRA

This monastery is the earliest (AD 963) and largest of the religious complexes on Mount Athos in Northern Greece. Many parts have been rebuilt, but its appearance remains essentially Byzantine. The monasteries became important centers of learning and religious art.

Defence of Thessaloníki

The fall of Thessaloníki to the Saracens in AD 904 was a blow to the Byzantine Empire. Many towns in Greece were heavily fortified against attack from that time on.

TIMELINE

578–86 Avars and Slavs invade Greece

Gold solidus of the Byzantine Empress Irene, who ruled AD 797–802

400 | 600 | 800

529 Aristotle's and Plato's schools of philosophy close as Christian and Orientalized culture supplants Classical thought

680 Bulgars cross Danube and establish empire in northern Greece

726 Iconoclasm introduced by Pope Leo III (abandoned in 843)

841 Parthenon becomes a cathedral

Constantine the Great
The first eastern emperor to recognize Christianity, Constantine founded the city of Constantinople in AD 324. Here he is shown with his mother, Helen.

Where to See Byzantine and Crusader Greece

In Athens, the Benáki Museum *(see p287)* contains icons, metalwork, sculpture, and textiles. On Pátmos, the treasury of the Monastery of St. John, founded in 1088 *(pp160–61)*, is the richest outside Mount Athos. The 11th-century convent of Néa Moní on Chíos *(pp146–7)* has magnificent gold-ground mosaics. The medieval architecture of the Palace of the Grand Masters and the Street of the Knights on Rhodes *(pp182–5)* is particularly fine. Buildings by the Knights on Kos *(pp166–9)* are also worth seeing. The Venetian castle on Páros *(p223)* dates from 1260.

Christ Pantokrátor
This 14th-century fresco of Christ as ruler of the world is in the Byzantine city and monastic center of Mystrás.

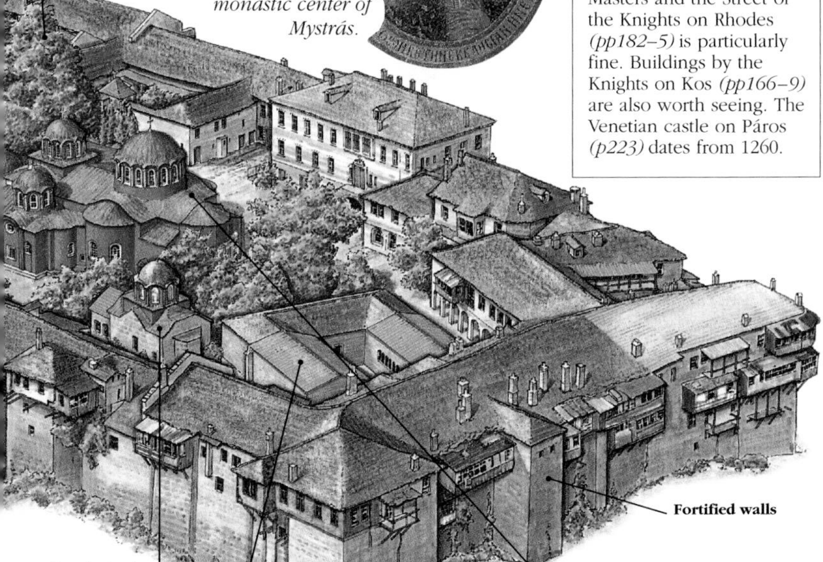

Cypress tree of Agios Athanásios

Fortified walls

Chapel of Agios Athanásios, founder of Great Lávra

Combined library and treasury

The katholikón, the main church in Great Lávra, has the most magnificent Byzantine murals on Mount Athos.

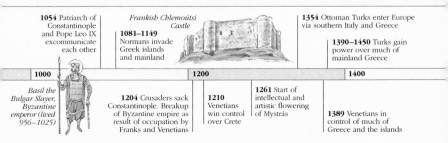

1054 Patriarch of Constantinople and Pope Leo IX excommunicate each other

Frankish Chlemoútsi Castle

1081–1149 Normans invade Greek islands and mainland

1354 Ottoman Turks enter Europe via southern Italy and Greece

1390–1450 Turks gain power over much of mainland Greece

1000 | **1200** | **1400**

Basil the Bulgar Slayer, Byzantine emperor (lived 956–1025)

1204 Crusaders sack Constantinople. Breakup of Byzantine empire as result of occupation by Franks and Venetians

1210 Venetians win control over Crete

1261 Start of intellectual and artistic flowering of Mystrás

1389 Venetians in control of much of Greece and the islands

Venetian and Ottoman Greece

Venetian lion of St Mark

FOLLOWING THE OTTOMANS' momentous capture of Constantinople in 1453, and their conquest of almost all the remaining Greek territory by 1460, the Greek state effectively ceased to exist for the next 350 years. Although the city became the capital of the vast Ottoman Empire, it remained the principal center of Greek population and the focus of Greek dreams of resurgence. The small Greek population of what today is modern Greece languished in an impoverished and underpopulated backwater, but even there rebellious bands of brigands and private militias were formed. The Ionian islands, Crete, and a few coastal enclaves were seized for long periods by the Venetians – an experience more intrusive than the inefficient tolerance of the Ottomans, but one that left a rich cultural and architectural legacy.

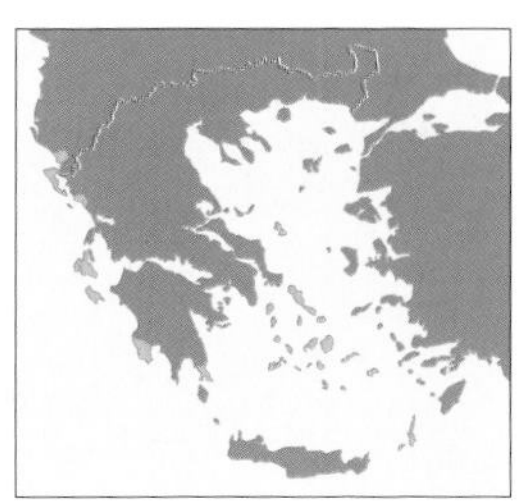
GREECE IN 1493

Areas occupied by Venetians

Areas occupied by Ottomans

Battle of Lepanto *(1571)*
The Christian fleet, under Don John of Austria, decisively defeated the Ottomans off Náfpaktos, halting their advance westward.

Cretan Painting
This 15th-century icon is typical of the style developed by Greek artists in the School of Crete, active until the Ottomans took Crete in 1669.

ARRIVAL OF TURKISH PRINCE CEM ON RHODES

Prince Cem, Ottoman rebel and son of Mehmet II, fled to Rhodes in 1481 and was welcomed by the Christian Knights of St. John *(see pp184–5)*. In 1522, however, Rhodes fell to the Ottomans after a siege.

TIMELINE

1453 Mehmet II captures Constantinopole, which is renamed Istanbul and made capital of the Ottoman Empire

1456 Ottoman Turks occupy Athens

1460 Turks capture Mystrás

1500

1503 Ottoman Turks win control of the Peloponnese apart from Monemvasía

1522 The Knights of St. John forced to cede Rhodes to the Ottomans

1550

Cretan chain mail armor from the 16th century

1571 Venetian and Spanish fleet defeats Ottoman Turks at the Battle of Lepanto

1600

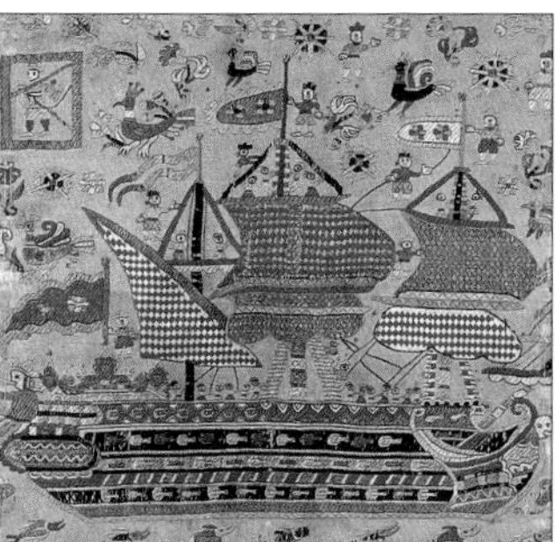

Shipping
Greek merchants traded throughout the Ottoman Empire. By 1800 there were merchant colonies in Constantinople and as far afield as London and Odessa. This 19th-century embroidery shows the Turkish influence on Greek decorative arts.

The Knights of St. John defied the Turks until 1522.

The massive fortifications eventually succumbed to Turkish artillery.

The Knights supported Turkish rebel, Prince Cem.

Where to See Venetian and Ottoman Architecture

The Ionian islands are particularly rich in buildings dating from the Venetian occupation. The old town of Corfu *(see pp70–73)* is dominated by its two Venetian fortresses. The citadel in Zákynthos *(p86)* is also Venetian. Crete has a number of Venetian buildings: the old port of Irákleio *(pp264–5)* and some of the back streets of Chaniá *(pp248–9)* convey an overwhelming feeling of Venice. Irákleio's fort withstood the Great Siege of 1648–69. Some Ottoman-era houses survive on Thásos *(p127)*. Several mosques and other Ottoman buildings, including a library and *hammam* (baths), can be seen in Rhodes old town *(pp178–87)*.

Dinner at a Greek House in 1801
Nearly four centuries of Ottoman rule profoundly affected Greek culture, ethnic composition, and patterns of everyday life. Greek cuisine incorporates Turkish dishes still found thoughout the old Ottoman empire.

1687 Parthenon seriously damaged during Venetian artillery attack on Turkish magazine

1715 Turks reconquer the Peloponnese

Ali Pasha (1741–1822), a governor of the Ottoman empire

1814 Britain gains possession of Ionian islands

1650 | 1700 | 1750 | 1800

Parthenon blown up

1684 Venetians reconquer the Peloponnese

1778 Ali Pasha becomes Vizier of Ioánnina and establishes powerful state in Albania and northern Greece

1801 Frieze on Parthenon removed by Lord Elgin

1814 Foundation of *Filikí Etaireía*, Greek liberation movement

The Making of Modern Greece

Flag with the symbols of the *Filikí Etaireía*

THE GREEK WAR of Independence marked the overthrow of the Ottomans and the start of the "Great Idea," an ambitious project to bring all Greek people under one flag *(Enosis)*. The plans for expansion were initially successful, and during the 19th century the Greeks succeeded in doubling their national territory and reasserting Greek sovereignty over many of the islands. However, an attempt to take the city of Constantinople by force after World War I ended in disaster: in 1922 millions of Greeks were expelled from Smyrna in Turkish Anatolia, ending thousands of years of Greek occupation in Asia Minor.

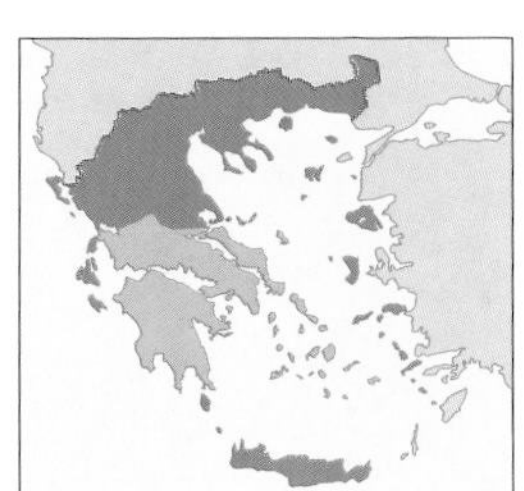

THE EMERGING GREEK STATE

- *Greece in 1832*
- *Areas gained 1832–1923*

Massacre at Chíos
This detail of Delacroix's shocking painting Scènes de Massacres de Scio *shows the events of 1822, when Turks took savage revenge for an earlier killing of Muslims.*

Klephts (mountain brigands) were the basis of the Independence movement.

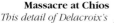

Weapons were family heirlooms or donated by philhellenes.

Declaration of the Constitution in Athens
Greece's Neo-Classical parliament building in Athens was the site of the Declaration of the Constitution in 1843. It was built as the Royal Palace for Greece's first monarch, King Otto, in the 1830s.

TIMELINE

1821 Greek flag of independence raised on March 25; Greeks massacre Turks at Tripolitsá in Morea

1824 The poet Lord Byron dies of a fever at Mesolóngi

1827 Battle of Navaríno

1828 Ioánnis Kapodístrias becomes first President of Greece

1831 President Kapodístrias assassinated

1832 Great Powers establish protectorate over Greece and accept Otto, Bavarian prince, as king

1834 Athens replaces Náfplio as capital

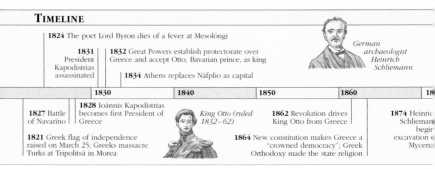

1830 | 1840 | 1850 | 1860 | 18

King Otto (ruled 1832–62)

German archaeologist Heinrich Schliemann

1862 Revolution drives King Otto from Greece

1864 New constitution makes Greece a "crowned democracy"; Greek Orthodoxy made the state religion

1874 Heinric Schlieman begir excavation Mycen

Life in Athens
By 1836 urban Greeks still wore a mixture of Greek traditional and Western dress. The Ottoman legacy had not totally disappeared and is visible in the fez worn by men.

Where to See 19th-Century Greece

In Crete, Moní Arkadíou *(see p256)* is the site of mass suicide by freedom fighters in 1866; the tomb of Venizélos is at Akrotíri *(p247)*. The harbor and surrounding buildings at Sýros *(p216)* are evidence of the importance of Greek seapower in the 19th century.

Flag Raising of 1821 Revolution

In 1821, the Greek secret society *Filikí Etaireía* was behind a revolt by Greek officers which led to anti-Turk uprisings throughout the Peloponnese. Tradition credits Archbishop Germanós of Pátra with raising the rebel flag near Kalávryta in the Peloponnese on March 25. The struggle for independence had begun.

Corinth Canal
This spectacular link between the Aegean and Ionian seas opened in 1893.

Elefthérios Venizélos
This great Cretan politician and advocate of liberal democracy doubled Greek territory during the Balkan Wars (1912–13) and joined the Allies in World War I.

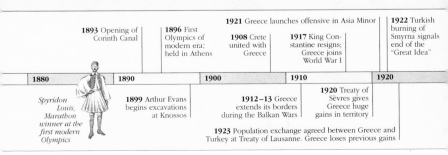

1893 Opening of Corinth Canal

1896 First Olympics of modern era; held in Athens

1908 Crete united with Greece

1921 Greece launches offensive in Asia Minor

1917 King Constantine resigns; Greece joins World War I

1922 Turkish burning of Smyrna signals end of the "Great Idea"

1880 | 1890 | 1900 | 1910 | 1920

Spyrídon Louis, Marathon winner at the first modern Olympics

1899 Arthur Evans begins excavations at Knossos

1912–13 Greece extends its borders during the Balkan Wars

1920 Treaty of Sèvres gives Greece huge gains in territory

1923 Population exchange agreed between Greece and Turkey at Treaty of Lausanne. Greece loses previous gains

Twentieth-Century Greece

THE YEARS after the 1922 defeat by Turkey were terrible ones for the Greek people. The influx of impoverished refugees contributed to the political instability of the interwar years. The dictatorship of Metaxás was followed by invasion in 1940, then Italian, German, and Bulgarian occupation and, finally, the bitter Civil War, between 1946 and 1949, with its legacy of division. After experiencing the Cyprus problem of the 1950s and the military dictatorship of 1967 to 1974, Greece is now an established democracy and a member of the European Union.

1947 Internationally acclaimed Greek artist, Giánnis Tsaroúchis, holds his first exhibition of set designs, in the Romvos Gallery, Athens

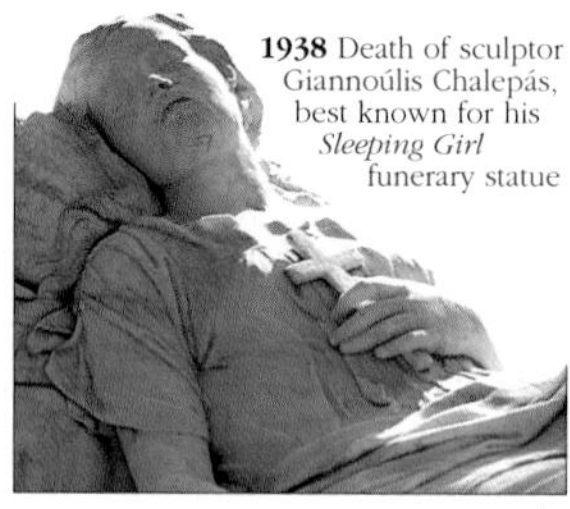

1938 Death of sculptor Giannoúlis Chalepás, best known for his *Sleeping Girl* funerary statue

1946 Government institutes "White Terror" against Communists

1945 Níkos Kazantzákis publishes *Zorba the Greek*, later made into a film

1958 USSR threatens Greece with economic sanctions if NATO missiles installed

1957 Mosaics found by chance at Philip II's 300 BC palace at Pélla

1925	1935	1945	1955

1925	1935	1945	1955

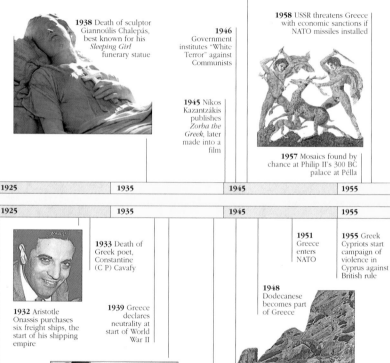

1933 Death of Greek poet, Constantine (C P) Cavafy

1951 Greece enters NATO

1955 Greek Cypriots start campaign of violence in Cyprus against British rule

1948 Dodecanese becomes part of Greece

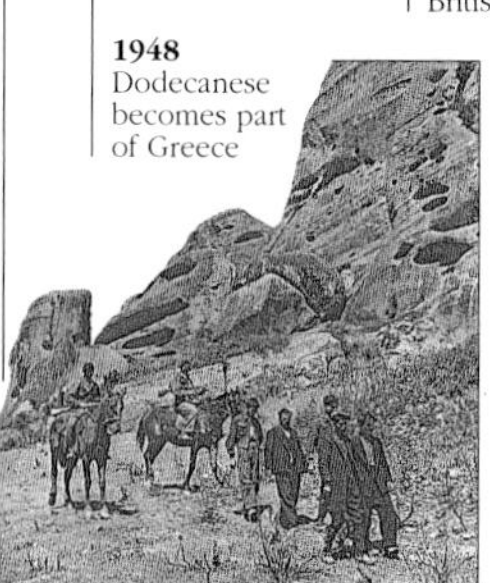

1946–9 Civil War between Greek government and the Communists who take to the mountains

1932 Aristotle Onassis purchases six freight ships, the start of his shipping empire

1939 Greece declares neutrality at start of World War II

1925 Birth of Chatzidákis, who wrote music for the 1960 film *Never on Sunday*

1944 Churchill visits Athens to show his support for Greek government against Communist Resistance

1960 Cyprus declared independent

1940 Italy invades Greece. Greek soldiers defend northern Greece. Greece enters World War II

1963 Geórgios Papandréou's center-left government voted into power

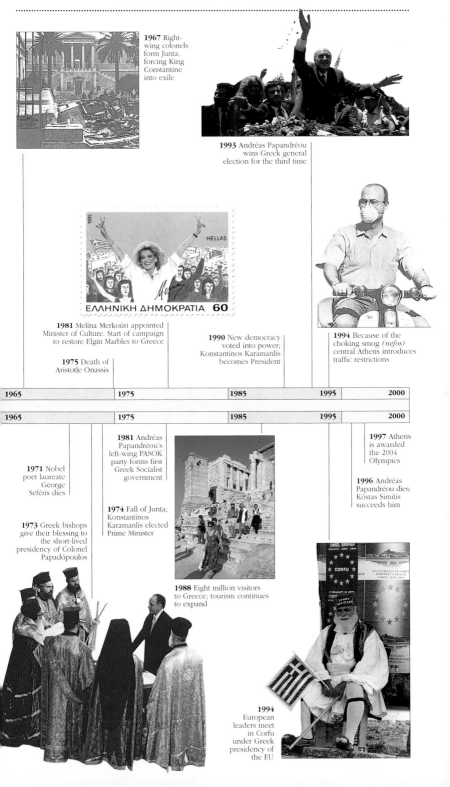

1967 Right-wing colonels form Junta, forcing King Constantine into exile

1993 Andréas Papandréou wins Greek general election for the third time

1981 Melína Merkoúri appointed Minister of Culture. Start of campaign to restore Elgin Marbles to Greece

1994 Because of the choking smog *(nefos)* central Athens introduces traffic restrictions

1990 New democracy voted into power; Konstantínos Karamanlís becomes President

1975 Death of Aristotle Onassis

1965	1975	1985	1995	2000

1965	1975	1985	1995	2000

1971 Nobel poet laureate George Seféris dies

1973 Greek bishops give their blessing to the short-lived presidency of Colonel Papadópoulos

1974 Fall of Junta; Konstantínos Karamanlís elected Prime Minister

1981 Andréas Papandréou's left-wing PASOK party forms first Greek Socialist government

1988 Eight million visitors to Greece; tourism continues to expand

1997 Athens is awarded the 2004 Olympics

1996 Andréas Papandréou dies; Kóstas Simítis succeeds him

1994 European leaders meet in Corfu under Greek presidency of the EU

The Greek Islands Through the Year

Greek island life revolves around the seasons, and is punctuated by saints' days and colorful religious festivals, or *panigýria*. Easter is the most important Orthodox festival of the year, but there are lively pre-Lenten carnivals on some islands as well. The Greeks mix piety and pleasure, with a great enthusiasm for their celebrations, from the most important to the smallest village fair. There are also festivals that have ancient roots in pagan revels. Other festivals celebrate harvests of local produce, such as grapes, olives, and grain, or re-enact various victories for Greece in its struggle for Independence.

May Day wreath

Spring

The Greek word for spring is *ánoixi* (the opening), and it heralds the beginning of the tourist season on the islands. After wintering in Athens or Rhodes, hoteliers and shopkeepers head for the smaller islands to open up. The islands in spring are at their most beautiful, carpeted with red poppies, camomile, and wild cyclamen. Fruit trees are in blossom, fishing boats and houses are freshly painted, and people are at their most welcoming. Orthodox Easter is the main spring event, preceded in late February or March with pre-Lenten carnivals. While northern island groups can be showery, by late April, Crete, the Dodecanese, and East Aegean islands are usually warm and sunny.

Children in national dress, March 25

March

Apókries, or Carnival Sunday *(first Sun before Lent)*. There are carnivals on many islands for three weeks leading up to this date, the culmination of pre-Lenten festivities. Celebrations are exuberant at Agiásos on Lésvos and on Kárpathos, while a goat dance is performed on Skýros.

Katharí Deftéra, or Clean Monday *(seven Sundays before Easter)*. This marks the start of Lent. Houses are spring-cleaned and the unleavened bread *lagána* is baked. Also, a huge kite-flying contest takes place in Chalkída on Evvoia.

Celebrating Easter in Greece

Greek Orthodox Easter can fall up to three weeks either side of Western Easter. It is the most important religious festival in Greece, and Holy Week is a time for Greek families to reunite. It is also a good time to visit Greece, to see the processions and church services and to sample the Easter food. The ceremony and symbolism is a direct link with Greece's Byzantine past, as well as with earlier more primitive beliefs. The festivities reach a climax at midnight on Easter Saturday when, as priests intone "Christ is risen," fireworks explode to usher in a Sunday of feasting, music, and dancing. The Sunday feasting on roast meat marks the end of the Lenten fast, and a belief in the renewal of life in spring. Particularly worthwhile visiting for the Holy Week processions and the Friday and Saturday night services are Olympos on Kárpathos, Ydra, Pátmos, and just about any village on Crete.

Priests in robes at the Easter parade of icons

***Christ's bier**, decorated with flowers and containing his effigy, is carried in solemn procession through the streets at dusk on Good Friday.*

***Candle lighting** takes place at the end of the Easter Saturday mass. In pitch darkness, a single flame is used to light the candles held by worshipers.*

A workers' rally in Athens on Labor Day, May 1

Independence Day and **Evangelismós** *(Mar 25).* A national holiday, with parades and dances nationwide to celebrate the 1821 revolt against the Ottoman empire. The religious festival, one of the Orthodox church's most important, marks the Angel Gabriel's announcement to the Virgin Mary that she was to become the Holy Mother. Name day for Evángelos and Evangelía.

April

Megáli Evdomáda, Holy Week *(Apr or May)*, including *Kyriakí ton Vaïón* (Palm Sunday), *Megáli Pémpti* (Maundy Thursday), *Megáli Paraskeví* (Good Friday), *Megáli Savváto* (Easter Saturday) and the most important date in the Orthodox calendar, *Páscha* (Easter Sunday).
Agios Geórgios, St. George's Day *(Apr 23).* A day for celebrating the patron saint of shepherds. This date traditionally marks the beginning of the grazing season in Greece.

Kite-flying competition in Chalkída, Evvoia

May

Protomagiá, May Day or Labor Day *(May 1).* Traditionally, wreaths made with wild flowers and garlic are hung up to ward off evil. In major towns and cities, the day is marked by workers' demonstrations and rallies.
Agios Konstantínos kai Agía Eléni *(May 21).* A nationwide celebration for the saint and his mother, the first Orthodox Byzantine rulers.
Análipsi, Ascension *(40 days after Easter, usually in May).* An important Orthodox feast day, celebrated across the nation.

***Easter dancing**, for young and old alike, continues the outdoor festivities after the midday meal on Sunday.*

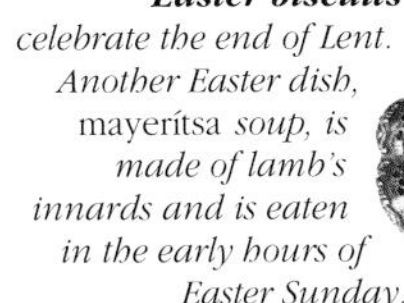
***Easter biscuits** celebrate the end of Lent. Another Easter dish,* mayerítsa *soup, is made of lamb's innards and is eaten in the early hours of Easter Sunday.*

***Egg loaves**, made of sweet plaited dough, contain eggs with shells dyed red to symbolize the blood of Christ. Red eggs are also traditionally given as presents on Easter Sunday.*

***Lamb roasting** is traditionally done in the open air on giant spits over charcoal, for lunch on Easter Sunday. The first retsina wine from last year's harvest is opened and for dessert there are sweet cinnamon-flavored pastries.*

Harvesting barley in July on the island of Folégandros

Summer

With islands parched and sizzling, the tourist season is now in full swing. Villagers with rooms to rent meet backpackers from the ferries and prices go up. The islands are sometimes cooled by the strong, blustery *meltémi*, a northerly wind from the Aegean, which can blow up at any time to disrupt ferry schedules and delight windsurfers.

In June, the grain is harvested and cherries, apricots, and peaches are at their best. In July herbs are gathered and dried, and figs begin to ripen. August sees the mass exodus from Athens to the islands, especially for the festival of the Assumption on August 15. By late summer the first of the grapes have ripened and temperatures soar.

Consecrated bread for religious festivals

June

Pentikostí, Pentecost, or Whitsunday *(seven weeks after Orthodox Easter)*. An important Orthodox feast day, celebrated throughout Greece.

Agíou Pnévmatos, Feast of the Holy Spirit, or Whitmonday *(the following day)*. A national holiday.

Athens Festival *(mid-Jun to mid-Sep)*, Athens. A cultural festival with modern and ancient theater and music.

Klídonas *(Jun 24)* Chaniá, Crete *(see pp248–9)*. A festival, celebrating the custom of water-divining for a husband. An amusing song is sung while locals dance.

Agios Ioánnis, St. John's Day *(Jun 24)*. On some islands bonfires are lit on the evening before. May wreaths are consigned to the flames, and youngsters jump over the fires.

Agioi Apóstoloi Pétros kai Pávlos, Apostles Peter and Paul *(Jun 29)*. There are festivals at dedicated churches, such as St. Paul's Bay, Líndos, Rhodes *(see p193)*.

Agioi Apóstoloi, Holy Apostles *(Jun 30)*. This time the celebrations are for anyone named after one of the 12 apostles.

July

Agios Nikódimos *(Jul 14)*, Náxos town. A small folk festival and procession for the town's patron saint.

One of the many local church celebrations during summer, Pátmos

Festivities on Tínos for Koímisis tis Theotókou, August 15

Agía Marína *(Jul 17)*. This day is widely celebrated in rural areas, with feasts to honor this saint. She is revered as an important protector of crops and healer of snakebites. There are festivals throughout Crete and at the town of Agía Marína, Léros.

Profítis Ilías, the Prophet Elijah *(Jul 18–20)*. There are high-altitude celebrations in the Cyclades, Rhodes, and on Evvoia at the mountain-top chapels dedicated to him. The chapels were built on former sites of Apollo temples.

Agíou Panteleïmonos Festival *(Jul 25–28)*, Tílos *(see p173)*. Three days of song and dance at Moní Agíou Panteleïmonos, culminating in "Dance of the Koupa," or Cup, at Taxiárchis, Megálo Chorió. There are also celebrations at Moní Panachrántou, Andros *(see p205)*.

Simonídeia Festival *(Aug 1–19)*, Kea. A celebration of the work of the island's famous lyric poet, Simonides (556–468 BC), with drama, exhibitions, and dance.

Réthymno Festival *(Jul and Aug)*, Réthymno, Crete. The event includes a wine festival and renaissance fair.

August

Ippokráteia, Hippokrates Cultural Festival *(throughout Aug)*, Kos *(see p166)*. Art exhibitions are combined with concerts and films, plus the ceremony of the Hippocratic Oath at the Asklepieion.

Dionysía Festival *(first week of Aug)*, Náxos town. A festival of folk dancing in traditional costume, with free food and plenty of wine.
Metamórfosi, Transfiguration of Christ *(Aug 6)*. An important day in the Orthodox calendar, celebrated throughout Greece. It is a day of fun in the Dodecanese, and particularly on the island of Chálki, where you may get pelted with eggs, flour, yogurt, and squid ink.
Koímisis tis Theotókou, Assumption of the Virgin Mary *(Aug 15)*. A national holiday, and the most important festival in the Orthodox calendar after Easter. Following the long liturgy on the night of the 14th, the icon of the Madonna is paraded and kissed. Then the celebrations proceed, and continue for days, providing an excellent opportunity to experience traditional music and spontaneous dance. There are spectacular celebrations at Olympos on Kárpathos *(see p199)*, with women wearing dazzling costumes, and at Panagía Evangelístria on Tínos *(see pp208–9)*.

Women in ceremonial costume, Kárpathos

Autumn

The wine-making months of September and October are still very warm in the Dodecanese, Crete, and the Cyclades, although they can be showery farther north and the sea can be rough. October sees the "little summer of St. Dimitrios," a pleasant heat wave when the first wine is ready to drink. The shooting season begins and hunters take to the hills in search of pigeon, partridge, and other game. The main fishing season begins, with fish such as bream and red mullet appearing on restaurant menus. By the end of October many islanders are heading for Athens, packing the ferries and wishing each other *Kaló Chimóna* (good winter). But traditional island life goes on: olives are harvested and strings of garlic, onions, and tomatoes are hung up to dry for the winter; flocks of sheep are brought down from the mountains; and fishing nets are mended.

The year's first wine

September

Génnisis tis Theotókou, birth of the Virgin Mary *(Sep 8)*. An important feast day in the Orthodox church calendar. Also on this day, there is a reenactment of the Battle of Spétses (1822) in the town's harbor *(see p97)*, followed by a fireworks display and feast.
Ypsosis tou Timíou Stavroú, Exaltation of the True Cross *(Sep 14)*. This end-of-season celebration is the last of Greece's summer festivals. The festivities are celebrated with fervor on Chálki.

Strings of tomatoes hanging out to dry in the autumn sunshine

October

Agios Dimítrios *(Oct 26)*. A popular and widely celebrated name day. It is also traditionally the day when the first wine of the year is ready to drink.
Ochi Day *(Oct 28)*. A national holiday, with patriotic parades in the cities and plenty of dancing. The day commemorates the famous reply by Greece's prime minister of the time, Metáxas, to Mussolini's 1940 call for Greek surrender: an emphatic no *(óchi)*.

Greek veterans on Ochi Day

November

Ton Taxiarchón Michaíl kai Gavriíl *(Nov 8)*. Ceremonies at many monasteries named after Archangels Gabriel and Michael, such as at Panormítis, on Sými *(see p175)*. This is an important name day throughout Greece.
Eisódia tis Theotókou, Presentation of the Virgin in the Temple *(Nov 21)*. A religious feast day, and one of the most important for the Orthodox church. Name day for Mariá, Máry, Panagióta.

Diving for the cross at Epiphany, Jan 6

Winter

Lashed by wild winds and high seas, the islands can be bleak in winter. *Kafeneía* are steamed up and full of men playing cards or backgammon. Women often embroider or crochet, and cook warming stews and soups. Fishermen celebrate Agios Nikólaos, their patron saint, and then preparations get underway for Christmas. The 12-day holiday begins on Christmas Eve, when the wicked goblins, *kallikántzaroi*, are about causing mischief, until the Epiphany in the new year, when they are banished. Pigs are slaughtered for Christmas pork, and cakes representing the swaddling clothes of the infant Christ are made. The Greek Santa Claus comes to visit on New Year's Day, and special cakes, called *vasilópita*, are baked with coins inside to bring good luck to the finder.

***Kourambiethes*, almond shortbread eaten at Christmas**

December

Agios Nikólaos *(Dec 6).* This is a celebration for the patron saint of sailors. *Panigýria* (religious ceremonies) are held at harborside churches, and decorated boats and icons are paraded on beaches.

Agios Spyrídon *(Dec 12)*, Corfu *(see pp70–75)*. A celebration for the patron saint of the island, with a parade of his relics.

Christoúgenna, Christmas *(Dec 25).* A national holiday. Though less significant than Easter in Greece, Christmas is still an important feast day.

Sýnaxis tis Theotókou, meeting of the Virgin's entourage *(Dec 26).* A religious celebration nationwide and a national holiday. The next day *(Dec 27)* is a popular name day for Stéfanos and Stéfania, commemorating the saint Agios Stéfanos.

January

Agios Vasíleios, also known as *Protochroniá (Jan 1).* A national holiday to celebrate this saint. The day combines with festivities for the arrival of the new year. Gifts are exchanged, and the new year greeting is *Kalí Chroniá.*

Theofánia, or Epiphany *(Jan 6).* A national holiday and an important feast day. There are special ceremonies to bless the waters at coastal locations throughout many of the islands. A priest at the harborside throws a crucifix into the water. Young men then dive into the sea for the honor of retrieving the cross.

Main Public Holidays

These are the dates when museums and public sites are closed nationwide.

Agios Vasíleios (Jan 1).
Evangelismós (Mar 25).
Protomagiá (May 1).
Paraskeví (Good Friday).
Megáli Páscha (Easter Sunday).
Christoúgenna (Dec 25).
Sýnaxis tis Theotókou (Dec 26).

February

Ypapantí, Candlemas *(Feb 2).* An important Orthodox feast day throughout Greece. This festival celebrates the presentation of the infant Christ at the temple.

Priests in ceremonial robes at Ypapantí, February 2

Name Days

Most Greeks do not celebrate their birthdays past the age of about 12. Instead they celebrate their name days, or *giortí*, the day of the saint after whom they were named at their baptism. Choice of names is very important in Greece, and children are usually named after their grandparents – though in recent years it has become fashionable to give children ancient names, from Greece's history and mythology. On St. George's day or St. Helen's day (May 21) the whole nation seems to celebrate, with visitors dropping in, bearing small gifts, and being given cakes and liqueurs in return. On a friend's name day you may be told, *Giortázo símera* (I'm celebrating today). The traditional greeting, by way of reply, is *Chrónia pollá* (many years), the equivalent of many happy returns.

The Climate of the Greek Islands

THROUGHOUT THE ISLANDS, the tendency is for long, dry summers and mild but rainy winters. The Dodecanese, Cyclades, and the Cretan coast are buffeted by a dry north wind called the *meltémi*, which can blow up at any time between June and September, moderating the high temperatures.

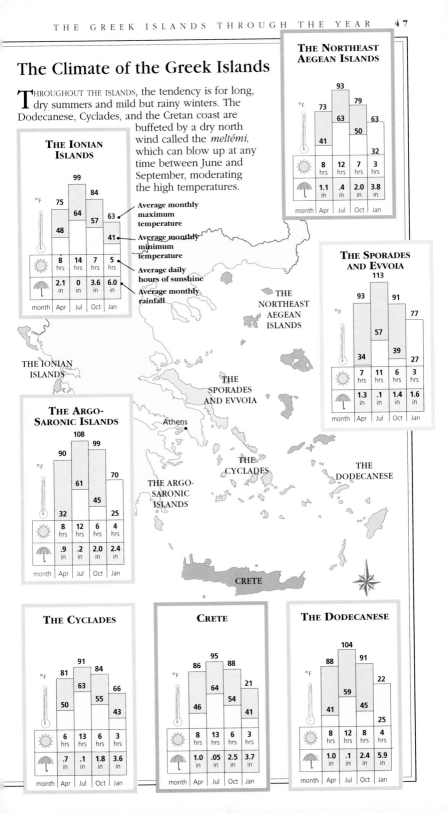

The Northeast Aegean Islands

month	Apr	Jul	Oct	Jan
°F max	73	93	79	63
°F min	41	63	50	32
sunshine	8 hrs	12 hrs	7 hrs	3 hrs
rainfall	1.1 in	.4 in	2.0 in	3.8 in

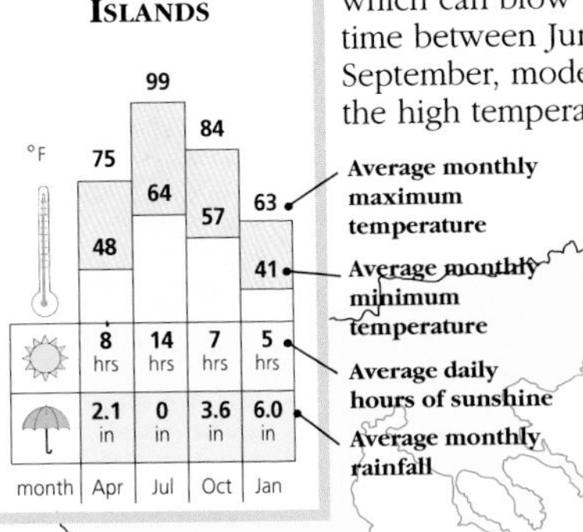

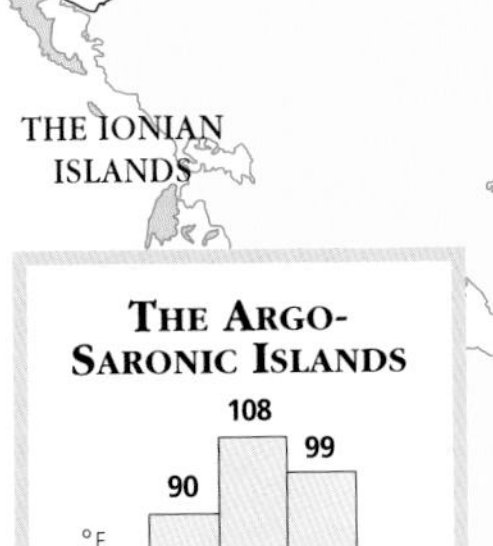

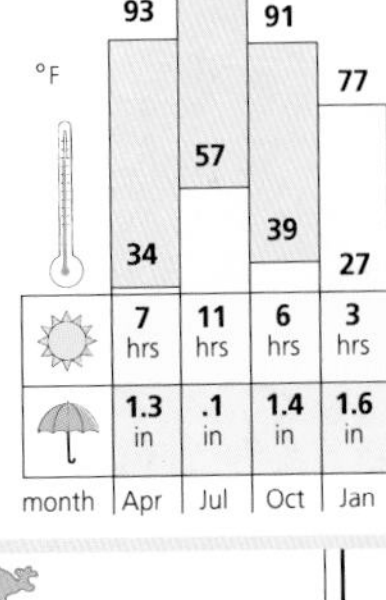

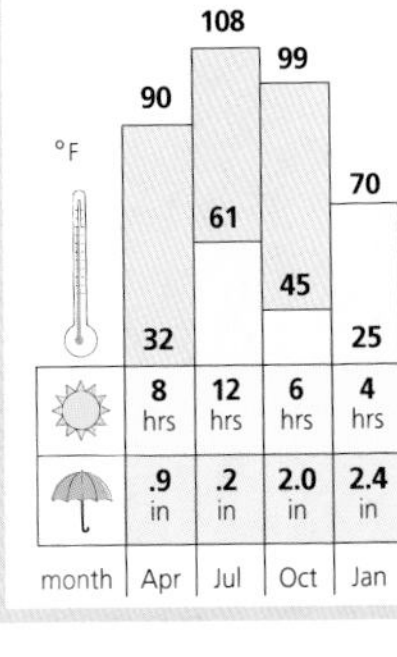

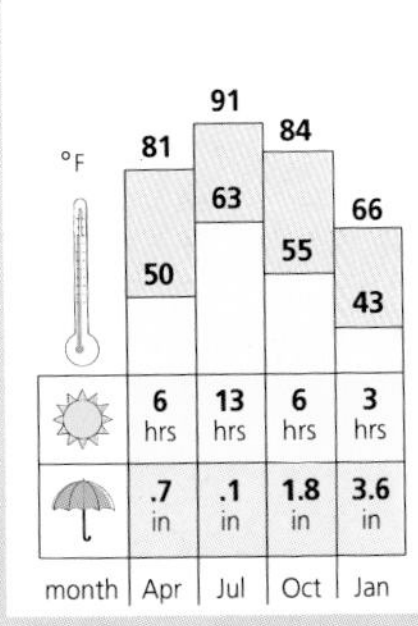

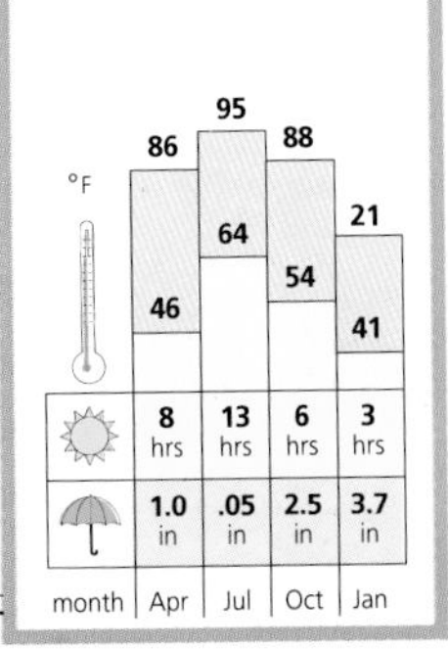

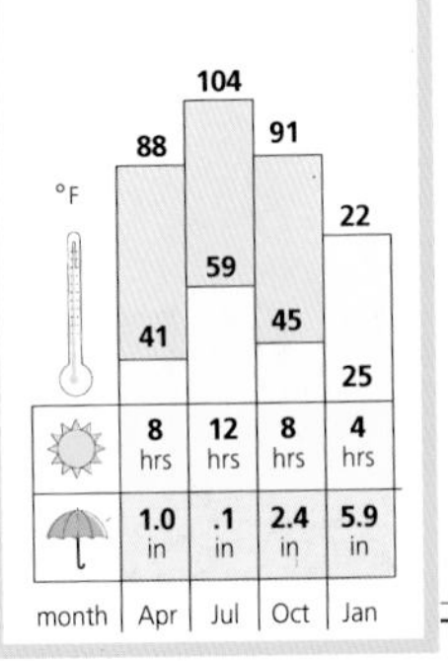

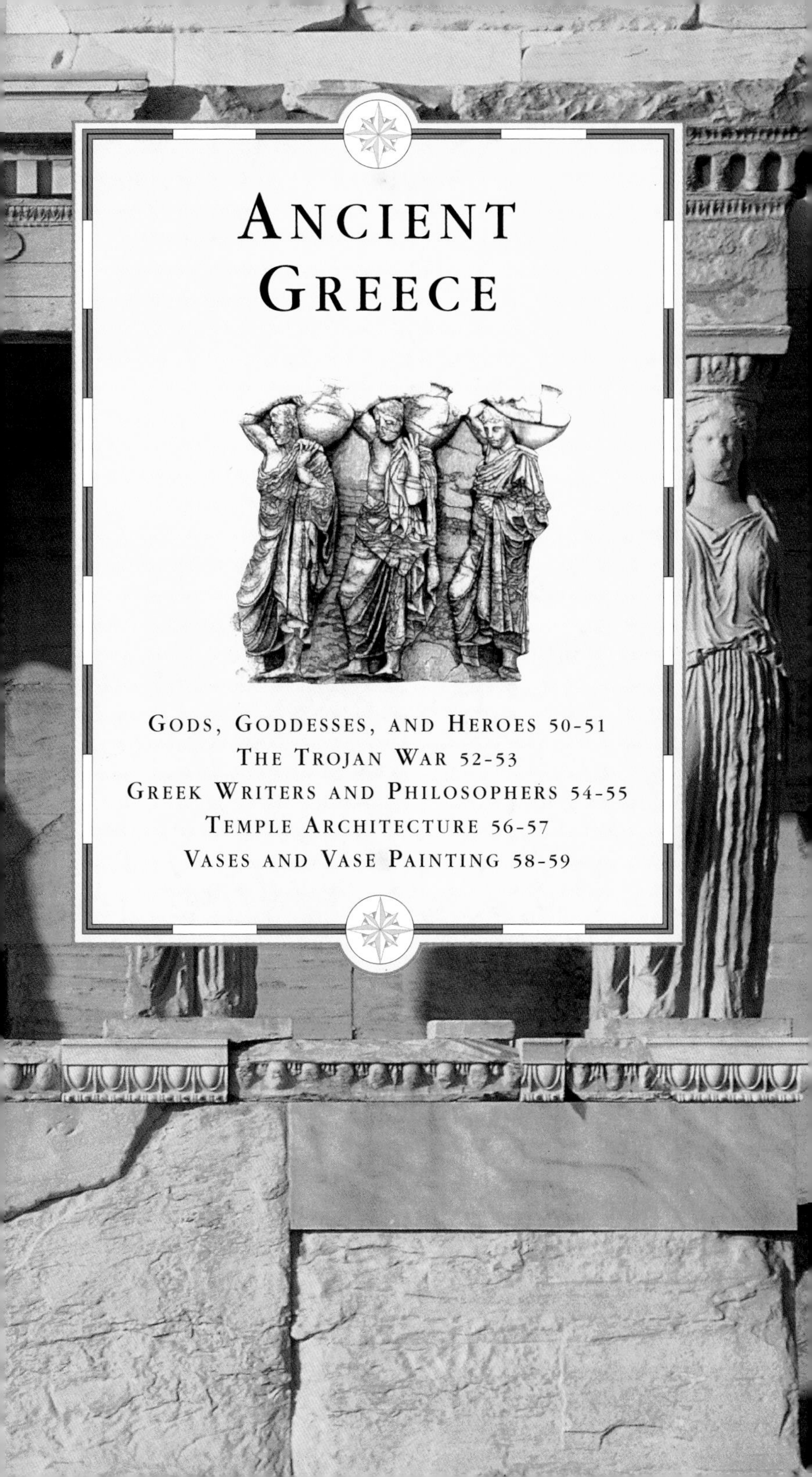

Ancient Greece

Gods, Goddesses, and Heroes

THE GREEK MYTHS that tell the stories of the gods, goddesses, and heroes date back to the Bronze Age when they were told aloud by poets. They were first written down in the early 6th century BC and have lived on in Western literature. Myths were closely bound up with Greek religion and gave meaning to the unpredictable workings of the natural world. They tell the story of the creation and the "golden age" of gods and mortals, as well as the age of semi-mythical heroes, such as Theseus and Herakles, whose exploits were an inspiration to ordinary men. The gods and goddesses were affected by human desires and failings and were part of a divine family presided over by Zeus. He had many offspring, both legitimate and illegitimate, each with a mythical role.

Hades and Persephone *were king and queen of the Underworld (land of the dead). Persephone was abducted from her mother Demeter, goddess of the harvest, by Hades. She was then only permitted to return to her mother for three months each year.*

Poseidon*, one of Zeus's brothers, was given control of the seas. The trident is his symbol of power, and he married the sea-goddess Amphitrite, to whom he was not entirely faithful. This statue is from the National Archaeological Museum in Athens* (see p282).

Zeus was the father of the gods and ruled over them and all mortals from Mount Olympos.

Eris was the goddess of strife.

Clymene, a nymph and daughter of Helios, was mother of Prometheus, creator of mankind.

Hera, sister and wife of Zeus, was famous for her jealousy.

Athena was born from Zeus's head in full armor.

Paris was asked to award the golden apple to the most beautiful goddess.

Paris's dog helped him herd cattle on Mount Ida, where the prince grew up.

A Divine Dispute

This vase painting shows the gods on Mount Ida, near Troy. Hera, Athena, and Aphrodite, quarreling over who was the most beautiful, were brought by Hermes to hear the judgment of a young herdsman, the Trojan prince, Paris. In choosing Aphrodite, he was rewarded with the love of Helen, the most beautiful woman in the world. Paris abducted her from her husband Menelaos, King of Sparta, and thus the Trojan War began *(see pp52–3)*.

Dionysos*, god of revelry and wine, was born from Zeus's thigh. In this 6th-century BC cup, painted by Exekias, he reclines in a ship whose mast has become a vine.*

◁ **The statues of the Caryatids on the Erechtheion, Athens**

***Artemis**, the virgin goddess of the hunt, was the daughter of Zeus and sister of Apollo. She can be identified by her bow and arrows, hounds, and group of nymphs with whom she lived in the forests. Although sworn to chastity, she was, in contrast, the goddess of childbirth.*

Happiness, here personified by two goddesses, waits with gold laurel leaves to garland the winner. Wreaths were the prizes in Greek athletic and musical contests.

Helios, the sun god, drove his four-horse chariot (the sun) daily across the sky.

Aphrodite, the goddess of love, was born from the sea. Here she has her son Eros (Cupid) with her.

Hermes was the gods' messenger.

***Apollo**, son of Zeus and brother of Artemis, was god of healing, plague, and also music. Here he is depicted holding a lyre. He was also famous for his dazzling beauty.*

The Labors of Herakles

Herakles (Hercules to the Romans) was the greatest of the Greek heroes, and the son of Zeus and Alkmene, a mortal woman. With superhuman strength he achieved success, against seemingly impossible odds in the "Twelve Labors" set by Eurystheus, King of Argos. For his first task he killed the Nemean lion, and wore its hide ever after.

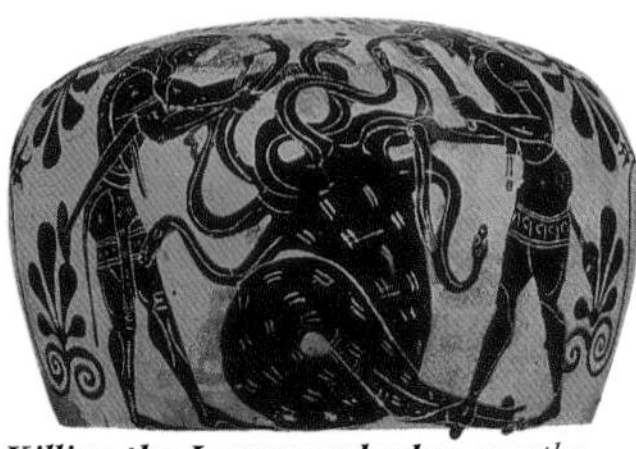

***Killing the Lernaean hydra** was the second labor of Herakles. The many heads of this venomous monster, raised by Hera, grew back as soon as they were chopped off. As in all his tasks, Herakles was helped by Athena.*

***The huge boar** that ravaged Mount Erymanthus was captured next. Herakles brought it back alive to King Eurystheus, who was so terrified that he hid in a storage jar.*

***Destroying the Stymfalian birds** was the sixth labor. Herakles rid Lake Stymfalia of these man-eating birds, which had brass beaks, by stoning them with a sling, having first frightened them off with a pair of bronze castanets.*

The Trojan War

Ajax carrying the body of the dead Achilles

THE STORY of the Trojan War, narrated in the *Iliad*, Homer's 8th-century BC epic poem, tells how the Greeks sought to avenge the capture of Helen, wife of Menelaos, King of Sparta, by the Trojan prince, Paris. The Roman writer Virgil takes up the story in the *Aeneid*, where he tells of the sack of Troy and the founding of Rome. Archaeological evidence of the remains of a city identified with ancient Troy in modern Turkey suggests that the myth may have a basis in fact. Many of the ancient sites in the Peloponnese, such as Mycenae and Pylos, are thought to be the cities of some of the heroes of the Trojan War.

Achilles binding up the battle wounds of his friend Patroklos

Gathering of the Heroes

WHEN PARIS *(see p50)* carries Helen back to Troy, her husband King Menelaos summons an army of Greek kings and heroes to avenge this crime. His brother, King Agamemnon of Mycenae, leads the force; its ranks include young Achilles, destined to die at Troy.

At Aulis their departure is delayed by a contrary wind. Only the sacrifice to Artemis of Iphigeneia, the youngest of Agamemnon's daughters, allows the fleet to depart.

Fighting at Troy

THE ILIAD OPENS with the Greek army outside Troy, maintaining a siege that has already been in progress for nine years. Tired of fighting, yet still hoping for a decisive victory, the Greek camp is torn apart by the fury of Achilles over Agamemnon's removal of his slave girl Briseis. The hero takes to his tent and refuses adamantly to fight.

Deprived of their greatest warrior, the Greeks are driven back by the Trojans. In desperation, Patroklos persuades his friend Achilles to let him borrow his armor. Achilles agrees and Patroklos leads the Myrmidons, Achilles's troops, into battle. The tide is turned, but Patroklos is killed in the fighting by Hector, son of King Priam of Troy, who mistakes him for Achilles. Filled with remorse at the news of his friend's death, Achilles returns to battle, finds Hector, and kills him in revenge.

King Priam begging Achilles for the body of his son

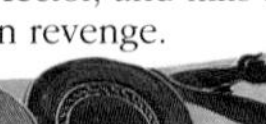

Greeks and Trojans, in bronze armor, locked in combat

Patroklos Avenged

REFUSING HECTOR'S dying wish to allow his body to be ransomed, Achilles instead hitches it up to his chariot by the ankles and drags it round the walls of Troy, then takes it back to the Greek camp. In contrast, Patroklos is given the most elaborate funeral possible with a huge pyre, sacrifices of animals and Trojan prisoners, and funeral games. Still unsatisfied, for 12 days Achilles drags the corpse of Hector around Patroklos's funeral mound until the gods are forced to intervene over his callous behavior.

Priam visits Achilles

ON THE INSTRUCTIONS of Zeus, Priam sets off for the Greek camp holding a ransom for the body of his dead son. With the help of the god Hermes he reaches Achilles's tent undetected. Entering, he pleads with Achilles to think of his own father and to show mercy. Achilles relents and allows Hector to be taken back to Troy for a funeral and burial.

Although the Greek heroes often seem superhuman, they were portrayed as fallible beings with human emotions who had to face universal moral dilemmas.

Achilles Kills the Amazon Queen

Penthesileia was the Queen of the Amazons, a tribe of warlike women reputed to cut off their right breasts to make it easier to wield their weapons. They come to the support of the Trojans. In the battle, Achilles finds himself face to face with Penthesileia and deals her a fatal blow. One version of the story has it that as their eyes meet at the moment of her death, they fall in love. The Greek idea of love and death would be explored 2,000 years later by the psychologists Jung and Freud.

Achilles killing the Amazon Queen Penthesileia in battle

The Wooden Horse of Troy

As was foretold, Achilles *(see p79)* is killed at Troy by an arrow in his heel from Paris's bow. With this weakening of their military strength, the Greeks resort to guile.

Before sailing away they build a great wooden horse, in which they conceal some of their best fighters. The rumor is put out that this is a gift to the goddess Athena and that if the horse enters Troy, the city can never be taken. After some doubts, but swayed by supernatural omens, the Trojans drag the horse inside the walls. That night, the Greeks sail back, the soldiers creep out of the horse, and Troy is put to the torch. Priam, with many others, is murdered. Among the Trojan survivors is Aeneas, who escapes to Italy and founds the race of Romans: a second Troy. The next part of the story (the *Odyssey*) tells of the heroes' adventures on their way home *(see p83)*.

An early image of the Trojan Horse, from a 7th-century BC clay vase

Death of Agamemnon

Klytemnestra, the wife of Agamemnon, had ruled Mycenae in the ten years that he had been away fighting in Troy. She was accompanied by Aigisthos, her lover. Intent on vengeance for the death of her daughter Iphigeneia, Klytemnestra receives her husband with a triumphal welcome and then brutally murders him, with the help of Agisthos. Agamemnon's fate was a result of a curse laid on his father, Atreus, which was finally expiated by the murder of both Klytemnestra and Aigisthos by her son Orestes and daughter Elektra. In these myths, the will of the gods both shapes and overrides that of heroes and mortals.

Greek Myths in Western Art

From the Renaissance onward, the Greek myths have been a powerful inspiration for artists and sculptors. Kings and queens have had themselves portrayed as gods and goddesses with their symbolic attributes of love or war. Myths have also been an inspiration for artists to paint the nude or Classically draped figure. This was true of the 19th-century artist Lord Leighton, whose depiction of the human body reflects the Classical ideals of beauty. His tragic figure of Elektra is shown here.

Elektra mourning the death of her father Agamemnon at his tomb

Greek Writers and Philosophers

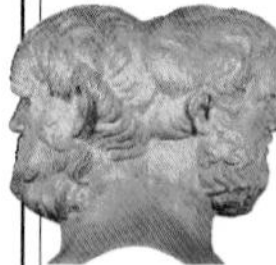

Playwrights Aristophanes and Sophocles

THE LITERATURE OF GREECE began with long epic poems, accounts of war and adventure, which established the relationship of the ancient Greeks to their gods. The tragedy and comedy, history and philosophical dialogues of the 5th and 4th centuries BC became the basis of Western literary culture. Much of our knowledge of the Greek world is derived from Greek literature. Pausanias's *Guide to Greece*, written in the Roman period and used by Roman tourists, is a key to the physical remains.

Hesiod with the nine Muses who inspired his poetry

EPIC POETRY

AS FAR BACK as the 2nd millennium BC, before even the building of the Mycenaean palaces, poets were reciting the stories of the Greek heroes and gods. Passed on from generation to generation, these poems, called *rhapsodes*, were never written down but were changed and embellished by successive poets. The oral tradition culminated in the *Iliad* and *Odyssey* *(see p83)*, composed around 700 BC. Both works are traditionally ascribed to the same poet, Homer, of whose life nothing reliable is known. Hesiod, whose most famous poems include the *Theogony*, a history of the gods, and the *Works and Days*, on how to live an honest life, also lived around 700 BC. Unlike Homer, Hesiod is thought to have written down his poems, although there is no firm evidence available to support this theory.

PASSIONATE POETRY

FOR PRIVATE OCCASIONS, and particularly to entertain guests at the cultivated drinking parties known as *symposia*, shorter poetic forms were developed. These poems were often full of passion, whether love or hatred, and could be personal or, often, highly political. Much of this poetry, by writers such as Archilochus, Alcaeus, Alcman, Hipponax, and Sappho, survives only in quotations by later writers or on scraps of papyrus that have been preserved by chance from private libraries in Hellenistic and Roman Egypt. Through these fragments we can gain glimpses of the life of a very competitive elite. Since *symposia* were an almost exclusively male domain, there is a strong element of misogyny in much of this poetry. In contrast, the fragments of poems discovered by the poetess Sappho, who lived on the island of Lésvos, are exceptional for showing a woman competing in a literary area in the male-dominated society of ancient Greece, and for describing with great intensity her passions for other women.

An unusual vase-painting of a *symposion* for women only

HISTORY

UNTIL THE 5th century BC little Greek literature was composed in prose – even early philosophy was in verse. In the latter part of the 5th century, a new tradition of lengthy prose histories, looking at recent or current events, was established with Herodotus's account of the great war between Greece and Persia (490–479 BC). Herodotus put the clash between Greeks and Persians into a context, and included an ethnographic account of the vast Persian Empire. He attempted to record objectively what people said about the past. Thucydides took a narrower view in his account of the long years of the Peloponnesian wars between Athens and Sparta (431–404 BC). He concentrated on the political history, and his aim was to work out the "truth" that lay behind the events of the war. The example of Thucydides dominated the later writing of Greek history, though few could match his acute insight into human nature.

Herodotus, the historian of the Persian wars

The orator Demosthenes in a Staffordshire figurine of 1790

ORATORY

PUBLIC ARGUMENT was basic to Greek political life even in the Archaic period. In the later part of the 5th century BC, the techniques of persuasive speech began to be studied in their own right. From that time on some orators began to publish their speeches. In particular, this included those wishing to advertise their skills in composing speeches for the law courts, such as Lysias and Demosthenes. The texts that survive give insights into both Athenian politics and the seamier side of Athenian private life. The verbal attacks on Philip of Macedon by Demosthenes, the 4th-century BC Athenian politician, became models for Roman politicians seeking to defeat their opponents. With the 18th-century European revival of interest in Classical times, Demosthenes again became a political role model.

DRAMA

ALMOST ALL the surviving tragedies come from the hands of the three great 5th-century BC Athenians; Aeschylus, Sophocles, and Euripides. The latter two playwrights developed an interest in individual psychology (as in Euripides's *Medea*). While 5th-century comedy is full of direct references to contemporary life and dirty jokes, the "new" comedy developed in the 4th century BC is essentially situation comedy employing character types.

Vase painting of two costumed actors from around 370 BC

GREEK PHILOSOPHERS

The Athenian Socrates was recognized in the late 5th century BC as a moral arbiter. He wrote nothing himself but we know of his views through the "Socratic dialogues," written by his pupil, Plato, examining the concepts of justice, virtue, and courage. Plato set up his academy in the suburbs of Athens. His pupil, Aristotle, founded the Lyceum, to teach subjects from biology to ethics and helped to turn Athens into one of the first university cities. In 1508–11 Raphael painted this vision of Athens in the Vatican.

Aristotle, author of the *Ethics*, had a genius for scientific observation.

Euclid laid the rules of geometry in around 300 BC.

Plato saw "the seat of ideas" in heaven.

Epicurus advocated moderation in all things.

Socrates taught by debating his ideas.

Diogenes, the Cynic, lived like a beggar.

Temple Architecture

Pheidias, sculptor of the Parthenon, at work

TEMPLES WERE THE most important public buildings in ancient Greece, largely because religion was a central part of everyday life. Often placed in prominent positions, temples were also statements about political and divine power. The earliest temples, in the 8th century BC, were built of wood and sun-dried bricks. Many of their features were copied in marble buildings from the 6th century BC onward.

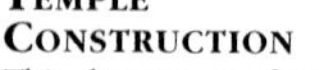

Temple Construction

This drawing is of an idealized Doric temple, showing how it was built and used.

The pediment, triangular in shape, often held sculpture.

The cella, or inner sanctum, housed the cult statue.

The cult statue was of the god or goddess to whom the temple was dedicated.

A ramp led up to the temple entrance.

The stepped platform was built on a stone foundation.

The column drums were initially carved with bosses for lifting them into place.

Fluting on th[e] columns was carved *i[n] situ*, guided by that on th[e] top and bottom drums

Timeline of Temple Construction

Detail of the Parthenon pediment

700 BC	600 BC	500 BC	400 BC	300 BC

522 Temple of Hera, Sámos (Ionic; *see p152*)

477–390 Athenian Temple of Apollo, Delos *(see pp214–15)*

447–405 Temples of the Acropolis, Athens: Athena Nike (Ionic), Parthenon (Doric), Erechtheion (Ionic) (*see pp284–6*)

490 Temple of Aphaia, Aígina (Doric; *see pp94–5*)

4th century BC Temple of Lindian Athena, Líndos Acropolis, Rhodes (Doric; *see pp192–3*)

Late 4th century BC Sanctuary of the Great Gods, Samothráki (Doric; *see pp128–9*)

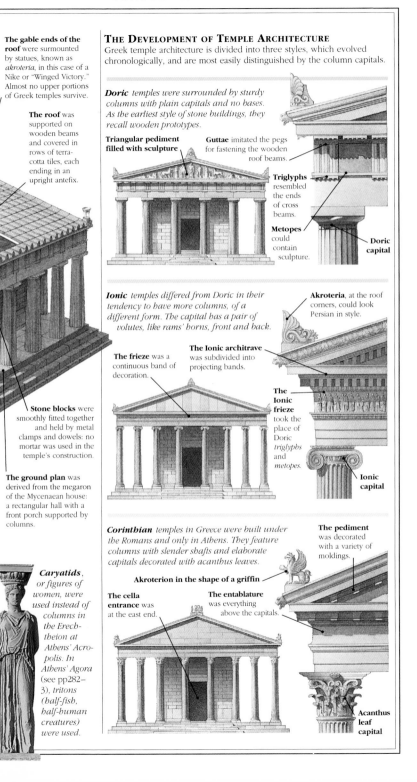

The gable ends of the roof were surmounted by statues, known as *akroteria*, in this case of a Nike or "Winged Victory." Almost no upper portions of Greek temples survive.

The roof was supported on wooden beams and covered in rows of terra-cotta tiles, each ending in an upright antefix.

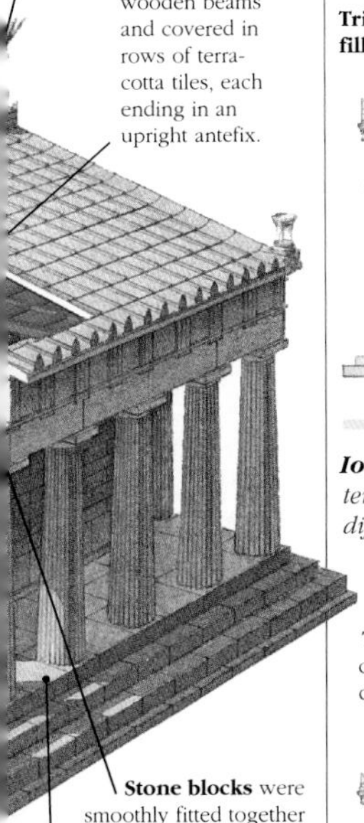

Stone blocks were smoothly fitted together and held by metal clamps and dowels: no mortar was used in the temple's construction.

The ground plan was derived from the megaron of the Mycenaean house: a rectangular hall with a front porch supported by columns.

Caryatids, *or figures of women, were used instead of columns in the Erechtheion at Athens' Acropolis. In Athens' Agora* (see pp282–3), *tritons (half-fish, half-human creatures) were used.*

The Development of Temple Architecture

Greek temple architecture is divided into three styles, which evolved chronologically, and are most easily distinguished by the column capitals.

Doric *temples were surrounded by sturdy columns with plain capitals and no bases. As the earliest style of stone buildings, they recall wooden prototypes.*

Triangular pediment filled with sculpture

Guttae imitated the pegs for fastening the wooden roof beams.

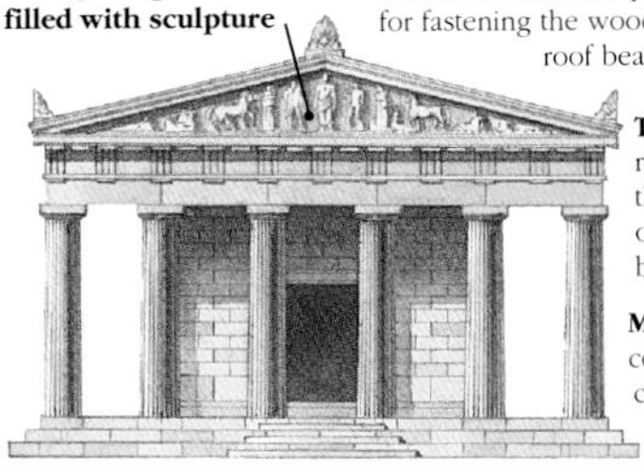

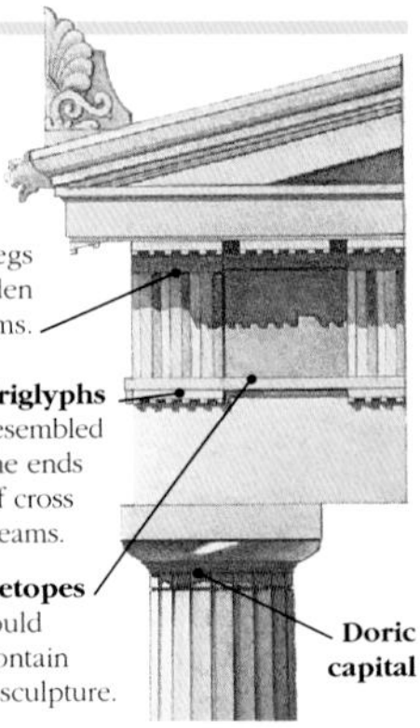

Triglyphs resembled the ends of cross beams.

Metopes could contain sculpture.

Doric capital

Ionic *temples differed from Doric in their tendency to have more columns, of a different form. The capital has a pair of volutes, like rams' horns, front and back.*

Akroteria, at the roof corners, could look Persian in style.

The frieze was a continuous band of decoration.

The Ionic architrave was subdivided into projecting bands.

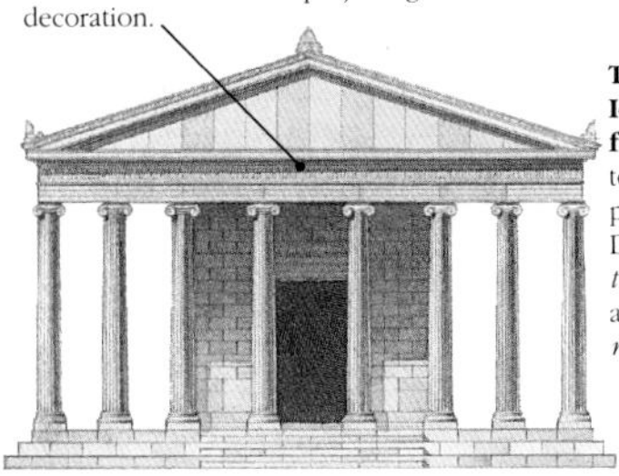

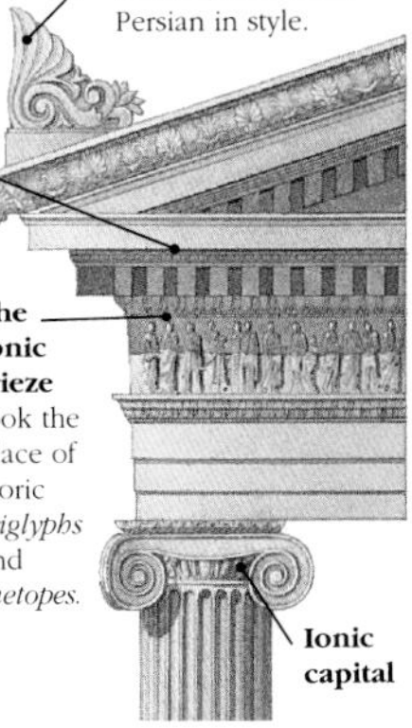

The Ionic frieze took the place of Doric *triglyphs* and *metopes*.

Ionic capital

Corinthian *temples in Greece were built under the Romans and only in Athens. They feature columns with slender shafts and elaborate capitals decorated with acanthus leaves.*

The pediment was decorated with a variety of moldings.

Akroterion in the shape of a griffin

The cella entrance was at the east end.

The entablature was everything above the capitals.

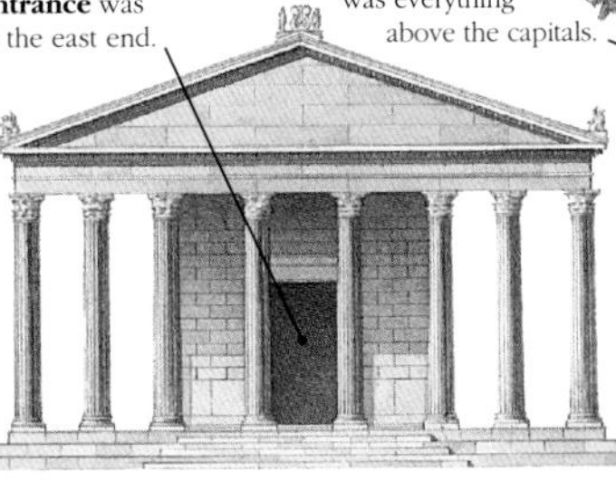

Acanthus leaf capital

Vases and Vase Painting

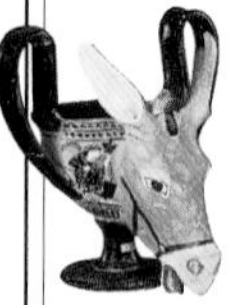

Donkey cup

This 6th-century BC black-figure vase *shows pots being used in an everyday situation. The vases depicted are* hydriai*. It was the womens' task to fill them with water from springs or public fountains.*

THE HISTORY OF GREEK vase painting continued without a break from 1000 BC to Hellenistic times. The main center of production was Athens, which was so successful that by the early 6th century BC it was sending its high-quality black- and red-figure wares to every part of the Greek world. The Athenian potters' quarter of Kerameikós, in the west of the city, can still be visited today. Beautiful works of art in their own right, the painted vases are the closest we can get to the vanished wall paintings with which ancient Greeks decorated their houses. Although vases could break during everyday use (for which they were intended) a huge number still survive intact or in reassembled pieces.

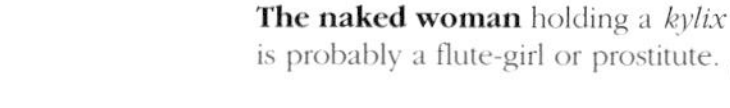

The naked woman holding a *kylix* is probably a flute-girl or prostitute.

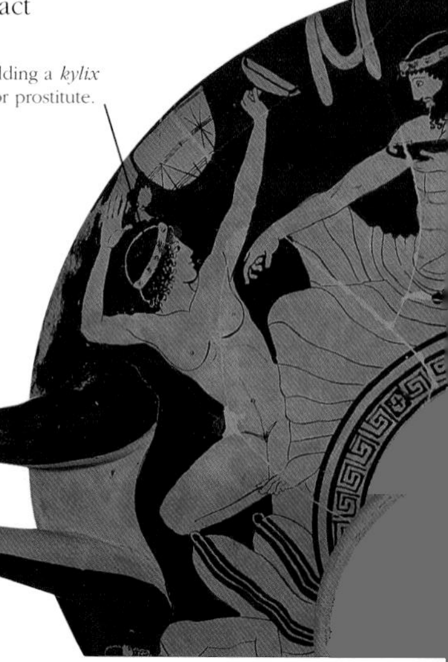

***The white-ground* lekythos** *was developed in the 5th century BC as an oil flask for grave offerings. They were usually decorated with funeral scenes, and this one, by the Achilles Painter, shows a woman placing flowers at a grave.*

The Symposion

These episodes of mostly male feasting and drinking were also occasions for playing the game of *kottabos*. On the exterior of this 5th-century BC *kylix* are depictions of men holding cups, ready to flick out the dregs at a target.

The Development of Painting Styles

Vase painting reached its peak in 6th- and 5th-century BC Athens. In the potter's workshop, a fired vase would be passed to a painter to be decorated. Archaeologists have been able to identify the varying styles of many individual painters of both black-figure and red-figure ware.

The body of the dead man is carried on a bier by mourners.

The geometric design is a prototype of the later "Greek-key" pattern.

Chariots and warriors form the funeral procession.

Geometric style *characterizes the earliest Greek vases, from around 1000 to 700 BC, in which the decoration is in bands of figures and geometric patterns. This 8th-century BC vase placed on a grave as a marker is more than 1 m (3 ft) high and depicts the bier and funeral rites of a dead man.*

Eye cups *were given an almost magical power by the painted eyes. The pointed base suggests that they were passed around during feasting.*

***The* rhyton**, *such as this one in the shape of a ram's head, was a drinking vessel for watered-down wine. The scene of the* symposion *around the rim indicates when it would have been used.*

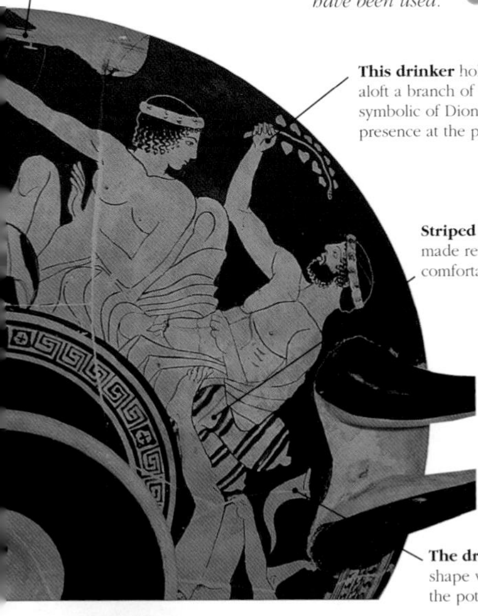

This *kylix* is being held by one handle by another woman feaster, ready to flick out the dregs at a *kottabos* target.

This drinker holds aloft a branch of a vine, symbolic of Dionysos's presence at the party.

Striped cushions made reclining more comfortable.

The drinking horn shape was copied in the pottery *rhyton.*

Black-figure style *was first used in Athens around 630 BC. The figures were painted in black liquid clay onto the iron-rich clay of the vase, which turned orange when fired. This vase is signed by the potter and painter Exekias.*

Red-figure style *was introduced in c.530 BC. The figures were left in the color of the clay, silhouetted against a black glaze. Here a woman pours from an* oinochoe *(wine-jug).*

Vase Shapes

Almost all Greek vases were made to be used; their shapes are closely related to their intended uses. Athenian potters had about 20 different forms to choose from. Below are some of the most commonly made shapes and their uses.

***The* amphora** *was a two-handled vessel used to store wine, olive oil, and foods preserved in liquid such as olives. It also held dried foods.*

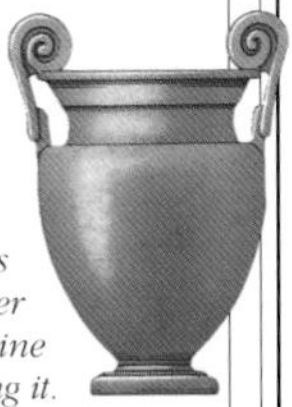

***This* krater** *with curled handles or "volutes" is a wide-mouthed vase in which the Greeks mixed water with their wine before drinking it.*

***The* hydria** *was used to carry water from the fountain. Of the three handles, one was vertical for holding and pouring, two horizontal for lifting.*

***The* lekythos** *could vary in height from 3 cm (1 in) to nearly 1 m (39 in). It was used to hold oil both in the home and as a funerary gift to the dead.*

***The* oinochoe**, *the standard wine jug, had a round or trefoil mouth for pouring, and just one handle.*

***The* kylix**, *a two-handled drinking cup, was one shape that could take interior decoration.*

The Greek Islands Area by Area

The Greek Islands at a Glance

THE GREEK ISLANDS range in size from tiny uninhabited rocks to the substantial islands of Crete and Evvoia. Over the centuries, the sea has brought settlers and invaders and provided the inhabitants with their way of life; it now attracts millions of visitors. Each island has developed its own character through a mix of landscape, climate, and cultural heritage. As well as the scattered historical sites, there is enough remote, rugged terrain to satisfy the most discerning walker and, of course, the variety of beaches is extraordinary.

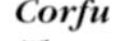

Skópelos
The capital of this rugged island (see pp108–9), *Skópelos town, spills down from the hilltop kástro to the sea.*

Corfu
The most visited of the Ionians, Corfu (see pp68–79) *is a green, fertile island. Corfu town, its capital, contains a maze of narrow streets overlooked by two Venetian fortresses.*

KEY

Athens

Aígina
Home to the spectacular and well-preserved ancient Temple of Aphaia, Aígina (see pp92–5) *has a rich history due to its proximity to Athens.*

Crete
The largest Greek island, Crete (see pp240–77) *encompasses historic cities, ancient Minoan palaces, such as Knosós, and dramatic landscapes, including the Samaria Gorge (right).*

◁ **Windmills in village of Olympos, Kárpathos**

Delos
This tiny island (see pp214–15) *is scattered with the ruins of an important ancient city. From its beginnings as a center for the worship of Apollo in 1000 BC until its sacking in the 1st century AD, Delos was a thriving cultural and religious center.*

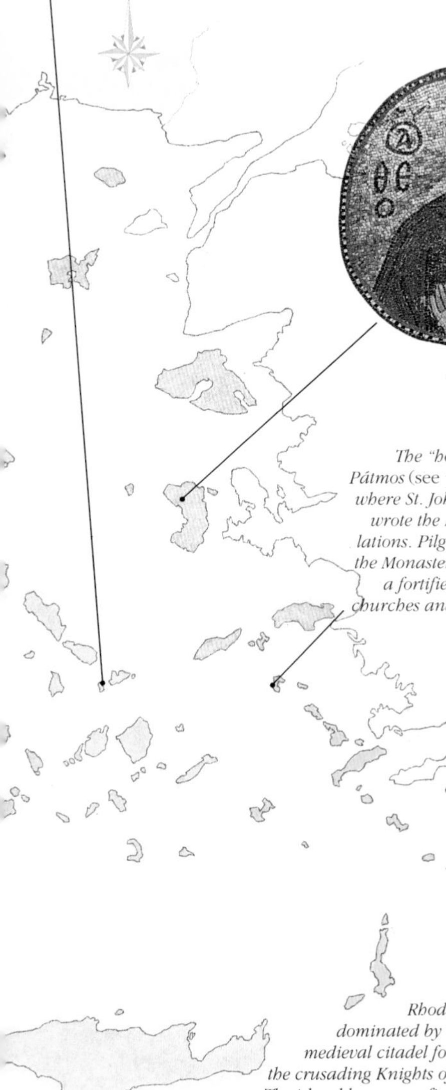

Chíos
The Byzantine monastery of Néa Moní in the center of the island (see pp142–9) *contains beautiful mosaics, which survived a severe earthquake in 1881. The mastic villages in the south of the island prospered from the wealth generated by the medieval trade in mastic gum.*

Pátmos
The "holy island" of Pátmos (see pp158–61) *is where St. John the Divine wrote the Book of Revelations. Pilgrims still visit the Monastery of St. John, a fortified complex of churches and courtyards.*

0 kilometers 100

0 miles 50

Rhodes
Rhodes town is dominated by its walled medieval citadel founded by the crusading Knights of St. John. The island has many fine beaches and, inland, some unspoiled villages and remote monasteries (see pp176–93).

The Ionian Islands

CORFU · PAXOS · LEFKADA · ITHACA · KEFALLONIA · ZAKYNTHOS

THE IONIAN ISLANDS *are the greenest and most fertile of all the island groups, characterized by olive groves and cypresses. Lying off the west coast of mainland Greece, these islands have been greatly influenced by Western Europe, in part because the Turks never managed to gain control here, except on the island of Lefkáda.*

Famous as the homeland of Homer's Odysseus, these islands were colonized by the Corinthians in the 8th century BC and flourished as a wealthy trading post. In the 5th century BC Corfu defeated Corinth and joined the Athenians, instigating the Peloponnesian Wars. The Ionians first became a holiday destination during the Roman era.

Gorgon pediment in Corfu town's Archaeological Museum

The islands were not politically grouped together until Byzantine times. They were later occupied by the Venetians whose rule began in 1363 and lasted until 1797. After a brief period of French rule the British took over in 1814. The islands were finally ceded to the Greek state in 1864.

Evidence of the various periods of occupation can be seen throughout the islands, especially in Corfu town, which contains a mixture of Italian, French, and British architecture.

Each island has its own distinct character, from tiny Paxos covered in olive groves, to rocky Ithaca, the rugged beauty of Kefalloniá and mountainous Corfu. The group historically includes Kýthira, but in this guide it is included under the Argo-Saronic islands because of easier transport connections. The islands lie on a fault line that runs south down Greece's west coast and have been subjected to much earthquake damage. Kefalloniá and Zákynthos in particular suffered massive destruction in the summer of 1953.

Summers are hot and dry but for the rest of the year the islands have a mild climate; the above-average rainfall supports the lush greenery. There is a huge variety of beaches throughout the Ionians, from resorts providing lively nightlife to quieter stretches, virtually untouched by tourism.

Watching from the shade as a ship comes into Sámi town, Kefalloniá

◁ **The islet of Vlachérne with its small convent, reached by a short causeway from Corfu island**

Exploring the Ionian Islands

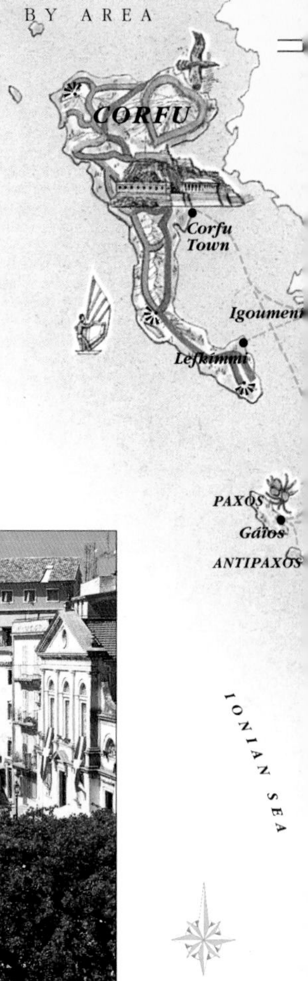

THE WIDELY SCATTERED Ionian Islands are not particularly well connected with each other, though most are easily reached from the mainland. Corfu is the best base for the northern islands and Kefalloniá for the southern islands. There are few archaeological remains, and museums tend to concentrate on folklore, culture, and historical European links. Today's tourists come mostly for beach vacations. The main islands are large enough to cater to those who like bars and discos, as well as those who prefer a quieter stay, in a family resort or simply in a small fishing village. Traditional Greek life does exist here, inland on the larger islands and on islands such as Meganísi off Lefkáda, or Mathráki, Othoní, and Erikoúsa off northern Corfu.

CORFU
Corfu Town
Igoumeni
Lefkímmi
PAXOS
Gáïos
ANTIPAXOS
IONIAN SEA

Islands at a Glance

Looking down on Plateía Dimarcheíou in Corfu town with the town hall on the left

See Also

• ***Where to Stay*** pp298–9
• ***Where to Eat*** pp322–3
• ***Travel Information*** pp356–9

A typical house by the roadside in Stávros village on Ithaca

Key

- Major road
- Paved road
- Unpaved road
- Scenic route
- Tourist-season, direct ferry route
- Viewpoint

0 kilometers 25

0 miles 25

The mountain landscape of Lefkáda

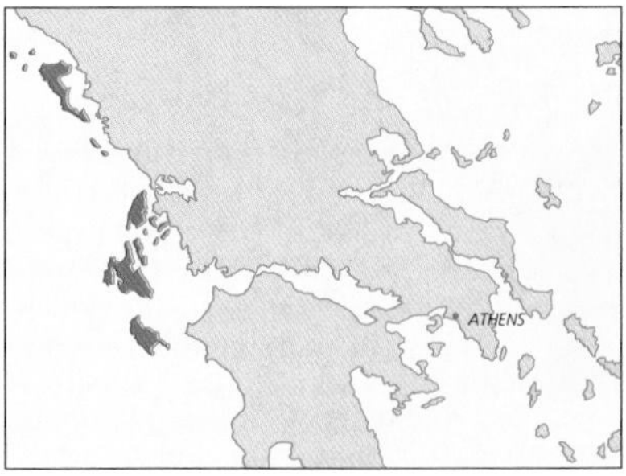

ATHENS

Locator Map

Getting Around

Aside from Ithaca and Paxos, all the main Ionians can be reached by air, Préveza airport serving Lefkáda, which is also connected to the mainland by a road bridge. Larger ferries often travel via the mainland, but smaller boats offer direct connections between the islands. Islands often have several ports, so check specific destinations. Buses in the capitals provide services radiating out around the islands, with taxis filling the gaps. Car and bike rental is widespread, but road standards vary considerably, as do local road maps.

An islander working on his boat in Gäïos harbor on Paxos

Vacation apartments at Fiskárdo on Kefalloniá

Corfu

Κέρκυρα

Detail from Corfu Town Hall

CORFU IS A GREEN ISLAND offering the diverse attractions of secluded coves, stretches of wild coast, bands of coast given over totally to resorts, and traditional hill villages. In 229 BC it was taken over by Rome, remaining so until AD 337. Byzantine rule then began, intermittently broken by Gothic, Norman, and Angevin rule. Situated between Italy and the Greek mainland, its strategic importance continued under Venetian rule (1386–1797). French rule (1807–14) saw the Greek language restored and the founding of the Ionian Academy, set up for the development of the arts. A period of British rule (1814–64) was followed by unification with Greece.

Angelókastro is a ruined 13th-century fortress that stands across the bay from Palaiokastrítsa *(see p77).*

Myrtiótissa is one of Corfu's finest beaches *(see p78).*

Sidári
Unusual rock formations, produced by the effect of sea on sandstone, give the resort of Sidári its appeal. Legend has it that any couple swimming through the Canal d'Amour will stay together forever ❺

Vátos
This traditional Greek hill village is set above the fertile Ropa plain ❼

Palaiokastrítsa
Three main coves cluster around a thickly wooded headland at Palaiokastrítsa. It is now one of the most popular spots on the island and is an ideal base for families, with water sports available and a friendly atmosphere ❻

Korisíon Lagoon
This lake is a haven for wildlife and is separated from the Ionian Sea only by some beautiful beaches ❽

KEY

For key to map see back flap

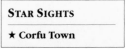

0 kilometers 5

0 miles 3

STAR SIGHTS

★ Corfu Town

Kassiópi
The unspoiled bay at Kassiópi is overlooked by an attractive wharf lined with tavernas, shops, and bars ❹

Visitors' Checklist

100,000. 3 km (1.5 miles) S of Corfu town. Xenofóntos Stratigoú, Corfu town. Corfu town (0661 37520). Cultural festival at Ano Korakiána: Aug 1–15; festival at Benítses: July 17.

Mount Pantokrátor
This is the highest point on Corfu and offers excellent views of the island and, on a clear day, as far as Italy ❸

Kalámi
Made famous by the author Lawrence Durrell, Kalámi remains an attractive coastal village ❷

★ Corfu Town
Corfu town is a delightful blend of European influences. The Liston, focus of café life, was built during the brief French rule. It overlooks the Esplanade that dates to Venetian rule in the town ❶

Achílleion Palace
The Empress Elizabeth of Austria built this palace (1890–91) ❿

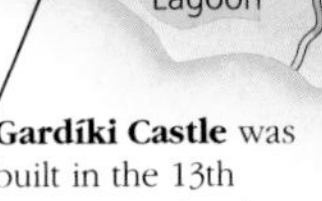

Gardíki Castle was built in the 13th century on the site of Paleolithic remains *(see p78)*.

Benítses
An archetypal package vacation resort, Benítses appeals to a young crowd. There is plenty of nightlife, and the beach offers every conceivable water sport ❾

Street-by-Street: Corfu Old Town ❶

Πόλις της Κέρκυρας

The 20th century has not spoiled Corfu town, and it continues to be a delightful blend of European influences. The Venetians ruled here for over four centuries, and elegant Italianate buildings, with balconies and shutters, can be seen above French-style colonnades. British rule left a wealth of monuments, public buildings, and also the cricket pitch, which is part of the Esplanade, or Spianáda *(see pp72–3)*. This large park, still a venue for cricket matches, is a focus for both locals and tourists, with park games and good walks. On its eastern side is the Old Fortress *(see p74)* standing guard over the town, a reminder that Corfu was never conquered by the Turks.

View of the Old Fortress from Corfu Old Town

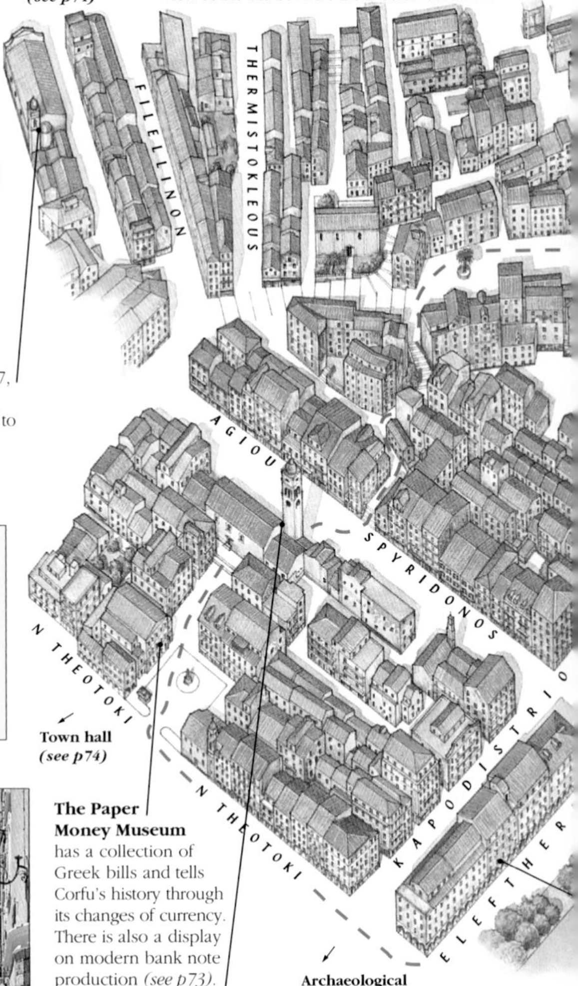

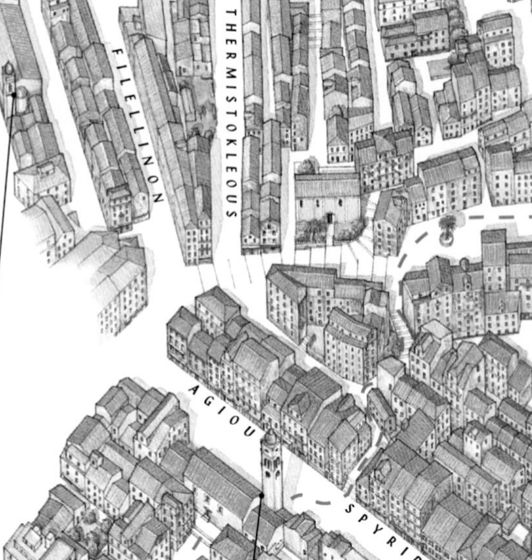

New Fortress ***(see p74)***

The Mitrópoli was built in 1577, and became Corfu's Orthodox cathedral in 1841. It is dedicated to St. Theodora, whose remains are housed here along with some impressive gold icons.

Star Sights

- ★ **Palace of St. Michael and St. George**
- ★ **The Liston**
- ★ **Agios Spyrídon**

Town hall ***(see p74)***

The Paper Money Museum has a collection of Greek bills and tells Corfu's history through its changes of currency. There is also a display on modern bank note production *(see p73)*.

Archaeological Museum ***(see pp74–5)***

★ Agios Spyrídon

The red-domed belfry of this church is the tallest on Corfu. It was built in 1589 and dedicated to the island's patron saint, whose sarcophagus is just to the right of the altar (see p72).

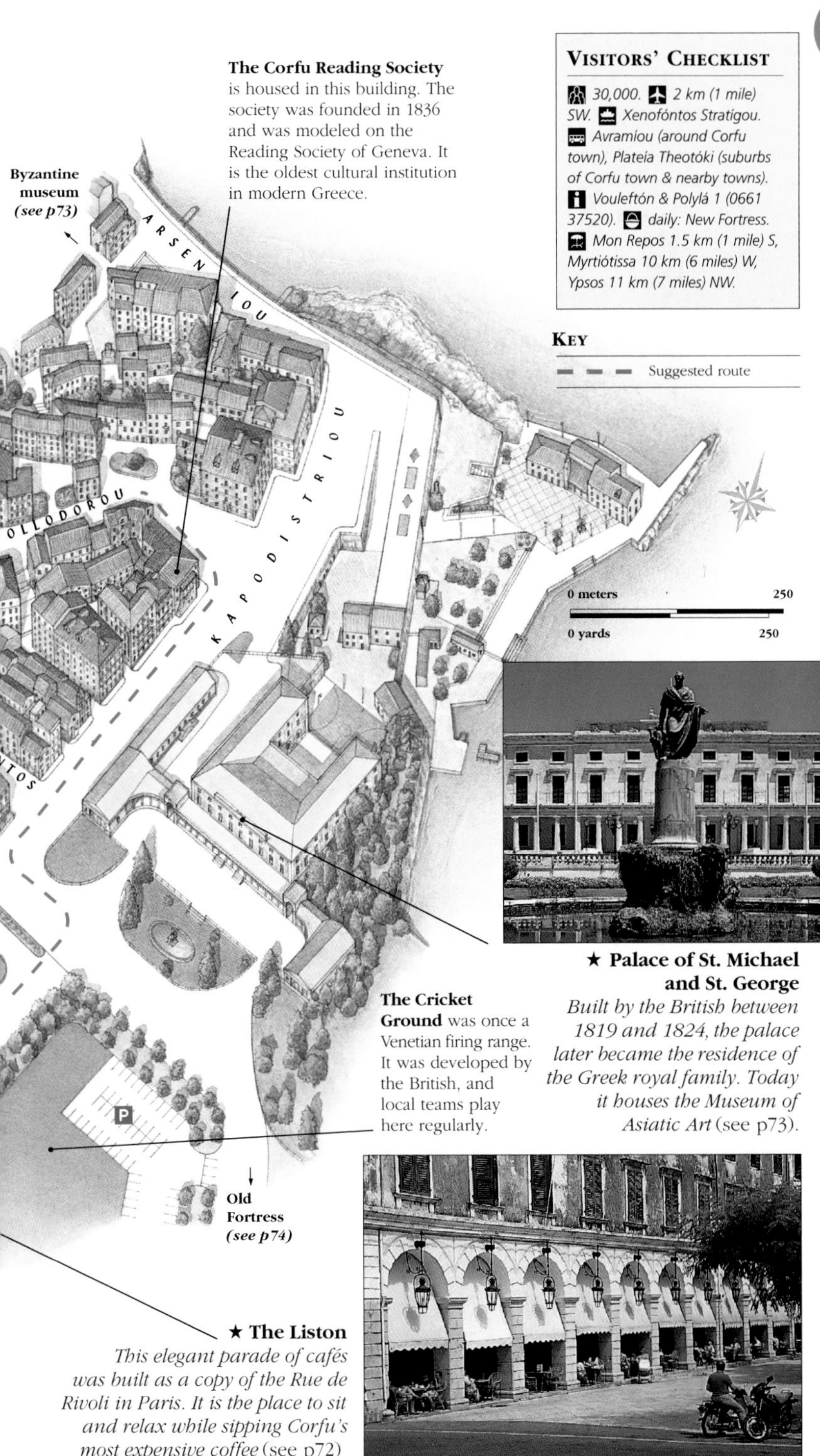

The Corfu Reading Society is housed in this building. The society was founded in 1836 and was modeled on the Reading Society of Geneva. It is the oldest cultural institution in modern Greece.

Byzantine museum *(see p73)*

Visitors' Checklist

30,000. 2 km (1 mile) SW. Xenofóntos Stratígou. Avramíou (around Corfu town), Plateía Theotóki (suburbs of Corfu town & nearby towns). Vouleftón & Polylá 1 (0661 37520). daily: New Fortress. Mon Repos 1.5 km (1 mile) S, Myrtiótissa 10 km (6 miles) W, Ypsos 11 km (7 miles) NW.

Key

Suggested route

★ Palace of St. Michael and St. George

Built by the British between 1819 and 1824, the palace later became the residence of the Greek royal family. Today it houses the Museum of Asiatic Art (see p73).

The Cricket Ground was once a Venetian firing range. It was developed by the British, and local teams play here regularly.

Old Fortress *(see p74)*

★ The Liston

This elegant parade of cafés was built as a copy of the Rue de Rivoli in Paris. It is the place to sit and relax while sipping Corfu's most expensive coffee (see p72)

Exploring Corfu Town

IN MIDSUMMER THE narrow streets of Corfu's old town may be packed with visitors, but there are always quiet places to be found down alleyways and shady cobbled squares. The Corfiot housewives string washing across the streets from their balconies and, below, silversmiths and wood-carvers' shops are hidden away in the maze of alleys. On Nikifórou Theotóki, the southern boundary of the old town, there are several elegant arcaded sections. Built by the French, they are now home to souvenir shops, chapels and churches. Parts of the surrounding new town are quite modern, but many of the buildings date back to French and British rule.

Corfu town by horse and trap

Agios Spyrídon

Agíou Spyrídonos. 0661 330759. *daily.*

The distinctive red-domed tower of Agios Spyrídon guides the visitor to this church, the holiest place on the island. Inside, in a silver casket, is the mummified body of the revered saint, after whom many Corfiot men are named.

Spyrídon himself was not from Corfu but from Cyprus, where he was raised as a shepherd. Later he entered the church and rose to the rank of bishop. He is believed to have performed many miracles before his death in AD 350, and others since – not least in 1716 when he is said to have helped drive the Turks from the island after a six-week siege. His body was smuggled from Constantinople just before the Turkish occupation of 1453. It was only by chance that it came to Corfu, where the present church was built in 1589 to house his coffin.

The church is also worth seeing for the immense amount of silverware brought by the constant stream of pilgrims. On four occasions each year (Palm Sunday, Easter Saturday, August 11, and the first Sunday in November) the saint's remains are carried aloft through the streets.

Esplanade

This mixture of park and town square is one of the reasons Corfu town remains such an attractive place. Known as the Esplanade, or Spianáda, it offers relief from the packed streets in summer, either on a park bench or in one of the elegant cafés lining the square on the **Liston**, overlooking the cricket pitch.

The Liston was designed by a Frenchman, Mathieu de Lesseps, who built it in 1807. The name Liston comes from the Venetian practice of having a "List" of noble families in the *Libro d'Oro* or Golden Book – only those on this list were allowed to promenade here.

There are a number of monuments in and around the Esplanade. Near the fountain is the **Enosis Monument**: the word *énosis* means unification, and this celebrates the 1864 union of the Ionian islands with the rest of Greece, when British rule came to an end. The marble monument has carvings of the symbols of each of the Ionian islands.

A statue of **Ioánnis Kapodístrias**, modern Greece's first president in 1827 and a native of Corfu, stands at the end of the street that flanks the Esplanade and bears

Agios Spyrídon, seen down one of the many small shopping alleyways

A game of cricket on the pitch by the Esplanade

his name. He was assassinated in Náfplio in the Peloponnese in 1831 by two Cretans whose uncle he had imprisoned.

Facing this is the **Maitland Rotunda** (1816), a memorial to Sir Thomas Maitland, who became Britain's first Lord High Commissioner to Corfu after the island became a British Protectorate in 1814, though neither he nor his policies were much liked.

Palace of St. Michael and St. George

Plateía Spianáda. 0661 30443. Tue–Sun. main public hols.

The Palace of St. Michael and St. George was built by the British between 1819–24 from Maltese limestone. It served as the residence of Sir Thomas Maitland, the High Commissioner, and as such is the oldest official building in Greece. When the British left Corfu in 1864 the palace was used for a short time by the Greek royal family, but it was later abandoned and left to fall into disrepair.

The palace was carefully renovated in the 1950s by Sir Charles Peake, British Ambassador to Greece, and now houses the traffic police, a library, and some government offices. Conferences and exhibitions are also held in the palace from time-to-time.

The Palace of St. Michael and St. George also houses the **Museum of Asiatic Art**. The core of the museum's collection is the 10,000 items that were collected by a Corfiot diplomat, Grigórios Mános (1850–1929), during his travels overseas. He offered his vast collection to the state on condition that he could retire and become curator of the museum. Unfortunately he died before he could realise his ambition. The exhibits include statues, screens, armor, silk, and ceramics from China, Japan, India and other Asiatic countries.

In front of the building is a statue of **Sir Frederick Adam**, the British High Commissioner to Corfu from 1824–31. He built the Mon Repos villa *(see p75)*, to the south of town and was also responsible for popularizing the west coast resort of Palaiokastrítsa *(see p77)*, one of his favorite spots on the island.

Statue of Sir Frederick Adam

Byzantine Museum

Prosfórou 30 & Arseníou. *0661 38313.* *Tue–Sun.* *main public hols.*

The Byzantine Museum opened in 1984 and is housed in the renovated church of Panagía Antivouniótissa, which provided some of the exhibits. The museum contains about 90 icons dating back to the 15th century. It also has work by artists from the Cretan School. Many of these artists worked and lived on Corfu, as it was a convenient stopping-off point on the journey between Crete and Venice from the 13th to the 17th centuries during the period of Venetian rule.

Paper Money Museum

Ionikí Trapéza, Plateía Iróon Kypriakoú Agóna. *0661 41552.* *Tue, Thu.* *main public hols.*

This complete collection of Greek bank notes traces the way in which the island's currency has altered as Corfu's society and rulers changed. The first bank note on the island was issued in British pounds, while later notes show the German and Italian currency of the war years. Another intriguing display shows the process of producing a note from the artistic design to engraving and printing.

Maitland Rotunda situated in the Esplanade

The Old Fortress towering above the sea on the eastern side of Corfu town

Old Fortress

0661 48310. daily. main public hols. except Sun. limited.

The ruined Old Fortress, or Palaió Froúrio, stands on a promontory believed to have been fortified since at least the 7th or 8th century AD; archaeological digs are still underway. The Old Fortress itself was constructed by the Venetians, who began building it in 1550 and completed it in 1559. The very top of the fortress gives magnificent views of the town and along the island's picturesque east coast. Lower down is the church of St. George, a British garrison church built in 1840. The fortress is also a venue for summer sound and light shows, preceded by Ionian folk dancing displays.

New Fortress

Plateía Solomoú. 0661 27477. Apr–Oct: daily.

The Venetians began building the New Fortress, or Néo Froúrio, in 1576 to further strengthen the town's defenses. It was not completed until 1589, 30 years after the Old Fortress, hence their respective names. The fortress is used by the Greek navy as a training base, while the surrounding moat is the setting for the town's market.

Mitrópoli

Mitropóleos. 0661 39409. daily.

The Greek Orthodox church of the Panagía Spiliótissa, or Virgin Mary of the Cave, was built in 1577. It became Corfu's cathedral in 1841, when the nave was extended. It is dedicated to St. Theodora, a former Byzantine Empress whose remains were brought to Corfu at the same time as those of St. Spyrídon. Her body is in a silver coffin near the altar.

The 17th-century Catholic cathedral Agios Iákovos in Plateía Dimarcheíou

Plateía Dimarcheíou

Town Hall 0661 40402. daily. main public hols.
Agios Iákovos daily.

Within this elegant square stands the **Town Hall**. It is a grand Venetian building that began life in 1663 as a single-story *loggia* or meeting place for the nobility. It was then converted into the San Giacomo Theater in 1720, which made it the first modern theater in Greece. The British added the second floor in 1903 when it became the Town Hall.

Adjacent to it is the Catholic cathedral **Agios Iákovos**, also known by its Italian name of San Giacomo. Built in 1588 and consecrated in 1633, it was badly damaged by bombing in 1943 with only the bell tower surviving intact. Services are held every day, with three masses on Sundays.

Archaeological Museum

Vraíla 1. 0661 30680. Tue–Sun. main public hols.

The Archaeological Museum is situated a pleasant stroll south from the center of town, along the waterfront. The museum's collection is not large, but a visit is worthwhile to see the centerpiece, the stunning Gorgon frieze.

The frieze, dating from the 6th century BC, originally formed part of the west pediment of the Temple of Artemis near Mon Repos Villa. The layout ensures that

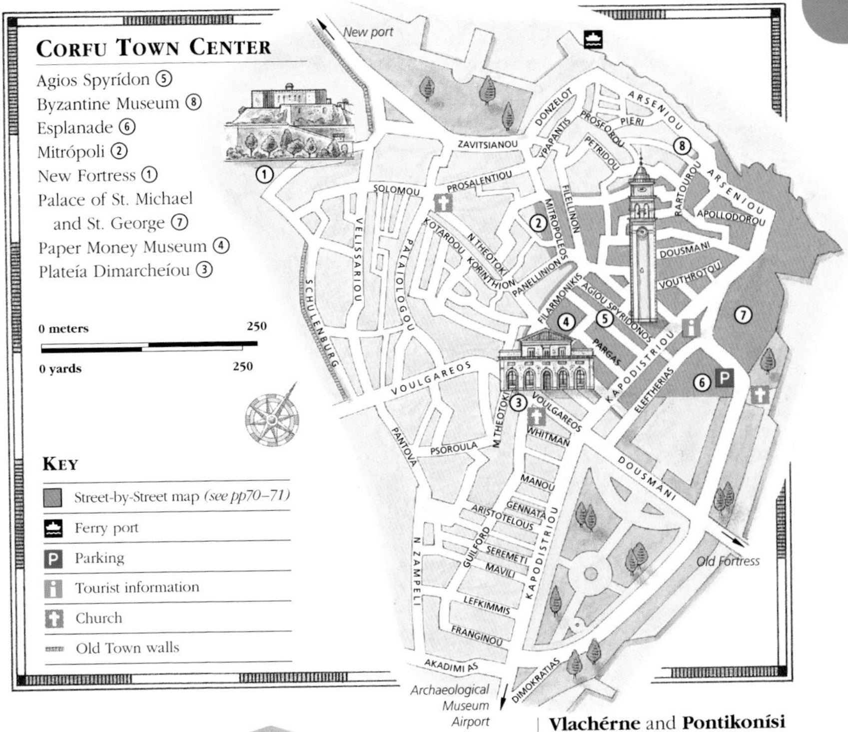

Corfu Town Center

Agios Spyrídon ⑤
Byzantine Museum ⑧
Esplanade ⑥
Mitrópoli ②
New Fortress ①
Palace of St. Michael and St. George ⑦
Paper Money Museum ④
Plateía Dimarcheíou ③

0 meters 250
0 yards 250

Key

Street-by-Street map (see pp70–71)
Ferry port
Parking
Tourist information
Church
Old Town walls

The Gorgon frieze in Corfu town's Archaeological Museum

the frieze, a massive 17 m (56 ft) long, is not seen until the final room. The museum also displays other finds from the Temple of Artemis and the excavations at Mon Repos Villa.

Environs: Garítsa Bay sweeps south of Corfu town, with the suburb of Anemómilos visible on the promontory. Here, in the street named after it, is the 11th-century church of **Agios Iásonos kai Sosipátrou** (Saints Jason and Sossipater). These disciples of St. Paul brought Christianity to Corfu in the 1st century AD. Inside are faded wall paintings, including an 11th-century fresco.

South of Anemómilos is **Mon Repos Villa.** It was built in 1824 by Sir Frederick Adam, the second High Commissioner of the Ionian state, as a present for his wife, and was later passed to the Greek royal family. The remains of the **Temple of Artemis** lie nearby. Opposite the villa are the 5th-century ruins of **Agía Kérkyra**, the church of the Old City.

An hour's walk or a short bus ride south of Corfu town is **Kanóni,** with the islands of **Vlachérne** and **Pontikonísi** just off the coast. Vlachérna, with its tiny white convent, is among Corfu's most famous landmarks and can be reached by a causeway. In summer boats go to Pontikonísi, or Mouse Island, said to be Odysseus's ship turned to stone by Poseidon. This caused Odysseus to be shipwrecked on Phaeacia, the island often closely identified with Corfu in Homer's Odyssey.

Mon Repos Villa
April–Oct: daily.

The church of Agios Iásonos kai Sosipátrou

Around Northern Corfu

NORTHERN CORFU, in particular the northeast coast, is emphatically vacation Corfu, with a string of resorts along the main coast road. These include popular spots such as Kassiópi and Sidári, though there are also quieter villages like Kalámi. In the northwest is one of Corfu's prettiest areas, Palaiokastrítsa, a jigsaw of bays and beaches. Inland stands Mount Pantokrátor, a reminder that there is also a rugged interior to explore.

View looking southward over the beach at Kalámi Bay

Kalámi ❷

Καλάμι

26 km (16 miles) NE of Corfu town.
18. to Kassiópi.

Kalámi village has retained its charm despite its popularity with visitors. A handful of tavernas lines its sand and shingle beach, while behind them cypress trees and olive groves climb up to the lower slopes of Mount Pantokrátor. The hills of Albania are a little over 2 km (1 mile) across Kalámi Bay.

Kalámi's obvious appeal attracted the author Lawrence Durrell to the village in 1939. Only during the day in tourist season, when visitors from resorts throng his "peaceful fishing village," might Durrell fail to recognize the place. In the evenings and outside the months of July and August, normalcy returns.

Mount Pantokrátor ❸

Ορος Παντοκράτωρ

29 km (18 miles) N of Corfu town.
to Petáleia.

Mount Pantokrátor, whose name means "the Almighty," dominates the northeast bulge of Corfu. It rises so steeply that its peak, at 906 m (2,972 ft), is less than 3 km (2 miles) from the beach resorts of Nisáki and Mparmpáti. The easiest approach is from the north, where a rough road goes all the way to the small monastery at the top. The mountain has great appeal to naturalists as well as walkers, but exploring its slopes is not something to be undertaken lightly, as Corfu's weather can change suddenly. However, the reward is a view to Albania and Epirus in the east, of Corfu town to the south, and even west to Italy when weather conditions are clear.

Kassiópi ❹

Κασσιόπι

37 km (23 miles) N of Corfu town.
600. Avláki 2 km (1 mile) S.

Kassiópi has developed into one of Corfu's busiest vacation centers without losing either its charm or character. It is set around a harbor that lies between two wooded headlands. Although there is plenty of nightlife to attract younger vacationers, there are no high-rise hotels to spoil the setting. The heart of the town is at its harbor, with tavernas and souvenir shops overlooking fishing boats moored alongside motor boats from the many water sports schools.

In the 1st century AD the Emperor Nero is said to have visited a Temple of Jupiter, which was situated on the western side of the harbor, where the church of **Kassiopítissa** now stands. The ruins of a 13th-century castle are a short walk farther west.

Fishing boats moored in Kassiópi harbor, east of the castle ruins

The caretaker monk of Moní Theotókou, Palaiokastrítsa

Sidári ❺

Σιδάρι

31 km (20 miles) NW of Corfu town. *300.* *Róda 6 km (4 miles) E.*

One of Corfu's first settlements, the village of Sidári has pre-Neolithic remains dating back to about 7000 BC. Today it is a bustling vacation center with the twin attractions of sandy beaches and unusual rock formations. Erosion of the sandstone has created a number of caves and tunnels, the most famous being a channel between two rocks known as the Canal d'Amour *(see p68)*.

Palaiokastrítsa ❻

Παλαιοκαστρίτσα

26 km (16 miles) NW of Corfu town.

 *600.*

Palaiokastrítsa is one of Corfu's most popular spots. Three main coves cluster around a wooded headland, dividing into numerous other beaches that are popular with families because swimming is safe. Water sports are available, as well as boat trips to the nearby grottoes. Until the early 19th century the place was noted for its beauty, but access was difficult. The British High Commissioner, Sir Frederick Adam *(see p73)*, loved to picnic here but did not like the difficult journey from Corfu town, so he had a road built between the two.

On the main headland stands **Moní Theotókou**, which dates from the 17th century, although the first monastery stood here in 1228. The church's ceiling features a fine carving of the *Tree of Life*.

Views from the monastery include **Angelókastro**, the ruined 13th-century fortress of Michaíl Angelos Komninós II, the Byzantine Despot of Epirus. Situated above the cliffs west of Palaiokastrítsa, the fortress was never taken, and in 1571 it sheltered locals from another failed Turkish attempt to conquer Corfu. The remains include a hilltop chapel and some hermit cells and caves.

Outlying Islands

Corfu has three offshore islands. **Mathráki** offers the simplest Greek island life, with two villages and only a few rooms to rent. **Ereikoússa** is the most popular island, because of its glorious sandy beaches. **Othonoí**, the largest island, has the best facilities but lacks the finer beaches.

Writers and Artists in Corfu

The poet Dionýsios Solomós lived on Corfu from 1828 until his death in 1857. He is best known for his poem Hymn to Freedom, part of which was adopted as the national anthem after Independence. Other writers have also found inspiration on Corfu, including the British poet and artist Edward Lear, who visited the island in the 19th century, and the Durrell brothers, who both wrote about Corfu. Gerald described his idyllic 1930s childhood in *My Family and Other Animals*, and Lawrence produced *Prospero's Cell* in 1945. He wrote this while staying in Kalámi, where he was visited by Henry Miller, whose 1941 book *The Colossus of Maroussi* is one of the most accurate and endearing books about Greece.

A view from the Benítses road near Gastoúri, by Edward Lear

Around Southern Corfu

Less mountainous but more varied than the north, southern Corfu encompasses Benítses' wild nightlife and the shy wildlife of the Korisíon Lagoon. Much of Corfu's produce grows in the fertile Rópa Plain north of Vátos. To the south lies Myrtiótissa, once described as the world's most beautiful beach. Bus services are good but to explore off the beaten track you will need your own car.

View inland over the freshwater Korisíon Lagoon

Vátos ❼

Βάτος

24 km (15 miles) W of Corfu town.
480. Myrtiótissa 2 km (1 mile) S, Ermones 2 km (1 mile) W.

In the hillside village of Vátos, the whitewashed houses with flower-bedecked balconies offer a traditional image of Greece. Vátos has only two tavernas and a handful of shops and has mostly remained untainted by the impact of tourism. From the village, a steep climb leads up the mountainside to the top of Agios Geórgios (392 m; 1,286 ft), while below lies the fertile Rópa Plain and the beach at busy Ermones.

Environs: The glorious beach at **Myrtiótissa**, 2 km (1 mile) south of Vátos, is named after the 14th-century monastery behind it dedicated to Panagía Myrtiótissa (Our Lady of the Myrtles). The beach is a long golden sweep of sand backed with cypress and olive trees. Lawrence Durrell was fond of the area and, in his book *Prospero's Cell*, referred to Myrtiótissa as "perhaps the loveliest beach in the world."

South of Vátos lies **Pélekas**, another picturesque and unspoiled hillside village. Its traditional houses tumble down wooded slopes to the small and secluded beach below. Above this is the **Kaiser's Throne**, the hilltop from which Kaiser Wilhelm II of Germany loved to watch the sunset while staying at the Achílleion Palace.

Korisíon Lagoon ❽

Λίμνι Κορισσίων

42 km (26 miles) S of Corfu town.
Gardiki 1 km (0.5 mile) N.

The Korisíon Lagoon is a 5-km (3-mile) stretch of water separated from the sea by some of the most beautiful dunes and beaches on Corfu. The lake remains a haven for wildlife, despite the Greek love of hunting. At the water's edge are a variety of waders such as sandpipers and avocets, egrets and ibis. Flowers include sea daffodils and Jersey orchids.

Almost 2 km (1 mile) north lies **Gardíki Castle**, built in the 13th century by Michaíl Angelos Komninós II *(see p77)*, with the ruined towers and outer castle walls still standing. The site is also known for a find of Paleolithic remains, now removed.

Benítses ❾

Μπενίτσες

14 km (9 miles) S of Corfu town.
1,400. Benitses.

Benítses has become the archetypal package resort. Its appeal is to young people and not to those seeking peace and quiet or a real flavor of Greece.

The beaches offer every conceivable water sport, and at the height of the season are extremely busy. The nightlife is also very lively: the bars and discos close about the same time as the local fishermen return from their night at sea.

There are few sights of interest in Benítses other than the remains of a Roman bathhouse near the harbor square.

A whitewashed house in the attractive village of Vátos

Achílleion Palace ⓾

Αχίλλειον

19 km (12 miles) SW of Corfu town.

0661 56210. **Palace & gardens** *daily.*

A popular day trip from any of Corfu's resorts is to the Achílleion Palace. It was built in 1890–91 by the Italian architect Raphael Carita for the Empress Elizabeth of Austria (1837–98), formerly Elizabeth of Bavaria. She used it as a personal retreat from the problems she was enduring at the Hapsburg court. Her health was poor and her husband, Emperor Franz Josef, notoriously unfaithful. After the assassination of the Empress Elizabeth by an Italian anarchist in 1898, the palace lay empty for nearly a decade until it was bought by Kaiser Wilhelm II in 1907. The Achílleion is famous as the set used for the casino in the James Bond movie *For Your Eyes Only.*

The outer entrance to the Achílleion's gardens

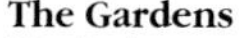

The Gardens

The lush green gardens below the palace are terraced on a slope that drops 150 m (492 ft) to the coast road. The views along the rugged coast both north and south are spectacular. In the grounds the walls are draped with colourful bougainvillea and a profusion of palm trees. The gardens are also dotted with numerous statues, especially of Achilles, who was the empress's hero, after whom the palace is named. One moving bronze of the *Dying Achilles* is by the German sculptor, Ernst Herter. The statue is thought to have appealed to the unhappy empress following the tragic suicide of her second son, the Archduke Rudolph, at Mayerling. Another impressive statue of the hero Achilles is the massive 15-m (49-ft) high, cast iron figure, which was commissioned by Kaiser Wilhelm II.

A 19th-century painting of Elizabeth of Bavaria by Franz Xavier

The Palace

There have been numerous attempts to describe the Achílleion's architectural style, ranging from Neo-Classical to Teutonic, although Lawrence Durrell was more forthright, and declared it "a monstrous building." The empress was not particularly pleased with the finished building, but her fondness for Corfu made her decide to stay.

The palace does however contain a number of interesting artifacts. Inside, some original furniture is on display, and on the walls there are some fine paintings of Achilles, echoing the bronze and stone statues seen in the gardens. Another exhibit is the strange saddle-seat that was used by Kaiser Wilhelm II whenever he was writing at his desk.

Visitors requiring a pick-me-up after touring the palace can try the Vasilákis Tastery, opposite the entrance, and sample this local distiller's many products, which include a number of Corfiot wines, ouzo and the specialty kumquat liqueur.

THE LEGEND OF ACHILLES

Shortly after his birth, Achilles was immersed in the River Styx by his mother Thetis. This left him invulnerable apart from the heel where she had held him. Achilles' destiny lay at Troy *(see pp52–3)*; Helen, the wife of King Menelaos of Sparta, was held by Paris at Troy where Menelaos and his allies laid siege. As the Greeks' mightiest warrior, it was Achilles who killed the Trojan hero Hektor. However, he did not live to see Troy fall, since he was struck in the heel by a fatal arrow from Paris's bow.

Achilles victoriously dragging the body of Hektor around the walls of Troy

Local fishing boats moored at the eastern end of the harbor at Gáïos

Paxós
Παξοί

2,700. Gáïos, Lákka. Gáïos. Gáïos (0622 22222). Mogonisi 3 km (2 miles) SE of Gáïos.

Paxós is green and wooded, with a few farming and fishing villages. The thick groves of olive trees are still a major part of the island's economy. In mythology, Poseidon created Paxós for his mistress, and its small size has saved it from the turbulent history of its larger neighbors. Paxós became part of the Greek State along with the other Ionians in 1864.

Gaios

Gáïos is a lively, if small-scale, vacation town with two harbors: the main port where ferries dock, and, a short walk away, the small harbor, lined with 19th-century houses with Venetian-style shutters and balconies. The waterfront statue is of Pyropolítis, a sailor who died heroically in the Greek War of Independence *(see pp38–9)*. The grandest house was once the residence of the British High Commissioner of Corfu. Behind it are narrow old streets, bars, and tavernas.

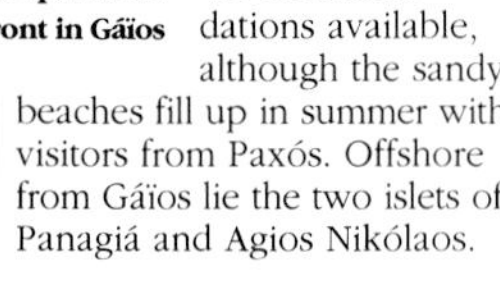
Statue of Pyropolítis on the waterfront in Gáïos

Around the Island

One main road goes from the south to the north of the island. There are few cars, and the best way to get about is by bicycle or moped. Many pleasant tracks lead through woods to high cliffs or secluded coves. At the end of a deep, almost circular inlet on Paxós's northern coast lies the town of **Lákka**. This pretty coastal town is backed by olive groves and pine-covered hills. Lákka is popular with day-trippers from Corfu, but at night it returns to being a quiet fishing village, with a few rooms to rent and only a scattering of restaurants and cafés.

To the east is the small village of **Pórto Longós**, which is the most attractive of the island's settlements. It has a pebble beach, a handful of houses, a few shops, and tavernas whose tables stand at the water's edge. Pórto Longós is a peaceful place where the arrival of the boat bringing fruit and vegetables every few days is a major event. Paths from the village lead through olive groves to several quiet coves, good for swimming.

Outlying Islands

Around 100 people live on **Antípaxos**, south of Paxós, and mostly in Agrapidiá, although there are a few hamlets inland. The island is unusual in that olive trees are easily outnumbered by grape vines, which produce Antípaxos's potent and good quality wine. There is little tourism and no accommodations available, although the sandy beaches fill up in summer with visitors from Paxós. Offshore from Gáïos lie the two islets of Panagiá and Agios Nikólaos.

View overlooking Lákka to the south

Houses on a hillside near Kalamítsi

Lefkáda

Λευκάδα

25,000. Nydrí, Vasilikí.
Dimitroú Golémi, Lefkáda town.
Lefkáda town (0645 26450).
Lefkáda town: daily.

Lefkada offers variety, from mountain villages to beach resorts. It has had a turbulent history, typical of the Ionian islands, since the Corinthians took control of the island from the Akarnanians in 640 BC, right up until the British left the island in 1864.

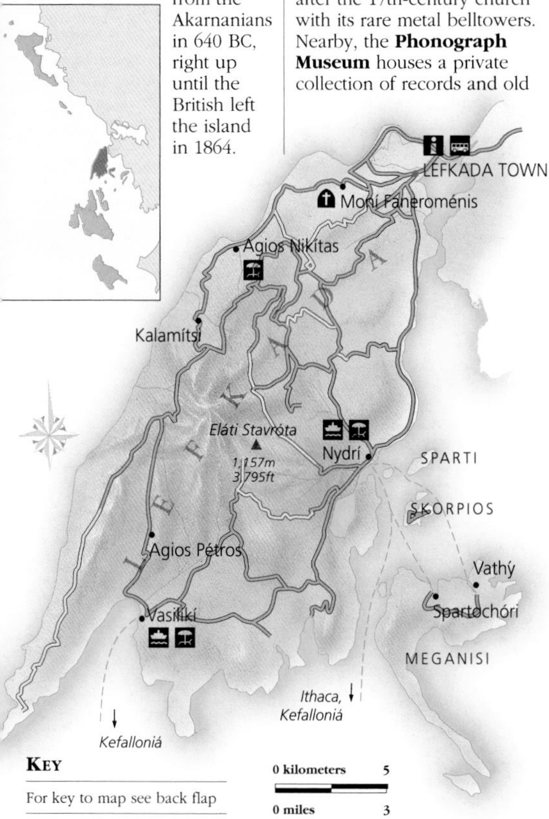

Lefkada Town

The town has suffered repeated earthquakes, but there are interesting back streets and views of the beautiful ruins of the 14th-century **Sánta Mávra fortress.** Situated on the mainland opposite, the fortress is connected to Lefkáda by a causeway. The main square, Plateía Agíou Spyrídona is named after the 17th-century church with its rare metal belltowers. Nearby, the **Phonograph Museum** houses a private collection of records and old phonographs. The small **Folk Museum** has local costumes and old photographs of island life. Above the town, **Moní Faneroménis** was founded in the 17th century; the present buildings date from the 19th-century. Its icon of the Panagía is also 19th century.

A bell at Moní Faneroménis

Phonograph Museum
Konstantínou Kalkáni 10.
0645 23433. daily. main public hols.

Folk Museum
Stefanítsi 2. *0645 22473.*
daily, May–Oct. main public hols.

Around the Island

The best way to see the island is to hire a moped or bike, although bus services operate from Lefkáda town. **Agios Nikítas** is a traditional small resort with a harbor and beach. To the south, **Kalamítsi** is a typical Lefkáda mountain village. In the south, the main hill village is **Agios Pétros,** still a rural community despite the nearby resort of **Vasilikí,** a windsurfers' paradise. **Nydrí** is the main resort on the east coast, with great views of the off-shore islands.

Outlying Islands

Meganísi has retained its rural lifestyle. Most boats from Nydrí stop at Vathý, the main port, whose harbor has chapels on each side and several tavernas. Uphill, the small village of Katoméri has the island's only hotel.

Sailing boats off the white sand beach at Vasilikí

Key

For key to map see back flap

0 kilometers 5
0 miles 3

The pebble beach of Pólis Bay on the northwest coast of Ithaca

Ithaca
Ιθάκη

4,000. Vathý. Vathý (0674 327 95). Pólis Bay 20 km (12 miles) NW of Vathý.

SMALL AND RUGGED, Ithaca is famous, according to Homer's epic the *Odyssey*, as the home of Odysseus. Finds on Ithaca date back as far as 4000–3000 BC, and by Mycenaean times it had developed into the capital of a kingdom that included its larger neighbor, Kefalloniá.

Vathy

The capital, also known as Ithaca town, is an attractive port, its brown-roofed houses huddled around an indented bay. The surrounding hills were the site for the first settlement, but the harbor itself was settled in the medieval period, and Vathý became the capital in the 17th century. Destroyed by an earthquake in 1953, it was reconstructed from the rubble and declared a traditional settlement, which requires all new buildings to match existing styles.

The **Archaeological Museum** contains a collection mainly of vases and votives from the Mycenaean period. In the church of **Taxiárchis** is a 17th-century icon of Christ, believed to have been painted by El Greco *(see p264)*.

Archaeological Museum
Kalliníkou. 0674 32200. Tue–Sun. main public hols.

Around the Island

With just one main town, high hills, a few pebble beaches, and little development, Ithaca is a pleasant island to explore. A twice-daily bus (four in season) links Vathý to villages in the north, and there are some taxis.

Stavrós, the largest village in northern Ithaca, has only 300 inhabitants but is a thriving hill community and market center. Nearby **Pólis Bay** is thought to have been the old port of ancient Ithaca and site of an important cave sanctuary to the nymphs. **Odysseus's Palace** may have stood above Stavrós on the hill known as Pilikáta. To find it, ask for directions at the one-room **Archaeological Museum**, whose curator gives guided tours in several languages. Among the varied local finds is a piece of a terra-cotta mask from Pólis cave bearing the inscription "Dedicated to Odysseus."

Archaeological Museum
Stavrós. 0674 31305. variable. main public hols.

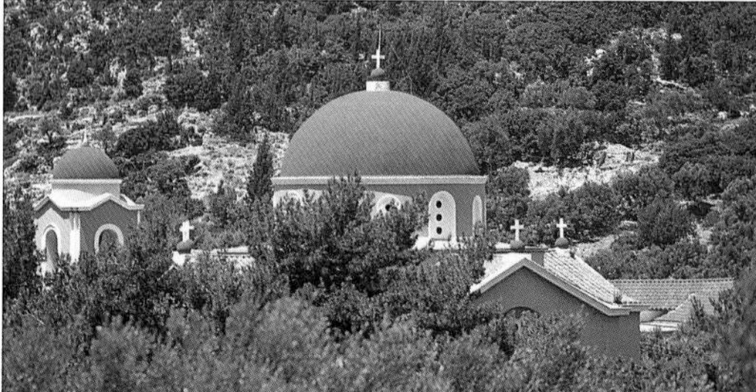

The red-domed roof of a church in Stavrós

KEY

For key to map see back flap

The Legend of Odysseus's Return to Ithaca

Odysseus, the king of Ithaca, had been unwilling to leave his wife Penelope and infant son Telemachos and join Agamemnon's expedition against Troy *(see pp52–3)*. But once there his skills as warrior and speaker, and his cunning, ensured he played a vital role. However, his journey home was fraught with such perils as the monstrous one-eyed Cyclops, the witch Circe, and the seductive Calypso. His blinding of the Cyclops angered the god Poseidon who saw to it that, despite the goddess Athena's support, Odysseus lost all his companions, before the kindly Phaeacians brought him home, 10 years after he left Troy. On Ithaca, Odysseus found Penelope besieged by suitors. Disguising himself as a beggar, and aided by his his loyal swineherd Eumaios and his son, he killed them all and returned to his marriage bed and to power.

Odysseus's homecoming *is depicted in this 15th-century painting attributed to Coracelli. Odysseus had been washed ashore on Phaeacia (Corfu), where King Alkinoös took pity and ferried him back to Ithaca.*

Penelope *wove a shroud for Odysseus's father Laertes, shown in this 1920 illustration by A F Gorguet. She refused to remarry until the shroud was finished; each night she would unpick the day's weaving.*

Eumaios, *Odysseus's faithful swineherd, gave his disguised master food and shelter for the night on his arrival in Ithaca. Eumaios then demonstrated his loyalty by praising his absent king while describing the situation on Ithaca to Odysseus. Their meeting is shown on this 5th-century BC Athenian vase.*

Argus*, Odysseus's aged dog, recognized his master without prompting, a feat matched only by Odysseus's old nurse, Eurykleia. Immediately after their meeting Argus died.*

Telemachos *had challenged Penelope's suitors to string Odysseus's bow and thereby to win his mother's hand in marriage. The suitors all failed the test. Odysseus locked them in the palace hall, strung the bow, and revealed his identity before slaughtering them.*

Kefalloniá

Κεφαλλονιά

ARCHAEOLOGISTS DATE Kefalloniá's first inhabitants to about 50,000 BC. The island flourished in Mycenaean times and remained Greek until the 2nd century BC, when it was captured by the Romans. It was squabbled over by many powers, but from 1500 to 1700 it shared the Ionians' history of Venetian occupation. Its attractions range from busy beach resorts to Mount Aínos National Park, which surrounds the Ionians' highest peak.

A church tower in the countryside between Argostóli and Kástro

Argostoli

A big, busy town with lush surrounding countryside, Kefalloniá's capital is situated by a bay with narrow streets rising up the headland on which it stands. Its traditional appearance is deceptive as Argostóli was destroyed in the 1953 earthquake and rebuilt with donations from emigrants. The destruction and rebuilding is shown in a photographic collection at the **Historical and Folk Museum**. Other exhibits range from rustic farming implements to traditional folk costumes.

The nearby **Archaeological Museum** includes finds from the Sanctuary of Pan, based at the Melissaní Cave-Lake and an impressive 3rd-century AD bronze head of a man found at Sámi. From the waterfront you can see the **Drápanos Bridge**, built during British rule in 1813.

Historical and Folk Museum
Ilía Zervoú 12. *0671 28835.*
Apr–Oct: Mon–Sat. *main public hols.*

Archaeological Museum
Rókkou Vergotí. *0671 28300.*
under renovation until at least summer 1999.

Around The Island

It takes time to travel around Kefalloniá, the largest of the Ionian islands. Despite this, driving is rewarding, with some beautiful spots to discover. The island's liveliest places are **Lássi** and the south-coast resorts; elsewhere there are quiet villages and the scenery is stunning. A bus service links Argostóli with most parts of the island.

Capital of Kefalloniá until 1757, the whitewashed village of **Kástro** still flourishes outside the Byzantine fortress of Agios Geórgios. The Venetians renovated the fortress in 1504 but it was damaged by earthquakes in 1636 and 1637, and the 1953 earthquake finally ruined it. The large and overgrown interior is a haven for swallowtail butterflies.

In 1264 there was a convent on the site of **Moní Agíou Andréa**. The original church was

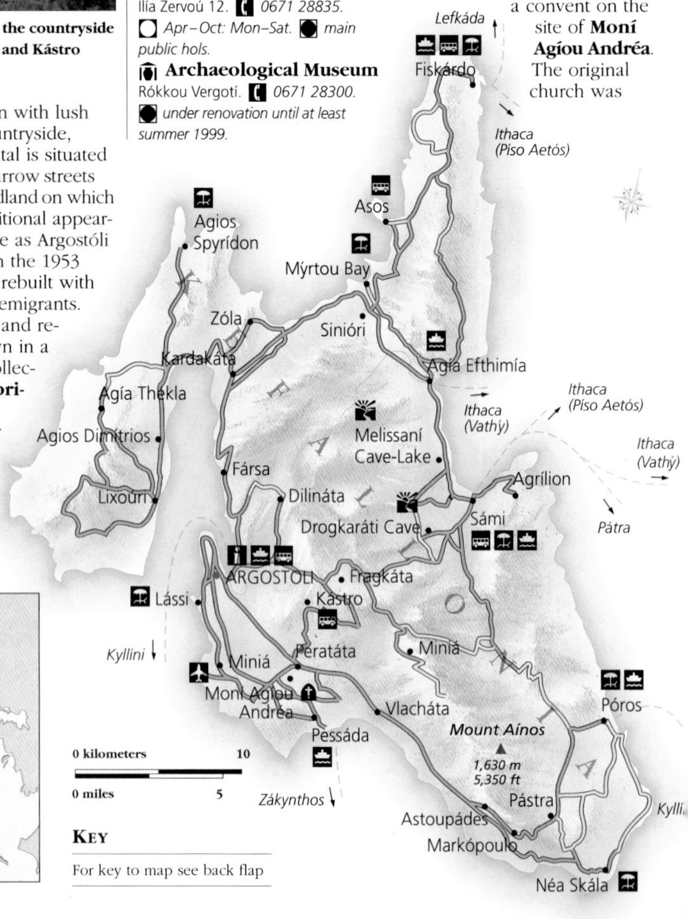

0 kilometers 10

0 miles 5

Key

For key to map see back flap

Visitors to the blue waters of the subterranean Melissaní Cave-Lake

VISITORS' CHECKLIST

31,000. 9 km (5.5 miles) S of Argostóli. Argostóli, Fiskárdo, Agía Efthimía, Sámi, Póros, Pessáda. Ioánnou Metaxá, Argostóli. Waterfront, Argostóli (0671 22248). daily, Argostóli. Panagía or Snake Festival at Markópoulo: Aug 15; Wine Festival at Fragáta: 1st Sat after Aug 15.

damaged in 1953, but has been restored as a museum to house icons and frescoes made homeless by the earthquake. The new church houses the monastery's holiest relic, supposedly the foot of the Apostle Andrew.

There was once a sanctuary to Aenios Zeus at the summit of **Mount Aínos**, which is 1,630 m (5,350 ft) high. Wild horses live in the Mount Aínos National Park, and the slopes of the mountain are covered with the native fir tree, *Abies cephalonica*. A road leads up toward the mountain's summit, but soon becomes a very rough track.

Apostle Andrew from the Moní Agíou Andréa

On the east coast, **Sámi** has ferry services to the Peloponnese and Ithaca. Nearby are two caves, Drogkaráti Cave, 3.5 km (2 miles) southwest and the Melissaní Cave-Lake, 2 km (1 mile) to the north. **Drogkaráti** drips with stalactites. It is the size of a large concert hall and is sometimes used as such due to its fine acoustics. The subterranean **Melissaní Cave-Lake** was a sanctuary of Pan in Mycenaean times. Part of its limestone ceiling has collapsed creating a haunting place with deep blue water. A channel leads to the enclosed section, where legend says that the nymph Melissaní drowned herself when she was spurned by Pan.

Fiskárdo is Kefalloniá's prettiest village, undamaged by the 1953 earthquake. Its pastel-painted 18th-century Venetian houses cluster by the harbor, which is a popular berth for yachts. It is also busy in the summer with daily ferry services and day trips from elsewhere on Kefalloniá. Despite the crowds and gift shops Fiskárdo retains its charm.

Asos is an unspoiled village on Kefalloniá's west coast. The surrounding hilly terrain is noted for its stone terracing, which once covered the island. On the peninsula across the isthmus from Asos is a ruined Venetian fortress, built in 1595, which has seen occupation by Venetians and stays by the French and Russians in the 19th century. Now Asos sees mostly day trippers, as there is little accommodation in the village. South of Asos is **Mýrtou Bay**, a lovely cove with the most beautiful beach on the island.

Moni Agíou Andréa
Peratáta village. 0671 69557.
daily. museum only.

A view overlooking Asos in the northwest of the island

Zákynthos

Ζάκυνθος

ZAKYNTHOS WAS INHABITED by Achaians until Athens took control in the 5th century BC. They were followed by a succession of rulers, including the Spartans, Macedonians, Romans, and Byzantines. The Venetians ruled from 1484 until 1797, and Zákynthos finally joined the rest of Greece in 1864. An attractive and green island, there are mountain villages, monasteries, fertile plains, and beautiful views to reward exploration.

Statue of the poet Solomós in the main square, Zákynthos town

Zakynthos Town

Completely destroyed in the 1953 earthquake that hit the Ionian islands, Zákynthos town has now been rebuilt with efforts to recapture its former grace. The traditional arcaded streets run parallel to the waterfront, where fishing boats arrive each morning to sell their catch. Farther down the waterfront the ferry boats dock alongside grand Mediterranean cruise ships.

At the southern end of the harbor is the impressive church of **Agios Dionýsios**, the island's patron saint (1547–1622). The church, which houses the body of St. Dionýsios in a silver coffin, was built in 1925 and survived the earthquake.

The **Byzantine Museum** has a scale model of the pre-earthquake town, an elegant city built by the Venetians. It also houses a breathtaking collection of icons and frescoes rescued from the island's destroyed churches and monasteries.

North of here is the **Solomós Museum**, which contains the tomb of the poet Dionýsios Solomós (1798–1857), author of the Greek national anthem. The collection details lives of prominent Zákynthiot citizens.

A short walk north from the town center, **Stráni hill** offers good views, while the Venetian kástro, above the town, has even more impressive views of the mainland. The ruined walls contain remnants of several churches and an abundance of plants and wildlife.

Byzantine Museum
0695 42714. Tue–Sun. main public hols.

Solomós Museum
0695 48982. daily. main public hols.

Around the Island

Outside the main resorts there is little tourist development on Zákynthos. It is possible to drive around the island in a day as most of the roads are in good condition. Renting a

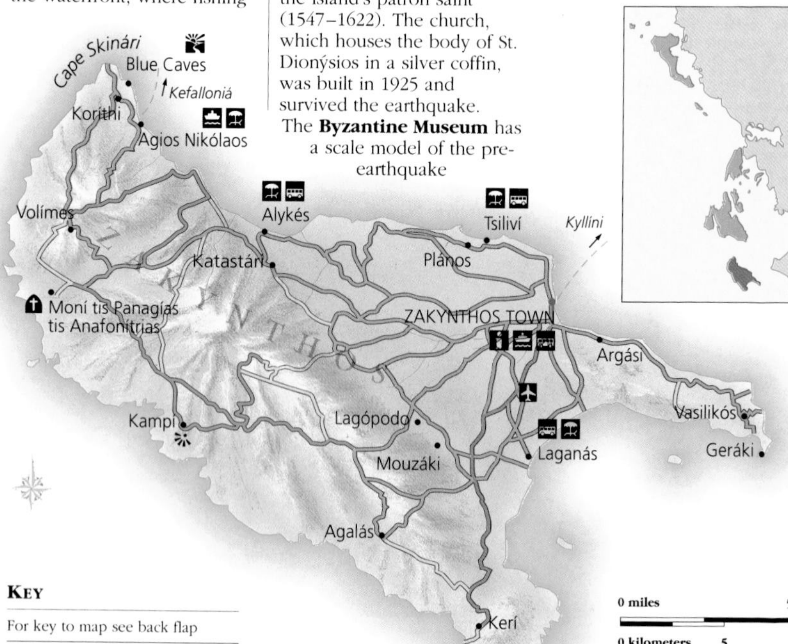

Key

For key to map see back flap

Loggerhead Turtles

The Mediterranean green loggerhead turtle *(Caretta caretta)* has been migrating from Africa to Laganás Bay, its principal nesting site, for many thousands of years. These giant sea creatures can weigh up to 180 kg (400 lb). They lay their eggs in the sand, said to be the softest in Greece, at night. However, disco and hotel lights disorient the turtles' navigation, and few now nest successfully. Of the eggs that are eventually laid, many are destroyed by vehicles or by the poles of beach umbrellas. The work of environmentalists has led to some protection for the turtles, with stretches of beach now off-limits, in an attempt to give the turtles a chance at least to stabilize their numbers.

Visitors' Checklist

30,000. 4 km (3 miles) S of Zákynthos town. Zákynthos town; Agios Nikólaos. Zákynthos town. Tzouláti 2, Zákynthos town (0695 27367). Zákynthos town Festival: Jul.

car or a powerful motorcycle is the best idea, though buses from Zákynthos town are frequent to resorts such as Alykés, Tsiliví, and Laganás.

The growth of tourism on Zákynthos has been heavily concentrated in **Laganás** and its 14-km (9-mile) sweep of soft sand. This unrestricted development has decimated the population of loggerhead turtles that nests here – only an estimated 800 remain. Efforts are now being made to protect the turtles and to ensure their future survival. Visitors may take trips out into the bay in glass-bottomed boats to see the turtles, and all sorts of turtle souvenirs fill the large number of trinket shops. An equally large number of bars and discos ensure the nightlife here continues till dawn.

Head to the north coast for the quieter beach resorts of **Tsiliví** and **Alykés**, the latter being especially good for windsurfing.

The 16th-century **Moní tis Panagías tis Anafonítrias** in the northwest has special appeal for locals as it was here the island's patron saint, Dionýsios, spent the last years of his life as an abbot. During his time here, it is said that Dionýsios heard a murderer's confession; the murderer received the saint's forgiveness, never knowing that his victim was the abbot's brother. When questioned by the authorities, Dionýsios denied seeing the man, which was the only lie he ever told. Dionýsios lived in a cell here that still stands and contains many of the saint's revered possessions. The three-aisled church and the tiny chapel alongside are rare in that they survived the 1953 earthquake.

Coat of arms at Moní tis Panagías tis Anafonítrias

At the northernmost tip of the island are the unusual **Blue Caves**, formed by the relentless action of the sea on the coastline. The principal cave, the Blue Grotto, lies directly underneath the lighthouse on Cape Skinári. It was discovered in 1897 and has become well known for its stunningly blue and clear water. The caves can be visited by boat from the resort of Agios Nikólaos, and the round-the-island boat trips from the main resorts also stop here.

The Blue Caves of Zákynthos on the northern tip of the island

THE ARGO-SARONIC ISLANDS

SALAMINA · AIGINA · POROS · YDRA · SPETSES · KYTHIRA

ALTHOUGH THE ARGO-SARONIC ISLANDS *have succumbed to some degree of tourism, they remain relatively untouched by progress and are quintessential Greek islands, still supporting fishing and farming communities. Kýthira, off the tip of the Peloponnese, shares its history of Venetian and British rule with the Ionians, but is today administered with the Argo-Saronics.*

The islands' location close to Athens has given them a rich history. Aígina was very prosperous in the 7th century BC as a maritime state that minted its own coins and built the magnificent temple of Aphaia. Salamína is famed as the site of the battle of Salamis (480 BC), when the Greek fleet defeated the Persians. Wealth gained from maritime trading also assured the Argo-Saronics' cultural and social development, seen today in the architectural beauty of Ydra and in the grand houses and public buildings of Aígina. Ydra and Spétses were important in the War of Independence *(see p38–9)*, both islands producing brave fighters, including the notorious Laskarína Mpoumpoulína and Admiral Miaoúlis.

Terra-cotta ornament

Salamína and Aígina are so easy to reach from the capital that they are often thought of as island suburbs of Athens. Póros hardly seems like an island at all, divided from the Peloponnese by a narrow channel. However, despite modern colonization peaceful spots can still be found. Póros and Spétses are lush and green, covered with pine forests and olive groves, in contrast to the other more barren and mountainous islands. Scenically, Kýthira's rugged coastline has more in common with the Ionians than the Argo-Saronics. The island's position on ancient shipping routes has led to some major finds, such as the bronze *Youth of Antikýthira*, now in the National Archaeological Museum *(see p282)*.

The chapel of Agios Nikólaos on Aígina

◁ **Póros town with the mountains of the Peloponnese in the background**

Exploring the Argo-Saronic Islands

Close proximity to Athens makes the Argo-Saronic islands suitable for short visits as well as longer stays. The islands have a lush landscape, with pine forests and crystal clear waters in secluded bays. Aígina is an ideal base and, like the other islands, has picturesque ports with cobbled streets and Neo-Classical buildings. Packed with stylish bars and shops, the cosmopolitan atmosphere of the Argo-Saronics is tempered by harborside caïques selling vegetables and horse-drawn carriages driving along the waterfront. Horse power is particularly evident in Póros, Ydra, and Spétses, where no cars are allowed. Kýthira remains a well-kept secret. This large island has beautiful villages and deserted beaches to explore.

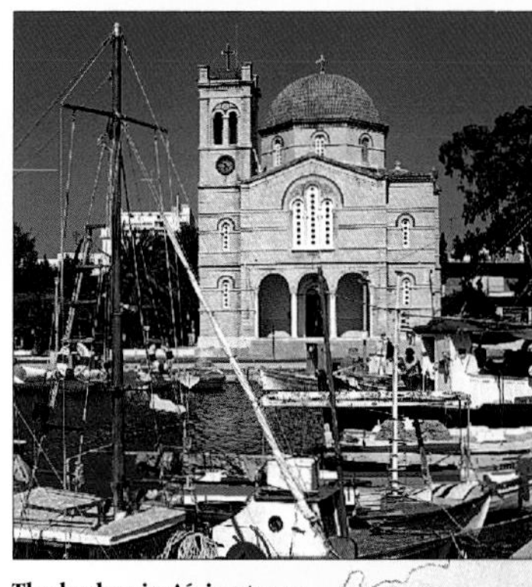

The harbor in Aígina town

Islands at a Glance

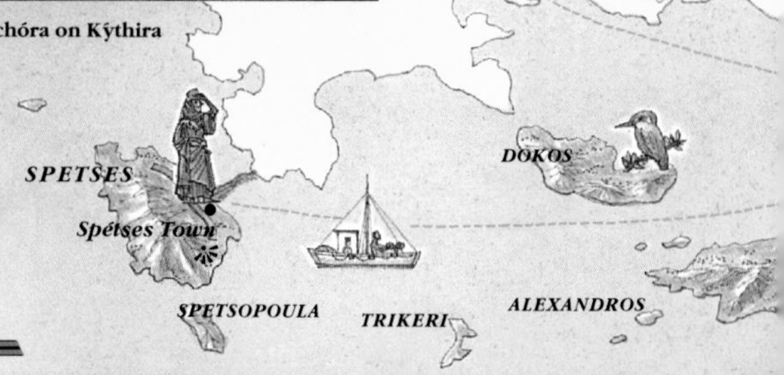

See Also

- ***Where to Stay*** p299
- ***Where to Eat*** p323
- ***Travel Information*** pp356–9

The rugged scenery of Palaiochóra on Kýthira

Key

- Paved road
- Unpaved road
- Scenic route
- Tourist season, direct ferry route
- Viewpoint

KOLPOS EPIDAVROU

Ermióni

SPETSES

Spétses Town

SPETSOPOULA

TRIKERI

DOKOS

ALEXANDROS

0 kilometers 20

0 miles 10

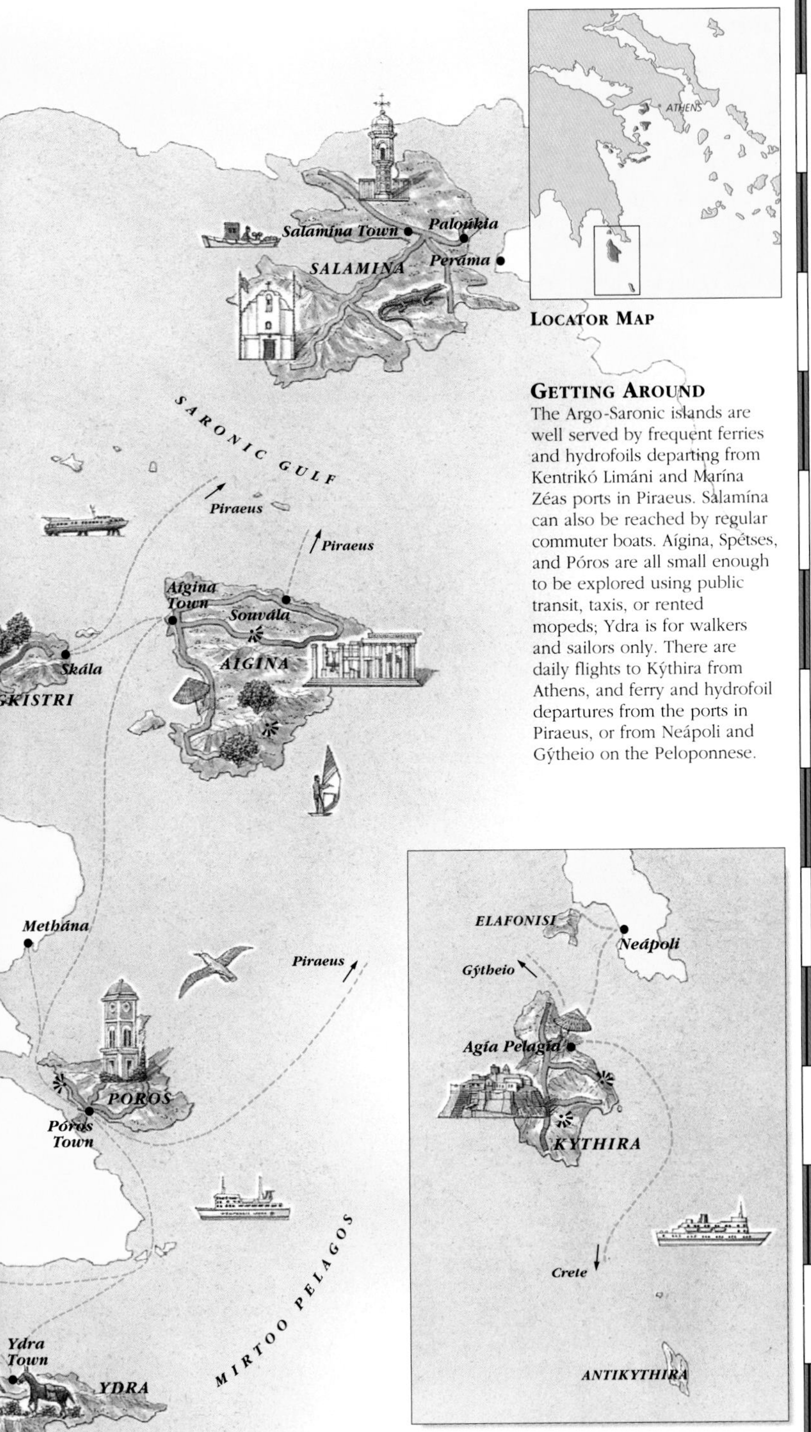

LOCATOR MAP

GETTING AROUND

The Argo-Saronic islands are well served by frequent ferries and hydrofoils departing from Kentrikó Limáni and Marína Zéas ports in Piraeus. Salamína can also be reached by regular commuter boats. Aígina, Spétses, and Póros are all small enough to be explored using public transit, taxis, or rented mopeds; Ydra is for walkers and sailors only. There are daily flights to Kýthira from Athens, and ferry and hydrofoil departures from the ports in Piraeus, or from Neápoli and Gýtheio on the Peloponnese.

Salamína
Σαλαμίνα

23,000. Paloúkia & Selínia. Salamína town. Thu at Salamína town, Sat at Aiánteio.

SALAMINA IS THE LARGEST of the Saronic Gulf islands, and so close to Athens that most Greeks consider it part of the mainland. The island is famed as the site of the decisive battle of Salamis in 480 BC, when the Greeks defeated the Persians. The king of Persia, Xerxes, watched the humiliating sight of his cumbersome ships being destroyed in Salamis Bay, trapped by the faster triremes of a smaller Greek fleet under Themistokles. The island today is a cheerful medley of vacation homes, immaculately whitewashed churches, and cheap tavernas, although its east coast is lined with a string of marine scrapyards and naval bases.

The west coast capital of **Salamína town** is a charmless place, straddling an isthmus of flat land filled with vineyards. Both the town and the island are known as Koúlouri, nicknamed after a biscuit that resembles the island's shape.

East of Salamína town **Agios Nikólaos** has far more character, with 19th-century mansions lining the dockside and small caïques off-loading their catch of fish. A road from Paloúkia meanders across the south of the island to the villages of Selínia, Aiánteio, and Peristéria.

In the northwest of the Salamína, the 17th-century **Moní Faneroménis** looks across a narrow gulf to Ancient Eleusis on the Attic coast. The monastery was used during the War of Independence *(see pp38–9)* as a hiding place for Greek freedom fighters. Its Byzantine church was restored by the Venetians and has fine 18th-century frescoes vividly depicting the *Last Judgment*. Today nuns welcome visitors and tend the gardens, home to a number of peacocks.

Shrine opposite Moní Faneroménis

Fishing boats sailing into Aígina harbor

Aígina
Αίγινα

12,400. Aígina town. Leonárdou Ladá, Aígina town (0297 27777).

ONLY 20 km (12 miles) southwest of the port of Piraeus, Aígina has been inhabited for over 4,000 years and has remained an important settlement throughout that time. Taking its name from early settlers from Phoenicia who called it Pigeon Island (*Ai* means island, *Gina* means pigeon), Aígina flourished and became a prosperous maritime state. By the 7th century BC the second largest Saronic island was the first place in Europe to mint its own silver coins, which became accepted currency throughout the Greek-speaking world. Plying the Mediterranean and the Black Sea, the people of Aígina controlled most foreign trade in Greece. However, their legendary nautical skills and vast wealth finally incurred the wrath of neighboring Athens, who settled the long-term rivalry by conquering the island in 456 BC. Aígina's most famous site is the well-preserved **Temple of Aphaia** *(see pp94–5)*, built in about 490 BC, prior to Athenian control. Later, the island declined during the centuries of alternating Turkish and Venetian rule and the constant plague of piracy. However, Aígina enjoyed fame again for a brief period in 1828 when Ioánnis Kapodístrias (1776–1857) declared it the first capital of modern Greece.

The ruined Venetian Pýrgos Markéllou in Aígina town

Aigina Town

This picturesque island town is home to many churches, including the pretty 19th-century **Agía Triáda**, situated to the right of the fish market, overlooking the harbor. At the dockside, horse-drawn carriages wait to take visitors through narrow streets of Neo-Classical mansions to the Venetian tower **Pýrgos Markéllou** near the cathedral. Caïques from the mainland sell fruit and vegetables at the water's edge. Octopuses are hung out to dry at tavernas in the cobbled street leading to the enclosed fish market. To the northwest, past shops

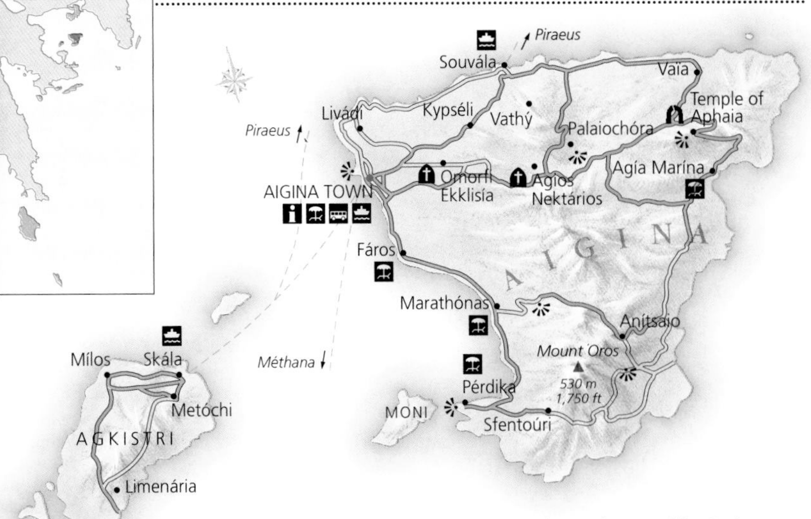

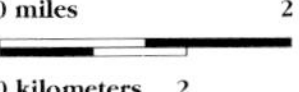

The church of Agía Triáda in Aígina town

selling local pistachio nuts and earthenware water jugs, are the remains of the 6th-century BC **Temple of Apollo**. The famous 6th-century BC Sphinx of Aígina, now in the **Aígina Museum**, was discovered here.

Aígina Museum
Kolóna 8. *0297 22637.* *Tue–Sun.* *main public hols.*

Environs: North of Aígina town, in Livádi, a plaque marks the house where Níkos Kazantzákis wrote *Zorba the Greek* *(see p272)*.

Around the Island

Aígina, at only 8 km (5 miles) across, is easy to explore by bicycle. Just off the main road east from Aígina town, is the

Key

For key to map see back flap

13th-century Byzantine church, **Omorfi Ekklisía**, which has some fine frescoes. Pilgrims take this road to pay homage at **Agios Nektários**. Archbishop Nektários (1846–1920) was the first man to be canonized in modern times (1961) by the Orthodox church. Visitors can see his quarters and the chapel where he rests.

On the opposite hillside are the remains of the deserted town of **Palaiochóra**. Populated since Byzantine times, it was destroyed by Barbarossa, the general of Sultan Suleiman I, in 1537. The area around the town was abandoned in 1826.

South from Aígina town, the road hugs the shore, beneath the shadow of **Mount Oros** at 530 m (1,740 ft). Passing the pistachio orchards and the fishing harbor of Fáros, this scenic route ends at **Pérdika** at the southwestern tip of the island. Overlooking the harbor, this small, picturesque fishing village has some excellent fish tavernas that are packed on weekends with Athenians over for a day trip.

Outlying Islands

Just 15 minutes by caïque from Pérdika is the island of **Moní**, popular for its emerald green waters, secluded coves, and hidden caves.

Agkístri is easily accessible by caïque from Aígina town or by ferry from Piraeus. Originally settled by Albanians, today this island is colonized by Germans who have bought most of the houses in the village of Metóchi, just above Skála port. Although many hotels, apartments, and bars have been built in Skála and Mílos, its other main port, the rest of this hilly, pineclad island remains largely unspoiled. Limenária, in the south of the island, is a more traditional, peaceful community of farmers and fishermen.

The scattered ruins of Byzantine chapels around the deserted town of Palaiochóra

Aígina: Temple of Aphaia

Ναός της Αφαίας

SURROUNDED BY PINE TREES, on a hilltop above the busy resort of Agía Marína, the Temple of Aphaia is one of the best-preserved Doric temples in Greece *(see pp56–7)*. The present temple dates from around 490 BC, but the site is known to have been a place of worship from the 13th century BC. In 1901 the German archaeologist Adolf Furtwängler found an inscription to the goddess Aphaia, disproving theories that the temple was dedicated to Athena. Although smaller, the building is similar to the temple of Zeus at Olympia that was built 30 years later.

Inner Walls
The inner wall was built with a thickened base and a minimal capital to correspond with the capitals of the colonnade.

Aerial view of the site from the south

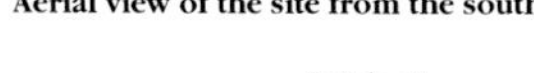

The east pediment sculptures, with Athena at the center, were replacements for an earlier set. The west pediment sculptures are Archaic in style.
Triglyph
Metope
Architrave
Ramp from altar to temple

Corner Columns
These columns were made thicker for emphasis and to counteract the appearance of thinness in a column that was seen against the sky.

Corner Architraves
Still in good condition, the stonework above the capitals consists of a plain architrave surmounted by a narrow band of plain metopes alternating with ornate triglyphs.

Inner Columns
The cella is enclosed by two stories of Doric columns, one on top of the other. The taper of the upper columns is continuous with that of the lower.

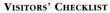

The roof was made of terra-cotta tiles with Parian marble tiles at the edges.

Opisthodomos, or rear porch

Visitors' Checklist

12 km (7.5 miles) E of Aígina town. ☎ *0297 32398.* **Site** ○ *Apr–Sep: 8:15am–7pm Mon–Fri, 8:30am–3pm Sat & Sun; Oct–Mar: 8:15am–5pm Mon–Fri, 8:30am–3pm Sat & Sun.* **Museum** ○ *9am–1pm daily.* ● *Jan 1, Mar 25, Good Fri am, Easter Sun, May 1, Dec 25, 26.*

View of the Cella
The cella was the inner room of the temple, and the home of the cult statue. Some temples had more than one, the back cella being reserved for the priestess alone.

Reconstruction of the Temple of Aphaia

Viewed from the northwest, this reconstruction shows the temple as it would have been in c.490 BC. Built of local limestone covered in stucco and painted, it was highly colorful.

Cult statue of the goddess Aphaia

The pool of olive oil was a collection of the many libations (offerings) made to the goddess.

Temple Pediments

The famous sculptures from the pediments of the temple of Aphaia were discovered by a group of British and German architects and artists, including John Foster, C R Cockerell, and Baron Haller von Hallerstein, in April 1811. They were later sold to the Crown Prince of Bavaria at auction and are now housed in the Glyptothek in Munich. They portray the struggles of various mythological heroes. The sculptures from the west pediment date from around 490 BC and are in the late Archaic style. Those from the east, with their more fluid movements and serious expressions, date from approximately 480 BC and foreshadow the Classical style.

Reconstruction of the *Warriors* sculpture from the west pediment

Póros
Πόρος

4,000. Póros town.
Póros town (0298 22256).
Fri (am) at Paidikí Chará.

Poros takes its name from the 400-m (1,300-ft) passage *(póros)* separating it from the mainland at Galatás. Póros is in fact two islands, joined by a causeway: pine-swathed Kalavreía to the north, and the smaller volcanic islet of Sfairía in the south, on which **Póros town** is built. In spite of much tourist development, the town is an appealing place, extending along the narrow straits, busy with shipping. Its 19th-century houses climb in tiers to its apex at a clock tower.

The **National Naval Academy**, northwest of the causeway and Póros town, was set up in 1849. An old battleship is usually at anchor there for training naval cadets.

The attractive 18th-century **Moní Zoödóchou Pigís** can be found on Kalavreía, built around the island's only spring. There are the ruins of a 6th-century BC hilltop **Temple of Poseidon** near the center of Kalavreía, next to which the orator Demosthenes poisoned himself in 322 BC rather than surrender to the Macedonians. In antiquity the site was linked to ancient Troezen in the Peloponnese. The temple has unlimited access.

The busy waterfront on Ydra

Ydra
Υδρα

3,000. Ydra town.
Ydra town (0298 52205).
Mandráki 1.5 km (1 mile) NE of Ydra town; Vlychós 2 km (1 mile) SW of Ydra town.

A long, narrow mass of barren rock, Ydra had little history before the 16th century, when it was settled by Orthodox Albanians, who then turned to the sea for a living. Ydra town was built in a brief period of prosperity in the late 18th and early 19th centuries, boosted by blockade running during the Napoleonic wars. After Independence, Ydra lapsed into obscurity again, until foreigners rediscovered it after World War II. By the 1960s, the trickle had become a flood of outsiders who set about restoring the old houses, transforming Ydra into one of the most exclusive resorts in Greece. Yet the island has retained its charm, thanks to an architectural preservation order that has kept the town's appearance as it was in the 1820s, along with a ban on motor vehicles. Donkey caravans perform all hauling on steep, stepped streets.

Bell tower of Ydra's Panagía church

Ydra Town

More than a dozen three- or four-storied mansions *(archontiká)* survive around the port, though none are regularly open to the public. Made from local stone, they were

Póros town, its houses clustered on the hillside of Sfairía

built by itinerant craftsmen between 1780 and 1820. On the east side of the harbor the **Tsamadoú mansion** is now the National Merchant Marine Academy. On the west, the **Tompázi mansion** is a School of Fine Arts. Just behind the center of the marble-paved wharf is the monastic church of the **Panagía**, built between 1760 and 1770 using masonry from Póros's Temple of Poseidon. The marble belfry is thought to have been erected by a master stonemason from Tínos.

The old harbor of Valtíza on Spétses

Around the Island

Visitors must walk virtually everywhere on Ydra, or hire water taxis to go along the coast. **Kamíni**, 15 minutes' walk southwest along the shore track, has been Ydra's main fishing port since the 16th century. The farm hamlet of **Episkopí**, in the far southwest of the island, used to be a summer refuge and a hunting resort for the upper classes. An hour's steep hike above the town, is the convent of **Agía Efpraxía** which still houses nuns, who are eager to sell you handicrafts. The adjacent 19th-century **Profítis Ilías** functions as a monastery. In the island's eastern half, visible from Profítis Ilías, are three uninhabited monasteries, dating from the 18th- and 19th-centuries. They mark the arduous 3-hour long route to **Moní Panagía**, situated out near Cape Zoúrvas to the northeast of the island.

Spétses
Σπέτσες

3,700. Spétses town.
Spétses town (0298 73744).
Wed at Kokinária.

Spetses is a corruption of Pityoússa, or "Piney," the ancient name for this round, green island. Its history is similar to that of Ydra: Albanian settlement during the 16th century, a flourishing maritime background, and fleets put at the disposal of the Greek revolutionary effort.

Possibly the most famous Spetsiot was Laskarína Mpoumpoulína, the admiral who menaced the Turks from her flagship *Agamemnon* and reputedly seduced men at gunpoint. She was shot in 1825 by the father of a girl her son had eloped with. During the 1920s and 30s, Spétses was a fashionable resort for British expatriates and anglophile Greeks. The ban on vehicles is not total: mopeds and horsecabs can be rented in town, and there are buses to the beaches.

Statue of Mpoumpoulína in Spétses town

Spetses Town

Spétses town runs along the coast for 2 km (1 mile). Its center lies at Ntápia dock, fringed by cafés. The *archontiká* of Chatzi-Giánnis Méxis, dating from 1795, is now the **Chatzi-Giánnis Méxis Museum**. Mpoumpoulína's coffin is on display as well as figureheads from her ship. Her former home is now the privately run **Mpoumpoulína Museum**. Southeast from here lies the old harbor at **Valtíza** inlet, where wooden boats are still built using the traditional methods. Above the harbor is the attractive 17th-century church of **Agios Nikólaos**, which has some fine pebble mosaics and a belfry made by craftsmen from Tinos.

Chatzi-Giánnis Méxis Museum
300 m (980 ft) from the port.
0298 72994. Tue–Sun.
main public hols.

Mpoumpoulína Museum
Behind Plateía Ntápia. 0298 72077.
Mar 25–Oct 28: daily.

Around the Island

A track, only partly paved, runs all the way round the island, and the best way to get around is by bicycle or moped. East of the town, stands the Anargýreios and Korgialéneios College, which is now closed. British novelist John Fowles taught briefly at the college in the early 1950s. He later used Spétses as the setting for *The Magus*. The pebble beaches on Spétses are the best in the Argo-Saronic group, including **Ligonéri**, **Vréllas**, and **Agía Paraskeví**. **Agioi Anárgyroi** is the only sandy one.

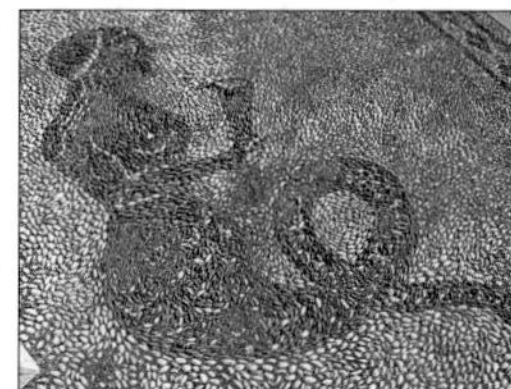

Pebble mosaic from the church of Agios Nikólaos, Spétses town

Kýthira

Κύθηρα

Called tserigo by the Venetians, Kýthira is one of the legendary birthplaces of Aphrodite. Historically, the island shared Venetian and British rule with the Ionian islands; today it is governed from Piraeus with the other Argo-Saronics. Clumps of eucalyptus seem emblematic of the island's modern alias of "Kangaroo Island"; return visits from 60,000 Australian Kythirans are central to Kythiran life. The island is also popular with Athenians seeking unspoiled beaches and vacation homes, many of which are the typical mix of Aegean and Venetian architecture.

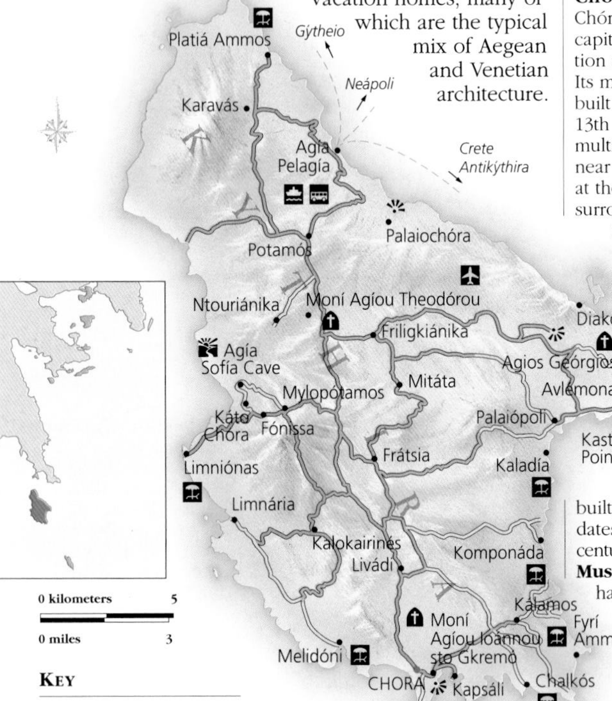

Key

For key to map see back flap

The houses of Chóra clustered on the hillside at dusk

Kapsáli harbor seen from Chóra

Chora

Chóra has been Kýthira's capital only since the destruction of Palaiochóra in 1537. Its magnificent **kástro** was built in two phases during the 13th and 15th centuries. A multidomed cistern lies intact near the bottom of the castle; at the summit, old cannons surround the church of **Panagía Myrtidiótissa**. The steepness of the drop to the sea below and Avgó islet, thought to be the birthplace of Aphrodite, is unrivaled throughout the Greek islands. A magnet for wealthy Athenians, the appealing lower town with its solidly built, flat-roofed mansions dates from the 17th to 19th centuries. The **Archaeological Museum** just outside Chóra has finds from Mycenaean and Minoan sites, plus gravestones dating from the British occupation of 1809–64.

Archaeological Museum

0735 31739. Tue–Sun. main public hols.

Environs: Yachts, hydrofoils, and, occasionally, large ferries drop anchor in the admirably well-protected harbor of **Kapsáli**, just east of Chóra. The beach is mediocre, but most foreigners stay here. In the cliff above the pine woods is the 16th-century **Moní Agíou Ioánnou sto Gkremó**, built onto the cliff edge. The nearest good beaches are pebbly **Fyrí Ammos**, 8 km (5 miles) northeast via Kálamos, with sea caves at its south end; and sandy **Chalkós**, 7 km (4.5 miles) south of Kálamos.

Whitewashed house in Mylopótamos

AROUND THE ISLAND

Like many Greek islands, the best way to get around Kýthira is by car, particularly as it is very mountainous. A bus runs to the main towns once a day during the summer from Agía Pelagía to Kapsáli. **Avlémonas**, with its vaulted warehouses and double harbor, forms an attractive fishing port at the east end of a stretch of rocky coast. Just offshore, the *Mentor*, carrying many of the Elgin Marbles, sank in 1802. Excellent beaches extend to either side of Kastrí point. The 6th-century hilltop church of **Agios Geórgios**, which has a mosaic floor, sits high above Avlémonas.

Roadside shrine on Kýthira

On the other side of the island is **Mylopótamos**. From here a track leads west to the small Fónissa waterfall, downstream from which is a mill-house and a tiny stone bridge.

In its blufftop situation with steep drops to the north and west, and a clutch of locked chapels, the Venetian kástro at **Káto Chóra** superficially resembles Palaiochóra. It was not a military stronghold but a refuge prepared in 1565 for the peasantry in unsettled times. The Lion of St. Mark presides over the entrance; nearby an English-built school of 1825 is being restored.

Agía Sofía Cave, 2.5 km (1.5 miles) from Káto Chóra and 150 m (500 ft) above the sea, has formed in black limestone strata. At the entrance, a frescoed shrine, painted by a 13th-century hermit, depicts Holy Wisdom and three attendant virtues. **Palaiochóra,** the Byzantine capital of Kýthira after 1248, was sited so as to be nearly invisible from the sea, but the pirate Barbarossa detected and destroyed it in 1537. The ruins of the town perch on top of a sheer 200-m (650-ft) bluff. Among six churches in Palaiochóra, the most striking and best preserved is the 14th-century **Agía Varvára**.

To the south, **Moní Agíou Theodórou** is the seat of Kýthira's bishop. The church, originally 12th-century, has been much altered, and the Baroque relief plaque over the door is a rarity in Greece.

To the north, the main port, **Agía Pelagía**, has a handful of hotels. **Karavás**, 5 km (3 miles) northwest is, in contrast, an attractive oasis village, with clusters of houses overhanging the steep banks of a stream valley.

VISITORS' CHECKLIST

3,000. 22 km (14 miles) NE of Chóra. Agía Pelagía & Kapsáli. runs between Agía Pelagía & Kapsáli. Sun at Potamós.

Agía Sofía Cave

Mylopótamos. *0735 33754.*

Tue–Sun. Nov–Mar.

Jul & Aug.

OUTLYING ISLANDS

Directly north of Kýthira, the barren islet of **Elafonísi** is visited mostly by Greeks for the sake of the best desert-island beaches in the country. The better of the two is Símos on the east side of a peninsula 5 km (3 miles) southeast of the port town. The remote island of **Antikýthira**, south-east of Kýthira, has a tiny population and no beaches.

View to the east across a gorge from Palaiochóra

THE SPORADES AND EVVOIA

SKIATHOS · SKOPELOS · ALONNISOS
SKYROS · EVVOIA

THE LUSH LANDSCAPE *of Evvoia and the Sporades comes as a surprise after barren and arid islands such as the Cyclades. Since ancient times, settlers and pirates alike have been lured by the pine-clad mountains, abundant springs and rivers, endless beaches, and hidden coves that are found throughout these islands.*

Being close to the mainland, the Sporades and Evvoia have been easily conquered throughout history. They were colonized in the prehistoric era by nearby Iolkos (Vólos), and also by the Minoans, who introduced vine and olive cultivation. More than any other island, Evvoia reveals its diverse history in the large number of buildings remaining from the long periods of Venetian and Turkish occupation. Susceptible to pirate raids, the inhabitants of the Sporades lived in the safety of fortified towns until as late as the 19th century. Even in Evvoia, when life proved too difficult in coastal villages such as Límni, the residents simply migrated to Skiáthos for a few generations. The islanders have a rich heritage of maritime trading around the Aegean and are still noted today as sailors. The islands' patchworked interiors of fertile fields and orchards, watered by ample springs and rivers, also encouraged agricultural self-sufficiency and wealth. Particularly on remote and rugged Skýros, such insularity has nurtured some unique folk art and colorful traditions. Its inaccessible coastline enables it to remain relatively unaffected by the numerous tourist hotel complexes that have sprung up on Skiáthos and Skópelos.

Mariner statue in Kárystos, Evvoia

The size of Evvoia also means it is one of the few places in the Greek islands where life carries on during the summer, undeterred by the annual invasion of vacationers.

Castel Rosso near Kárystos on Evvoia

◁ **The harbor of Agnóntas on Skópelos in the evening sun**

Exploring the Sporades and Evvoia

THE RICH AND FAMOUS first flocked in their yachts to the deserted beaches of Skiáthos, Skópelos, and Alónnisos in the 1960s and 1970s. Although no longer so exclusive, the beautiful coastlines of these islands still lure Greek and foreign vacationers alike. There are facilities for windsurfing and boats for rent on most beaches. Skópelos and Skiáthos have a sophisticated array of nightclubs and bars. Quieter Skýros and Evvoia, offering a varied culture and landscape, are perfect for rambling vacations, punctuated by visits to local folk art museums and lingering days on the fine beaches.

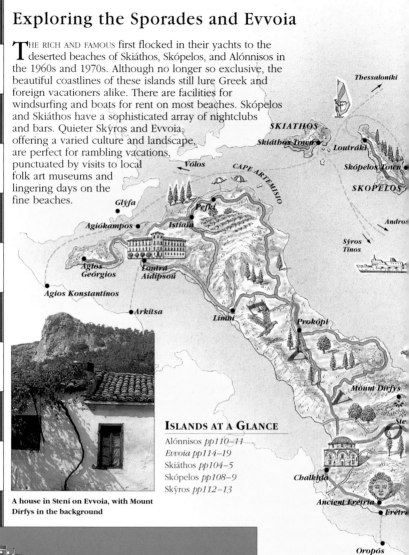

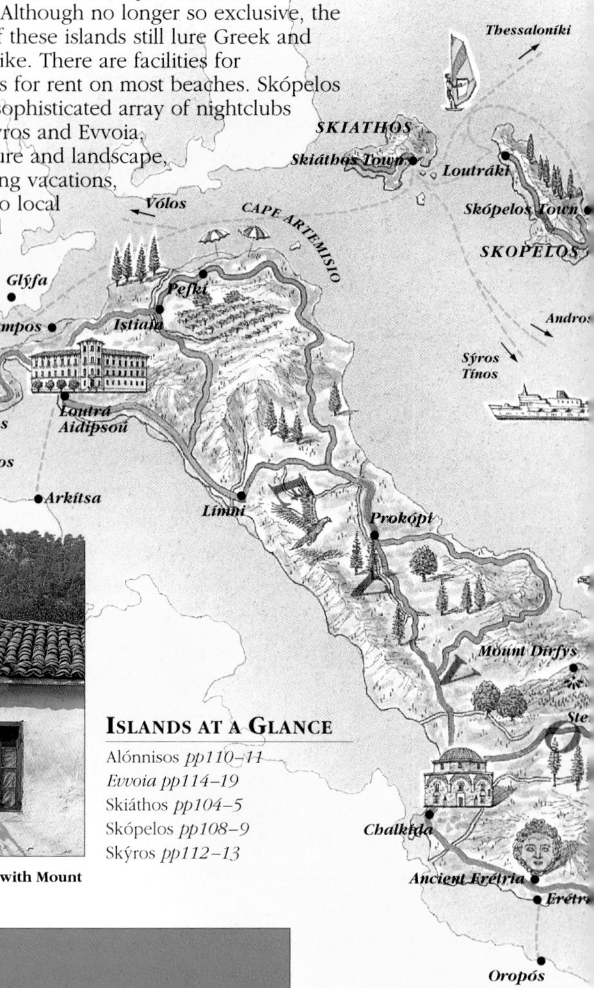

A house in Stení on Evvoia, with Mount Dírfys in the background

ISLANDS AT A GLANCE

Alónnisos *pp110–11*
Evvoia pp114–19
Skiáthos *pp104–5*
Skópelos *pp108–9*
Skýros *pp112–13*

The harbor of Skiáthos town

SEE ALSO

• ***Where to Stay*** p300
• ***Where to Eat*** p324
• ***Travel Information*** pp356–9

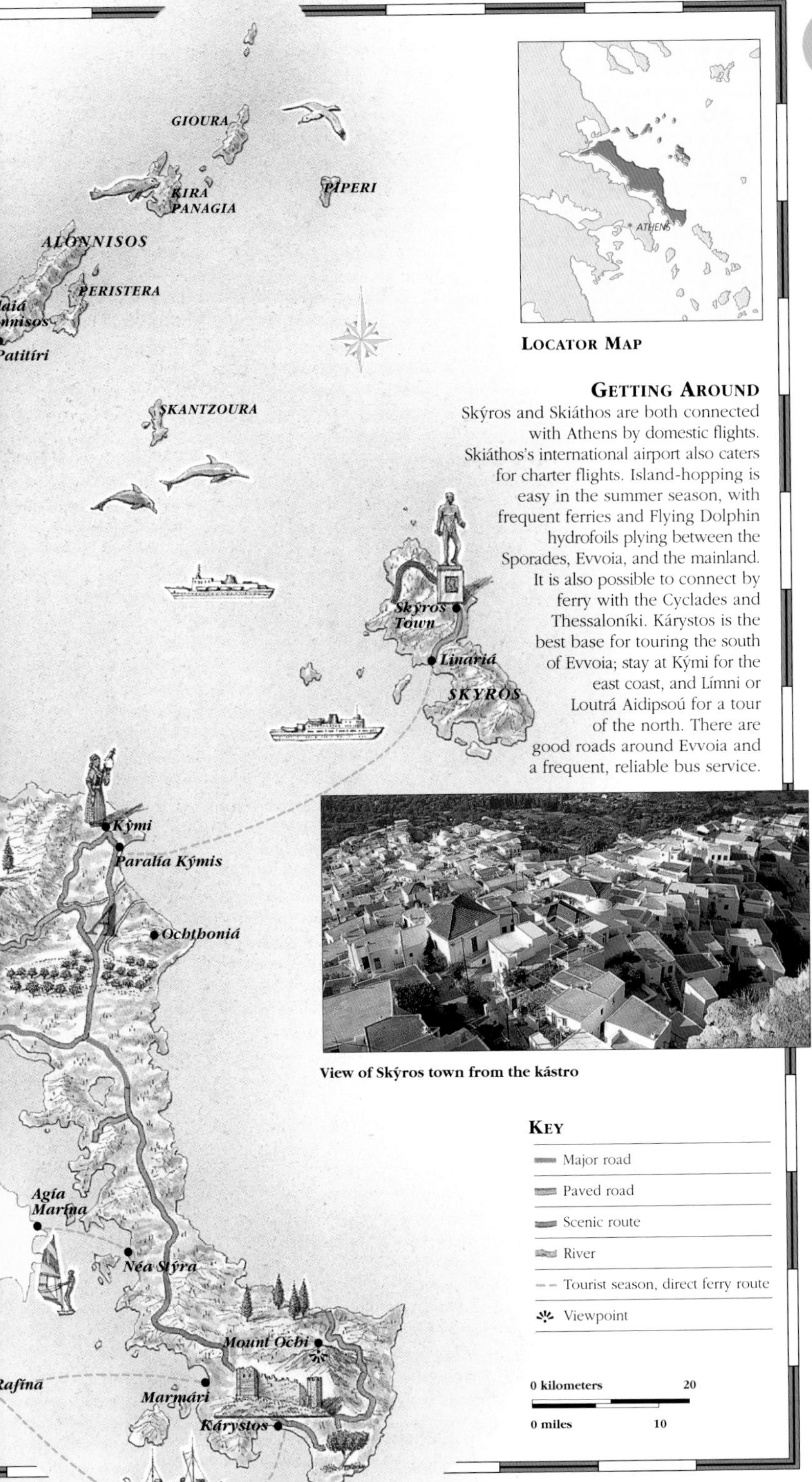

Locator Map

Getting Around

Skýros and Skiáthos are both connected with Athens by domestic flights. Skiáthos's international airport also caters for charter flights. Island-hopping is easy in the summer season, with frequent ferries and Flying Dolphin hydrofoils plying between the Sporades, Evvoia, and the mainland. It is also possible to connect by ferry with the Cyclades and Thessaloníki. Kárystos is the best base for touring the south of Evvoia; stay at Kými for the east coast, and Límni or Loutrá Aidipsoú for a tour of the north. There are good roads around Evvoia and a frequent, reliable bus service.

View of Skýros town from the kástro

Key

- Major road
- Paved road
- Scenic route
- River
- Tourist season, direct ferry route
- Viewpoint

0 kilometers 20

0 miles 10

Skiáthos

Σκιάθος

Skiathos has always been an unashamedly hedonistic island from its early tourist development in the 1960s, when it attracted the rich and famous with its legendary beaches, to its current role as pail and shovel paradise for family package tours. Although the introduction of direct package flights has diminished Skiáthos's exclusive status, the luxury yachts are still in evidence off Koukounariés beach. In spite of the tourism, the island retains its scenic beauty and a scattering of atmospheric churches and monasteries.

The sweeping bay of Koukounariés

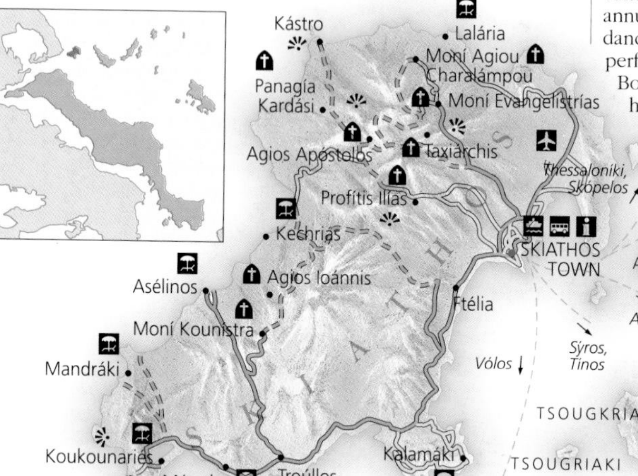

Key

For key to map see back flap

0 kilometers 2

0 miles 1

Skiathos Town

Still picturesque, the island town is a charming place with its red-tiled roofs and maze of cobblestone back streets. It is built on two small hills, dominated by the large 19th-century churches of **Trión Ierarchón** and **Panagía Limniá**, that offer excellent views of the bustling harbor below. The main street winds up between the two hills to the old quarter of Limniá, a quiet neighborhood of restored sea captains' houses covered with trailing bougainvillea and trellised vines. The town is excellent for shopping, full of aromatic bakeries, chic boutiques, and antique shops, some of which specialize in genuine folk artifacts, including ceramics, icons, jewelry, and embroidery.

The town has twin harbors, separated by **Boúrtzi** islet, which is reached by a narrow causeway. The pine-covered islet, once a fortress, is now a cultural center and hosts the annual Aegean festival of dance, theater, and concert performances each summer.

Boúrtzi is dominated by a handsome Neo-Classical building, with a statue of the famous Greek novelist Aléxandros Papadiamántis standing guard. Life in Skiáthos town centers on the long, sweeping wharves lined with numerous *kafeneía* specializing in *loukoumádes* (small honeyed fritters). In the evenings the waterfront attracts many people for a stroll in the cool night air. During the day there is the spectacle of arriving and departing flotilla yachts, ferries, and hydrofoils. The western end of the wharf has a good fish market and an *ouzerí* frequented by locals. It is also where small boats and caïques depart for day trips to some of the island's famous beaches,

View of Skiáthos town from the church of Profítis Ilías

An ornate fresco in the Christós church

such as Koukounariés and Lalária, or to the nearby islands of Tsougkriá and Arkos.

Behind the harbor is the **Papadiamántis Museum**, former home of the locally-born novelist whose name it takes. Although tiny, the museum shows the simplicity of local island life prior to the invasion of tourism.

Papadiamántis Museum
0427 23843. May–Oct.

Moní Agíou Charalámpou, set in the hills above Skiáthos town

Around the Island

The interior of the northern side of the island, with its verdant landscape of pine and olive trees, reveals deserted monasteries and churches, springs, and plenty of birdlife. This is in contrast to the overdeveloped southern coast. It is still possible to find deserted beaches and coves scattered along the northern coast. Many of these, such as **Kechriás** and **Mandráki**, can be visited only when the excursions stop for a few hours on their day trips around the island.

The main road south from Skiáthos town passes Ftélia and branches to the west just before Troúllos for Asélinos beach and **Moní Kounístra**. The monk who built this 17th-century monastery, originally called Panagía Eikonístria, found a miraculous icon in a nearby tree. Today, the icon is kept in Trión Ierarchón in Skiáthos town.

The path north from here leads to **Agios Ioánnis**, where it is customary to stop and ring the church bell after completing the steep walk through pine trees.

Farther north still is the tiny 19th-century **Panagía Kardási** chapel, with its blue ceiling covered in stars, which perches high above **Kástro**. Abandoned in 1829, remains of the 300 houses are still visible in this deserted town, and three churches have been restored – the 17th-century **Christós** church has a fine iconostasis.

On the road heading northwest out of Skiáthos town lies the barrel-vaulted 20th-century church of **Profítis Ilías**, which has a good taverna nearby with stunning views of the town. Continuing north, past rich farms and the 20th-century **Agios Apóstolos** church, the track descends through sage and bracken to **Moní Agiou Charalámpou**, built in 1809. Aléxandros Moraïtidis, the writer, spent his last days here as a monk in the early 1920s. Just south of here is **Moní Evangelistrías**. Founded in 1775 by monks from Mount Athos, it played a crucial role in the War of Independence *(see pp38–9)*, hiding many freedom fighters.

To the south of Moní Agíou Charalámpou, on the way back to Skiáthos town, is the beautiful church of **Taxiárchis**. It is covered in plates in the shape of a cross, and the best mineral spring water on the island flows out of a tap that is by the church.

Visitors' Checklist

5,000. 2 km (1 mile) NE of Skiáthos town. Harborfront, Skiáthos town. 0427 23172. Aegean Festival of Dance, Skiáthos town: Jul.

Alexandros Papadiamantis

The island's most famous native is one of Greece's outstanding literary figures. Aléxandros Papadiamántis spent his early childhood on the island, with five brothers and sisters, before leaving to study in Athens, where he began his career in journalism. He wrote more than 100 novellas and short stories, all set against the backdrop of island life. Among his best known works are *The Gypsy*, *The Murderess*, a compulsive psychological drama, and *The Man Who Went to Another Country*. In 1908 he returned to Skiáthos where he died a few years later in 1911 at age 60.

Kalamáki beach, Skiáthos ▷

Skópelos

Σκόπελος

Surprisingly, given its close proximity to Skiáthos, Skópelos has not totally succumbed to tourism. It is known to have been colonized by the Minoans as far back as 1600 BC and was used as a place of exile by the Byzantines. The Venetians held power for about 300 years after 1204. Famed for its wine in ancient times, Skópelos is still renowned for its fruit today. It offers many good beaches and has a beautiful pine-covered interior.

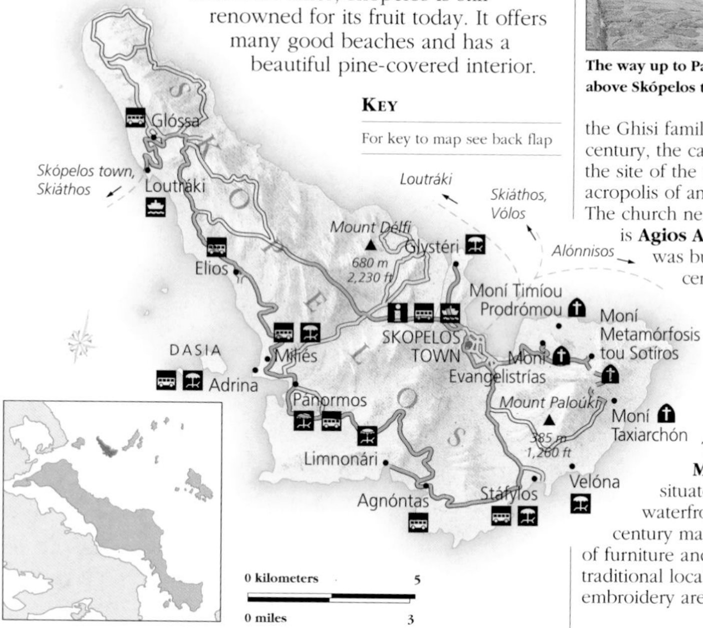

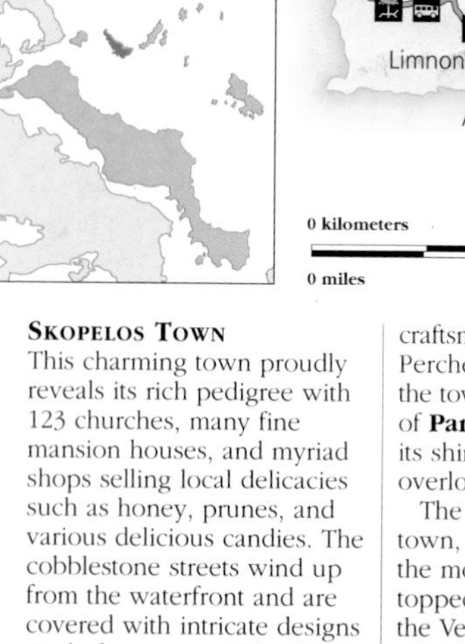

Key

For key to map see back flap

Skopelos Town

This charming town proudly reveals its rich pedigree with 123 churches, many fine mansion houses, and myriad shops selling local delicacies such as honey, prunes, and various delicious candies. The cobblestone streets wind up from the waterfront and are covered with intricate designs made from sea pebbles and shells. There are numerous classic examples of the old Sporadan town house, with its wooden balcony and fish-scale, slate-tiled roof.

In the upper town the cruciform church of **Panagía Papameletíou** is particularly splendid. Built in 1662, it is also known as Koímisis tis Theotókou. It has a well-kept interior, with an interesting display case of ecclesiastical *objets d'art* and a carved iconostasis by the Cretan craftsman Antónios Agorastós. Perched on a cliff top above the town, the landmark church of **Panagía tou Pýrgou**, with its shining fish-scale roof, overlooks the harbor.

The old quarter of Skópelos town, the Kástro, sits above the modern town and is topped by the remains of the Venetian **castle**. Built by the Ghisi family in the 13th century, the castle stands on the site of the 5th-century BC acropolis of ancient Skópelos. The church nearest the castle is **Agios Athanásios**. It was built in the 11th century, but the foundations date from the 9th century. There are some fine 16th-century frescoes inside. The **Folk Art Museum** is situated behind the waterfront in a 19th-century mansion. Pieces of furniture and examples of traditional local costumes and embroidery are on display.

The way up to Panagía tou Pýrgou above Skópelos town

Folk Art Museum

Chatzistamáti. 0424 23494.

daily.

Environs: In the hills above Skópelos town there are numerous impressive monasteries. Reached by the road going east out of the town, they all have immaculate churches with carved iconostases and icons. The fine

The attractive bay of Skópelos town, viewed from the Kástro

Fish tavernas around the bay at Agnóntas in the late afternoon

Visitors' Checklist

5,000. Skópelos town.
Harborfront (0424 23220).
Panagia: Aug 15.

Moní Evangelistrías (also known as Evangelismós) was built in 1712 and is one of the largest on the island. The nuns sell their handicrafts, including weavings, embroidery, and food. Farther up the road is **Metamórfosis tou Sotíros**, one of the oldest monasteries on Skópelos. It was built in the 16th century and is now inhabited by a solitary monk.

Moní Timíou Prodrómou, north of Moní Metamórfosis tou Sotíros, was restored in 1721. It has been inhabited by nuns, who also sell crafts, since the 1920s, and has a commanding view down over Skópelos town below. From here a rough track leads up to **Mount Paloúki**. The deserted **Moní Taxiarchón** is reached by a track from Mount Paloúki that hugs the *sares*, the local name for the steep cliffs facing Alónissos.

Around the Island

The island is easy to explore, with its main road traversing the developed southern coast, and continuing as far as Glóssa to the northwest. It has a beautiful interior, full of plum orchards, pine forests, and *kalívia* (farmhouses), but beware of the lack of signposts when traveling inland.

A steep road leads down to the popular beaches south of Skópelos town, Stáfylos and Velóna. **Agnóntas**, which serves as a port for ferries in rough weather, is quieter than Skópelos town. It is popular with locals who come for the fish tavernas beside its pebble beach. Nearby **Limnonári**, with its stunning pebble beach and azure-colored water, is reached by boat or along the narrow cliff top road.

Whitewashed houses in Glóssa, with colorful doors and shutters

Before reaching the modern village of Elios, there are two thriving resorts at Miliés and Pánormos. For a quieter location, the tiny beach of **Adrina** nearby is often deserted. Sitting oposite the beach is wooded Dasiá island, named after a female pirate who drowned there long ago.

Glóssa is the other major settlement on the island and sits directly opposite Skiáthos. Reminders of the Venetian occupation of Skópelos are evident in the picturesque remains of Venetian towers and houses. The small port of **Loutráki** below Glóssa is a sleepy place with little charm, but most ferries stop here as well as at Skópelos town.

On the north coast, caïques shuttle every half hour between the pebbled **Glystéri** beach and Skópelos town. From Glystéri a winding road leads inland to the wooded region just east of the island's highest peak, **Mount Délfi**. A short walk through the enchanting pine forest leads to four mysterious niches, signposted as *sentoúkia*, literally "crates," that are carved in the rocks. Believed to be Neolithic tombs, their position offers fine views of the island.

Kalivia

Skópelos's interior is covered with an unusual array of beautiful *kalívia* (farmhouses). Some of these traditional stone buildings are still occupied all year round; others are only used during important seasonal harvests or for celebratory feasts on local saints' days. They all have distinctive outdoor prune ovens – a legacy from the days when Skópelos was renowned for its prunes. They provide a rare insight into the rural life that has virtually disappeared on neighboring islands.

A traditional *kalívi* among olive and cypress trees

Two of the old houses in Palaiá Alónnisos in the process of restoration

Alónnisos
Αλόννησος

3,000. Patitíri. Kokkinókastro 6 km (3.5 miles) N of Patitíri.

SHARING a history of attacks by the pirate Barbarossa with the other Sporades and having endured earthquake damage in 1965, Alónnisos has suffered much over the years. However, the island is relatively unspoiled by tourism, and most of the development is centered in the main towns of Patitíri and Palaiá Alónnisos.

Patitiri

The port of Patitíri is a center of bustling activity. Boats are available for day trips to the neighboring islands, and there is excellent swimming off the rocks, northeast of the port. The picturesque backstreets display typical Greek pride in the home, evident in the immaculate whitewashed courtyards and pots of flowers.

Fishing vessels and cargo boats moored in Patitíri harbor

Rousoúm Gialós and Vótsi, 3–4 km (1–2 miles) north of Patitíri, are quieter alternatives with their natural cliff-faced harbors and tavernas.

Around the Island

This quiet island has a surfeit of beaches and coves, and the interior is crisscrossed by dirt tracks accessible only to intrepid shepherds and motorcycles. The old capital of **Palaiá Alónnisos**, west of Patitíri, perches precariously on a cliff top. There are ruins of a 15th-century Venetian castle and a beautiful small chapel, tou Christoú, that has a fish-scale roof. The town was seriously damaged by the earthquake in 1965, and the inhabitants were forced to leave their homes. They were rehoused initially in makeshift concrete homes at Patitíri. Today, the houses of Palaiá Alónnisos have been bought and restored by German and British families, and the town retains all the architectural beauty of a traditional Sporadhan village.

The road across the island, northeast from Patitíri, reveals a surprisingly fertile land of pine, olive, and arbutus trees. At **Kokkinókastro**, a popular pebble beach edged by red cliffs and pines, there are scant remains of the site of ancient Ikos – the old name of the island. The main center of the **HSSPMS** (Hellenic Society for the Study and Protection of the Monk Seal) is located at Stení Vála, where there are information displays and a video show. From here, a road snakes toward **Gérakas**, at the wild northern tip of the island. This lovely deserted beach has a research center for the HSSPMS and is good for snorkeling.

Hellenic Society for the Study and Protection of the Monk Seal (HSSPMS)
Stení Vála. 0424 65084. Apr–Oct: daily; Nov–Mar: on request.

Taverna at Stení Vála

Two endangered Mediterranean monk seals

Sporades Marine Park

Θαλάσσιο Πάρκο

from Skiáthos, Skópelos, Alónnisos.

FOUNDED IN 1992, the National Marine Park of Alónnisos and the Northern Sporades, to give it its full name, is an area of great environmental importance. It is the only such park in the Aegean and includes not just Alónnisos but also its uninhabited outlying islands of Peristéra, Skantzoúra, and Gioúra. Day trips by boat are possible, but access is limited.

The park was created to protect an important breeding colony of the endangered Mediterranean monk seal and a fragile marine ecosystem of other rare wildlife, flora, and fauna. Thanks to the pioneering efforts of marine biologists from the University of Athens, who first formed the Hellenic Society for the Study and Protection of the Monk Seal in 1988, Greece's largest population of the elusive Mediterranean monk seal is now scientifically monitored. Fewer than 500 of these seals exist worldwide, making it one of the world's most endangered species. There is an estimated population of 250 seals around the Aegean, with about 47 in the marine park. A recent campaign to promote awareness of the endangered status of the seals and restrictions on fishing in the area seems to be paying off.

Sightings of seals are not always guaranteed and sadly there is no longer access for the public to view the wild goats on Gioúra, Audouin's gull or Eleonora's falcons on the islet of Skantzoúra: only scientists are now permitted.

The marine park is also an important route and staging post for many migrant birds during the spring and autumn. Land birds, ranging in size from tiny warblers through to elegant pallid harriers, pass through the region in large numbers to and from their breeding grounds in northeast Europe.

Marine Wildlife in the Sporades

Visitors can observe a wide range of other wildlife in the Sporades while watching out for monk seals. Gray herons and kingfishers are both birds of the coast here, a surprise for many birdwatchers from northern Europe who usually associate them with freshwater habitats. Spring and autumn in particular are good times for seeing several species of gull, and tern and, when venturing close to sea cliffs, keep an eye out for the Eleonora's falcons that nest on the inaccessible ledges; in the air, they are breathtakingly acrobatic birds.

Farther out to sea, look for jellyfish in the water and the occasional group of common dolphins that may accompany the boat for a while. Cory's shearwaters fly with rigid wings close to the waves and head toward the shore in high winds and as dusk approaches. If you are at sea after dark, you are likely to see a glowing bioluminescence on the surface of the waves, caused by microscopic marine animals.

Cory's shearwaters glide low over the water. They are a common sight around Alónnisos.

Jellyfish flourish in the seas off the Sporadic islands. This is a *Pelagia noctiluca.*

Common dolphins can sometimes be seen in small groups diving in and out of the waves around the boat's wake or swimming alongside.

Mediterranean gulls are easily recognized by the pure white wings and black hood that characterize their summer plumage.

Skýros

Σκύρος

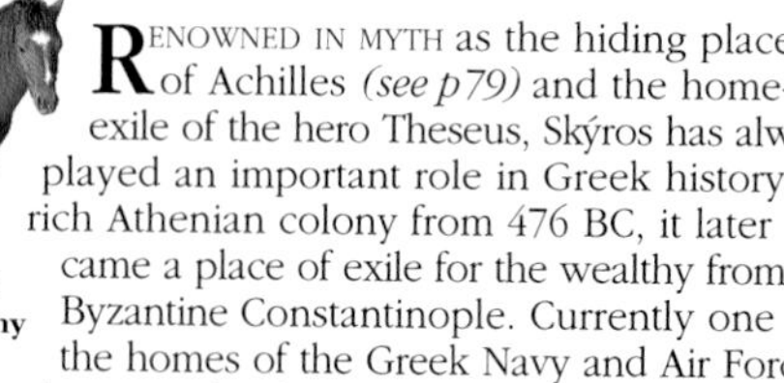

Skýrian pony

RENOWNED IN MYTH as the hiding place of Achilles *(see p79)* and the home-in-exile of the hero Theseus, Skýros has always played an important role in Greek history. A rich Athenian colony from 476 BC, it later became a place of exile for the wealthy from Byzantine Constantinople. Currently one of the homes of the Greek Navy and Air Force, its unique heritage, landscape, and architecture bear more resemblance to the Dodecanese than the Sporades.

An example of traditional Skýrian embroidery in the Fáltaïts Museum

SKYROS TOWN

The main town is architecturally unusual in the Aegean; it has a fascinating mixture of cube-shaped houses, Byzantine churches, and spacious squares. Although its main street has been spoiled by loud tavernas and bars, many backstreets give glimpses into Skýrian homes. Traditional ceramics, wood carving, copper, and embroidery are always proudly on display.

Topping the kástro of the old town with its impressive mansion houses are the remains of the **Castle of Lykomedes**, site of both an ancient acropolis and later a Venetian fortress. It is reached through a tunnel underneath the whitewashed **Moní Agíou Geórgiou**, which contains a fine painting of St. George killing the dragon. The views from the kástro of the bay below are quite breathtaking. Nearby are the remains of two Byzantine churches and three tiny chapels, with colorful pastel pink and blue interiors.

Immortal Poetry in Plateía Rupert Brooke

The town has three good museums. The **Municipal Museum** presents a traditional Skýrian town house that has been accurately recreated with local furnishings. In the **Archaeological Museum** are some bracelets and pottery that were discovered during excavations of minor Neolithic and Mycenaean sites around the island.

Housed in an old mansion owned by the Fáltaïts family, the excellent **Fáltaïts Museum** was opened in 1964 by one of their descendants, Manos Fáltaïts. It has a diverse collection of folk art including rare books and manuscripts, photographs, and paintings, which reveal much about Skýrian history and culture. It shows not only how craftsmen absorbed influences from the Byzantine, Venetian, and Ottoman occupations, but also how the development of a wealthy aristocracy actively helped transform the island's woodcarving, embroidery, ceramics, and copperware into highly sophisticated artforms.

One place to learn some of these crafts is the **Skýros Center**, a unique vacation center which also has courses in such wide-ranging subjects as yoga, reflexology, creative writing, and windsurfing. The main branch is in Skýros town, with another branch at Atsítsa, on the west coast of the island.

Plateía Rupert Brooke, above the town, is famous for its controversial statue of a naked man by M. Tómpros. Erected in 1930 in memory of the British poet Rupert Brooke, who died on the island, the statue is known as *Immortal Poetry*.

Municipal Museum
Megálou Stratoú. 0222 91256.
daily. *Nov–Mar.*

Archaeological Museum
Plateía Brooke. *0222 91327.*
Tue–Sun. *main public hols.*

Fáltaïts Museum
Palaiópyrgos. *0222 91232.*
daily. *Nov–Mar.*

Skýros Center
0171-267 4424 (contact London office for bookings). *Apr–Oct.*

The Castle of Lykomedes towering above Skýros town

ENVIRONS: Below Skýros town are the resorts of **Mólos** and **Magaziá**. Around these two resorts there are plenty of decent hotels, tavernas, and rooms to rent. Farther along the coast from Mólos, there is another sandy stretch of beach at **Pouriá**, which offers excellent spearfishing and snorkeling. At **Cape Pouriá** itself, the chapel of Agios Nikólaos is built into a cave. Just off the coast are the islets of Vrikolakonísia where the incurably ill were sent during the 17th century.

Visitors' Checklist

3,000. 18 km (11 miles) NW of Skýros town. Linariá. Skýros town. 0222 92789. Carnival around island: end Feb–early Mar.

Around the Island

The island divides into two distinct halves bisected by the road from Skýros town to the port of Linariá. Méroi, the northern part of the island, is where most people live and farm on the fertile plains of Kámpos and Trachý.

Skýros is famous for its indigenous ponies, thought by some to be the same breed as the horses that appear on the Parthenon frieze *(see p286)*. It is certainly known that the animals have been bred exclusively on Skýros since ancient times and can still be seen in the wild on the island today, particularly in the south, near the grave of Rupert Brooke.

The road running north from Skýros town leads first to the airport and then west around the island through pine forests to **Kalogriá** and **Kyrá Panagiá**, two leeward beaches sheltered from the *meltémi* (north wind). From here, the road leads to the small village and pine-fringed beach of **Atsítsa**, where there are rooms to rent and a good taverna. As noted above, Atsítsa is also home to the other branch of the Skýros Center, the island retreat offering alternative vacations. A little way south are the two beaches of **Agios Fokás** and **Péfkos**. The road loops back from Péfkos to the port of **Linariá**. Caïques depart from here to the inaccessible sea caves at Pentekáli and Diatrýpti on the east coast.

Access to Vounó, the mountainous southern part of the island, is through a narrow fertile valley south of **Ormos Achíli** between the island's two halves. The road continues south to **Kalamítsa** bay, and beyond to **Treís Mpoúkes**, a natural, deep-water harbor used by pirates in the past and the Greek Navy today. Reached by a dirt road, this is also the site of poet Rupert Brooke's simple marble grave, set in an olive grove. Brooke (1887–1915) died on a hospital ship that was about to set sail to fight at Gallipoli.

The azure waters and tree-lined sand of Péfkos beach

The Skyros Goat Dance

This famous goat dance is one of Greece's few rites that have their roots in pagan festivals. It forms the centerpiece of the pre-Lenten festivities in Skýros, celebrated with dancing and feasting. Groups of masquerading men parade noisily around the narrow streets of Skýros town. Each group is led by three central characters, the *géros* (old man), wearing a traditional shepherd's outfit and a goatskin mask and weighed down with noisy bells, the *koréla*, a young man in Skýrian women's clothing, and the *frángos*, or foreigner, a comic figure wearing disheveled clothes.

The *géros* in full costume

Evvoia
Εύβοια

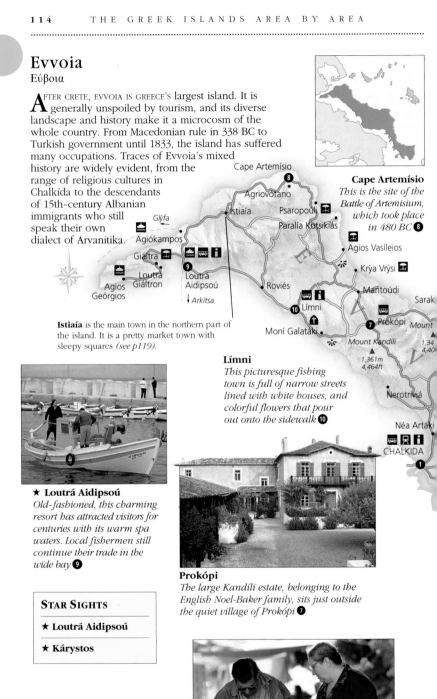

After Crete, Evvoia is Greece's largest island. It is generally unspoiled by tourism, and its diverse landscape and history make it a microcosm of the whole country. From Macedonian rule in 338 BC to Turkish government until 1833, the island has suffered many occupations. Traces of Evvoia's mixed history are widely evident, from the range of religious cultures in Chalkída to the descendants of 15th-century Albanian immigrants who still speak their own dialect of Arvanitika.

Cape Artemísio
This is the site of the Battle of Artemisium, which took place in 480 BC 8

Istiaía is the main town in the northern part of the island. It is a pretty market town with sleepy squares *(see p119)*.

Límni
This picturesque fishing town is full of narrow streets lined with white houses, and colorful flowers that pour out onto the sidewalk 10

★ Loutrá Aidipsoú
Old-fashioned, this charming resort has attracted visitors for centuries with its warm spa waters. Local fishermen still continue their trade in the wide bay 9

Prokópi
The large Kandíli estate, belonging to the English Noel-Baker family, sits just outside the quiet village of Prokópi 7

Star Sights

- ★ **Loutrá Aidipsoú**
- ★ **Kárystos**

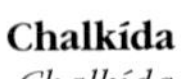

Chalkída
A modern town, Chalkída is the capital of the island, and has a mixed populace of Muslims, Jews, and Orthodox Greeks. By the waterfront is a flourishing market 1

Stení

Nestling in the green hills of Mount Dírfys, Stení's cool climate makes it a pleasant escape from the summer heat and a popular place for a day trip 6

Visitors' Checklist

208,000. Agiókampos, Erétria, Kárystos, Loutrá Aidipsoú, Marmári, Néa Stýra, Paralía Kýmis. Chalkída. Chalkída (0221 77777). Summer Drama Festival in Chalkída: May–Sep.

Kými

A wealthy port in the 1880s, Kými is quieter today, with a fine Folk Museum displaying traditional crafts such as this embroidered picture frame 5

Ochthoniá

The wild and exposed beaches surrounding Ochthoniá are quiet and often deserted, offering a relaxing break from the busy village 4

Mount Dírfys, the highest point on Evvoia, is a trekker's paradise *(see p118).*

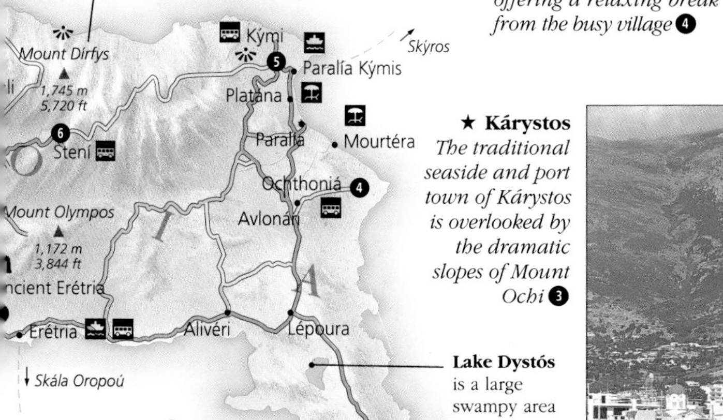

Mount Dírfys 1,745 m 5,720 ft
Kými
Skýros
Paralía Kýmis
Platána
Stení
Paralía
Mourtéra
Ochthoniá
Mount Olympos 1,172 m 3,844 ft
Avlonári
Ancient Erétria
Erétria
Alivéri
Lépoura
Skála Oropoú
Néa Stýra
Agía Marína
Stýra
Kalérgo
Mount Ochi 1,398 m 4,585 ft
Marmári
Rafína
Kárystos
Rafína

★ Kárystos

The traditional seaside and port town of Kárystos is overlooked by the dramatic slopes of Mount Ochi 3

Lake Dystós is a large swampy area on the road to Néa Stýra *(see p117).*

Mount Ochi provides a scenic day's trek with excellent views *(see p117).*

Ancient Erétria

Finds from ancient Erétria, such as this statue of the goddess Athena, are displayed in the modern town's Archaeological Museum 2

Néa Stýra is one of the minor ports on the island for ferries to the mainland *(see p117).*

Key

For key to map see back flap

0 kilometers 15

0 miles 5

Chalkída 1

Χαλκίδα

Ancient Chalkis was one of the major independent city-states until it was taken by Athens in 506 BC, and it remained an Athenian ally until 411 BC. Briefly Macedonian, the town was under Roman rule by 200 BC. There followed the same history of Byzantine, Frankish, and Venetian rule that exists in the Sporades. A bridge has spanned the fast-flowing Evripos channel since the 6th century BC. According to legend, Aristotle was so frustrated at his inability to understand the ever-changing currents that he threw himself into the water.

Visitors' Checklist

75,000. Athinón. corner of Athanasíou Diákou & Frizi. 0221 77777. Mon–Sat. Agía Paraskeví celebrations: Jul 26–Aug 1.

Chalkída's waterfront market

Exploring Chalkída

Although much of modern Chalkída is dominated by commercial activity, there are two areas of the town that are worth a visit: the waterfront that overlooks the Evripos channel, and the old Kástro quarter, on the slopes overlooking the seafront.

The Waterfront

Lined with old-fashioned hotels, cafés, and restaurants, Chalkída's waterfront also has a bustling enclosed market where farmers from the neighboring villages sell their produce. This often leads to chaotic traffic jams in the surrounding narrow streets, an area still known by its Turkish name of Pazári, where there are interesting shops devoted to bee-keeping (6 Neofýtou) and other fascinating rural activities.

Kástro

In the old Kástro quarter, southeast of the Evripos bridge, the deserted streets reveal a fascinating architectural history. Many houses still bear the traces of their Venetian and Turkish ancestry, with timbered façades or marble heraldic carving. Now inhabited by Thracian Muslims who settled here in the 1980s, and the surviving members of the oldest Jewish community in Greece, the Kástro also has an imposing variety of religious buildings. Three examples of these include the 19th-century **synagogue** on Kótsou, a beautiful 15th-century mosque, **Emir Zade**, in the square marking the entrance to the Kástro, and the church of **Agía Paraskeví**. The mosque is usually closed, but outside there is an interesting marble fountain with an Arabic inscription.

Agía Paraskeví, situated near the Folk Museum, reveals the diverse history of Evvoia more than any other building in Chalkída. This huge 13th-century basilica is built on the site of a much earlier Byzantine church. Its exterior resembles a Gothic cathedral, but the interior is a patchwork of different styles, a result of years of modification by invading peoples, including the Franks and the Turks. It has a marble iconostasis, a carved wooden pulpit, brown stone walls, and a lofty wooden ceiling. Opposite the church on a house lintel is a carving of St. Mark's winged lion, the symbol of Venice.

Housed in the vaults of the old Venetian fortress at the top of the Kástro quarter, the **Folk Museum** presents a jumble of local costumes, engravings, and a bizarre set of uniforms from a brass band, suspended with their instruments from the ceiling. The **Archaeological Museum** is a more organized collection of finds from ancient Evvoian sites such as Kárystos. Exhibits include some 5th-century BC gravestones and vases.

Roman horse head in Archaeological Museum

Folk Museum
Skalkóta 4. *0221 21817. Wed–Sun.*

Archaeological Museum
Venizélou 13. *0221 76131. Tue–Sun. main public hols.*

The 15th-century mosque in the Kástro, home to some Byzantine relics

Around Evvoia

THE FORESTS OF PINE and chestnut trees, rivers, and deserted beaches in the fertile north contrast dramatically with the dry and scrubby south. Separated by the central mountains, the south becomes rough and dusty with sheep grazing in flinty fields, snaking roads along cliff tops, and the scree slopes of Mount Ochi.

Picturesque Kárystos harbor, with Mount Ochi in the background

Ancient Erétria ❷

Αρχαία Ερέτρια

22 km (14 miles) SE of Chalkída.

Excavations begun in the 1890s in the town of Néa Psará have revealed the sophistication of the ancient city-state of Erétria, which was destroyed in 87 BC during the First Mithridatic War. At the height of its power it had colonies in both Italy and Asia Minor. Although the ancient harbor is silted up, evidence of its maritime wealth can be seen in the ruined agora, temples, gymnasium, theater, and sanctuary, which still remain around the modern town.

Artifacts from the ancient city are housed in the **Archaeological Museum**. The tomb finds include some bronze cauldrons and funerary urns. There are votive offerings from the Temple of Apollo, gold jewelry and a terra-cotta gorgon's head, which was found in a 4th-century BC Macedonian villa.

Archaeologists have also restored the **House with Mosaics** (ask for the key at the museum). Its floor mosaics are of lions attacking horses, sphinxes, and panthers.

Archaeological Museum
On the road from Chalkída to Alivéri.
0229 62206. *Tue–Sun.*

ENVIRONS: Past **Alivéri**, with its medieval castle and ugly power station, the road forks at the village of **Lépoura**. Venetian towers can be seen on the hillside here, and also around the Dýstos plain northward to Kými and south to Kárystos. A road twists through tiny villages such as **Stýra**, with their surrounding wheat fields and olive trees. Below lie the seaside resorts of Néa Stýra and Marmári, both of which provide ferry services to the mainland port of Rafína.

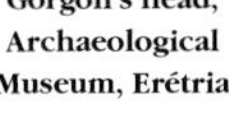

Gorgon's head, Archaeological Museum, Erétria

Kárystos ❸

Κάρυστος

130 km (80 miles) SE of Chalkída.
4,600.

Kárystos, overlooked by the imposing Castel Rosso and the village of Mýloi where plane trees surround the *kafeneía*, is a picturesque town. The modern part of the town dates from the 19th century and was built during the reign of King Otto. Kárystos has five Neo-Classical municipal buildings, excellent waterfront fish tavernas close to its Venetian Bourtzi fortress, and a **Folk Museum**. Set up as a typical Karystian house, the museum contains examples of rural life – copper pots and pans, oil amphorae, and ornate 19th-century furniture and embroidery. Kárystos is also famed for its green and white marble and green slate roof and floor tiles.

Folk Museum
50 m (165 ft) from the town square.
0224 22472.
Apr–Oct: Tue–Sun; Nov–Mar: Wed.
main public hols.

ENVIRONS: Southeast of Kárystos, remote villages, such as Platonistós and Amigdaliá, hug the slopes of Mount Ochi. Caïques from these villages take passengers on boat trips to visit nearby coves where there are prehistoric archaeological sites.

DRAGON HOUSES

Off the main road at Stýra, a signpost points the way to the enigmatic dragon houses, known locally as *drakóspita*. Red arrows mark the trail that leads to these low structures. Constructed with huge slabs of stone, they take their name from the only creatures thought capable of carrying the heavy slabs. There are many theories about the *drakóspita*, but the most plausible links them to two other similar sites, on the summits of Mount Ochi and Mount Ymittós in Attica. All three are near marble quarries, and it is believed that Carian slaves from Asia Minor (where there are similiar structures) built them as temples in about the 6th century BC.

Scenic road running through olive groves between Ochthoniá and Avlonári

Ochthoniá ❹

Οχθονιά

90 km (56 miles) E of Chalkída.

1,140.

Both Ochthoniá and its neighboring village of Avlonári, with their Neo-Classical houses clustered around ruined Venetian towers, are reminiscent of protected Umbrian hill towns.

A Frankish castle overlooks the village of Ochthoniá, and just west of Avlonári is the distinctive 14th-century basilica of Agios Dimítrios, which is the largest Byzantine church in Evvoia. Beyond the fertile fields that surround these villages, wild beaches, such as those at Agios Merkoúris and Mourterá, stretch out toward the forbidding cliffs of Cape Ochthoniá.

Kými ❺

Κύμη

90 km (56 miles) NE of Chalkída.

4,000. *Sat.* *Platána 7 km (4.5 miles) S.*

Four km (2.5 miles) above Paralía Kýmis lies the thriving town of Kými. With a commanding view of the sea, this remote settlement had surprisingly rich resources, derived from silk production and maritime trading, in the 19th century. In the 1880s, 45 ships from Kými plied the Aegean sea routes. The narrow streets of elegant Neo-Classical houses testify to its past wealth. It is known today mainly for the medicinal spring water from nearby Choneftikó, and a statue in the main square of Dr. Geórgios Papanikoláou, the town's most famous son and inventor of the cervical smear or "Pap Test." A large and well-organized **Folk Museum** contains many exhibits from Kymian life, such as a fine collection of unique cocoon embroideries and costumes. On the road north of Kými, the 17th-century **Moní Sotíra**, now inhabited by nuns, perches on the cliff edge.

Dr. Papanikoláou (1883–1962)

Folk Museum

0222 23668. *daily.* *main public hols.*

Stení ❻

Στενή

31 km (19 miles) NE of Chalkída.

1,250.

This mountain resort is much loved by Greeks who come for the cool climate and fine scenery. Stení is also popular with hikers setting their sights on Mount Dírfys, the island's highest peak at 1,740 m (5,720 ft), with spectacular views from the summit. A brisk walk followed by a lazy lunch of classic mountain cuisine – grilled meats and oven-baked beans – make for a pleasant day. The main square is also good for shops selling local specialties, such as wild herbs and mountain tea.

The road from Stení to the northern coast snakes up the mountain. It passes through spectacular scenery of narrow gorges filled with waterfalls and pine trees, and wheat fields that stretch down to the sea.

Moní Sotíra in the mountains near Kými overlooking the sea

Prokópi 7

Προκόπη

52 km (32 miles) NW of Chalkída.
1,200. *Sun.* *Krýa Vrýsi 15 km (9 miles) N.*

Sleepy at most hours, Prokópi only wakes when the tourist buses arrive with pilgrims coming to worship the remains of St. John the Russian (Agios Ioánnis o Rósos), housed in the modern church of Agíou Ioánnou tou Rósou. Souvenir shops and hotels around the village square cater fully to the visiting pilgrims. In reality a Ukranian, John was captured in the 18th century by the Turks and taken to Prokópi (present-day Ürgüp) in central Turkey. After his death, his miracle-working remains were brought over to Evvoia by the Greeks during the exodus from Asia Minor in 1923.

Prokópi is also famous for the English Noel-Baker family, who own the nearby Kandíli estate and most of the local land. Although the family have done much for the region, local feeling is mixed about the once-feudal status of this estate. Many locals, however, now accept the important role Kandíli plays in its latest incarnation as a vacation spot, by bringing money into the local economy.

Environs: The road between Prokópi and Mantoúdi runs by the river Kiréa, and a path leads to one of the oldest trees in Greece, said to be over 2,000 years old. This huge plane tree has a circumference of over 4.5 m (15 ft). Sadly, it is sinking into the sludge created by a nearby mine.

Façade of the mansion on the Noel-Baker Kandíli estate, Prokópi

View across the beach at Cape Artemísio

Cape Artemísio 8

Ακρη Αρτεμίσιο

105 km (65 miles) NW of Chalkída.
to Agriovótano. *Agriovótano (0226 23333).* *Psaropoúli 15 km (9 miles) SE.*

Below the picturesque village of Agriovótano sits Cape Artemísio, site of the Battle of Artemisium. Here the Persians, led by King Xerxes, defeated the Greeks in 480 BC. In 1928, local fishermen hauled the famous bronze statue of Poseidon out of the sea at the cape. It is now on show in the National Archaeological Museum in Athens *(see p282)*.

Old Mercedes truck delivering produce

Environs: About 20 km (12.5 miles) east lies **Istiaía**, a pleasant market town with sleepy squares, white chapels, and ocher-colored houses.

Loutrá Aidipsoú 9

Λουτρά Αιδιψού

90 km (56 miles) NW of Chalkída.
5,000. *0226 22456.* *Mon–Sat.* *Giáltra 20 km (12 miles) SW.*

Loutrá Aidipsoú is Greece's largest spa town, popular since antiquity for its cure-all sulfurous waters. These waters bubble up all over the town, and many hotels are built directly over hot springs to provide a supply to their treatment rooms. In the rock pools of the public baths by the sea, the steam rises in winter, scalding the red rocks. The old hotel Thérmai Sýlla has a rickety elevator and a marble staircase down to its splendid basement treatment rooms. These luxuries are reminders of the days when the rich and famous came to take the cure. Other faded Neo-Classical hotels along the waterfront also recall the town's days of glory in the late 19th century. The town has a relaxed atmosphere, and in summer the beach is popular with Greek families.

Environs: In the summer a ferry service goes across the bay to **Loutrá Giáltron** where warm spring water mixes with the shallows of a quiet beach edged by tavernas.

Límni 10

Λίμνη

87 km (54 miles) NW of Chalkída.
2,100. *0227 31215.*

Once a wealthy 19th-century seafaring power, the pleasant town of Límni has elegant houses, cobblestone streets, and a charming waterfront. Just south of the town is the magnificent Byzantine **Moní Galatáki**, the oldest monastery on Evvoia, etched into the cliffs of Mount Kandíli. Inhabited by nuns since the 1940s, its church is filled with beautiful frescoes. The *Last Judgment* is shown in particularly gory detail, with some souls frantically climbing the ladder to heaven while others are dragged mercilessly into the Leviathan's jaws.

THE NORTHEAST AEGEAN ISLANDS

THASOS · SAMOTHRAKI · LIMNOS · LESVOS
CHIOS · IKARIA · SAMOS

MORE THAN ANY OTHER ARCHIPELAGO IN GREECE, *the seven major islands of the Northeast Aegean defy easy categorization. Though they are neighbors, sharing a common history of rule by the Genoese and lively fishing industries, the islands are culturally distinct, encompassing a range of landscapes and lifestyles.*

Although Sámos and Chíos were prominent in ancient times, few traces of that former glory remain. Chíos offers the region's most compelling medieval monuments, including the Byzantine monastery of Néa Moní and the mastic villages, while Sámos has a fascinating museum of artifacts from the long-venerated Heraion shrine. In Límnos's capital, Mýrina, you encounter evidence of the Genoese and Ottoman occupations, in the form of its castle and domestic architecture.

Assumption of the Virgin **by Theófilos (1873–1934), Mytilíni's Byzantine Museum, Lésvos**

Lésvos shares the fortifications and volcanic origin of Límnos, though the former's monuments are grander and its topography more dramatic. To the south, the islands of Sámos, Chíos, and Ikaría have mountainous profiles and are forested with pine, olive, and cypress trees. Most of the pines of Thásos were devastated by forest fires in the 1980s, though Samothráki remains unspoiled; its numerous hot springs and waterfalls, as well as the brooding summit of Mount Fengári, are a counterpoint to the long-hallowed Sanctuary of the Great Gods.

Beaches come in all sizes and consistencies, from the finest sand to melon-sized volcanic shingle. Apart from Thásos, Sámos, and Lésvos, package tourism is scarce in the north where summers are short. Wild Ikaría, historically a backwater, will appeal mostly to spa-plungers and beachcombers, while its tiny dependency, Foúrnoi, is an ideal do-nothing retreat owing to its convenient beaches and abundant seafood.

Mólyvos harbor, Lésvos, overlooked by the town's 14th-century Genoese castle

◁ **The broad, sandy beach near the village of Kámpos, Ikaría**

Exploring the Northeast Aegean Islands

FOR ITS BEACHES AND ANCIENT RUINS, both composed of white marble, Thásos is hard to fault, while Samothráki has long been a destination for hardy nature-lovers. Less energetic visitors will find Límnos ideal, with picturesque villages and beaches close to the main town. Olive-rich Lésvos offers the greatest variety of scenery but requires time and effort to tour. For first-time visitors to the eastern isles, Sámos is the best touring base, though the cooler climate of Chíos is more attractive, and its main town offers good shopping. Connoisseurs of relatively unspoiled islands will want to sample a slower pace of life on Ikaría, Psará, or Foúrnoi.

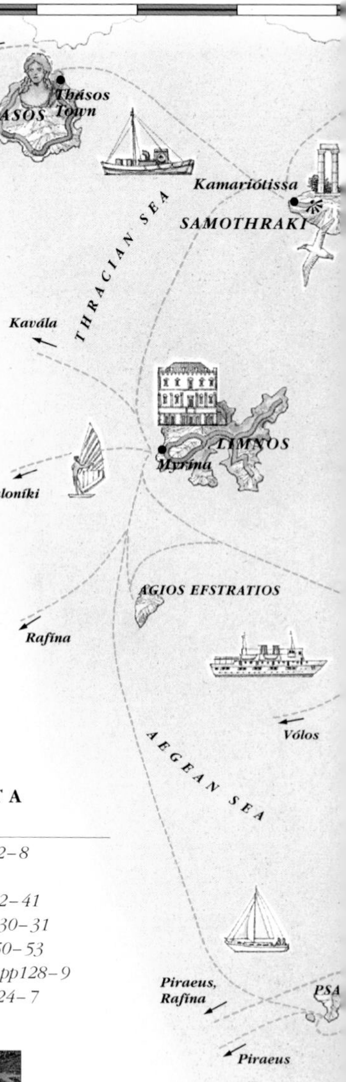

Fishing boat in Mólyvos harbor, Lésvos

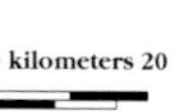

ISLANDS AT A GLANCE

Chíos *see pp142–8*
Ikaría *see p149*
Lésvos see pp132–41
Límnos *see pp130–31*
Sámos *see pp150–53*
Samothráki *see pp128–9*
Thásos *see pp124–7*

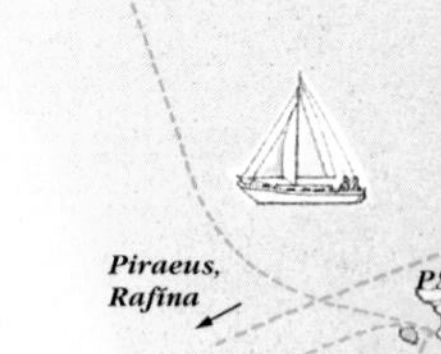

Piraeus

Piraeus, Sýros

Byzantine monastery of Néa Moní, Chíos, seen from the southwest

KEY

- Minor road
- Unpaved road
- Scenic route
- Tourist-season, direct ferry route
- Viewpoint

Alexandroúpoli

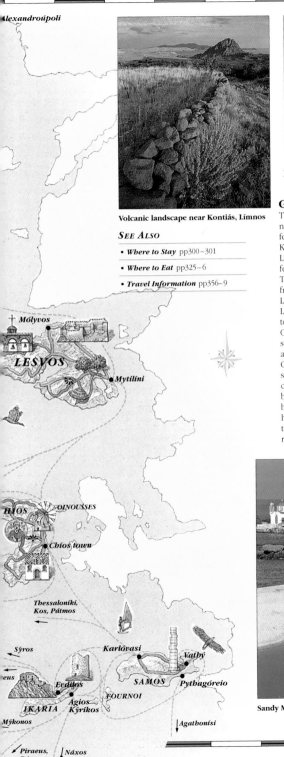

Volcanic landscape near Kontiás, Límnos

See Also

- ***Where to Stay*** pp300–301
- ***Where to Eat*** pp325–6
- ***Travel Information*** pp356–9

Locator Map

Getting Around

Thásos and Samothráki have no airports, but are served by ferries from Alexandroúpoli and Kavála on the mainland, while Límnos and Lésvos have air and ferry links with Athens and Thessaloníki. Bus services vary from virtually nonexistent on Límnos and Samothráki, or Lésvos's functional schedules, to Thásos's frequent buses. Chíos, Ikaría, and Sámos are served by flights from Athens and are connected by ferry. Chíos has an adequate bus service but is best explored by car; Sámos has more frequent buses and is small enough to be toured by motorbike; Ikaría has skeletal public transportation and steep roads requiring sturdy vehicles.

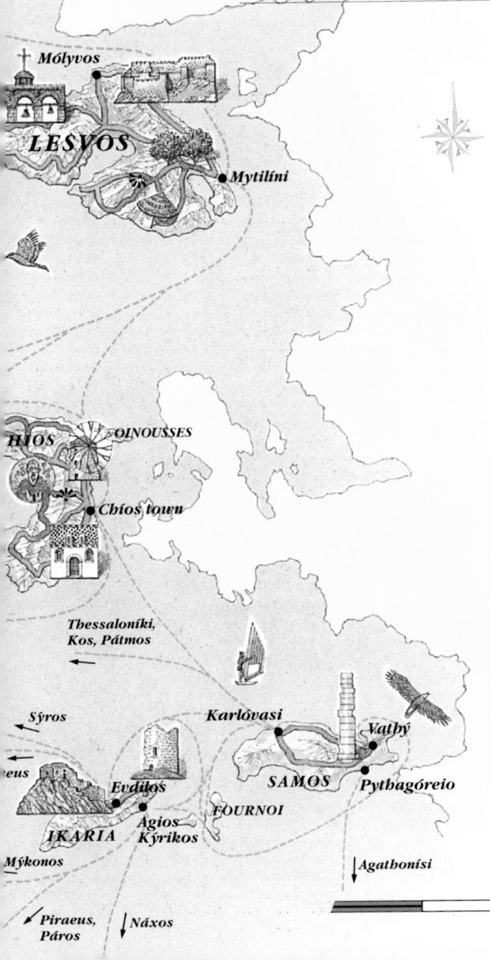

Mólyvos
LESVOS
Mytilíni
OINOUSSES
HIOS
Chíos town
Thessaloníki, Kos, Pátmos
Sýros
Karlóvasi
Vathý
SAMOS
Pythagóreio
Evdilos
Agios Kýrikos
FOURNOI
IKARIA
Mýkonos
Agathonísi
Piraeus, Páros
Náxos

Sandy Messaktí beach, Ikaría

Thásos

Θάσος

THASOS HAS BEEN INHABITED since the Stone Age, with settlers from Páros colonizing the east coast during the 7th century BC. Spurred by revenues from gold deposits near modern Thásos town, ancient Thásos became the seat of a seafaring empire, though its autonomy was lost to the Athenians in 462 BC. The town thrived in Roman times but lapsed into medieval obscurity. Today, the island's last source of mineral wealth is delicate white marble, cut from quarries whose scars are prominent on the hillsides south of Thásos town.

Exterior of the Archaeological Museum, Thásos

Thásos town harbor, viewed from the agora

Thásos Town ❶

Λιμένας

3,000. 0593 22500. daily. Pachý s 9 km (6 miles) W.

Modern Liménas, also known as Thásos town, is an undistinguished resort on the coastal plain that has been settled for nearly three millennia. Interest lies in the vestiges of the ancient city and the manner in which they blend into the modern town. Foundations of a Byzantine basilica take up part of the central square, and the road to Panagía cuts across a vast shrine of Herakles before passing a monumental gateway.

Ancient Thásos

Site & Museum 0593 22180. daily. Mon (museum only), main public hols. museum only.

Founded in the 7th century BC, ancient Thásos is a complex series of buildings, only the remains of which can be seen today. French archaeologists have conducted excavations here since 1911; digs were recently resumed at a number of locations in Thásos town. The **Archaeological Museum**, next to the agora, houses the latest treasures to have been unearthed.

Well defined by the ruins of four stoas, the Hellenistic and Roman **agora** covers a vast area behind the ancient military harbor, today the picturesque Limanáki, or fishing port. Though only a few columns

Sights at a Glance

Alykí ❸
Kástro ❻
Megálo Kazavíti ❽
Moní tou Archangélou Michaïl ❹
Potamiá ❷
Sotíros ❼
Thásos Town ❶
Theológos ❺

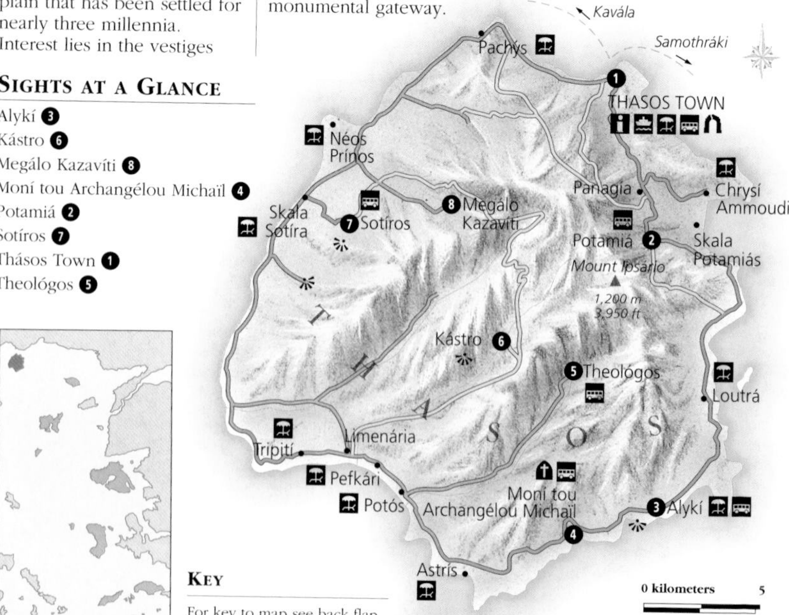

Key

For key to map see back flap

Plan of Ancient Thasos

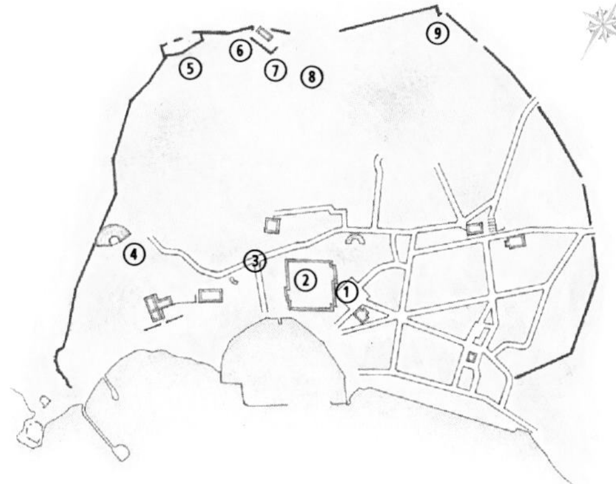

Key to Plan

1. Archaeological Museum
2. Agora
3. Temple of Dionysos
4. Theater
5. Citadel
6. Walls
7. Temple to Athena Poliouchou
8. Shrine to Pan
9. Gate of Parmenon

have been reerected, it is easy to trace the essentials of ancient civic life, including several temples to gods and deified Roman emperors, foundations of heroes' monuments, and the extensive drainage system.

Foundations of a **Temple of Dionysos**, where a 3rd-century BC marble head of the god was found, mark the start of the path up to the acropolis. Partly overgrown by oaks, the Hellenistic **theater** has spectacular views out to sea. The Romans adapted the stage area for their bloody spectacles; it is now being excavated with the intent of complete restoration.

The ancient **citadel**, once the location of an Apollo temple, was rebuilt during the 13th century by the Venetians and Byzantines. It was then ceded by Emperor Manuel II Palaiológos to the Genoese Gatelluzi clan in 1414, who enlarged and occupied it until 1455. Recycled ancient masonry is conspicuous at the south gateway. By the late 5th century BC, substantial walls of more than 4 km (2.5 miles) surrounded the city, the sections by the sea having been mostly wrecked on the orders of victorious besiegers in 492 and 462 BC.

Foundations of a **Temple to Athena Poliouchou** (Protector of the City), dated to the early 5th century BC, are just below the acropolis summit; massive retaining walls support the site terrace. A cavity hewn in the rocky outcrop beyond served as a **shrine to Pan** in the 3rd century BC; he is depicted in faint relief playing his pipes.

Behind the summit point, a steep 6th-century BC stairway descends to the **Gate of Parmenon** in the city wall. The gate retains its lintel and takes its name from an inscription "Parmenon Made Me" (denoting its mason), on a nearby wall slab.

Visitors' Checklist

16,000. Thásos town.
Panagía: Aug 15.

The Gate of Parmenon in the south wall of ancient Thásos

Columns of the agora, with the town church in the background

Around Thásos Island

Thasos is just small enough to explore by motorcycle, though the bus service along the coastal ring road is good and daily hydrofoils link Thásos town with the western resorts. The best beaches are in the south and east, though the coastal settlements are mostly modern annexes of inland villages, built after the suppression of piracy in the 19th century.

Sculpture at the Vagis Museum

Boats in the peaceful harbor of Skála Potamiás

Potamiá ❷

Ποταμιά

9 km (6 miles) S of Thásos town.
1,000. daily. Loutrá 12 km (7 miles) S; Chrysí Ammoudiá 5 km (3 miles) E.

Named after the perennial river in the valley behind, Potamiá is a small village with one of the most popular paths leading to the 1,204-m (3,950-ft) summit of Mount Ipsário. Following bulldozer tracks upstream brings you to the trailhead for the ascent, which is a seven-hour excursion; although the path is marked by the Greek alpine club, it is in a poor condition.

The sculptor and painter Polýgnotos Vagis (1894–1965) was a native of the town, although he emigrated to America at an early age. Before his death, the artist bequeathed most of his works to the Greek state, and they are now on display at the small **Vagis Museum**, situated in the village center. His work has a mythic, dreamlike quality; the most compelling sculptures are representations of birds, fish, turtles, and ghostly faces that he carved onto boulders or smaller stones.

Vagis Museum
0593 61400. Tue–Sun.

Blue-washed house in Panagía

Environs: Many visitors stay and enjoy the traditional Greek food at **Skála Potamiás,** 3 km (2 miles) east of Potamiá, though **Panagía,** 2 km (1 mile) north, is the most visited of the inland villages. It is superbly situated above a sandy bay, has a lively square, and many of its 19th-century houses have been preserved or restored.

Alykí ❸

Αλυκή

29 km (18 miles) S of Thásos town.
Astrís 12 km (7 miles) W.

Perhaps the most scenic spot on the Thasian shore, the headland at Alykí is tethered to the body of the island by a slender spit, with beaches on either side. The westerly cove is fringed by the hamlet of Alykí, which has well-preserved 19th-century vernacular architecture due to its official classification as an archaeological zone. A Doric temple stands over the eastern bay, and behind it, on the headland, are two fine Christian basilicas, dating from the 5th-century, with a few of their columns reerected.

Local marble was highly prized in ancient times; now all that is left of Alykí's quarries are overgrown depressions on the headland. At sea level, "bathtubs" (trenches scooped out of the rock strata) were once used as evaporators for salt-harvesting.

Moní tou Archangélou Michaïl, perched on its clifftop

Moní tou Archangélou Michaïl ❹

Μονί του Αρχαγγέλου Μιχαήλ

34 km (18 miles) S of Thásos town.
0593 51275. daily.

Overhanging the sea 3 km (2 miles) west of Alykí, Moní tou

Archangélou Michaïl was founded early in the 12th century by a hermit called Luke, on the spot where a spring had appeared at the behest of the Archangel. Now a dependency of Moní Filothéou on Mount Athos in northern Greece, its most treasured relic is a holy nail from the Cross. Nuns have occupied the grounds since 1974.

Slate-roofed house with characteristically large chimney pots, Theológos

Theológos 5

Θεολόγος

50 km (31 miles) S of Thásos town. *900.* *daily.* *Potós 10 km (6 miles) SW.*

Well inland at a pirate-safe location, Theológos was the Ottoman-era capital of Thásos. Tiered houses still exhibit their typically large chimneys and slate roofs. Generous gardens and courtyards give the village a green and open aspect. A ruined tower and low walls on the hillside opposite are evidence of Theológos's original 16th-century foundation by Greek refugees from Constantinople.

Kástro 6

Κάστρο

45 km (28 miles) SW of Thásos town. *6.* *Triptí 13 km (8 miles) W of Limenária.*

At the center of Thásos, 500 m (1,640 ft) up in the mountains, the village of Kástro was even more secure than Theológos. Founded in 1403 by Byzantine Emperor Manuel II Palaiológos, it became a stronghold of the Genoese, who fortified the local hill, which is now the cemetery. Kástro was slowly abandoned after 1850, when a German mining operation created jobs at Limenária, on the coast below.

This inland hamlet has now been reinhabited on a seasonal basis by sheep farmers. The *kafeneío*, on the ground floor of the former school, beside the church, shelters the single telephone; there is no public electricity.

Sotíros 7

Σοτίρος

23 km (14 miles) SW of Thásos town. *12* *Skála Sotíra 3 km (2 miles) E.*

Facing the sunset, Sotíros has the most alluring site of all the inland villages – a fact not lost on the dozens of foreigners who have made their homes here. Under gigantic plane trees watered by a triple fountain, the tables of a small taverna fill the relaxed balcony-like square. The ruin above the church was a lodge for German miners, whose exploratory shafts still yawn on the ridge opposite.

Taverna overhung by plane trees in Sotíros village

Traditional stone houses with timber balconies, Megálo Kazavíti

Megálo Kazavíti 8

Μεγάλο Καζαβίτι

22 km (14 miles) SW of Thásos town. *1,650.* *daily.* *Néos Prínos 6 km (4 miles) NE.*

Greenery-shrouded Megálo Kazavíti (officially Ano Prínos) surrounds a central square, which is a rarity on Thásos. There is no better place to find examples of traditional domestic Thasian architecture with its characteristic mainland Macedonian influence: original house features include narrow-arched doorways, balconies, and overhanging upper stories, with traces of the indigo, magenta, and ocher plaster pigment that was once commonly used across the Balkans.

Samothráki
Σαμοθράκι

2,700. Kamariótissa. Pachiá Ammos 15 km (9 miles) SW of Kamariótissa.

WITH VIRTUALLY NO level terrain, except for the western cape, Samothráki is synonymous with the bulk of Mount Fengári. In the Bronze Age the island was occupied by settlers from Thrace. Their religion of the Great Gods was incorporated into the culture of the Greek colonists in 700 BC and survived under Roman patronage until the 4th century AD. The rawness of the weather seems to go hand in hand with the brooding landscape, making it easy to see how belief in the Great Gods endured.

Chora

Lying 5 km (3 miles) east of Kamariótissa, the main port of the island, Chóra is the capital of Samothráki. The town almost fills a pine-flecked hollow that renders it invisible from the sea.

With its labyrinthine bazaar, and cobblestone streets threading past sturdy, tile-roofed houses, Chóra is the most handsome village on the island. A broad central square with two tavernas provides an elegant vantage point, looking out to sea beyond the Genoese **castle**. Adapted from an earlier Byzantine fort, little other than the castle's gateway remains, though more substantial fortifications can be found downhill at Chóra's predecessor, **Palaiópoli**; here

The town of Chóra with the remains of its Genoese castle in the background

Sanctuary of the Great Gods
Ερείπια του Ιερού των Μεγάλων

THE SANCTUARY of the Great Gods on Samothráki was, for almost a millennium, the major religious center of ancient Aeolia, Thrace, and Macedonia. There were similar shrines on Límnos and Ténedos, but neither commanded the following or observed the same rites as the one here. Its position in a canyon at the base of savage, plunging crags on the northeast slope of Mount Fengári was perhaps calculated to inspire awe; today, though thickly overgrown, it is scarcely less impressive. The sanctuary was expanded and improved in Hellenistic times by Alexander's descendants, and most of the ruins visible today date from that period.

Nike Fountain
A marble centerpiece, the Winged Victory of Samothráki, once decorated the fountain. It was discovered by the French in 1863 and is now displayed in the Louvre, Paris.

The stoa is 90 m (295 ft) long and dates to the early 3rd century BC.

Hall for votive offerings

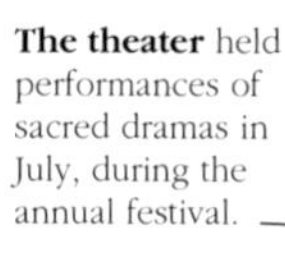

The theater held performances of sacred dramas in July, during the annual festival.

Hieron
The second stage of initiation, epopteia, *took place here. In a foreshadowing of Christianity, this involved confession and absolution followed by baptism in the blood of a sacrificed bull or ram. Rites took place in an old Thracian dialect until 200 BC.*

three Gatelluzi *(see p134)* towers of 1431 protrude above the extensive walls of the ancient town.

Around the Island

Easy to get around by bike or on foot, Samothráki has several villages worth visiting on its southwest flank, lost in olive groves or poplars. The north coast is moister, with plane, chestnut, and oak trees lining the banks of several rivers. Springs are abundant, and waterfalls meet the sea at Kremastá Nerá to the south. Stormy conditions compound the lack of adequate harbors.

Thermá has been the island's premier resort since the Roman era, due to its hot springs and lush greenery. You can choose among two rustic outdoor pools of about 34° C (93° F), under wooden shelters; an extremely hot tub of 48° C (118° F) in a cottage, only for groups; and the rather sterile modern bathhouse at 39° C (102° C). Cold-plunge fans will find rock pools and low waterfalls 1.5 km (1 mile) east at **Gría Váthra**. These are not as impressive or cold as the ones only 45 minutes' walk up the Foniás canyon, 5 km (3 miles) east of Thérma.

The highest summit in the Aegean, at 1,600 m (5,250 ft), is the granite mass of **Mount Fengári**. Although often covered with cloud, it serves year round as a seafaring landmark, and the views from the top are superb. In legend, the god Poseidon watched the Trojan war from this mountain. The peak is usually climbed from Thermá as a six-hour round trip, although there is a longer and easier route up from Profítis Ilías village on its southwest flank.

Three Gatelluzi towers at ancient Palaiópoli

Arsinoeion

At over 20 m (66 ft) across, this rotunda is the largest circular building known to have been built by the Greeks. It was dedicated to the Great Gods in the 3rd century BC.

Visitors' Checklist

6 km (4 miles) NE of Kamariótissa. to Palaiópoli. **Site & Museum** 0551 41474. 8:30am–3pm Tue–Sun. main public hols.

Anaktoron

This building was where myesis, *the first stage of initiation into the cult, took place. This involved contact with the* kabiri *mediated by prior initiates.*

The Temenos is a rectangular space where feasts were probably held.

Small theater

The Propylaion (monumental gate) was dedicated by Ptolemy II of Egypt in 288 BC.

Museum

Deities and Mysteries of Samothraki

When Samothráki was colonized by Greeks in 700 BC, the settlers combined later Olympian deities with those they found here. The principal deity of Thrace was Axieros, the Great Mother, an earth goddess whom the Greeks identified with Demeter, Aphrodite, and Hekate. Her consort was the fertility god Kadmilos and their twin offspring were the *kabiri* – a Semitic word meaning "Great Ones" that soon came to mean the entire divine family. These two deities were later recognized as the *dioskouroi* Castor and Pollux, whose emblems were snakes and a star. The cult was open to all comers of any age or gender, free or slave, Greek or barbarian. Details of the mysteries are unknown as adherents honored a vow of silence.

The twin *kabiri*, Castor and Pollux

Límnos

Λήμνος

THE MYTHOLOGICAL LANDING PLACE OF HEPHAISTOS, the god of metalworking down from Olympos by Zeus, Límnos is appropriately volcanic; the lava soil crumbles into broad beaches and grows excellent wine and herbal honey. Controlling the approaches to the Dardanelles, the island was an important outpost to both the Byzantines and the Turks, under whom it prospered as a trading station. The Greek military still controls much of the island, but otherwise it is hard to imagine a more peaceful place.

Visitors' Checklist

12,000. 22 km (14 miles) NE of Mýrina. Mýrina. Plateía Kída, Mýrina. Town Hall, on the waterfront Mýrina (0254 22208). Aug 15.

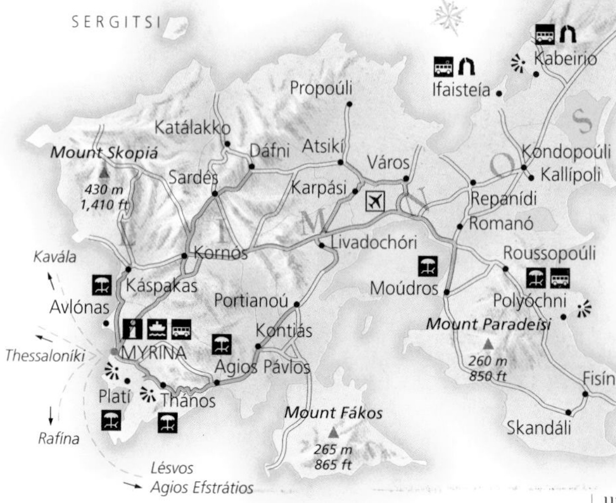

KEY

For key to map see back flap

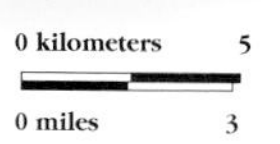

MYRINA

Successor to ancient Myrina, Límnos's second town in antiquity, modern Mýrina sprawls between two sandy bays at the foot of a rocky promontory. Not especially touristy, it is one of the more pleasant island capitals in the North Aegean, with cobblestone streets, an unpretentious bazaar, and imposing, late Ottoman houses. The most ornate of these cluster behind the northerly beach, Romaíikos Gialós, which is also the center of the town's nightlife. The south beach, Toúrkikos Gialós, extends beyond the compact fishing port with its half dozen dockside tavernas. The only explicitly Turkish relic is a fountain on Kída, inscribed with Turkish calligraphy, from which delicious potable water can still be drawn.

Housed in an imposing 19th-century mansion behind Romaíikos Gialós, the recently redesigned **Archaeological Museum** is exemplary in its display of artifacts belonging to the four main ancient cities of Límnos. The most prestigious items have been sent to Athens, however, leaving a collection dominated by pottery shards that may interest only a specialist. The most compelling ceramic exhibits are a pair of votive lamps in the form of Sirens from the temple at Ifaisteía, while metalwork from Polyóchni is represented by bronze tools and a number of decorative articles.

Spread across the headland, and overshadowing Mýrina, the **kástro** boasts the most dramatic position of any North Aegean stronghold. Like others in the region, it was in turn an ancient acropolis and a Byzantine fort, fought over and refurbished by Venetians and Genoese until the Ottomans took the island in 1478. Though dilapidated, the kástro makes a rewarding evening climb for views of western Límnos.

Archaeological Museum

Romaíikos Gialós. *0254 22990.*

Tue–Sun. main public hols.

Mýrina harbor, overlooked by the kástro in the background

The volcanic landscape of Límnos, viewed from the village of Kontiás

Around the Island

Though buses run from Mýrina to most villages in summer, the best way to travel around Límnos is by car or motorbike; both can be hired at Mýrina. Southeast from Mýrina, the road leads to **Kontiás**, the third largest settlement on Límnos, sited between two volcanic outcrops supporting the only pinewoods on the island. Sturdily constructed, red-tiled houses, including some fine Belle Epoque mansions, combine with the landscape to make this the island's most appealing inland village.

The bay of **Moúdros** was Commonwealth headquarters during the ill-fated 1915 Gallipoli campaign. Many casualties were evacuated to the hospital here; the unlucky ones were laid to rest a short walk east of Moúdros town on the road to Roussopoúli. With 887 graves, this ranks as the largest Commonwealth cemetery from either world war in the Greek islands; 348 more English-speaking servicemen lie in another graveyard across the bay at **Portianoú**.

Founded just before 3000 BC, occupying a clifftop site near the village of Kamínia, the fortified town of **Polyóchni** predates Troy on the Turkish coast just across the water. Like Troy, which may have been a colony, it was leveled in 2100 BC by an earthquake. It was never resettled. The suddenness of the catastrophe gave many people no time to leave their homes – skeletons were unearthed among the ruins. Polyóchni was noted for its metalsmiths, who refined and worked raw ore from Black Sea deposits and shipped the finished objects to the Cyclades and Crete. A hoard of gold jewelry, now displayed in Athens, was found in one of the houses. Italian archaeologists continue the excavations every summer and have penetrated four distinct layers since 1930.

The patron deity of Límnos was honored at **Ifaisteía**, situated on the shores of Tigáni Bay. This was the largest city on the island until the Byzantine era. Most of the site has yet to be completely revealed. Currently, all that is visible are outlines of the Roman theater, parts of a necropolis, and foundations of Hephaistos's temple.

Looking down on the remains of a Roman theater, Ifaisteía

Rich grave offerings and pottery found on the site can be seen in the Mýrina Archaeological Museum.

The ancient site of the **Kabeirio** (Kavírio in modern Greek) lies across Tigáni Bay from Ifaisteía and has been more thoroughly excavated. The Kabeirioi, or Great Gods, were worshiped on Límnos in the same manner as on Samothráki *(see pp128–9)*, though at this sanctuary little remains of the former shrine and its adjacent stoa other than a number of column stumps and bases.

Below the sanctuary ruins, steps lead down to a sea grotto known as the Cave of Philoctetes. It takes its name from the wounded Homeric warrior who was abandoned here by his Greek comrades on their way to Troy because of his putrefying leg injury.

Outlying Islands

Certainly the loneliest outpost of the North Aegean, tiny, oak-covered **Agios Efstrátios** (named after the saint who was exiled and died here) has scarcely a handful of tourists in any summer. The single port town was damaged by an earthquake in 1967, with dozens of islanders killed; some pre-quake buildings survive above the ferry jetty. Deserted beaches can be found an hour's walk to either side of the port.

Lésvos

Λέσβος

Ouzo from Plomári

ONCE A FAVORED SETTING for Roman holidays, Lésvos, with its thick southern forests and idyllic orchards, was known as the "Garden of the Aegean" to the Ottomans. Following conquest by them, in 1462, much of the Greek population was enslaved or deported to Constantinople, and most physical traces of Genoese or Byzantine rule were obliterated by both the Turks and the earthquakes the island is prone to. Lésvos has been the birthplace of a number of artists, its most famous child being the great 7th-century BC lyric poet Sappho.

★ Mólyvos

The tourist capital of the island, Mólyvos has a harbor overlooked by a Genoese castle with fine views of Turkey 6

Pétra

This popular resort takes its name from the huge perpendicular rock at its heart. Steps in the rock lead to an 18th-century church on the summit 7

Kalloní

Known mainly for the sardines caught off the coast of nearby Skála Kallonís, this is a cross-roads for most of the island's bus routes 8

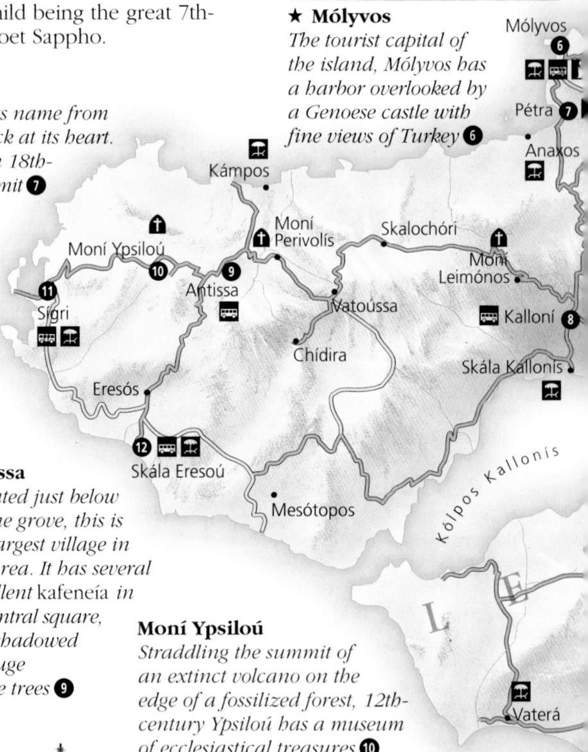

Antissa

Situated just below a pine grove, this is the largest village in the area. It has several excellent kafeneía *in its central square, overshadowed by huge plane trees* 9

Moní Ypsiloú

Straddling the summit of an extinct volcano on the edge of a fossilized forest, 12th-century Ypsiloú has a museum of ecclesiastical treasures 10

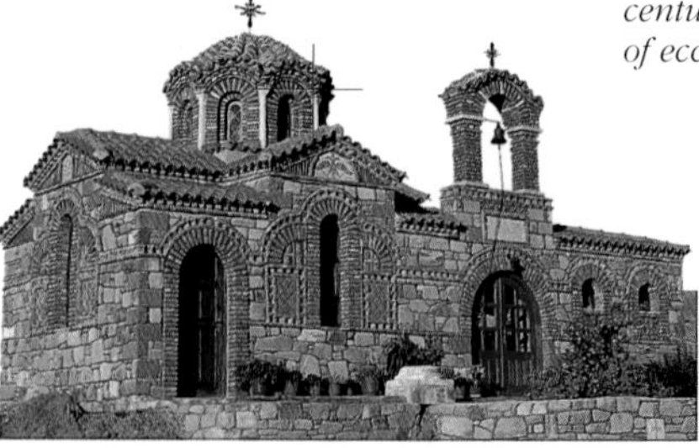

Sígri

Near the westernmost point of the island, this small chapel stands at the waterfront on the edge of the remote village of Sígri 11

Skála Eresoú

One of the largest resorts on the island, the beach at Eresoú lies only a short walk from the birthplace of the poet Sappho 12

Visitors' Checklist

90,000. 8 km (5 miles) S of Mytilíni. Pávlou Kountourióti, Mytilíni.
Mytilíni (around island).
Mytilíni (0251 28661).
Panigýri at Agiásos: Aug 15.

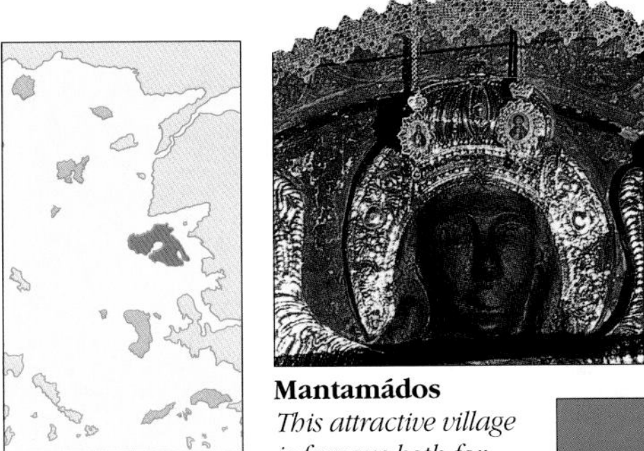

Mantamádos
This attractive village is famous both for its pottery and the "black" icon at the enormous Moní ton Taxiarchón 4

Sykaminiá
The harbor below the hill town of Sykaminiá, birthplace of modern novelist Stratís Myrivílis, is one of the most picturesque in Greece 5

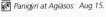

★ Mytilíni
Just outside Mytilíni is a museum devoted to the work of modern artist Theófilos Chatzimichaïl 1

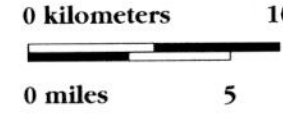

Plomári
This large coastal resort, with its Varvagiánnis distillery, is the ouzo capital of Lésvos 2

Agiásos
Widely regarded as the most beautiful hill town of the island, Agiásos's main church has an icon supposedly painted by St. Luke 3

Star Sights

- ★ **Mólyvos**
- ★ **Mytilíni**

Key

For key to map see back flap

Mytilíni ❶

Μυτιλήνη

Ottoman inscription above the castle gate

MODERN MYTILINI has assumed both the name and site of the ancient town. It stands on a slope descending to an isthmus bracketed by a pair of harbors. An examination of Ermoú reveals the heart of a lively bazaar. Its south end is home to a fish market selling species rarely seen elsewhere, while at the north end the roofless shell of the Gení Tzamí marks the edge of the former Turkish quarter. The Turks ruled from 1462 to 1912, and Ottoman houses still line the narrow lanes between Ermoú and the castle rise. The silhouettes of such Belle Epoque churches as Agioi Theódoroi and Agios Therápon pierce the tile-roofed skyline.

The dome of Agios Therápon

Kástro

Ermoú 201. 0251 27970. Tue–Sun. main public hols.

Surrounded by pine groves, this Byzantine foundation of emperor Justinian (527–65) still impresses with its huge curtain walls, but it was even larger during the Genoese era. Many ramparts and towers were destroyed during the Ottoman siege of 1462 – an Ottoman Turkish inscription can be seen at the south gate. Over the inner gate the initials of María Palaiologína and her husband Francesco Gatelluzi – a Genoan who helped John Palaiológos regain the Byzantine throne – complete the list of the castle's renowned occupants. Ruined foundations include those of the Gatelluzi palace, a Turkish *medresse* (school), and a dervish cell; a Byzantine cistern stands by the north gate.

Archaeological Museum

Argýris Eftaliótis. **New wing:** Corner of 8 Noemvríou & Melínas Merkoúri. 0251 28032. Tue–Sun. main public hols.

Lésvos's archaeological collection occupies a Belle Epoque mansion and a small annex in its back yard. The most famous exhibits are Roman villa mosaics. Neolithic finds from the 1929–33 British excavations at Thermí, just north of town, can also be seen, and the garden contains grave stelae. A new building nearby displays additional finds.

Byzantine Museum

Agios Therápon. 0251 28916. mid-May–mid-Oct: Mon–Sat.

This ecclesiastical museum is devoted almost entirely to exhibiting icons. The collection ranges from the 13th to the 18th century and also includes a more recent, folk-style icon by Theófilos Chatzimichaïl.

ENVIRONS: The **Theófilos Museum**, 3 km (2 miles) south in Vareiá village, offers four rooms of canvases by Theófilos Chatzimichaïl (1873–1934), the Mytilíni-born artist. All were commissioned by his patron Tériade in 1927 and created over the last seven years of the painter's life. Theófilos detailed the fishermen, bakers, and harvesters of rural Lésvos, and executed creditable portraits of personalities he met on his travels. For his depictions of historical episodes or landscapes beyond his experience, Theófilos relied on his imagination. The only traces of our age are occasional airplanes or steamboats in the background of his landscapes.

Just along the road is the **Tériade Museum**, housing the collection of Stratís Eleftheriádis – a local who emigrated to Paris at the turn of the century, adopting the name Tériade. He became a publisher of avant-garde art and literature. Miró, Chagall, Picasso, Léger, and Villon were some of the artists who took part in his projects.

Theófilos Museum

Mikrás Asías, Vareiá. 0251 41644. Tue–Sun. main public hols.

Tériade Museum

Mikrás Asías, Vareiá. 0251 23372. Tue–Sun. main public hols.

VISITORS' CHECKLIST

30,000. 8 km (5 miles) S. Pávlou Koudourióti. Aristárchou 6 (0251 42511). Agios Ermogénis 12 km (7 miles) S; Charamída 14 km (9 miles) S. Jul 15–Aug 15.

Daphnis and Chloe, by Marc Chagall (1887–1984), in the Tériade Museum

Olive Growing in Greece

THE CRETAN MINOANS are thought to have been the first people to have cultivated the olive tree, around 3800 BC. The magnificent olive groves of modern Greece date back to 700 BC, when olive oil became a valuable export commodity. According to Greek legend, Athena, goddess of peace as well as war, planted the first olive tree on the Athenian Acropolis – the olive has thus become a Greek symbol for peace. The 11 million or so olive trees on Lésvos are reputed to be the most productive oil-bearing trees in the Greek Islands; Crete produces more and better quality oil, but no other island is so dominated by olive monoculture. The fruits can be cured for eating throughout the year or pressed to provide a nutritious and versatile oil; further crushing yields oil for soap and lanterns, and the pulp is a good fertilizer.

Branch of ripening olives

In myth, *the olive is a virgin tree, tended only by virgin males. Its abundant harvest has been celebrated in verse, song, and art ever since antiquity. This vase shows three men shaking olives from a tree while a fourth gathers the harvest into a basket.*

Olive groves *on Lésvos date mostly from after a killing frost in 1851. The best olives come from the hillside plantations between Plomári and Agiásos, founded in the 18th century by local farmers desiring land relatively inaccessible to tax collectors.*

The olive harvest *on Lésvos takes place from late November to late December. Each batch is brought to the local* elaiotriveío *(olive mill), ideally within 24 hours of being picked, pressed separately, and tested for quality.*

Greek olive oil, *greenish-yellow after pressing, is believed by the Greeks to be of a higher quality than its Spanish and Italian counterparts, because of hotter, drier summers that promote low acid levels in olive fruit.*

Types of Olive

From the mild fruits of the Ionians to the small, rich olives of Crete, the Greek islands are a paradise for olive-lovers.

Kalamáta, the most famous Greek olive, is glossy-black, almond-shaped, and cured in red wine vinegar.

Elítses are small, sweet-flavored olives from the island of Crete.

Thásos olives are salt-cured and have a strong flavor that goes well with cheese.

Tsakistés are picked young and lightly cracked before curing in brine.

Ionian greens are mild, mellow-flavored olives, lightly brine-cured.

Throúmpes are a true taste of the countryside, very good as a simple *mezés* with olive-oil bread.

Around Eastern Lésvos

Miraculous icon of Agiásos

Eastern Lesvos is dominated by the two peaks of Lepétymnos in the north and Olympos in the south, both reaching the same height of 968 m (3,176 ft). Most of the island's pine forests and olive groves are found here, as well as the two major resort areas and the most populous villages after the port and capital. There are also several thermal spas, the most enjoyable being at Loutrá Eftaloús, near Mólyvos. With an early start from Mytilíni, which provides bus connections to all main towns and villages, the east of the island can be toured in a single day.

Plomári ❷
Πλωμάρι

42 km (26 miles) SW of Mytilíni.
3,600. Mon–Sat.
Agios Isídoros, 3 km (2 miles) NE; Melínta, 6 km (4 miles) NW.

Plomári's attractive houses spill off the slope above its harbor and stretch to the banks of the usually dry Sedoúntas River that runs through the central commercial district. The houses date mostly from the 19th century, when Plomári became wealthy through its role as a major shipbuilding center. Today, Plomári is known as the island's ouzo capital, with five distilleries, the most famous being Varvagiánnis.

Agiásos ❸
Αγιάσος

28 km (17 miles) W of Mytilíni.
3,500. Mon–Sat.
Vaterá, 31 km (19 miles) S.

Hidden in a forested ravine beneath Mount Olympos, Agiásos is possibly the most beautiful hill town on Lésvos. It began life in the 12th century as a dependency of the central monastic church of the **Panagía Vrefokratoússa**, which was constructed to enshrine a miraculous icon reputed to have been painted by St. Luke.

After exemption from taxes by the Sultan during the 18th century, Agiásos swelled rapidly with Greeks fleeing hardship elsewhere on the island. The town's tiled houses and narrow, cobblestone lanes have changed little in recent years, except for stands of locally crafted souvenirs that line the way to the church with its belfry and surrounding bazaar. The presence of shops built into the church's foundations, with rents going toward its upkeep, is an ancient arrangement. It echoes the country fair element of the traditional religious *panigýria* (festivals), where pilgrims once came to buy and sell as well as perform devotions. Agiásos musicians are hailed as the best on Lésvos – they are out in force during the August 15 festival of the Assumption of the Virgin, considered one of the liveliest in Greece. The pre-Lenten carnival is also celebrated with verve at Agiásos; there is a special club devoted to organizing it.

Ouzo

Ouzo is the Greek version of a spirit found throughout the Mediterranean. The residue of grape skins left over from wine-pressing is boiled in a copper still to make a distillate originally called raki. The term ouzo may derive from the Italian *uso Massalia*, used to label early shipments leaving the Ottoman Empire for Marseille. Today it means a base of raki flavored with star anise or fennel. Ouzo's alcohol content varies from 38–48 percent, with 44 percent considered the minimum for a quality product. When water is added, ouzo turns milky white – this results from the binding of anethole, an aromatic compound found in fennel and anise.

Mantamádos ❹
Μανταμάδος

36 km (22 miles) NW of Mytilíni.
1,500. Mon–Sat.
Tsónia, 12 km (7 miles) N.

The attractive village of Mantamádos is famous for its pottery industry and the adjacent **Moní Taxiarchón**. The existing monastery dates from the 17th century and houses a black icon of the Archangel Michael, reputedly made from mud and the blood of monks slaughtered in an Ottoman raid. A bull is publicly sacrificed here on the third Sunday after Easter and its meat eaten in a communal stew, the first of several such rites on the island's summer festival calendar. Mantamádos ceramics come in a wide

Plomári, viewed from the extended jetty

Fishing boats at Mólyvos harbor with the castle in the background

range of sizes and colors, from giant *pythária* (olive oil containers) to smaller *koumária* (ceramic water jugs).

Sykaminiá ❺

Συκαμινιά

46 km (23 miles) NW of Mytilíni. *300.* *Mon–Sat.* *Kágia 4 km (2 miles) E; Skála Sykaminiás, 2 km (1 mile) N.*

Flanked by a deep valley and overlooking the straits to the Asia Minor coast, Sykaminiá has the most spectacular position of any village on Mount Lepétymnos, which stands at a height of 968 m (3,176 ft). Novelist Efstrátios Stamatópoulos (1892–1969), known as Stratís Myrivílis, was born close to the atmospheric central square. The jetty church, which featured in his novel *The Mermaid Madonna*, can be seen down in Skála Sykaminiás. One of Skála's tavernas is named after the *mouriá* or mulberry tree in which Myrivílis slept on hot summer nights.

Mólyvos ❻

Μόλυβος

61 km (38 miles) NW of Mytilíni. *1,500.* *0253 71313.* *Mon–Sat.*

Situated in a region celebrated in antiquity for its vineyards, Mólyvos is the most popular and picturesque town on Lésvos. It was the birthplace of Arion, the 7th-century BC poet, and the site of the grave of Palamedes, the Achaian warrior buried by Achilles. According to legend, Achilles besieged the city until the king's daughter fell in love with him and opened the gates – though he killed her for her treachery. There is little left of the ancient town apart from the tombs excavated near the tourist office, but its ancient name, Míthymna, has been revived and is used as an alternative to Mólyvos (a Hellenization of the Turkish "Molova").

Before 1923 over a third of the population was Muslim, forming a landed gentry who built many sumptuous three-story town houses and graced Mólyvos with a dozen street fountains, some of which retain original ornate inscriptions. The mansions, or *archontiká*, are clearly influenced by eastern architecture *(see p18)*; the living spaces are arranged on the top floor around a central stairwell, or *chagiáti* – a design which had symbolic, cosmological meaning in the original Turkish mansions from which it was taken. The picturesque harbor and cobblestone lanes of tiered stone houses are all protected by law; any new development must conform architecturally with the rest of the town.

Overlooking the town, and affording splendid views of the Turkish coast, stands a sizeable Byzantine **kástro**. The castle was modified by the Genoese adventurer Francesco Gatelluzi *(see p134)* in 1373, though it fell into Turkish hands during the campaign of Mohammed the Conqueror in 1462. Restored in 1995, the castle still retains its wood and iron medieval door and a Turkish inscription over the lintel. During summer, the interior often serves as a venue for concerts and plays.

As you head down to the port, the **Archaeological Museum** is worth visiting for its artifacts from ancient Míthymna. A boatyard operates at the fishing harbor, a reminder of the days when Mólyvos was one of the island's major commercial ports.

Kástro
0253 71803. *Tue–Sun.* *main public hols.*

Archaeological Museum
0253 71059. *Tue–Sun.* *main public hols.*

Colorfully restored Ottoman-style houses in Mólyvos

Tiered stone houses rising above the picturesque harbor of Mólyvos ▷

Around Western Lésvos

THOUGH MOSTLY TREELESS AND CRAGGY, western Lésvos has a severe natural beauty, broken by inland villages, beach resorts, and three of Lésvos's most important monasteries. Many of the island's famous horses are bred in this region, and where the streams draining the valleys meet the sea, reedy oases form behind the sand, providing a haven for bird-watchers during spring. Bus schedules are too infrequent for touring the area, but cars can be rented at Mólyvos.

Tiered houses of the village of Skalochóri

Pétra ❼

Πέτρα

55 km (34 miles) NW of Mytilíni.
1,000. *Anaxos 3 km (2 miles) W.*

The village of Pétra takes its name (meaning "rock") from the volcanic monolith at its center. By its base is the 16th-century basilica of **Agios Nikólaos**, still with its original frescoes, and a flight of 103 steps climbs to the 18th-century church of **Panagía Glykofiloúsa** church. The **Archontikó Vareltzídaina**, one of the last of the Ottoman dwellings once widespread on Lésvos *(see p137)*, is also 18th-century.

Archontikó Vareltzídaina
Sapphous. *0253 41510.*
Tue–Sun. *main public hols.*

ENVIRONS: In 1527, the abbot Ignatios founded the rambling complex of **Moní Leimónos**, the second most important monastery on Lésvos. You can still view his cell, maintained as a shrine. A carved wood ceiling, interior arcades, and a holy spring trickling from the foundations distinguish the central church. Leimónos also has various rest homes, a minizoo, and two museums: one ecclesiastical and one of folkloric miscellany.

Moní Leimónos
5 km (3 miles) NW of Kalloní. *0253 22289.* **Ecclesiastical Museum** *daily.* **Folk Museum** *on request.*

Kalloní ❽

Καλλονή

40 km (25 miles) NW of Mytilíni.
1,600. *Mon–Sat.*
Skála Kallonís 2 km (1 mile) S.

An important crossroads and market town, Kalloní lies 2 km (1 mile) inland from its namesake gulf. Sardines are netted at the beach of **Skála Kallonís**.

Antissa ❾

Αντισσα

76 km (47 miles) NW of Mytilíni.
1,410. *daily.*
Kámpos 4 km (2.5 miles) S.

The largest village of this part of Lésvos, Antissa merits a halt for its fine central square alone, in which a number of cafés and tavernas stand overshadowed by three huge plane trees. The ruins of the eponymous ancient city, destroyed by the Romans in 168 BC, lie 8 km (5 miles) down the road, near the remains of the Genoese **Ovriókastro**. This castle stands on the shore, east of the tiny fishing port of Gavathás and the long sandy beach of Kámpos.

ENVIRONS: Although, unlike Antissa, there is no view of the sea, **Vatoússa**, 10 km (6 miles) east, is the area's most attractive village. Tiered **Skalochóri**, another 3 km (2 miles) north, does overlook the north coast and – like most local villages – has a ruined mosque dating to the days before the 1923 Treaty of Lausanne *(see p39)*.

Hidden in a lush river valley, 3 km (2 miles) east of Antissa, stands the 16th-century **Moní Perivolís**, situated in the middle of a riverside orchard. The narthex features three 16th-century frescoes, restored in the 1960s: the apocalyptic the *Earth and Sea Yield Up Their Dead*, the *Penitent Thief of Calvary*, and the *Virgin* (flanked by Abraham). The interior is lit by daylight only, so it is advisable to visit the monastery well before dusk.

Frescoes adorning the narthex of Moní Perivolís

Moní Ypsiloú ⑩
Μονή Υψηλού

62 km (38 miles) NW of Mytilíni.
0253 56259. daily.

Spread across the 511-m (1,676-ft) summit of Mount Ordymnos, an extinct volcano, Moní Ypsiloú was founded in the 12th century and is now home to just four monks. It has a handsome double gate and a fine, wood-lattice ceiling in its *katholikón* (main church), beside which a rich exhibition of ecclesiastical treasures can be found. In the courtyard outside stand a number of fragments of petrified trees. The patron saint of the monastery is John the Divine (author of the *Book of Revelations*), a typical dedication for religious communities located in such wild, forbidding scenery.

Triple belltower of Moní Ypsiloú

Environs: The main entry to Lésvos's **petrified forest** is just west of Ypsiloú. Some 15 to 20 million years ago, Mount Ordymnos erupted, beginning the process whereby huge stands of sequoias, buried in the volcanic ash, were transformed into stone.

Sígri ⑪
Σίγρι

93 km (58 miles) NW of Mytilíni.
400.

An 18th-century Ottoman **castle** and the church of **Agía Triáda** dominate this sleepy port, protected from severe weather by long, narrow Nisópi Island. Sígri's continuing status as a naval base has discouraged tourist development, though it has a couple of small beaches; emptier ones are only a short drive away.

The peaceful harbor of Sígri

Skála Eresoú ⑫
Σκάλα Ερεσού

89 km (55 miles) W of Mytilíni.
1,500.

Extended beneath the acropolis of ancient Eresoú, the wonderful, long beach at Skála Eresoú supports the island's third largest resort. By climbing the acropolis hill, you can spot the ancient jetty submerged in the modern fishing anchorage. Little remains at the summit, but the Byzantine era is represented in the ancient center by the foundations of the basilica of **Agios Andreás**; its 5th-century mosaics await restoration.

Environs: The village of **Eresoú**, 11 km (7 miles) inland, grew up as a refuge from medieval pirate raids; a vast, fertile plain extends between the two settlements. Two of Eresoú's most famous natives were the philosopher Theophrastos, a pupil of Aristotle *(see p55)*, and Sappho, one of the greatest poets of the ancient world.

Sappho, the Poet of Lesvos

One of the finest lyric poets of any era, Sappho (c.615–562 BC) was born, probably at Eresoú, into an aristocratic family and a society that gave women substantial freedom. In her own day, Sappho's poems were known across the Mediterranean, though Sappho's poetry was to be suppressed by the church in late antiquity and now survives only in short quotations and on papyrus scraps. Many of her poems were also addressed to women, which has prompted speculation about Sappho's sexual orientation. Much of her work was inspired by female companions: discreet homosexuality was unremarkable in her time. Even less certain is the manner of her death; legend asserts that she fell in love with a younger man whom she pursued as far as the isle of Lefkáda. Assured that unrequited love could be cured by leaping from a cliff, she did so and drowned in the sea: an unlikely, and unfortunate, end for a poet reputed to be the first literary lesbian.

Chíos

Χίος

Although Chios has been prosperous since antiquity, today's island is largely a product of the Middle Ages. Under the Genoese, who controlled the highly profitable trade in gum mastic *(see pp144–5)*, the island became one of the richest in the Mediterranean. It continued to flourish under the Ottomans until March 1822, when the Chians became the victims of one the worst massacres *(see p147)* of the independence uprising. Chíos had only partly recovered when an earthquake in 1881 caused severe damage, particularly in the south.

Storefront in Chíos town bazaar

Chíos Town ❶

Χίος

25,000. Polytechníou (around island), Dimokratías (environs). Kanári 18 (0271 44389). Mon–Sat. Karfás 7 km (4 miles) S.

Chíos town, like the island, was settled in the Bronze Age and was colonized by the Ionians from Asia Minor by the 9th century BC. The site was chosen for its convenient position for traveling to the mainland opposite, rather than as a good anchorage: a series of rulers have been obliged to construct long breakwaters as a consequence. Though it is a modernized island capital (few buildings predate the earthquake of 1881), there are a number of museums and other scattered relics from the town's eventful past. Besides the kástro, the most interesting sights are the lively bazaar at the top of Roïdou and an ornate Ottoman fountain dating to 1768 at the junction of Martýron and Dimarchías.

Kástro

Maggiora. 0271 22819. daily.

The most prominent medieval feature of the town is the kástro, a Byzantine foundation improved by the Genoese after they acquired Chíos in 1346. Today the kástro lacks the southeasterly sea rampart, which fell prey to developers after the devastating earthquake in 1881. Its most impressive gate is the southwesterly Porta Maggiora; a deep dry moat runs from here around to the northwest side of the walls. Behind the walls, Ottoman-era houses line narrow lanes of what were once the Muslim and Jewish quarters of the town; after the Ottoman conquest, in 1566, Orthodox and Catholics were required to live outside the walls. Also inside, an abandoned mosque, ruined Turkish baths, and

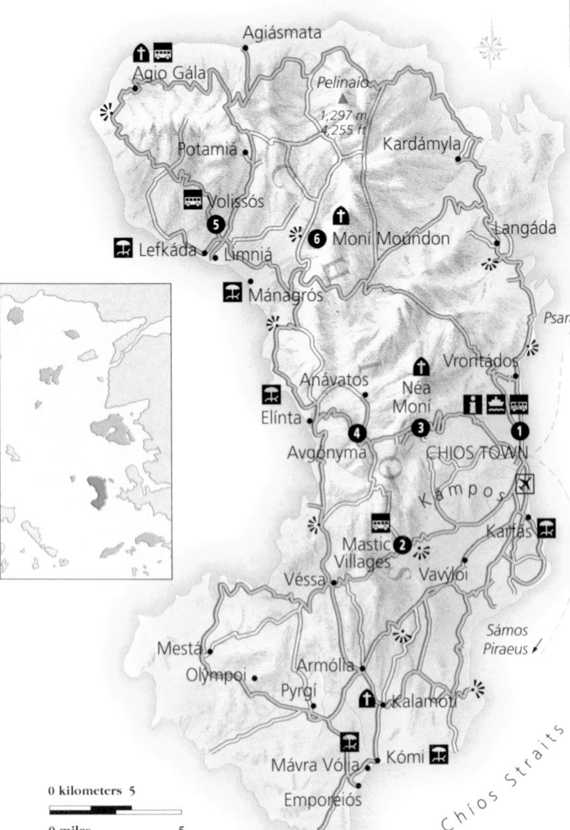

Key

For key to map see back flap

Sights at a Glance

Avgónyma ❹
Chíos Town ❶
Mastic Villages ❷
Moní Moúndon ❻
Néa Moní ❸
Volissós ❺

Chíos town waterfront with the dome and minaret of the Mecidiye mosque

a small Ottoman cemetery can be found. The latter contains the grave and headstone of Admiral Kara Ali, who commanded the massacre of 1822. He was killed aboard his flagship when it was destroyed by the Greek captain Kanarís.

Porta Maggiora, the southwesterly entrance to the kástro

Justiniani Museum

John Kennedy 6. 0271 22819.
Tue–Sun. main public hols.

This collection is devoted to religious art and includes a 5th-century AD floor mosaic rescued from a neglected Chian chapel. The saints featured on the icons and frescoes include Isídoros, who is said to have taught the islanders how to make liqueur from mastic *(see pp144–5)*, and Matrona, a martyr of Roman Ankara whose veneration here was introduced by refugees from Asia Minor after 1923.

Byzantine Museum

Plateía Vounakíou. 0271 26866.
Tue–Sun. main public hols.

Though called the Byzantine Museum, this is little more than an archaeological warehouse and restoration workshop. It is housed within the only mosque to have survived intact in the East Aegean, the former Mecidiye Cami, which still retains its minaret. A number of Jewish, Turkish, and Armenian gravestones stand propped up in the courtyard, attesting to the multiethnic population of the island during the medieval period.

Philip Argénti Museum

Koraïs 2. 0271 44246.
8am–2pm Mon–Fri, 5–7:30pm Fri, 8:30am–12:30pm Sat.

Endowed in 1932 by a member of a leading Chian family and occupying the floor above the Koraïs library, this collection features rural wooden implements, plus examples of traditional embroidery and costumes. Also on display, alongside a number of portraits of the Argénti family, are rare engravings of islanders and numerous copies of the *Massacre at Chíos* by Delacroix (1798–1863). This painting, as much as any journalistic dispatch, aroused the sympathy of Western Europe for the Greek revolutionary cause *(see pp38–9)*. The main core of the Koraïs library, situated on the ground floor, consists of a number of books and manuscripts bequeathed by the revolutionary hero and intellectual Adamántios Koraïs (1748–1833); these include works given by Napoleon.

Environs: The fertile plain known as the **Kámpos** extends 6 km (4 miles) south of Chíos town. The land is crisscrossed by a network of unmarked lanes which stretch between high stone walls that betray nothing of what lies behind. However, through an ornately arched gateway left open, you may catch a glimpse of what were once the summer estates of the medieval Chian aristocracy.

Several of the mansions were devastated by the 1881 earthquake, but some have been restored with their blocks of multicolored sandstone arranged so that the different shades alternate. Many of them still have their own waterwheels, which were once donkey-powered and drew water up from 30-m (98-ft) deep wells into open cisterns shaded by a pergola and stocked with fish. These freshwater pools, which are today filled by electric pumps, still irrigate the vast orange, lemon, and tangerine orchards for which the region is widely known.

Detail of Delacroix's *Massacre at Chíos* (1824) in the Philip Argénti Museum

Visitors' Checklist

45,000. 4 km (2 miles) S of Chíos town.
Chíos town.
Chíos town (0271 44389).

Mastic Villages ❷

Μαστιχοχώρια

Ammólian pottery

The 20 settlements in southern Chíos known as the *mastichochória*, or "mastic villages," received their name from their most lucrative medieval product. Genoese overlords founded the villages well inland as an antipirate measure during the 14th and 15th centuries. Constructed to a design unique in Greece, they share common defensive features made all the more necessary by the island's proximity to the Turks. Though they were the only villages to be spared in the 1822 massacres *(see p147)*, most have had their architecture compromised by both earthquake damage and ill-advised modernization.

Main Mastic Villages

Véssa

This is the one village whose regular street plan can easily be seen from above while descending from Agios Geórgios Sykoúsis or Eláta.

Fortification towers guarded each corner of the village.

Houses reached three stories, with vaulted ceilings except on the top floor.

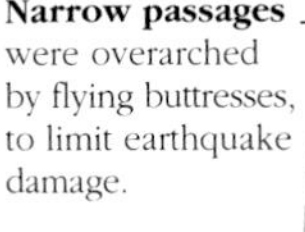

Narrow passages were overarched by flying buttresses, to limit earthquake damage.

Streets followed an intricate grid plan designed to confuse strangers.

Flat roofs of adjacent buildings were ideally of the same height to facilitate escape.

Pyrgí

Pyrgí is renowned for its bright houses, many patterned with xystá *("grating") decoration. Outer walls are plastered using black sand and coated with whitewash. This is then carefully scraped off in repetitive geometric patterns, revealing the black undercoat. An example of this is the church of Agioi Apóstoloi, which also has medieval frescoes.*

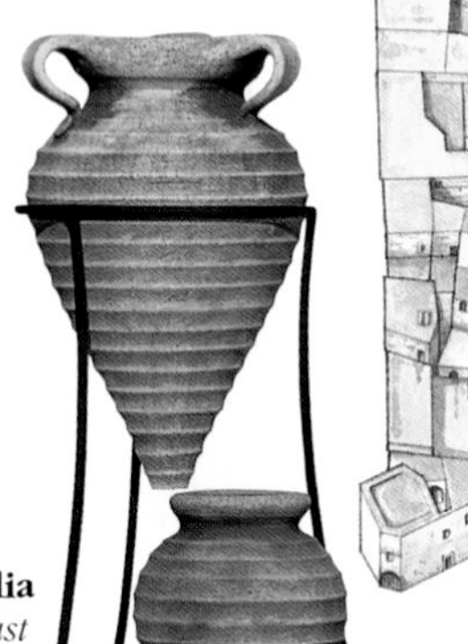

Armólia

One of the smallest and least elaborate of the mastichória, *Armólia is renowned for its pottery industry.*

Olýmpoi
Olýmpoi is almost square in layout. Its central tower has survived to nearly its original height, and today two cafés occupy its ground floor. Here local men and women can be seen winnowing mastic.

Visitors' Checklist

28 km (17 miles) SW of Chíos town. *Pyrgí: 1,200; Mestá: 400; Olýmpoi: 350.* *Mestá.* *Mávra Vólia & Kómi 5 km (3 miles) SE of Pyrgí.*

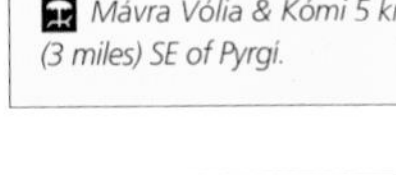

Vavýloi
The 13th-century Byzantine church of Panagía Krína, on the edge of the village, is famed for its frescoes and its alternating courses of stone- and brickwork.

A square tower in the center of the village was the last refuge in troubled times.

The outer circuit of houses doubled as a perimeter wall.

Mastic Production

The mastic bush of southern Chíos secretes a resin or gum that, before the advent of petroleum-based products, formed the basis of paints, cosmetics, and medicines. Today it is made into chewing gum, liqueur, and even toothpaste. About 300 tons of gum are harvested each summer through incisions in the bark, which weep resin "tears"; once solidified a day later, the resin is scraped off and spread to air-cure on large trays.

Mastic bush bark and crystals

Crystals separated from the bark

Mesta

Viewed here from the southwest, Mestá is considered the best-preserved of the mastic villages. It has the most even roof heights and still retains its perimeter corner towers.

Taxiárchis Church
Mestá's 19th-century church, the largest on Chíos, dominates the central square. The atmospheric interior has a fine carved altar screen.

Néa Moní ❸

Νέα Μονή

St. Anne mosaic, inner narthex

Hidden in a wooded valley 11 km (7 miles) west of Chíos town, the monastery of Néa Moní and its mosaics – some of Greece's finest – both date from the 11th century. It was established by Byzantine Emperor Constantine IX Monomáchos in 1042 on the site where three hermits found an icon of the Virgin. It reached the height of its power after the fall of the Byzantine empire and remained influential until the Ottoman reprisals of 1822. Néa Moní has now been a convent for decades, but when the last nun dies will be taken over again by monks.

Néa Moní, viewed from the west

Narthex
Seen here with the main church dome in the background, the narthex contains the most complex mosaics. Twenty-eight saints are depicted, including St. Anne, the only woman. The Virgin with Child *adorns the central dome.*

The belfry is a modern structure, added after the 1881 earthquake.

St. Joachim mosaic

Ornate marble inlays were highly prized in the Byzantine empire.

★ Christ Washing the Disciples' Feet
Here Christ washes the feet of Peter, who indicates he wishes his head and hands also to be bathed.

Star Features

- **★ Anástasis**
- **★ Christ Washing the Disciples' Feet**

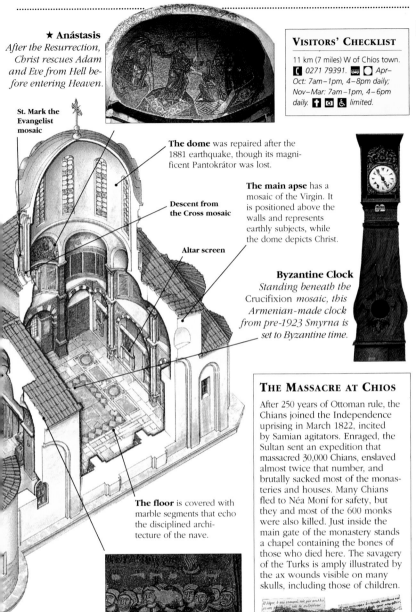

★ Anástasis

After the Resurrection, Christ rescues Adam and Eve from Hell before entering Heaven.

Visitors' Checklist

11 km (7 miles) W of Chíos town. *0271 79391.* *Apr–Oct: 7am–1pm, 4–8pm daily; Nov–Mar: 7am–1pm, 4–6pm daily.* *limited.*

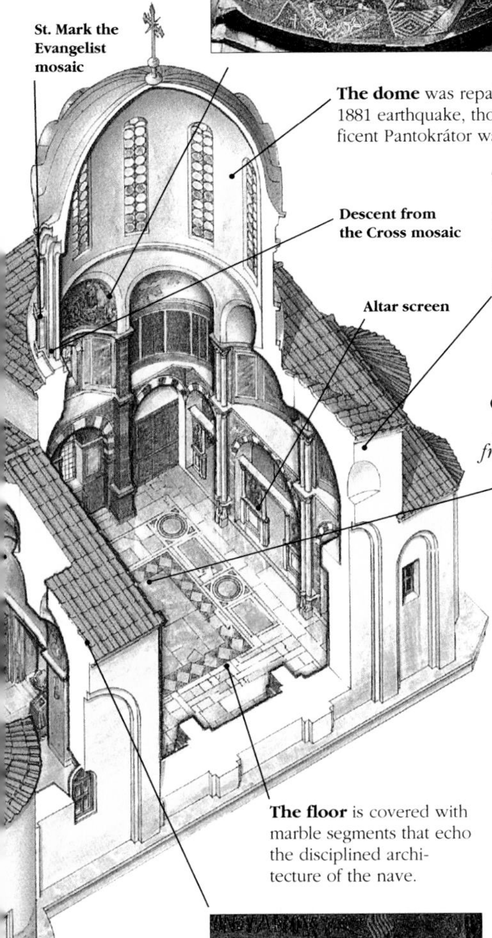

St. Mark the Evangelist mosaic

The dome was repaired after the 1881 earthquake, though its magnificent Pantokrátor was lost.

Descent from the Cross mosaic

The main apse has a mosaic of the Virgin. It is positioned above the walls and represents earthly subjects, while the dome depicts Christ.

Altar screen

Byzantine Clock

Standing beneath the Crucifixion *mosaic, this Armenian-made clock from pre-1923 Smyrna is set to Byzantine time.*

The floor is covered with marble segments that echo the disciplined architecture of the nave.

Betrayal in the Garden

A detail of this mosaic shows Peter lopping off the centurian's ear following the betrayal of Jesus in Gethsemane. Unfortunately, the Kiss of Judas *has been damaged.*

The Massacre at Chios

After 250 years of Ottoman rule, the Chians joined the Independence uprising in March 1822, incited by Samian agitators. Enraged, the Sultan sent an expedition that massacred 30,000 Chians, enslaved almost twice that number, and brutally sacked most of the monasteries and houses. Many Chians fled to Néa Moní for safety, but they and most of the 600 monks were also killed. Just inside the main gate of the monastery stands a chapel containing the bones of those who died here. The savagery of the Turks is amply illustrated by the ax wounds visible on many skulls, including those of children.

Cabinet containing the skulls of the Chian martyrs of 1822

Around Chíos Island

Ceiling detail at Moúndon

With its verdant, semimountainous terrain, edged by rocky cliffs in the south and sandy beaches to the northwest, Chíos is one of the Aegean's most beautiful islands. Roads and public transportation radiate in all directions from Chíos town, and the best bus service is to be found on the densely populated southeast coast; to explore anywhere else you need to rent a taxi, car, or powerful motorbike.

Avgónyma ❹

Αυγώνυμα

20 km (12 miles) W of Chíos town.
15. Elínta 7 km (4 miles) W.

This is the closest settlement to Néa Moní (see pp146–7) and the most beautiful of the central Chian villages, built in a distinct style: less labyrinthine and claustrophobic than the Mastic Villages, and more elegant than the houses of northern Chíos. The town's name means "clutch of eggs," perhaps after its clustered appearance when viewed from the ridge above. Virtually every house has been tastefully restored in recent years by Greek-Americans with roots here. The medieval *pýrgos* (tower) on the main square, with its interior arcades, is home to the excellent central taverna.

Environs: Few Chian villages are as striking glimpsed from a distance as **Anávatos**, 4 km (2 miles) north of Avgónyma. Unlike Avgónyma, Anávatos has scarcely changed in recent decades; shells of houses blend into the palisade on which they perch, overlooking occasionally tended pistachio orchards. The village was the scene of a particularly traumatic incident during the atrocities of 1822 (see p147). Some 400 Greeks threw themselves into a ravine from the 300-m (985-ft) bluff above the village, choosing suicide rather than death at the hands of the Turks.

Volissós ❺

Βολισσός

40 km (25 miles) NW of Chíos town.
500. Mánagros 2 km (1 mile) SW.

Volissós was once the primary market town for the 20 smaller villages of northwestern Chíos, but today the only vestige of its former commercial standing is a single saddlery on the western edge of town. The strategic importance of medieval Volissós is borne out by the crumbled hilltop castle, erected by the Byzantines in the 11th century and repaired by the Genoese in the 14th. The town's stone houses stretch along the south and east flanks of the fortified hill; many have been bought and restored by Volissós's growing expatriate population.

One of the many restored stone houses of Avgónyma

Environs: Close to the village of **Agio Gála**, 26 km (16 miles) northwest of Volissós, two 15th-century chapels can be found lodged in a deep cavern near the top of a cliff. The smaller one at the rear is the more interesting of the two; it is built entirely within the grotto and features a sophisticated and mysterious fresco of the *Virgin and Child* in its apse. The larger chapel, which stands at the entrance to the cave, boasts an intricate carved *témblon*, or altar screen. Agio Gála can be reached by bus from Volissós, and admission to the churches should be made via the resident warden who holds the keys.

The largely deserted town of Anávatos with the few inhabited dwellings in the foreground

Moní Moúndon ❻

Μονί Μούνδων

35 km (21 miles) NW of Chíos town.
0274 21230. *to Volissós.*
daily.

Founded late in the 16th century, this picturesque monastery was once second in importance to Néa Moní *(see pp146–7)*. The *katholikón* (or central church) has a number of interesting late medieval murals, the most famous being the *Salvation of Souls on the Ladder to Heaven*. Although the church is open to the public only during the monastery's festival (August 29), the romantic setting on the barren hillside makes the stop worthwhile.

Moúndon's mural *Salvation of Souls on the Ladder to Heaven*

Outlying Islands

Domestic architecture on the peaceful islet of **Oinoússes**, a few miles east of Chíos town, is deceptively humble, for it is the wealthiest territory in Greece. Good beaches can be found on either side of the port, and in the northwest of the island is the Evangelismoú convent, endowed by the Pateras family.

Much of **Psará**, 71 km (44 miles) to the west, was ruined in the Greek War of Independence *(see pp38–9)*; as a result, the single town, built in a pastiche of island architectural styles, is a product of the last 100 years. The landscape is still desolate and infertile, though there are good beaches to visit east of the harbor, and Moní Koímisis tis Theotókou in the far north.

The remains of a Hellenistic tower near Fanári, Ikaría

Ikaría

Ικαρία

9,000. *Agios Kýrikos.*
Fanári 16 km (10 miles) NE of Agios Kýrikos.

Lying 244 km (152 miles) south of Chíos, Ikaría is named after the Ikaros of legend who flew too near the sun on artificial wings and plunged to his death in the sea when his wax bindings melted.

Agios Kýrikos, the capital and main port, is a pleasant town flanked by two spas, one of them dating to Roman times and still popular with an older Greek clientele. A number of hot baths can be visited at **Thérma**, a short walk to the northeast, while at **Thérma Lefkádas**, to the southwest, the springs still well up among the boulders in the shallows of the sea.

About 2 km (1.5 miles) west of Evdilos, a village port on the north coast, lies the village of **Kámpos**. It boasts a broad, sandy beach and, beside the ruins of a 12th-century church, the remains of a Byzantine manor house can be seen. The building recalls a time when the island was considered a humane place of exile for disgraced noblemen; there was a large settlement of such officials in Kámpos. A small museum contains artifacts from the town of Oinoë, Kámpos's ancient predecessor.

Standing above Kosoíkia village, 5 km (3 miles) inland, the Byzantine castle of **Nikariás** was built during the 10th century to guard a pass on the road to Oinoë. The only other well-preserved fortification is a 3rd-century BC **Hellenistic tower**, once an ancient lighthouse, near Fanári.

Tiny **Armenistís**, with its surrounding forests and fine beaches, such as Livádi and Messaktí to the east, is Ikaría's main resort. The foundations of a temple to the goddess Artemis Tauropolë, Artemis incarnated as the patroness of bulls, lie 4 km (2 miles) west.

Home to the most active fishing fleet in the East Aegean, the island of **Foúrnoi**, due east of Ikaría, is far more populous and lively than its small size suggests. The main street of the port town, lined with mulberry trees, links the dock with a square well inland, where an ancient sarcophagus sits between the two cafés. Within walking distance lie Kampí and Psilí Ammos beaches.

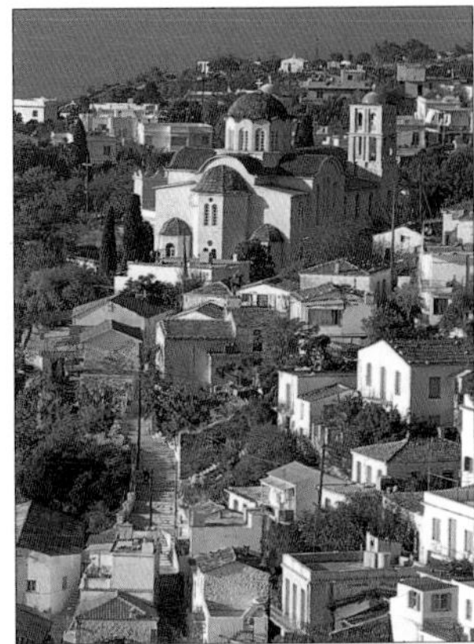

Coastal town of Agios Kýrikos, the capital of Ikaría

Sámos
Σάμος

SETTLED EARLY, because of its natural richness and easy access from Asia, Sámos was a major maritime power by the 7th century BC and enjoyed a golden age under the rule of Polykrates (538–522 BC). After the collapse of the Byzantine empire, most of the islanders fled from pirates and Sámos lay deserted until 1562, when Ottoman Admiral Kiliç Ali repopulated it with returned Samians and other Orthodox settlers. The 19th century saw an upsurge in fortunes made in tobacco trading and shipping. Union with Greece came in 1912.

Visitors' Checklist

32,000. 4 km (2.5 miles) W of Pythagóreio. Vathý, Karlóvasi, Pythagóreio. Vathý (0273 28530). Wine Festival: August; Fishermen's Festival, Pythagóreio: June or July.

Fishermen at Vathý harbor

Sights at a Glance

Vathý 1
Βαθύ

5,700. Ioánnou Lekáti. 25 Martíou (0273 28530). daily. Psilí Ammos 8 km (5 miles) SE; Mykáli 6 km (4 miles) S.

Though the old village of Ano Vathý existed in the 1600s, today's town is recent; the harbor quarter grew up only after 1832, when the town became the capital of the island. Just large enough to provide all amenities in its bazaar, lower Vathý caters to tourists while cobble-laned Ano Vathý carries on oblivious to the commerce in the streets below.

The Sámos **Archaeological Museum** contains artifacts from the excavations at the Heraion sanctuary *(see p152)*. Because of the far-flung origins of the pilgrims who visited the shrine, the collection of small votive offerings is one of the richest in Greece – among them are a bronze statuette of an Urartian god, Assyrian figurines, and an ivory miniature of Perseus and Medusa. The largest free-standing sculpture to have survived from ancient Greece is the star exhibit: a 5-m (16-ft) tall marble *koúros* dating from 580 BC and dedicated to the god Apollo.

Assyrian bronze horse figurine, Vathý Archaeological Museum

Archaeological Museum
Kapetán Gymnasiárchou Katevání. *0273 27469. Tue–Sun. main public hols.*

Key

For key to map see back flap

Around Sámos Island

SAMOS HAS A PAVED ROAD around the island, but buses are frequent only between Pythagóreio and Karlóvasi, via Vathý. Car rental is easy, though many points can be reached only by jeep or foot. In the south and west there are many rough dirt roads where caution is necessary.

Efpalíneio Orygma ❷

Ευπαλίνειο Ορυγμα

15 km (9 miles) SW of Vathý. 0273 61400. Tue–Sun. main public hols.

Efpalíneio Orygma (Eupalinos's tunnel) is a 1,040-m (3,412-ft) aqueduct, ranking as one of the premier engineering feats of the ancient world. Designed by the engineer Eupalinos and built by hundreds of slaves between 529 and 524 BC, the tunnel guaranteed ancient Samos a water supply in times of siege, and remained in use until this century. Eupalinos's surveying was so accurate that, when the work crews met, having begun from opposite sides of the mountain, their vertical error was nil.

Visitors may walk along the ledge used to remove rubble from the channel far below. Half the total length is open to the public, with fences to protect you from the worst drops.

Pythagóreio ❸

Πυθαγόρειο

13 km (9 miles) SW of Vathý. 1,500. Lykoúrgou Logothéti (0273 61389). Potokáki 3 km (2 miles) W.

Cobblestoned Pythagóreio, named after the philosopher Pythagoras, who was born here in 580 BC, has long been the lodestone of Samian tourism. The extensive foundations and walls of ancient Sámos act as a brake on high-rise construction; the only genuine tower is the 19th-century manor of **Lykoúrgos Logothétis**, the local chieftain who organized a decisive naval victory over the Turks on August 6, 1824, the date of the Feast of the Transfiguration. Next to this stronghold is the church of the **Metamórfosis**, built to celebrate the victory. At the far western edge of town are the extensive remains of

Pythagoras statue (1989) by Nikoláos Ikaris, Pythagóreio

Roman Baths, with a few doorways still intact. Farther west, the Doryssa Bay luxury complex stands above the silted-in area of the Archaic harbor; all that remains is Glyfáda lake.

Roman Baths
W of Pythagóreio. 0273 61400. variable.

ENVIRONS: Polykrates protected Pythagóreio by constructing a circuit of walls enclosing Kastrí hill, to a circumference of more than 6 km (4 miles), with 12 gates. The walls were damaged by an Athenian siege of 439 BC, and today are most intact just above Glyfáda, where a fortification tower still stands. Enclosed by the walls, just above the ancient theater, sits **Moní Panagías Spilianís** with its 100-m (330-ft) cave containing a shrine to the Virgin.

Moní Megális Panagías ❹

Μονή Μεγάλης Παναγίας

27 km (17 miles) W of Vathý. May–Oct: daily.

Founded in 1586 by Nílos and Dionýsios, two hermits from Asia Minor, the monastery of Megális Panayías is the second oldest on Sámos and contains the island's best surviving frescoes from that period. The central church is oriented diagonally within the square compound of cells, now restored, probably built directly above a temple of Artemis, which it replaced. Sadly, the area was ravaged by fire in 1990, shortly after the last monk died. Visiting hours depend on the whim of the caretaker.

Fresco of Jesus washing the Apostles' feet, Moní Megális Panagías

The single remaining column of Polykrates' temple, the Heraion

Heraion ❺
Ηραίο

21 km (14 miles) SW of Vathý. ☎ 0273 27469. 🚌 *Iraío.* ○ *Tue–Sun.* ● *main public hols.*

A fertility goddess was worshiped here from Neolithic times, though the cult only became identified with Hera after the arrival of Mycenaean colonists *(see pp24–5)*, who brought their worship of the Olympian deities with them. The sanctuary's site on flood-prone ground honored the legend that Hera was born under a sacred osier (willow tree) on the banks of the Imvrasos and celebrated her nuptials with Zeus among the osiers here, in the dangerous pre-Olympian days when Kronos still ruled.

A 30-m (100-ft) long temple built in the 8th century BC was replaced in the 6th century BC by a stone one of the Ionic order, planned by Rhoikos, a local architect. Owing to earthquakes, or a design fault, this collapsed during the reign of Polykrates, who ordered a grand replacement designed by Rhoikos's son, Theodoros. He began the new temple in 525 BC, 40 m (130 ft) west of his father's, recycling building materials from its predecessor. Building continued off and on for many centuries, but the vast structure was never completed. The interior, full of votive offerings, was described by visitors in its heyday as a veritable art gallery.

Most of the finds on display at the Archaeological Museum in Vathý *(see p150)* date from the 8th to the 6th centuries BC, when the sanctuary was at the height of its prestige. The precinct was walled and contained several temples to other deities, though only Hera herself had a sacrificial altar. Pilgrims could approach from the ancient capital along a 4,800-m (15,750-ft) Sacred Way.

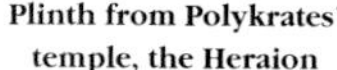

Plinth from Polykrates' temple, the Heraion

Despite diligent German excavations this century, much of the sanctuary is confusing. Byzantine and medieval masons removed ready-cut stone for reuse in their buildings, leaving only one column untouched as a landmark. Early in the 5th century, Christian masons built a basilica dedicated to a new mother figure: the Virgin Mary. Its foundations lie to east of the Great Temple.

Kokkári ❻
Κοκκάρι

10 km (6 miles) W of Vathý. *1,000.* *Agíou Nikoláou (0273 92333).* *Tsamadoú & Lemonákia 2 km (1.5 miles) W.*

Built on and behind twin headlands, this charming little port takes its name from the shallotlike onions once cultivated just inland. Today it is the island's third resort after Pythagóreio and Vathý, with its windblown location turned to advantage by a multitude of windsurfers. The town's two beaches are stony and often

The Cult of Hera

Hera was worshipped as the main cult of a number of Greek cities, including Argos on the mainland, and always at out-of-town sanctuaries. Before the first millennium BC, she was venerated in the form of a simple wooden board that was later augmented with a copper statue. One annual rite, the Tonaia, commemorated a foiled kidnapping of the wooden statue by Argive and Etruscan pirates. During the Tonaia, the idol would be paraded to the river mouth, bound on a litter of osiers (sacred to Hera), bathed in the sea, and draped with gifts. The other annual festival, the Heraia, when the copper statue was dressed in wedding finery, celebrated Hera's union with Zeus and was accompanied by concerts and athletic contests. Housed in a special shrine after the 8th century, the statue of Hera was flanked by a number of live peacocks and sprigs from an osier tree. Both are shown on Samian coins of the Roman era stamped with the image of the richly dressed goddess.

Hera, led by peacocks, and depicted on Samian coins

The beach and harbor of Kokkári, flanked by its twin headlands

surf-battered, but the paved dock and its waterside cafés and tavernas are the busy focus of nightlife.

Environs: Though many of Sámos's hill villages are becoming deserted, **Vourliótes** is an exception, thriving thanks to its orchards and vineyards. The picturesque central square is one of the most beautiful on the island, with outdoor seating at its four tavernas. Vourliótes is situated at a major junction in the area's network of hiking trails; paths come up from Kokkári, descend to Agios Konstantínos, and climb to Manoláтes, which is the trailhead for the ascent of Mount Ampelos, a five-hour round trip.

Karlóvasi 7

Καρλόβασι

33 km (20 miles) NW of Vathý. 5,000. Potámi 2 km (1 mile) W.

Sprawling, domestic Karlóvasi, gateway to western Sámos and the island's second town, divides into four separate districts. Néo Karlóvasi served as a major leather production center between the world wars, and abandoned tanneries and ornate mansions built on shoe-wealth can still be seen down by the sea. Meséo Karlóvasi, on a hill across the river, is more attractive, but most visitors stay at the harbor of Limín, with its tavernas and lively boatyard. Immediately above the port, Ano, or Palaió Karlóvasi is tucked into a wooded ravine, overlooked by the landmark hilltop church of **Agía Triáda**, the only structure in Ano visible from the sea.

Environs: An hour's walk from Ano Karlóvasi, inland from Potámi beach, is the site of a medieval settlement. Its most substantial traces include the 11th-century church of **Metamórfosis**, the oldest on the island, and a Byzantine castle immediately above.

Mount Kérkis 8

Ορος Κέρκις

50 km (30 miles) W of Vathý. to Marathókampos. Votsalákia, 2 km (1 mile) S of Marathókampos; Limniónas, 5 km (3 miles) SW of Marathókampos.

Dominating the western tip of Sámos, 1,437-m (4,715-ft) Mount Kérkis is the second highest peak in the Aegean after Sáos on Samothráki. On an island otherwise composed of smooth sedimentary rock, the partly volcanic mountain is an anomaly, with jagged rocks and bottomless chasms.

Kérkis was first documented in Byzantine times, when religious hermits occupied some of its caves. Nocturnal glowings at the cave mouths were interpreted by sailors as the spirits of departed saints, or the aura of some holy icon awaiting discovery. Today, two monasteries remain on Kérkis: the 16th-century **Moní Evangelistrías**, perched on the south slope, and **Koímisis tis Theotókou**, built in 1887, tucked into a valley on the northeast side.

Despite recent forest fires and the paving of a road to remote villages west of the summit, Mount Kérkis still boasts magnificent scenery, with ample opportunities for hiking. At Seïtáni Bay on the north coast, a marine preserve protects the Mediterranean monk seal *(see p111)*.

Mount Kérkis, seen from the island of Ikaría

The Dodecanese

Patmos · Lipsi · Leros · Kalymnos · Kos · Astypalaia · Nisyros
Tilos · Symi · Rhodes · Chalki · Kastellorizo · Karpathos

Scattered along the coast of Turkey, *the Dodecanese are the most southerly group of Greek islands, their hot climate and fine beaches attracting many visitors. They are the most cosmopolitan archipelago, with an eastern influence present in their architecture. They were the last territories to be incorporated into modern Greece.*

Due to their distance from Athens and mainland Greece, these islands have been subject to a number of invasions, with traces of occupation left behind on every island. The Classical temples built by the Dorians can be seen on Rhodes. The Knights of St. John were the most famous invaders, arriving in 1309 and staying until they were defeated by Suleiman the Magnificent in 1522.

A statue at Mandráki harbor in Rhodes

Ottoman architecture is most prominent on larger, wealthier islands, such as Kos and Rhodes. After centuries of Turkish rule, the Italians arrived in 1912 and began a regime of persecution. Mussolini built many imposing public buildings, notably in the town of Lakkí on Léros. After years of occupation, the islands were finally united with the Greek state in 1948.

Geographically, the Dodecanese vary dramatically in character: some are dry, stark, and barren, such as Chálki and Kásos, while Tílos and volcanic Nísyros are fertile and green. Astypálaia and Pátmos, with their whitewashed houses, closely resemble Cycladic islands; the pale houses of Chóra, on Pátmos, are spectacularly overshadowed by the dark monastery of St. John. Rhodes is the the capital of the island group, and is one of the most popular holiday destinations due to its endless sandy beaches and many sights.

The climate of these islands stays hot well into the autumn, providing a long season in which to enjoy the beaches. These vary from black pebbles to silver sands, and deserted bays to shingle strips packed with sunbathers.

One monk's method of traveling around on the holy island of Pátmos

◁ **A façade on the waterfront of Sými town's harbor**

Exploring the Dodecanese

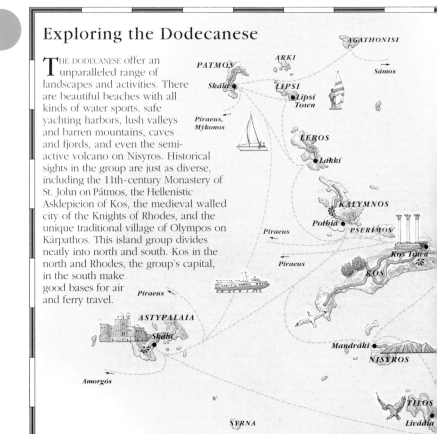

The Dodecanese offer an unparalleled range of landscapes and activities. There are beautiful beaches with all kinds of water sports, safe yachting harbors, lush valleys and barren mountains, caves and fjords, and even the semi-active volcano on Nísyros. Historical sights in the group are just as diverse, including the 11th-century Monastery of St. John on Pátmos, the Hellenistic Asklepieion of Kos, the medieval walled city of the Knights of Rhodes, and the unique traditional village of Olympos on Kárpathos. This island group divides neatly into north and south. Kos in the north and Rhodes, the group's capital, in the south make good bases for air and ferry travel.

The domed entrance to the New Market in Rhodes town

Islands at a Glance

Astypálaia *p170*
Chálki *pp194–5*
Kálymnos *pp164–5*
Kárpathos *pp198–9*
Kastellórizo *p195*
Kos *pp166–9*
Pátmos *pp158–61*
Léros *pp162–3*
Lipsí *p162*
Nísyros *pp170–72*
Rhodes pp176–93
Sými *pp174–5*
Tílos *p173*

Getting Around

Kos, Rhodes, and Kárpathos have international airports; those at Léros, Astypálaia, and Kásos are domestic. Traveling by sea, it is wise to plan where you want to go, as some islands do not share direct connections even when quite close. Also journeys can be long – it takes nine hours from Rhodes to Pátmos. If possible, allow time for changes in the weather. The cooling *meltémi* wind is welcome in the high summer but, if strong, can mean ferries will not operate and even leave you stranded. Bus services are good, especially on the larger islands, and there are always cars and bikes for rent or taxis available, though the standard of roads can vary.

Locator Map

An aerial view of Sými town with its Neo-Classical houses

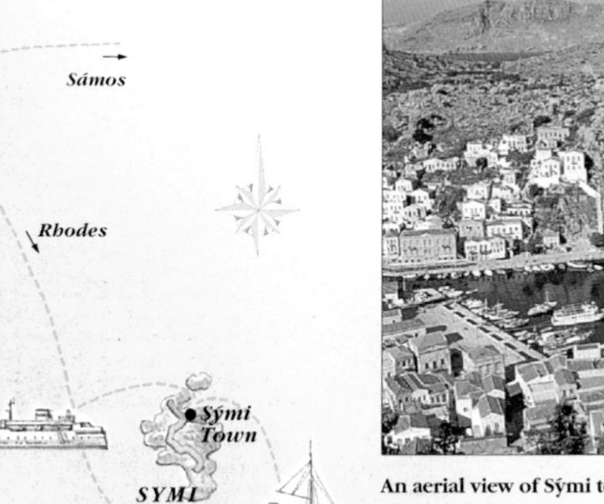

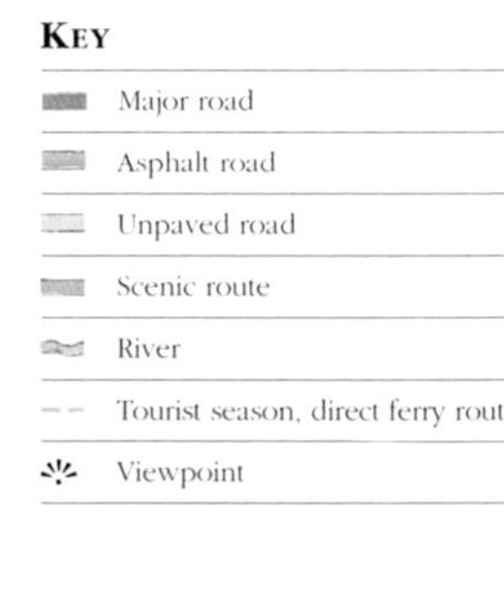

Key

- Major road
- Asphalt road
- Unpaved road
- Scenic route
- River
- Tourist season, direct ferry route
- Viewpoint

0 kilometers 25

0 miles 15

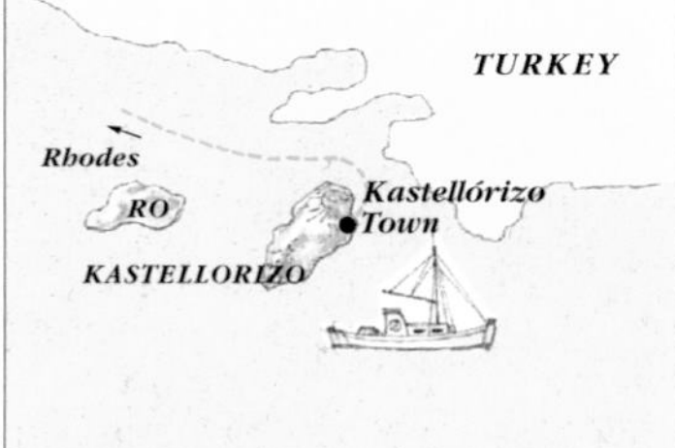

See Also

- ***Where to Stay*** pp302–4
- ***Where to Eat*** pp326–8
- ***Travel Information*** pp356–9

Pátmos

Πάτμος

KNOWN AS THE JERUSALEM of the Aegean, Pátmos's religous significance dates from St. John's arrival in AD 95 and the founding of the Monastery of St. John *(see pp160–61)* in 1088. Monastic control declined as the islanders grew rich through shipbuilding and trade, and in 1720 the laymen and monks divided the land. Today Pátmos tries to maintain itself as a center for both pilgrims and tourists.

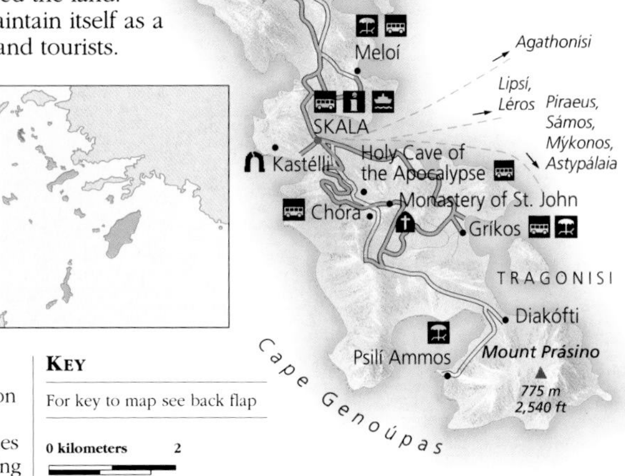

KEY

For key to map see back flap

0 kilometers 2

0 miles 1

SKALA

Ferries, yachts, and cruise ships dock at Skála, the island's port and main town, which stretches around a wide sheltered bay. As there are many exculsive gift shops and boutiques, Skála has a stylish, upscale feel. There are several travel and shipping agencies along the harborfront.

Skála's social life centers on the café-bar *Aríon*, a Neo-Classical building that doubles as a meeting place and waiting point for ferries. From the harborfront caïques and small cruise boats leave daily for the island's main beaches.

ENVIRONS: The sandy town beach can get very crowded. To the north, around the bay, lies the shingly, shaded beach at **Meloí**. There is an excellent campsite and taverna, and taxi boats also run back to Skála. Above Skála lie the ruins of the ancient acropolis at **Kastélli**. The remains include a Hellenistic wall. The little chapel of **Agios Konstantínos** is perched on the summit where the wonderful views at sunset make the hike up from Mérichas Bay well worthwhile.

CHORA

From Skála an old cobblestone pathway leads up to the Monastery of St. John *(see pp160–61)*, which crowns Chóra. The panoramic views to Sámos and Ikaría are ample reward for the long trek. A maze of dazzling white narrow lanes with over 40 monasteries and chapels, Chóra is a gem of Byzantine architecture. Many of the buildings have distinctive window moldings, or *mantomáta*, decorated with a Byzantine cross. Along the twisting alleys, some doorways lead into vast sea captains' mansions, or *archontiká*, that were built to keep marauding pirates at bay.

View of Skála from the Monastery of St. John

Stall owners selling souvenirs on the pathway to the Monastery of St. John

Visitors' Checklist

3,500. Skála. Skála. Dímou, Skála (0247 31666). Níptiras at the Monastery of St. John: Maundy Thu; Panagía at Kámpos: Aug 15.

Down the path to Skála is the church of **Agía Anna**. Steps decked with flowers lead down from the path to the church (1090) which is dedicated to the mother of the Virgin Mary. Inside the church is the **Holy Cave of the Apocalypse**, where St. John saw the vision of fire and brimstone and dictated the book of *Revelation* to his disciple, Próchoros. The visitor can see the rock where the book of *Revelation* was written, and the indentation where the saint is said to have rested his head. There are 12th-century wall paintings and icons from 1596 of St. John and the Blessed Christódoulos *(see p160)* by the Cretan painter Thomás Vathás. St. John is said to have heard the voice of God coming from the cleft in the rock, still visible today. The rock is divided into three, symbolizing the Trinity.

Near Plateía Xánthos is an *archontikó*, **Simantíri House**, preserved as a Folk Museum. Built in 1625 by Aglaïnós Mousodákis, a wealthy merchant, it still has the original furnishings and contains objects from Mousodákis's travels, such as Russian samovars and four-poster beds.

Nearby, the tranquil convent of **Zoödóchou Pigís**, built in 1607, has some fine frescoes and icons and is set in peaceful gardens.

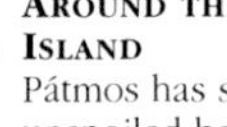
Votive offerings from pilgrims to Pátmos

Holy Cave of the Apocalypse
Between Skála and Chóra.
0247 31234. *daily.*

Simantíri House
Chóra. *daily.*

Around the Island

Pátmos has some unspoiled beaches and a rugged interior with fertile valleys. Excursion boats run to most beaches, and buses from Skála serve Kámpos, and also Gríkos and Chóra.

The island's main resort is **Gríkos**, set in a magnificent bay east of Chóra. It has a shingly beach with fishing boats, water sports facilities, and a handful of tavernas. From here the bay curves past the uninhabited Tragonísi islet south to the curious Kallikátsou rock, perched on a sand spit, which looks like the cormorant it is named after. The rock has been hollowed out to make rooms, possibly by 4th-century monks, or it could have been the 11th-century hermitage mentioned in the writings of Christódoulos.

On the southwestern coast is the island's best beach, **Psilí Ammos**, with its stretch of fine sand and sweeping dunes. It is the unofficial nudist beach and is also popular with campers. Across the bay, the Rock of Génoupas is marked by a red buoy. This is where, according to legend, the evil magician Génoupas challenged St. John to a duel of miracles. Génoupas plunged into the sea to bring back effigies of the dead, but God then turned him to stone. Cape Génoupas has a grotto that is said to be where the wizard lived.

Situated in the more fertile farming region in the north of the island, **Kámpos** beach, reached via the little hill village of Kámpos, is another popular beach with water sports and a few tavernas. From Kámpos a track leads eastward to the good pebble beaches at **Vagiá** and **Livádi Geranoú**.

Windy **Lámpi** on the north coast is famous for its colored and multipatterned pebbles. There are two garden tavernas and a little chapel set back from the reed beds. You can walk here from the hamlet of Christós above Kámpos.

Holy Cave of the Apocalypse where St. John lived and worked

Pátmos: Monastery of St. John

Μονή του Αγίου Ιωάννου του Θεολόγου

THE 11TH-CENTURY Monastery of St. John is one of the most important places of worship among Orthodox and Western Christian faithful alike. It was founded in 1088 by a monk, the Blessed Christodoulos, in honor of St. John the Divine, author of the Book of Revelations. One of the richest and most influential monasteries in Greece, its towers and buttresses make it look like a fairy-tale castle, but were built to protect its trove of religious treasures, which are now the star attraction for the thousands of pilgrims and tourists.

Monastery of St. John above Chóra

The Hospitality of Abraham
This is one of the most important of the 12th-century frescoes found in the chapel of the Panagía. They had been painted over but were revealed after an earthquake in 1956.

Kitchens

Inner courtyard

Chapel of John the Baptist

The monks' refectory has two tables made of marble taken from the temple of Artemis that originally occupied the site.

★ Icon of St. John
This 12th-century icon is the most revered in the monastery and is housed in the katholikón, *the monastery's main church.*

The Chapel of Christodoulos contains the tomb and silver reliquary of the Blessed Christodoulos.

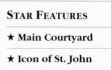

STAR FEATURES

- **★ Main Courtyard**
- **★ Icon of St. John**

Chapel of the Holy Cross
This is one of the monastery's ten chapels built because church law forbade mass being heard more than once a day in the same chapel.

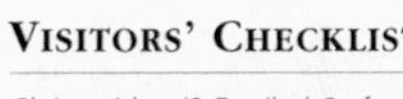

VISITORS' CHECKLIST

Chóra, 4 km (2.5 miles) S of Skála. *0247 31398.*
Monastery & Treasury
Apr–Oct: 8am–1pm Mon, Wed, Fri & Sat, 8am–1pm, 4–6 Tue & Thu, 10am–noon, 4–6 Sun. *treasury only.*

Chrysobull
This scroll of 1088 in the treasury is the monastery's foundation deed, sealed in gold by the Byzantine Emperor Alexios I Comnenos.

The treasury houses over 200 icons, 300 pieces of silverware, and a dazzling collection of jewels.

★ **Main Courtyard**
Frescoes of St. John from the 18th century adorn the outer narthex of the katholikón, *whose arcades form an integral part of the courtyard.*

The Chapel of the Holy Apostles lies just outside the gate of the monastery.

The main entrance has slits for pouring boiling oil over marauders. This 17th-century gateway leads to the cobblestone main courtyard.

NIPTIRAS CEREMONY

The Orthodox Easter celebrations on Pátmos are some of the most important in Greece. Hundreds of people pack Chóra to watch the *Niptíras* (washing) ceremony on Maundy Thursday. The abbot of the Monastery of St. John publicly washes the feet of 12 monks, re-enacting Christ's washing of his disciples' feet before the Last Supper. The rite was once performed by the Byzantine emperors as an act of humility.

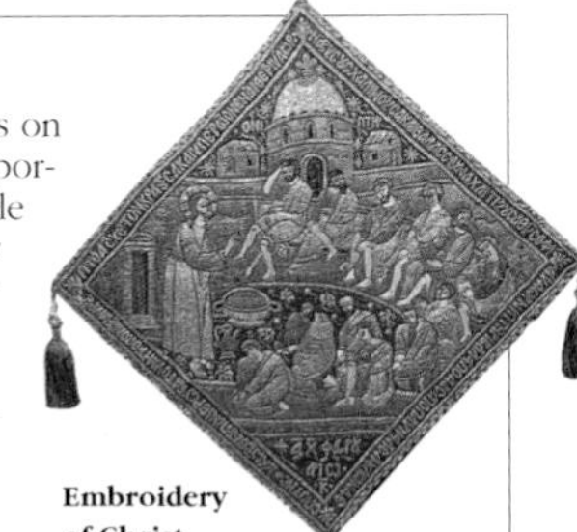

Embroidery of Christ washing the disciples' feet

Agios Ioánnis church in Lipsí village

Lipsí
Λειψοί

650. Lipsí town. Town hall, Lipsí (0247 41209). Platýs Gialós 4 km (2.5 miles) N of Lipsí town.

LITTLE LIPSI is a magical island characterized by green hills dotted with blue and white chapels, and village houses painted in a riot of colors. It is one of many islands claiming to be the enchanted place where Calypso beguiled Odysseus. Officially owned by the monastery at Pátmos since Byzantine times, Lipsí has excellent beaches and is popular for day excursions from Pátmos and Kálymnos.

The island is only 10 sq km (4 sq miles) and remains a haven for traditional Greek island life, producing some good local wines and cheeses.

The main settlement, **Lipsí town** is based around the harbor. Here the blue-domed church of **Agios Ioánnis** holds a famous icon of the Panagía. Ancient lilies within the frame miraculously spring into bloom on August 23, the feast of the Yielding of the Annunciation. In the town hall the **Nikóforeion Ecclesiastical Museum** features an odd collection of finds, from neatly labeled bottles of holy water to traditional costumes.

These sights are all marked from the harbor, and there are informal taxi services to the more distant bays and beaches of **Platýs Gialós**, **Monodéntri** and the string of sandy coves at **Katsadiá**.

Nikóforeion Ecclesiastical Museum
May–Sep: daily.

Léros
Λέρος

8,000. Parthéni. Lakkí, Agia Marína (hydrofoils). Plateía Plátanos, Plátanos. Harborfront, Lakkí (0247 22937).

ONCE FAMOUS AS the island of Artemis, Léros has since become infamous as the home of Greece's most notorious mental institutions.

Priests escorting Greece's president during a visit to Léros

The island was occupied by the Knights of St. John in 1309, by the Turks from 1522 to 1831, and by the Italians in 1912 when they built naval bases in Lakkí bay. Under German rule from 1943 until the Allied liberation, Léros was eventually united with Greece in 1948. When the military Junta took power in 1967 they exiled political dissidents to a Léros prison camp.

Today tourism is low-key, with the hospitals still providing the main source of employment and income. Life is traditional, and the people are welcoming and friendly.

Léros has always had a strong cultural and educational heritage. The island is famous for its musicians and poets. Its traditional folk dance and music have been preserved through Artemis, the youth cultural society.

Lakki

Lakkí, the main port and former capital, has one of the best natural harbors in the Aegean, an anchorage in turn for the Italian, German and British fleets. Now it resembles an unused movie set full of derelict Art Deco buildings, the remains of Mussolini's vision of a Fascist dream town. Lakkí is a ghost town by day, but the waterfront cafés come to life in the evening. Around the bay at Lépida, the former Italian naval base now houses the State Therapeutical Hospital

The Art Deco Architecture of Lakki

Mussolini's vision of a new Roman Empire took shape here in 1923 when Italian architects and town planners turned their energies to building the new town. A quite remarkable example of Art Deco architecture, Lakkí was built around wide boulevards by the engineers Sardeli and Caesar Lois, an Austrian. The model town was all curves and featured a saucer-shaped market building with a clock tower, completed in 1936; a cylindrical Town Hall and Fascist center, dating to 1933–34; and the vast Albergo Romana, later the Léros Palace Hotel. The Albergo, with the cinema and theater complex, was completed in 1937 for visiting Italian performers. These days the majority of the buildings are crumbling and neglected.

Lakkí's Art Deco movie theater

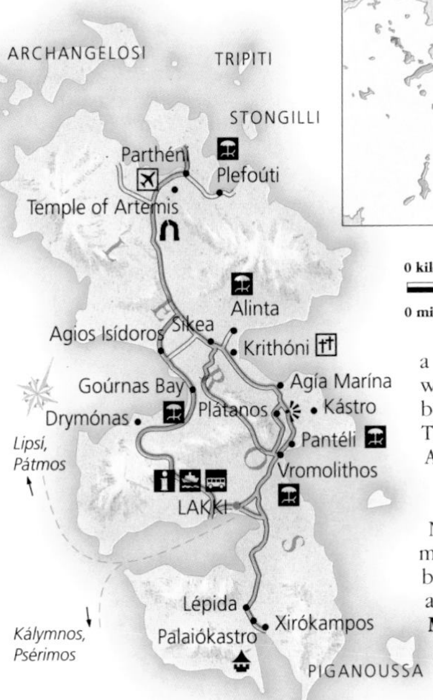

0 kilometers 4

0 miles 2

Key

For key to map see back flap

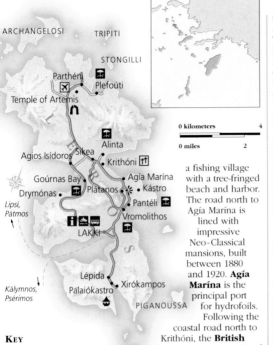

and within the complex is a mansion once used as Mussolini's summer residence. Also in Lépida is the 11th-century church of **Agios Ioánnis Theológos** (St. John the Divine), built over the remains of a Byzantine church by the monk Christódoulos *(see p160)*.

Around the Island

Léros is a pretty, green island with an indented coastline sweeping into vast gulfs, the "four seas" of Léros. With craggy hills and fertile valleys, it is good walking country.

To defy the Italians, the Lerians abandoned Lakkí and made the village of **Plátanos** the capital. Straddling a hilltop, its houses spill down to the little port of Pantéli and to the fishing village of Agía Marína.

Perched above Plátanos, the Byzantine kástro offers fine views. Renovated by the Venetians and the Knights of St. John, it houses the church of **Megalóchari tis Kyrás tou Kástrou** (the Madonna of the Castle) famous for its miraculous icon. Nearby Pantéli is a fishing village with a tree-fringed beach and harbor. The road north to Agía Marína is lined with impressive Neo-Classical mansions, built between 1880 and 1920. **Agía Marína** is the principal port for hydrofoils. Following the coastal road north to Krithóni, the **British War Cemetery** is a site of pilgrimage for those who lost relatives in the 1943 Battle of Léros.

Beaches line the road farther north to **Alinta**, the island's main resort, which has a long beach with water sports and seafront cafés. Alinta's **Historic and Folk Museum** is housed in the twin-towered Bellini Castle, built by an expatriate benefactor, Paríssis Bellínis. Little remains of the once-powerful Temple of Artemis, now overlooking the airport at Parthéni in the north. There are a few carved blocks of stone and fragments of pillars. The goddess still has some influence in Léros, however, as property passes down the female family line.

Neo-Classical façade of Maliamate villa, Agía Marína

Early Christian basilicas have been found in the area, and south of the airport the 11th-century church of **Agios Geórgios**, built by the monk Christódoulos *(see p160)* using temple columns, has a fresco of the saint.

Agios Isídoros, on the west coast above Goúrnas Bay, has a white chapel on an islet that can be reached by means of a narrow causeway.

At Drymónas, with its coves and oleander gorge, is the church of the **Panagía Gourlómata**, or goggle-eyed Virgin. Reconstructed in 1327 from an 11th-century chapel, the church is named after the face in one of its frescoes.

The resort of **Xirókampos**, lying in a bay to the south of the island, is overlooked by ancient Palaiókastro, former site of the 3rd-century castle of Lépida; the huge Cyclopean walls remain. Inside, the church of Agía Panagía is home to some fine mosaics.

Historic and Folk Museum

Bellini Castle, Alínda. *May–Sep: daily.*

Plátanos village with the kástro in the background

Kálymnos
Κάλυμνος

FAMOUS TODAY AS THE sponge-fishing island, Kálymnos's history can be traced back to a Neolithic settlement in Vothini, near Póthia; it was colonized after the 1450 BC devastation of Crete. The people have been known for their resilience since the 11th-century massacre by the Seljuk Turks, which a few survived in fortified Kastélli.

KEY

For key to map see back flap

0 kilometers 5

0 miles 3

POTHIA

The capital and main port of the island is a busy working harbor. Wedged between two mountains, the town's brightly painted houses curve around the bay.

Póthia is home to Greece's last sponge fleet, and there is a sponge-diving school on the eastern side of the harbor. The waterfront is lined with cafés, and the main landmarks are the pink, domed Italianate buildings, including the old **Governor's Palace,** which now houses the market, and the silver-domed cathedral of **Agios Christós** (Holy Christ). This 19th-century cathedral has a reredos (screen) behind the altar by Giannoúlis Chalepás *(see p40)*. The *Mermaid* at the harbor is one of 43 works that were donated to the island by local sculptors Irene and Michális Kókkinos.

The **Archaeological Museum**, housed in a Neo-Classical mansion, has been lavishly reconstructed, and there is a collection of Neolithic and Bronze Age finds from the island, plus local memorabilia. The **Sponge Factory**, just off Plateía Eleftherías, has a complete history of sponges.

Archaeological Museum
Near Plateía Kyprou. *0243 23113.*
Tue–Sun. *main public hols.*

Sponge Factory
Plateía Eleftherías. *0243 28501.*
daily. *main public hols.*

AROUND THE ISLAND

Kálymnos is easy to get around, with good bus service to the villages and numerous taxis. This rocky island has three mountain ranges, the peaks offset by deep, fjordlike inlets.

Northwest of Póthia the suburb of Mýloi, with its three derelict windmills, blends into **Chorió**, the pretty white town and former capital. On the way, standing to the left, is the ruined **Castle of the Knights**, and above, via steps from Chorió, is the citadel of **Péra Kástro**. Following a Turkish attack, this fortified village was inhabited from the 11th to the 18th century. It has good views, and nine white chapels stand on the crags.

The Mermaid at Póthia harbor

The **Cave of Seven Virgins**, (Eptá Parthénon), shows traces of nymph worship. Legend has it that the seven virgins hid here from pirates, but disappeared in the bottomless channel below.

The main resorts on the island are strung out along the

View of Póthia and harbor

The deep Vathý inlet with the settlement of Rína at its head

west coast. The sunset over the islet of Telendos from **Myrtiés** is one of Kálymnos's most famous sights. Although Myrtiés and neighboring Masoúri have now grown into noisy tourist centers, the Armeó end of Masoúri is less frenetic. To the north is the fortified **Kastélli**, the refuge of survivors from the 11th-century Turkish massacre. The coast road from here is spectacular, passing fish farms, inlets, and the fjordlike beach at **Arginónta**. A visit to the northernmost fishing hamlet, **Emporeió**, makes a good day out and is in craggy walking country. You can walk to **Kolonóstilo** (the Cyclops Cave), which is named after its massive stalactites.

In the southeast is the most beautiful area of Kálymnos: the lush Vathý valley which has three small villages at the head of a stunning blue inlet. Backed by citrus groves, **Rína**, named after St. Irene, is a pretty hamlet with a working boatyard. **Plátanos**, the next village, has a huge plane tree and the remains of Cyclopean walls. There is a three-hour trail from here via **Metóchi**, the third Vathý village, across the island to Arginónta.

Visitors' Checklist

14,000. Póthia. behind marketplace, Póthia. Plateía Charalámpous, Póthia (0243 329301). Póthia: Mon–Sat. Easter celebrations around island: Easter Sat; Sponge week at Póthia: week following Greek Easter.

Caïques from Rína take trips to the **Daskalió Cave** in the side of the sheer inlet, and to Armies, Drasonía, and Palónissos beaches on the east coast.

Outlying Islands

Excursion boats leave Póthia daily for **Psérimos** and the islet of **Nerá** with its Moní Stavroú. Psérimos has an often busy sandy beach and a popular festival of the Assumption on August 15.

Télendos, reached from Myrtiés, is perfect for a hideaway vacation, with a few rooms to rent and a handful of tavernas, plus shingly beaches. There are Roman ruins, a derelict fort, and the ruined Moní Agios Vasíleos, dating from the Middle Ages. The Byzantine castle of Agios Konstantínos also stands here.

Sponge-Fishing Around Kalymnos

Sea sponge

Kálymnos has been a sponge-fishing center since ancient times, although fishing restrictions and sponge blight have hit the trade in recent years. Once in great demand, sponges were used for the Sultan's harem, for padding in armor, and later for cosmetic and industrial purposes. Divers were weighed down with rocks or used crude air apparatus, and many men were drowned or died of the bends. The week before Kálymnos's fleet sets out to fish is the *Ipogros* or Sponge Week Festival. Divers are given a celebratory send-off with food, drink, and dancing in traditional costume.

***This black-figure** Greek vase depicts an early sponge-diving scene. The diver, pictured standing at the front of the boat, is preparing to enter the sea to search for sponges. The vase dates back to around 500 BC.*

A stone was used to weigh divers to keep them near the seabed.

***Diving equipment** varied greatly over the years. Early diving suits were made from rubber and canvas with huge helmets. You can see some on display in the sponge factory at Póthia and on stalls where divers sell their wares.*

Kos

Κως

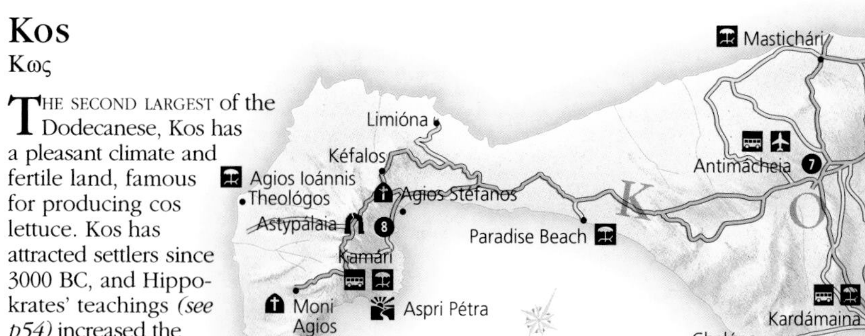

THE SECOND LARGEST of the Dodecanese, Kos has a pleasant climate and fertile land, famous for producing cos lettuce. Kos has attracted settlers since 3000 BC, and Hippokrates' teachings *(see p54)* increased the island's renown. By the 4th century BC Kos was a strong trading power, though it declined after the Romans arrived in 130 BC. The Knights of St. John ruled from 1315, and the Turks governed from 1522–1912. Italian and German occupation followed until unification with Greece in 1948.

Yachts moored in the harbor at Kos town

Kos Town 1

Κως

15,000. Aktí Koundouriotou. Vasiléos Georgíou 1 (0242 28724). daily. Kos town.

Dominated by its Castle of the Knights, old Kos town was destroyed in the 1933 earthquake. This revealed many ancient ruins that the Italians excavated and restored.

The harbor bristles with yachts and excursion boats, and pavement cafés line the street. At night in tourist season you can almost get swept along by the crowds. There are palm trees, pines, and gardens full of jasmine. Ancient and modern sit oddly side by side: Nafklírou, the "street of bars," runs beside the ancient agora, at night lit up by strobes and lasers. Hippokrates' ancient plane tree, in Plateía Platánou, is said to have been planted by him 2,400 years ago. Despite its 14-m (46-ft) diameter, the present tree is only about 560 years old and is probably a descendent of the original. The nearby fountain was built in 1792 by the Turkish governor Hadji Hassan, to serve the Mosque of the Loggia. The water gushed into an ancient marble sarcophagus.

The water fountain near Hippokrates' plane tree

KEY

For key to map see back flap

Castle of Knights

Plateía Platánou. *0242 28326. Tue–Sun. main public hols.*

The 16th-century castle gateway is carved with gargoyles and an earlier coat of arms of Fernández De Heredia the Grand Master from 1376 to 1396. The outer keep and battlements were built between 1450 and 1478 from stone and marble, including blocks from the Asklepieion *(see p168)*. The fortress was an important defense for the Knights of Rhodes against Ottoman attack, and the ramparts still offer great views.

Ancient Agora

South of Plateía Platánou.

This site is made up of a series of ruins, from the original Hellenistic city to Byzantine buildings. Built over by the Knights, the ancient remains were revealed in the 1933 earthquake. Highlights include

Sights at a Glance

the 3rd-century BC stoa Kamára tou Fórou (Arcade of the Forum), the 3rd-century BC Temple of Herakles, mosaic floors depicting Orpheus and Herakles, and ruins of the Temple of Pandemós Aphrodite. A 5th-century Christian basilica was also discovered, along with the Roman Agora.

Archaeological Museum

Plateía Eleftherías. 0242 28326. Tue–Sun. main public hols.
The museum has an excellent collection of the island's Hellenistic and Roman finds, including a 4th-century BC marble statue of Hippokrates. The main hall displays a 3rd-century AD mosaic of Asklepios surrounded by 2nd-century statues of Dionysos with Pan and a satyr. The east wing exhibits Roman statues and the north Hellenistic finds, while the west room has later gigantic statuary.

Roman Remains

Grigoríou E. Tue–Sun.
The most impressive of these ruins is the Casa Romana, built in the Pompeiian style. It had 26 rooms and three pools surrounded by shady courtyards lined with Ionian and Corinthian columns. There are mosaics of dolphins, pouncing lions, and leopards. The dining room has decorated marble walls, and several rooms are painted. In the grounds are the excavated thermal baths and part of the main Roman road, covered with ancient capitals and Hellenistic fragments. Set back off the road down an avenue of cypresses is the ancient odeion or theater. It has rows of marble benches – the first class seats – and limestone blocks for the plebeians.

The western excavations opposite reveal a mix of historical periods. There are Mycenaean remains, a tomb dating from the Geometric period, and Roman houses with some fine mosaics. One of the most impressive sights is the gym or *xystó* with its 17 restored Doric pillars.

Visitors' Checklist

27,000. 27 km (16 miles) W of Kos town. Aktí Koundouriótou, Kos town. Kos town. Kos town (0242 28724). Hippocrates Cultural Festival: Jul–Sep; Panagía at Kardámaina: Sep 8, Agios Geórgios Festival at Palaió Pylí: Apr 23 .

Cos lettuce (romaine) on a market stall in Plateía Eleftherías

Rows of marble benches for the Roman audiences that came to the ancient odeion

Around Kos Island

Carving at the Asklepieion

MAINLY FLAT AND FERTILE, Kos is known as the "Floating Garden." It has a wealth of archaeological sites and antiquities, Hellenistic and Roman ruins, and Byzantine and Venetian castles. Most visitors, however, come for Kos's sandy beaches. Those on the southwest shore are some of the finest in the Dodecanese, while the northwest bays are ideal for water sports. Much of the coast has been developed, but inland you can still see remnants of Kos's traditional lifestyle.

The seven restored columns of the Temple of Apollo at the Asklepieion

Asklepieion ❷

Ασκληπιείο

4 km (2.5 miles) NW of Kos town.

 Tue–Sun.

With its white marble terraces cut into a pine-clad hill, the Asklepieion site was chosen in the 4th century BC for rest and recuperation and still exudes an air of tranquillity. The views from the sanctuary are breathtaking, and it is one of Greece's most important Classical sites.

Temple, school, and medical center combined, it was built after the death of Hippocrates and was the most famous of ancient Greece's 300 Asklepieia dedicated to Asklepios, god of healing. The doctors were priests of the Asklepiada and became practitioners of Hippocrates's methods of diagnosis and treatment. The cult's symbol was the snake, once used to seek healing herbs, and it remains the emblem of modern Western medicine today.

There are three levels linked by a staircase. The lowest one has a 3rd-century BC porch and 1st-century AD Roman baths. The second has a 4th-century BC altar of Apollo and a 2nd to 3rd-century AD temple of Apollo. On the third level is the Doric temple of Asklepios from the 2nd century BC.

Asfendíou Villages ❸

Ασφενδίου

14 km (8 miles) W of Kos town.

The Asfendíou villages of Ziá, Asómatos, Lagoúdi, Evangelístria, and Agios Dimítrios are a cluster of picturesque hamlets on the wooded slopes of Mount Dikaíos. These mountain villages have managed to retain their traditional character, with whitewashed houses and attractive Byzantine churches. The highest village, **Ziá**, has become the epitome of a traditional Greek village, at least to the organizers of the many bus tours that regularly descend upon it. The more adventurous traveler can take the very rough track from the Asklepieíon via tiny Asómatos to Ziá. The lowest village, **Lagoúdi**, is less commercialized, and a road leads from here to Palaió Pylí.

Tigkáki ❹

Τιγκάκι

12 km (7 miles) W of Kos town.

Tigkáki.

The popular resorts of Tigkáki and neighboring Marmári have long white sand beaches ideal for windsurfing and other water sports. Boat trips are available from Tigkáki to the island of Pserimós opposite. The nearby **Alikés saltpans** are a perfect place for bird-watching. The many wetland species here include small waders like the avocet, and the black-winged stilt with its long pink legs.

HIPPOKRATES

The first holistic healer and "father of modern medicine," Hippokrates was born on Kos in 460 BC and died in Thessaly in about 375 BC. He supposedly came from a line of healing demigods and he learned medicine from his father and grandfather: his father was supposedly a direct descendant of Asklepios, the god of healing, his mother of Herakles. He was the first physician to classify diseases and introduced new methods of diagnosis and treatment. He taught at the site of the Asklepieion in Kos, and wrote the Hippocratic Oath, to cure rather than harm, still sworn by medical practitioners worldwide.

Palaió Pylí castle perched precariously on a cliff's edge

Palaió Pylí ❺

Παλαιό Πυλί

15 km (9 miles) W of Kos town.

to Pylí.

The deserted Byzantine town of Palaió Pylí is perched on a crag 4 km (2 miles) above the farming village of Pylí, with the remains of its castle walls built into the rock. Here the Blessed Christódoulos built the 11th-century church of the Ipapandís (Presentation of Jesus), before he went to Pátmos *(see p160)*. In Pylí lies the Classical *thólos* tomb of the mythical hero-king Charmýlos. It has 12 underground crypts, which are now surmounted by the church of Stávros.

Kardámaina ❻

Καρδάμαινα

26 km (16 miles) SW of Kos town.

Kardámaina.

Once a quiet fishing village noted for its ceramics, Kardámaina is the island's biggest resort – brash, loud, and packed with young British and Scandinavian tourists. It has miles of crowded golden sands and a swinging nightlife. It is quieter farther south with some exclusive developments. Sights include a Byzantine church and the remains of a Hellenistic theater.

Antimácheia ❼

Αντιμάχεια

25 km (15 miles) W of Kos town.

The village of Antimácheia is dominated by its Venetian castle and windmills. The castle, located near the airport, was built by the Knights of Rhodes *(see pp184–5)* as a prison in the 14th century and was constantly bombarded by pirates. Its massive crenellated battlements and squat tower now overlook an army base, and there are good views toward Kardámaina. The inner gateway still bears the coat of arms of the Grand Master Pierre d'Aubusson (1476–1503), and there are two small chapels within the walls.

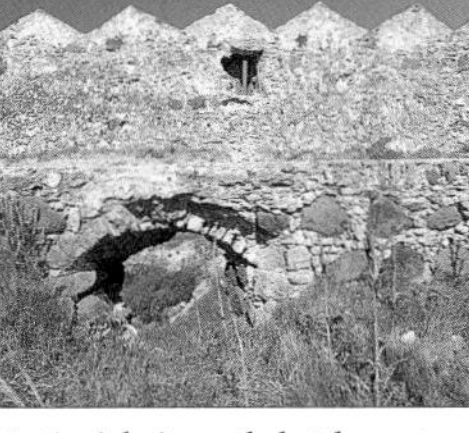

Antimácheia castle battlements

Environs: The road north from Antimácheia leads to the charming port of **Mastichári**. There are good fish tavernas here and a long sandy beach that sweeps into dunes at the western end. On the way to the dunes, the ruins of an early Christian basilica, with good mosaics, can be seen.

Kamári ❽

Καμάρι

15 km (9 miles) SW of Kos town.

Paradise 7 km (4 miles) E.

Kamári is a good base for exploring the southwest coast, where the island's best beaches can be found. Mostly reached via steep tracks from the main road, the most famous is Paradise beach with fine white sands. Kamári beach leads to the 5th-century AD Christian basilica of Agios Stéfanos, which has mosaics and Ionic columns.

Environs: Kéfalos, on the mountainous peninsula inland from Kamári, is known for its thyme, honey, and cheeses. Sights include the ruined Castle of the Knights, said to be the lair of a dragon. According to legend, Hippokrates' daughter was transformed into a dragon by Artemis and awaits the kiss of a knight to resume human form. Above Kéfalos is the windmill of Papavasílis, and nearby at Palátia are the remains of **Astypálaia**, the birthplace of Hippokrates. Neighboring Aspri Pétra cave has yielded remains.

The journey to **Moní Agios Ioánnis**, 6 km (4 miles) south of Kéfalos, passes through dramatic scenery, and a track leads to the beach of Agios Ioánnis Theológos.

Music bars and clubs in the resort of Kardámaina

Chóra overlooking Astypálaia's main harbor, Skála

Astypálaia
Αστυπάλαια

1,100. 11 km (7 miles) E of Astypálaia town. Astypálaia town. Skála dockside, Astypálaia town (0243 61206).

With its dazzling white fortified town of Chóra and its scenic coastline, the island of Astypálaia retains an exquisite charm. A backwater in Classical times, Astypálaia flourished in the Middle Ages when the Venetian Quirini family ruled from 1207 to 1522.

The most westerly of the Dodecanese, it is a remote island with high cliffs and a hilly interior. There are many coves and sandy bays along the coast, which was once the lair of Maltese pirates.

Astypálaia town incorporates the island's original capital, Chóra, which forms its mazelike upper town. The splendid Venetian kástro of the Quirini family is on the site of the ancient acropolis. Houses were built into the kástro's walls for protection, and the Quirini coat of arms can still be seen on the gateway. Within its walls are two churches: the silver-domed, 14th-century Panagía Portaítissa (Madonna of the Castle Gates), and the 14th-century Agios Geórgios (St. George), built on the site of an ancient temple.

A two-hour hike westward from the derelict windmills above Chóra leads to **Agios Ioánnis** and its gushing waterfall. **Livádi**, the main resort, lies south of Chóra in a fertile valley with citrus groves and cornfields. It has a long beach. The nudist haunt of **Tzanakí** lies a short distance to the south. From Livádi a dirt track leads north to **Agios Andréas**, a remote and attractive cove, an hour and a half's trek away.

North of Chóra, on the narrow land bridge between the two sides of the island, lies **Maltezána** (also known as Análipsi), the fastest growing resort on the island. Named after the marauding pirates who once frequented it, Maltezána was where the French Captain Bigot set fire to his ship in 1827 to prevent it being captured.

On the northeastern peninsula is the "lost lagoon," a deep inlet at the hamlet of **Vathý**. From here you can visit the caves of Drákou and Negrí by boat, or the Italian Kastellano fortress, built in 1912, 3 km (2 miles) to the south.

A typical housefront in Mandráki on Nísyros

Nísyros
Νίσυρος

1,000. Mandráki harbor. Gyaliskári 2 km (0.5 miles) E of Mandráki; Páloi 4 km (2 miles) E of Mandráki.

Almost circular, Nísyros is on a volcanic line that passes through Aígina, Póros, Mílos, and Santoríni. In 1422 there was a violent eruption and its 1,400-m (4,593-ft) high peak exploded, leaving a huge caldera *(see p172)*. Everything flourishes in the volcanic soil and there are some unique flora and fauna.

According to mythology, Nísyros was formed when the enraged Poseidon threw a chunk of Kos on the warring giant, Polybetes, who was submerged beneath it, fiery and fuming. In ancient times, it was famous for its millstones, often known as the "stones of Nísyros." Now the island prospers from pumice mining on the islet of Gyalí to the north.

Mandraki

Boats dock at Mandráki, the capital, with waterfront tavernas, ticket agencies, and buses shuttling tourists to the volcano. Mandráki's narrow two-story houses have brightly painted wooden balconies, often hung with strings of drying tomatoes and onions. A maze of lanes congregates at Plateía Iróon, with its war memorial. Other roads weave south, away from the sea, past the *kípos* (public

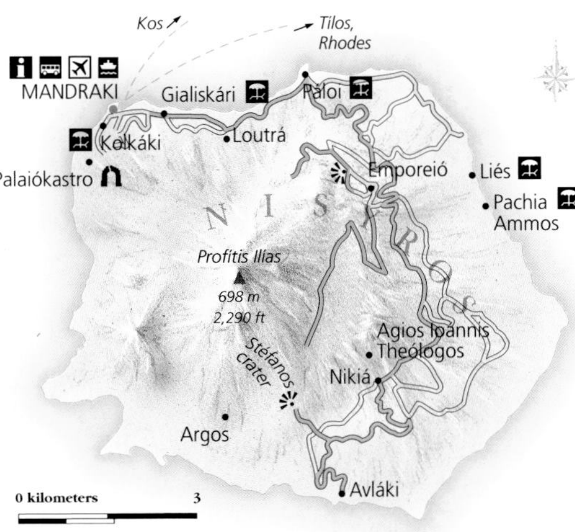

Key

For key to map see back flap

orchard) to the main square, Plateía Ilikioménon. At night, the area is bustling: shops that resemble houses are open, with traditional painted signs depicting their wares. The lanes become narrow and more winding as you approach the medieval Chóra district. In the nearby Langádi area, the balconies on the houses almost touch across the street.

The major attractions in Mandráki are the 14th-century kástro and the monastery. The former is the castle of the Knights of St. John *(see pp184–5)*, built in 1325 high up the cliff face. The monastery, **Moní Panagía Spilianís,** lies within the kástro and dates from around 1600. Inside, a finely carved iconostasis holds a Russian-style icon, decked in gold and silver offerings, of the Virgin and Child. The fame of the church grew after Saracens failed to find its trove of silver, hidden by being worked into the Byzantine icons. The library holds rare editions and a number of ecclesiastical treasures.

The main square in Nikiá with its *choklákia* mosaic

The **Historical and Folk Museum**, on the way up to the kástro, has a reconstructed traditional island kitchen, embroideries, and a small collection of local photographs.

Excursion boats offer trips from Mandráki to **Gyalí** and the tiny **Agios Antónios** islet beyond. Both destinations have white sandy beaches.

Historical and Folk Museum

Kástro. *May–Sep: daily.*

Around the Island

Nísyros is lush and green with terraces of olives, figs, and almond trees contrasting with the strange gray and yellow moonscape of the craters. No visit would be complete without an excursion to the volcano, and by day the island is swamped with visitors from Kos. However, it is quiet when the excursion boats have left.

Above Mandráki lies the **Palaiókastro**, the acropolis of ancient Nísyros, dating back 2,600 years. Remains include Cyclopean walls made from massive blocks carved from the volcanic rock, and Doric columns.

Nísyros is pleasant for walking. Visits to the volcano must include the pretty village of **Nikiá** *(see p172)*, with its *choklákia* mosaic in the square, and abandoned **Emporeió**, which clings to the rim of the crater.

To the east of Mandráki, **Páloi** is a pretty fishing village with good tavernas and a string of dark volcanic sand beaches. Two kilometers (1 mile) west of the village, at **Loutrá**, an abandoned spa can be found.

The *meltémi* wind blows fiercely on Nísyros in tourist season, and the beaches east of Páloi can often be littered with debris.

View of Mandráki, the capital of Nísyros

The Geology of Nísyros

Crystals in a steam vent

FUMING and smelling of rotten eggs, the center of Nísyros is a semiactive caldera – a crater formed by an imploded mountain. Its eruption, around 24,000 years ago, was accompanied by an outpouring of pumice, forming a blanket 100 m (328 ft) thick on the upper slopes of the island. When formed, the caldera was 3 km (2 miles) in diameter. It is now occupied by two craters and five solidified lava domes, forced upward in the last few thousand years, including Profítis Ilías, the largest in Europe. Further eruptions in 1873 built cones of ash 100 m (328 ft) high.

Steep paths *descend to the crater floor, where the surface is hot enough to melt rubber-soled shoes. Gas vents let off steam at 98° C (208° F), which bubbles away beneath the earth's crust.*

Paths lead visitors around the caldera.

Profítis Ilías dome is almost 600 m (1970 ft) high.

Ash cones have been produced in the recent life of the caldera.

Original caldera wall

Lava dome

The Stéfanos crater, which is 300 m (984 ft) wide and 25 m (82 ft) deep, was created by an explosion of pressurized water and superheated steam.

NÍSYROS CALDERA

This huge caldera contains several water-filled smaller craters. The largest is the still active Stéfanos crater, which has a number of hot springs, boiling mud pots, and gas vents. There is a stench of sulfur and numerous pure sulfur crystals are eagerly snapped up by would-be geologists.

Nikiá *is the more appealing of Nísyros's two rim villages with its brightly painted houses and* chokläkia *pebble mosaics. There are good views from Nikiá of the crater, and a path down to the caldera.*

The oldest volcanic *minerals found on Nísyros date back 200,000 years. There are vast amounts of pumice around the caldera, and rich deposits of sulfur and kaolin.*

Sulfur

Kaolin

Pumice

Tílos
Τήλος

300. Livádia. Megálo Chorió (0241 44212). Eristós 10 km (6 miles) NW of Livádia.

Remote Tilos is a tranquil island with good walking and, as a resting stop on migration paths, it offers rich rewards for birdwatchers. Away from the barren beaches, Tílos has a lush heartland, with small farms growing everything from tobacco to almonds. Its hills are scattered with chapels and ruins of Crusader castles, outposts of the Knights of St. John, who ruled from 1309 until 1522.

There is a strong tradition of music and poetry on the island – the poet Erinna, famous for the *Distaff*, was born here in the 4th century BC. In the 18th and 19th centuries Tílos was known for weaving cloth for women's costumes, still worn by some islanders today.

Livadia

Livádia, the main settlement, has a tree-fringed pebble beach sweeping round its bay. The blue and white church of **Agios Nikólaos** dominates the waterfront and has an iconostasis carved in 1953 by Katasáris from Rhodes. On the beach road, the tiny, early Christian basilica of **Agios Panteleïmon kai Polýkarpos** has an attractive mosaic floor.

The pebble beach at Livádia

Around the Island

Buses run from Livádia to Megálo Chorió and Eristos, and mopeds can be rented; otherwise you are on foot.

Built on the site of the ancient city of Telos, **Megálo Chorió** is 8 km (5 miles) uphill from Livádia. The kástro was built by the Venetians, who incorporated a Classical gateway and stone from the ancient acropolis. The **Palaeontological Museum** has midget fossilized mastodon (elephant) bones from the Mesariá region, and a gold treasure trove, found in a Hellenistic tomb in the Kená region of the island.

Detail of the War Memorial at Livádia

The church of Archángelos Michaïl (1827) was built against the kástro walls. It has silver icons from the original Taxiárchis church, a gilded 19th-century iconostasis, and the remains of 16th-century frescoes.

South of Megálo Chorió lies **Eristos,** a long sandy beach. **Agios Antónis** beach to the west of Megálo Chorió has the petrified remains of human skeletons. These "beach rocks" are thought to be of sailors caught in the lava when Nísyros erupted in 600 BC.

One of many almond orchards on Tílos

Perched on a cliff on the west coast, the Byzantine **Moní Agios Panteleïmon** is the island's main sight. In a cluster of trees, this fortified monastery with red tiled roofs is famous for its sunset views. Built in 1470 it has circular chapels, a mosaic courtyard, and medieval monks' cells. The dome of the church has a vision of *Christ Pantokrátor* (1776) by Gregory of Sými. Other important artifacts include 15th-century paintings of Paradise and the apostles, and a carved iconostasis that dates from 1714.

The fossilized bones of miniature mastodons from 7000 BC were discovered in the **Charkádi Grotto**, a ravine in the Mesariá area. The ruined fortress of Mesariá marks the spot.

Mikró Chorió, below Mesariá, has about 220 roofless, abandoned houses. Those residents who had stone roofs took them with them to Livádia when the population abandoned the village in the 1950s. Quiet during the day, at night the ruins are illuminated, and one house has been restored as a bar. There is also the mid 17th-century church of **Tímia Zoní**, which has 18th-century frescoes, and the chapels of **Sotíros**, **Eléousas**, and **Pródromos**, with 15th-century paintings.

Palaeontological Museum

Megálo Chorió. 0241 44212.
Apr–Oct: daily; request key at town hall. Nov–Mar.

Sými

Σύμη

A prayer in a bottle at Moní Taxiárchi

Ever since classical times, rocky, barren Sými has thrived on the success of its sponge-diving fleet and boat-building industry, which once launched 500 ships a year. By the 17th century it was the third richest island in the Dodecanese. The Italian occupation in 1912 and the arrival of artificial sponges and steam power ended Sými's good fortunes. Its population had fallen from 23,000 to 6,000 by World War II, and the mansions built in its heyday crumbled.

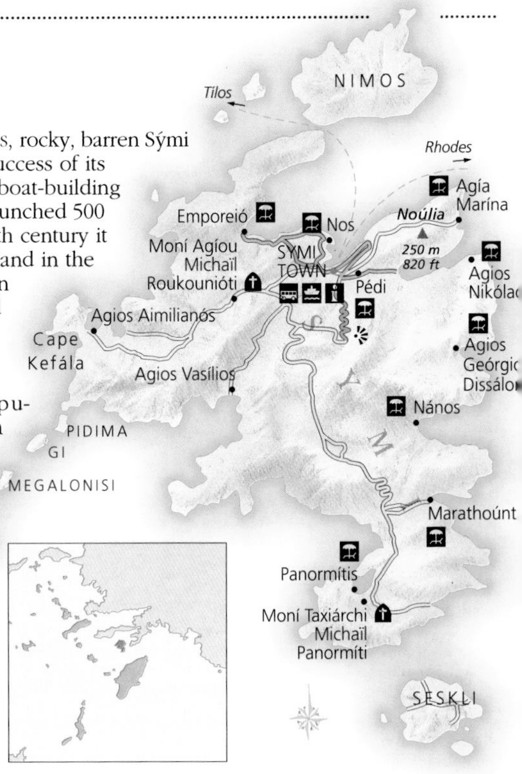

Key

For key to map see back flap

0 kilometers 4

0 miles 2

Symi Town

The harbor area, Gialós, is one of the most beautiful in Greece, surrounded by Neo-Classical houses and elaborate churches built on the hillside. Gialós is often busy with day trippers, particularly late morning and early afternoon.

A clock tower (1884) stands on the western side of the harbor where the ferries dock; beyond is the shingle bay of Nos beach. Next door to the town hall, the **Maritime Museum** has an interesting record of Sými's seafaring past.

Gialós is linked to the upper town, Chorió, by a road and also by 375 marble steps. Chorió comprises a maze of lanes and distinctive houses, often with traditional interiors. The late 19th-century church of **Agios Geórgios** has an unusual pebble mosaic of fierce mermaids who, in Greek folklore, are responsible for storms that sink ships. The **Sými Museum**, high up in Chorió, has a small but interesting collection of costumes and traditional items plus some Hellenistic finds. Beyond the museum is the ruined Byzantine **kástro** and medieval walls. Megáli Panagía church, the jewel of the kástro, has an important post-Byzantine icon of the *Last Judgment*, from the late 16th century, by the painter Geórgios Klontzás.

Maritime Museum
Plateía Ogdóis Maïou. *0241 71114.*
Apr–Oct: daily. *Nov–Apr.*

Sými Museum
Chorió. *0241 71114.*
Tue–Sun. *main public hols.*

The pastel-colored houses of Chorió on the ancient acropolis overlooking Sými's harbor

The traditional craft of boat building in Sými town

Environs: The road from Gialós to Chorió passes the hill of **Noúlia,** also known as Pontikókastro. On the hill are the remains of 20 windmills and an ancient tomb monument believed to have been erected by the Spartans in 412–411 BC.

Around the Island

Sými's road network is limited, but there are plenty of tracks over its rocky terrain. East of Sými town, an avenue of eucalyptus trees leads down through farmland to **Pédi** bay, a beach popular with local families. From here taxi boats run to **Agios Nikólaos** beach, and there are paths to Agios Nikólaos and **Agía Marína**.

The 18th-century church of **Moní Agíou Michaïl Roukounióti,** 3 km (2 miles) west of Sými town, is built like a desert fortress in Gothic and folk architecture. It houses 14th-century frescoes and a rare 15th-century, semicircular icon of the *Hospitality of Abraham* by Cretan artist Stylianós Génis.

Sými's most popular sight is **Moní Taxiárchi Michaïl Panormíti** in Panormítis bay, a place of pilgrimage for Greek sailors worldwide. Its white buildings, spanning the 18th to 20th centuries, line the water's edge. The pleasant horseshoe-shaped harbor is dominated by the elaborate mock-Baroque bell tower, a 1905 copy of Turkey's famous bell tower of Agía Foteiní in Izmir.

The monastery is famous for its icon of the Archangel Michael, Sými's patron saint and guardian of seafarers. Despite being removed to Gialós it mysteriously kept returning to Panormítis so the monastery was founded here. The single-nave *katholikón* was built in 1783 on the remains of an early Byzantine chapel also dedicated to the saint.

According to tradition, if you ask a favor of St. Michael, you must vow to give something in return. As a result, the interior is a dazzling array of votive offerings, or *támata*, from pilgrims, including small model ships in silver and gold.

The mock-Baroque bell tower of Moní Taxiárchi Michaïl Panormíti

Visitors' Checklist

2,500. Gialós, Sými town. Sými town (0241 71111). *Orthodox Easter celebrations around the island; Parade for signing of Dodecanese Treaty at Gialós: May 8.*

The intricate Baroque iconostasis by Mastrodiákis Taliadoúros is a remarkable piece of woodcarving. The walls and ceiling are covered in smoke-blackened 18th-century frescoes by the two Symiot brothers Nikítas and Michaïl Karakostís.

The sacristy museum is full of treasures, including a post-Byzantine painting of the ten saints, Agioi Déka, by the Cretan Theódoros Poulákis. There are prayers in bottles, that have floated miraculously into Panormítis, containing money for the monastery from faithful sailors. The cloister has a *chokláki*a courtyard of zigzag pebble mosaics *(see p194)* and an arcaded balcony.

West of the monastery, past the taverna, is a memorial to the former abbot, two monks, and two teachers executed by the Germans in 1944 for running a spy radio for British commandos. Small Panormítis beach is here, and there are woodland walks to **Marathoúnta.**

Moní Taxiárchi Michaïl Panormíti

Panormítis bay. *Tue–Sun.*

The Treaty of the Dodecanese

A plaque outside Les Katerinettes Restaurant, on the dockside in Gialós, marks the end of Nazi occupation on May 8, 1945, when the islands were handed over to the Allies at the end of World War II. The islands officially became part of Greece on March 7, 1948, having been under Italian rule since 1912. Farther along the dockside a bas-relief of an ancient trireme commemorates the liberation of the islands. It is a copy of an original at the base of the Acropolis at Líndos, on Rhodes island *(see pp192–3)*.

The bas-relief of a trireme on the dockside at Sými town

Rhodes

Ρόδος

RHODES, THE CAPITAL of the Dodecanese, was an important center in the 5th to 3rd centuries BC. It was part of both the Roman and Byzantine empires before being conquered by the Knights of St. John. They occupied Rhodes from 1306 to 1519, and their medieval walled city still dominates Rhodes town. Ottoman and Italian rulers followed. Fringed by sandy beaches, and with good hiking and lively nightlife, Rhodes attracts thousands of tourists each year.

KEY

For key to map see back flap

Ancient Kámeiros

The stunning ruins of this once-thriving Doric city include a 6th-century BC Temple of Athena Polias 5

Skála Kameírou

A pleasant place to relax, Skála Kameírou is an attractive harbor that once served the ancient city of Kámeiros 6

Kritinía castle, built by the Knights of Rhodes, was one of their larger strongholds *(see p189).*

Siána is a pretty traditional hill village, known for its locally distilled spirit, *soúma (see p189).*

Emponas

The slopes around this traditional town have been cultivated with vines by the Emery winery since the 1920s 7

Monólithos

The village is dominated by the 15th-century castle, perched high on a massive rock. It was built by the Knights of Rhodes 8

Moní Skiádi

This monastery was built in the 18th and 19th centuries and is famous for its icon of the Panagía, or the Blessed Virgin 9

Moní Thárri

Hidden away in the countryside, this monastery has a domed church that is home to several frescoes, some dating to the 12th century 10

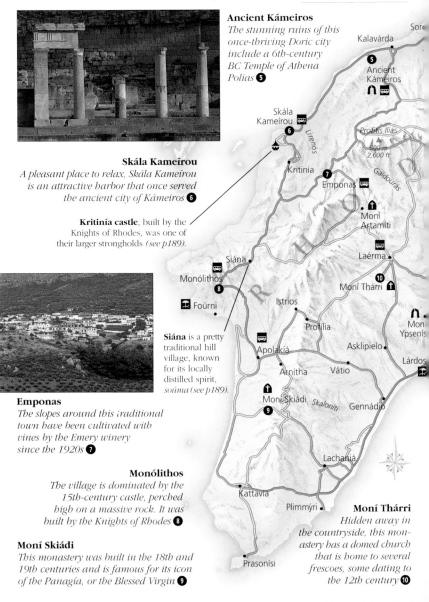

Petaloúdes
Called butterfly valley, this tranquil place is, in fact, home to thousands of moths during the summer ❹

Moní Filérimos
Filérimos monastery is set on the beautiful hillsides of Mount Filérimos. The main church dates back to the 14th century ❸

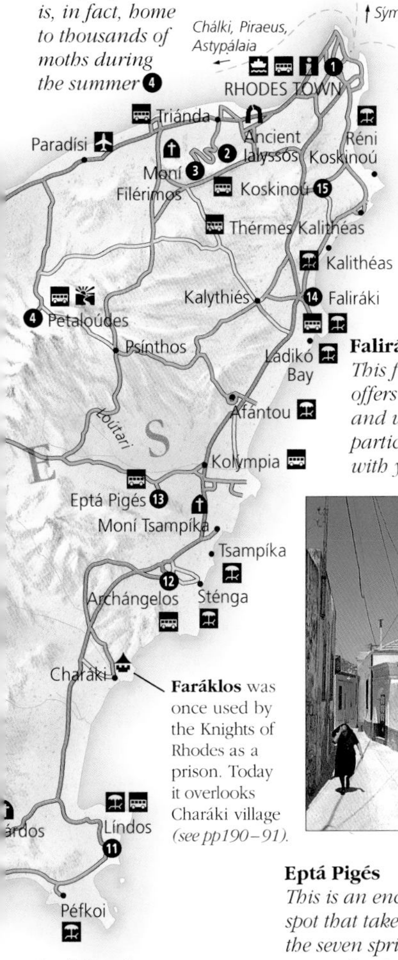

Visitors' Checklist

100,000. 25 km (15 miles) SW of Rhodes town. Commercial harbor, Rhodes town. Rhodes town (0241 23255). Rodíni Park Wine Festival, outskirts of Rhodes town: end Aug.

Ancient Ialyssós
Set on a plateau with commanding views, this ancient site dates back to 2500 BC. The ruins include remains of a 3rd-century BC acropolis ❷

★ Rhodes Town
Mandráki harbor is at the center of Rhodes town, which is one of Greece's most popular tourist destinations ❶

Faliráki
This fun-packed resort offers all sorts of nightlife and water sports and is particularly popular with young people. ⓮

Faráklos was once used by the Knights of Rhodes as a prison. Today it overlooks Charáki village *(see pp190–91).*

Koskinoú
This small village offers visitors the opportunity to see traditional Rhodian houses and choklákia pebble mosaics (see p194) ⓯

Eptá Pigés
This is an enchanting beauty spot that takes its name from the seven springs that are the source for the area's central reservoir ⓭

Star Sights

★ Rhodes Town

★ Líndos

Archángelos
A popular place to visit, Archángelos is set in attractive countryside and maintains a tradition of handicraft production ⓬

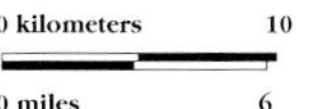

★ Líndos
One of the island's most visited sites, the acropolis at Líndos towers over the town from its clifftop position ⓫

Street-by-Street: Rhodes Old Town ❶

Πόλη Ροδού

THE TOWN OF RHODES has been inhabited for more than 2,400 years. A city was first built here in 408 BC, and when the Knights of St. John arrived in 1309 they built their citadel over these ancient remains. The Knights' medieval citadel, dominated by the towers of the Palace of the Grand Masters, forms the center of the Old Town. The new town *(see pp186–7)* lies beyond the original walls. Of the walls' 11 gates, Koskinoú (St. John's) gate, which leads into the Bourg quarter *(see p181)*, has the best view of the city's defenses.

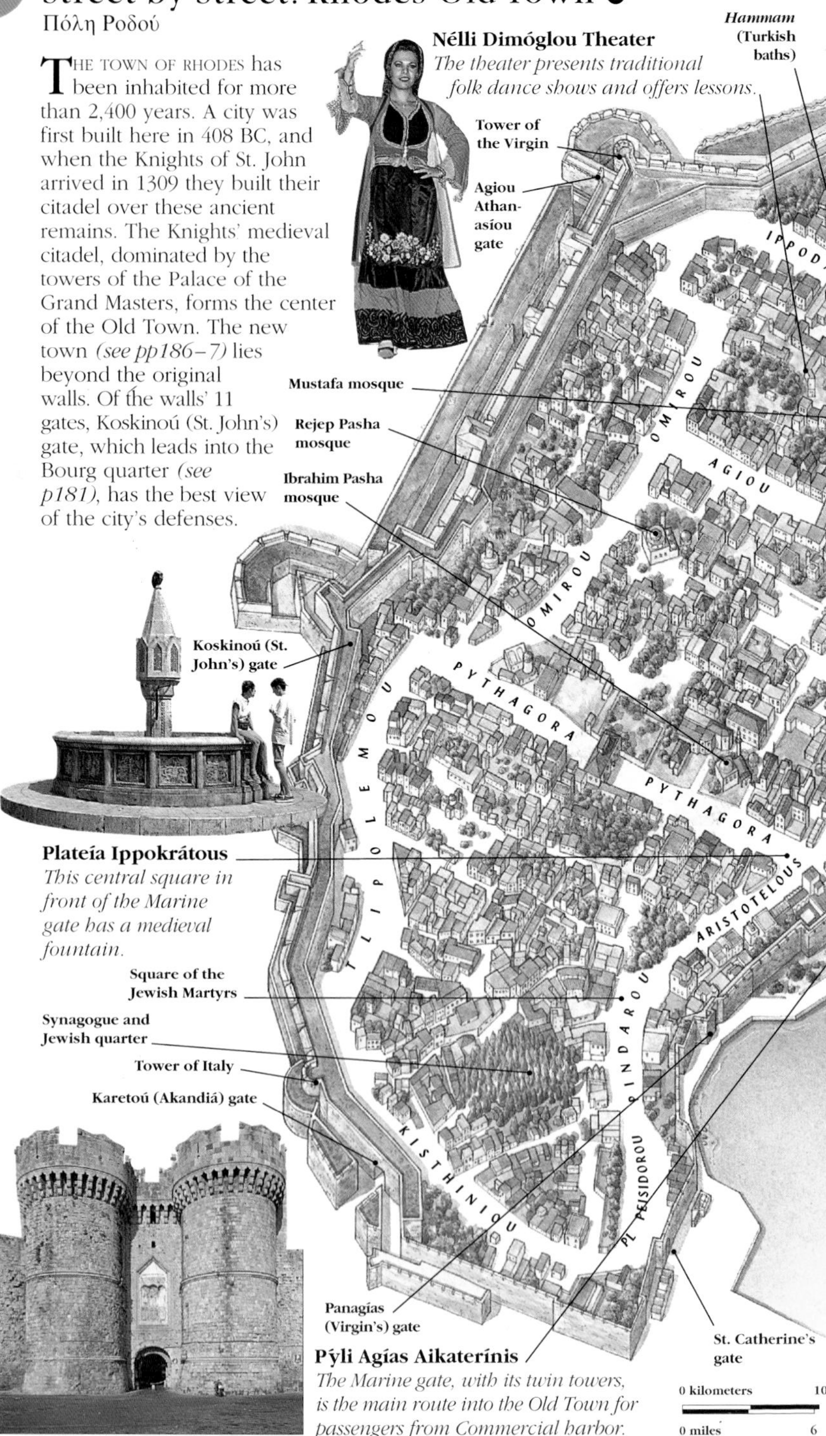

Nélli Dimóglou Theater
The theater presents traditional folk dance shows and offers lessons.

Plateía Ippokrátous
This central square in front of the Marine gate has a medieval fountain.

Pýli Agías Aikaterínis
The Marine gate, with its twin towers, is the main route into the Old Town for passengers from Commercial harbor.

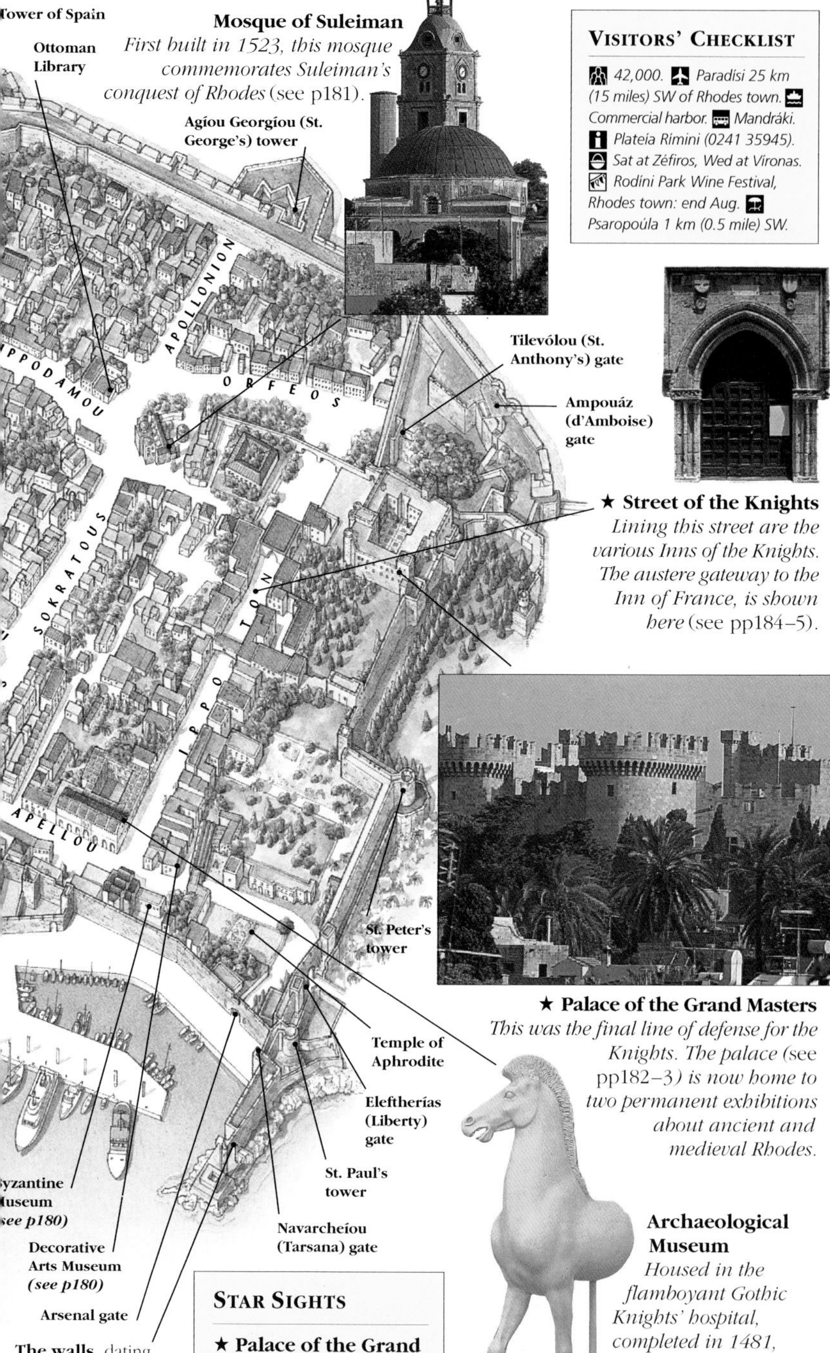

Mosque of Suleiman
First built in 1523, this mosque commemorates Suleiman's conquest of Rhodes (see p181).

Visitors' Checklist

42,000. Paradísi 25 km (15 miles) SW of Rhodes town. Commercial harbor. Mandráki. Plateía Rímini (0241 35945). Sat at Zéfiros, Wed at Víronas. Rodíni Park Wine Festival, Rhodes town: end Aug. Psaropoúla 1 km (0.5 mile) SW.

★ Street of the Knights
Lining this street are the various Inns of the Knights. The austere gateway to the Inn of France, is shown here (see pp184–5).

★ Palace of the Grand Masters
This was the final line of defense for the Knights. The palace (see pp182–3*) is now home to two permanent exhibitions about ancient and medieval Rhodes.*

Archaeological Museum
Housed in the flamboyant Gothic Knights' hospital, completed in 1481, the museum displays a large collection, including this Hellenistic statue of a horse (see p180).

The walls, dating from 1330, are up to 12 m (40 ft) thick and 4 km (2.5 miles) long. Tours start at the Palace of the Grand Masters.

Star Sights

- ★ **Palace of the Grand Masters**
- ★ **Street of the Knights**

Exploring Rhodes Old Town

Dominated by the Palace of the Grand Masters, this medieval citadel is surrounded by moats and 3 km (2 miles) of walls. Eleven gates give access to the Old Town, which is divided into the Collachium and the Bourg. The Collachium was the Knights' quarter, and dates from 1309. The Bourg housed the rest of the population, that included Jews and Turks as well as Greeks. As one of the finest walled cities in existence, the Old Town is now a World Heritage Site.

The imposing 16th-century d'Amboise gate

The Collachium

This area includes the Street of the Knights *(see pp184–5)* and the Palace of the Grand Masters *(see pp182–3)*. The main gates of entry from the new town are d'Amboise gate and the Eleftherías (Liberty) gate. The former was built in 1512 by Grand Master d'Amboise, leading from Dimokratías to the palace. The Eleftherías gate was built by the Italians and leads from Eleftherías to Plateía Sýmis. An archway leads from here into Apéllou.

Archaeological Museum

Plateía Mouseíou. 0241 27657. *Tue–Sun.* *main public hols.*

The museum is housed in the Gothic Hospital of the Knights, built in 1440–81. Most famous of the exhibits is the 1st-century BC marble *Aphrodite of Rhodes*. Other gems include a 2nd-century BC head of Helios the Sun God, discovered at the Temple of Helios on the nearby hill of Monte Smith. The grave *stelae* from the necropolis of Kámeiros give a good insight into 5th-century BC life. Exhibits also include *koúroi* (550–525 BC) from Kámeiros, and coins, jewelry, and ceramics from the Mycenaean graves at nearby Ialyssós.

***Aphrodite of Rhodes*, Archaeological Museum**

Decorative Arts Museum

Plateía Argyrokástrou.
0241 21954. *Tue–Sun.* *main public hols.*

This is an excellent folk museum featuring Lindian plates and tiles, a wide range of island costumes, and a reconstructed traditional Rhodian house.

An arched street in the Old Town

Medieval Rhodes and Ancient Rhodes Exhibitions

Palace of the Grand Masters.
0241 23359. *Tue–Sun.* *main public hols.*

Both of these permanent exhibitions can be seen as part of a tour of the Palace of the Grand Masters *(see pp182–3)*. The medieval Rhodes exhibition is titled: Rhodes from the 4th century AD to the Turkish Conquest (1522). It gives an insight into trade and everyday life in Byzantine and medieval times, with Byzantine icons, Italian and Spanish ceramics, armor, and militaria.

The Ancient Rhodes exhibition, entitled Ancient Rhodes: 2,400 years, is situated off the inner court. It details 45 years of archaeological investigations on the island with a marvelous collection of finds.

Byzantine Museum

Apéllou. 0241 27657. *Tue–Sun.* *main public hols.*

Dating from the 11th century, this Byzantine church became the Knights' cathedral, but was converted under Turkish rule into the Mosque of Enderum, known locally as the Red Mosque. Now a museum, it houses a fine collection of icons and frescoes. Among the exhibits are striking examples of 12th-century paintings in the dynamic Comnenian style from Moní Thárri *(see p190)* and late 14th-century frescoes from the abandoned church of Agios Zachárias on Chálki.

Courtyard at the Knights' Hospital, now the Archaeological Museum

Medieval City Walls

Tours from the Palace of the Grand Masters. *Tue & Fri: 2.45pm.*

A masterpiece of medieval military architecture, the huge walls run for 4 km (2.5 miles) and display 151 escutcheons of Grand Masters and Knights.

The Bourg's clock tower

The Bourg

Close to d'Amboise gate is the restored clock tower, has excellent views. It was built in 1852 on the site of a Byzantine tower and marks the end of the Collachium. The Bourg's labyrinth of streets begins at Sokrátous, the Golden Mile of bazaar-style shops, off which lie shady squares with sidewalk cafés and tavernas. The architecture is a mix of Neo-Classical, medieval, and middle Eastern. Between the houses, with their rickety wooden balconies, Ottoman mosques can be found.

Other than the major sights listed below, the Hospice of the Tongue of Italy (1392) on Kisthiníou is worth a visit, as is the Panagía tis Níkis (Our Lady of Victory). It stands near St. Catherine's gate and was built by the Knights in 1480 after the Virgin had appeared to them, inspiring victory over the Turks.

Mosque of Suleiman the Magnificent

Orféos Sokrátous. *for renovation.*

The pink mosque was constructed in 1522 to commemorate the Sultan's victory over the Knights. Rebuilt in 1808, using material from the original mosque, it remains one of the town's major landmarks. Its superb, but unsafe, minaret had to be removed in 1989, and the once-mighty mosque is now crumbling. It is closed to the public.

Library of Ahmet Havuz

Orféos Sokrátous. *0241 74090.* *May–Sep: by request, call to arrange.* *Oct–Apr; main public hols.*

The Library of Ahmet Havuz (1793) houses the chronicle of the siege of Rhodes in 1522. This is a collection of very rare Arabic and Persian manuscripts, including beautifully illuminated 15th- and 16th-century Korans, that were restored to the library in the early 1990s, having been stolen then rediscovered in London.

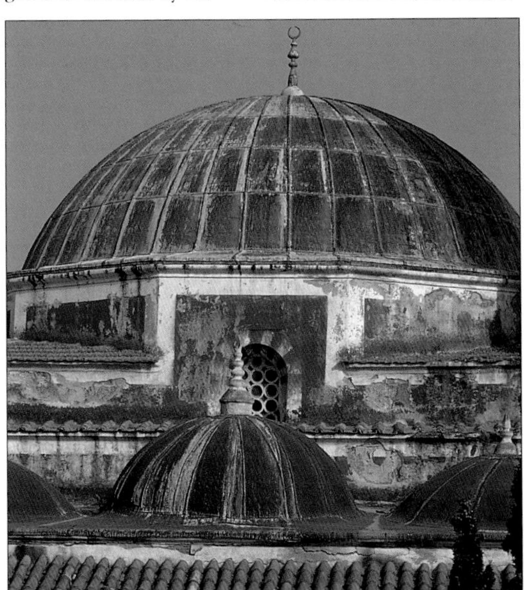

The dome of the Mosque of Suleiman the Magnificent

Nélly Dimóglou Theater

7 Andrónikou. *0241 20157.* *mid-May–mid-Oct: Mon, Wed & Fri.*

The Nélly Dimóglou Theater offers lessons in authentic Greek folk dancing. Its gardens are open all day for refreshments, and performances begin at 9:20 every evening from Monday to Friday.

Hammam

Plateía Aríonos. *0241 27739.* *Mon & Sun.*

The *hammam*, or Turkish baths, were built by Mustapha Pasha in 1765. For decades a famous place of rest and relaxation for Eastern nobility, the *hammam* is now used by Greeks, tourists, and the Turkish minority. Your own soap and towels are essential, and sexes are segregated.

Mosque of Ibrahim Pasha

Plátanos. *0241 73410.* *daily.* *donation.*

Situated off Sofokléous, the Mosque of Ibrahim Pasha was built in 1531 and refurbished in 1928. The mosque has an exquisite interior.

Mosque of Rejep Pasha

Ekátonos. *for renovation.*

Built in 1588, Rejep Pasha is one of the most striking of the 14 or so mosques to be found in the Old Town. The mosque, which has a fountain made from Byzantine and medieval church columns, contains the sarcophagus of the Pasha. The tiny Byzantine church of Agios Fanouríos is situated close by.

The Jewish Quarter

East from Hippocrates Square, the Bourg embraces Evraiakí. This was the Jewish Quarter from the 1st century AD until German occupation in 1944, when the Jewish population was transported to Auschwitz.

East along Aristotélous is **Plateía Evraíon Martýron** (Square of the Jewish Martyrs), named in memory of all those who perished in the concentration camps. There is a bronze sea horse fountain in the center, and to the north is Admiralty House, an imposing medieval building. The Synagogue is on Simíou.

Rhodes: Palace of the Grand Masters

Παλάτι του Μεγάλου Μαγίστρου

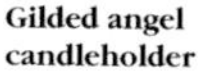

Gilded angel candleholder

A FORTRESS WITHIN a fortress, this was the seat of 19 Grand Masters, the nerve center of the Collachium, or Knights' Quarter, and last refuge for the population in times of danger. Built in the 14th century, it survived earthquake and siege but was blown up by an accidental explosion in 1856. It was restored by the Italians in the 1930s for Mussolini and King Victor Emmanuel III. The palace has some priceless mosaics from sites in Kos, after which some of the rooms are named. It also houses two exhibitions: Medieval and Ancient Rhodes *(see p180)*.

Chamber with Colonnades
Two elegant colonnades support the roof, and there is a 5th-century AD early Christian mosaic.

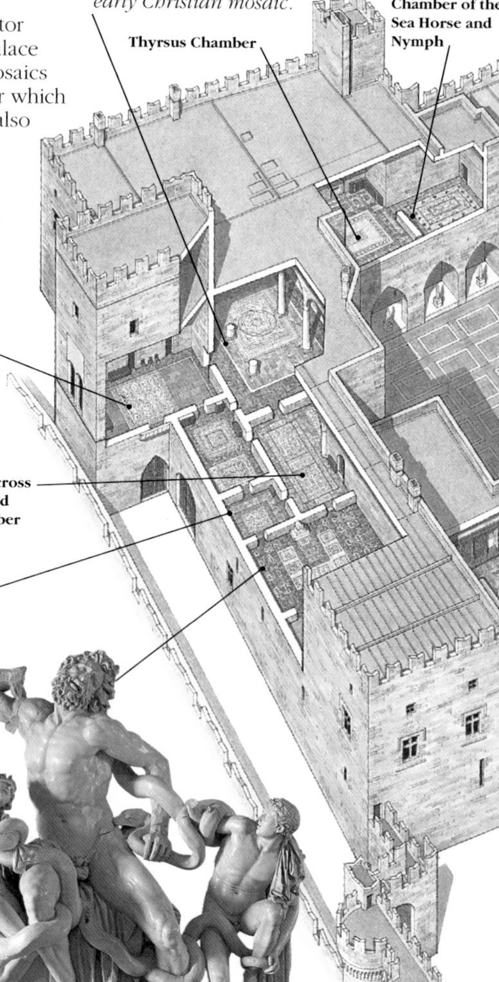

Thyrsus Chamber

Chamber of the Sea Horse and Nymph

The second cross vaulted chamber, once used as the governor's office, is paved with an intricately decorated, early Christian mosaic of the 5th century AD from Kos.

First cross vaulted chamber

★ Medusa Chamber
The mythical Gorgon Medusa, with hair of writhing serpents, forms the centerpiece of this important late Hellenistic mosaic. The chamber also features Chinese and Islamic vases.

Laocoön Chamber
A copy of the sculpture of the death of the Trojan Laocoön and his sons dominates the hall. The 1st-century BC original by Rhodian masters Athenodoros, Agesandros, and Polydoros is in the Vatican.

The battlements and heavy fortifications of the palace were to be the last line of defense in the event of the city walls being breached.

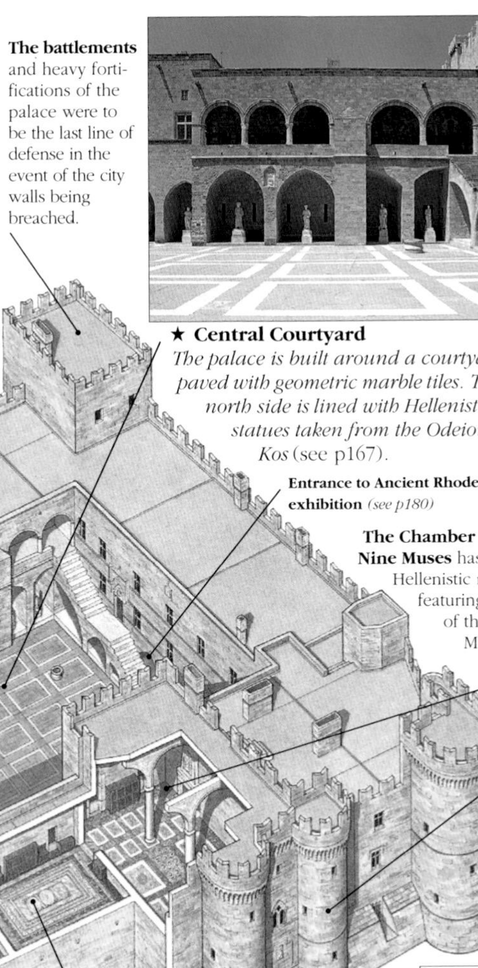

★ Central Courtyard
The palace is built around a courtyard paved with geometric marble tiles. The north side is lined with Hellenistic statues taken from the Odeion in Kos (see p167).

Entrance to Ancient Rhodes exhibition *(see p180)*

The Chamber of the Nine Muses has a late Hellenistic mosaic featuring busts of the Nine Muses of Greek myth.

Entrance

Street of the Knights → *(see pp184–5)*

The First Chamber, with its 16th-century choir stalls, features a late Hellenistic mosaic.

Grand staircase

Entrance to Medieval Rhodes exhibition *(see p180)*

The Second Chamber has a late Hellenistic mosaic and carved choir stalls.

Visitors' Checklist

Ippotón. *0241 23359.*
Aug–Sep: 8am–6pm Tue–Sun; Oct–Jul: 8:30am–3pm Tue–Sun; 12–3pm Good Fri.
Jan 1, Mar 25, Easter Sun, May 1, Dec 25, 26.
limited.

★ Main Gate
This imposing entrance, built by the Knights, has twin horseshoe-shaped towers with swallowtail turrets. The coat of arms is that of Grand Master del Villeneuwe, who ruled from 1319 to 1346.

The First Grand Master

The first Grand Master, or Magnus Magister, of the Knights was Foulkes de Villaret (1305–19), a French knight. He negotiated to buy Rhodes from the Lord of the Dodecanese, Admiral Vignolo de Vignoli. This left the Knights with the task of conquering the island's inhabitants. The Knights of Rhodes *(see pp184–5)*, as they became, remained here until their expulsion in 1522. The Villaret name lives on in Villare, one of the island's white wines.

Foulkes de Villaret

Star Features

- ★ **Central Courtyard**
- ★ **Medusa Chamber**
- ★ **Main Gate**

Rhodes: Street of the Knights

ONE OF THE OLD TOWN's most famous sights, the medieval Street of the Knights (Odos Ippotón) is situated between the harbor and the Palace of the Grand Masters *(see pp182–3)*. It is lined by the Inns of the Tongues, or nationalities, of the Order of St. John. Begun in the 14th century in Gothic style, the Inns were used as meeting places for the Knights. The site of the German Inn is unknown, but the others were largely restored by the Italians in the early 20th century.

This residence was built for the head of the Tongue of Aragon, Diomede de Vilaragut.

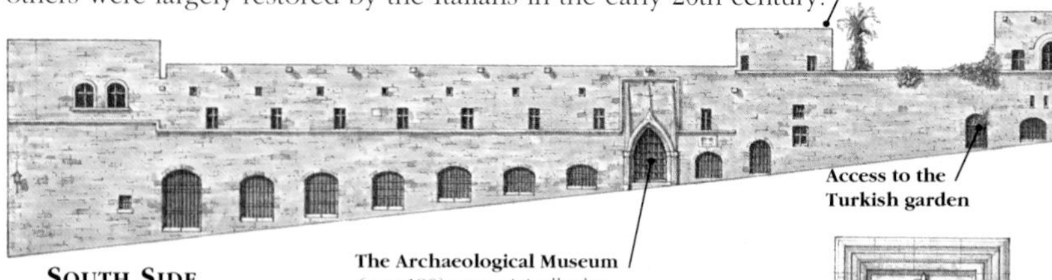

Access to the Turkish garden

The Archaeological Museum *(see p180)*, was originally the New Hospital of the Knights.

SOUTH SIDE

←
To Inn of England

The Inn of Provence *has coats of arms set in the wall. They represent the Order of the Knights of St. John, the Royal House of France, Grand Master del Carretto, and the Knight de Flota.*

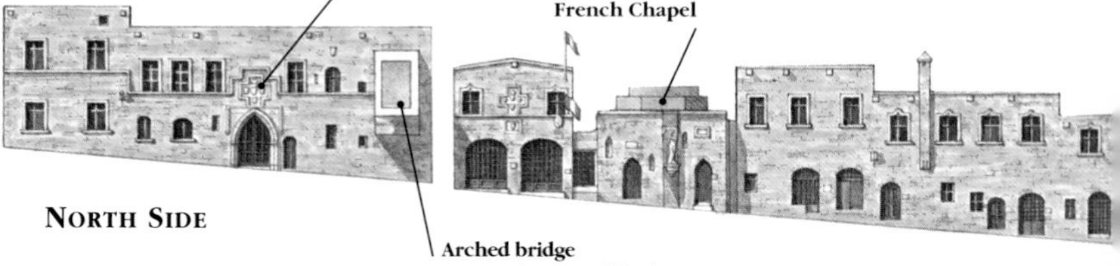

Agía Triáda, or French Chapel

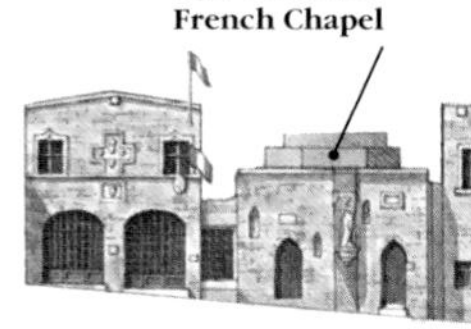

NORTH SIDE

Arched bridge connecting Inn of Spain and Inn of Provence

Palace of the Grand Masters
←

The Knights of Rhodes

Coat of arms of Foulkes de Villaret, first Grand Master

FOUNDED IN THE 11th century by merchants from Amalfi, the Order of Hospitallers of the Knights of St. John guarded the Holy Sepulcher and tended Christian pilgrims in Jerusalem. They became a military order after the First Crusade (1096–9) but had to take refuge in Cyprus when Jerusalem fell in 1291. They then bought Rhodes from the Genoese pirate Admiral Vignoli in 1306 and eventually conquered the Rhodians in 1309. A Grand Master was elected for life to govern the Order, which was divided into seven Tongues, or nationalities: France, Italy, England, Germany, Provence, Spain, and Auvergne. Each Tongue protected an area of city wall known as a Curtain. The Knights fortified the Dodecanese with about 30 castles, and their defenses are some of the finest examples of medieval military architecture.

The Knights *were drawn from noble Roman Catholic families. Those who entered the Order of the Knights of St. John swore vows of chastity, obedience, and poverty. Although knights held all the major offices, there were also lay brothers.*

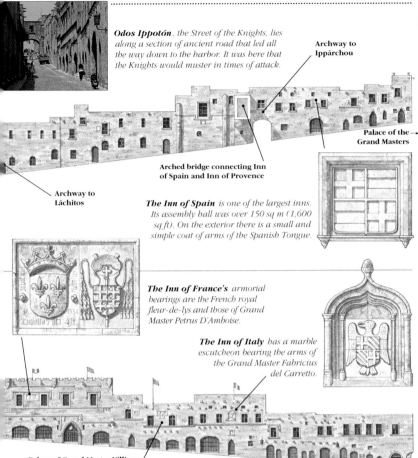

Odos Ippotón, *the Street of the Knights, lies along a section of ancient road that led all the way down to the harbor. It was here that the Knights would muster in times of attack.*

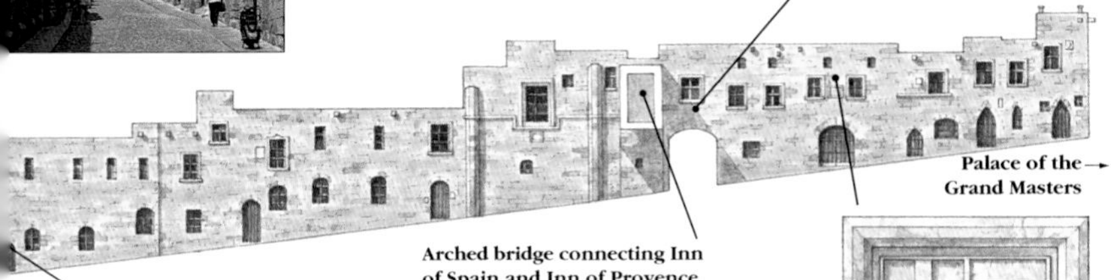

Archway to Ippárchou

Palace of the Grand Masters →

Arched bridge connecting Inn of Spain and Inn of Provence

Archway to Láchitos

The Inn of Spain *is one of the largest inns. Its assembly hall was over 150 sq m (1,600 sq ft). On the exterior there is a small and simple coat of arms of the Spanish Tongue.*

The Inn of France's *armorial bearings are the French royal fleur-de-lys and those of Grand Master Petrus D'Amboise.*

The Inn of Italy *has a marble escutcheon bearing the arms of the Grand Master Fabricius del Carretto.*

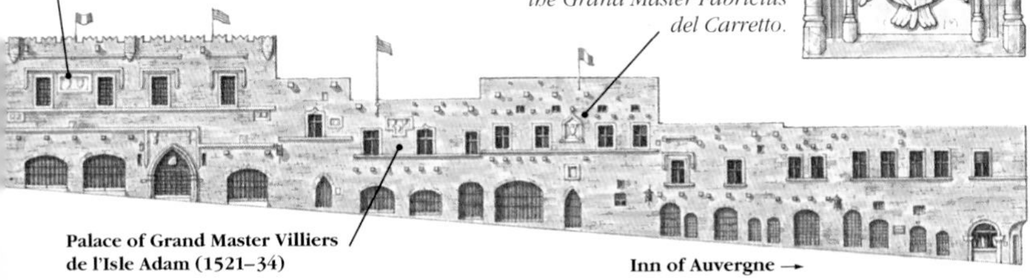

Palace of Grand Master Villiers de l'Isle Adam (1521–34)

Inn of Auvergne →

The Great Siege of Rhodes *in 1522 resulted in the Knights being defeated by the Turks. From a garrison of 650 Knights, only 180 survived. They negotiated a safe departure, although the Rhodians who fought with them were slaughtered. Seven years later, the Knights found sanctuary on the island of Malta. Their final defeat came in 1798 when Malta was annexed by Napoleon.*

Pierre d'Aubusson, *Grand Master from 1476 to 1503, is featured in this market scene. He oversaw a highly productive time in terms of building in Rhodes, including completion of the Hospital (now the Archaeological Museum).*

Exploring Rhodes New Town

THE NEW TOWN grew steadily over the last century, and became firmly established during the Italian Fascist occupation of the 1920s with the construction of the grandiose public buildings by the harbor. The New Town is made up of a number of areas including Néa Agora and Mandráki harbor in the eastern half of town. The Italian influence remains in these areas with everything from pizzerias to Gucci shops. The town's west coast is a busy tourist center, with lively streets and a crammed beach.

Mandráki harbor with the two statues of deer at its entrance

Mandráki Harbor

The harbor is the hub of life, the link between the Old and New towns where locals go for their evening stroll, or *vólta*. It is lined with yachts and excursion boats for which you can book a variety of trips in advance.

A bronze doe and stag guard the harbor entrance, where the Colossus was believed to have stood. The harbor sweeps around to the ruined 15th-century fortress of **Agios Nikólaos**, now a lighthouse, on the promontory past the three medieval windmills.

Elegant public buildings, built by the Italians in the 1920s, line Mandráki harbor: the post office, law courts, town hall, police station, and the National Theater all stand in a row. The **National Theater** often shows Rhodian character plays based on folk customs.

Nearby, on Plateía Eleftherías, is the splendid church of the **Evangelismoú**

Government House, previously the Italian Governor's Palace

(Annunciation), a 1925 replica of the Knight's Church of St. John, which has a lavishly decorated interior. The Archbishop's Palace is next door beside a giant fountain, which is a copy of the Fontana Grande in Viterbo, Italy. Farther along, the mock Venetian Gothic **Government House** (Nomarchía) is ornately decorated and surrounded by fine vaulted arcades. Unfortunately, there is no access for tourists or the general public.

At the north end of Plateía Eleftherías is the attractive **Mosque of Murad Reis**, with its graceful minaret. It was named after a Turkish admiral serving under Suleiman who was killed during the 1522 siege of Rhodes. Situated within the grounds is the Villa Kleoboulos, which was the home of the British writer Lawrence Durrell between 1945 and 1947. Also in the grounds is a cemetery reserved for Ottoman notables.

The minaret of the Mosque of Murad Reis

Heading north from the area around Mandráki harbor, a pleasant stroll along the waterfront via the crowded Elli beach leads to the northern tip of the New Town. The Hydrobiological Institute is situated on the coastal tip, housing the **Aquarium**. Set in a subterranean grotto, this is the only major aquarium in Greece, displaying nearly 40 tanks of fish. Opposite, on the north point of the island is Aquarium Beach, which is particularly good for windsurfing and paragliding.

Aquarium

Hydrobiological Institute, Kássou.

0241 27308. *daily.* *main public hols.*

THE COLOSSUS OF RHODES

Painting of the Colossus by Fischer von Erlach, 1700

One of the Seven Wonders of the Ancient World, the Colossus was a huge statue of Helios, the sun god, standing at 32–40 m (105–131 ft). Built in 305 BC to celebrate Rhodian victory over Demetriuos, the Macedonian besieger, it was sculpted by Chares of Líndos. It took 12 years to build, using bronze from the battle weapons, and cost 9 tons (10 imperial tons) of silver. Traditionally pictured straddling Mandráki Harbor, it probably stood at the Temple of Apollo, now the site of the Palace of the Grand Masters in the Old Town *(see pp182–3)*. An earthquake in 227 BC caused it to topple over.

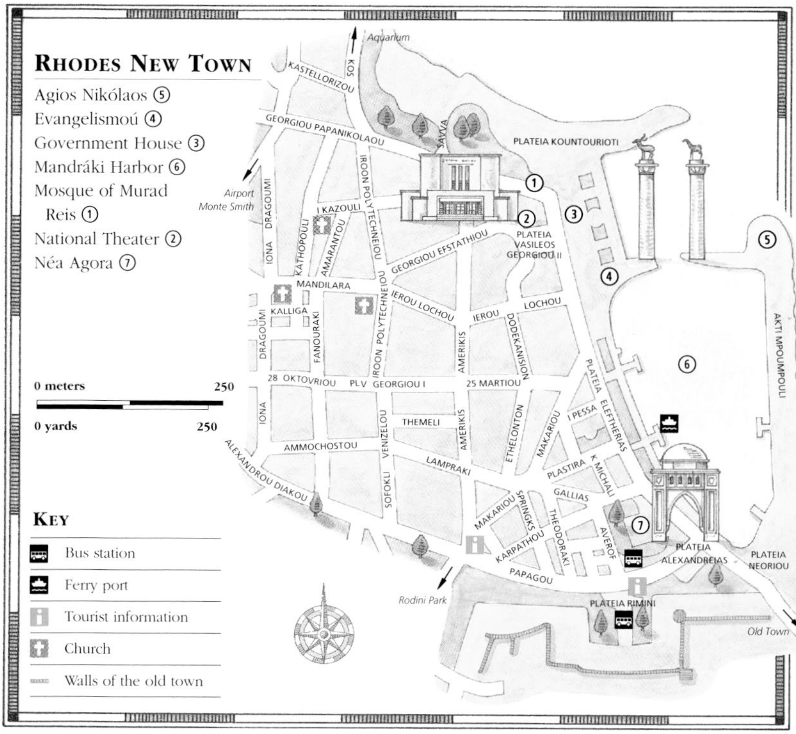

Rhodes New Town

Agios Nikólaos ⑤
Evangelismoú ④
Government House ③
Mandráki Harbor ⑥
Mosque of Murad Reis ①
National Theater ②
Néa Agora ⑦

0 meters 250
0 yards 250

Key

- Bus station
- Ferry port
- Tourist information
- Church
- Walls of the old town

Néa Agora
Mandráki is backed by the New Market or Néa Agora with its Moorish domes and lively cafés. Inside the market are food stalls, gift shops, small *souvláki* bars, and cafés. It is popular as a meeting place for people coming from outlying villages and islands. Behind the Néa Agora, on the grounds of the Palace of the Grand Masters, a sound and light show is held. This takes place daily in one of four languages and tells the story of the overthrow of the Knights by Suleiman the Magnificent in 1522.

A view of the domed centerpiece of the New Market from Mandráki Harbor

Monte Smith
Monte Smith, a hill to the west of town, offers panoramic views over Rhodes town and the coast. It is named Monte Smith after the English Admiral Sir Sidney Smith, who kept watch from there for Napoleon's fleet in 1802. It is also known as Agios Stéphanos.

The hill is the site of a 3rd-century BC Hellenistic city that was excavated by the Italians. They restored the 3rd-century BC stadium, the 2nd-century BC acropolis, and a small theater or odeion. This was built in a unusual square shape and is used for performances of ancient drama in the summer. Only three columns remain of the once-mighty Temple of Pythian Apollo, and there are other ruins of the temples of Athena Polias and Zeus. Nearby, on Voreíou Ipeírou, are the remains of the Asklepieion, a temple dedicated to the god of healing, Asklepios.

Rodíni Park
The beautiful Rodíni Park, 3 km (2 miles) to the south of Rhodes town, is now home to the Rhodian deer sanctuary, and perfect for a break away from the crowded center. It is the site where the orator Aeschines built the School of Rhetoric in 330 BC, attended by both Julius Caesar and Cassius, although there are no remains to visit. Sights include a 3rd-century BC necropolis with Doric rock tombs and the tomb of one of the Ptolemies. In medieval times the Knights grew their herbs at Rodíni.

Exploring Western Rhodes

An icon at Our Lady of Filérimos

THE WINDSWEPT WEST COAST is a busy strip of hotels, bars, and restaurants, along gravelly beaches from Rhodes town to the airport at Paradísi. But head south and the landscape becomes green and fertile, with vineyards and wooded mountain slopes dotted with traditional farming villages. The attractions include Moní Filérimos, Ancient Kámeiros, the wine-making village of Emponas, and the enchanting valley of Petaloúdes, the place that gives Rhodes its name as the "Island of Butterflies." Farther south is a dramatic mix of scenery with castle-topped crags and sea views to the islands of Chálki and Alimiá.

Ancient Ialyssós 2

Αρχαία Ιαλυσός

15 km (9 miles) SW of Rhodes town. *to Triánda.* *Tue–Sun.* *main public hols.*

Named after a grandson of the sun god Helios, Ialyssós fused with two other Doric city-states, Líndos and Kámeiros, to create one capital, Rhodes, in 408 BC. As this new center grew, Ialyssós, Líndos, and Kámeiros lost their former importance. However, Ialyssós proved a much fought over site: the Byzantines were besieged by the Genoese there in 1248; the Knights *(see pp184–5)* used it as a base before taking Rhodes in 1309; and it was Suleiman's headquarters before his assault on the Knights in 1522. The Italians used it again for gun positions during World War II.

The only remnant of the acropolis is the 3rd-century BC **Temple of Athena Polias and Zeus Polios** by the church of Agios Geórgios. The restored lion-head fountain, to the south, is 4th century BC.

Moní Filérimos 3

Μονή Φιλέρημος

15 km (9 miles) SW of Rhodes town. *0241 92202.* *to Triánda.* *Tue–Sun.* *main public hols.*

One of Rhodes' beauty spots, the hillsides of Filérimos are home to cypresses and pines. Among the trees sits Moní Filérimos, its domed chapels decorated with the cross of the Knights and the coat-of-arms of Grand Master Pierre d'Aubusson. A place of worship for 2,000 years, layers of history and traditions can be seen, from Phoenician to Byzantine, Orthodox, and Catholic.

The main attraction is Our Lady of Filérimos, the Italian reconstruction of the Knights' 14th-century church of the Virgin Mary. The church is a complex of four chapels: the main one, built in 1306, leads to three others. The innermost chapel has a Byzantine floor decorated with a red mosaic fish.

The Italians erected a Calvary, from the entrance of the monastery, in the form of an avenue with the Stations of the Cross illustrated on plaques. On the headland stands a giant 18-m (59-ft) cross.

Moní Filérimos in its woodland setting

Petaloúdes 4

Πεταλούδες

26 km (16 miles) SW of Rhodes town.

Petaloúdes, or Butterfly Valley, is a narrow leafy valley with a stream crisscrossed by wooden bridges. It teems not with butterflies, but with Jersey tiger moths from June to September. Thousands are attracted by the golden resin of the storax trees, which exude vanilla-scented gum used for incense. Cool and pleasant, Petaloúdes attracts walkers as well as lepidopterists and is at its most peaceful in the early morning before all the tour buses arrive.

There is a walk along the valley up to the **Moní Panagía Kalópetra**. This rural church, built in 1782, is a tranquil resting place, and the fine views are well worth the climb.

Jersey tiger moth

Ancient Kámeiros 5

Αρχαία Κάμειρος

36 km (22 miles) SW of Rhodes town. *0241 40037.* *Tue–Sun.* *main public hols.* *to lower sections only.*

Discovered in 1859, this Doric city was a thriving community during the 5th century BC. Founded by Althaimenes of Crete, the city was probably destroyed in a large earthquake in 142 BC. In spite of this, it remains one of the best-preserved Classical Greek cities.

There are remains of a 3rd-century BC Doric temple, an altar to Helios, public baths, and a 6th-century BC cistern that supplied 400 families. The 6th-century BC Temple of Athena Polias is on the top terrace, below which are remains of the Doric stoa, 206 m (675 ft) long.

Monólithos castle in its precarious position overlooking the sea

Skála Kameírou ❻

Σκάλα Καμείρου

50 km (30 miles) SW of Rhodes town.

100.

The fishing harbor of Skála Kameírou makes a good place for lunch. It was the Doric city of an ancient port, and the outline of a Lycian tomb remains on the cliff side. Nearby, **Kritínia castle** is one of the Knights' more impressive ruins. Its three levels are attributed to different Grand Masters. Clinging to the hillside, a cluster of white houses form the picturesque village of **Kritínia**.

Emponas ❼

Εμπονας

55 km (34 miles) SW of Rhodes town.

1,500.

Situated in the wild foothills of Mount Attáviros, the atmospheric village of Emponas has been home to the Cair winery since the 1920s and is also famous for its folk-dancing and festivals. Although the village is popular for organized Greek nights, Emponas has maintained its traditional ways.

Monólithos ❽

Μονόλιθος

80 km (50 miles) SW of Rhodes town.

250. Foúrni 5 km (3 miles) SW.

Named after its monolith, a crag with a dramatic 235-m (770-ft) drop to the sea, Monólithos is the most important village in the southwest.

Situated at the foot of Mount Akramýtis, the village is 2 km (1 mile) from **Monólithos castle**. This impregnable 15th-century fortress, built by Grand Master d'Aubusson, is perched spectacularly on the vast gray rock. Its massive walls enclose two small 15th-century chapels, Agios Panteleïmon and Agios Geórgios, both decorated with frescoes. Views from the top are impressive, and the sheer drop hair-raising.

Down a rough road south from the castle is the sheltered sandy beach of **Foúrni**, which has a seasonal taverna.

Environs: Between Emponas and Monólithos, the pretty hill village of **Siána** is famous for its honey and fiery *soúma* – a kind of grape spirit, like the Cretan raki. The villagers were granted a licence by the Italians to make the spirit, and you can sample both the firewater and honey at the roadside cafés. The village houses have traditional clay roofs, and the domed church of **Agios Panteleïmon** has restored 18th-century frescoes.

Moní Skiádi ❾

Μονή Σκιάδι

8 km (5 miles) S of Apolakiá.

0244 46006. to Apolakiá.

daily.

Moní Skiádi is famous for its miraculous icon of the Panagía or the Blessed Virgin. When a 15th-century heretic stabbed the Virgin's cheek it was supposed to have bled, and the brown stains are still visible. The present monastery was built during the 18th and 19th centuries around the 13th-century church of Agios Stavrós, or the Holy Cross. At Easter the holy icon is carried from village to village until finally coming to rest for a month on the island of Chálki.

Sunset over the village of Emponas and Mount Attáviros

Exploring Eastern Rhodes

THE SHELTERED EAST COAST has miles of beaches and rocky coves, the crowded vacation playgrounds of Faliráki and Líndos contrasting with the deserted sands in the southeast. For sightseeing purposes the way east divides into two sections: from the southern tip of the island at Prasonísi up to Péfkoi, and then from Líndos up to Rhodes town. The landscape is a rich patchwork, from the oasis of Eptá Pigés and the orange groves near Archángelos, to the stretches of rugged coastline and sandy bays.

Fountain in Lárdos village

Moní Thárri ⓾
Μονή Θάρρι

40 km (25 miles) S of Rhodes town. *to Laérma.* *daily.*

From the inland resort of Lárdos follow signs to Laérma, which is just north of Moní Thárri, famous for its 12th-century frescoes. Reached through a forest, the domed church was hidden from view in order to escape the attention of marauding pirates.

According to legend, it was built in the 9th century by a mortally ill Byzantine princess, who miraculously recovered when it was completed.

The 12th-century north and south walls remain, and there are vestiges of the 9th-century building in the grounds. The nave, apse, and dome are covered with frescoes. Some walls have four layers of paintings, the earliest dating as far back as 1100, while there are three layers in the apse dating from the 12th–16th centuries. These are more distinct, and depict a group of prophets and a horse's head. The monastery has been extended and has basic accommodations for visitors.

Asklipieío village

About 8 km (5 miles) south along a rough track is the pleasant village of **Asklipieío**, with the frescoed church of Kímisis tis Theotókou.

Líndos ⓫
See pp192–3.

Archángelos ⓬
Αρχάγγελος

33 km (20 miles) S of Rhodes town. 3,000. *Sténga 3 km (2 miles) E.*

The island's largest village, Archángelos lies in the Valley of Aíthona, which is famous for its oranges. The town itself is known for pottery, handwoven rugs, and leather boots. Traditionally worn as protection from snakes while in the fields working, they are made of sturdy cowhide for the feet, with soft goatskin leggings. The townspeople have their own dialect and are fiercely patriotic – some graves are even painted blue and white.

In the center, the church of **Archángelos Michaïl and Gavriíl**, the village's patron saints, is distinguished by a tiered bell tower and pebble mosaic courtyard.

Above the town are ruins of the **Crusader castle**, built by Grand Master Orsini in 1467 as part of the Knights' defenses against the Turks. Inside, the chapel of Agios Geórgios has a modern fresco of the saint in action against the dragon. To the east of the town, at the end of a minor road, lies the bay of **Sténga**, a quiet and sheltered stretch of sand.

Environs: South past Malónas is the castle of **Faraklós**. It was a pirate stronghold before the Knights defeated them and turned it into a prison. The fortress overlooks Charáki,

Charáki village with the castle of Faraklós in the background

The sandy beach at Tsampíka

a pleasant fishing hamlet, now growing into a resort with a pebble beach that is lined with fish tavernas.

Eptá Pigés ⓭

Επτά Πηγές

26 km (16 miles) S of Rhodes town. *to Kolýmpia.* *Tsampíka 5 km (3 miles) SE.*

Eptá Pigés, or Seven Springs, is one of the island's leading woodland beauty spots. Peacocks strut beside streams and waterfalls, where the seven springs feed a central reservoir. The springs were harnessed to irrigate the orange groves of Kolýmpia to the east. The lake can be reached either by a woodland trail, or you can shuffle ankle-deep in water through a 186-m (610-ft) tunnel.

Peacock at Eptá Pigés

Environs: Farther east along the coast, the Byzantine **Moní Tsampíka** perches on a mountain top at 300 m (984 ft). Legend has it that the 11th-century icon in the chapel was found by an infertile couple, who later conceived a child. The chapel hence became a place of pilgrimage for childless women, who still walk there barefoot, and pray to the icon of the Virgin. They also pledge to name their child Tsampíka or Tsampíkos, names unique to the Dodecanese.

Below the monastery lies **Tsampíka** beach, a superb stretch of sand that becomes very crowded in tourist season. Various water sports are also available here.

Faliráki ⓮

Φαληράκι

15 km (9 miles) S of Rhodes town. *400.*

Faliráki, the island's most popular resort, consists of long sandy beaches surrounded by whitewashed hotels, vacation apartments, and restaurants. Also a good base for families who like a lively vacation with plenty of activities, it is a brash and loud resort that caters mostly to a younger crowd. As well as a waterslide complex, there are all types of water sports to enjoy. There are bars and discos, and numerous places to eat, from fish and chips to Chinese. Other diversions include bungee-jumping or a visit to the **Faliráki Snake House**.

Faliráki Snake House

Faliráki. *0241 85841.* *Apr–Oct: daily.*

Environs: Slightly inland, the village of **Kalythiés** offers a more traditional break. Its attractive Byzantine church, **Agía Eleoúsa**, contains some interesting frescoes. Farther southeast, rocky **Ladikó Bay** is worth a visit. It was used as a location for filming *The Guns of Navarone.*

Golfers can visit the 18-hole course at **Afántou** village, with its pebbly coves and beaches, popular for boat trips from Rhodes town. Set in apricot orchards, Afántou is known as the "hidden village," and is noted for hand-woven carpets.

Koskinoú ⓯

Κοσκινού

10 km (6 miles) S of Rhodes town. *1,200.* *Réni Koskinoú 2 km (1 mile) NE.*

The old village of Koskinoú is characterized by its traditional Rhodian houses featuring the *choklákia* pebble mosaic floors and courtyards. There is an attractive church of **Eisódia tis Theotókou**, which has a multitiered bell tower. Nearby, **Réni Koskinoú** has good hotels, restaurants, and beaches.

Environs: South of Koskinoú lies **Thérmes Kalithéas**, Kalithea Spa, once popular for its healing waters. Now abandoned, the domed pavilions, pink-marbled pillars, and Moorish archways look quite bizarre. Often used in films, the spa is set in lovely gardens, reached through pinewoods. There is now a busy lido here, and the rocky coves are popular for scuba-diving and snorkeling.

A church with a tiered bell tower in Koskinoú village

Líndos ⓫

Λίνδος

Carved stones of stoa

LINDOS WAS FIRST INHABITED around 3000 BC. Its twin harbors gave it a head start over Rhodes' other ancient cities of Kámeiros and Ialyssós as a naval power. In the 6th century BC, under the benevolent tyrant Kleoboulos, Líndos thrived and grew rich from its many foreign colonies. With its dazzling white houses, Crusader castle, and acropolis dramatically overlooking the sea, Líndos is a magnet for tourists. Second only to Rhodes town as a holiday resort, it is now a National Historic Landmark, with development strictly controlled.

A traditional Líndian doorway

Exploring Líndos Village

Líndos is the most popular excursion from Rhodes town, and the best way to arrive is by boat. The narrow cobblestone streets can be shoulder to shoulder with tourists in high summer, so spring or autumn are more relaxed times to visit. Líndos is a sun trap and is known for consistently recording the highest temperatures on the island.

Traffic is banned so the village retains much of its charm, and donkeys carry people up to the acropolis. But it is very busy, with a bazaar of gift shops and fast food outlets. Happily there are also several good tavernas, and, at the other end of the scale, there are a number of stylish restaurants offering international cuisine.

Líndos lace seller on the steps to the acropolis

The village's winding lanes are fronted by imposing doorways that lead into the flower-filled courtyards of the unique Líndian houses. Mainly built by rich sea-captains between the 15th and 18th centuries, these traditional houses are called *archontiká*. They have distinctive carvings on the stonework, like ship's cables or chains, and are built round *choklákia* pebble mosaic courtyards *(see p194)*. The older houses mix Byzantine and Arabic styles and a few have small captains' rooms built over the doorway. Some of the *archontiká* have been converted into apartments and restaurants.

In the center of the village lies the Byzantine church of the **Panagías**. It has a graceful bell tower and tiled domes. Originally a 10th-century basilica, it was rebuilt beween 1489 and 1490. The frescoes inside were painted by Gregory of Sými in 1779.

On the road that leads up to the acropolis is the **Pántheon**, a waxwork museum of characters in mythology, including gods and heroes, such as Perseus and Herakles. There are sound and light shows accompanying each character and a souvenir shop.

Also on the path leading to the acropolis, are a number of women selling the lace for which Líndos is renowned. Lindian stitchwork is sought after by museums throughout the world; even Alexander the Great wore a cloak stitched by Lindian women.

Líndos Stoa
This colonnade or stoa was built in the Hellenistic period around 200 BC.

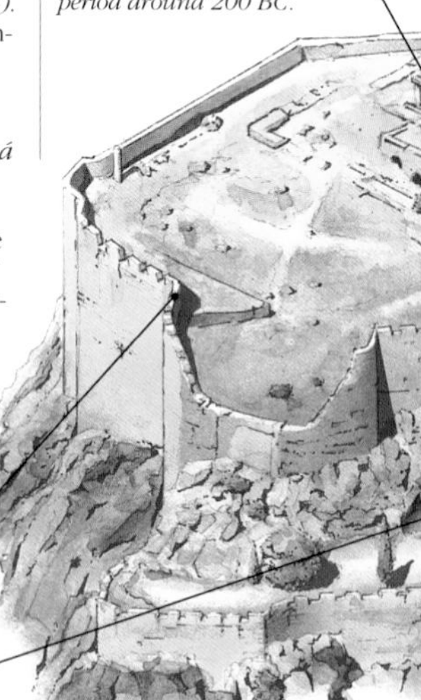

The battlements were built in the 13th century by the Knights of Rhodes.

A trireme warship is carved into the rock.

The Acropolis at Lindos

Perched on a sheer precipice 125 m (410 ft) above the village, the acropolis is crowned by the 4th-century BC Temple of Lindian Athena, its remaining columns etched against the skyline. The temple site was among the most sacred spots in the ancient world, visited by Alexander the Great and supposedly by Helen of Troy and Herakles. In the 13th century, the Knights Hospitallers of St. John fortified the city with battlements much higher than the original walls.

The acropolis overlooking Líndos town and bay

The main beach at Líndos, **Megálos Gialós**, is where the Líndian fleet once anchored, and it sweeps north of the village round Líndos bay. It is a popular beach and it tends to get very crowded in summer, but a wide selection of water sports are available. It is also safe for children, and several tavernas can be found along the beachfront.

Pántheon

Along the road to the acropolis.
Apr–Oct: daily.

Visitors' Checklist

1 km (0.5 mile) E of Líndos village.
0244 31258. *Jul–Sep: 8am–6:40pm Tue–Sun; Oct–Jun: 8:30am–2:45pm Tue–Sun.*
Jan 1, Mar 25, Easter Sun, May 1, Dec 25 & 26.

Environs: Tiny, trendy **Pallás** beach is linked to Líndos's main beach by a walkway. Nudists make for the headland, around which is the more exclusive **St. Paul's Bay**, where the Apostle landed in AD 43, bringing Christianity to Rhodes. An idyllic, almost enclosed cove, it has azure waters and a white chapel dedicated to St. Paul, with a festival on June 28.

Although called the **Tomb of Kleoboulos**, the stone monument on the promontory north of the main beach at Líndos bay had nothing to do with the great Rhodian tyrant. The circular mausoleum, made from huge blocks of stone, was constructed around the 1st century BC, several centuries after his death. In early Christian times the tomb was converted into the church of Agios Aimilianós, but who was originally buried here still remains a mystery.

Péfkos, 3km (1.8 miles) south of Líndos, has small sandy beaches fringed by pine trees and is fast developing as a popular resort.

Lárdos is a quiet inland village, 7 km (4 miles) west of Líndos. **Lárdos Bay**, 1 km (0.5 mile) south of the village, has sand dunes bordered by reeds and is being developed with upscale village-style hotels.

Reconstruction of the Acropolis (c.AD 300)

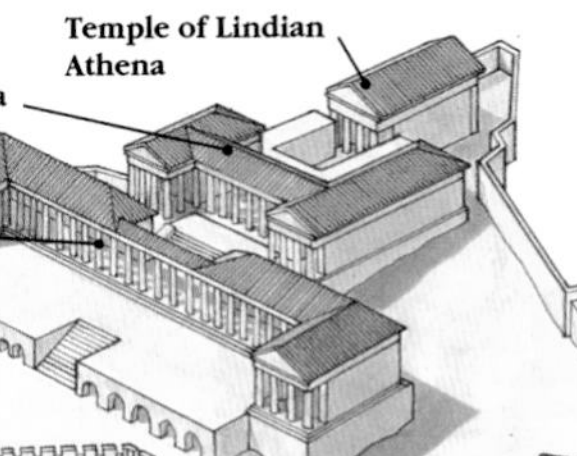

Nimporió with Agios Nikólaos church towering above the surrounding buildings

Chálki
Χάλκη

280. Nimporió. Piátsa, Nimporió (0241 45213). Chorió: Panagía 15 Aug. Nimporió.

CHALKI WAS ONCE a thriving sponge-fishing island but was virtually abandoned when its sponge divers emigrated to Florida in search of work in the early 1900s. Tourism has grown steadily as the island has been spruced up. Once fertile, Chálki's water table was infiltrated by seawater, and the island is now barren with fresh water shipped in by tanker. Sheep and goats roam the rocky hillside, but there is little cultivation, and produce is imported from Rhodes.

NIMPORIO

Chálki's harbor and only settlement, Nimporió is a quiet and picturesque village with a Neo-Classical flavor.

A goat farmer in Chálki on his journey home

The main sight in Nimporió is the church of **Agios Nikólaos** with its elegant bell tower, the highest in the Dodecanese, tiered like a wedding cake. The church is also known for its magnificent black and white *choklákia* pebble mosaic courtyard depicting birds and the tree of life. The watchful eye painted over the main door is to ward off evil spirits.

A row of ruined windmills stands above the harbor, which also boasts an Italianate town hall and post office plus a fine stone clock tower. Nearby is sandy **Póntamos** beach, which is quiet and shallow and suitable for children.

AROUND THE ISLAND

The island is almost traffic-free so it is ideal for walkers. An hour's walk uphill from Nimporió is the abandoned former capital of **Chorió**. Its Crusader castle perches high on a crag, worth a visit for the coat of arms and Byzantine

CHOKLAKIA MOSAICS

A distinctive characteristic of the Dodecanese, these decorative mosaics were used for floors from Byzantine times onward. An exquisite art form as well as a functional piece of architecture, they were made from small sea pebbles, usually black and white but occasionally reddish, wedged together to form a kaleidoscope of raised patterns. Kept wet, the mosaics also helped to keep houses cool in the heat.

Early examples featured abstract, formal, and mainly geometric designs such as circles. Later on the decorations became more flamboyant with floral patterns and symbols depicting the lives of the householders with ships, fish, and trees. Aside from Chálki, the houses of Líndos also have fine mosaics *(see pp192–3)*. On Sými the church of Agios Geórgios *(see p174)* depicts a furious mermaid about to dash a ship beneath the waves.

A *choklákia* mosaic outside Moní Taxiárchi in Sými

Circular *choklákia* mosaic in Chálki

frescoes in the ruined chapel. On a clear day you can see Crete. The Knights of St. John *(see pp184–5)* built it on an ancient acropolis, using much of the earlier stone.

The Byzantine church of the **Panagía** below the castle has some interesting frescoes and is the center for a giant festival on August 15. Clinging to the mountainside opposite is the church of **Stávros** (the Cross).

From Chorió you can follow the newly constructed road west to the Byzantine **Moní Agíou Ioánnou Prodrómou** (St. John the Baptist). The walk takes three to five hours, or it is a one hour drive. The monastery has an attractive shaded courtyard. It is best to visit in the early morning or to stay overnight: the caretakers will offer you a cell. You can walk from here to the pebbly beaches of **Kánia** and **Gialí** or take a taxi boat.

The interior of Moni Agíou Ioánnis Prodrómou

Outlying Islands

Excursions run east from Nimporió to deserted **Alímia** island, where Italy berthed some submarines in World War II. There are several small chapels and a ruined castle.

Kastellórizo

Καστελλόριζω

275. 2.5 km (1.5 miles) S of Kastellórizo town. Kastellórizo town. 500 m (1,640 ft) N of port (0241 49333).

Remote Kastellórizo is the most far-flung Greek island, just 2.5 km (1.5 miles) from Turkey but 118 km (73 miles) from Rhodes. It was very isolated until the airport opened up tourism in 1987. Kastellórizo has no beaches, but clear seas full of marine life, including monk seals, and it is excellent for snorkeling. Known locally as Megísti (the biggest), it is the largest of 14 islets.

The island's population has declined from 15,000 in the 19th century to barely 300 today. From 1920 it was severely oppressed by the Italians who occupied the Dodecanese, and in World War II it was evacuated and looted.

Despite hardships, the waterfront bustles with tavernas and sometimes impromptu music and dancing. It is a strange backwater, but the indomitable character of the islanders is famous throughout Greece.

Kastellórizo town is the island's only settlement, with reputedly the best natural harbor between Piraeus and Beirut. Above the town is the ruined fort or **kástro** with spectacular views of the islands and the coast of Turkey. It was named the Red Castle (Kastello Rosso) by the Knights of St. John due to its red stone, and this name was adopted by the islanders. The **Castle Museum** contains costumes, frescoes, and photographs. Nearby, cut into the rock, is Greece's only **Lycian Tomb**, from the ancient Lycian civilization of Asia Minor. It is noted for its Doric columns.

Most of the old Neo-Classical houses stand in ruins, bombed during World War II or destroyed by earthquakes.

A traditional housefront in Kastellórizo town

However, buildings are being restored as tourism develops. The Italian film *Mediterraneo* was set here, and since then the island has attracted many Italian tourists.

Highlights worth seeing include the elegant cathedral of **Agios Konstantínos kai Eléni**, built with granite columns from the Temple of Apollo in Patara, Anatolia.

From town a path leads up to four white churches and the **Palaiokástro**. This Doric fortress and acropolis has a 3rd-century BC inscription on the gate referring to Megísti.

A boat trip southeast from Kastellórizo town to the spectacular **Perásta Cave** should not be missed; it is famed for its stalactites and the strange light effects on the vivid blue waters.

Castle Museum

Kastellórizo town. *0241 49283. Tue–Sun. main public hols.*

Kastellórizo town with Turkey in the background

ΞΕΝΟΔΟΧΕΙΟΝ Ο ΠΟΣΕΙΔΩΝ
POSIDON PENSION

Kárpathos

Κάρπαθος

WILD, RUGGED KARPATHOS is the third largest island in the Dodecanese. Dramatically beautiful, it has remained largely unspoiled despite the recent increase in tourism. Like most of the Dodecanese, it has had a checkered history including periods of domination by both the Romans and Byzantines. Once known as Porfiris, after the red dye that is manufactured locally, the island's name today is thought to derive from the word *arpákatos* ("robbery"), as the island was a popular pirate lair in medieval times.

Folk reliefs on a taverna in Diafáni

KEY

For key to map see back flap

SARIA
Chálki, Rhodes
Vrykoúnda
Avlóna
Olympos
Diafáni
KARPATHOS
Apélla
Lefkós
Kalí Límni
685 m 2,250 ft
Kyrá Panagiá
Apéri
Othos
KARPATHOS TOWN
Menetés
Arkása
Profítis Ilías
Ammopí
510 m 1,670 ft
Crete (Siteía)
ARMATHIA
Frý
Agía Marína
KASOS
Crete (Siteía, Irákleio)
Chélathros Bay
0 kilometers 5
0 miles 3

KARPATHOS TOWN

Kárpathos town, also known as Pigádia, is the island's main port and capital, sheltered in the southeast of Vróntis bay. Once an ordinary working town, it now has hotels strung out all around the previously deserted bay. The waterfront is bustling with sidewalk cafés and restaurants that serve international fare. Opposite the Italianate town hall, **Kárpathos park** has an open-air display of ancient objects. Exhibits include an early Christian marble font and objects discovered in 5th-century BC Mycenaean tombs on the island.

ENVIRONS: South of Kárpathos town there is a pretty walk through olive groves to the main resort of **Ammopí**, 7 km (4 miles) away, with its string of sandy beaches. Above Ammopí, the village of **Menetés**, nestling at 350 m (1,150 ft) on the slopes of Mount Profítis Ilías, has quaint vine-covered streets. The traditional pastel-colored houses have attractive courtyards and gardens. Inside the village church is an interesting carved wooden iconostasis.

AROUND THE ISLAND

A mountainous spine divides the wild north from the softer, fertile south. On the west coast, 8 km (5 miles) from Menetés, the village of **Arkása** has been transformed into a resort. In 1923, the 4th-century church of Agía Anastasía was discovered. It contained some fine early Byzantine mosaics, the best of which depicts two deer gazing into a water jug, now in the Rhodes's Archaeological Museum *(see p180)*.

Apéri, 8 km (5 miles) north of Kárpathos town, was the island's capital until 1892, and is said to be one of the richest villages in Greece. It sits 300 m (984 ft) up Mount Kalí Límni and has fountains and fine houses with exquisite gardens dating from the 1800s.

Othos, just to the west of Apéri is the highest village on the island, at 450 m (1,476 ft) above sea level. It is also one

The white mansions of Apéri, clustered on the hillside

◁ **The historical village of Olympos, sitting high in the hills of northern Kárpathos**

Windmills in the traditional village of Olympos

of the oldest, with traditional Karpathian houses. One of the houses is a **Folk Museum** with textiles and pottery on display. There is also a family loom and tools for traditional crafts.

The west coast resort of **Lefkós** is considered to be the jewel of the island by the Karpathians, with its three horseshoe bays of white sand. On the east coast, **Kyrá Panagiá**, with its pink-domed church, is another beautiful cove of fine white sand. **Apélla**, the next beach along, is a stunning crescent of sand with azure water.

Diafáni, a small, colorful village on the northeast coast, has a handful of tavernas and hotels and both sand and pebble beaches. A 20-minute bus-ride away is the village of **Olympos**, which spills down from a bleak ridge 600 m (1,969 ft) up. Founded in 1420, and virtually cut off from the rest of the island for centuries by its remote location, this village is now a strange mix of medieval and modern. The painted houses huddle together in a maze of steps and alleys just wide enough for mules. One traditional house, with just a single room containing many embroideries and bric-a-brac, is open to visitors. Customs and village life are carefully preserved and traditional dress is daily wear for the older women who still bake their bread in outdoor ovens.

From Olympos a rough track leads north to **Avlóna**, inhabited only in the harvest season by local farmers. From here, **Vrykoúnda**, the site of a 6th-century BC city, is a short walk away. Remains of the protective city walls can be seen, as can burial chambers cut into the cliffs.

Folk Museum
Othos village. 0245 31338.
Apr–Oct: daily.

Visitors' Checklist

5,000. 17 km (11 miles) S of Kárpathos town. Kárpathos town, Diáfani. corner of Oktovríou & Dimokratías, Kárpathos town. Kárpathos town (0245 22222.) Panagía at Ólympos: Aug 15.

Outlying Islands

North of Avlóna is the island of **Sária**, site of ancient Nísyros, where the ruins of the ancient city can be seen. Excursion boats go there from Diafáni.

Barely touched by tourism, **Kásos**, off the south coast of Kárpathos, was the site of a massacre by the Turks in 1824, commemorated annually on June 7 in the capital, Frý. Near the village of Agía Marína are two fine caves, Ellinokamára and Sellái, both with stalactites and stalagmites. Chélathros Bay is ideal for sun lovers, as are the quiet beaches of the tiny offshore islet of **Armathiá.**

The Traditions of Olympos

Caretaker of the Olympos windmills

The costume of the women of Olympos consists of white pantaloons with an embroidered tunic or a dark skirt with a long patterned apron. Fabrics are heavily embroidered in lime green, silver, and bright pinks. Daughters wear a collar of gold coins and chains to indicate their status and attract suitors. The society was once strictly matriarchal. Today the mother passes on her property to the first-born daughter and the father to his son, ensuring that the personal fortunes of each parent are preserved through the generations.

Traditional houses in Olympos often have decorative balconies and the initials of the owners sculpted above the entrance. Consisting of one room built around a central pillar with fold-away bedding, they are full of photographs and souvenirs. People flock to Olympos from all over the world for the Festival of the Assumption of the Virgin Mary, on August 15, one of the most important festivals in the Orthodox church. The village celebrations of music and dance last three days. Traditional instruments are played, including the *lýra,* which stems from the ancient lyre, the bagpipelike goat-skin *tsampourás,* and the *láouto,* which is similar to a mandolin.

Interior of an Olympos house

THE CYCLADES

ANDROS · TINOS · MYKONOS · DELOS · SYROS · KEA
KYTHNOS · SERIFOS · SIFNOS · PAROS · NAXOS · AMORGOS
IOS · SIKINOS · FOLEGANDROS · MILOS · SANTORINI

DERIVING THEIR NAME FROM THE WORD "KYKLOS," *meaning circle, because they surround the sacred island of Delos, the Cyclades are the most visited island group. They are everyone's Greek island ideal, with their dazzling white houses, twisting cobbled alleyways, blue-domed churches, hilltop windmills, and stunning beaches.*

The islands were the cradle of the Cycladic civilization (3000–1000 BC). The early Cycladic culture developed in the Bronze Age and has inspired artists ever since with its white marble figurines. The Minoans from Crete colonized the islands during the middle Cycladic era, making Akrotíri on Santoríni a major trading center. During the late Cycladic period the Mycenaeans dominated, and Delos became their religious capital. The Dorians invaded the islands in the 11th century BC, a calamity that marked the start of the Dark Ages.

Venetian rule (1204–1453) had a strong influence, evident today in the medieval kástra seen on many islands and the Catholic communities on Tínos, Náxos, and Sýros.

Traditional mule transport

There are 56 islands in the group, 24 inhabited, some tiny and undisturbed, others famous holiday playgrounds. They are the ultimate islands for sun, sea, and sand vacations, with good nightlife on Mýkonos and Ios. Sýros, the regional and commercial capital, is one of the few islands in the group where tourism is not the mainstay. Cycladic life is generally centered on the village, which is typically divided between the harbor and the upper village, or Chóra, often topped with a kástro.

Most of the Cyclades are rocky and arid, with the exceptions of wooded and lush-valleyed Andros, Kéa, and Náxos. This variety ensures the islands are popular with artists, walkers, and those seeking quiet relaxation.

The sandy cove of Kolymbíthres beach, Páros

◁ **The tiered, whitewashed houses of Triandáros village, Tínos**

Exploring the Cyclades

THE CYCLADES ARE BEST KNOWN for their beaches and whitewashed cliff-top villages with stunning views; most famously, Firá on Santoríni. Mýkonos and Ios are well-established beach destinations, while more remote islands such as Mílos and Amorgós also have beautiful stretches of sand. Packed in July and August, these usually arid islands are beautiful in spring when they are carpeted with wildflowers. Varying in character, some of the islands, such as Síkinos, are quiet and traditional whereas others, such as Ios, are more nightlife-oriented. The Cyclades also offer a rich ancient history, evident in the ruins of ancient Delos.

Getting Around

Páros and Sýros are the travel hub of the Cyclades. Ferries serve most of the islands from here and link to Crete and the Dodecanese. The islands are buffeted by the strong *meltémi* wind from July to September. It provides relief from the heat but can play havoc with ferry timetables.

Mýkonos and Santoríni have international airports, and islands with domestic airports include Sýros, Mílos, Páros and Náxos.

See Also

- **Where to Stay** pp304–6
- **Where to Eat** pp328–30
- **Travel Information** pp356–9

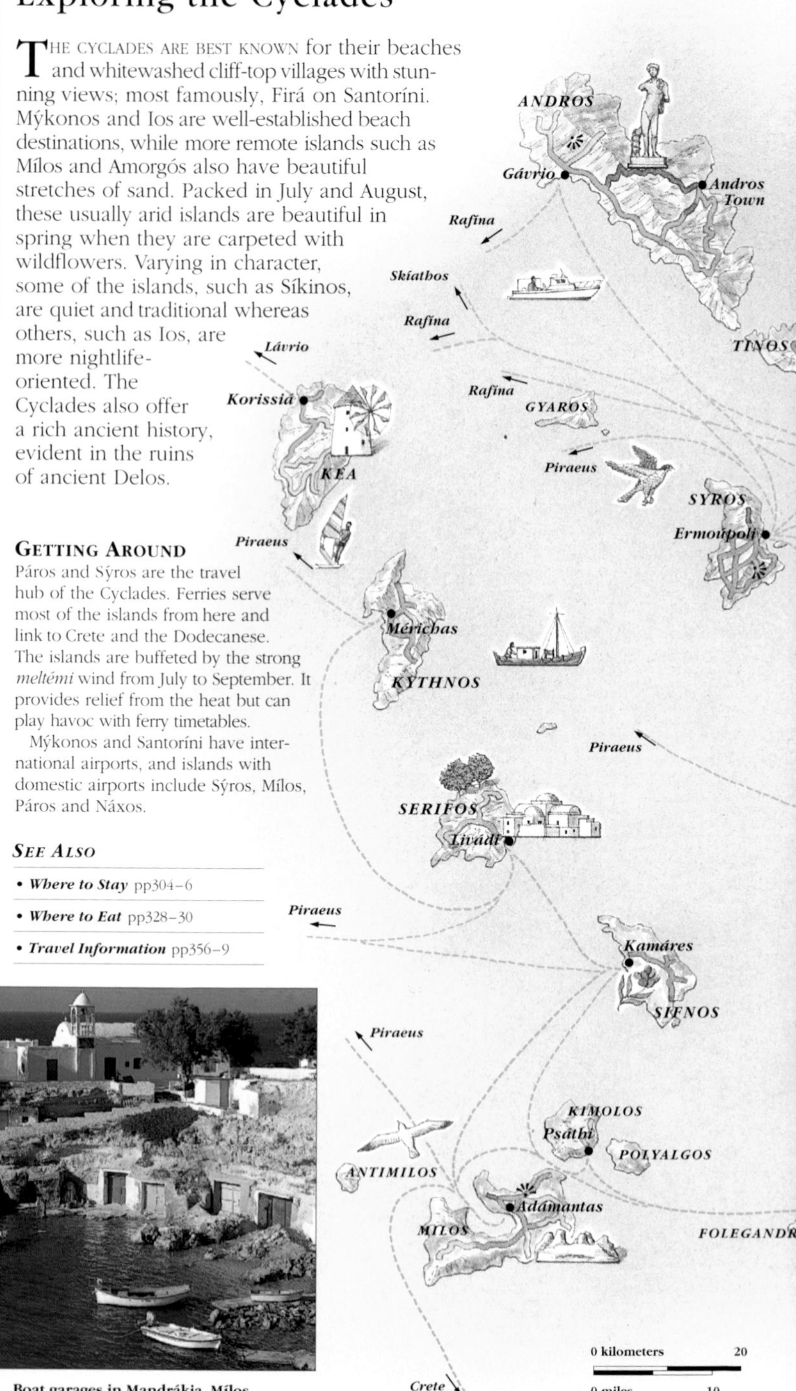

Boat garages in Mandrákia, Mílos

Islands at a Glance

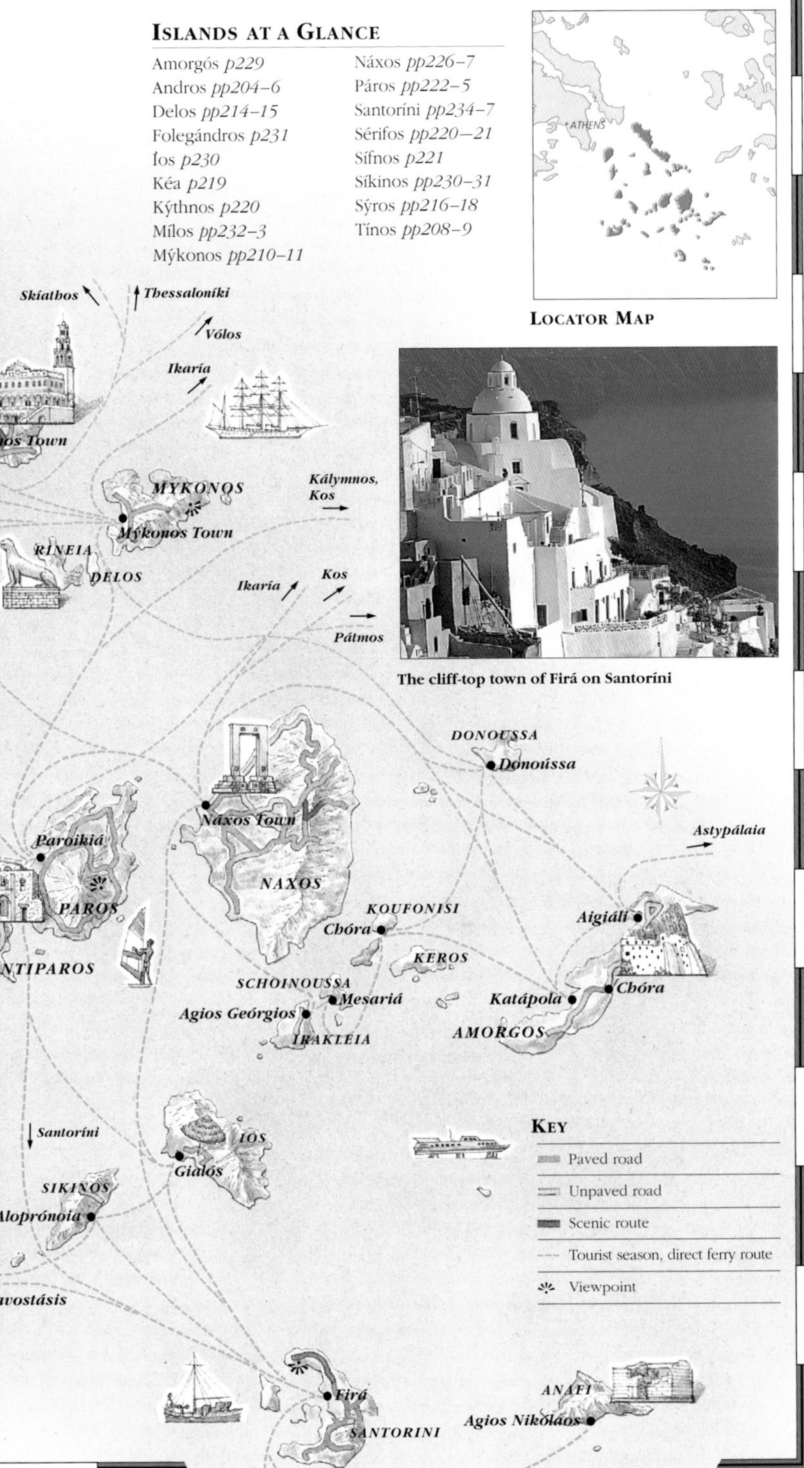

The cliff-top town of Firá on Santoríni

Key

- Paved road
- Unpaved road
- Scenic route
- Tourist season, direct ferry route
- Viewpoint

Andros

Ανδρος

THE NORTHERNMOST OF THE CYCLADES, Andros is lush and green in the south, scorched and barren in the north. The fields are divided by distinctive dry-stone walls. The island was first colonized by the Ionians in 1000 BC. In the 5th century BC, Andros sided with Sparta during the Peloponnesian Wars *(see p28)*. After Venetian rule, the Turks took power in 1566 until the War of Independence. Andros has long been the vacation haunt of wealthy Athenian shipping families.

Andros Town ❶

Χώρα

1,680. Plateía Agía Olga. 0282 22316.

The capital, Andros town, or Chóra, is located on the east coast of the island 20 km (12 miles) from the island's main port at Gávrio.

An elegant town with magnificient Neo-Classical buildings, it is the home of some of Greece's wealthiest shipowners. The pedestrianized main street is paved with marble slabs and lined with old mansions converted into public offices among the *kafeneía* and small shops.

The *Hermes of Andros*, in the Archaeological Museum

Plateía Kaïri

This is the main square in the town's Ríva district and is home to the **Archaeological Museum**, built in 1981. The museum's most famous exhibit is the 2nd-century BC *Hermes of Andros*, a fine marble copy of the 4th-century BC bronze original. Other exhibits include the *Matron of Herculaneum*, which was found with the Hermes, and finds from the 10th-century BC city at Zagorá. There are also finds from ancient Palaiópoli *(see p206)* near Mpatsí, architectural illustrations, and a large collection of ceramics.

The **Museum of Modern Art**, which was endowed by the Gouländri family, has an excellent collection of paintings by 20th-century artists such as Picasso and Braque and leading Greek artists such as Alékos Fasianós. The sculpture garden has works by Michális Tómpros (1889–1974).

Archaeological Museum
Plateía Kaïri. 0282 23664. Tue–Sun. Mon, main public hols.

Museum of Modern Art
Plateía Kaïri. 0282 22650. Apr–Sep: Wed–Mon; Oct–Mar: Sat–Mon. main public hols. except Sun.

Typical white houses and a small church in Káto Kástro

Káto Kástro and Plateía Riva

From Plateía Kaïri an archway leads into the maze of streets that form the medieval city, Káto Kástro, wedged between Parapórti and Nimporió bays. The narrow lanes lead to windswept Plateía Ríva at the end of the peninsula, jutting into the sea and dominated by the heroic statue of the *Unknown Sailor* by Michális Tómpros. Just below, a precarious stone bridge leads to the islet opposite. Here stands the Venetian castle, **Mésa Kástro**, built between 1207 and 1233. The **Maritime Museum**, with model ships, photographs, and a collection of nautical instruments on display, is situated on the corner of the square.

On the way back to the center of the town is the church of **Panagía Theoskepastí,** built in 1555 and dedicated to the Virgin Mary. Legend has it that the priest could not afford the wood for the church roof, so the ship delivering the wood set sail again. It ran into a storm and the crew prayed to the Virgin for help, promising to return the cargo to Andros. The seas were miraculously calmed and the church became known as Theoskepastí, meaning "sheltered by God."

Statue of the *Unknown Sailor*

Maritime Museum
Plateia Ríva. 0282 22444. Apr–Sep: Wed–Mon; Oct–Mar: Fri–Sun. main public hols.

ENVIRONS: Steniés, 6 km (3.5 miles) northwest of Andros town, is very beautiful and popular with wealthy shipping families. Fifteen minutes' walk southwest of Steniés, the 17th-century Mpístis-Mouvelá tower is a fine example of an Andriot house.

Below Steniés lies **Gyália** beach, which is shaded with eucalyptus trees and has a fish taverna. Above Steniés, 3 km (2 miles) west, in **Apoikía**, mineral water is bottled from the Sáriza spring. You can taste the waters at the spring.

Around Andros Island

Lion's head fountain in Ménites

PROSPEROUS, neat, and dotted with many white dovecotes first built by the Venetians, Andros retains its traditional charm while playing host to international vacationers. There are a number of unspoiled sandy beaches, water sports facilities, wild mountains, and a good network of footpaths. However, unless you are an avid trekker, car or bike rental is essential because the bus service is quite limited.

Mesariá ❷

Μεσαριά

8 km (5 miles) SW of Andros town. 850.

From Andros town the road passes through the medieval village of Mesariá with ruined tower houses and the pantiled Byzantine church of the **Taxiárchis**, built by Emperor Emanuel Comnenus in 1158 and recently restored.

Springs gush from marble lion's head fountains in the leafy village of **Ménites**, just above Mesariá. Ménites is known both for its nightingales and for the taverna overlooking a stream. Steps lead up to the pretty restored church of **Panagía i Koúmoulos** (the Virgin of the Plentiful) thought to be built on the site of an ancient temple of Dionysos.

SIGHTS AT A GLANCE

Andros Town ❶
Gávrio ❻
Mesariá ❷
Moní Panachrántou ❸
Mpatsí ❺
Palaiókastro ❹

Moní Panachrántou overlooking the valley

VISITORS' CHECKLIST

9,000. Gávrio. 0282 22275. Agios Panteleïmon Festival at Moní Panachrántou: Jul 27.

Moní Panachrántou ❸

Μονή Παναχράντου

12 km (7 miles) SW of Andros town. 0282 51090. *daily.*

This spectacular monastery is perched 230 m (750 ft) above sea level in the mountains southwest of Andros town. It can be reached either by a two-hour steep walk from Mesariá or a three-hour trek from Andros town.

It was founded in 961 by Nikifóros Fokás, who later became Byzantine Emperor as reward for his help in the liberation of Crete from Arab occupation. The fortified monastery is built in Byzantine style and today houses just three monks. The church holds many treasures, including the skull of Agios Panteleïmon, believed to have healing powers. Visitors flock here to see the skull on the saint's annual festival day.

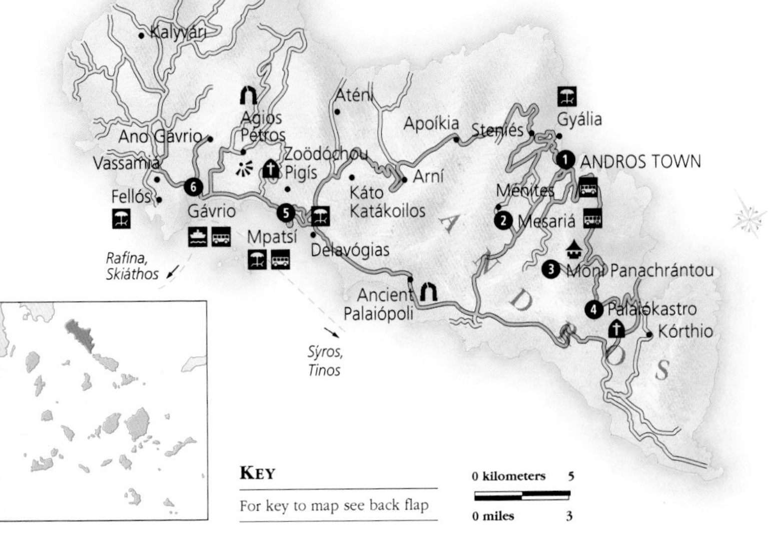

Palaiókastro ❹

Παλαιόκαστρο

18 km (11 miles) SW of Andros town.
unrestricted access.

High on a rocky plateau inland is the ruined Venetian Palaiókastro built between 1207 and 1233. Its alternative name, the Castle of the Old Woman, is after a woman who betrayed the Venetians to the Turks in the 16th century. After tricking her way inside the castle she opened the gates for the Ottoman Turks. Appalled by the bloody massacre that followed, she hurled herself off the cliffs near Kórthio, 5 km (3 miles) to the southeast, in remorse. The rock from which she jumped is known as Tis Griás to Pídima, or Old Lady's Leap.

Mpatsí ❺

Μπατσί

8 km (5 miles) S of Gávrio.
200.

Built around a sweeping sandy bay, Mpatsí is a pretty resort. It has a small fishing harbor and a maze of narrow lanes reached by white steps from the café-lined waterfront. Despite the lively nightlife, Mpatsí has retained its village atmosphere. The main beach is popular with families while **Delavógias** beach, south along the coastal track, is a favourite with nudists. Agía Marína, farther along, has a friendly, family-run taverna.

Environs: South of Mpatsí the original capital of Andros, **Ancient Palaiópoli,** was inhabited until around AD 1000 when the people moved to Mesariá *(see p205)*. It was largely destroyed in the 4th-century AD by an earthquake, but part of the acropolis is still visible as are the remains of some of the temples under the sea.

Inland lies **Káto Katákoilos** village, known for its island music and dance festivals. A rough track leads north from here to remote **Aténi**, a hamlet at the head of a lush valley. Two beautiful beaches lie farther to the windy north-east, in the bay of Aténi. The garden village of **Arní**, high on the slopes of the Kouvára mountain range, has flowing springs and is one of the island's greenest spots. The area has many dry-stone walls and is spectacular walking country.

Ancient Palaiópoli

9 km (6 miles) S of Mpatsí.
unrestricted access. *limited.*

Gávrio ❻

Γάυριο

450. *Fellós 4 km (2.5 miles) NW.*

Gávrio is a rather character-less port that, on weekends, becomes packed with Athenians heading for their vacation homes. There is a beach, a good campsite, and plenty of tavernas. During the tourist season it can be the only place with rooms available since Mpatsí is often prebooked by package companies.

Agios Pétros tower near Gávrio

Environs: From Gávrio, it takes an hour or so to walk up to the tower of **Agios Pétros,** the island's best-preserved ancient monument. Dating from the Hellenistic era, the tower stands 20 m (65 ft) high in an olive grove below the hamlet of Káto Agios Pétros. The upper stories of the tower were reached by footholds and an internal ladder, and its inner hall was once crowned by a corbeled dome. The purpose of the tower remains a mystery, although it may have been built to serve as a watchtower to guard the nearby mines from attack by marauding pirates.

North of Gávrio there are good beaches beyond the village of Vassamiá, which has two sandy coves. **Fellós** beach is the best but is fast being developed with vacation villas.

A turn-off from the coastal road, 8 km (5 miles) south of Gávrio, leads to the 14th-century convent, **Zoödóchou Pigís**, the Spring of Life. Only a handful of nuns remain where there were 1,000 monks, but they are happy to show visitors their collection of icons and Byzantine tapestries.

The beach at Mpatsí Bay on Andros

Cycladic Art

WITH THEIR SIMPLE geometric shapes and purity of line, Cycladic marble figurines are the legacy of the islands' Bronze Age civilization *(see pp24–5)* and the first real expression of Greek art. They all come from graves and are thought to represent, or be offerings to, an ancient deity. The earliest figures, from before 3000 BC, are slim and violin-shaped. By the time of the Keros-Sýros culture of 2700–2300 BC, the forms are recognizably human and usually female. They range from palm-sized up to life-size, the proportions remaining consistent. Obsidian blades, marble bowls prefiguring later Greek art, abstract jewelry and pottery, including the strange "frying pans," also survive. The examples of Cycladic art shown here are from the Museum of Cycladic Art in Athens *(see p287)*. Cycladic artifacts are also in many museums throughout the Cyclades.

"Violin" figurines*, such as this one, date from the early Cycladic period of 3300–2700 BC. Often no bigger than a hand, the purpose of these highly schematic representations of the human form is unknown. In some graves up to 14 of these figurines were found; other graves had none.*

"Frying pan" *pottery vessels take their name from their shape, but their function is unknown. They may have been used as mirrors or trays. Decorated with spirals or suns, they belong to the mature phase of Cycladic art.*

Collared vases*, or* kandelas, *carved from marble, are one of the high points of Cycladic art. Probably used for food storage, the four lugs on the sides would have allowed them to be hung from a support.*

This male figurine, *found together with a female figurine, is one of the few male figures to have been found. He is also atypical in having one arm raised and a band slung across his chest.*

This female figurine *with folded arms is typical of Cycladic sculpture. The head is slightly tipped back, with only minimal markings for arms, legs, and features.*

Influence on Modern Art

Considered crude and ugly when first discovered in the 19th century, the simplicity of both form and decoration of Cycladic art exerted a strong influence on 20th-century artists and sculptors such as Picasso, Modigliani, Henry Moore, and Constantin Brancusi.

Henry Moore's *Three Standing Figures*

***The Kiss* by Brancusi**

Tínos
Τήνος

A CRAGGY YET GREEN ISLAND, Tínos was first settled by Ionians in Archaic times. In the 4th century BC it became known for its Sanctuary of Poseidon and Amphitrite. Under Venetian rule from medieval times, Tínos became the Ottoman Empire's last conquest in 1715. Tínos has over 800 chapels, and in the 1960s the military Junta declared it a holy island. Many Greek Orthodox pilgrims come to the church of the Panagía Evangelístria (Annunciation) in Tínos town. The island is also known for its many dovecotes *(peristeriónas)*, scattered across the landscape.

Tínos town and the small harborfront

Tinos Town

A typical island capital, Tínos town has narrow streets, whitewashed houses, and a bustling port lined with restaurants and hotels.

Panagía Evangelístria
Church & museums daily.
0283 22256.

Situated at the top of Megalóchari, the main street that runs up from the ferry, Panagía Evangelístria, the church of the Annunciation dominates Tínos town. The pedestrianized Evangelistrías, which runs parallel to Megalóchari, is packed with stalls full of icons and votive offerings. Built in 1830, the church houses the island's miraculous icon. In 1822, during the Greek War of Independence, Sister Pelagía, a nun at Moní Kechrovouníou, had visions of the Virgin Mary showing where an icon had been buried. In 1823, acting on the nun's directions, excavations revealed the icon of the Annunciation of the Archangel Gabriel, unscathed after 850 years underground. Known in Greece as the Megalóchari (the Great Joy) the icon was found to have healing powers, and the church became a pilgrimage center for Orthodox Christians. Tínos becomes very busy during the festivals of the Annunciation and the Assumption, when the icon is paraded through the streets *(see pp44–5)* and the devout often crawl to Panagía Evangelístria.

Archaeological Museum exhibit from Exómpourgko

The church is a treasury of offerings, such as an orange tree made of gold and silver, from pilgrims whose prayers have been answered. The icon itself is so smothered in gold and jewels it is hard to see the painting. The crypt where it was found is known as the chapel of Evresis, or Discovery. Where the icon lay is now lined with silver and the holy spring here, Zoödóchos Pigí, is said to have healing powers.

The vestry has gold-threaded ecclesiastical robes and valuable copies of the gospels.

Pilgrim crawling to the Panagía Evangelístria

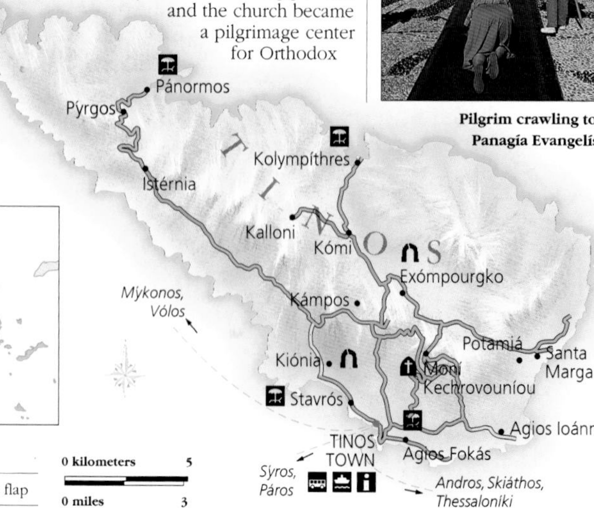

Key

For key to map see back flap

0 kilometers 5

0 miles 3

The pretty village of Pýrgos in the north of the island

Also within the church complex is a museum, displaying items by local sculptors and painters, including works by sculptors Antónios Sóchos, Geórgios Vitális, and Ioánnis Voúlgaris. The art gallery has works of the Ionian school, a Rubens, a Rembrandt, and 19th-century works by international artists.

Archaeological Museum

Megalóchari 0283 22670.
Tue–Sun. main public hols.
On Megalóchari near the church, is the Archaeological Museum, which has displays of sculptures of nereids (sea-nymphs) and dolphins found at the Sanctuary of Poseidon and Amphitrite. There is also a 1st-century BC sundial by Andronikos Kyrrestes, who designed Athens' Tower of the Winds *(see p283)*, and some huge 8th-century BC storage jars from ancient Tínos on the rock of Exómpourgko.

ENVIRONS: East of town, the closest beach is shingly **Agios Fokás.** To the west is the popular beach at **Stavrós,** with a jetty that was built in Classical times. To the north near Kiónia are the foundations of the 4th-century BC **Sanctuary of Poseidon and Amphitrite,** his seanymph bride. The excavations here have yielded many columns, or *kiónia*, after which the surrounding area is named.

AROUND THE ISLAND

Tínos is easy to explore, as there are plenty of taxis and a good bus service around the island. North of Tínos town is the 12th-century walled **Moní Kechrovouníou,** one of the largest convents in Greece. You can visit the cell where Sister Pelagía had her visions and the chest where her embalmed head is kept.

At 640 m (2,100 ft) high, the great rock of **Exómpourgko** was the site of the Archaic city of Tínos and later became home to the Venetian fortress of St. Elena. Built by the Ghisi family after the Doge handed over the island to them in 1207, the fortress was the toughest stronghold in the Cyclades until it surrendered to the Turks in 1714. You can see remains of a few ancient walls on the crag, medieval houses, a fountain and three churches.

The interior of the 12th-century Moní Kechrovouníou

VISITORS' CHECKLIST

9,000. Tínos town. Quay, Tínos town. corner of Kionion & Vlacháki, Tínos town (0283 22255). Annunciation & Panagía at Panagía Evangelístrias, Tínos town: Mar 25 & Aug 15.

From Kómi, to the north, a valley runs down to the sea at **Kolympíthres,** with two sandy bays: one is deserted; the other has rooms and tavernas.

Overlooking the harbor of Pánormos in the northwest of the island, the pretty village of **Pýrgos** is famous for its sculpture school. The area is known for its green marble, and the stonework here is among the finest in the islands. Distinctive, carved marble fanlights and balconies decorate the island villages. There are examples at the **Giannoúli Chalepá Museum**, housed in the former home of the island's renowned sculptor (1851–1938). The old grammar school is now the School of Fine Arts, and a shop in the main square exhibits and sells works by the students.

Giannoúli Chalepá Museum

Pýrgos. daily. Oct–Apr.

THE PERISTERIONAS (DOVECOTES) OF TINOS

The villages of Tínos are studded with around 1,300 beautiful white dovecotes *(peristeriónas)*, all elaborately decorated. They have two stories: the lower floor is for storage, the upper houses the doves and is usually topped with stylized winged finials or mock doves. The breeding of doves was introduced by the Venetians. Although also found on the islands of Andros and Sífnos, the *peristeriónas* of Tínos are considered the finest.

A dovecote in Kámpos with traditional elaborate patterns

Mýkonos

Μύκονος

Pétros the Pelican, the island mascot

ALTHOUGH MYKONOS IS DRY AND BARREN, its sandy beaches and dynamic nightlife make this island one of the most popular in the Cyclades. Under Venetian rule from 1207, the islanders later set up the Community of Mykonians in 1615 and flourished as a self-sufficient society. Visited by intellectuals in the early days of tourism, today Mýkonos thrives on its reputation as the glitziest island in Greece.

Mýkonos harbor in the early morning

Mykonos Town

Mýkonos town (or Chóra) is the supreme example of a Cycladic village – a tangle of dazzling white alleys and cube-shaped houses. Built in a maze of narrow lanes to defy the wind and pirate raids, the bustling port is one of the most photographed in Greece. Many visitors still get lost around the lanes today.

Taxi boats for the island of Delos *(see pp214–15)* leave from the dock. The island's mascot, Pétros the Pelican, may be seen near the dock, hunting for fish.

Adjacent to the harbor is Plateía Mavrogénous, overlooked by the bust of revolutionary heroine Mantó Mavrogénous (1796–1848). She was awarded the rank of General for her victorious battle against the Turks on Mýkonos during the War of Independence in 1821.

Mantó Mavrogénous

The **Archaeological Museum**, housed in a Neo-Classical building south of the ferry port, has a large collection of Roman and Hellenistic carvings, 6th- and 7th-century BC ceramics, jewelry, and gravestones, as well as many finds from the ancient site on Delos.

Kástro, the oldest part of the town, sits high up above the waterside district. Built on part of the ancient castle wall is the excellent **Folk Museum**, one of the best in Greece. It is housed in an elegant sea captain's mansion and has a fine collection of ceramics, embroidery, and ancient and modern Mykonian textiles. Among the more unusual exhibits is the original Pétros the Pelican, now stuffed, who was the island's mascot for 29 years. The 16th-century Vonís Windmill is part of the Folk Museum and has been restored to full working order. It was one of the 30 windmills that were used by families all over the island to grind corn. There is also a small threshing floor and a dovecote on the grounds around the windmill.

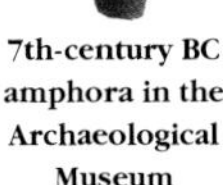

7th-century BC amphora in the Archaeological Museum

The most famous church on the island, familiar from postcards, is the extraordinary **Panagía Paraportianí**, in the Kástro. Built on the site of the postern gate *(parapórti)* of the medieval fortress, it is made up of four chapels at ground level with another above. Part of it dates from 1425 and the rest was built in the 16th and 17th centuries.

From Kástro, the lanes run down into Venetía, or **Little Venice** (officially known as Alefkándras), the artists' quarter. The tall houses have painted balconies jutting out over the sea. The main square, Plateía Aléfkandra, is home to the large Orthodox cathedral of Panagía Pigadiótissa (Our Lady of the Little Wells).

The **Maritime Museum of the Aegean**, at the end of Matogiánni, features a collection of model ships from pre-Minoan times to the 19th century, maritime instruments, paintings, and 5th-century BC coins with nautical themes.

Next door, **Lena's House**, a 19th-century mansion, evokes the life of a Mykonian lady, Léna Skrivánou. Everything is preserved, from her needlework to her chamber pot.

Works of Greek and international artists are on display at the **Municipal Art Gallery** on Matogiánni and include an exhibition of works by local Mykonian painters.

Working 16th-century windmill, part of the Folk Museum

The famous Paraportianí church

Archaeological Museum
Harborfront. 0289 22325.
Tue–Sun. *main public hols.*

Folk Museum
Harborfront. 0289 22591.
Apr–Oct: Mon–Sat.

Maritime Museum of the Aegean
Enoplón Dynaméon. 0289 22700.
Apr–Oct: daily. *main public hols.*

Lena's House
Enoplón Dynaméon. *Apr–Oct: daily.* *limited.*

Municipal Art Gallery
Matogiánni. 0289 22615.
Apr–Oct: daily.

Around the Island

Mýkonos is popular primarily for its beaches; it has no lush countryside. The best ones are along the south coast. At stylish **Platýs Gialós**, 3.5 km (2 miles) south of the town, regular taxi boats are available to ferry sun-worshipers from bay to bay. Backed by hotels and restaurants, this is the main family beach on the island, with water sports and a long sweep of sand. Serious sun-lovers head southeast to the famous nudist beaches. First is **Parágka**, or Agía Anna, a quiet spot with a good taverna. Next is **Paradise**, with its neighboring camping site, disco music, and water sports. The cove of **Super Paradise** is gay and nudist. **Eliá**, at the end of the boat line is also nudist and busy in tourist season.

In contrast to Mýkonos town, the inland village of **Ano Merá**, 7.5 km (4.5 miles) east, is traditional and largely unspoiled by tourism. The main attraction is the 16th-century **Panagía i Tourlianí**, dedicated to the island's protectress. Founded by two monks from Páros, the red-domed monastery was restored in 1767. The ornate marble tower was sculpted by Tíniot craftsmen. The monastery houses some fine 16th-century icons, vestments, and embroideries. Northwest of the village is Palaiókastro hill, once crowned by a Venetian castle. It is thought to be the site of one of the ancient cities of Mýkonos. Today it is home to the 17th-century working **Moní Palaiokástrou**. To the northwest, in the pretty village of **Maráthi**, is Moní Agíou Panteleïmona, founded in 1665. From here, the road leads to **Pánormos Bay** and **Fteliá**, a windsurfers' paradise.

Visitors' Checklist

4,500. 3 km (1.5 mile) SE of Mýkonos town. Mýkonos town. Polykandrióti, Mýkonos town (for north of island); on road to Ornós, Mýkonos town (for south of island). Harborfront, Mýkonos town (0289 22482). Fishermen's Festival, Mýkonos town: Jun 30.

Platýs Gialós beach, one of the best on Mýkonos

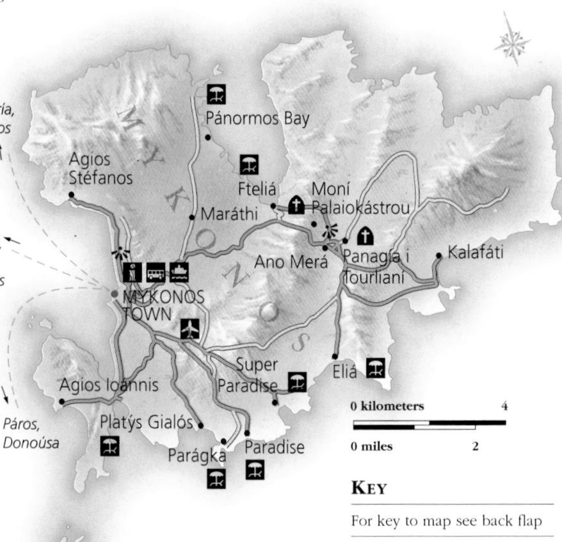

Key

For key to map see back flap

The old houses of Little Venice, Mýkonos town ▷

Katerinas
BAR

Delos

Δήλος

Tiny, uninhabited Delos is one of the most important archaeological sites in Greece. According to legend, Leto gave birth to Artemis and Apollo here. The Ionians arrived in about 1000 BC, bringing the worship of Apollo and founding the annual Delian Festival, during which games and music were played in his honor. By 700 BC, Delos was a major religious center. First a place of pilgrimage, it later became a thriving commercial port particularly in the 3rd and 2nd centuries BC. It is now an open-air archaeological museum with mosaics and marble ruins covered in wildflowers in spring.

Artemis of Delos

Archaeological Museum
This displays most of the finds from the island, including storage pots used for offerings and koúroi *dating from the 7th-century BC.*

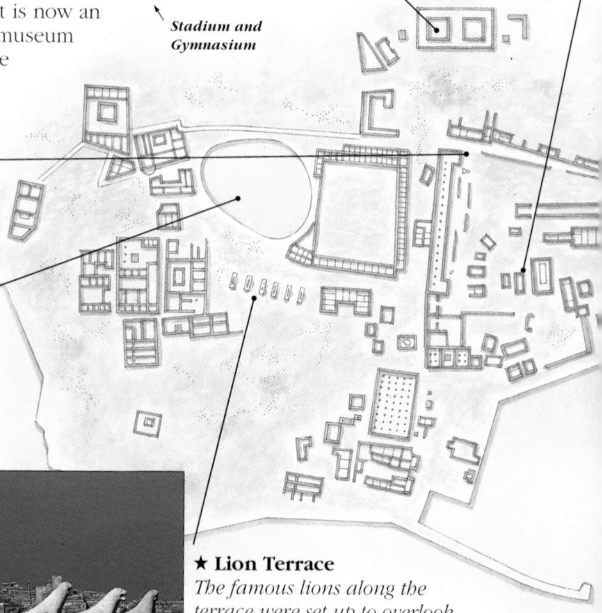

The Sanctuary of Apollo has three temples: one dating from the 6th century BC and two dating from the 5th century BC.

Stadium and Gymnasium

The Sanctuary of Dionysos has remains of huge phallic monuments dating back to 300 BC.

The Sacred Lake, now dried up, was so-called because it had witnessed Apollo's birth. A wall marks the lake's Hellenistic boundaries.

★ Lion Terrace
The famous lions along the terrace were set up to overlook and protect the Sacred Lake. They were carved from Naxian marble at the end of the 7th century BC. Originally there were nine, but now only five remain.

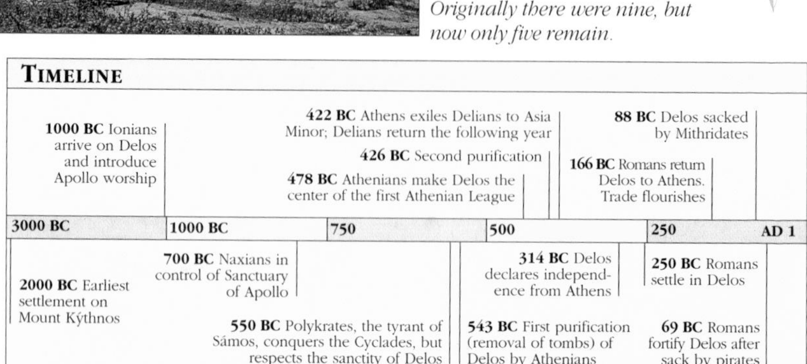

Timeline

3000 BC | 1000 BC | 750 | 500 | 250 | AD 1

- **2000 BC** Earliest settlement on Mount Kýthnos
- **1000 BC** Ionians arrive on Delos and introduce Apollo worship
- **700 BC** Naxians in control of Sanctuary of Apollo
- **550 BC** Polykrates, the tyrant of Sámos, conquers the Cyclades, but respects the sanctity of Delos
- **543 BC** First purification (removal of tombs) of Delos by Athenians
- **478 BC** Athenians make Delos the center of the first Athenian League
- **426 BC** Second purification
- **422 BC** Athens exiles Delians to Asia Minor; Delians return the following year
- **314 BC** Delos declares independence from Athens
- **250 BC** Romans settle in Delos
- **166 BC** Romans return Delos to Athens. Trade flourishes
- **88 BC** Delos sacked by Mithridates
- **69 BC** Romans fortify Delos after sack by pirates

House of the Dolphins
This house of the 2nd century BC contains a mosaic of two dolphins with an elaborate Greek key design and waved borders.

Visitors' Checklist

2.5 km (1 mile) SW of Mýkonos town. 0289 22259.
8–10am daily from Mýkonos town returning 12–2pm.
8:30am–3pm Tue–Sun.
Jan 1, Mar 25, Good Fri am, Easter Sun, Mon, May 1, Dec 25, 26.

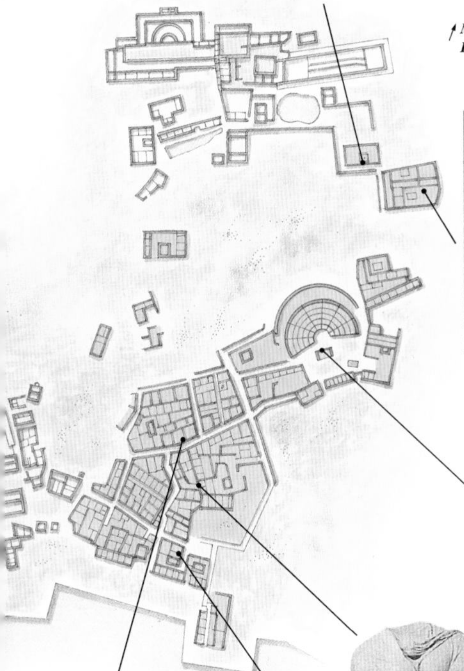

Mount Kýthnos

House of the Masks
Probably a hostelry for actors, this house contains a 2nd-century BC mosaic of Dionysos, god of theater, riding a panther.

★ Theater
Built in 300 BC to hold 5,500 spectators, the theater was sited in a natural amphitheater. On its west side, a huge, vaulted cistern collected rainwater draining from the theater and supplied part of the town.

★ Theater Quarter
In Hellenistic and Roman times the wealthy built houses near the theater, many with opulent, colonnaded courtyards.

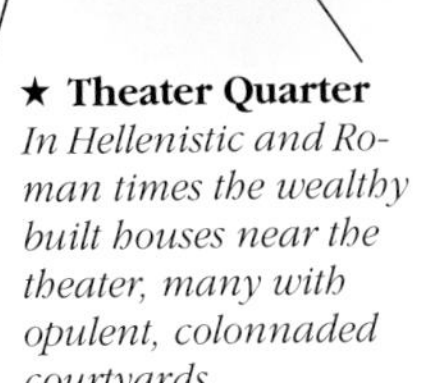

House of Cleopatra
Two headless statues represent Cleopatra and her husband Dioscourides, owners of the house in the 2nd century BC.

Key

Theater quarter

House of Dionysos
Inside the house is a mosaic depicting Dionysos riding a leopard. Twenty-nine tesserae *are used just to make up the animal's eye.*

Star Sights

- **★ Theater**
- **★ Lion Terrace**
- **★ Theater Quarter**

Sýros
Σύρος

ROCKY SYROS, or Sýra, is the commercial, administrative, and cultural center of the Cyclades. Archaeological digs have revealed finds of the Cycladic civilization dating from 2800 to 2300 BC. The inhabitants converted to Catholicism under the French Capuchins in the Middle Ages. The 19th century saw Sýros become a wealthy and powerful port in the eastern Mediterranean. Though Sýros does not live off tourism, more visitors arrive each year, attracted by its traditional charm.

The twin peaks of Ermoúpoli: Ano Sýros and Vrondádo

Ermoúpoli ❶
Ερμούπολη

13,000. Aktí Ethnikís Antistássis. Plateía Miaoúli (0281 82610).

Elegant Ermoúpoli, named after Hermes, the god of commerce, is the largest city in the Cyclades. In the 19th century it was Greece's leading port and a major coaling station with a huge natural harbor and thriving shipyard. Crowned by the twin peaks of Catholic Ano Sýros to the north and the Orthodox Vrondádo to the south, the city is built like an amphitheater around the harbor.

The Lower Town
The architectural glories of central **Plateía Miaoúli** have led to the town becoming a National Historical Landmark. Paved with marble and lined with palm-shaded cafés and pizzerias, the grand square is the city's hub and meeting place, especially for the evening stroll, or *vólta*. There is also a marble bandstand and a statue dedicated to the revolutionary hero Admiral Andréas Miaoúli. The square is dominated by the vast Neo-Classical **town hall** (1876), designed by the German architect Ernst Ziller.

Town hall, designed by Ernst Ziller

The **Archaeological Museum**, up the steps to the left of the town hall, houses bronze and marble utensils from the 3000 BC Cycladic settlement of Chalandrianí. Also on display are Cycladic statuettes and Roman finds. Left of the town hall is the **Historical Archives Office**.

Nearby, on Plateía Vardáka, is the **Apollo Theater**, designed in 1864 by French architect Chabeau as a copy of La Scala, Milan. The first opera house in Greece, it is noted for its

Statue of Andréas Miaoúli

Sights at a Glance
Ermoúpoli ❶
Galissás ❸
Kíni ❷
Poseidonía ❹
Vári ❺

Key
For key to map see back flap

0 kilometers 4

0 miles 2

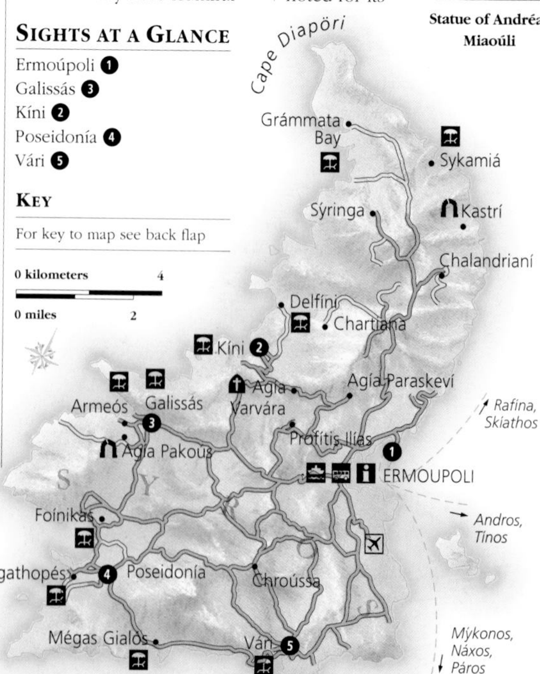

Markos Vamvakaris

One of the greatest exponents of *rempétika*, the Greek blues, Márkos Vamvakáris (1905–72) was born in Ano Sýros. Synonymous with hash dens and the low-life, *rempétika* was the music of the urban underclass. With strong Byzantine and Islamic influences it is often played on the *baglama* or bouzouki. Vamvakáris was a master of the bouzouki as well as a noted composer. Over 20 recordings have been made of his music, the earliest of which dates back to the 1930s. A bust of Vamvakáris looks out to sea from the small square named after him in Ano Sýros.

fine wall paintings of Mozart and Verdi and is still used for plays and concerts.

Across the street the 1871 **Velissarópoulos Mansion**, now housing the Labor Union, has an elaborate marble façade and splendid painted ceilings and murals. Beyond here is the church of **Agios Nikólaos** (1848) with a marble iconostasis by the 19th-century sculptor Vitális. Also by Vitális is the world's first monument of the unknown soldier, in front of the church.

The Upper Town

The twin bell towers and distinctive blue and gold dome of Agios Nikólaos mark the start of the **Vapória** district. Here Sýros's shipowners built their Neo-Classical mansions, with some of the finest plasterwork, frescoes, and marble carvings in

Marble iconostasis by Vitális, in the church of Agios Nikólaos

Greece. The houses cling to the coastline above the town's docks and moorings at Táliro, Evangelídi, and Agios Nikólaos.

The charming district of **Vrondádo,** on the eastern peak, has a number of excellent tavernas spread out on its slopes at night. The Byzantine church of the **Anástasis** on top of the hill has views to Tínos and Mýkonos.

A ceiling in one of Ermoúpoli's mansions

A half hour's climb along Omiroú, or a brief bus ride, is the fortified medieval quarter of **Ano Sýros,** on the western peak. It is also known as Apáno Chóra or Kástro. On the way is the Orthodox cemetery of **Agios Geórgios** with its elaborate marble mausoleums. Ano Sýros is a maze of whitewashed passages, arches, and steps forming a huddle of interlinking houses. The architecture is unique, making the most of minimal space with *stegádia* (slate or straw roofs) and tight corners. The main entrance into Ano Sýros is Kamára, an ancient passageway leading into the main road, or Piatsa. The **Vamvakáris Museum**, dedicated to the life and work of Márkos Vamvakáris, is situated just off this road. At the top of Ano Sýros, the Baroque **Aï-Giórgi**, known as the cathedral of St. George, was built on the site of a 13th-century church. The basilica contains fine icons. The Jesuit cloister was founded in 1744 around the church of Our Lady of Karmilou (1581) and houses 6,000 books and manuscripts in its library. Below it, the Capuchin convent of **Agios Ioánnis** was a meeting place and a refuge from pirates. Its church was founded by Louis XIII of France as a poorhouse.

Visitors' Checklist

23,000. 1 km (0.5 miles) SE of Ermoúpoli. Ermoúpoli. Ermoúpoli (0281 82375). Ermoúpoli Maritime Festival: Jul; Agios Nikólaos processions at Ermoúpoli: Dec 6.

Archaeological Museum
Plateía Miaoúli. *0281 88487. Tue–Sun. main public hols. limited.*

Historical Archives Office
Plateía Miaoúli. *0281 86891. Mon–Fri. main public hols.*

Vamvakáris Museum
Plateía Vamvakáris, Ano Sýros. *0281 82934. Jun–Sep: daily. main public hols.*

A typical street in the Ano Sýros quarter

Around Sýros Island

Syros has numerous attractive coves as well as popular resorts like Galissás and Kíni. The landscape is varied, with palm trees and terraced fields. In the northern region of Apáno Meriá the traditional farms built to house both families and animals are in total contrast to the Italianate mansions and vacation homes of the south. Sýros has good roads, especially in the south, and is easy to explore by car or bike. There is a regular bus from the harbor to Ano Sýros, the main resorts, and outlying villages.

Kíni Bay and the town's harbor

Kíni ❷
Κίνι

9 km (6 miles) NW of Ermoúpoli.
300. Delfíni 3 km (2 miles) N.

The fishing village of Kíni is set in a horseshoe-shaped bay with two good sandy beaches. Kíni is a popular meeting place for watching the sunset over an ouzo, and it has some excellent fish tavernas.

North, over the headland, is the award-winning **Delfíni** beach – the largest on Sýros and popular with nudists.

Between Ermoúpoli and Kíni, set in pine-covered hills, is the red-domed convent of **Agía Varvára**. With spectacular views to the west, the Orthodox convent was once a girls' orphanage. The nuns run a weaving school, and their knitwear and woven goods are on sale at the convent. The frescoes in the church depict the saint's martyrdom.

The red-tiled roofs of Agía Varvára convent near Kíni

Environs: Boat services run from Kíni to some of the island's remote northern beaches. **Grámmata Bay** is one of the most spectacular, a deep, sheltered inlet with golden sands where sea lilies grow in autumn. Some of the rocks here have a Hellenistic inscription carved on them, seeking protection for ships from sinking.

A boat trip around the tip of the island past Cape Diapóri to the east coast takes you to **Sykamiá** beach. Here there is a cave where the Syriot philosopher Pherekydes is thought to have lived during the summer months. A physicist and astronomer, Pherekydes pioneered philosophical thought in the mid-6th century BC and was the inventor of the heliotrope, an early sundial. From Sykamiá you can see the remains of the Bronze Age citadel of **Kastrí** with its six towers perched on a steep rock.

Galissás ❸
Γαλησσάς

7 km (4 miles) W of Ermoúpoli.
500. Armeós beach 1 km (0.5 miles) N.

Lively Galissás has the most sheltered beach on the island, fringed by tamarisk trees and, across the headland to the north, **Armeós** beach is a haven for nudists. Galissás has both the island's campsites, making it popular with backpackers. In tourist season it can be a noisy place to stay and is often full of bikers. To the south of the bay lies **Agía Pakoús**, which is the site of the Classical city of Galissás.

Huge **Foínikas** bay, 3 km (2 miles) farther south, was originally settled by the Phoenicians, and now houses more than 1,000 people. Foínikas is a popular resort with a pier and moorings for yachts and fishing boats.

Sweeping Foínikas bay on the southwest coast of Sýros

Poseidonía ❹
Ποσειδονία

12 km (8 miles) SW of Ermoúpoli.
700. Agathopés 1 km (0.5 miles) S.

Poseidonía, or Dellagrázia, is one of the largest tourist sites on the island, with cosmopolitan hotels and restaurants. The island's first main road

An Italianate mansion in Poseidonía

was built in 1855 from Ermoúpoli through Poseidonía to Foínikas. The affluent village contains some Italianate mansions that are the country retreats of wealthy islanders. A short walk to the southwest, quieter **Agathopés** is one of the island's best beaches with safe waters protected by an islet opposite. Mégas Gialós, 3.5 km (2 miles) away on the west coast, is a pretty beach shaded by tamarisk trees.

Vári ❺

Βάρη

8 km (5 miles) S of Ermoúpoli.
1,150. Vári.

Quaint, sheltered Vári has become a major resort, but it still has traditional houses. On the Chontrá peninsula, east of the beach, is the site of the island's oldest prehistoric settlement (4000–3000 BC).

Kéa

Κέα

1,600. Korissía. 0288 21100. Gialiskári 6 km (4 miles) NW of Ioulís

KEA WAS FIRST inhabited in 3000 BC and later settled by Phoenicians and Cretans. In Classical times it had four cities: Ioulís, Korissía, Poiíssa, and Karthaía. The remains of Karthaía can be seen on the headland opposite Kýthnos. It is a favorite spot for rich Athenians due to its proximity to Attica. Mountainous, with fertile valleys, Kéa has been known since ancient times for its wine, honey, and almonds.

Ioulis

The capital, Ioulís, or Ioulída, with its red terra-cotta-tiled roofs and winding alleyways, is perched on a hillside 5 km (3 miles) above Korissía. Ioulís has 26 windmills situated on the Mountain of the Mills. The town is a maze of tunnel-like alleys and has a spectacular Neo-Classical **town hall** (1902) topped with statues of Apollo and Athena. On the west side are ancient bas-relief sculptures and in the entrance a sculpture of a woman and child found at ancient Karthaía.

The Kástro quarter is reached through a white archway that stands on the site of the ancient acropolis. The Venetians built their castle in 1210 with stones from the ancient walls and original Temple of Apollo. There are panoramic views from here. The **Archaeological Museum** is based in a Neo-Classical house. Its displays include an interesting collection of Minoan finds from Agía Eiríni; artifacts from the four ancient cities; Cycladic figurines and ceramics; and a copy of the stunning, marble, 6th-century BC *koúros* of Kéa. The smiling 6th-century BC **Lion of Kéa** is carved into the rock 400 m (1,300 ft) north of the town.

Archaeological Museum
0288 22079. Tue–Sun. main public hols.

Around the Island

The port of **Korissía** can be packed with Greek families on vacation, as can **Vourkári,** an attractive and popular resort farther north on the island that is famous for its fish tavernas.

The archaeological site of **Agía Eiríni** is topped by the chapel of the same name. The Bronze Age settlement was destroyed by an earthquake in 1450 BC and was excavated from 1960 to 1968. First occupied at the end of the Neolithic period, around 3000 BC, the town was fortified twice in the Bronze Age, and there are still remains of the great wall with a gate, a tower, and traces of streets. Many of the finds are displayed in the Archaeological Museum in Ioulís. The most spectacular monument on Kéa is the Hellenistic tower at Moní Agía Marína, 5 km (3 miles) southwest of Ioulís.

A Hellenistic tower at Moní Agía Marína on Kéa

Kýthnos
Κύθνος

1,500. *Mérichas.*
0281 31201.

BARREN KYTHNOS attracts more Greek visitors than foreign tourists, although it is a popular anchorage for flotilla vacations. Its dramatic, rugged interior and the sparsity of visitors make it an ideal location for walkers.

The local clay was traditionally used for pottery and ceramics, but is also used to make the red roofing tiles that characterize all the island's villages.

Known locally as Thermiá because of the island's hot springs, Kýthnos attracts visitors to the thermal spa at Loutrá. Since the closure of the iron mines in the 1940s, the islanders have lived off fishing, farming, and basket-weaving. To celebrate festivals such as the major pre-Lenten carnival, the islanders often wear traditional costumes.

Chora

Also known as Messariá, the capital is a charming mix of red roofs and Cycladic cube-shaped houses. Also worth visiting is the church of **Agios Sávvas**, founded in 1613 by the Venetian Cozzadini family whose coat of arms it bears. The oldest church is **Agía Triáda** (Holy Trinity), a domed, single-aisle basilica.

Interior of the church of Panagía Kanála in Kanála town on Kýthnos

Around the Island

The road network is limited, but buses connect the port of Mérichas with Kanála in the south and Loutrá in the north. The remaining areas of the island are mostly within a walkable distance of these points. **Mérichas**, on the west coast, has a small marina and tree-fringed beach, lined with small hotels and tavernas. Just to the north, the sandy beach of **Martinákia** is popular with families. Farther along the coast are the lovely beaches at **Episkopí** and **Apókrousi**, overlooked by **Vryókastro,** the Hellenistic ruins of ancient Kýthnos.

The red-roofed village of Dryopída on Kýthnos

You can walk to **Dryopída**, a good hour south of Chóra, down the ancient cobbled way with dramatic views. The town was named after the ancient Dryopes tribe whose king, Kýthnos, gave the island its name. The charming red-roofed village is divided into two districts by the river valley: Péra Roúga is lush with crops, while Galatás was once a center for ceramics, but only one pottery remains.

At **Kanála**, 5 km (3 miles) to the south, vacation homes have sprung up by the church of Panagía Kanála, dedicated to the Virgin Mary, the island's patron saint. Set in attractive shaded picnic grounds, the church houses Kýthnos's most venerated icon of the Virgin. It is probably by master iconographer, Skordílis, as Kýthnos was a center for icon-painting in the 17th century. Kanála beach has views of Sérifos and Sýros, and there are good beaches nearby.

Potter at work in Dryopída

Loutrá is a straggling resort on the northeast coast with windswept beaches. Its spa waters are saturated with iron, and since ancient times the springs of Kákavos and Agioi Anárgyroi have been used as a cure for ailments ranging from gout, rheumatism, and eczema to gynecological problems. The Xenía Hotel, situated next door to the excellent Hydrotherapy Center, has late 19th-century marble baths inside. A Mesolithic settlement to the north, dating from 7500–6000 BC, is the oldest in the Cyclades.

Sérifos
Σέριφος

1,100. *Livádi.*
0281 51300.

IN MYTHOLOGY, the infant Perseus and his mother Danae were washed up on the shores of rocky Sérifos, known as "the barren one." Once rich in iron and copper mines, the island has bare hills

The whitewashed village of Chóra on Sérifos

with small fertile valleys, and long sandy beaches.

Ferries dock at **Livádi** on the southeast coast. The town is situated on a sandy, tree-fringed bay backed by hotels and tavernas. Follow the stone steps up from Livádi, or use the sporadic bus service to reach the dazzling white **Chóra** high above on the steep hillside. It is topped by the ruins of a 15th-century Venetian kástro. Many of its medieval cube-shaped houses, some incorporating stone from the castle, have been renovated as vacation homes by Greek artists and architects. It is an attractive town with chapels and windmills perched precariously, offering breathtaking views of the island.

Near to the northern inland village of Galaní, the fortified **Moní Taxiarchón** (Archangel), built in 1500, is run by a single monk. The monastery contains fine 18th-century frescoes by Skordílis and some valuable Byzantine manuscripts.

Sífnos
Σίφνος

1,950. Kamáres.
0284 31210.

FAMOUS FOR its pottery, poets, and chefs, Sífnos has become the most popular destination in the Western Cyclades. Visitors in their thousands flock to the island in summer lured by its charming villages, terraced countryside dotted with ancient towers, Venetian dovecotes, and long sandy beaches. In ancient times Sífnos was renowned for its gold mines. The islanders paid yearly homage to the Delphic sanctuary of Apollo with a solid gold egg. But one year they cheated and sent a gilded rock instead, incurring Apollo's curse. The gold mines were flooded, the island was ruined, and from then on was known as *sífnos*, meaning empty.

A fountain in Kástro, Sífnos

Apollonia

The capital is set above Kamáres port and is a Cycladic labyrinth of white houses, flowers, and belfries. It is named after the 7th-century BC Temple of Apollo, which overlooked the town, now the site of the 18th-century church of the **Panagía Ouranofóra**. The **Museum of Popular Arts and Folklore** in the main square has a good collection of local pottery and embroideries.

Museum of Popular Arts and Folklore
Plateía Iróou. *Apr–Oct: daily.*

Around the Island

Sífnos is a small, hilly island, popular with walkers. Buses from Kamáres port connect it with Apollonía and Kástro, on the east coast. **Artemónas** is Apollonía's twin village, the second largest on Sífnos, with impressive Venetian houses sporting distinctive chimneys. The 17th-century church, Agios Geórgios tou Aféndi, contains several fine icons from the period. The church of Panagía Kónchi, with its cluster of domes, was built on the site of a temple of Artemis.

Kástro, 3 km (2 miles) east of Artemónas, overlooks the sea, the backs of its houses forming massive outer walls *(see pp18–19)*. Some buildings in the narrow, buttressed alleys bear Venetian coats of arms. There are ruins of a Classical acropolis in the village. The **Archaeological Museum** has a collection of Archaic and Hellenistic sculpture, and Geometric and Byzantine pottery.

The port of **Kamáres** is a straggling resort, with waterside cafés and tavernas. The north of the harbor was once lined with pottery shops making Sífnos's distinctive blue and brown ceramics, but only two remain. Taxis-boats go from Kamáres to the pretty pottery hamlet of **Vathý**, in the south. An hour's walk to the east is the busy resort of **Platýs Gialós**, with its long sandy beach. This is also connected by bus to Apollonía and Kamáres.

Archaeological Museum
Kástro. 0284 31022. *Tue–Sun.* *main public hols.*

A chapel with steps leading down to a small wharf at Platýs Gialós

Páros
Πάρος

FERTILE, THYME-SCENTED Páros is the third largest Cycladic island. Since antiquity it has been famous for its white marble, which ensured the island's prosperity from the early Cycladic age through to Roman times. In the 13th century Páros was ruled by the Venetian Dukes of Náxos, then by the Turks from 1537 until the Greek War of Independence *(see pp38–9)*. Páros is the hub of the Cycladic ferry system and is busy in tourist season. Buffeted by strong winds in July and August, it is a windsurfer's paradise. There are several resorts, but it retains its charm with hill villages, vineyards, and olive groves.

An ornate chandelier in the interior of Ekatontapylianí

The famous windmill beside Paroikía's busy port

Paroikía ❶
Παροικία

3,000. harbor.
0284 21673. Apr–Oct.
Kriós 3 km (2 miles) N.

The port of Paroikía, or Chóra, owes its foundations to the marble trade. Standing on the site of a leading early Cycladic city, it became a major Roman marble center. Traces of Byzantine and Venetian rule remain, although earthquakes have caused much damage.

Today it prospers as a resort town, with its dockside windmill and commercialized waterfront crammed with ticket agencies, cafés, and bars. The area behind the harbor is an enchanting Cycladic town, with narrow paved alleys, archways dating from medieval times, and white houses overhung with cascading jasmine.

Ekatontapylianí

W Paroikía. 0284 21243. daily.

The Ekatontapylianí (Church of a Hundred Doors) in the west of town is the oldest in Greece in continuous use and a major Byzantine monument. Its official name is the Dormition of the Virgin.

According to legend, the church was founded by St. Helen, mother of Constantine, the first Christian Byzantine emperor. After having a vision here showing the path to the True Cross, she vowed to build a church on the site but died before fulfilling her promise. In the 6th century AD the Emperor Justinian carried out her wish, commissioning the architect Ignatius to design a cathedral. He was the apprentice of Isidore of Miletus, master builder of Agía Sofía in Constantinople. The result was so impressive that Isidore, consumed with jealously, pushed his pupil off the roof. Ignatius grabbed his master's foot and they both fell to their deaths. The pair are immortalized in stone in the north of courtyard in front of the church.

Theoktísti's footprint

Ekatontapylianí is made up of three interlocking buildings. It is meant to have 99 doors and windows. According to legend, when the 100th door is found, Constantinople (Istanbul) will return to the Greeks. Many earthquakes have forced much reconstruction, and the main church building was restyled in the 10th century in the shape of a Greek cross. The sanctuary columns date from the pre-Christian era and the marble screen, capitals, and iconostasis are of Byzantine origin.

On the carved wooden iconostasis is an icon of the Virgin, worshiped for its healing virtues. Nearby a footprint, set in stone, is claimed

Fishing boats, Paroikía harbor

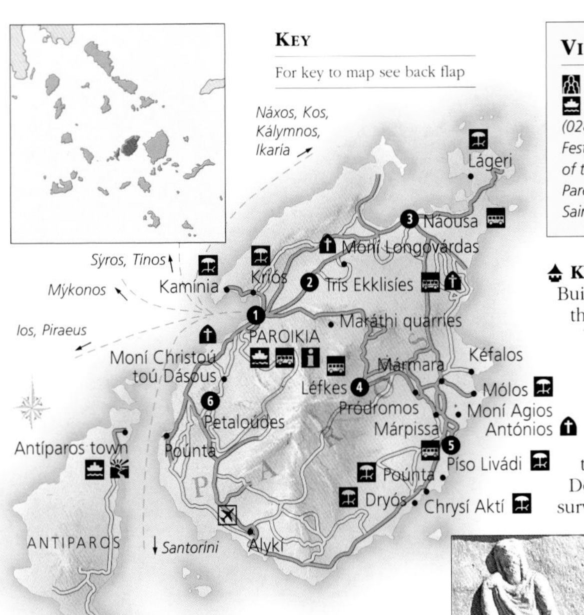

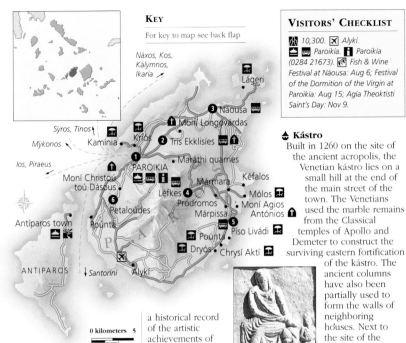

Key

For key to map see back flap

Visitors' Checklist

10,300. Alykí. Paroikía. Paroikía (0284 21673). Fish & Wine Festival at Náousa: Aug 6; Festival of the Dormition of the Virgin at Paroikía: Aug 15; Agía Theoktísti Saint's Day: Nov 9.

Sights at a Glance

Léfkes 4
Náousa 3
Paroikía 1
Petaloúdes 6
Píso Livádi 5
Tris Ekklisíes 2

to be that of Agía Theoktísti, the island's patron saint. The Greeks fit their feet into the print to bring them luck. Also displayed is her severed hand.

From the back of the church a door leads to the chapel of Agios Nikólaos, an adapted 4th-century BC Roman building. It has a double row of Doric columns, a marble throne, and a 17th-century iconostasis. Next door, the 11th-century baptistry has a marble font with a frieze of Greek crosses. Ekatontapylianí has no bell tower and instead the bells are hung from a tree outside.

Archaeological Museum

W Paroikía. 0284 21231.
Tue–Sun. main public hols.

The museum can be found behind Ekatontapylianí. One of its main exhibits is part of the priceless Parian Chronicle, a historical record of the artistic achievements of ancient Greece up to 264 BC. It is carved on a marble tablet and was discovered in the kástro walls during the 17th century.

Also on display are finds from the Temple of Apollo including a 5th-century BC Winged Victory, a mosaic depicting Herakles hunting, and a frieze of Archilochus, the 7th-century BC poet and soldier from Páros.

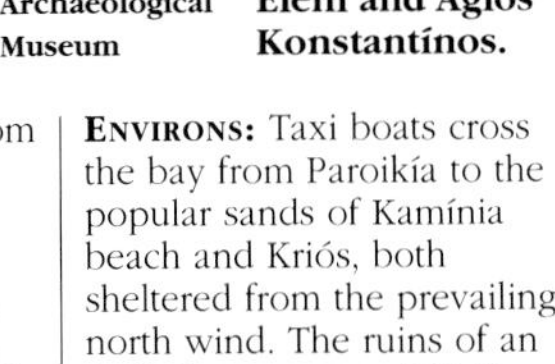
A Greco-Roman frieze in the Archaeological Museum

Kástro

Built in 1260 on the site of the ancient acropolis, the Venetian kástro lies on a small hill at the end of the main street of the town. The Venetians used the marble remains from the Classical temples of Apollo and Demeter to construct the surviving eastern fortification of the kástro. The ancient columns have also been partially used to form the walls of neighboring houses. Next to the site of the Temple of Apollo stands the 300-year-old blue-domed church of **Agía Eléni and Agios Konstantínos.**

Environs: Taxi boats cross the bay from Paroikía to the popular sands of Kamínia beach and Kriós, both sheltered from the prevailing north wind. The ruins of an Archaic sanctuary of Delian Apollo stand on the hill above.

The Legend of Agia Theoktisti

Páros's patron saint, Theoktísti, was a young woman captured by pirates in the 9th century. She escaped to Páros and lived alone in the woods for 35 years, leading a pious and frugal life. Found by a hunter, she asked him to bring her some communion bread. When he returned with the bread she lay down and died. Realizing she was a saint, he cut off her hand to take as a relic but found he could not leave Páros until he reunited her hand with her body.

Around Páros Island

PAROS IS AN EASY ISLAND to explore, with an excellent bus service linking the three main towns: the capital Paroikía, the trendy fishing village resort of Náousa in the north, and the central mountain town of Léfkes. There are plenty of cars and bikes for rent to get to the beaches and villages off the beaten track, and boat excursions and caïques to tour the remoter shores.

The mountain village of Léfkes, the medieval capital of Páros

Tris Ekklisíes ❷

Τρείς Εκκλησιές

3 km (2 miles) NE of Paroikía.

North of Paroikía the road to Náousa passes the remains of three 17th-century churches, Tris Ekklisíes, adapted from an original 7th-century basilica. That was in turn built from the marble of a 4th-century BC *heróon*, or hero's shrine, tomb of the Parian poet Archilochus.

In the mountains farther north, the remote, 17th-century **Moní Longovárdas** is a hive of activity. The monks make wine and books and work in the fields, and the abbot is famous for his icon-painting. Visitors are, however, discouraged and women are banned.

Náousa ❸

Νάουσα

12 km (7 miles) NE of Paroikía.
2,100. *Lageri 5 km (3 miles) NE.*

With its brightly painted fishing boats and winding white alleyways, Náousa has become a cosmopolitan destination for the jet set, with expensive boutiques and relaxed bars. It is the island's second largest town and the place to sit and watch the rich and the beautiful parade chic designer clothes along the waterfront.

Main door at Moní Longovárdas

The colorful harbor has a unique breakwater in the half-submerged ruin of a Venetian castle that has slowly been sinking with the coastline.

Every year, on the evening of August 23, 100 torch-lit fishing boats assemble to reenact the battle of 1536 between the islanders and the pirate Barbarossa, ending with celebrations of music and dancing.

Caïques at the attractive fishing harbor at Náousa

Léfkes ❹

Λεύκες

10 km (6 miles) SE of Paroikía.
850.

The mountain road to Léfkes, the island's highest village, passes the abandoned marble quarries at Maráthi, last worked for Napoleon's tomb. It is possible to explore the ancient tunnels with a flashlight.

Léfkes, named after the local poplar trees, was the capital under Ottoman rule. It is a charming, unspoiled village with medieval houses, a labyrinth of alleys, *kafeneía* in shaded squares, and restaurants with terraces overlooking the green valley below. Shops stock local weaving and ceramic handicrafts, and the town has a tiny Folk Museum.

Folk Museum

Apr–Oct: daily; Nov–Mar: key at town hall.

ENVIRONS: From the windmills overlooking Léfkes, a Byzantine marble pathway leads 3 km (2 miles) southeast to **Pródromos**, an old fortified farming village. Walk a further 15 minutes past olive groves to reach **Mármara** village with its marble-paved streets. The pretty hamlet of **Márpissa** lies about 1.5 km (1 mile) south.

On Kéfalos hill, 2 km (1 mile) east of Márpissa, are the ruins of a 15th-century Venetian fortress and the 16th-century **Moní Agios Antónios**. The monastery, which is often shut, is built from Classical remains. It has a fine 17th-century fresco of the *Second Coming*.

The convent of Moní Christoú tou Dásous near Petaloúdes

Píso Livadi ❺

Πίσω Λιβάδι

15 km (9 miles) SE of Paroikía. 50. to Márpissa. Poúnta 1 km (0.5 mile) S.

Situated below Léfkes on the east coast of the island, the fishing village of Píso Livádi, with its sheltered sandy beach, has grown into a lively small resort. It was once the port for Páros's hill villages and the island's marble quarries; today there are services operated over to nearby Agía Anna *(see p226)* on Náxos island. The small harbor has a wide range of bars and tavernas with a disco nearby and occasional local activities and entertainments.

The beautiful and fashionable beach at Poúnta

Environs: Mólos, 6 km (4 miles) north, has a long sandy beach with dunes, tavernas, and a windsurfing center. Just to the south lies **Poúnta** (not to be confused with the village of Poúnta on the west coast), one of the best and most fashionable beaches in the Cyclades, with a trendy laid-back beach bar. The island's most famous east coast beach, 3 km (2 miles) south, is **Chrysí Aktí** (Golden Beach). With 700 m (2,300 ft) of golden sand, it is perfect for families. It is also a well-known center for water sports and has hosted the world windsurfing championships.

Dryós, 2 km (1 mile) farther southwest, is an expanding resort, but at its heart is a pretty village with a duck pond, tavernas, a small harbor with a pebbly beach, and a string of sandy coves.

Petaloúdes ❻

Πεταλούδες

6 km (4 miles) SW of Paroikía. 1 Jun–20 Sep: daily.

Petaloúdes, or the Valley of the Butterflies, on the slopes of Psychopianí, is easily reached from Paroikía. This lush green oasis is home to swarms of Jersey tiger moths, from May to August, that flutter from the foliage when disturbed. There are mule treks along the donkey paths that cross the valley. About 2 km (1 mile) north of Petaloúdes, the 18th-century convent of **Moní Christoú tou Dásous**, Christ of the Woods, is worth the walk, although only women are allowed into the sanctuary. Páros's second patron saint, Agios Arsénios, teacher and abbot, is also buried here.

Outlying Islands

The island of **Antíparos** used to be joined to Páros by a causeway. These days a small ferry links the two from the west coast resort of Poúnta, and there are also caïque trips from Paroikía. Antíparos town has a relaxed and stylish café society, good for escaping from the Páros crowds. Activity centers around the dock and the Venetian **kástro** area. The kástro is a good example of a 15th-century fortress town, designed with inner courtyards and narrow streets to impede pirate attacks *(see pp18–19)*. The village also has two 17th-century churches, Agios Nikólaos and Evangelismós.

The island has fine beaches, but the star attraction is the massive **Cave of Antíparos**, with a breathtaking array of stalactites and stalagmites, discovered during Alexander the Great's reign. In summer, boats run to the cave from Antíparos town and Poúnta on Páros. From where the boat docks, it is a half-hour walk up the hill of Mount Ioánnis to the cave mouth, then a dramatic 70 m (230 ft) descent into the cavern. Lord Byron and other visitors have carved their names on the walls. In 1673 the French ambassador, the Marquis de Nointel, held a Christmas mass here for 500 friends. The church outside, Agios Ioánnis Spiliótis, was built in 1774.

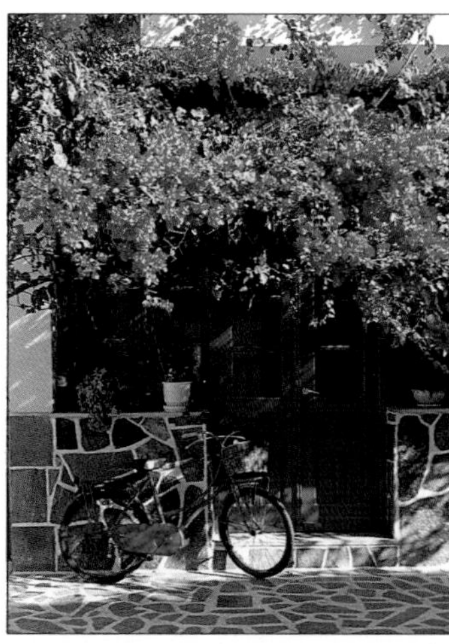

Bougainvillea on a house in Antíparos town

Náxos

Νάξος

The largest of the Cyclades, Náxos was first settled in 3000 BC. A major center of the Cycladic civilization *(see pp24–5)*, it was one of the first islands to use marble. Náxos fell to the Venetians in 1207, and the numerous fortified towers *(pýrgoi)* were built, still evident across the island today. Its landscape is rich with citrus orchards and olive groves, and it is famous in myth as the place where Theseus abandoned the Cretan princess Ariadne.

The Portára gateway from the unfinished Temple of Apollo

Náxos Town ❶

Χώρα

15,000. waterfront
waterfront (0285 22717).

North of the port and reached by a causeway is the huge marble Portára gateway on the islet of Paláteia, which dominates the harbor of Náxos town, or Chóra. Built in 522 BC, it was to be the entrance to the unfinished Temple of Apollo.

The town is made up of four distinct areas. The harbor bustles with its cafés and fishermen at work. To the south is Neá Chóra, or Agios Geórgios, a concrete mass of hotels, apartments, and restaurants. Above the harbor, the old town divides into the Venetian Kástro, once home of the Catholic nobility, and the medieval Bourg, where the Greeks lived.

The twisting alleys of the Bourg market area are lined with restaurants and gift shops. The Orthodox cathedral in the Bourg, the fine 18th-century **Mitrópoli Zoödóchou Pigís**, has an iconostasis, painted by Dimítrios Válvis of the Cretan school in 1786.

Uphill lies the imposing medieval north gate of the fortified Kástro, built in 1207. Only two of the original seven gate-towers remain. Little is left of the 13th-century outer walls, but the inner walls still stand, protecting 19 impressive Venetian houses. The houses bear the coats of arms of the Venetian nobles who lived there, and many of the present-day residents are descended from these families. Their remains are housed in the 13th-century Catholic **cathedral**, in the Kástro, beneath marble slabs dating back to 1619.

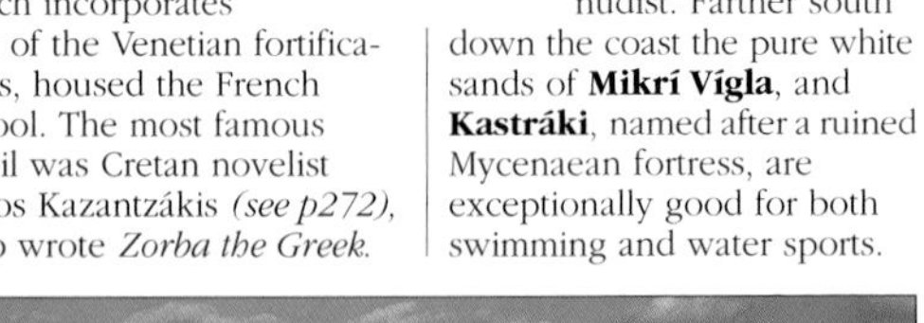

Angel from the Roman Catholic cathedral

During the Turkish occupation, Náxos was famous for its schools. The magnificent Palace of Sanoúdo, dating from 1627, which incorporates part of the Venetian fortifications, housed the French school. The most famous pupil was Cretan novelist Níkos Kazantzákis *(see p272)*, who wrote *Zorba the Greek*.

Mosaic from the Archaeological Museum in Náxos town

The building now houses the **Archaeological Museum**, which has one of the best collections of Cycladic marble figurines *(see p207)* in the Greek islands, as well as some beautiful Roman mosaics.

Archaeological Museum
Palace of Sanoúdo. *0285 22725.*
Tue–Sun. *main public hols.*

Environs: A causeway leads to the **Gkrótta** area, north of Náxos town, named after its numerous sea caves. To the south the lagoonlike bay of **Agios Geórgios** is the main vacation center, with golden sands and shallow water.

The best beaches are out of town along the west coast. **Agía Anna** is a pleasant small resort with silver sands and water sports. For more solitude, head south 3 km (2 miles) over the dunes to **Pláka**, the best beach on the island and mainly nudist. Farther south down the coast the pure white sands of **Mikrí Vígla**, and **Kastráki**, named after a ruined Mycenaean fortress, are exceptionally good for both swimming and water sports.

The remote and beautiful Pláka beach south of Naxos town

Around Náxos Island

INLAND, NAXOS is a dramatic patchwork of rich gardens, vineyards, orchards, and villages. These are backed by wild crags and dotted with Venetian watchtowers and a wealth of historical sites. Although there are organized tours from Náxos town and a good local bus service, a rented car is advisable to explore the island fully. The Tragaía region is, however, a walker's paradise.

Moní village in the Tragaía valley, surrounded by olive groves

Visitors' Checklist

20,000. 2 km (1 mile) S of Náxos town. Náxos town. Náxos town (0285 22717). Agios Nikódimos Folk Festival, Náxos town: Jul 14; Dionysiac Festival, Náxos town: 1st week of Aug; Diorvoia Festival: Jul–Aug.

Mélanes Valley 2

Κοιλάδα Μέλανες

10 km (6 miles) S of Náxos town. *to Kinídaros.*

The road south of Náxos town passes through the Livádi valley, the heart of ancient marble country, to the Mélanes villages. In **Kourounochóri**, the first village, is the Venetian Della Rocca tower. At **Mýloi**, near the ancient marble quarry at Flério, lie two 6th-century BC *koúroi*, huge marble statues. One, 8 m (26 ft) long, lies in a private garden, open to visitors. The other, 5.5 m (18 ft) long, lies in a nearby field.

***Koúros* in a private garden in Mýloi in the Mélanes valley**

ENVIRONS: Southeast of Náxos town is **Glinádo**, a market town, home to the Venetian Bellonias tower, first of the fortified mansions on Náxos. The chapel of Agios Ioánnis Gýroulas in **Ano Sagkrí**, south of Glinádo, is built over the ruins of a temple of Demeter.

Tragaía Valley 3

Κοιλάδα Τραγαία

15 km (9 miles) SE of Náxos town.

From Ano Sagkrí the road twists to the Tragaía Valley. The first village in the valley, **Chalkí**, is the most picturesque with its Venetian architecture and the old Byzantine Fragkópoulos tower in its center.

From Chalkí a road leads up to Moní, home of the most unusual church on Náxos, **Panagía Drosianí**. Dating from the 6th century, its domes are made from field stones.

Filóti is a traditional village, the largest in the region. It sits on the slopes of Mount Zas, which, at 1,000 m (3,300 ft), is the highest in the Cyclades.

Sights at a Glance

Apeíranthos 4
Apóllon 6
Komiakí 5
Mélanes Valley 2
Náxos town 1
Tragaía Valley 3

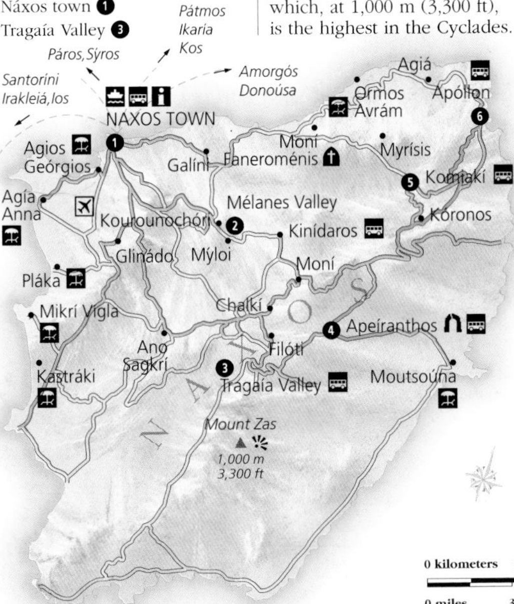

Key

For key to map see back flap

Terraced fields outside the village of Komiáki

Apeíranthos ❹
Απειράνθος

25 km (15 miles) SE of Náxos town. 1,500.

Apeíranthos was originally settled in the 17th and 18th centuries by Cretan refugees fleeing Turkish oppression and coming to work in the nearby emery mine. It is the island's most atmospheric village, with marble-paved streets and 14th-century towers *(pýrgoi)* built by the Venetian Crispi family. Locals still wear traditional costume, women weave on looms, and farmers sell their wares from donkeys.

The small **Archaeological Museum** has a collection of proto-Cycladic marble plaques depicting scenes from daily life as well as Neolithic finds. There is also a small **Geological Museum** on the second floor of the village school. Below the village is the port of **Moutsoúna** where ships were once loaded with emery before the industry's decline. The fine beach is now lined with vacation homes.

Archaeological Museum
Off main road. *daily.* *main public hols.*

Geological Museum
Village school. *daily.* *main public hols.*

Komiáki ❺
Κωμιάκη

42 km (26 miles) E of Náxos town. 500.

Approaching from Kóronos the road becomes a tortuous succession of hairpin turns before finally arriving in pretty Komiáki (also known as Koronída). This is the highest village on Náxos and a former home of the emery miners. It is covered with vines and is known for being the place where the local *kítrou* liqueur originated. There are wonderful views of the surrounding terraced vineyards. The village is the start of one of the finest walks on Náxos. The walk takes you down into the lush valley and the charming oasis hamlet of **Myrísis**.

Apóllon ❻
Απόλλων

49 km (30 miles) NE of Náxos town. 100.

Originally a fishing village that is slowly turning into a resort, Apóllon gets busy in the summer with bus trips of people coming to visit the fish tavernas and the huge *koúros* found here. Steps lead up the hillside above the village to ancient marble quarries where the vast unfinished statue has lain abandoned since 600 BC. The bearded marble figure, which is believed to represent the god Apollo, is 10.5 m (35 ft) long and weighs 30 tons. There is also a lively festival in the village for St. John the Baptist on August 28.

ENVIRONS: At Agía, 10 km (6 miles) west of Apóllon, stands the **Cocco Pýrgos**, built by the Venetian Cocco clan at the beginning of their rule of northern Náxos in 1770. *Pýrgoi* are fortified watchtowers that were built during the Venetian occupation of Náxos. Farther along the north coast road lies the idyllic beach at **Ormos Avráam** with a good family-run taverna.

Dating from 1606, the abandoned **Moní Faneroménis** is 13 km (8 miles) south on the road winding down the west coast from Apóllon. Slightly farther south toward Galíni, a road leads up to the most famous *pýrgos,* the **High Tower** of the Cocco clan. It was built in 1660 in a commanding position overlooking a valley. During the 17th century a family feud between the Orthodox Cocco and the Catholic Barozzi

The harbor at Moutsoúna, Náxos

The huge *koúros* in Apóllon's ancient quarries

families broke out as a result of an insult. The feud led to the bombardment of the High Tower when a Barozzi woman persuaded her husband, who was a Maltese privateer, to besiege it. The Cocco clan managed to hold out, but the vendetta continued to rage for another 20 years until a marriage eventually united the two families.

A Venetian fortified watchtower, or *pýrgos*, west of Apóllon

Outlying Islands

Between Náxos and Amorgós lie **Donoússa**, **Koufoníssi**, **Iráklia**, and **Schinoússa**, the "Back Islands." The islands all have rooms to rent, a post office, and OTE, but no banks.

Iráklia, the largest, boasts impressive stalactites in the Cave of Aï-Iánni as well as Cycladic remains. Koufoníssi consists of two islands, Ano (upper), the most developed of the Back Islands, with good sandy beaches, and the uninhabited Káto (lower). Schinoússa has wild beaches and great walking over cobblestone mule tracks. Dónoussa, the most northerly of the chain, is more isolated and food can be scarce. A settlement from the Geometric era was excavated on the island, but most of its visitors come for the fine sandy beaches at **Kéntros** and **Livádi**.

Amorgós
Αμοργός

1,800. Katápola & Aigiáli. Katápola & Aigiali harbors. Katápola quay (0285 71278). Ormos Aigialis 12 km (7 miles) NE of Amorgós town.

DRAMATICALLY RUGGED, the small island of Amorgós is narrow and long with a few beaches. Inhabited from as early as 3300 BC, its peak was during the Cycladic civilization, when there were three cities: Minoa, Arkesini, and Egiali. In 1885 a find of ceramics and marble was taken to the Archaeological Museum in Athens *(see p282)*.

Chora

The capital, Chóra, or Amorgós town, is a dazzling clutch of whitewashed houses with windmills standing nearby. Above the town is **Apáno Kástro**, a Venetian fortress, which was built by Geremia Ghisi in 1290. Chóra also boasts the smallest church in Greece, the tiny **Agios Fanoúrios**.

ENVIRONS: The main attraction on the island is the spectacular Byzantine **Moní Panagía Chozoviótissa**, below Chóra on the east coast. The stark white monastery clings to the 180-m (590-ft) cliffs. It is a huge fortress, built into the rock, housing the miraculous icon of the Virgin Mary. Founded in 1088 by the Byzantine Emperor Alexis Comnenus, the monastery has a library with a collection of ancient manuscripts.

Around the Island

The best way to get around the island is by boat or walking, although there is a limited bus service. The main port of **Katápola** in the southwest is set in a horseshoe-shaped bay with tavernas, pensions, fishing boats, and a small pebbly beach. The harbor area links three villages: Katápola in the middle where the ferries dock, quieter **Xylokeratídi** to the north, and **Rachídi** on the hillside above. A track leads from Katápola to the hilltop ruins of the ancient city of **Minoa**. All that remain are the Cyclopean walls, the gymnasium, and the foundations of the temple of Apollo.

The northern port of **Ormos Aigiális** is the island's main resort, popular for its good sandy beach. It is worth following the mule paths north to the hill villages of **Tholária**, which has vaulted Roman *tholos* tombs, and **Lagkáda**, which is one of the prettiest villages on the island, with a stepped main street that is painted with daisies.

The clifftop Moní Chozoviótissa

The white walls and blue domed churches of Ios town

Ios
Ιος

1,654. Gialós. Ios town. Ano Chóra, Ios town (0286 91222). Mylopótas 2 km (1 mile) E of Ios town.

In ancient times Ios was covered in oak woods, later used for shipbuilding. The Ionians built cities at the port of Gialós and at Ios town, later to be used as Venetian strongholds. Ios is also known as the burial place of Homer, and May 15 is the Omíria, or Homer festival. A local specialty is its cheese, *myzíthra*, similar to a soft cream cheese.

Ios is renowned for its nightlife and as a result is a magnet for the young. However, it remains a beautiful island. Its mountainous coastline has over 400 chapels and some of the finest sands in the Cyclades.

Ios town, also known as the Village, is a dazzling mix of white houses and blue-domed churches fast being swamped by discos and bars. There are ruins of the Venetian fortress, built in 1400 by Marco Crispi, remains of ancient walls, and 12 windmills above the town.

The port of **Gialós**, or Ormos, has a busy harbor, with yachts and fishing boats, good fish tavernas, and quieter accommodations than Ios town. The beach here is windy, but a 20-minute walk west leads to the sandy cove at Koumpará. A bus service runs from here to Ios town and the superb **Mylopótas** beach, which has two campsites. Excursion boats run from Gialós to the beach at **Manganári** bay, in the south, and **Psáthi** bay in the east.

On the northeast coast the beach at **Agía Theodóti** is overlooked by the medieval ruins of Palaiokástro fortress. A festival is held at nearby **Moní Agías Theodótis** on September 8 to mark the islanders' victory over medieval pirates. You can see the door the pirates broke through only to be scalded to death by boiling oil.

Windmill above Ios town

Homer's tomb is supposed in the north at **Plakotós**, an ancient Ionian town that has slipped down the cliffs over the ages. Homer died on the island after his ship was forced to dock en route to Athens. The tomb entrance, ruined houses, and the remains of the Hellenistic **Psarópyrgos tower** can be seen today.

Síkinos
Σίκινος

300. Aloprónia. Síkinos town. Kástro, Síkinos town (0286 51222). Agios Geórgios 7 km (3 miles) NE of Síkinos town.

Síkinos is quiet, very Greek, and one of the most ruggedly beautiful islands in the Cyclades. Known in Classical Greece as an *oinie* (wine island), it has remained a traditional backwater throughout history. Fishing and farming are the main occupations of the 300 or so islanders and, although there are some vacation homes, there is little mass tourism.

Síkinos town is divided into twin villages: Kástro and the pretty and unspoilted Chóra perched high up on a ridge overlooking the sea. Kástro is a maze of lanes and *kafeneía*. At the entrance to the village is Plateía Kástrou, where the walls of 18th-century stone mansions formed a bastion of defense. The church of the Pantánassa forms the focal point, and among the ruined houses is a huge marble portico.

The partly ruined Moní Zoödóchou Pigís, fortified against pirate raids, looms down from the crag above Chóra and has icons by the 18th-century master Skordílis.

In medieval Chóra there is a private **Folk Museum**, which is in the family home of an American expatriate. It has an olive press and a wide range of local domestic and agricultural artifacts.

From Chóra a path leads past the ruined ancient Cyclopean walls southwest to **Moní Episkopís**, a good hour's trek. With Doric

The golden sands of Mylopótas beach, Ios

columns and inscriptions it is thought to be a 3rd-century AD mausoleum, converted in the 7th century to the Byzantine church of Koímisis Theotókou. A monastery was added in the 17th century, but is now abandoned.

On the east coast 3 km (2 miles) southeast of Síkinos town, the port of **Aloprónoia**, also known as Skála, has a few small cafés that double as shops, a modern hotel complex, and a wide sandy beach that is safe for children.

Folk Museum
Ano Chorió, Síkinos town.
May–Sep: daily.

The sleepy port of Aloprónoia

Folégandros
Φολέγανδρος

650. Karavostásis.
Chóra (0286 41249).
Agkális 2 km (1 mile) W of Folégandros town.

Bleak and arid, Folégandros is one of the smallest inhabited islands in the Cyclades. It aptly takes its name from the Phoenician for rocky. Traditionally a place of exile, this remote island passed quietly under the Aegean's various rulers, suffering only from the threat of pirate attack. Popular with photographers and artists for its sheer cliffs, terraced fields, and striking Chóra, it can be busy in tourist season, but is still a good place for walkers, with a wild beauty

Koímisis tis Theotókou in Folégandros town

and unspoiled beaches.

Folégandros town or Chóra, perched 300 m (984 ft) above the sea to avoid pirates, is spectacular. It divides into the fortified Kástro quarter *(see p18)* and Chóra, or main village. Kástro, built in the 13th century by Marco Sanudo, Duke of Náxos, is reached through an arcade. The tall stone houses back onto the sea forming a stronghold along the ridge of the cliff with a sheer drop below. Within its maze of crazy-paved alleys full of geraniums are the distinctive two-story cube houses with brightly painted wooden balconies.

In Chóra village life centers on four squares with craft shops and lively tavernas and bars. The path from the central bus stop leads to the church of Koímisis tis Theotókou, (Assumption of the Virgin Mary). It was built after a silver icon was miraculously saved by an islander from medieval pirates who drowned in a storm. Forming part of the ancient town walls, it is thought to have once been the site of a Classical temple of Artemis.

Ferries dock at **Karavostási** on the east coast, a tiny harbor with a tree-fringed pebble beach, restaurants, hotels, and rooms. There is a bus to Chóra, and **Livádi** beach is a short walk from the port. In season there are excursions available to the western beaches at **Agkáli**, **Agios Nikoláos**, and **Latináki**, as well as to the island's most popular sight, the **Chrysospiliá**, or Golden Cave. Named after the golden shade of its stalactites and stalagmites, the grotto lies just below sea level in the northeast cliffs.

Ano Meriá, 5 km (3 miles) to the west of Folegándros town, is a string of farming hamlets on either side of the road, surrounded by terraced fields. There are wonderful sunset views from here, and on a clear day it is possible to see Crete in the distance. There is a good **Ecology and Folk Museum** with a display of farming implements, and reconstructions of traditional peasant life. On July 27 a major local festival is held for Agios Panteleïmon.

From Ano Meriá steep paths weave down to the remote beaches at **Agios Geórgios** bay and **Vígla**.

Ecology and Folk Museum
Ano Meriá. *Jul–mid-Sep: daily.*

Traditional houses in Kástro, Folégandros town

Mílos

Μήλος

VOLCANIC MILOS is the most dramatic of the Cyclades with its extraordinary rock formations, hot springs, and white villages perched on multicolored cliffs. Under the Minoans and Mycenaeans the island became rich from trading obsidian. However, the Athenians brutally captured and colonized Mílos in the 4th century BC. Festooned with pirates, the island was ruled by the Crispi dynasty during the Middle Ages and was claimed by the Turks in 1580. Minerals are now the main source of the island's wealth, although tourism is growing.

View across the houses of Pláka in the mid-morning sun

Plaka

On a clifftop 4 km (2.5 miles) above the port of Adámas, Pláka is a pretty mix of churches and white cube houses. These blend into the suburb of Trypití, which is topped by windmills.

It is believed that Pláka is sited on the acropolis of ancient Mílos, built by the Dorians between 1100 and 800 BC. The town was then destroyed by the Athenians and later settled by the Romans.

The principal sight is the **Archaeological Museum**, its entrance hall dominated by a plaster copy of the *Venus de Milo*, found on Mílos. The collection includes Neolithic finds, particularly obsidian, Mycenaean pottery, painted ceramics, and terra-cotta animals from 3500 BC, found at the ancient city of Philakopi. The most famous of the ceramics is the *Lady of Phylakopi*, an early Cycladic goddess decorated in Minoan style. However, the Hellenistic 4th-century BC statue of Poseidon and the *koúros* of Mílos (560 BC) are now in the National Archaeological Museum in Athens *(see p282)*. There are also finds from the neighboring island of Kímolos.

The *Lady of Philakopi*, in the Archaeological Museum

The **History and Folk Museum** is housed in a 19th-century mansion in the center of Pláka. It has costumes, four-poster beds, and handicrafts.

Steps lead to the ruined **kástro**, which was built by the Venetians on a volcanic plug 280 m (920 ft) above sea level. Only the houses that formed the outer walls of the fortress remain.

Above the kástro, the church of Mésa Panagía was bombed during World War II. It was rebuilt and renamed **Panagía Schoiniótissa** (Our Lady of the Bushes) after an icon of the Virgin Mary appeared in a bush where the old church used to stand.

Just below, the church of **Panagía Thalassítra** (Our Lady of the Sea), built in 1728, has icons of Christ, the Virgin Mary, and Agios Elefthérios.

The massive stone blocks of the Cyclopean walls that formed the city's East Gate in 450 BC remain, and 15 m (50 ft) west there are marble relics

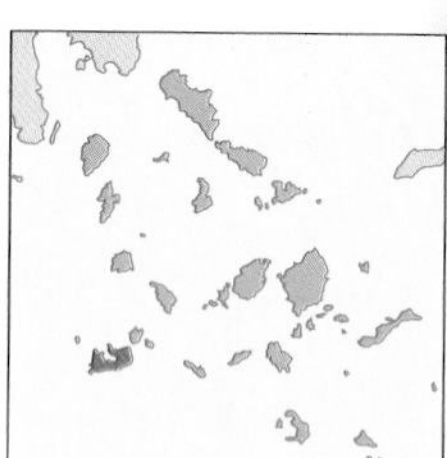

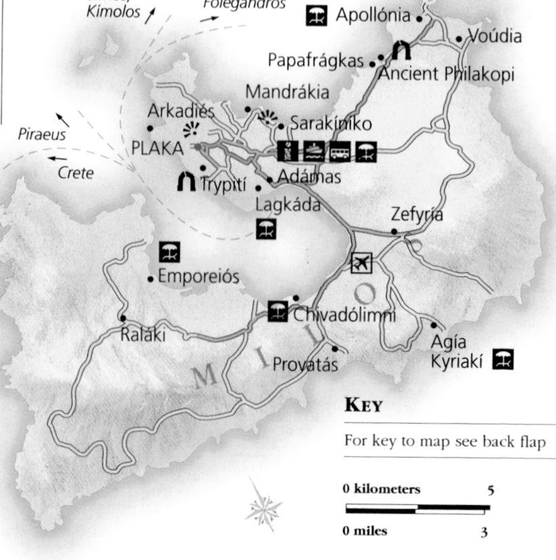

The twin rocks, known as The Bears, on the approach to Adámas

and a Christian baptismal font from a Byzantine basilica. A Roman amphitheater nearby is still used for performances.

Archaeological Museum
Main square. 0287 21620. Tue–Sun. May 1.

History and Folk Museum
Pláka. 0287 21292. Tue–Sat & Sun am. main public hols.

Inside the Christian Catacombs

ENVIRONS: In the nearby town of Trypití are the well-preserved 1st-century AD **Christian Catacombs**, which are unique in Greece. Carved into the hillside, the massive complex of galleries has tombs in arched niches, each one containing up to seven bodies. The catacomb network is 184 m (600 ft) long, with 291 tombs. Archaeologists believe that as many as 8,000 bodies were interred here.

From the catacombs, a track leads to the place where the *Venus de Milo* was discovered, now marked by a plaque. It was found on April 8, 1820, by a farmer, Geórgios Kentrótas. He uncovered a cave in the corner of his field with half of the ancient marble statue inside. The other half was found by a visiting French officer, and both halves were bought as a gift for Louis XVIII, on March 1, 1821. The statue is now displayed in the Louvre, Paris. The missing arms are thought to have been lost in the struggle for possession.

Christian Catacombs
Trypití, 2 km (1 mile) SE of Pláka. 0287 21625. Tue–Sun.

AROUND THE ISLAND

The rugged island is scattered with volcanic relics and long stretches of beach. The vast Bay of Mílos, the site of the volcano's central vent, is one of the finest natural harbors in the Mediterranean and has some of Mílos's best sights.

West of Adámas, the small and sandy **Lagkáda** beach is popular with families. On the way to the beach are the municipal baths with their warm mineral waters.

South of Adámas, the Bay of Mílos has a succession of attractive beaches, including **Chivadólimni**, backed by a turquoise saltwater lake. On the south coast is the lovely beach of Agía Kyriakí, near the village of Próvatas.

Situated on the northeast tip of the island is **Apollónia**, a popular resort with a tree-fringed beach. Water taxis leave here for the island of **Kímolos**, named after the chalk *(kimoliá)* mined there.

Once an important center of civilization, little remains now of **Ancient Philakopi**, just southwest of Apollónia. You can make out the old Mycenaean city walls, ruined houses and grave sites, but a large part of the city has been submerged under the sea.

VISITORS' CHECKLIST

4,500. 7 km (4 miles) SE of Adámas. Adámas. Adámas. Harborfront, Adámas (0287 22445). Nautical week: end Jun–beg Jul; Panagía at Zefyría: Aug 15.

GEOLOGY OF MILOS

Due to its volcanic origins, Mílos is rich in minerals and has some spectacular rock formations. Boat tours from Adámas go to the eerie pumice moonscape of Sarakinikó, formed two to three million years ago, the lava formations known as the "organ-pipes" of Glaronísia (offshore near Philakopi), and the sulfurous blue water at Papafrágkas. Geothermal action has provided a wealth of hot springs, in some areas, such as off the Mávra Gkrémna cliffs, the sea can reach 100° C (212° F) only 30 cm (12 inches) below the surface.

Mineral mine at Voúdia, still in operation

The white pumice landscape at Sarakinikó

The sulfurous blue water at Papafrágkas

Santoríni

Σαντορίνη

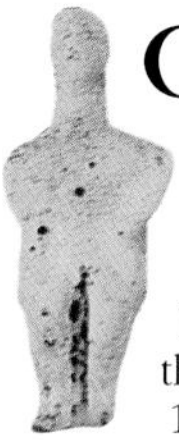

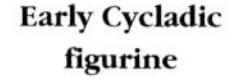

Early Cycladic figurine

COLONIZED BY THE Minoans in 3000 BC, this volcanic island erupted in 1450 BC, forming Santoríni's crescent shape. The island is widely believed to be a candidate for the lost kingdom of Atlantis. Named Thíra by the Dorians when they settled here in the 8th century BC, it was renamed Santoríni, after St. Irene, by the Venetians who conquered the island in the 13th century. Despite tourism, Santoríni remains a stunning island with its white villages clinging to volcanic cliffs above black sand beaches.

One of the many cliffside bars in Firá, with views over the caldera

Firá 1

Φηρά

1,550. 50 m (160 ft) S of main square. 0286 22649. Monólithos 5 km (2.5 miles) E.

Firá, or Thíra, overlooking the caldera and the island of Néa Kaméni, is the island's capital. It was founded in the late 18th century when islanders moved from the Venetian citadel of Skáros, near present day Imerovígli, to the cliff-top plains for easier access to the sea.

Devastated by an earthquake in 1956, Firá has been rebuilt, terraced into the volcanic cliffs with domed churches and barrel-roofed cave houses *(skaftá)*. The terraces are packed with hotels, bars, and restaurants in good positions along the lip of the caldera to enjoy the magnificent views, especially at sunset. The tiny port of Skála Firá is 270 m (890 ft) below Firá, connected by cable car or by mule up the 580 steps. Firá is largely pedestrianized, and its winding cobblestoned alleys are just wide enough for mules to pass. The town's main square, Plateía Theotokópoulou, is the bus terminal and hub of the road network. All the roads running north from here

Firá's whitewashed buildings lining the cliff top

Sights at a Glance

Akrotíri 4

Ancient Thíra 3

Firá 1

Oía 2

Key

For key to map see back flap

0 kilometers 5

0 miles 3

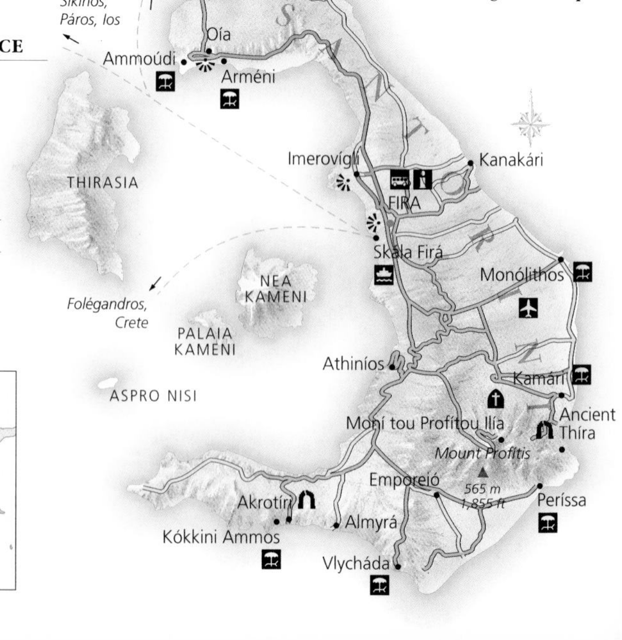

and from the harbor eventually merge in the attractive Plateía Firostefáni. The most spectacular street, Agíou Miná, runs south along the edge of the caldera to the 18th-century church of **Agíou Miná**. With its distinctive blue dome and its white bell tower, it has become the symbol of Santoríni.

Detail of bright orange volcanic cliff in Firá

Opposite the cable car station is the **Archaeological Museum**, which houses finds from Akrotíri *(see p237)* and the ancient city of Mésa Vounó *(see p236)*, including early Cycladic figurines found in local pumice mines. There is also a collection of 6th-century BC Attic black-figure vases.

Housed in a beautiful 17th-century mansion, the **Mégaro Ghisi Museum**, in the northern part of the town, holds manuscripts from the 16th to 19th centuries, maps, paintings, and photographs of Firá before and after the earthquake.

Despite the 1956 earthquake you can still see vestiges of Firá's architectural glory from the 17th and 18th centuries, on Nomikoú and Erythroú Stavroú where several mansions have been restored.

The pretty ocher chapel of **Agios Stylianós**, clinging to the edge of the cliff, is worth a visit on the way to the Frangiuka, or Frankish quarter, with its maze of arcaded streets. To the south, the Orthodox **cathedral** is dedicated to the Ypapantí (the Presentation of Christ in the Temple). Built in 1827, it is an imposing ocher building with two bell towers and murals by 19th-century artist, Christóforos Asímis. The bell tower of the **Dómos** dominates the north of town on Agíou Ioánnou. Though severely damaged in the earthquake, much of its elaborate Baroque interior has now been well restored.

A donkey ride up the steps from Skála Firá to Firá

Visitors' Checklist

12,500. 5 km (3 miles) SE of Firá. Skála Firá. Firá (0286 22649). Classical Music, Firá: Aug & Sep.

Archaeological Museum
Opposite cable car station.
0286 22217. Tue–Sun. main public hols.

Mégaro Ghisi Museum
Opposite Archaeological Museum.
0286 23077. May–late Oct: daily.

Geological History of Santorini

Santoríni is one of several ancient volcanoes lying on the southern Aegean volcanic arc. During the Minoan era, around 1450 BC, there was a huge eruption that began Santoríni's transformation to the way we see it today.

1 *Santoríni was a circular volcanic island before the massive eruption that blew out its middle.*

The volcano was active for centuries, building up to the 1450 BC explosion.

Clouds containing molten rock spread over 30 km (18 miles).

Crater of 22 sq km (8.5 sq miles)

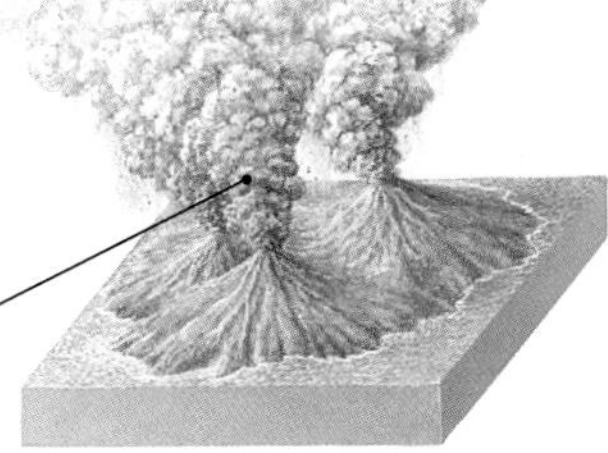

2 *The eruption left a huge crater, or caldera. The rush of water into the void created a tidal wave, or* tsunami, *that devastated Minoan Crete.*

A huge volume of lava was ejected, burying Akrotíri *(see p237)*.

Néa Kaméni and its active volcanic cone

Volcano walls up to 300 m (985 ft) high

3 *The islands of Néa Kaméni and Palaiá Kaméni, visible today, emerged after more recent volcanic activity in 197 BC and 1707. They are still volcanically active.*

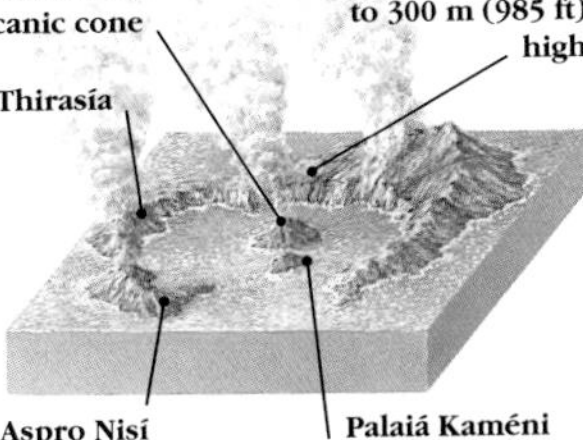

Thirasía

Aspro Nisí

Palaiá Kaméni

Around Santoríni Island

SANTORINI HAS MUCH TO OFFER apart from the frequently photographed attractions of Firá. There are some charming inland villages and excellent beaches at Kamári and Períssa with their long stretches of black sand. You can also visit some of Santoríni's wineries or take a ferry or boat to the smaller islands. There are good bus services, but a car or bike will allow you more freedom to explore. Major sites such as Ancient Thíra and Akrotíri have frequent bus and organized tour services.

A blue and ocher painted housefront in Oía

Oía ❷

Οία

11 km (7 miles) NW of Firá.
400. main road (0286 71234).

At the northern tip of the island, the beautiful town of Oía is famous for its spectacular sunsets. A popular island excursion is to have dinner in one of the many restaurants at the edge of the abyss as the sun sinks behind the caldera. According to legend, the atmospheric town is haunted and home to vampires.

Reached by one of the most tortuous roads in the Cyclades, Oía is the island's third port and was an important and wealthy commercial center before it was badly damaged in the 1956 earthquake.

Today Oía is designated a traditional settlement, having been carefully reconstructed after the earthquake. Its white and pastel-colored houses with red pebble walls cling to the cliff-face with the famous *skaftá* cave houses and blue-domed churches. Some of the Neo-Classical mansions built by ship owners can still be seen. A marble-paved pathway skirts the edge of the caldera to Firá. Staircases lead down to Arméni and the nearby fishing harbor at **Ammoúdi** with its floating pumice stones and red pebble beach. The tradition of boat-building continues at Arméni's small ferry dock at the base of the cliff, although the port is now mainly used by tourist boats departing daily for the small island of Thirasía.

Rock carving in Ancient Thíra

Ammoúdi fishing village overlooked by Oía on the cliff top above

Ancient Thíra, situated at the end of the Mésa Vounó peninsula

Ancient Thíra ❸

Αρχαία Θήρα

11 km (7 miles) SW of Firá.
to Kamári. Tue–Sun. main public hols. Períssa 200 m (600 ft) below.

Commanding the rocky headland of Mésa Vounó, 370 m (1,210 ft) up on the southeast coast, the ruins of the Dorian town of Ancient Thíra are still visible. Recolonized after the great eruption *(see p235)*, the ruins stand on terraces overlooking the sea.

Excavated by the German archaeologist Hiller von Gortringen in the 1860s, most of the ruins date from the Ptolemies, who built temples to the Egyptian gods in the 4th and 3rd centuries BC. There are also Hellenistic and Roman remains. The 7th-century Santoríni vases that were discovered here are now housed in Firá's Archaeological Museum *(see p235)*.

A path through the site passes an early Christian basilica, remains of private houses, some with mosaics, the agora (or market), and a theater, with a sheer view down to the sea. On the far west is a 3rd-century BC sanctuary cut into the rock, founded by Artemídoros of Perge, an admiral of the Ptolemaic fleet. It features relief carvings of an eagle, a lion, a dolphin, and a phallus symbolizing the gods Zeus, Apollo, Poseidon, and Priapus.

To the east, on the Terrace of Celebrations, you can find

The view from ancient Thíra down to Kamári

graffiti that dates back as far as 800 BC. The messages praise the competitors and dancers of the *gymnopedíes* – festivals in which boys danced naked and sang hymns to Apollo, or competed in feats of physical strength.

Environs: The headland of Mésa Vounó, which rises to the peak of Mount Profítis, juts out into the sea between the popular beaches of Kamári and Períssa. **Kamári** is situated below ancient Thíra to the north and is the island's main resort. The beach is a mix of stone and black volcanic sand and is backed by bars, tavernas, and apartments. **Períssa** has 8 km (5 miles) of black volcanic sand, a wide range of water sports, and a campsite. A modern church stands on the site of the Byzantine chapel of Irene, after whom the island is named.

Akrotíri ❹

Ακρωτήρι

12 km (7 miles) SW of Firá.
350. *Kókkini Ammos 1 km (0.5 miles) S.*

Akrotíri was once a Minoan outpost on the southwest tip of the island and is one of the most inspiring archaeological sites in the Cyclades. After an eruption in 1866, French archaeologists discovered Minoan pots at Akrotíri, although it was Professor Spyrídon Marinátos who, digging in 1967, unearthed the complete city; it was wonderfully preserved after some 3,500 years of burial under tons of volcanic ash. The highlight was the discovery of frescoes that are now displayed at the National Archaeological Museum in Athens *(see p282)*. Marinátos was killed in a fall on the site in 1974 and his grave is beside his life's work. Covered by a modern roof, the excavations include late 16th-century BC houses on the Telchínes road, two and three stories high, many still containing huge *pithoi*, or ceramic storage jars. The lanes were covered in ash, and it was here that the well-known fresco of the two boys boxing was uncovered. Farther along there is a mill and a pottery. A overpass-style bridge enables you to see the town's layout, including a storeroom for *pithoi* that held grain, flour, and oil. The three-story House of the Ladies is named after the fresco of two voluptuous dark women. The Triangle Square has large houses that were originally decorated with frescoes of fisher-boys and ships, now removed to Firá's Archaeological Museum.

The city's drainage system demonstrates how sophisticated and advanced the civilization was. No human or animal remains or treasure were ever found, suggesting that the inhabitants were probably warned by tremors before the catastrophe and fled in good time.

Outlying Islands

From Athiniós, 12 km (7 miles) south of Firá, excursion boats run to the neighboring islands. The nearest are **Palaiá Kaméni** and **Néa Kaméni**, known as the Burnt Islands. You can take a hot mud bath in the springs off Palaiá Kaméni and walk up the volcanic cone and crater of Néa Kaméni. **Thirasía** has a few tavernas and hotels. Its main town, the picturesque Manolás, has fine views across the caldera to Firá. Remote **Anáfi** is the most southerly of the Cyclades and shares the history of the other islands in the group. It is a peaceful retreat with good beaches. There are a few ancient ruins, but nothing remains of the sanctuaries of Apollo and Artemis that once stood here.

Storage jars found at Akrotíri

Frescoes of Akrotiri

Painted around 1500 BC, these Minoan-style murals are similar to those found at Knosós *(see p268–71)*. The best known are *The Young Fisherman*, depicting a youth holding blue and yellow fish, and *The Young Boxers*, showing two young sparring partners with long black hair and almond-shaped eyes. Preserved by the lava, the frescoes have kept their color. Many of them are now on display in the National Archaeological Museum in Athens *(see p282)*.

The dramatic setting of Firá on the cliffs of Santoríni ▷

CRETE

CHANIA · RETHYMNO · IRAKLEIO · LASITHI

THE ISLAND OF CRETE *is dominated by harsh, soaring mountains whose uncompromising impregnability is etched deep into the Cretan psyche. For centuries, cut off by these mountains and isolated by sea, the character of the island people has been proudly independent. Many conquerors have come and gone, but the Cretan passion for individuality and freedom has never been extinguished.*

For nearly 3,000 years the ruins of an ancient Minoan civilization lay buried and forgotten beneath the coastal plains of Crete. It was not until early this century that the remains of great Minoan palaces at Knossos, Phaestos, Mália, and Zákros were unearthed. Their magnificence demonstrates the level of sophistication and artistic imagination of the Minoan civilization, now considered the wellspring of European culture.

Rug detail, Anógeia

Historically, the island and its people have endured occupation by foreign powers and the hardships of religious persecution. The Romans brought their administrative expertise to the island, and the ancient city-state of Górtys became capital of the Roman province of Crete in 65 BC. Byzantine rule was followed by the Venetians (1204–1669), whose formidable fortresses, such as Fragkokástello, and elegant buildings in Réthymno and Chaniá testify to 400 years of rule. Oppression and religious persecution by the Ottoman Turks (1669–1898) encouraged a strong independence movement. By 1913, led by Elefthérios Venizélos (1864–1936), Crete became a province of Greece. The island was again occupied by German forces during World War II.

Today, mountains, sparkling seas, and ancient history combine with the Cretans' relaxed outlook on life to make the island an idyllic destination for thousands of vacationers.

A local in Réthymno wearing traditional Cretan boots and headdress

◁ **A palm-fringed estuary meets the sea at Préveli Beach on Crete's southern coast**

The Flora and Fauna of Crete

CRETE'S WILDLIFE is as varied as its landscape. In spring, flowers cover the coastal strip and appear inland in the patchwork of olive groves, meadows, and orchards. Stony, arid *phrygana* habitat is widespread, and pockets of native evergreen forests still persist in remote gorges. Freshwater marshes act as magnets for waterbirds, while Crete's position between North Africa and the Greek mainland makes it a key staging post for migrant birds in spring and autumn. Its comparative isolation has meant that several unique species of plant have evolved.

The Samariá Gorge (see pp250–51) *has been carved out by winter torrents washing down from the Omalós Plateau. Visitors should look out for peonies, cyclamens, and Cretan ebony. Watch out as well for wild goats, called* kri-kri, *whose sure-footed confidence enables them to scale the precipitous slopes and cliffs.*

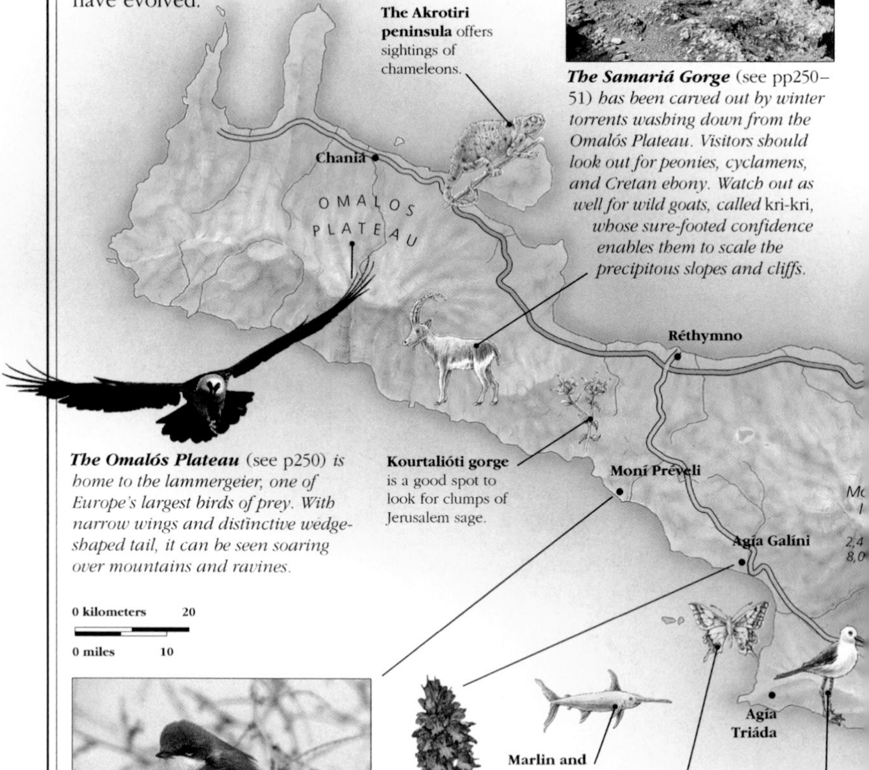

The Akrotiri peninsula offers sightings of chameleons.

Chania

OMALOS PLATEAU

Réthymno

Moní Préveli

Agía Galíni

Agía Triáda

The Omalós Plateau (see p250) *is home to the lammergeier, one of Europe's largest birds of prey. With narrow wings and distinctive wedge-shaped tail, it can be seen soaring over mountains and ravines.*

Kourtalióti gorge is a good spot to look for clumps of Jerusalem sage.

0 kilometers **20**

0 miles **10**

Marlin and swordfish are the largest fish in the seas around Crete.

The Gulf of Mesará has a rough, grassy shoreline that is home to butterflies like the swallowtail.

Agía Triáda's wetlands are the haunt of black-winged stilts.

Moní Préveli (see p256) *is visited by the migrant Ruppell's warbler between May and August. With his bold black and white head markings and beady red eyes, the male is a striking bird.*

Agía Galíni (see p259) *is an excellent spot for spring flowers, and in particular the stunning giant orchid. It stands more than 60 cm (24 inches) tall and can bloom as early as February or early March.*

The colorful yellow bee orchid

The catchfly with its sticky stems

Cretan ebony, endemic to Crete

Wild Flowers on Crete

Botanists visit Crete in the thousands each year to enjoy the spectacular display of wild flowers. They are at their best, and in greatest profusion, from February to May. By late June, with the sun at its highest in the sky, many have withered and turned brown. Most of those that undergo this transformation survive the summer as underground bulbs or tubers.

Wildlife Tour Operators

Field Guides, Inc.
(Limosa Holidays),
P.O. Box 160723, Austin, TX 78716.
(800) 728-4953.
FAX *(512) 327-9231.*

Guaranteed Travel
83 South Street,
Morristown, NJ 07960.
(201) 540-1770.
FAX *(201) 540-8602.*

Raymond & Whitcomb
400 Madison Ave.,
New York, NY 10017.
(212) 759-3960.
(800) 245-9005 (outside NY).

Wings, Inc.
1643 N. Alvernon, Suite 105,
Tucson, AZ 85712.
(520) 749-1967.

Mália (see pp272–3) *is one of the many coastal resorts on Crete that provide a temporary home for migrant waders in spring and autumn. This wood sandpiper will stay and feed for a day or so around the margins of pools and marshes.*

Mount Díkti's slopes are covered in wild flowers in spring, including Cretan bee orchids.

Dolphins can be spotted from northern headlands.

Eloúnta has salt pans that are much favored by avocets.

Siteía's *precipitous cliffs* (see p276) *are the habitat for Cretan ebony, a shrub unique to the island that produces pinkish purple spikes of flowers in the spring.*

Lasíthi's fields are feeding grounds for colorful hoopoes.

Agios Nikólaos is a stopping-off place for migrants such as wagtails.

Geckos can be found on stone walls beside many roads in eastern Crete.

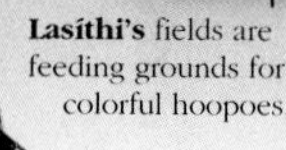
Ierápetra (see p275) *attracts the migrant woodchat shrike in summer. Woodchats feed on insects and small lizards that they sometimes impale on thorns to make them easier to eat.*

Zákros (see p277), *with its high cliffs, is where you find Eleonora's falcons performing aerobatic displays in summer.*

Exploring Crete

THE SOUTHERNMOST of the Greek islands, Crete boasts clear blue seas, sandy beaches, and glorious sunshine. Its north coast bustles with thriving resorts as well as historic towns such as Réthymno and Chaniá. Its rugged southern coast, in particular the southwest, is less developed. Four great mountain ranges stretch from east to west, forming the spine of the 250-km (155-mile) long island. A hiker's paradise, they offer magnificent scenery and some spectacular gorges. The island's capital, Irákleio, is famous for its Archaeological Museum and is also a good base for exploring the greatest of Crete's Minoan palaces, Knossos.

Card players in the vine-canopied streets of Réthymno's old town

Kythira, Gýtheio
GRAMVOUSA
RODOPOS
AKROTIRI PENINSULA
Piraeus
Piraeus
5 SOUDA
4 CHANIA
MALEME
1 KASTELLI KISAMOU
FALASARNA
POLIRINIA
GEORGIOPOLI
RETHYMNO 7
MONI ARKADIOU 12
ARCHAIA ELEFTHIRA
ANOGE
LAKE KOURNAS
IRINI GORGE
MONI CHRISOSKALITISSI
SAMARIA 6 GORGE
ARMENOI CEMETERY
MOUNT IDA 14
ELAFONISI BEACH
3 SOUGIA
IMBROS GORGE
AMARI 13 VALLEY
IDEO ANTRO
2 PALAIOCHORA
AGIA ROUMELI
LOUTRO
SFAKIA 8
9
10 PLAKIAS
FRAGKOKASTELLO
11 MONI PREVELI
AGIA GALINI 16
AGIA TRIADA 17
PHAESTOS 19
PAXIMADIA
18 MATALA
GAVDOPOULA
GAVDOS

View of the harbor, Sfakiá

SEE ALSO

• ***Where to Stay*** pp307–9

• ***Where to Eat*** pp330–32

• ***Travel Information*** pp356–9

GETTING AROUND

The provincial capitals of Chaniá, Réthymno, Irákleio, and Agios Nikólaos act as the main transport hub for each region. Crete's bus service is quite well developed, with regular buses running along the north coast road. For touring the island a car is the most convenient mode of transportation, though taxi fares are reasonable. Mountain roads between villages are now largely paved.

Large domed mosque inside Réthymno's Venetian Fortétsa

Sights at a Glance

Locator Map

The north entrance to the Palace of Knossos

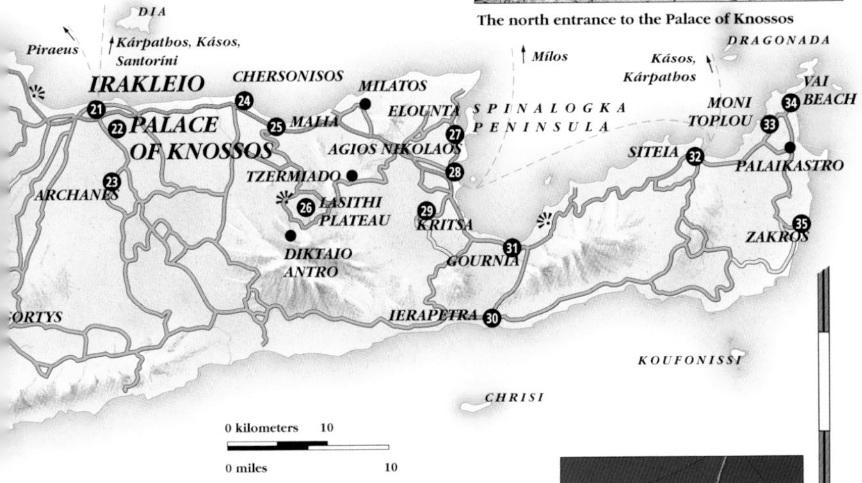

A pelican in the picturesque harbor at Siteía

A stone windmill at the entrance to the Lasithí Plateau

Key

For key to map see back flap

The magnificent beach of Falásarna with its long stretch of sand and turquoise waters

Kastélli Kisámou ❶
Καστέλλι Κισάμου

Chaniá. 3,000. Kastélli Kisámou.

The small, unassuming town of Kastélli Kisámou, also known simply as Kastélli, sits at the eastern base of the virtually uninhabited Gramvoúsa Peninsula, once a stronghold of pirates. While not a tourist-oriented town, it has a scattering of hotels and restaurants along its pebbly shore and is a good base from which to explore the west coast of Crete. Boat trips run to the tip of the **Gramvoúsa Peninsula**, where there are some isolated, and beautiful sandy beaches.

Environs: Some 7 km (4 miles) south of Kastélli, the ruins of the ancient city of **Polyríneia** are scattered above the village of Ano Palaiókastro (also known as Polyríneia). Dating from the 6th century BC, the fortified city-state was developed by the Romans and later the Byzantines and Venetians. Post-Roman walls, towers, and foundations can still be seen. The present church of **Enneninta-ennéa Martýron** (Ninety-nine Martyrs), built in 1894, stands on the site of a large Hellenistic building.

On the west coast of the Gramvoúsa Peninsula, 16 km (10 miles) west of Kastélli, a winding road descends to the spectacular and isolated beach at **Falásarna**. Once the site of a Hellenistic city-state of that name, earthquakes have obliterated almost all trace of the once-thriving harbor and town. Today a few small guesthouses and tavernas are scattered along the northern end of the beach. Small roads zigzag south from here, linking some of the isolated fishing villages along the island's spectacular west coast.

About 20 km (12 miles) east of Kastélli, at the base of the massive Rodopós Peninsula, lies the picturesque fishing village of **Kolympári**. Head 1 km (0.6 miles) north of Kolympári for the impressive 17th-century **Moní Panagías Goniás**, with a magnificent seaside setting and a fine collection of 17th-century icons. Every year on 29 August (Feast of St John the Baptist), hundreds of pilgrims make the three-hour walk up the peninsula to the church of **Agios Ioánnis Gíonis** for the mass baptism of boys named John (Ioánnis).

Palaióchora ❷
Παλαιόχωρα

Chaniá. 1,800. Venizélou (0823 41507). Elafónisos 14 km (9 miles) W.

First discovered in the 1960s by the hippie community, Palaióchora has become a haven for backpackers and package tour vacationers. This small port began life as a castle built by the Venetians in 1279. Today the remains of the fort, destroyed by pirate attacks in 1539, stand guard on a little headland dividing the village's two excellent beaches. To the west is a wide sandy beach with a windsurfing school, while to the east is a rocky but sheltered beach.

Environs: Winding up through the Lefká Ori (White Mountains), a network of roads passes through a stunning

Moní Chrysoskalítisas near Palaióchora

The Battle of Crete (1941)

Following the occupation of Greece in World War II, German forces invaded Crete. Thousands of German troops were parachuted into the Chaniá district, where they seized Máleme airport on 20 May 1941. The Battle of Crete raged fiercely for ten days, with high casualties on both sides. Allied troops retreated through the Lefká Ori (White Mountains) to the south where, with the help of locals, they were evacuated from the island. Four years of German occupation followed, during which time implacable local resistance kept up the pressure on the invaders, until their final surrender in 1945.

German parachutists in Crete, 1941

landscape of terraced hills and mountain villages, noted for their Byzantine churches. The closest of these is **Anydroi**, 5 km (3 miles) east of Palaióchora, with the 14th-century double-naved church of **Agios Geórgios** containing frescoes by Ioánnis Pagoménos (John the Frozen) from 1323.

In summer, a daily boat service runs to **Elafónisos**, a lagoon-like beach of golden sand and brilliant blue water. From here, a 5-km (3-mile) walk north takes you to **Moní Chrysoskalítisas** (Golden Step), named for the 90 steps leading up to its church, one of which is said to appear golden, at least in the eyes of the virtuous. It can also be reached by road 28 km (17 miles) south of Kastélli Kisámou. From Palaióchora, boat trips make the rough, 64-km (40-mile) crossing to **Gávdos** island, Europe's southernmost point.

Soúgia ❸
Σούγια

Chaniá. 270. Soúgia; Lissós 3 km (1.5 miles) W.

Once isolated from the rest of the world at the mouth of the Agía Eiríni Gorge, the hamlet of Soúgia is now linked with Chaniá and the north coast by a good road. Still growing as a resort, the village has rooms to rent, and a few tavernas and bars. The beach is long and pebbly. It is overlooked by the village church which is built on top of a Byzantine structure, whose mosaic floors have been largely removed.

Fresco by Ioánnis Pagoménos, Agios Geórgios

Environs: Just over an hour's walk west of Sougia, the ancient city-state of **Lissós** was a flourishing commercial center in Hellenistic and Roman times. Among the remains are two fine 13th-century Christian basilicas, a 3rd-century BC Asklepieion (temple of healing) and a sanctuary. The route to Lissós leads up through the **Agía Eiríni Gorge**. Popular with experienced hikers, plans are under way to develop the gorge along the lines of the Samariá Gorge.

Chaniá ❹

See pp248–9.

Akrotíri Peninsula ❺
Χερσόνησος Ακρωτήρι

6 km (3.5 miles) NW of Chaniá. Soúda. Chaniá & Soúda. Stavrós 14 km (9 miles) N of Chaniá. Maráthi 10 km (6 miles) E of Chaniá.

Relatively flat by Cretan standards, the Akrotíri Peninsula lies between Réthymno *(see pp254–5)* and Chaniá *(see pp248–9)*. At its base, on top of Profítis Ilías hill, is a shrine to Crete's national hero, Eleftheríos Venizélos *(see p39)*. His tomb is a place of pilgrimage, for it was here that Cretan rebels raised the Greek flag in 1897 in defiance of the Great Powers.

There are several monasteries in the northeastern hills of the peninsula. **Moní Agías Triádas**, which has an impressive multidomed church, is 17th century, while **Moní Gouvernétou** dates back to the early Venetian occupation. Monks still inhabit both. Nearby, but accessible only on foot, the abandoned **Moní Katholikoú**, is partly carved out of the rock.

Situated at the neck of the peninsula is a military base and the **Commonwealth War Cemetery**, burial ground of over 1,500 British, Australian and New Zealand soldiers killed in the Battle of Crete.

Commonwealth War Cemetery
4 km (2.5 miles) SE of Chaniá
daily.

Goats grazing on the Akrotíri Peninsula

Chaniá ❹

Χανιά

Olive oil, Chaniá covered market

Set against a spectacular backdrop of majestic mountains and aquamarine seas, Chaniá is one of the island's most appealing cities and a good base from which to explore western Crete. Its stately Neo-Classical mansions and massive Venetian fortifications testify to the city's turbulent and diverse past. Once the Minoan settlement of ancient Kydonia, Chaniá has been fought over and controlled by Romans, Byzantines, Venetians, Genoese, Turks, and Egyptians. Following unification with Greece in 1913, the island saw yet another invasion during World War II – this time by the German army in 1941, when the Battle of Crete raged around Chaniá *(see p247)*.

The Venetian Fort Firkás overlooking Chaniá's outer harbor

The Mosque of the Janissaries

The Harbor

Most of the city's interesting sights are to be found in the old Venetian quarter, around the harbor and surrounding alleyways. At the northwest point of the outer harbor, the **Naval Museum**'s collection of model ships and other maritime artifacts is displayed in the well-restored Venetian Fort Firkás – also the setting for theater and evenings of traditional dance in summer.

On the other side of the outer harbor, the **Mosque of the Janissaries** dates back to the arrival of the Turks in 1645 and is the oldest Ottoman building on the island. It was damaged during World War II and reconstructed soon after. Behind the mosque rises the hilltop quarter of Kastélli, the oldest part of the city, where the Minoan settlement of **Kydonia** is undergoing excavation. The site, closed to the public but clearly visible from the road, is approached along Líthinon, a street lined with ornate Venetian doorways. Many of the finds from the site are on display in Chaniá's Archaeological Museum, including a collection of clay tablets inscribed with Minoan Linear A script.

By the inner harbor stand the now derelict 16th-century Venetian arsenals, where ships were once stored and repaired. The Venetian lighthouse, at the end of the sea wall, offers superb views of Chaniá.

Naval Museum

Fort Firkás, Aktí Kountourióti.

daily. main public hols.

Around the Covered Market

Connected to the harbor by Chalídon, this turn-of-the-century covered market has a wide variety of local fruit and vegetables on sale each day, as well as Cretan souvenirs. Alongside the covered market, the bustling Skrýdlot, or Stilvanádika,

A tranquil view of Chanía's old harbor at dawn

The atmospheric backstreets of the old Spiántza quarter

abounds in shops selling a miscellany of leather goods, including traditional Cretan boots and made-to-measure sandals. The nearby **Archaeological Museum** is housed in the Venetian church of San Francesco and displays artifacts from western Crete including coins, mosaics, sculpture, and pottery that date from Neolithic times to the Roman era. Situated next to the museum is a small garden that contains a Turkish fountain. Set back in the square on the opposite side to the museum is the 19th-century cathedral of **Agía Triáda**.

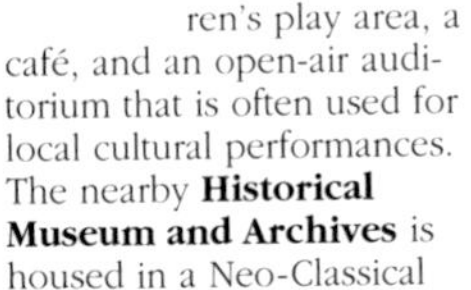

Dionysos and Ariadne mosaic, Chaniá Archaeological Museum

Archaeological Museum

Chalidón 21. 0821 90334.
May–Oct: daily; Nov–Apr: Tue–Sun. main public hols.

The Spiántza Quarter

Northeast of the market, the Spiántza quarter is a picturesque area of the old town, where houses with wooden balconies overhang the cobblestone backstreets. The tree-lined square known as **Plateía 1821** commemorates a rebellion against the occupying Turks, during which an Orthodox bishop was hanged on the spot. Overlooking the square stands the Venetian church of **Agios Nikólaos** with its truncated minaret, and nearby are the 16th-century church of **Agioi Anárgyroi**, with its early icons and paintings, and the church of **San Rocco**, which was built in 1630.

Outside the City Walls

South of the covered market along Tzanakáki are the **Public Gardens**. They were laid out in the 19th century by a Turkish *pasha*. The gardens include a zoo, which houses a few animals, including the *kri-kri* (the Cretan wild goat). The gardens also offer a children's play area, a café, and an open-air auditorium that is often used for local cultural performances. The nearby **Historical Museum and Archives** is housed in a Neo-Classical building and is devoted to the Cretan preoccupation with rebellions and invasions. Its exhibits include photographs and letters of the famous statesman Eleftérios Venizélos (1864–1936), and many other historical records.

Visitors' Checklist

Chaniá. *50,000. 16 km (10 miles) E of Chaniá. Soúda bay. Kydonías (long distance), Plateía Agoras (around Chaniá). Kriári 40 (0821 92943). Mon–Thu, Sat (veg & clothes). Nautical Week (end June). Agía Marína 9 km (6 miles) W; Plataniás 11 km (7 miles) W.*

Historical Museum and Archives

Sfakianáki 20. *0821 52606.*
Mon–Fri. main public hols.

Environs: A series of sandy beaches stretches west from Chaniá all the way to the agricultural town of Tavronítis, 21 km (13 miles) away. A short walk west of Chaniá, the sandy beach of **Agioi Apóstoloi** is quieter and less developed than the city beaches.

Farther west, the well-tended **German War Cemetery** stands witness to the airborne landing at Máleme of the German army in 1941 *(see p247)*. Built into the side of a hill, the peaceful setting is home to over 4,000 graves whose simple stone markers look out over the Mediterranean. A small pavilion by the entrance to the cemetery houses a display commemorating the event.

German War Cemetery

19 km (12 miles) W of Chaniá.
0821 62296. daily.

The sandy beach of Agioi Apóstoloi, a short walk west of Chaniá

Samariá Gorge ❻

Φαράγγι της Σαμαριάς

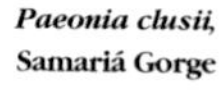

***Paeonia clusii*, Samariá Gorge**

THE MOST spectacular landscape in Crete lies along the Samariá Gorge, the longest ravine in Europe. When the gorge was established as a national park in 1962, the inhabitants of pastoral Samariá village moved elsewhere, leaving behind the tiny chapels seen today Starting from the Xylóskalo, 44 km (27 miles) south of Chaniá, a well-trodden trail leads down a tortuous 18-km (11-mile) course to the seaside village of Agía Rouméli. The walk takes from five to seven hours. Water fountains can be found en route and sturdy shoes should be worn.

Facing east across the spectacular Samariá Gorge

Omalós Plateau

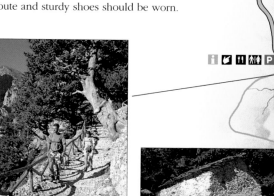

★ Xylóskalo (Wooden Stairs)

The Samariá Gorge is reached via the Xylóskalo, a zigzag path with wooden handrails that drops a staggering 1,000 m (3,280 ft) in the first 2 km (1 mile) of the walk.

Agios Nikólaos

This tiny chapel nestles under the shade of pines and cypresses near the bottom of the Xylóskalo.

THE KRI-KRI (CRETAN WILD GOAT)

Found in only a few areas of Crete, notably the Samariá Gorge, the Cretan wild goat is thought to be a truly wild relative of the all-too-numerous feral goats that are found throughout the Mediterranean region, as well as in other parts of the world. The Cretan wild goat is nimble and sure-footed on rugged terrain, an attribute that helps guard against attacks by predators. Mature adults have attractively marked coats and horns with three rings along their length.

A kri-kri on rocky terrain

0 kilometers 2

0 miles 1

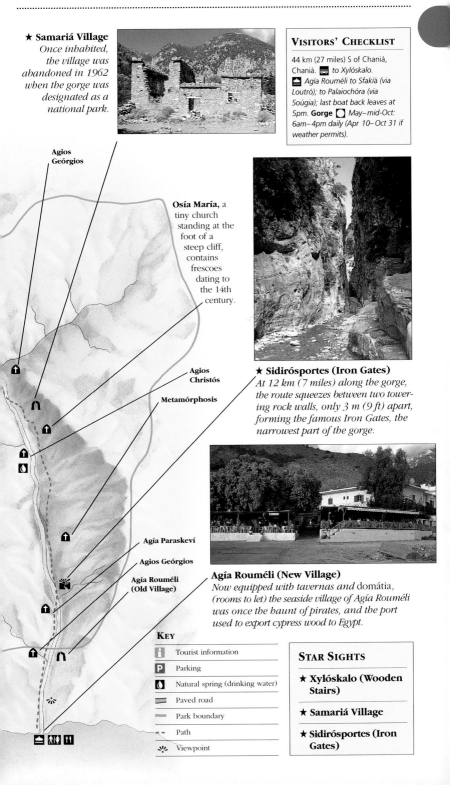

★ Samariá Village
Once inhabited, the village was abandoned in 1962 when the gorge was designated as a national park.

VISITORS' CHECKLIST

44 km (27 miles) S of Chaniá, Chaniá. *to Xylóskalo.* *Agía Rouméli to Sfakiá (via Loutró); to Palaiochóra (via Soúgia); last boat back leaves at 5pm.* **Gorge** *May–mid-Oct: 6am–4pm daily (Apr 10–Oct 31 if weather permits).*

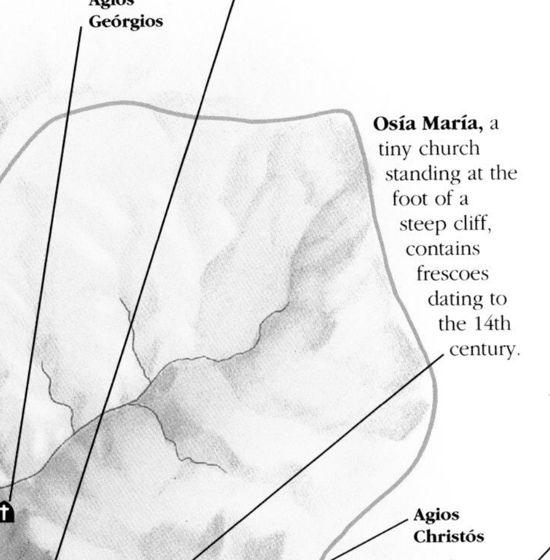

Osía María, a tiny church standing at the foot of a steep cliff, contains frescoes dating to the 14th century.

★ Sidirósportes (Iron Gates)
At 12 km (7 miles) along the gorge, the route squeezes between two towering rock walls, only 3 m (9 ft) apart, forming the famous Iron Gates, the narrowest part of the gorge.

Agía Rouméli (New Village)
Now equipped with tavernas and domátia, *(rooms to let) the seaside village of Agía Rouméli was once the haunt of pirates, and the port used to export cypress wood to Egypt.*

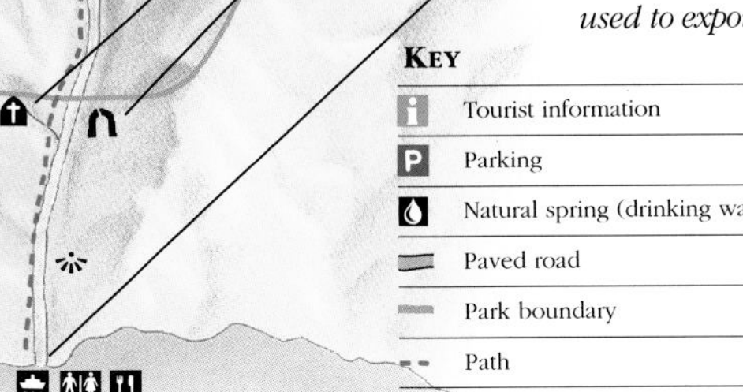

KEY

- Tourist information
- Parking
- Natural spring (drinking water)
- Paved road
- Park boundary
- Path
- Viewpoint

STAR SIGHTS

- **★ Xylóskalo (Wooden Stairs)**
- **★ Samariá Village**
- **★ Sidirósportes (Iron Gates)**

EROTOKRITOS
EROTOCRITOS

Réthymno 7

Ρέθυμνο

Once the Greco-Roman town of Rithymna, the site of today's Réthymno has been occupied since Minoan times. The city flourished under Venetian rule during the 16th century, developing into a literary and artistic center and becoming a haven for scholars fleeing Constantinople. Despite modern development and tourism, the city today has retained much of its charm and remains the intellectual capital of Crete. The old quarter is rich in elegant, well-preserved Venetian and Ottoman architecture. The huge Venetian Fortétsa, built in the 16th century to defend the island against the increasing attacks by pirates, overlooks the picturesque harbor with its charming 13th-century lighthouse.

The 17th-century Nerantzís Mosque

Exploring Réthymno

Réthymno's bustling harborfront serves as one great outdoor café, catering almost exclusively to tourists. It is skirted along most of its length by a good sandy beach, but at its western end lies a small inner harbor. A restored 13th-century **lighthouse** stands on its breakwater.

The **Fortétsa** dominates the town, above the inner harbor. Designed by Pallavicini in the 1570s, it was built to defend the port against pirate attacks (Barbarossa had devastated the town in 1538) and the threat of expansionist Turks. The ramparts are still largely intact. Within them, a mosque, a small church, and parts of the governor's quarters can still be seen, though most are now in ruins. During the summer there are open-air concerts.

Traditional weaving in the Historical and Folk Art Museum

Directly opposite the main entrance to the Fortétsa, the **Archaeological Museum** occupies a converted Turkish bastion. Its collection is set out chronologically from Neolithic through Minoan to Roman times and includes artifacts from cemeteries, sanctuaries, and caves in the region. Highlights include the late Minoan burial caskets *(larnakes)* and grave goods.

The old town clusters behind the Fortétsa, characterized by a maze of narrow vine-canopied streets and Venetian and Ottoman houses with wrought iron balconies. Off Plateía Títou Peocháki is the **Nerantzís Mosque.** This 17th-century mosque is the best preserved in the city. Built as a church by the Venetians, it was converted into a mosque by the Turks. It now serves as the city's concert hall.

On Palaiológou, the 17th-century Venetian **Rimóndi Fountain**, with lion-headed spouts, stands alongside busy cafés and stores selling fresh produce. The elegant 16th-century Venetian **Lótzia** (Loggia) can also be seen here.

The small **Historical and Folk Art Museum** is housed in a Venetian mansion. On display here are local crafts, including some brilliantly colored weaving, pottery, lace, and jewelry.

Fortétsa

Katecháki. *0831 28101.* *May–Oct: daily.* *main public hols.*

Archaeological Museum

Cheimáras. *0831 54668.* *Tue–Sun.* *main public hols.*

Lótzia

Palaiológou & Arkadíou. *0831 53270.* *Mar–Sep: Mon–Fri.* *main public hols.*

Historical and Folk Art Museum

Verdánou 30. *0831 23398.* *May–Oct: Mon–Sat.* *main public hols.*

Tavernas and bars along Réthymno's waterfront, the focus of the town's activity

◁ **Fishing boats lining the picturesque Venetian harbor of Réthymno**

Visitors' Checklist

Réthymno. 24,000. *off Plateía Karaóli.* *Kefalogiánnidon.* *Eleftheriou Venizélou (0831 29148).* *Mon at Askoútsi.* *Wine Festival: mid-Jul; Renaissance festival: mid–end Jul.*

Environs: East of Réthymno, toward Pánormos, the resort developments flow one into another, while west of the city a 20-km (12-mile) stretch of uncrowded beach ends in the village of **Georgioúpoli**. Despite wholesale tourist development, this small community retains some of its traditional atmosphere. Massive eucalyptus trees line the streets, and a picturesque, turtle-inhabited river flows down to the sea. **Lake Kournás**, 5 km (3 miles) inland from Giorgioúpoli, is set in a hollow among the steeply rising hills. Pedal boats, windsurfing gear, and canoes can be rented at the lake, and a few shady tavernas offer refreshments.

In Arménoi, on the main Réthymno–Agía Galíni road, there is an extensive late **Minoan cemetery** where a large number of graves have been excavated. Among the contents unearthed are bronze weapons, vases, and burial caskets *(larnakes)*, now on view in the archaeological museums of Chaniá *(see p249)* and Réthymno.

Minoan Cemetery
9 km (5.5 miles) S of Réthymno.
Tue–Sun. *main public hols.*

Sfakiá 8
Σφακιά

Chaniá. 400. 0825 91205. *Sweetwater 3 km (2 miles) W of Loutró.*

Overlooking the Libyan Sea at the mouth of the breathtaking Impros Gorge, Sfakiá (also known as Chóra Sfakíon) enjoys a commanding position as the last coastal community of any size until Palaiochóra *(see p246)*. Cut off from the outside world until recently, it is little wonder that historically the local Sfakiot clansmen enjoy their reputation for rugged self-sufficiency and individualism, albeit accompanied by notorious feuding and vendetta. The village today is largely devoted to tourism and makes a good stepping-off point for the southwest coast.

A Sfakiot in traditional dress

The magnificent shell of Fragkokástello set against a dramatic backdrop

Environs: West of Sfakiá, almost impregnable mountains plummet into the Libyan Sea, allowing space for just a couple of tiny settlements accessible only by boat or on foot along the E4 coastal path. The closest of these is **Loutró**, a charming and remote spot whose sheltered cove, curving beach, and little white houses with blue shutters fulfil every traveler's fantasy of a "real" Greek village. In summer a dozen tavernas and houses provide rooms and meals for tourists. Small boats are available to take tourists to nearby Gávdos island and the breathtaking bay around Sweetwater beach.

The quiet bay and whitewashed houses of Loutró

Fragkokástello 9
Φραγκοκάστελλο

14 km (9 miles) E of Sfakiá, Chaniá.
daily.

At the time of its completion in 1371 Fragkokástello stood alone on the flat coastal plain east of Sfakiá. Though little now remains of its interior, its curtain walls are well preserved. From above the south entrance, the Venetian Lion of St. Mark looks out to sea.

The fortress was designed by the Venetians as a bulwark against pirates and rebellious Sfakiots. In 1770 the Sfakiot leader, Ioánnis Daskalogiánnis, surrendered here and was flayed alive in Irákleio by his Turkish captors. Fifty years later Chatzimichális Daliánis, a Greek campaigner for independence, wrested the fort from the Turks and tried to hold it with an army of just 385 men. Hopelessly outnumbered, he and all his followers were massacred by the pitiless Turks.

Directly below the fortress is a sandy beach whose waters are shallow and warm, an ideal spot for families with children. A scattering of hotels and tavernas cater to vacationers and passing motorists.

Boats lining the small harbor at Plakiás

Plakiás ⓾
Πλακιάς

Réthymno. *100.* *Damnóni 3 km (2 miles) E.*

UNTIL RECENTLY just a simple fishing harbor serving the villages of Mýrthios and Selliá, Plakiás has grown into a full-scale resort with all the usual facilities. Its gray sandy beach is nearly 2 km (1 mile) long. Sited at the mouth of the Kotsyfoú Gorge, Plakiás makes an excellent base for exploring the region, as it has good road connections in all directions.

ENVIRONS: A 5-minute drive, or a scenic walk around the headland, leads east to **Damnóni** beach. Tiny coves beyond it offer good swimming. Vacation apartments are being built on the adjoining hill. Quiet **Soúda** beach lies 3 km (2 miles) west of Plakiás.

Moní Préveli ⓫
Μονή Πρέβελη

14 km (9 miles) E of Plakiás, Réthymno. *0832 31246.* *daily.* *museum only.*

ACCESSIBLE BY road through the Kourtaliótiko Gorge, the working monastery of Préveli stands in an isolated but beautiful spot overlooking the sea. It played a prominent role in the evacuation of Allied forces from nearby beaches during World War II *(see p247)*.

The buildings cluster around a large central courtyard dating from 1731. There is a 19th-century church and a small museum displaying religious artifacts, including silver candlesticks and some highly decorative robes. Farther inland, the original 16th-century **Moní Agíou Ioánnou** (now known as Káto Préveli) was founded by Abbot Préveli and abandoned in the 17th century in favor of the more strategic position of the present monastery. About 1 km (0.5 mile) east of Moní Préveli, a steep path leads to **Préveli** beach (also known as Kourtaliótiko or Palm Beach), a crystal clear, palm-fringed oasis.

Venetian façade of the church at Moní Arkadíou

Moní Arkadíou ⓬
Μονή Αρκαδίου

24 km (15 miles) SE of Réthymno, Réthymno. *to Réthymno.* *daily.* *museum only.* *monastery only.*

THE 5TH-CENTURY monastery of Arkadíou stands at the top of a winding gorge, at the edge of a fertile region of fruit trees and cypresses. Largely rebuilt at the end of the 16th century, the most impressive of its buildings is the double-naved church with an ornate Venetian façade which dates back to 1587.

The monastery provided a safe haven for its followers in times of religious persecution by local Muslims. On November 9, 1866, when its buildings were crowded with hundreds of refugees, it came under attack by the Ottoman army. Choosing death over surrender, the Cretans torched the gunpowder storeroom, killing Christian and Muslim alike. The ensuing carnage created instant martyrs for freedom whose sacrifice is not forgotten. A sculpture outside the monastery depicts the only surviving girl and the abbot who lit the gunpowder. Today, a museum displays sacramental vessels, icons, prayer books, vestments, and tributes to the martyrs.

ENVIRONS: At Archaía Eléftherna, 10 km (6 miles) northeast of Moní Arkadíou, lie the ruins of the ancient city-state of **Eléftherna**. Founded in 700 BC, all that remains is a tower on a rocky ridge and a derelict Hellenistic bridge in the valley below. Northeast of Eléftherna the village of **Margarítes** is well known for its pottery.

The isolated buildings of Moní Préveli, nestled into the rocks

Tour of the Amári Valley ⓭

Dominated by the peaks of Mount Ida to its east, the Amári Valley offers staggering views over the region's rock-strewn peaks, broad green valleys, and dramatic gorges. Twisting but well-paved roads link the many small agricultural communities of the Amári where, even today, moustachioed men in knee-high boots and baggy trousers *(vrákes)* can be seen outside the local tavernas. The area is dotted with shrines, churches, and monasteries harboring Byzantine frescoes and icons. Traditionally an area of Cretan resistance, many of the Amári villages were destroyed during World War II.

Detail from the church of the Panagía at Mýronas

Olive groves in the Amári Valley

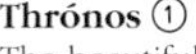

Thrónos ①
The beautifully frescoed church of the Panagía at Thrónos dates back to the 14th century. It still bears traces of mosaics from an early Christian basilica built in the 4th century.

Moní Asomáton ②
The Venetian buildings of **Moní Asomáton**, now an agricultural college, stand in a lush oasis of palm, plane, and eucalyptus trees.

Amári ③
Sweeping views of Mount Ida can be seen from the Venetian clocktower in the center of Amári. Just outside the village, the church of Agía Anna shelters the island's oldest frescoes, dated 1225.

Vizári ④
Just west of the village of Vizári are the ruins of an early Christian basilica dating from the 6th century.

Ano Méros ⑤
A large marble war memorial just outside Ano Méros depicts a woman hewing out the names of World War II resistance heroes.

Kardáki ⑥
The 13th-century ruined church of Agios Ioánnis Theológos stands by the roadside north of Kardáki.

Gerakári ⑦
Gerakári is famous for its fresh and bottled cherries and cherry brandy.

Mýronas ⑧
At the center of Mýronas is the Venetian-style church of the Panagía with its early 14th-century frescoes.

RETHYMNO
Agía Foteiní
Monastiráki
Opsigiás
Plátania
Fourfourás
Vrýses
Plat̄ys
SPILI
AGIA GALINI
Apodoúlou

Key

Tour route

Other roads

Viewpoint

0 kilometers 5

0 miles 2

Tips for Drivers

Length: *92 km (57 miles).*
Stopping-off points: *There are local tavernas in every village en route. The taverna at Ano Méros offers spectacular views over the valley. Opposite the ruined church outside Kardáki is a shaded area and water fountain, an ideal stop in the heat of summer* (see also p360).

Mount Ida ⓮

Ψηλορείτης

Réthymno. 🚌 *to Anógeia & Kamáres.*

At 2,456 m (8,060 ft) the soaring peaks of Mount Ida (or Psiloreítis) are the crowning glory of the massive Psiloreítis range. The highest mountain in Crete, it is home to many sanctuaries, including the famous Idaian Cave.

From Anógeia, a paved road leads to the **Nída Plateau,** a journey of 23 km (14 miles) through rocky terrain, punctuated by the occasional stone shepherd's hut. Here a lone taverna caters to visitors en route to the **Idaian Cave**, a further 20-minute hike up the hill. This huge cavern, where Zeus was reared, has yielded artifacts, including some remarkable bronze shields dating from c.700 BC. Some of the artifacts can be seen in the Irákleio Archaeological Museum *(see pp266–7)*. From the plateau, marked trails lead up to the peak of **Mount Ida,** and a short distance away a tiny ski resort operates on weekends, conditions permitting, from December to March.

On the mountain's southern face, a 3-hour scramble from Kamáres village leads to the **Kamáres Cave**. Here the famous Minoan pottery known as Kamáres ware was discovered, and examples are now on display in the Irákleio Archaeological Museum.

Cretan Caves and the Myth of Zeus

The island of Crete is home to 4,700 caves and potholes of which some 2,000 have been explored. From Neolithic times, caves have been used as cult centers by successive religions and have yielded many archaeological treasures. Bound up with ancient Cretan mythology, the Diktian *(see p273)* and Idaian caves are two of the island's most visited. According to legend, Rhea gave birth to the infant god Zeus in the Diktian Cave where he was protected by *kourítes* (warriors) and nurtured by a goat. He was then concealed and raised in the Idaian Cave to protect him from his father, Kronos, who had swallowed his other offspring after a warning that he would be dethroned by one of his sons. The Idaian Cave was an important pilgrimage center during Classical times.

Stalagmites in the Diktian Cave *(see p273)*, Lasíthi

Anógeia ⓯

Ανώγεια

Réthymno. 👥 *2,300.* 🚌

High up in the Psiloreítis mountain range, the small village of Anógeia dates back to the 13th century. The village has suffered a turbulent past, having been destroyed by the Turks in 1821 and 1826, and then completely rebuilt after destruction by the German army in 1944.

Modern Anógeia runs along a rocky ridge, with its own square and **war memorial** – a bronze statue of a Cretan hero in traditional dress. Inscribed on the memorial are the most significant dates in Crete's recent past: 1821, Greek Independence; 1866, slaughter of Christian refugees at Moní Arkadíou *(see p256)*; 1944, liberation from German occupation. Tavernas, shops, and banks are also situated in this part of town.

The old village tumbles down the steep slopes into a warren of narrow stepped alleys, ultimately converging on a little square of stalls and tavernas. Here, a marble bust

The Nída Plateau between Anógeia village and the Idaian Cave, Mount Ida

Woman selling locally-made rugs and lace in Anógeia

of local politician Vasíleios Skoulás stands next to a less formal woodcarving of his friend Venizélos *(see p39)*, by local artist Manólis Skoulás.

The stalls in the old part of the village abound in locally made embroidery, lace, and brightly colored rugs, forming one of Crete's main centers for woven and embroidered goods. Nearby tavernas serve grilled goat meat and other Cretan specialties. Music enthusiasts can pay their respects at the shrine of Níkos Xyloúris, a 1970s folk singer who died at an early age and whose little whitewashed house overlooks the main square.

Agía Galíni ⓰

Αγία Γαλήνη

Réthymno. 1,040. Agía Galíni.

FORMERLY A FISHING village situated at the southern end of the Amári Valley, Agía Galíni is today a full-blown tourist resort. The original village, now only a handful of old houses and narrow streets, is dwarfed by the mass of vacation apartments stretching up the coast. The harbor front is alive with busy tavernas snuggled between the water and cliffs. Just beyond the harbor, the small sandy beach is popular with sunbathers.

ENVIRONS: Taxi boat trips sail daily from Agía Galíni's harbor to the neighboring beaches of **Agios Geórgios** and **Agios Pávlos** and, farther still, to **Préveli** beach at Moní Préveli *(see p256)*. There are also daily excursions to the **Paximádia Islands**, where there are good sandy beaches.

Agía Triáda ⓱

Αγία Τριάδα

3 km (2 miles) W of Phaestos, Irákleio. to Phaestos. 0892 91360. daily. main public hols. Kómo 10 km (6 miles) SW; Mátala 15 km (9 miles) SW.

THE MINOAN VILLA of Agía Triáda was excavated by the Italians from 1902 to 1914. An L-shaped structure, it was built around 1700 BC, the time of the Second Palace Period *(see p271)*, over earlier houses. Its private apartments and public reception rooms are located in the angle of the L, overlooking a road that may have led to the sea. Gypsum facing and magnificent frescoes used to adorn the walls of these rooms. Rich Minoan treasures, including the carved stone Harvester Vase, Boxer Rhyton (jug), and Chieftain Cup, were all found in this area and are on display at the Irákleio Archaeological Museum *(see pp266–7)*. Evidence of the villa's importance is provided by a find of clay seals and rare tablets bearing the undeciphered Minoan Linear A script.

Following the villa's destruction by fire in around 1400 BC, a Mycenaean megaron (hall) was built on the site. The ruined settlement to the north, with its unique porticoed row of shops, dates mostly from this period, as does the magnificent painted sarcophagus that was found in the cemetery to the north. The paintwork on the sarcophagus depicts a burial procession; it can be seen in the Irákleio Archaeological Museum.

Agía Triáda archaeological site

ENVIRONS: At the village of Vóroi, 6 km (4 miles) northeast of Agía Triáda, is the fascinating **Museum of Cretan Ethnology**. Displayed here is a well-labeled collection of tools and materials used in the everyday life of rural Crete up to the early 20th century.

Museum of Cretan Ethnology

0892 91394. Apr–Oct: daily; Nov–Mar: Mon–Fri. main public hols.

Agía Galíni resort, nestled into the rocks at the foot of the Amári Valley

Mátala's town beach flanked by sandstone cliffs

Mátala 18

Μάταλα

Irákleio. *132.* *Kalamáki 5 km (3 miles) N; Léntas 24 km (15 miles) SE.*

CLUSTERED AROUND an idyllic sweeping bay, Mátala remained a small fishing hamlet until the tourist boom of the 1960s, when it was transformed into a pulsating resort. Hotels, bars, and restaurants abound in the lively town center, and development here is steadily on the increase.

Despite present appearances, Mátala has not passed untouched by history. Homer described Menelaos, husband of Helen of Troy *(see p50)*, being shipwrecked here on his way home from Troy. During Hellenistic times, around 220 BC, Mátala served as the port for the ancient city-state of Górtys. The resort's pitted sandstone cliffs, looming dramatically over the town beach, were originally carved out for use as tombs in the Roman era. Later they were extended as cave dwellings for early Christians, shepherds, and recently hippies.

ENVIRONS: The area around Mátala has some beautiful beaches, including the bay of **Kaloí Liménes** to the southeast. This was said to have been the landing place of St. Paul the Apostle on his way to Egypt. To the north, a sandy track leads to **Kómmos**, one of the best sandy beaches on the south coast. In this magnificent setting lay the Minoan settlement of Kómmos, thought to have been a major port serving Phaestos *(see pp262–3)*. The extensive site is currently under excavation.

Boat excursions run daily from Mátala to the Paximádia islands in the bay and to palm-fringed Préveli beach *(see p256)* farther west. There are also several bus tours to the important archaeological sites of Phaestos, Agía Triáda *(see p259)*, and Górtys.

Phaestos 19

See pp262–3.

Górtys 20

Γόρτυς

Irákleio. *0892 31144.* *daily.* *main public hols.*

A SETTLEMENT from Minoan through to Christian times, the ancient city-state of Górtys began to flourish under Dorian rule during the 6th century BC. Following its defeat of Phaestos in the 2nd century BC, Górtys became the most important city on Crete. Its preeminence was sealed following the Roman invasion of 65 BC, when Górtys was appointed capital of the newly created Roman province of Crete and Cyrene (modern-day Libya). Górtys continued to flourish under Byzantine rule, strategically sited at the point where a tributary of the ancient river Lethe (today's Mitropolianós) flowed into the fertile Messará Plain, with coastal ports to the west and south. It was not until the late 7th century AD that the great city was destroyed by Arab invaders.

Statue at the ancient site of Górtys

Today, the most visited ruins of this very extensive site lie to the north of the main road.

THE LAW CODE OF GORTYS

Section of the Law Code of Górtys, housed in the odeion, Górtys

The most extensive set of early written laws in the Greek world was found at the archaeological site of ancient Górtys and dates from c.500 BC. Each stone slab of the Górtys Code contains 12 columns of inscriptions in a Doric Cretan dialect. There is a total of 600 lines which read alternately from left to right and from right to left (a style known as *boustrophedon*, literally "ox-turning"). The laws were on display to the public and related to domestic matters including marriage, divorce, adoption, the obligations and rights of slaves, and the sale and division of property.

The *bema* (area behind altar) of Agios Títos basilica, Górtys

Exploring the Ruins

A parking area, ticket booth, and café are located near the entrance to the site. Immediately beyond stand the remains of the 6th-century basilica of **Agios Títos**, once an impressive, three-aisled edifice whose floor plan is still clearly visible. In its heyday it was the premier Christian church of Crete, traditionally held to be the burial place of St. Titus, first bishop and patron saint of Crete, who was sent by St. Paul to convert the heathens. Behind the basilica is an area thought to be a Greek **agora** (market place). Beyond this stand the semicircular tiered benches of the Roman **odeion**, originally used for concerts and now home to the famous stone slabs inscribed with the Law Code of Górtys.

Behind the odeion, a path leads up to the **acropolis** hill above Górtys, where a post-Minoan settlement was built around 1000 BC. Parts of the fortifications still remain. On the east slope of the hill are the foundations of the 7th-century BC **Temple of Athena**. A statue and other votive objects found at a sacrificial altar lower down are in Irákleio Historical Museum *(see p264)*.

To the south of the main road, an extensive area of Roman Górtys remains only partially excavated. Standing in a grove of old olive trees is the 7th-century BC **Temple of Pythian Apollo**, to which a monumental altar was added in Hellenistic times. The temple was converted into a Christian basilica in the 2nd century AD and remained important until AD 600, when it was superseded by the basilica of Agios Títos. At the far end of the site are the ruins of the 1st-century AD **praetorium**, the grand palace of the Roman provincial governor.

Environs: East of Górtys, in the nearby village of **Agioi Déka**, is the 13th-century Byzantine church of the same name. It was built on the spot where ten early Christian Cretans were martyred in AD 250 for their opposition to the Roman emperor, Decius. In the nave of the church is an icon portraying the ten marytrs.

13th-century icon of the ten martyrs, Agioi Déka church

North of Górtys, a scenic drive heads to the mountain village of **Zarós**, a surprisingly green oasis famous for its clear spring water. From here, a clearly marked trail leads north through the spectacular **Zarós Gorge**. About 3 km (2 miles) northwest of Zarós village is **Moní Vrontísi**. The monastery's icons by Michaïl Damaskinós (c.1530–91), a famous painter of the Cretan School, are now on display in the Museum of Religious Art in Irákleio *(see p264)*.

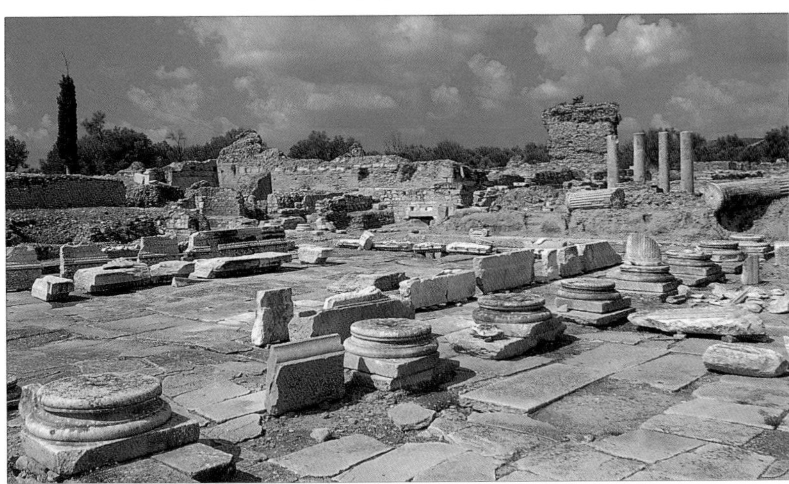

The ruins of the *praetorium*, the once-grand palace complex of the governor of the province, Górtys

Phaestos ⓳

Το Ανάκτορο της Φαιστού

Spectacularly situated on a ridge overlooking the fertile Messará Plain, Phaestos was one of the most important Minoan palaces in Crete. Excavations by the Italian archaeologist Frederico Halbherr, in 1900, unearthed two palaces. Remains of the first palace, constructed around 1900 BC and destroyed by an earthquake in 1700 BC, are still visible. However, most of the present ruins are of the second palace, which was severely damaged around 1450 BC, possibly by a tidal wave. The city-state was finally destroyed by Górtys *(see pp260–61)* in the 2nd century BC. Today, the superimposed ruins of both palaces make interpretation of the site difficult.

View of the Messará Plain from the north court

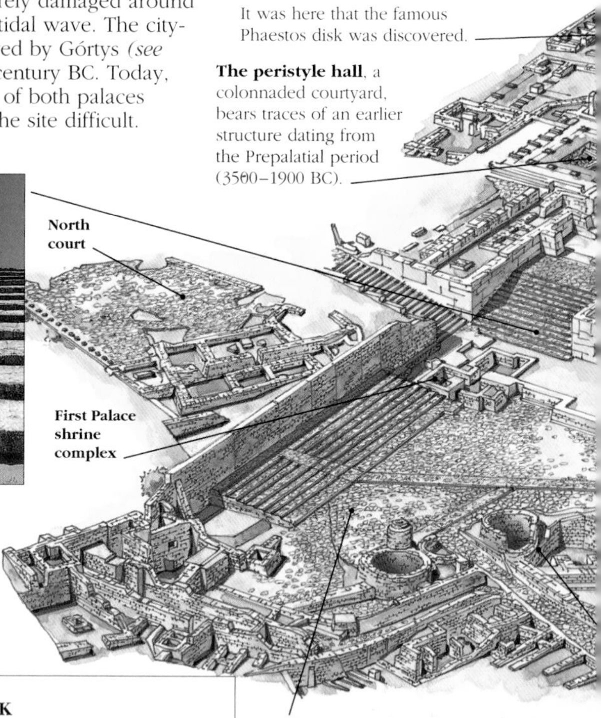

The archives room consists of a series of mudbrick chests. It was here that the famous Phaestos disk was discovered.

The peristyle hall, a colonnaded courtyard, bears traces of an earlier structure dating from the Prepalatial period (3500–1900 BC).

North court

First Palace shrine complex

★ Grand Staircase

This monumental staircase, which leads up to a propylon *(porch) and colonnaded lightwell, was the main entrance to the palace.*

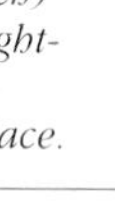

The Phaestos Disk

This round clay disk, measuring 16 cm (6 in) in diameter, was discovered at Phaestos in 1903. Inscribed on both sides with pictorial symbols that spiral from the circumference into the center, no one has yet been able to decipher its meaning or identify its origins, though it is possibly a sacred hymn. The disk is one of the most important exhibits at the Irákleio Archaeological Museum *(see pp266–7)*.

West Courtyard and Theatric Area

The ruins of the west court date to c.1900 BC, the First Palace period. The seats on its north side were used for viewing rituals and ceremonies.

Royal Apartments
Now fenced, these rooms were the most elaborate, consisting of the Queen's Megaron or chamber (left), the King's Megaron, a lavatory, and a lustral basin (covered pool)

Visitors' Checklist

65 km (40 miles) SW of Irákleio. *0892 91315.* *Apr–Sep: 8am–7pm daily; Oct–Mar: 8am–5pm daily.* *Jan 1, Mar 25, Good Fri am, Easter Sun, May 1, Dec 25, 26.*

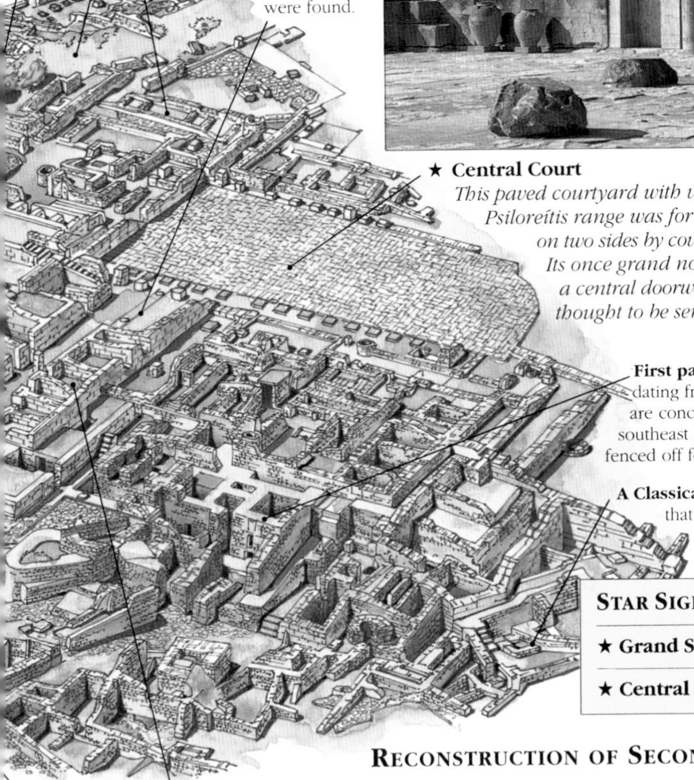

Northeast quarter

Workshops

The main hall is where clay seals dating to c.1900 BC were found.

★ Central Court
This paved courtyard with views of the Psiloreítis range was formerly flanked on two sides by covered walkways. Its once grand north façade has a central doorway and recesses thought to be sentry boxes.

First palace remains, dating from c.1900 BC, are concentrated in the southeast of the site, fenced off for protection.

A Classical temple shows that the site was still occupied after Minoan times.

Star Sights

★ Grand Staircase

★ Central Court

Storerooms

Storage Pits
Dating from around 1900 BC, these circular walled pits were used for storing the palace's grain.

Reconstruction of Second Palace

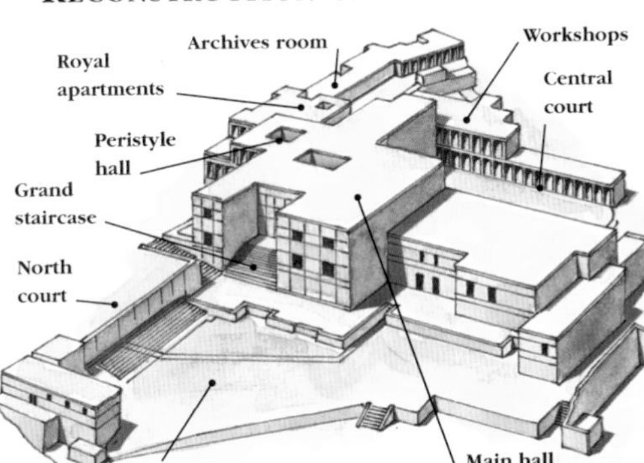

Irákleio ㉑

Ηράκλειο

A SETTLEMENT SINCE the Neolithic era, Irákleio served as the port for Knossos in Roman times. Under Venetian rule in the 13th century, it became known as Candia, the capital of the Aegean territories. Today the sprawl of traffic-jammed streets and concrete apartment buildings detracts from Irákleio's appeal. Yet, despite first impressions, the island's capital harbors a wealth of Venetian architecture, including the city walls and fortress. Its Archaeological Museum houses the world's greatest collection of Minoan art, and the city provides easy access to the Palace of Knossos *(see pp268–71)*.

Façade of the Venetian church of Agios Títos

Exploring Irákleio

At the heart of Irákleio is Plateía Eleftheríou Venizélou, a pedestrian zone with cafés and shops grouped around the ornate 17th-century **Morosini fountain**. Facing the square, the restored church of **Agios Márkos** was built by the Venetians in 1239 and is now used as a venue for concerts and exhibitions. From here, 25 Avgoústou (25 August Street) leads north to the Venetian harbor. On this street, the elegantly restored 17th-century **Loggia** was a meeting place for the island's nobility and now serves as Irákleio's city hall. Beyond the Loggia, in a small square set back from the road, is the refurbished 16th-century church of **Agios Títos**, dedicated to the island's patron saint. On the other side of 25 Avgoustou, the tiny **El Greco Park** is named after Crete's most famous painter.

At the northern end of 25 Avgoustou, the old harbor is dominated by the Venetian **fortress**, whose dauntingly massive structure successfully repulsed prolonged assaults by the invading Turks in the 17th century. Named the *Rocca al Mare* (Fort on the Sea) by the Venetians and *Koules* by the Turks, it was erected by the Venetians between 1523 and 1540. Opposite the fortress are the arcades of the 16th-century Venetian **Arsenali** where ships were built and repaired. West along the waterfront, the **Historical Museum** traces the history of Crete since early Christian times. Its displays include Byzantine icons and friezes, sculptures, and archives of the Battle of Crete *(see p247)*. Pride of place is given to the only El Greco painting in Crete, *The Landscape of the Gods-Trodden Mount Sinai* (c.1570).

Lion of St. Mark detail, fortress

A short walk two blocks southwest of Plateía Venizélou, on Plateía Agías Aikaterínis, is the 16th-century Venetian church of Agía Aikateríni of Sinai. Once a monastic foundation famous as a center of art and learning, it now houses the **Museum of Religious Art**, a magnificent collection of Byzantine icons, frescoes, and manuscripts. The most significant exhibits are six icons by Michaíl Damaskinós, a 16th-century Cretan artist who learned his craft here at Agía Aikateríni along with El Greco. Next door, the 19th-century cathedral of **Agios Minás** towers over the square.

To the east, the street market in 1866 Street leads south to Plateía Kornárou. Here, coffee is served from a charming converted Turkish pump-house, next to which a headless Roman statue graces the

EL GRECO

Domínikos Theotokópoulos (alias El Greco) was born in Crete in 1545. His art was rooted in the Cretan school of painting, an influence that permeates his highly individualistic use of dramatic color and elongated human forms. In Italy, El Greco became a disciple of Titian before moving to Spain. He died in 1614, and his works can to be seen in major collections around the world. Ironically, only one exists in Crete, at Irákleio's Historical Museum.

El Greco's *The Landscape of the Gods-Trodden Mount Sinai* (c. 1570), Historical Museum

Irákleio's boat-lined harbor, dominated by the vast Venetian fortress

The Bembo drinking fountain, Plateía Kornárou

16th-century **Bembo fountain**. East, along Avérof, Plateía Eleftherías (Freedom Square) is dominated by a statue of Elefthérios Venizélos (1864–1936), the politician central to Crete's union with Greece. Off the square, the pedestrianized Daidálou is good for shops and restaurants. Just to the north is the **Irákleio Archaeological Museum** *(see pp266–7)* and main tourist office. The east side of the square abuts the Venetian ramparts, from which there are good views.

South of the town, beyond the old city walls, the small **Museum of Natural History** deals with the natural environment of the Aegean. Exhibits include fossils, vegetation, and live and stuffed animals.

Loggia
25 Avgoústou. *081 245245.* *Mon–Sat.* *main public hols.*

Fortress
Venetian harbor. *Tue–Sun.* *main public hols.*

Historical Museum
Lysimáchou Kalokairinoú 7. *081 288708.* *Apr–Nov: Mon–Sat.* *main public hols.*

Museum of Religious Art
Agía Aikateríni of Sinai, Plateía Agías Aikatérinis. *081 288825.* *Mon–Sat.* *main public hols.*

Visitors' Checklist

Irákleio. 116,000. 5 km (3 miles) E. E of Venetian harbor. Leofóros Papadimitríou (for Réthymno, Chaniá, Agios Nikólaos and Ierápetra); Plateía Koráka (for Mátala). Xanthoudídou 1 (081 228203). Sat. Summer Festival: Jul–Sep. Amoudára 10 km (6 miles) W.

Museum of Natural History
Neória. *081 324366.* *daily.*

Environs: Traveling east by the main Irákleio–Réthymno road, a turn-off to Anógeia *(see pp258–9)* climbs to the village of **Týlissos**, where the remains of three Minoan villas were found in 1902. West of Irákleio, the road hugs the coast, passing above **Agía Pelagía**, a small resort on a sandy cove. Farther along, the picturesque village of **Fódele** claims to be the birthplace of El Greco. His house is above the Byzantine church just northwest of the village.

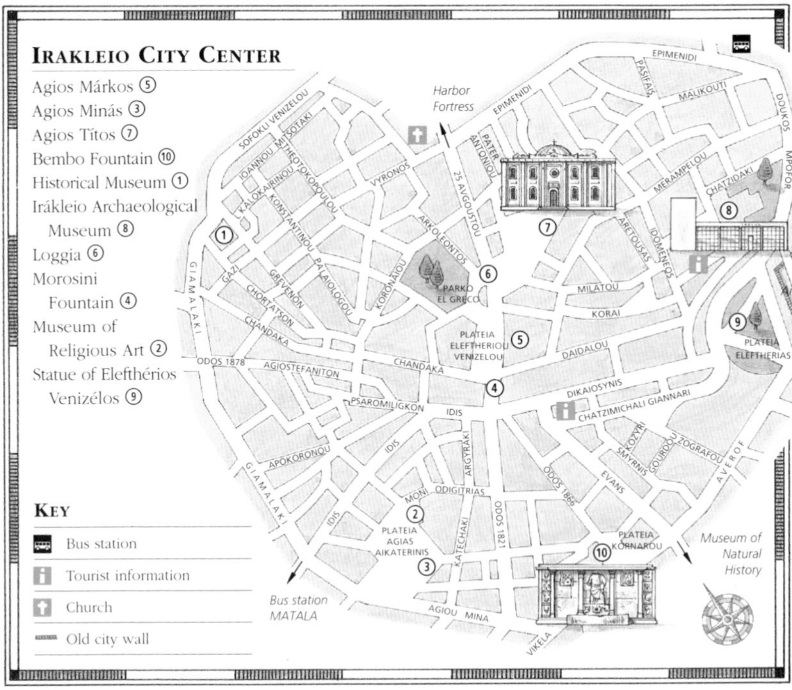

Irakleio City Center

Agios Márkos ⑤
Agios Minás ③
Agios Títos ⑦
Bembo Fountain ⑩
Historical Museum ①
Irákleio Archaeological Museum ⑧
Loggia ⑥
Morosini Fountain ④
Museum of Religious Art ②
Statue of Elefthérios Venizélos ⑨

Key

Bus station
Tourist information
Church
Old city wall

Irákleio Archaeological Museum

Αρχαιολογικό Μουσείο Ηρακλείου

THE IRAKLEIO ARCHAEOLOGICAL museum houses the world's most important collection of Minoan artifacts, giving a unique insight into a highly sophisticated civilization that existed on Crete over 3,000 years ago. On display are exhibits from all over Crete amassed since 1883, including the famous Minoan frescoes from Knossos *(see pp268–71)* and the Phaestos Disk *(see p262)*, among the most important finds from the ancient world. Finely carved stone vessels, exquisite jewelry, Minoan double axes, and the other artifacts make up only part of the museum's vast collection.

Gold Bee Pendant
Found in the Chrysólakkos cemetery at Mália (see p273), *this exquisite gold pendant of two bees joined together dates from the 17th century BC.*

★ Bull's Head Rhyton
This 16th-century BC vessel (see p59) *was used for the pouring of ritual wines. Found at Knossos, it is carved from steatite, a black stone, with rock crystal and mother-of-pearl insets.*

★ Phaestos Disk
Made of clay, the disk was found at the Palace of Phaestos in 1903.

STAR EXHIBITS

- ★ The Hall of the Frescoes
- ★ Phaestos Disk
- ★ Bull's Head Rhyton
- ★ Snake Goddesses

Octopus Vase
This fine late Minoan vase from Palaíkastro (see p277) *is decorated with images from the sea.*

Minoan vase with double ax motif

THE MINOAN DOUBLE AX

The Minoan double ax served both as a common tool used by carpenters, masons, and shipbuilders, and as an extremely powerful sacred symbol thought to have been a cult object connected with the Mother Goddess. The famous Labyrinth at Knossos *(see pp268–71)* is believed to have been the "dwelling place of the double ax", the word *labrys* being the ancient Greek name for double ax. Evidence of the importance of the ax for the Minoans is clear from the many vases, *larnakes* (clay coffins), seals, frescoes, and pillars that were inscribed or painted with the ceremonial double ax, including the walls of the Palace of Knossos. The ceremonial ax is often depicted between sacred horns or in the hands of a priest. Votive axes (ritual offerings) were highly decorated and made of gold, silver, copper, or bronze. A stylized version of the double ax also features in early Linear A and B scripts.

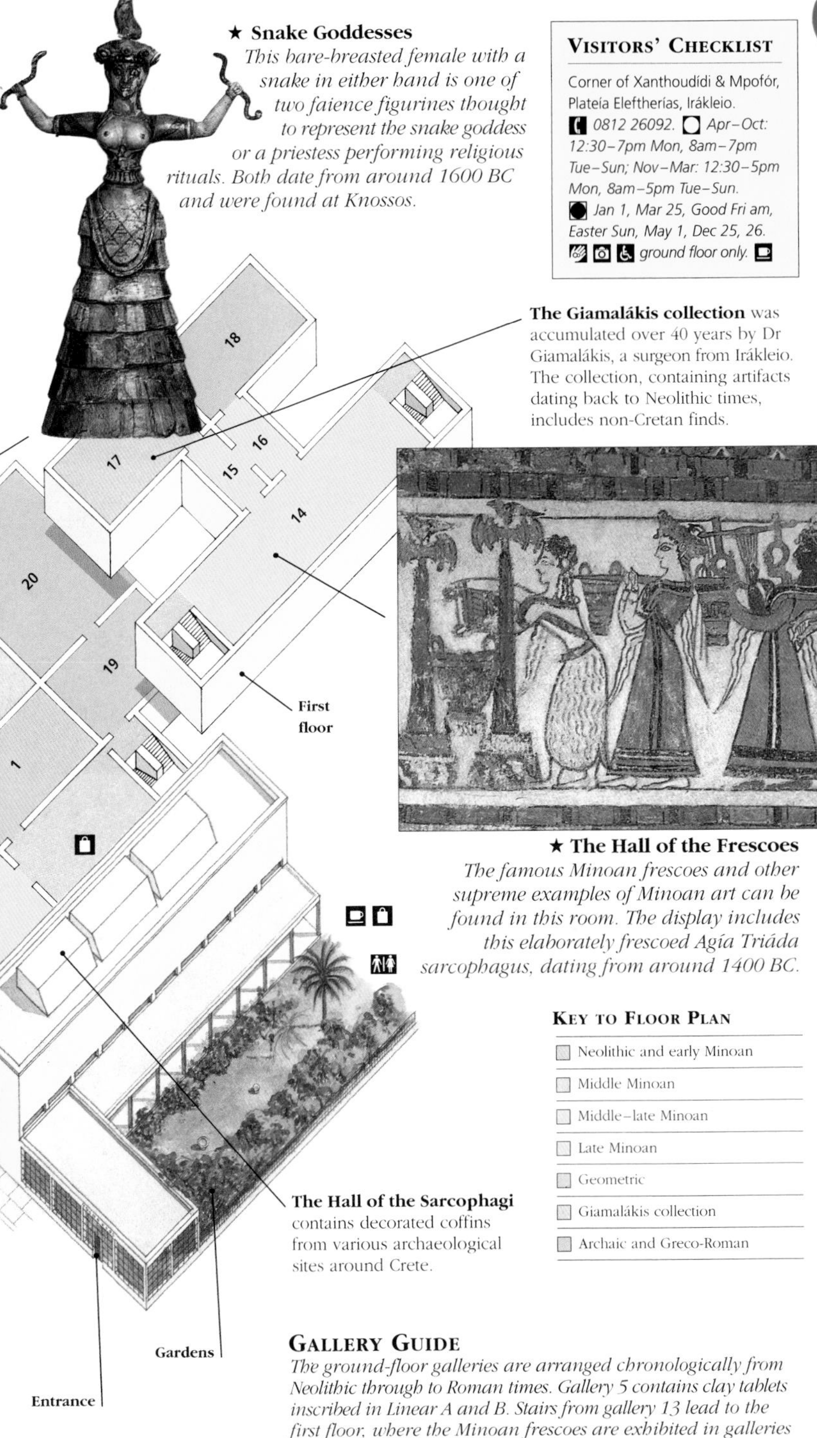

★ **Snake Goddesses**
This bare-breasted female with a snake in either hand is one of two faience figurines thought to represent the snake goddess or a priestess performing religious rituals. Both date from around 1600 BC and were found at Knossos.

The Giamalákis collection was accumulated over 40 years by Dr Giamalákis, a surgeon from Irákleio. The collection, containing artifacts dating back to Neolithic times, includes non-Cretan finds.

★ **The Hall of the Frescoes**
The famous Minoan frescoes and other supreme examples of Minoan art can be found in this room. The display includes this elaborately frescoed Agía Triáda sarcophagus, dating from around 1400 BC.

The Hall of the Sarcophagi contains decorated coffins from various archaeological sites around Crete.

Visitors' Checklist

Corner of Xanthoudídi & Mpofór, Plateía Eleftherías, Irákleio.
0812 26092. Apr–Oct: 12:30–7pm Mon, 8am–7pm Tue–Sun; Nov–Mar: 12:30–5pm Mon, 8am–5pm Tue–Sun.
Jan 1, Mar 25, Good Fri am, Easter Sun, May 1, Dec 25, 26.
ground floor only.

Key to Floor Plan

- Neolithic and early Minoan
- Middle Minoan
- Middle–late Minoan
- Late Minoan
- Geometric
- Giamalákis collection
- Archaic and Greco-Roman

Gallery Guide

The ground-floor galleries are arranged chronologically from Neolithic through to Roman times. Gallery 5 contains clay tablets inscribed in Linear A and B. Stairs from gallery 13 lead to the first floor, where the Minoan frescoes are exhibited in galleries 14, 15, and 16. Gallery 14, known as the Hall of the Frescoes, houses a model of the Palace of Knossos.

The Palace of Knossos ㉒

Ανάκτορο της Κνωσού

BUILT AROUND 1900 BC, the first palace of Knossos was destroyed by an earthquake in about 1700 BC and was soon completely rebuilt. The restored ruins visible today are almost entirely from this second palace. The focal point of the site is its vast north–south aligned Central Court, off which lie many of the palace's most important areas *(see pp270–71)*. The original frescoes are in the Archaeological Museum of Irákleio *(see pp266–7)*.

View across the Central Court toward the northeast

To Theater and Royal Road

Stairs to Piano Nobile (upper floor)

The Tripartite Shrine, formerly protected by a roof, was one of many shrines facing onto the Central Court.

West Court

Koulourás (storage pits)

West Magazines

Modern entrance

Bust of Arthur Evans

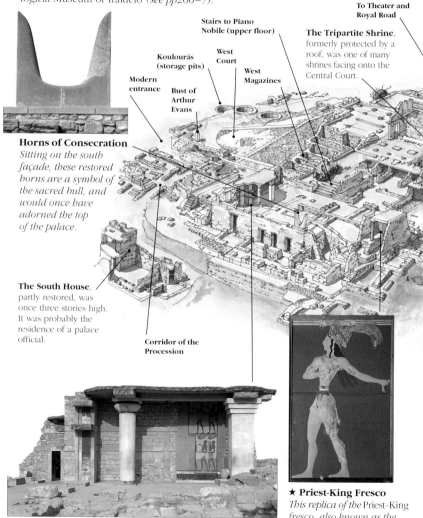

Horns of Consecration
Sitting on the south façade, these restored horns are a symbol of the sacred bull, and would once have adorned the top of the palace.

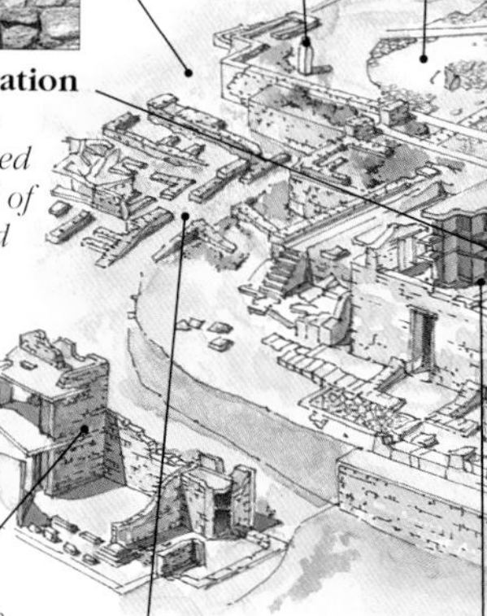

The South House, partly restored, was once three stories high. It was probably the residence of a palace official.

Corridor of the Procession

South Propylon
Entrance to the palace was through this monumental pillared gateway, decorated with a replica of the Cup-Bearer *figure, a detail from the* Procession *fresco.*

★ Priest-King Fresco
This replica of the Priest-King *fresco, also known as the* Prince of the Lilies, *is a detail from the* Procession *fresco and depicts a figure wearing a crown of lilies and feathers.*

★ Throne Room
With its adjoining antechamber and lustral basin, the Throne Room is believed to have served as a shrine. The original stone throne, thought to be that of a priestess, is guarded by a restored fresco of griffins, sacred symbols in Minoan times.

Visitors' Checklist

5 km (3 miles) S of Irákleio, Irákleio. *0812 31940.* *Mar–Oct: 8am–7pm daily; Nov–Apr: 8am–5pm daily.* *Jan 1, Mar 25, Good Fri am, Easter Sun, May 1, Dec 25, 26.*

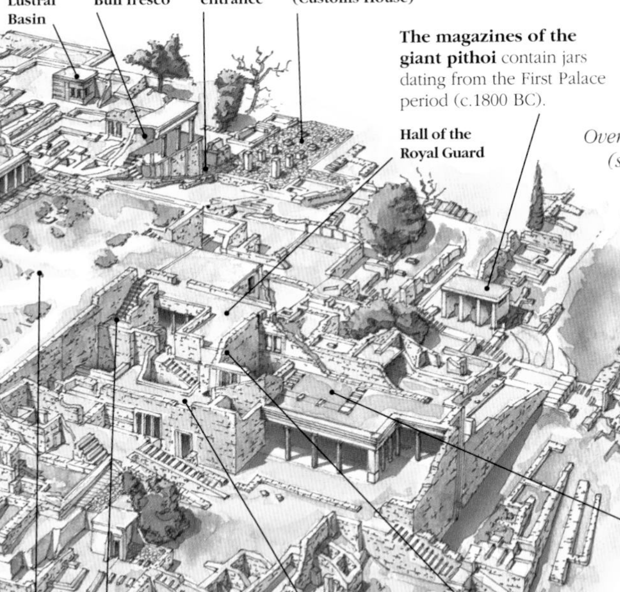

The magazines of the giant pithoi contain jars dating from the First Palace period (c.1800 BC).

★ Giant Pithoi
Over 100 giant pithoi *(storage jars) were unearthed at Knossos. The jars were used to store palace supplies.*

★ Royal Apartments
These rooms include the King's Megaron, also known as the Hall of the Double Axes; the Queen's Megaron, which is decorated with a copy of the famous dolphin fresco and has an adjoining bathroom; and the Grand Staircase.

Star Features

- ★ **Priest-King Fresco**
- ★ **Throne Room**
- ★ **Giant Pithoi**
- ★ **Royal Apartments**

Exploring the Palace of Knossos

UNLIKE OTHER Minoan sites, the Palace of Knossos was imaginatively restored by Sir Arthur Evans between 1900 and 1929. While his interpretations are the subject of academic controversy, his reconstructions of the second palace give the visitor an impression of life in Minoan Crete that cannot so easily be gained from the other palaces on the island.

AROUND THE SOUTH PROPYLON

THE PALACE complex is entered via the **West Court,** the original ceremonial entrance now marked by a bust of Sir Arthur Evans. To the left are three circular pits known as *koulourás*, which probably served as granaries. Ahead, along the length of the west façade, are the **West Magazines**. These contained numerous large storage jars *(pithoi)*, and, along with the granaries, give an impression of how important the control of resources and storage was as a basis for the power of the palace.

At the far right-hand corner of the West Court the west entrance leads to the **Corridor of the Procession**. Now cut short by erosion of the hillside, the corridor's frescoes, depicting a series of gift-bearers, seem to reflect the ceremony that accompanied state and religious events at the palace. This is further revealed in the frescoes of the **South Propylon**, to which one branch of the corridor led. From the South Propylon, steps lead up to the reconstructed **Piano Nobile**, the name given by Sir Arthur Evans to the probable location of the grand state apartments and reception halls. Stone vases found in this part of the palace were used for ritual purposes and indicate the centrality of religion to palace life. The close link between secular and sacred power is also reinforced by the **Throne Room**, where ritual bathing in a lustral basin (sunken bath) is thought to have taken place. Steps lead from the Throne Room to the once paved **Central Court**. Now open to the elements, this would have once been flanked by high buildings on all four sides.

Shield motif, Knossos

THE ROYAL APARTMENTS

ON THE EAST SIDE of the Central Court lie rooms of such size and elegance that they have been identified as the Royal Apartments. The apartments are built into the side of the hill and accessed by the **Grand Staircase**, one of the most impressive surviving architectural features of the palace. The flights of gypsum stairs descend to a colonnaded courtyard, providing a source of light to the lower stories. These light-wells were a typical feature of Minoan architecture.

Restored clay bath tub adjacent to the Queen's Megaron

A drainage system was provided for the toilet beside the **Queen's Megaron**, which enjoyed the luxury of an in-room bathroom complete with clay bathtub. Corridors and rooms in this area were decorated with frescoes of floral and animal motifs. The walls of the **Hall of the Royal Guard**, a heavily guarded landing leading to the Royal Apartments, were decorated with a shield motif. The **King's Megaron**, also known as the Hall of the Double Axes, takes its name from the double-ax symbols incised into its stone walls. The largest of the rooms in the Royal Apartments, the King's Megaron could be divided by multiple doors, giving it great spatial flexibility. Remains of what may have been a plaster throne were found here, suggesting that the room was also used for state functions.

NORTH AND WEST OF THE CENTRAL COURT

THE NORTH ENTRANCE of the Central Court was adorned with remarkable figurative decoration. Today, a replica of the *Charging Bull* fresco can be seen on site. The north

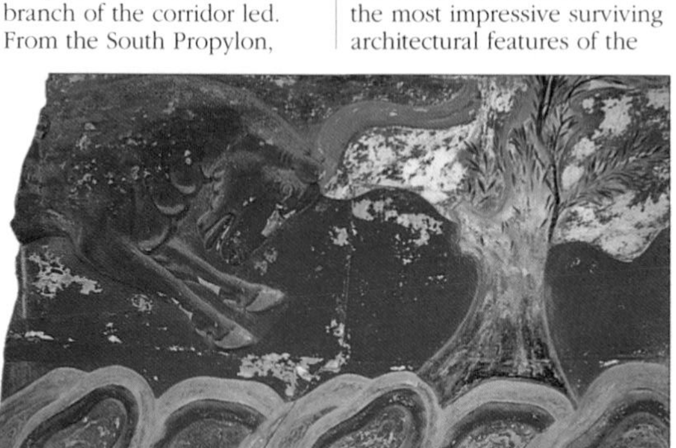

Replica of the celebrated *Charging Bull* fresco

entrance leads to the **North Pillar Hall**, named as the Customs House by Sir Arthur Evans, who believed merchandise was inspected here. The hall is an addition of the Second Palace period (c.1700 BC). Immediately to the west is a room with restored steps leading into a pool, known as the **North Lustral Basin.** Traces of burning and finds of oil jars suggest that those coming to the palace were purified and annointed here before entering. Farther west is the **Theater**, a stepped court whose position at the end of the Royal Road suggests that rituals connected with the reception of visitors may have occurred here. The **Royal Road,** which leads away from the Palace to the Minoan town of Knossos, was lined with houses. Just off the Royal Road lies the so-called **Little Palace**. This building has been excavated but is not open to the public. It is architecturally very similar to the main palace and was destroyed at the same time.

The stepped court of the theater

The History of Knossos

The capital of Minoan Crete, Knossos was the largest and most sophisticated of the palaces on the island. It contained over 1,000 rooms and enjoyed the comforts of an elaborate drainage system, flushing toilets, and paved roads. In legend, Knossos was believed to be the setting of an underground labyrinth designed to imprison the Minotaur. This half-man, half-bull was born of King Minos's wife, Pasiphaë, and slain by Theseus. This reconstruction shows the second palace as it might have looked in about 1700 BC.

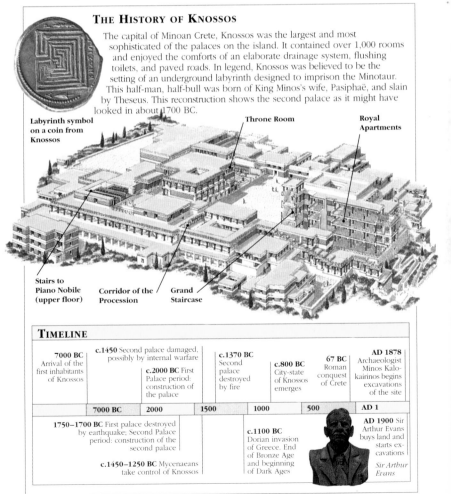

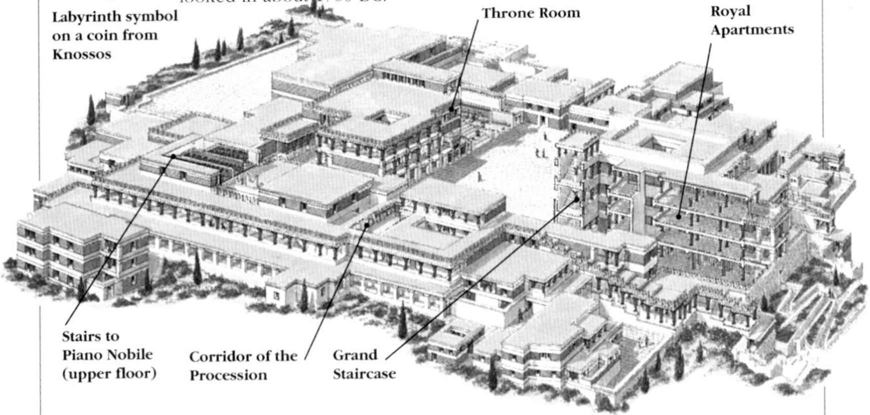

Labyrinth symbol on a coin from Knossos

Throne Room

Royal Apartments

Stairs to Piano Nobile (upper floor)

Corridor of the Procession

Grand Staircase

Timeline

7000 BC Arrival of the first inhabitants of Knossos

c.1450 Second palace damaged, possibly by internal warfare

c.2000 BC First Palace period: construction of the palace

c.1370 BC Second palace destroyed by fire

c.800 BC City-state of Knossos emerges

67 BC Roman conquest of Crete

AD 1878 Archaeologist Minos Kalokairinos begins excavations of the site

7000 BC | 2000 | 1500 | 1000 | 500 | AD 1

1750–1700 BC First palace destroyed by earthquake; Second Palace period: construction of the second palace

c.1450–1250 BC Mycenaeans take control of Knossos

c.1100 BC Dorian invasion of Greece. End of Bronze Age and beginning of Dark Ages

AD 1900 Sir Arthur Evans buys land and starts excavations

Sir Arthur Evans

The modern waterfront of Chersónisos, the busiest of Crete's package-tour resorts

Archánes ㉓

Αρχάνες

Irákleio. 4,000. 0817 51488.

AWAY FROM Crete's coastal resorts, Archánes is a down-to-earth farming center, where olive groves and small vineyards checker the rolling landscape. Lying at the foot of the sacred **Mount Gioúchtas** (burial place of Zeus, according to local tradition), Archánes was a thriving and important settlement in Minoan times.

In 1964, the remains of a Minoan **palace** were found in the town of Tourkogeitoniá. A short walk out of town, on Fourní hill to the north, lies an extensive **Minoan cemetery**. Among the treasures unearthed here was the tomb of a princess with mirror and gold diadem in place, as well as exquisitely engraved signet rings. Some of these are now on display at the **Archaeological Museum** of Archánes.

Minoan cemetery
Fourní hill. *Mon, Wed–Sun.* *main public hols.*

Archaeological Museum
Kalochristianáki. *Mon, Wed–Sun.* *main public hols.*

ENVIRONS: On the north slope of Mount Gioúchtas is the site of a Minoan sanctuary at **Anemospiliá**. Excavations unearthed a shocking scene of human sacrifice here, seemingly interrupted by an earthquake around 1700 BC that killed all four participants. Though little remains to be seen today, sensational views of Mount Ida *(see p258)* can be enjoyed from the sanctuary.

The **Kazantzákis Museum** at Myrtiá displays memorabilia of the author of *Zorba the Greek*.

Kazantzákis Museum
Myrtiá, 14 km (9 miles) E of Archánes. *0817 42451.* *Mar–Oct: Fri–Wed; Nov–Feb: Sun.* *main public hols.*

Chersónisos ㉔

Χερσόνησος

Irákleio. 4,050. 0897 22764. *Chersónisos.*

A FLOURISHING and busy port from Classical to early Byzantine times, Chersónisos (strictly, Liménas Chersonísou) is today the center of the package tour business. Amid the plethora of tavernas, souvenir shops, and discos, the harbor still retains faint intimations of the old Chersónisos. Along the waterfront a pyramid-shaped Roman **fountain** with fish mosaics dates from the 2nd–3rd century AD. Some remains of the **Roman harbor**, now mostly submerged, can also be seen here. Traditional Cretan life is recreated at the **Cretan Open Air Museum** or "Lychnostátis," where exhibits include a windmill, a stone house and a gallery. The **Museum of Rural Life**, housed in a 19th-century olive oil mill, displays a range of traditional farming tools used before the introduction of modern technology. To cool off, the **Aqua Splash Water Park** is a playground of pools, waterslides, and waterfalls.

Hard Rock Café sign at Chersónisos

Cretan Open Air Museum
Lychnostátis. *0897 23660.* *Apr–Oct: Tue–Sun.* *main public hols.*

Museum of Rural Life
Piskopianó. *0897 23303.* *Apr–Oct: Tue–Sun.*

Aqua Splash Water Park
5 km (3 miles) S of National Highway. *0897 24950.* *Apr–Oct: daily.*

NIKOS KAZANTZAKIS

From the village of Myrtiá, Níkos Kazantzákis (1883–1957) was Crete's greatest writer. Dedicated to the Cretan struggle for freedom from Turkish rule, he wrote poems, philosophical essays, plays, and novels, including *Zorba the Greek* and *The Last Temptation of Christ* (both made into movies). Excommunicated by the Orthodox church, the epitaph on his grave in Irákleio consists of his own words: "I hope for nothing. I fear nothing. I am free."

Poster of the 1960s film version of *Zorba the Greek*

Mália 25

Μάλια

36 km (22 miles) E of Irákleio. 2,700. Stalida 3 km (2 miles) NW.

THE MALIA of package-tour fame bustles noisily with sun-seekers hell-bent on enjoying the crowded beaches by day and the cacophony of competing discos by night.

In marked contrast, the less visited Minoan **Palace of Mália** lies in quiet ruins along the coastal plain to the east. The first palace was built in 1900 BC but, like all the other major palaces, it suffered destruction in 1700 BC and again in 1450 BC *(see p271)*. The site incorporates many features characteristic of other Minoan palaces – the great central court with its sacrificial altar, royal apartments, lustral basins (water pools), and light-wells (courtyards). In a small sanctuary in the west wing of the palace, the Minoan religious symbol of the double ax *(labrys)* can be seen inscribed on twin pillars.

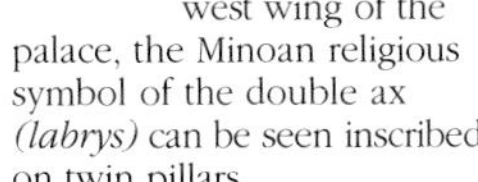

Giant *pithos* at the Palace of Mália

Beyond the palace, remains thought to be of a town are currently under excavation, and farther north lies the burial site of **Chrysólakkos** (pit of gold). Important treasures have been recovered here, including the famous gold bee pendant displayed in the Irákleio Archaeological Museum *(see pp266–7)*.

The checkered landscape of the agricultural plateau of Lasíthi

Palace of Mália

3 km (2 miles) E of Mália. 0897 31597. Tue–Sun. Oct 28, main public hols.

ENVIRONS: The fast developing village of **Sísi** is situated 6.5 km (4 miles) east of Mália. Continuing eastward, stunning views mark the descent to Mílatos. From here a well signposted trail leads to the **Mílatos Cave**, where a shrine and glass-fronted casket of bones are a memorial to those massacred here by the Turks in 1823 during the Greek War of Independence.

Lasíthi Plateau 26

Ωροπέδιο Λασιθίου

Díkti mountains, Irákleio. to Tzermiádo.

HIGH UP in the formidable Díkti mountains, the bowl-shaped plain of Lasíthi was for centuries shut off from the outside world. A row of stone windmills at the Séli Ampélou Pass marks the main entry to the plateau, a flat agricultural area lying 800 m (2,600 ft) above sea level and encircled by mountains. Fruit, potatoes, and grain are the main crops produced here, thanks to the fertile alluvial soil washed down from the mountains. A few cloth-sailed windmills are still used today to pump irrigation water.

Along the perimeter of the plain are several villages, the largest of which is **Tzermiádo**, with good tourist facilities. A path from Tzermiádo to the **Trápeza Cave** (also known as Króneion Cave) is signposted from the village center. At the west end of the village a rough road (just over an hour's walk) leads up to the archaeological site of **Karfí**, the last retreat of Minoan civilization. On the southern edge of the plain, the village of **Agios Geórgios** has a small **Folk Museum** set in two old village houses and displaying a collection of embroidery, paintings, and Kazantzákis memorabilia.

The highlight of a visit to Lasíthi is the climb to the **Diktian Cave** at Psychró, birthplace of Zeus *(see p258)*. A wealth of artifacts has been unearthed here, including votive offerings, double axes, and bronze statuettes, now in the Irákleio Archaeological Museum *(see pp266–7)*.

Folk Museum

Agios Geórgios. Mar–Oct: daily.

Diktian Cave

Psychró. daily. Sep 27, Oct 28, main public hols.

A small shrine in the multichambered Mílatos Cave

The fortified islet of Spinalógka off the coast of Eloúnta

Eloúnta ㉗

Ελούντα

Lasíthi. 1,500. 0841 41346. Tue. Eloúnta.

ONCE THE SITE of the ancient city-state of Oloús, the town of Eloúnta was developed by the Venetians in 1579 as a fortified port. Today, the town is a well-established resort idyllically situated on the Bay of Mirabello. The town is blessed with attractive sandy coves and offers a good range of accommodations.

East of the village an isthmus joins the mainland to the long strip of land forming the Spinalógka peninsula. Here, remains of the Greco-Roman city-state of **Oloús** can be discerned just below the water's surface. To the north of the peninsula is the small island of **Spinalógka** (pronounced Spinalonga) where a forbidding 16th-century Venetian fortress now stands deserted. Having withstood assault from the Turks for many years, its last function was as a leper colony until the mid-1950s. Today, boats regularly ferry tourists to the island from Eloúnta and elsewhere.

ENVIRONS: The small hamlet of **Pláka**, 5 km (3 miles) north of Eloúnta, makes for a pleasant retreat from the bustle of Eloúnta. Fresh fish is served at small tavernas on the waterfront, where boat trips are available to Spinalógka island.

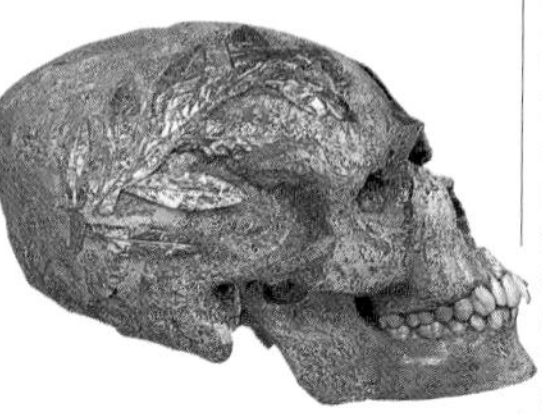

Skull and wreath, Archaeological Museum, Agios Nikólaos

Agios Nikólaos ㉘

Αγιος Νικόλαος

Lasíthi. 10,000. Koundoúrou 21 (0841 22357). Wed. Almyrós 2 km (1.5 miles) E; Chavánia 3 km (2 miles) W.

ONE OF THE MOST delightful vacation centers in Crete, Agios Nikólaos boasts a superb setting on the Bay of Mirabello. The origins of the town date back to Hellenistic times when, as Lató "pros Kamára" (towards the arch), it was the port for the city-state of nearby Lató. Having declined in importance under the Venetians, it was not until the 19th century that modern Agios Nikoláos began to develop.

Now a thriving resort, its center is the harbor and, with a depth of 64 m (210 ft), the so-called "Bottomless Lake" of Voulisméni. Overlooking the lake, the **Folk Museum** houses a colorful display of traditional Cretan crafts and domestic items. Just north of town, in the grounds of the Mínos Palace Hotel, is the tiny 10th–11th-century church of **Agios Nikólaos**, after which the town is named.

Close to several important Minoan sites, the **Archaeological Museum** at Agios Nikólaos possesses a treasure-trove of artifacts from Lasíthi Province. Pieces housed here include carved stone vases, gold jewelry from the Minoan site of Móchlos near Gourniá, and pottery, including the drinking vessel known as the Goddess of Mýrtos. One unique exhibit is the skull of a man thought to be an athlete, complete with a wreath made of gold laurel leaves and a silver coin for his fare across the mythical River Styx.

In summer, boat trips run to Spinalógka island and Agioi Pántes, an island refuge for the Cretan wild goat, the *kri-kri* *(see p250)*.

Folk Museum
Koundoúrou 23. 0841 25093. Apr–Oct: Sun–Fri. main public hols.

Archaeological Museum
Palaiológou 68. 0841 24943. Tue–Sun. main public hols.

The attractive inner harbor of Agios Nikólaos, with Lake Voulisméni in the foreground

Section of the *Paradise* fresco at Panagía Kerá in Kritsá

Kritsá ㉙
Κριτσά

Lasíthi. *2,500.* *Kritsá (0841 51205).* *Mon.* *Ammoudára 11 km (7 miles) E; Istro 15 km (9 miles) SE.*

SET AT THE FOOT of the Lasíthi mountains, Kritsá is a small village known throughout Crete for its famous Byzantine church. Also a popular center for Cretan crafts, its main street is awash with lace, elaborately woven rugs, and embroidered tablecloths during the summer months. From the cafés and tavernas along the main street, fine views of the valley leading down to the coast can be enjoyed. By November, Kritsá reverts back to life as a workaday Greek village.

East of Kritsá, situated just off the road among olive groves, the hallowed 13th-century church of **Panagía Kerá** contains some of the finest frescoes in Crete, dating from the 13th to mid-14th century. The building is triple-aisled, with the central aisle being the oldest. Beautiful representations of the life of Christ and the Virgin Mary cover the interior.

ENVIRONS: A fortified Dorian city-state dating from the 7th century BC, **Lató** flourished until Classical times. Its fortunes declined under Roman rule, when it was superseded by the more accessible port of Lató pros Kamára (today's Agios Nikólaos). Perched on a saddle between two peaks, the ancient site offers fine views of the Bay of Mirabello. A paved road with workshops and houses clustered on the right climbs up to a central agora, or marketplace, with a cistern to collect rainwater and a shrine. On the north side of the agora, a staircase flanked by two towers leads up to the *prytaneion* (town hall) where the city's archives would once have been stored. To the south of the agora a temple and a theater can be seen.

Lató
4 km (2 miles) N of Kritsá.
Tue–Sun. *main public hols.*

Lace shop on Kritsá's main street

Ierápetra ㉚
Ιεράπετρα

Lasíthi. *15,000.* *Adrianoú (0842 22562).* *Sat.* *Agiá Fotiá 17 km (10 miles) E; Makrýs Gialós 30 km (18 miles) E.*

SITUATED ON THE southeast coast of Crete, Ierápetra boasts of its position as the most southerly city in Europe. A settlement since pre-Minoan times, trade and cultural connections with North Africa and the Middle East were an important basis of the city's existence. Sir Arthur Evans *(see p270)* declared it the "crossroads of Minoan and Achaian civilizations." Once a flourishing city with villas, temples, amphitheaters, and imposing buildings, the town today has an air of decline. Gone are all signs of its ancient history, thanks partly to past pillage and, more recently, to modern "development."

The entrance to the old harbor is guarded by an early 13th-century Venetian **fortress**. West of the fortress is the attractive Turkish quarter where a restored **mosque** and elegant Ottoman fountain can be seen. Also in this area, on Kougioumoutzáki, is the 14th-century church of **Aféntis Christós** and, off Samouíl, **Napoleon's House**, where he is said to have spent a night en route to Egypt in 1798. Today it is not open to the public.

The small **Archaeological Museum** in the center of town displays a collection of local artifacts that managed to survive marauders and various archaeological predators. The exhibits date from Minoan to Roman times and include *larnakes* (burial caskets), *pithoi* (storage jars), statues, bronze axes, and stone carvings.

An almost unbroken line of sandy beaches stretches eastward from Ierápetra, overlooked by the inevitable plethora of hotels and restaurants. From Ierápetra's harbor, a daily boat service runs to the idyllic white sands and cedar forests of the uninhabited **Chrysí** island.

Fortress
Old port. *daily.* *main public hols.*

Archaeological Museum
Adrianoú Koustoúla. *0842 28721.* *Tue–Sun.* *main public hols.*

Mosque and Ottoman fountain in Ierápetra's old Turkish quarter

Goúrnia archaeological site

Goúrnia ㉛

Γουρνιά

18.5 km (11 miles) E of Agios Nikólaos, Lasíthi. *Tue–Sun.* *main public hols.* *Istro 8 km (5 miles) W.*

THE MINOAN SITE of Goúrnia stands on a low hill overlooking the peaceful Bay of Mirampéllou. Excavated by the American archaeologist Harriet Boyd-Hawes between 1901 and 1904, Goúrnia is the best preserved Minoan town in Crete. A very small palace (one tenth the size of Knosós) marks its center, surrounded by a labyrinth of narrow, stepped streets and one-room dwellings. The site was inhabited as early as the 3rd millennium BC, though what remains dates from the Second Palace period, around 1700 BC *(see p271)*. A fire, caused by seismic activity in about 1450 BC, destroyed the settlement at Goúrnia.

ENVIRONS: Along the National Highway, 2 km (1.5 miles) west of Goúrnia, an old concrete road turns left up a spectacular 6-km (4-mile) climb to **Moní Faneroménis**. Here, the 15th-century chapel of the **Panagía** has been built into a deep cave and is the repository for sacred (and some say miraculous) icons.

East along the National Highway, a left turning from Sfáka leads down to the delightful fishing village of **Móchlos**. The small island of Móchlos, once joined to the mainland by a narrow isthmus, is the site of a Minoan settlement and cemetery.

Siteía ㉜

Σητεία

Lasíthi. *7,500.* *Tue.* *Siteía.*

SNAKING ITS WAY through the mountains between Goúrnia and Siteía, the National Highway traverses some of the most magnificent scenery in Crete. Toward Siteía, the landscape gives way to barren hills and vineyards.

Although there is evidence of a large Greco-Roman city in the region, modern Siteía dates from the 4th century AD. It flourished under Byzantine and early Venetian rule, but its fortunes took a downturn in the 16th century as a result of earthquakes and pirate attacks. When rebuilding took place in the 1870s, Siteía began to prosper once again.

Today, the production of wine and olive oil is important to the town's economy, and the mid-August Raisin Festival celebrates its success as a raisin exporter.

At the center of Siteía's old quarter lies a picturesque harbor, with tavernas and cafés clustering around its edges. Above the north end of the harbor the restored Venetian **fort** (now used as an open-air theater) is all that remains of the once extensive fortifications of the town. Occupying a renovated old house near the harbor, the **Folk Museum** displays an interesting collection of local costumes and weaving.

On the southern outskirts of town, the **Archaeological Museum** displays artifacts from the Siteía district. Exhibits range from Neolithic to Roman times and include an exquisite Minoan ivory statuette known as the *Palaíkastro Koúros.* There are pottery finds from all over the region including a large collection of material from Zákros Palace.

Folk Museum

Kapetán Sífi 33. *0843 22861.* *May–Sep: Mon–Sat.* *main public hols.* *ground floor.*

Archaeological Museum

Piskokéfalou 3. *0843 23917.* *Tue–Sun.* *main public hols.*

Siteía's old quarter on the hillside overlooking the tree-lined harbor

Zákros archaeological site, situated behind the hamlet of Káto Zákros

Moní Toploú ㉝
Μονή Τοπλού

16 km (10 miles) W of Siteía, Lasíthi. *0843 61226.* *to Váï.*
Site & Museum *daily.*
Itanos 7.5 km (4.5 miles) NE.

FOUNDED IN THE 14th century, Moní Toploú is now one of the wealthiest and most influential monasteries in Crete. The present buildings date from Venetian times, when the monastery was fortified against pirate attacks. The Turkish name "Toplou" refers to the cannon installed here. During World War II, resistance radio broadcasts were transmitted from the monastery, an act for which the Abbot Siligknákis was executed by German forces near Chaniá.

Three levels of cells overlook the inner courtyard, where a small 14th-century church contains frescoes and icons. The most famous of these is the *Lord, Thou Art Great* icon, completed in 1770 by the artist Ioánnis Kornáros. On the façade of the church, an inscription records the Arbitration of Magnesia in 132 BC. This was an order that settled a dispute between the rival city-states of Ierapytna (today's Ierápetra) and Itanos, over the control of the Temple of Zeus Diktaios at Palaíkastro. The inscription stone was used originally as a tombstone. The monastery's small museum houses etchings and 15th- to 18th-century icons.

***Lord, Thou Art Great* icon by Ioánnis Kornáros, Moní Toploú**

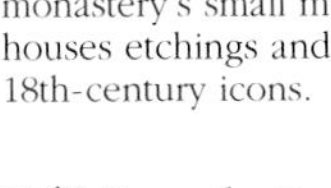

Váï Beach ㉞
Παραλία Βάϊ

28 km (17 miles) NE of Siteía, Lasíthi.

THE EXOTIC VAI BEACH is a tropical paradise of dense palm trees known to have existed in Classical times and reputedly unique in Europe. This inviting sandy cove is tremendously popular with vacationers. Although thoroughly commercialized, with overpriced tavernas and the constant arrival of tour buses, great care is taken to protect the palm trees.

ENVIRONS: In the desolate landscape 2 km (1 mile) north of Váï, the ruins of the ancient city-state of **Itanos** stand on a small hill between two sandy coves. Minoan, Greco-Roman, and Byzantine remains have been excavated (the scant traces of which can be seen today), including a Byzantine basilica and the sparse ruins of some Classical temples.

The agricultural town of **Palaíkastro**, 10 km (6 miles) south of Váï, is the center of an expanding olive business. At the south end of Chióna beach, 2 km (1 mile) to the east, the Minoan site of Palaíkastro is presently under excavation.

Zákros ㉟
Ζάκρος

Káto Zákros, Lasíthi. *0843 93338.*
Tue–Sun. *main public hols.* *Káto Zákros; Xerókampos 13 km (8 miles) S.*

IN 1961, CRETAN archaeologist Nikólaos Pláton discovered the unplundered Minoan palace of Zákros. The fourth largest of the palaces, it was built around 1700 BC and destroyed in the island-wide disaster of 1450 BC. Its ideal location made it a center of trade with the Middle East.

The two-storied palace was arranged around a central courtyard, the east side of which contained the royal apartments. Remains of a colonnaded cistern hall can still be seen, and a stone-lined well in which some perfectly preserved 3,000-year-old olives were found in 1964. The main hall, workshops, and storerooms are in the west wing. Finds from the palace include an exquisite rock crystal jug and numerous vases, now in the Irákleio Archaeological Museum *(see p266–7)*.

Váï Beach with its calm waters and native palms

A Short Stay in Athens

A VAST, SPRAWLING METROPOLIS *surrounded by rocky mountains, Athens covers 457 sq km (176 sq miles) and has a population of four million people. The city prides itself on being home to the 2,500-year-old temple of Athena, the Parthenon, as well as some superb museums. A stopover in Athens en route to the islands offers the ideal opportunity to visit the best sights in the city.*

The birthplace of European civilization, Athens has been inhabited for 7,000 years, since the Neolithic era. Ancient Athens reached its high point in the 5th century BC, when Perikles commissioned many fine new buildings, including some of the temples on the Acropolis. Other relics from the Classical period can be seen in the ancient Agora, a complex of public buildings dominated by the reconstructed Stoa of Attalos, a long, covered colonnade.

Evzone in Plateía Syntágmatos

There is little architectural evidence of the city's more recent history of occupation. With the exception of some fine Byzantine churches, particularly those in historic Pláka, one of the oldest areas of Athens, nothing of importance has survived from the years of Frankish, Venetian, and Ottoman rule. In 1834, inspired by the Classical buildings of the Acropolis, King Otto declared Athens the new capital of Greece, and his German town planners and architects created a modern city of Neo-Classical municipal buildings, wide boulevards, and elegant squares around the ancient "Sacred Rock."

The rich cultural heritage of Athens can be appreciated in some of its magnificent museums, including the National Archaeological Museum, where an unrivaled collection beautifully illustrates the glories of ancient Greece. The National Gallery of Art has a fine selection of paintings, including well-known works by both Greek and European artists.

The nightlife in Athens is excellent, with tavernas, clubs, and bars open until the early hours. Open-air movies and theaters, such as the Theater of Herodes Atticus at the foot of the Acropolis, are popular entertainment spots in summer. There is music to suit every taste, from traditional Greek to pop, jazz, and classical concerts. Shopping ranges from the flea market and the antique and bric-a-brac shops in Monastiráki, to the designer boutiques in Kolonáki, such as Armani and DKNY.

View of the Acropolis from Filopáppos hill

◁ **Lykavittós Hill rising above the spread of concrete apartment houses and Byzantine churches in Athens**

Exploring Athens

Even with only an afternoon to spend in Athens, it is possible to visit a few of the main sights. The Acropolis is the most popular attraction, along with the Ancient Agora. The National Archaeological Museum houses many finds from these sites in its fine collection of ancient Greek art. The recently renovated Benáki Museum houses a glittering array of jewelry, costumes, and ceramics from Greece and the Middle East. Shopping provides an alternative to sightseeing, whether it is exploring the bric-a-brac in Pláka or the designer stores in Kolonáki. For information on getting around Athens, see pp288–91.

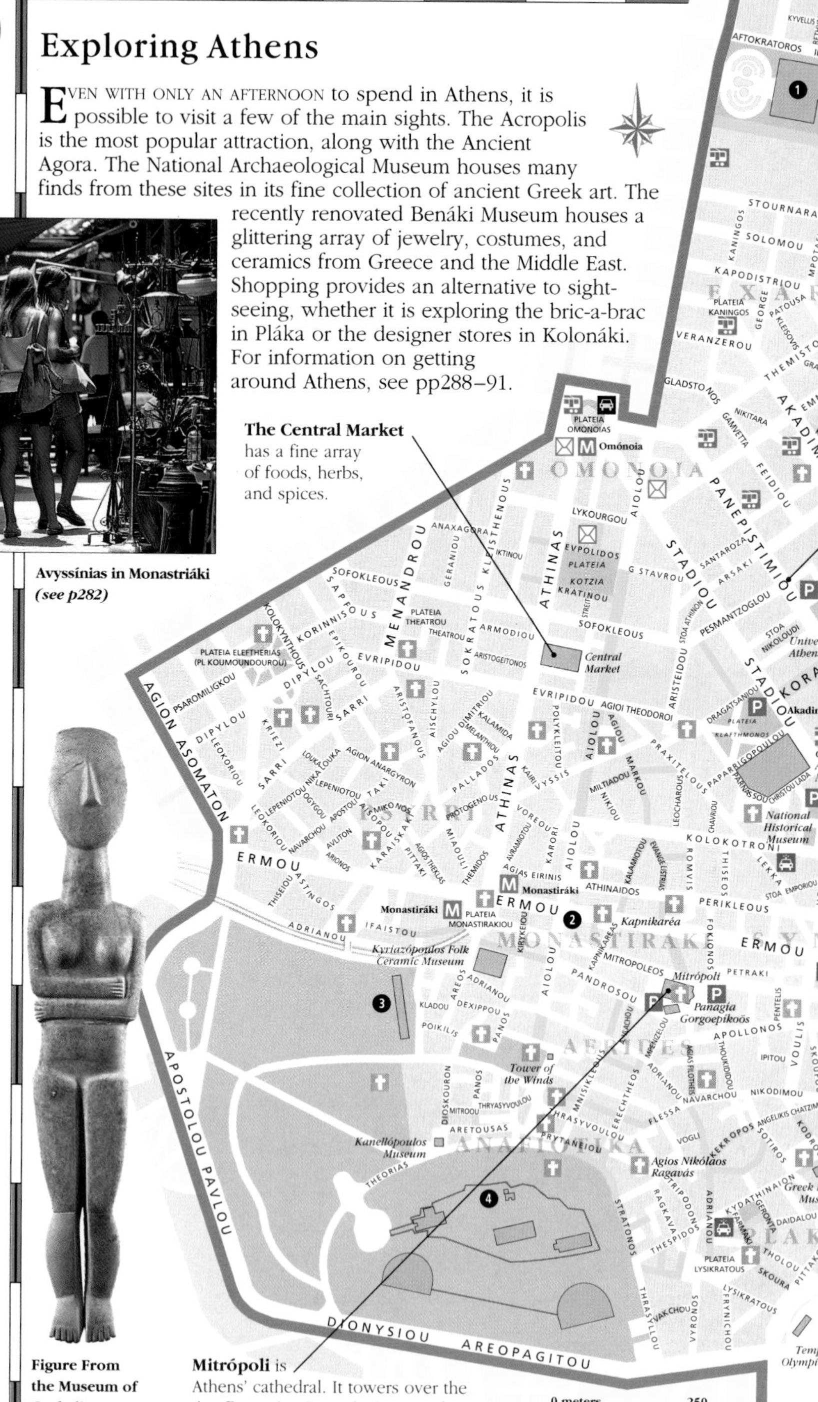

The Central Market has a fine array of foods, herbs, and spices.

Avyssínias in Monastiráki *(see p282)*

Figure From the Museum of Cycladic Art *(see p287)*

Mitrópoli is Athens' cathedral. It towers over the tiny Byzantine Panagía Gorgoepíkoös (or Little Cathedral) next to it.

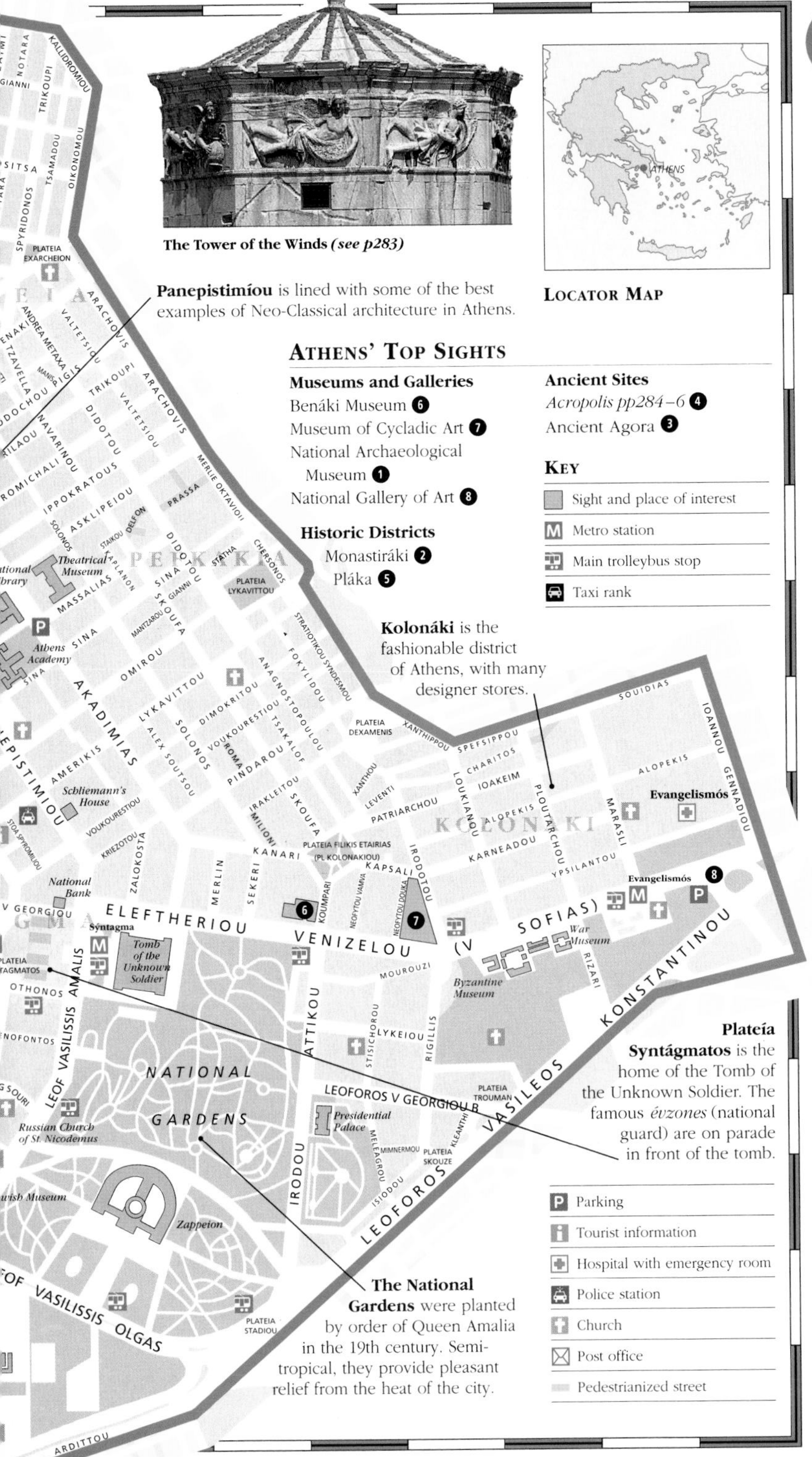

The Tower of the Winds *(see p283)*

Panepistimíou is lined with some of the best examples of Neo-Classical architecture in Athens.

Locator Map

Athens' Top Sights

Museums and Galleries

Benáki Museum ❻
Museum of Cycladic Art ❼
National Archaeological Museum ❶
National Gallery of Art ❽

Historic Districts

Monastiráki ❷
Pláka ❺

Ancient Sites

Acropolis pp284–6 ❹
Ancient Agora ❸

Key

- Sight and place of interest
- Metro station
- Main trolleybus stop
- Taxi rank
- Parking
- Tourist information
- Hospital with emergency room
- Police station
- Church
- Post office
- Pedestrianized street

Kolonáki is the fashionable district of Athens, with many designer stores.

Plateía Syntágmatos is the home of the Tomb of the Unknown Soldier. The famous *évzones* (national guard) are on parade in front of the tomb.

The National Gardens were planted by order of Queen Amalia in the 19th century. Semi-tropical, they provide pleasant relief from the heat of the city.

National Archaeological Museum ❶
Μουσείο Αρχαιολόγικο της Ελλάδος

Patissíon 44, Exárcheia. *01 821 7717.* *Omónoia, Viktória.* *mid-Apr–mid-Oct: 12:30–7pm Mon, 8am–7pm Tue–Fri, 8:30am–3pm Sat & Sun; Oct–Mar: 10:30am–5pm Mon, 8:30am–3pm Tue–Sun.* *main public hols.*

When it was opened in 1891, this museum brought together a collection that had previously been stored all over the city. New wings were added in 1939, but during World War II this priceless collection was dispersed and buried underground to protect it from possible damage. The museum reopened in 1946, but it has taken another 50 years of renovation and reorganization to finally do justice to its formidable collection. With its comprehensive assembly of pottery, sculpture and jewelry, it definitely deserves ranking as one of the finest museums in the world. It is a good idea to plan ahead and be selective when visiting the museum and not attempt to cover everything in one visit.

The museum's exhibits can be divided into seven main collections: Neolithic and Cycladic, Mycenaean, Geometric and Archaic sculpture, Classical sculpture, Roman and Hellenistic sculpture, the pottery collections and the Thíra frescoes. There are also other smaller collections that are well worth seeing. These include the stunning Eléni Stathátou jewelry collection and the recently opened Egyptian rooms.

High points of the museum include the unique finds from the grave circle at Mycenae, in particular the gold *Mask of Agamemnon*. Also not to be missed are the Archaic *kouroi* statues and the unrivaled collection of Classical and Hellenistic statues. Two of the most important and finest of the bronzes are the *Horse with the Little Jockey* and the *Poseidon*. One of the world's largest collections of ancient ceramics can also be found here, comprising the vast array of elegant red- and black-figure vases from the 6th and 5th centuries BC *(see pp58–59)* and some Geometric funerary vases that date back as far as 1000 BC.

Shoppers browsing in Athens' lively Monastiráki market

The *Mask of Agamemnon* in the National Archaeological Museum

Monastiráki ❷
Μοναστιράκι

Monastiráki. **Market** *daily.*

This area, which is named after the little monastery in Plateía Monastirakíou, is synonymous with Athens' famous flea-market. Located next to the ancient Agora, it is bounded by Sari in the west and Aiólou in the east. The streets of Pandrósou, Ifaístou, and Areos leading off Plateía Monastirakíou are full of shops, selling a range of goods from expensive antiques, leather, and silver to tourist trinkets.

The heart of the flea market is in Plateía Avyssínias, east of Plateía Monastirákiou, where every morning junk dealers arrive with pieces of furniture and various odds and ends. During the week the shops and stalls are filled with antiques, second-hand books, rugs, leatherware, taverna chairs, army surplus gear, and tools.

On Sunday mornings, when the shops are closed, the market itself still flourishes along Adriánou and in Plateía Agíou Filippoú. There are always numerous bargains to be had. Items particularly worth investing in include some of the colorful woven and embroidered cloths and an abundance of good silver jewelry.

Ancient Agora ❸
Αρχαία Αγορά

Main entrance at Adriánoú, Monastiráki. *01 321 0185.* *Thiseio, Monastiráki.* **Museum and site** *8:30 am–3pm Tue–Sun, noon–3pm Good Fri.* *main public hols.* *limited.*

The American School of Archaeology comenced excavations of the ancient Agora in the 1930s, and since then a complex array of public buildings and temples has been revealed. The democratically governed Agora was the political and religious heart of ancient Athens. Also the center of commercial and daily life, it abounded with schools and elegant stoas filled with shops. The state prison was

The rooftop of the church of Agios Nikólaos Ragavás above the streets of Pláka

here, as was the mint, which was used to make the city's coins inscribed with the famous owl symbol. Even the remains of an olive oil mill have been found here.

The main building standing today is the impressive two-storey stoa of Attalos. This was rebuilt between 1953 and 1956 on the original foundations and using ancient building materials. Founded by King Attalos of Pergamon (ruled 159–138 BC), it dominated the eastern quarter of the Agora until it was destroyed in AD 267. It is used today as a museum, exhibiting the finds from the Agora. These include legal finds, such as a *klepsydra* (a water clock that was used for timing plaintiffs' speeches), bronze ballots, and items from everyday life such as some terra-cotta toys and leather sandals. The best-preserved ruins on the site are the Odeion of Agrippa, a covered theater, and the Hephaisteion, a temple to Hephaistos, which is also known as the Theseion.

Acropolis ❹

See pp284–6.

Pláka ❺
Πλάκα

M Monastiráki. 1, 2, 4, 5, 9, 10, 11, 12, 15, 18.

THE AREA OF PLAKA is the historic heart of Athens. Even though only a few buildings date back farther than the Ottoman period, it remains the oldest continually inhabited area in the city. One probable explanation of its name comes from the word used by Albanian soldiers in the service of the Turks who settled here in the 16th century – *pliaka* (old) was how they used to describe the area. Despite the constant swarm of tourists and Athenians, who come to eat in old-fashioned tavernas or browse in the antique and icon shops, Plaka still retains the atmosphere of a traditional neighborhood. The only choregic monument still intact in Athens is the **Lysikrates Monument** in Plateía Lysikrátous. Built to commemorate the victors at the annual choral and dramatic festival at the Theater of Dionysos, these monuments take their name from the sponsor *(choregos)* of the winning team.

Detail from a terra-cotta roof, Pláka

Many churches are worth a visit: the 11th-century **Agios Nikólaos Ragavás** has ancient columns built into the walls.

The **Tower of the Winds**, in the far west of Plaka, lies in the grounds of the Roman Agora. It was built by the Syrian astronomer Andronikos Kyrrestes in the 2nd century BC as a weather vane and water clock. On each of its marble sides one of the eight mythological winds is depicted.

Tower of the Winds
Plateía Aérides. *01 324 5220.*
Tue–Sun. main public hols.

The façade of the Hephaisteion in the ancient Agora

Acropolis 4

Ακρόπολη

In the mid-5th century BC, Perikles persuaded the Athenians to begin a great program of new building work in Athens that has come to represent the political and cultural achievements of Greece. The work transformed the Acropolis with three contrasting temples and a monumental gateway. The Theater of Dionysos on the south slope was developed further in the 4th century BC, and the Theater of Herodes Atticus was added in the 2nd century AD.

The Acropolis with the Temple of Olympian Zeus in the foreground

★ Porch of the Caryatids
These statues of women were used in place of columns on the south porch of the Erechtheion. The originals, four of which can be seen in the Acropolis Museum, have been replaced by casts.

An olive tree now grows where Athena first planted her tree in a competition against Poseidon.

The Propylaia was built in 437–432 BC to form a new entrance to the Acropolis.

★ Temple of Athena Nike
This temple to Athena of Victory is on the west side of the Propylaia. It was built in 427–424 BC.

The Beule Gate was the first entrance to the Acropolis.

Pathway to Acropolis from ticket office

Theater of Herodes Atticus
Also known as the Odeion of Herodes Atticus, this superb theater was originally built in AD 161. It was restored in 1955 and is used today for outdoor concerts.

Star Sights

- ★ **Parthenon**
- ★ **Porch of the Caryatids**
- ★ **Temple of Athena Nike**

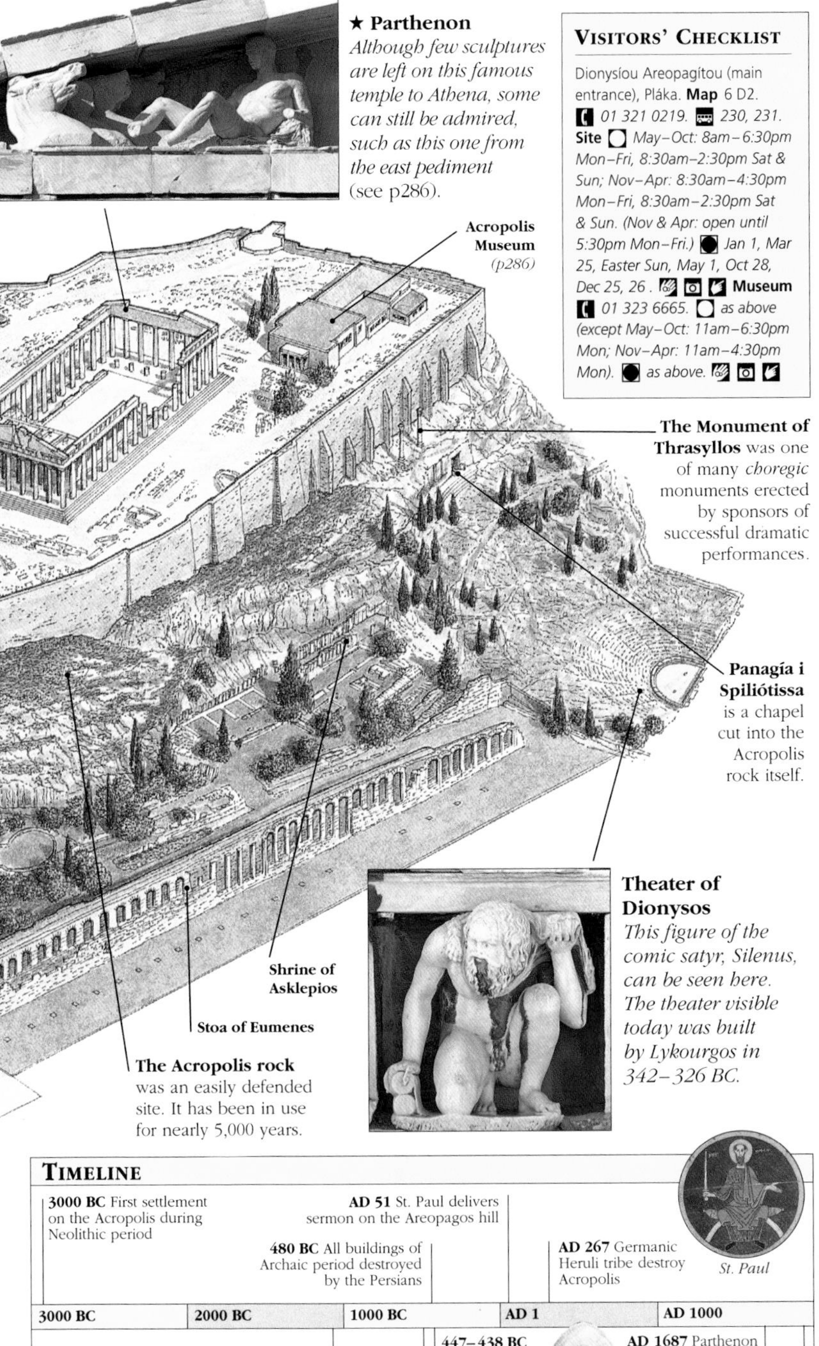

★ Parthenon
Although few sculptures are left on this famous temple to Athena, some can still be admired, such as this one from the east pediment (see p286).

Acropolis Museum *(p286)*

The Monument of Thrasyllos was one of many *choregic* monuments erected by sponsors of successful dramatic performances.

Panagía i Spiliótissa is a chapel cut into the Acropolis rock itself.

Theater of Dionysos
This figure of the comic satyr, Silenus, can be seen here. The theater visible today was built by Lykourgos in 342–326 BC.

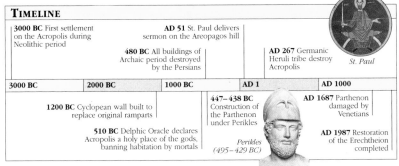

Shrine of Asklepios

Stoa of Eumenes

The Acropolis rock was an easily defended site. It has been in use for nearly 5,000 years.

Visitors' Checklist

Dionysíou Areopagítou (main entrance), Pláka. **Map** 6 D2. *01 321 0219. 230, 231.* **Site** *May–Oct: 8am–6:30pm Mon–Fri, 8:30am–2:30pm Sat & Sun; Nov–Apr: 8:30am–4:30pm Mon–Fri, 8:30am–2:30pm Sat & Sun. (Nov & Apr: open until 5:30pm Mon–Fri.) Jan 1, Mar 25, Easter Sun, May 1, Oct 28, Dec 25, 26 .* **Museum** *01 323 6665. as above (except May–Oct: 11am–6:30pm Mon; Nov–Apr: 11am–4:30pm Mon). as above.*

Timeline

3000 BC First settlement on the Acropolis during Neolithic period

1200 BC Cyclopean wall built to replace original ramparts

510 BC Delphic Oracle declares Acropolis a holy place of the gods, banning habitation by mortals

480 BC All buildings of Archaic period destroyed by the Persians

447–438 BC Construction of the Parthenon under Perikles

AD 51 St. Paul delivers sermon on the Areopagos hill

AD 267 Germanic Heruli tribe destroy Acropolis

AD 1687 Parthenon damaged by Venetians

AD 1987 Restoration of the Erechtheion completed

3000 BC | 2000 BC | 1000 BC | AD 1 | AD 1000

St. Paul

Perikles (495–429 BC)

Exploring the Acropolis

ONCE THROUGH THE PROPYLAIA, the grand entrance to the site, the Parthenon exerts an overwhelming fascination. The other fine temples on "the Rock" include the Erechtheion and the Temple of Athena Nike. Since 1975, access to all the temple precincts has been banned. However, it is a miracle that anything remains at all. The ravages of war, the removal of treasures, and pollution have all taken their irrevocable toll on the Acropolis.

A section from the north frieze of the Parthenon

The Parthenon

One of the world's most famous buildings, the Parthenon was commissioned by Perikles as part of his rebuilding plan. Work began in 447 BC when the sculptor Pheidias was entrusted with supervising the building of a magnificent new Doric temple to Athena, the patron goddess of the city. It was built on the site of earlier Archaic temples, and was designed primarily to house the *Parthenos*, Pheidias's impressive 12-m (40-ft) high cult statue of Athena covered in ivory and gold.

Taking just nine years to complete, the temple was dedicated to the goddess during the Great Panathenaia festival of 438 BC. Designed and constructed in Pentelic marble by the architects Kallikrates and Iktinos, the complex architecture of the Parthenon replaces straight lines with slight curves. This is generally thought to have been done to prevent visual distortion or perhaps to increase the impression of grandeur. All the columns swell in the middle and all lean slightly inward, while the foundation platform rises toward the center.

For the pediments and the friezes that ran all the way around the temple, an army of sculptors and painters was employed. Agorakritos and Alkamenes, both pupils of Pheidias, are two of the sculptors who worked on the frieze, which represented the people and horses in the Panathenaic procession.

Despite much damage and alterations made to adapt to its various uses, which include a church, a mosque, and even an arsenal, the Parthenon remains a majestic sight today – a powerful symbol of the glories of ancient Greece.

View of the Parthenon from the southwest at sunrise

The *Moschophoros* (or Calf-bearer) in the Acropolis Museum

Acropolis Museum

Built below the level of the Parthenon, this museum is located in the southeast corner of the site. Opened in 1878, it was reconstructed after World War II to accommodate a collection that was devoted solely to finds from the Acropolis. Among the treasures are some beautiful statues dating from the 5th century BC and segments of the Parthenon frieze.

The collection begins chronologically with 6th-century BC works in **Rooms I**, **II**, and **III** where the *Moschophoros* or Calf-bearer (c.570 BC) is displayed along with fragments of pedimental statues of mythological scenes. In **Room V** there is a pediment from the old Temple of Athena. **Rooms IV** and **VI** display a unique collection of *kórai* (550–500 BC), votive statues of maidens offered to the goddess Athena.

Rooms VII and **VIII** contain, among other exhibits, fragments from the Erechtheion frieze and a well-preserved *metope* from the south side of the Parthenon. The collection ends in **Room IX** with the four remaining caryatids from the Erechtheion, carefully kept behind glass in a temperature-controlled environment.

Benáki Museum ❻
Μουσείο Μπενάκη

Corner of Koumpári & Vasilíssis Sofías, Kolonáki. 01 361 1617. 3, 7, 8, 13. ring for opening hours. main public hols. limited.

THIS OUTSTANDING museum contains a diverse collection of Greek art and crafts, jewelry, regional costumes, and political memorabilia from the 3rd century BC to the 20th century. It was founded by Antónis Benáki (1873–1954), the son of Emmanouíl Benáki, a wealthy Greek who made his fortune in Egypt. Antónis Benáki was interested in Greek, Persian, Egyptian, and Ottoman art from an early age and started collecting while living in Alexandria. When he moved to Athens in 1926, he donated his collection to the Greek State, using the family house as a museum which was opened to the public in 1931. The elegant Neo-Classical mansion was built toward the end of the 19th century by Anastásios Metaxás, who was also the architect of the Panathenaic stadium.

A major part of the Benáki collection is made up of gold jewelry, some dating from as far back as 3000 BC. Also on display are icons, pieces of liturgical silverware, Egyptian artifacts, and Greek embroideries. The Chatzikyriákos-Gkíkas gallery is devoted entirely to the late artist's paintings and sculptures.

Museum of Cycladic Art ❼
Μουσείο Κυκλαδικής και Αρχαίας Ελληνικής Τέχνης

Neofýtou Doúka 4 (new wing at Irodótou 1), Kolonáki. 01 722 8321. 3, 7, 8, 13. 10am–4pm Mon & Wed–Fri, 10am–3pm Sat. main public hols.

OPENED IN 1986, this modern museum offers the visitor the world's finest collection of Cycladic art. Assembled by Nikólas and Dolly Goulandrí and helped by the donations of other wealthy Greeks, it has brought together a fine selection of ancient Greek art, spanning 5,000 years of history.

The museum is clearly laid out and provides a relaxed atmosphere in which to view the exhibits. Spread over five floors, the displays start on the first floor, which is home to the Cycladic collection. Dating back to the 3rd millennium BC, the Cycladic figurines were found mostly in graves, although their exact usage remains a mystery. One of the finest examples is the *Harp Player*. Ancient Greek art is exhibited on the second floor and the Charles Polítis collection of Classical and Prehistoric art on the fourth floor, highlights of which include some terracotta figurines of women from Tanágra, central Greece. The third floor of the museum is used for temporary, visiting exhibitions.

A new wing was opened in the adjoining Stathátos Mansion in 1992, named after its original inhabitants, Otto and Athiná Stathátos. It houses the Greek Art Collection of the Athens Academy. Temporary exhibitions are also on display on the first floor of the Stathátos Mansion.

Seated Cycladic figure

National Gallery of Art ❽
Εθνική Πινακοθήκη

Vasiléos Konstantínou 50, Ilísia. 01 723 5937. 3, 13. 9am–3pm Mon & Wed–Sat, 10am–2pm Sun. main public hols.

THIS MODERN low-rise building houses a permanent collection of European and Greek art. Opened to the public in 1971, the first floor is devoted mainly to European art and includes a number of works by Van Dyck, Dürer, Cézanne, and Rembrandt. Others include Picasso's *Woman in a White Dress* (1939) and Caravaggio's *Singer* (1620). The majority of the collection is made up of Greek art from the 18th to 20th centuries. The 1800s are largely represented by paintings of the War of Independence *(see pp38–9)* and a selection of seascapes. There are also some excellent portraits including *The Loser of the Bet* (1878) by Nikólaos Gýzis (1842–1901), and *Waiting* (1900) and *The Straw Hat* (1925) by Nikifóros Lýtras (1883–1927).

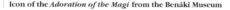

Icon of the *Adoration of the Magi* from the Benáki Museum

Getting Around Athens

Trolleybus stop sign

THE SIGHTS OF ATHENS' city center are closely packed, and almost everything of interest can be reached on foot. This is the best way of sightseeing, especially in view of the appalling traffic congestion, which can make both public and private transportation slow and inefficient. The expansion of the metro system should go some way to relieve these traffic problems but, until its completion, the bus and trolleybus network provides the majority of public transit in the capital for Athenians and visitors alike. Taxis are an alternative and, with the lowest tariffs of any EU capital, are worth considering even for longer journeys.

Orange and white regional bus for the Attica area

One of the large fleet of blue and white buses

Bus Services in Athens

ATHENS IS SERVED by an extensive bus network. Bus journeys are inexpensive, but can be slow and uncomfortably crowded, particularly in the city center and during rush hours; the worst times are from 7am to 8:30am, 2pm to 3:30pm, and 7:30pm to 9pm.

Tickets can be bought individually or in a book of ten, but either way, they must be purchased in advance from a *períptero* (street kiosk), a transit booth, or certain other designated places. The brown, red, and white logo, with the words *eisitíria edó*, indicates where you can buy bus tickets. The same ticket can be used on any bus or trolleybus, and must be stamped in a special ticket machine to cancel it when you board. There is a penalty fine for not stamping your ticket. Tickets are valid for one ride only, regardless of the distance and, within the central area, are not transferable from one vehicle to another.

Athens bus ticket booth

Useful Routes in Athens

Metro stations at Kerameikós, Plateía Syntágmatos, and the National Gallery of Art are due to be in operation by 2003, in time for the 2004 Olympic Games.

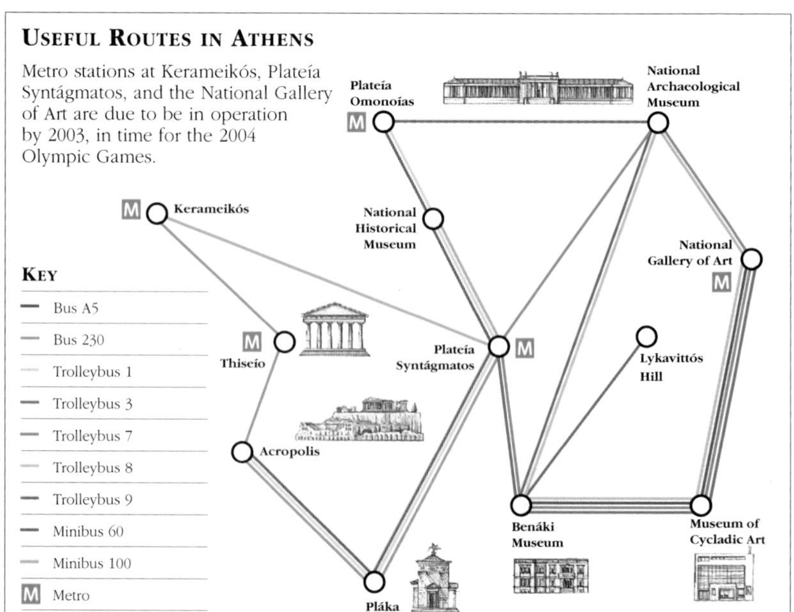

ΜΟΝΑΣΤΗΡΙΟΝ
Monastirion

Monastiráki metro sign

Athens Bus Networks

There are four principal bus networks serving greater Athens and the Attica region. They are individually color coded: blue and white, red, orange and white, and green. Blue and white buses run an extensive network of over 300 routes in greater Athens, connecting districts to each other and to central Athens. A small complementary network of minibuses with red stop signs also operates, but in the central area only.

Orange and white buses serve the area around Athens. On these you pay the conductor and, as distances are greater, fares are more expensive as well. The two terminals for orange and white buses are both situated on Mavrommataión, by Pedío tou Areos (Areos Park). Though you can board at any designated orange stop, usually you cannot get off until you are outside the city area. These buses are less frequent than the blue and white service, and on some routes buses stop running in the early evening.

Green express buses, the fourth category, travel between central Athens and Piraeus. Numbers 040 and 049 are very frequent – about every 6 minutes – running from Athinas, by Plateía Omonoías, to various stops in Piraeus, including Plateía Karaïskáki, at the main harbor.

Trolleybuses in Athens

Complementing the bus system is a network of trolleybuses, which are color-coded yellow. There are about 19 trolleybus routes that crisscross the city center. They provide a good way of getting around the sights of central Athens. Most routes pass the Pláka area, but route 3 is useful for getting to the National Archaeological Museum from Plateía Syntágmatos, and route 1 links Lárissis railroad station with Plateía Omonoías and Plateía Syntágmatos, the heart of Athens' city center.

Front view of an Athens trolleybus

Athens' Metro

The metro is a fast and reliable means of transportation in Athens. However, its usefulness is limited by the fact that, now, there is just one line. It runs from Kifisiá in the north to Piraeus in the south, with central stations at Thiseío, Monastiráki, Omónoia, and Victoria. The majority of the line is overland and only runs underground between Attikí and Monastiráki stations through the city center. The line is used mainly by commuters, but can be useful for tourists, especially to reach the port of Piraeus.

Metro tickets

The ticket price of 100 Dr increases a little if the trip passes through Omónoia station in either direction. Tickets can be bought at any metro station and must be validated before entering the train – use the machines at the entrances to all platforms. Trains run every five minutes, and operate from 5am to midnight.

Expansion of Athens' metro is well under way, with two additional lines and 18 new stations planned. The routes will extend the network diagonally from northwest to southeast, and laterally from east to west, with connecting points at Omónoia and Monastiráki. These lines will be 20 m (66 ft) underground, in order to avoid material of archaeological interest. The excavations that have begun as a result of the expansion project are impeding the metro lines' development, however, and the projected opening date of the end of 1998 has been severely delayed. The aim now is to open them in time for the Olympics in 2004.

Piraeus metro station

Driving in Athens

Driving in Athens can be a nerve-racking experience, especially if you are not accustomed to the Greek way of driving. Many streets in the center are pedestrianized, and there are also plenty of one-way streets, so you need to plan routes carefully. Finding a parking space can also be very difficult. Despite appearances to the contrary, parking in front of a no-parking sign or on a single yellow line is illegal. There are parking meters and pay and display machines, as well as underground lots, though they fill up quickly.

In an attempt to reduce dangerously high air pollution levels, there is an "odd-even" driving system in effect. Cars with an odd number at the end of their licence plates can enter the central grid *(daktýlio)* only on dates with an odd number, and cars with an even number on their plates are allowed only on even dates. The rule does not apply to foreign cars but, if possible, avoid taking your car into the city center.

Parking meter in Athens

No parking on odd-numbered days of the month

No parking on even-numbered days of the month

Yellow Athens taxi

Athenian Taxis

Swarms of yellow taxis can be seen cruising around Athens at most times of the day or night. However, trying to persuade one to stop for you can be difficult, especially from 2pm to 3pm when taxi drivers change shifts. Then, they will only pick you up if you happen to be going in a direction convenient for them.

To hail a taxi, stand on the edge of the pavement and shout out your destination to any cab that slows down. If a cab's "TAXI" sign is lit up then it is definitely for hire (but often a taxi is also for hire when the sign is not lit). It is also common practice for drivers to pick up extra passengers along the way, so do not ignore the occupied cabs. If you are not the first passenger, take note of the meter reading immediately: there is no fare-sharing, so you should be charged for your portion of the journey only (or the minimum fare of 200 Dr, whichever is greater).

Athenian taxis are extremely cheap by European standards – depending on traffic, you should not have to pay more than 1,000 Dr to go anywhere in the downtown area, and between 1,600 Dr and 2,200 Dr from the center to Piraeus or the airport. Double fares come into effect between midnight and 5am, and for journeys that exceed certain distances from the city center. There are also small surcharges for extra pieces of luggage weighing over 10 kg (22 lbs), and for trips from the airport, ferry, or railroad terminals. Taxi fares are increased around the Christmas holiday and during Easter.

For a small extra charge, you can make a phone call to a radio taxi company and arrange for a car to pick you up at an appointed place and time. Radio taxis are plentiful in the Athens area. Listed below are the telephone numbers of a few companies:

Express
01 993 4812.

Kosmos
1300.

Hellas
01 645 7000.

Walking

The center of Athens is very compact, and almost all major sights and museums are to be found within a 20- or 25-minute walk of Plateía Syntágmatos, which is generally regarded as the city's center. This is worth bearing in mind, particularly when traffic is congested, all buses are full, and no taxi will stop. Athens is still one of the safest European cities in which to walk around, though, as in any sizeable metropolis, it pays to be vigilant, especially at night.

Sign for a pedestrianized area

Visitors to Athens, walking up Areopagos hill

ATHENS TRANSIT LINKS

The hub of Athens' city transit is the area around Plateía Syntágmatos and Plateía Omonoías. From this central area trolleybuses or buses can be taken to the airport, the harbor at Piraeus, Athens' two train stations, and its domestic and international bus terminals.

Bus 091 provides a service that links the city center with the airport's East, West, and Charter terminals. Buses 040 and 049 link the harbor at Piraeus with the city center at Syntágmatos and Omonoías. The metro also extends to Piraeus harbor. Piraeus is linked directly to the airport: bus 19 goes from Piraeus to all the airport terminals and also operates a limited service throughout the night.

Trolleybus route 1 goes past Lárissis train station (with the Peloponnísou station a short walk away), while bus 024 goes to bus terminal B, on Liosíou, and bus 051 to bus terminal A, on Kifisoú.

Although it is more expensive than public transportation, the most convenient way of getting to and from any of these destinations is by taxi. The journey times can vary greatly but, if traffic is light, from the city center to the airport it takes between 25 and 30 minutes; the trip from the city center to Piraeus takes about 30 to 40 minutes; and the trip from Piraeus to the airport also takes in the region of 30 to 40 minutes.

Bus from Piraeus to Perâma, the port for Salamína island

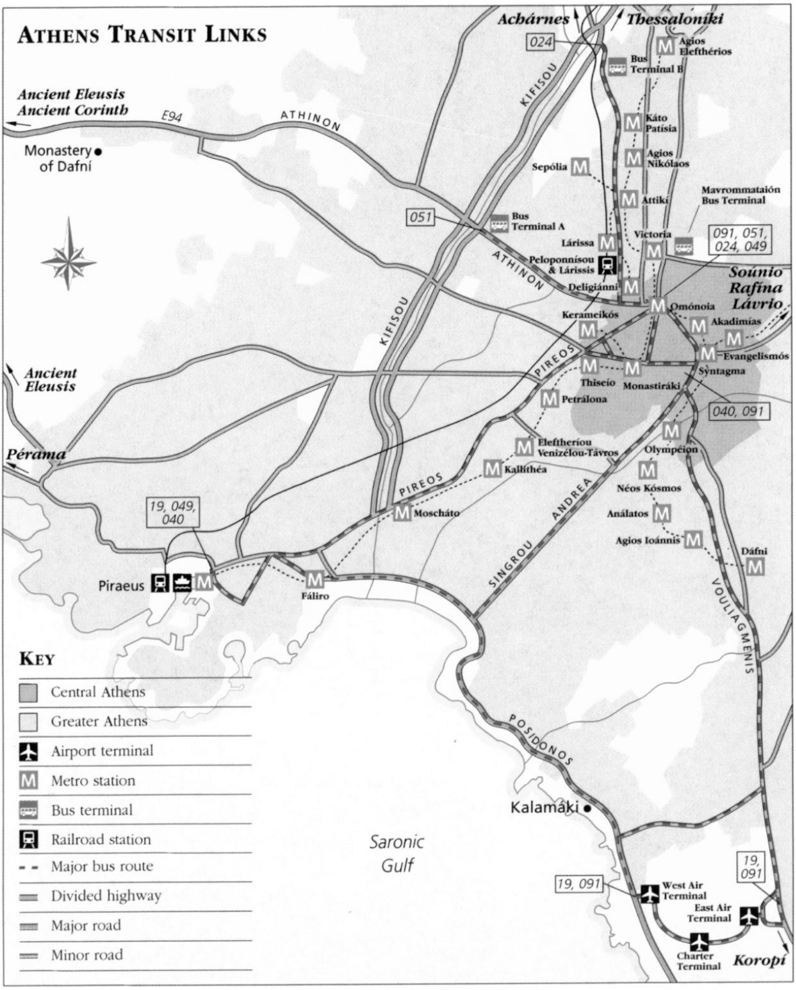

ATHENS TRANSIT LINKS

KEY

- Central Athens
- Greater Athens
- Airport terminal
- Metro station
- Bus terminal
- Railroad station
- Major bus route
- Divided highway
- Major road
- Minor road

Travelers' Needs

Where to Stay

Accommodations in the Greek islands are functional in most cases, and occasionally inspired. They are always abundant in a country that depends so heavily on tourism, and consequently are a bargain compared with most other European destinations. Despite inroads of commercialization in the busier resorts, hospitality off the beaten track can still be warm and heartfelt. Various types of accommodations are described over the next four pages. Information is also given for camping and hosteling. The listings section on pages 298–311 includes over 150 places to stay, ranging from informal *domátia* (rooms) and alpine refuges to luxurious hotels and accommodations in restored buildings.

Tourist apartment sign, Ionian Islands

Hotels

Most Greek hotels are of standard Mediterranean concrete architecture, though in coastal resorts height limits restrict the building of vast towering structures. Many surviving hotels date from the 1967–74 Junta era, when massive investment in "modern" tourism was encouraged. A very few Neo-Classical, or older, hotels remain – now benefiting from government preservation orders.

Hotels built since the 1980s are generally designed with greater imagination and sensitivity to the environment. The more expensive hotels will have a correspondingly higher level of service, offered by trained personnel.

Chain Hotels

Greece, with its tradition of family business ownership, has not taken to the idea of chain hotels. Among the few that operate on the islands, the oldest is the formerly state-run Xenía, founded during the 1950s. Most of their hotels, with well-worn facilities and indifferent service, are worth avoiding. Newer chains, such as **Grecotel** on Crete and **Chandris Hotels** on Corfu and Chíos, are a better bet. Grecotel has essentially consolidated the management of previously existing hotels.

Hotel Alýki *(see p304)*, with boats at the waterfront, on Sými

◁ **Steni Valá Taverna on the island of Alónnisos**

Restored Settlements and Buildings

During the 1970s, the EOT (Greek Tourist Office) began sponsoring the restoration of derelict buildings in vernacular style for accommodation. They usually offer a good value for your money and an exceptionally atmospheric environment. Preservation considerations, however, often mean that bathrooms are in the hall, not private. Such developments are found at Psará and at Mestá, on the island of Chíos. The complex at Mestá, however, has now been privatized, reflecting the growing commercial interest in such developments.

Private entrepreneurs have also successfully installed many small and medium-sized hotels in centuries-old buildings. Ventures that have worked well can be found on the islands of Ydra, Crete (at Chaniá and Réthymno), Sými, Mýkonos, Sýros, Lésvos, Folégandros, and Kálymnos.

Domatia

A large proportion of Greek accommodations, especially on the small islands, is in *domátia*, or rented rooms. Formerly these would often be in the home of the managing family, but nowadays they

Skiáthos Palace Hotel *(see p300)*

are far more likely to be in a separate, custom-built, modern structure. They are generally a good value compared to hotels of the same comfort. Increasingly they have private bathrooms, are well appointed with neutral pine furniture, and often have a kitchen for guests' use. There is usually no communal area, however, and hot water is provided either by an electric immersion heater or by a solar energy device.

Grading

Hotels and domatia are graded by the EOT. Hotel categories range from E-class up to A-class, plus deluxe. *Domátia* range from C-class to A-class. There is supposed to be a direct correlation between amenities and the classification, but there are often deviations – usually the result of a dispute with the local authorities.

E-class hotels, with the most basic facilities and narrow profit margins, are almost extinct. D-class still survive, and these should have at least some private baths. In a C-class hotel, all rooms must have private bathrooms, and the hotel must have some sort of common area, if only a small combination bar and breakfast area where a basic continental breakfast can be served. B-class hotels must have extra amenities such as a full-service restaurant, a more substantial breakfast, and at least one sports facility, such as a pool or tennis court. A-class hotels are usually at beach-front locations and offer all conceivable diversions, as well as aids for the business traveler, such as conference halls or telecommunications facilities. Deluxe hotels are the same, only more so – effectively self-contained resort complexes.

C-class *domátia,* offering baths down the hall and "jail-like" decor, are on the way out, supplanted by B-class blocks with guaranteed in-room plumbing and often a shared kitchen. A-class rooms are nearly synonymous with apartments; landscaping is usually superior, and kitchens are fitted into each unit.

Prices

The price of hotel rooms and *domátia* should correspond to their official category, although rates are variable, depending on high or low season and location. For 4,000 Dr or under, it is possible to find a C-class *domátio* for two without bathroom, or an E/D-class hotel; 6,000 Dr should cover a B-class double *domátio,* while A-class *domátia* and C-class hotels charge between 7,000 and 9,000 Dr. B-class hotels ask 9,000 to 13,000 Dr per double room, while A-class hotels typically cost from 13,000 Dr to 17,000 Dr. Deluxe resorts are exempt from the EOT price control and can easily run in excess of 22,000 Dr per night. These rates are only approximations for the tourist season, including sales and municipal taxes; prices can drop by as much as 50 percent in early spring or late autumn. Rates include breakfast, but stays of less than 3 nights can be penalized by surcharges in peak season.

Dodecanese window

Opening Seasons

Most island hotels, and all island *domátia,* operate only during peak season (late April to late October). But if Orthodox Easter falls early in April, many facilities may open then. *Domátia* are, in fact, forbidden by law to be open during winter. At such times your options may be limited to a single hotel at an island's main port. The listings in this guide indicate when hotels are closed.

Booking

The most common and cost-effective method of booking accommodation is by reserving in advance through a package tour or travel agency. If, however, you contact a hotel direct, it is better to do so by fax so that the transaction is properly recorded in writing.

You may also be asked to provide a credit card number, or forward travelers' checks equivalent to the value of the first night's stay in advance. If you fail to show up this sum is subject to forfeit.

Stélla Tsakíri *(see p301)* at Volissós, Chíos

Efficiency Apartments and Villas

Efficiency apartments or villas are known as *garsoniéres*, and are the logical outgrowth of *domátia*. The main differences are that kitchens are built into each studio or multibedroom unit, and many have swimming pools and landscaped gardens.

With few exceptions, these are far better equipped and easy to reserve through overseas package tour companies. Many villas are block-booked yearly by particular companies and are essentially not available to independent travelers. But in slow years, where this is not the case, the best strategy is personally to visit travel agencies in the island town concerned – they will know of any current vacancies and place you in a villa for a modest commission. In the off-season it is sometimes possible to get a villa or apartment long term, by direct negotiation with the owners.

Youth Hostels

The Greek islands have seven youth hostels *(xenón neótitos)* recognized by the IYHF (International Youth Hostel Federation). The hostels are found on Santoríni, Corfu, and on Crete at Irákleio, Réthymno, Plakiás, Siteía and Myrtiá. Greek hostels are not nearly as regimented as their northern European equivalents. Even without an IYHF membership card, it is usually possible to stay at a hostel, providing a vacancy is available, by paying a supplement.

Monastery of Agios Giórgos on Skýros ***(see pp112–13)***

There are also a handful of unofficial hostels that operate on the islands. These can be very good and are often better equipped than the IYHF-recognized hostels.

Alpine Refuges

Among the islands, only Crete has bona fide alpine refuges, or *katafýgia*. There are three on the island: one on Mount Psiloreítis and two in Chaniá's White Mountains. The refuge at Kallérgi, above the Samariá Gorge in the White Mountains, is the only one staffed most of the year round. For the other two, keys must be rented from Irákleio and Chaniá respectively, at branches of the **EOS** (Greek Alpine Club). This will, however, prove an expensive undertaking unless you are part of a large group.

Erevos ***(see p305)*** **at Imerovígli, Santoríni**

Rural Tourism

Conceived during the 1980s to give women in the Greek provinces a measure of financial independence, rural tourism allows foreigners to stay on a bed-and-breakfast basis in a village house, and also provides the opportunity to participate, if desired, in the daily life of a farming community. There are two such programs on the Greek islands, at Pyrgí (Chíos) and Pétra (Lésvos), each managed by a **Women's Rural Tourism Cooperative**. The Pétra cooperative runs a centrally located, bargain restaurant, featuring regional cuisine. Booking is made to each local cooperative directly.

Monasteries

The less visited monasteries and convents in Greece operate *xenónes*, or hostels, intended primarily for Greek Orthodox pilgrims on weekend visits. They will always have priority, but it is often possible to find a vacancy at short notice.

Accommodation is of the spartan dormitory variety, with a frugal evening meal and morning coffee also provided; it is customary to leave a donation in the *katholikón* (main church).

On the islands the tradition of hospitality, dating back to ancient times, is on the wane – a victim of mass tourism and its attendant commercialization. However, especially in the remoter parts of Rhodes, Crete, and other large islands, it is possible to stay in staffed monasteries.

Camping

The Greek islands have nearly 80 officially recognized campsites. Most of these are in attractive beachfront settings, and also cater to RVS. A small minority are owned and managed by the EOT (although they are soon to be privatised), or by the local municipality; the rest are privately run. All but the most primitive sites have solar-heated hot showers, shady landscaping, a snack bar or café, and power hookups available for an extra fee. The most luxurious campsites are miniature vacation villages, with swimming pool, tennis courts, laundry rooms, banking and postal facilities, and bungalows for the tentless. The ground at the sites is generally hard, so short pegs are best. For a regularly updated booklet covering campsites and their amenities, contact the **Greek Camping Association**.

Green hotel *(see p308)* in Spíli, Crete

Disabled Travelers

Facilities for disabled travelers are far less elaborate in Greece than in Western Europe. **Access-Able**

Lakka Paxi Camping, on the Ionian Islands

Travel Source maintains a web site (*http://www.access-able.com*) that provides general information on travel for the disabled, as well as links to many other Internet sites. In Greece, **Hermes** or the Tourist Guide of Greece in Athens can be contacted for advice. In the hotel listings of this guide we have indicated which establishments have facilities such as elevators and ramps for the disabled.

Greek information sources for disabled travelers tend to be rudimentary: the EOT only publishes a questionnaire, which can be sent to specific establishments to assess the suitability of their facilities.

Further Information

The invaluable *Guide to Hotels* is published by, and available from, the EOT (Greek Tourist Office). It covers all officially registered hotels – though not villas or *domátia* – indicating prices, facilities, and the operating season. *Camping in Greece*, published free by the Greek Camping Association is also available from EOT offices. There are two other, privately issued, publications, the monthly *Greek Travel Pages* (GTP) and the quarterly *Tourist Guide of Greece*. Both offer skeletal information unless the hotel concerned has purchased advertising space.

Directory

Chain Hotels

Chandris Hotels
Syngroú 385, 17564 Paléo Fáliron, Athens.
01 930 8000.

Club Mediterranée Hellas SA
Omírou 8, 10564 Athens.
01 325 4110.

Divani Hotels
Parthenónos 19–25, 11742 Athens.
01 922 9650.

Grecotel
PO Box 25, 74100 Réthymno, Crete.
0831 71602 (Crete).
01 725 0920 (Athens).

Holiday Company
Voulís 31–33, 10557 Athens.
01 323 9476.

Mamidakis Hotels of Greece
Panepistimíou 56, 10678 Athens.
01 381 9781-6.

Zante Hotels
PO Box 191, Laganás 29100, Zákynthos.
0695 51948.

Hostels

Hosteling International – American Youth Hostels
733 15th St. NW, Ste 840 Washington, DC 20005.
(202) 783-6161.

IYHF (Greece)
Dragatsaníou 4, 10559 Athens.
01 323 4107.

Alpine Refuges

EOS (Ellinikós Orivatikós Sýndesmos)
(Greek Alpine Club) Filadelfías 126, 13671 Acharnés, Attica.
01 246 1528.

Women's Rural Tourism Cooperatives

Pétra, Lésvos
0253 41238.

Pyrgí, Chíos
0271 72496.

Camping

Greek Camping Association
Sólonos 76, 10680 Athens.
01 362 1560.

Disabled Travelers

Hermes
Patriárchou Grigoríou toú Pémptou 13, 16452 Argyroúpoli, Attica.
01 996 1887.

SATH
347 Fifth Ave, Suite 610 New York, NY 10016.
(212) 447-7284.

Further Information

Greek Travel Pages
Psýlla 6, 10557 Athens.
01 324 7511.

Tourist Guide of Greece
Patissíon 137, 11251 Athens.
01 864 1688.

Choosing a Hotel

THESE HOTELS have been selected across a wide price range for their good value, facilities, and location; they are listed by area, starting with the Ionian Islands. Use the color-coded thumb tabs, which indicate the regions covered on each page, to guide you to the relevant section of the chart. For more information on hotels see pages 294–7.

THE IONIAN ISLANDS

Hotel	Number of Rooms	Restaurant	Close to Beach	Swimming Pool	Air-Conditioning
CORFU: *Bella Venezia* (Dr)(Dr)(Dr)(Dr) N Zampéli 4, Corfu town, 49100. *0661 46500.* FAX *0661 20708.* Close to the town center, this Neo-Classical mansion has high-ceilinged rooms which are comfortable and tasteful without being extravagant. Hospitable and courteous staff.	32		■		■
CORFU: *Akrotíri Beach* (Dr)(Dr)(Dr)(Dr)(Dr) Aristeídis Polyímas, Palaiokastrítsa, 49083. *0663 41237.* FAX *0663 41277.* One of the best hotels in this popular resort, the Akrotíri Beach enjoys a lovely setting on a headland. *Nov–Apr.*	127	●	■	●	■
CORFU: *Corfu Palace* (Dr)(Dr)(Dr)(Dr)(Dr) Leofóros Demokratías 2, Corfu town, 49100. *0661 39485-7.* FAX *0661 31749.* This luxury hotel is set in beautiful tropical gardens, with a peaceful, seafront location and views to the Greek mainland. *Nov–Mar.*	112	●	■	●	■
CORFU: *Divani Palace* (Dr)(Dr)(Dr)(Dr)(Dr) Naysikás 20, Corfu town, 49100. *0661 38996-8.* FAX *0661 711124.* A chic hotel, situated 3 km (2 miles) outside Corfu town, on a wooded hillside overlooking the lagoon of Kanóni. *Nov–Mar.*	165	●	■	●	■
CORFU: *San Stéfano* (Dr)(Dr)(Dr)(Dr)(Dr) Waterfront, Benítses, 49081. *0661 71112.* FAX *0661 71124.* This stylish hotel was once used to accommodate European politicians at a conference, so facilities are excellent. *Nov–Feb.*	259	●	■	●	■
ITHACA: *Méntor* (Dr)(Dr)(Dr) Vathý waterfront, 28300. *0674 32433.* FAX *0674 32293.* A small, chic hotel, it is kept spotless by family owners. There is a bar in the roof garden, ideal for watching the sun go down.	38	●	■		
KEFALLONIA: *Kefalloniá Star* (Dr)(Dr)(Dr) Ioánnou Metaxá 50, Argostóli, 28100. *0671 23181.* FAX *0671 23180.* A long-established hotel on the main harbor road, it has some balconied front rooms and fine sea views. A comfortable place to stay.	42		■		■
KEFALLONIA: *Tourist* (Dr)(Dr)(Dr) Ioánnou Metaxá 94, Argostóli, 28100. *0671 22510.* Blue and white decor gives a very Greek look to this pleasant hotel on the waterfront. The rooms are comfortable and reasonably priced.	20	●	■		
KEFALLONIA: *Filoxenía Guest House* (Dr)(Dr)(Dr)(Dr) On the waterfront, Fiskárdo, 28084. *0674 41319.* FAX *0674 41319.* Modern facilities mix with traditional furniture in this restored villa. Rooms are spacious and have use of a shared, well-appointed kitchen. The hotel is centrally situated in this busy harbor village. *Dec–Mar.*	6		■		
LEFKADA: *Lefkás* (Dr)(Dr)(Dr)(Dr) Papágou 2, Lefkáda town, 31100. *0645 23916.* FAX *0645 24579.* A large, centrally located hotel, with friendly staff and a relaxed atmosphere. All the rooms are airy and spacious.	186		■		
LEFKADA: *Nydrío Aktí* (Dr)(Dr)(Dr)(Dr) Waterfront, Nydrí, 31100. *0645 92400.* FAX *0645 92151.* Situated on the waterfront, overlooking the nearby islands, this hotel offers well-equipped rooms with balconies. There is also a beach bar.	39		■		■
MEGANISI: *Meganísi* (Dr)(Dr) North of main square, Katoméri, 31083. *0645 51240.* FAX *0645 51639.* This family-run hotel is the only one on the island. It offers simple but comfortable accommodation in a rural setting.	18	●			

Price categories are for a standard double room for one night in peak season, including tax, service charges, and breakfast:
Dr up to 8,000 Dr
DrDr 8–12,000 Dr
DrDrDr 12–16,000 Dr
DrDrDrDr 16–21,000 Dr
DrDrDrDrDr over 21,000 Dr.

Restaurant
Restaurant within the hotel sometimes reserved for residents only.

Close to Beach
Within walking distance of the beach.

Swimming Pool
Hotel swimming pools are usually quite small and outdoors unless otherwise stated.

Air-Conditioning
Hotel with air-conditioning in all the rooms.

Hotel	Number of Rooms	Restaurant	Close to Beach	Swimming Pool	Air-Conditioning
Zakynthos: *Montreal* DrDr Alykés, 29090. *0695 83241.* FAX *0695 83342.* Right on the busy beach of this popular holiday resort, all of the rooms have sea views and are modern and well kept. *Nov–Mar.*	35	●	■		
Zakynthos: *Strada Marína* DrDrDrDr Lomvárdou 14, Chóra, 29090. *0695 42761.* The town's best hotel is right on the waterfront and its rooms offer all modern facilities. There is also a relaxing roof garden.	112	●	■		
The Argo-Saronic Islands					
Aigina: *Aiginítiko Archontikó* DrDrDr Agíou Nikoláou & Eakou 1, Aígina town, 18010. *0297 24968.* FAX *0297 24968.* A Neo-Classical mansion with two courtyards and a roof garden. The public rooms are beautifully restored, and the simple guest rooms contain brass beds and antique furniture.	10.				■
Aigina: *Nafsiká* DrDrDr Near the Temple of Apollo, Aígina town, 18010. *0297 22333.* This small, quiet family-run hotel is situated by the sea just outside town. It provides easy access to the archaeological site. *Apr–Oct.*	36	●	■		
Kythira: *Margaríta* DrDrDrDr Town center, Chóra, 80100. *0735 31711.* FAX *0735 31325.* Housed in a converted 19th-century mansion, this is Chóra's most elegant accommodation. Rooms do not have balconies. *Sep–May.*	12				
Kythira: *Rigas Apartments* DrDrDrDr Kapsáli bay, 80100. *0735 31265.* FAX *0735 31265.* These modern, self-sufficient apartments are built in the traditional island style, each with a kitchen, bathroom and balcony. *Nov–Mar.*	15		■		■
Ydra: *Hydra* DrDrDr Voúlgari 8, Ydra town, 18040. *0298 52102.* FAX *0298 52102.* A converted mansion, set on the top of a hill in the west of the town. The most attractive rooms are those facing the harbor. *Nov–Feb.*	13				
Ydra: *Neféli* DrDrDr Tsamadoú 814, Ydra town, 18040. *0298 53297.* This western hillside conversion has three terraces on which breakfast is served. The climb up is steep but the views are rewarding. *Nov–Feb.*	10		■		
Ydra: *Mistral* DrDrDrDr Ydra town, 18040. *0298 52509.* FAX *0298 53412.* Situated at the southeast corner of town the hotel does not have port views, but it is quiet with, friendly staff and generous breakfasts. *Dec–Feb.*	20				■
Ydra: *Ydroússa* DrDrDrDr Behind park, Ydra town, 18040. *0298 52217.* FAX *0298 52161.* Formerly the state-run Xenía, this rambling mansion has benefited from privatization. It is situated in the town center.	36	●			
Spetses: *Poseidónion* DrDrDrDrDr On waterfront, Ntápia, Spétses town, 18050. *0298 72006.* FAX *0298 72208.* This Edwardian hotel offers somewhat faded elegance especially in its ground-floor common areas. Insist on a seaward room with tall windows and views across to the Peloponnese. *Nov–Apr.*	52		■		
Spetses: *Spétses* DrDrDrDrDr West of Ntápia, Spétses town, 18050. *0298 72602.* FAX *0298 72494.* One of few high-quality hotels on the island at only a fraction more than most hotels here. All the rooms have views of the sea. *Nov–Mar.*	77	●	■		

For key to symbols see back flap

Price categories are for a standard double room for one night in peak season, including tax, service charges, and breakfast:
(Dr) up to 8,000 Dr
(Dr)(Dr) 8–12,000 Dr
(Dr)(Dr)(Dr) 12–16,000 Dr
(Dr)(Dr)(Dr)(Dr) 16–21,000 Dr
(Dr)(Dr)(Dr)(Dr)(Dr) over 21,000 Dr.

Restaurant
Restaurant within the hotel sometimes reserved for residents only.

Close to Beach
Within walking distance of the beach.

Swimming Pool
Hotel swimming pools are usually quite small and outdoors unless otherwise stated.

Air-Conditioning
Hotel with air-conditioning in all the rooms.

The Sporades and Evvoia

Hotel	Number of Rooms	Restaurant	Close to Beach	Swimming Pool	Air-Conditioning
Alonnisos: *Charavgí* (Dr)(Dr) Waterfront, Patitíri. *0424 65090.* Wonderful views of the whole village can be enjoyed from this reasonably priced hotel. All rooms have balconies. ● *Nov–Feb.*	12		■		
Evvoia: *Beis* (Dr)(Dr) Kými beach, 34003. *0222 22604.* FAX *0224 22049.* This comfortable hotel offers rooms with a view of the port. There is also an excellent restaurant serving freshly caught fish.	40	●	■		
Evvoia: *Apollon* (Dr)(Dr)(Dr)(Dr)(Dr) Kárystos bay, 34001. *0224 22045-8.* FAX *0222 22870.* Situated on the edge of a lush bay, this modern hotel consists of suites overlooking the sea. Suites sleep five comfortably. ● *Nov–Mar.*	36	●	■	●	■
Evvoia: *Kandíli* (Dr)(Dr)(Dr)(Dr)(Dr) 1 km (0.5 miles) from seafront, Prokópi, 34004. *0227 41381.* FAX *0227 41190.* Set in a splendid estate, this hotel and seminar center offers various courses such as mosaics and painting. A Landrover is available for use.	12			●	
Skiathos: *Atrium Hotel* (Dr)(Dr)(Dr)(Dr)(Dr) Plataniás beach, Agía Paraskeví, 73002. *0427 49345.* FAX *0427 49444.* A smart, newly built hotel set on a wooded hill above the sandy beach of Plataniás. All rooms have private balconies. ● *Oct–May.*	75	●	■	●	■
Skiathos: *Esperídes* (Dr)(Dr)(Dr)(Dr)(Dr) Achladiá, 6 km (4 miles) S of Skiáthos town, 73002. *0427 22245.* FAX *0427 21580.* Achladiá bay's resort hotel has excellent facilities including tennis courts. The rooms are spacious and overlook a sandy beach. ● *Nov–Feb.*	180	●	■	●	■
Skiathos: *Palace* (Dr)(Dr)(Dr)(Dr)(Dr) Koukounariés beach, 37002. *0427 49700.* FAX *01 323 3667.* Situated on a sandy beach backed by pine trees, the rooms of this resort-type hotel all enjoy good sea views. ● *Oct 25.*	220	●	■	●	■
Skopelos: *Thea Home* (Dr)(Dr)(Dr) Waterfront, Skópelos town, 37003. *0424 22859.* FAX *01 647 5692.* This small, family-run hotel has a warm atmosphere and friendly staff. Rooms have balconies overlooking Skópelos bay. ● *Oct–Apr.*	12		■		
Skopelos: *Zanétta* (Dr)(Dr)(Dr) 300 m (990 ft) from the seafront, Elios, 37003. *0424 33140.* FAX *0424 33717.* Consisting of 60 well-furnished apartments with kitchen units, the Zanétta is surrounded by beautiful woodland. ● *mid-Oct–Jun.*	60	●		●	■
Skyros: *Neféli* (Dr)(Dr)(Dr) Plagiá area, Skýros town, 34007. *0222 91964.* FAX *0222 92061.* This traditional-style hotel situated on the edge of Skýros town, has ten independent rooms and nine separate flats.	19		■		

The Northeast Aegean Islands

Hotel	Number of Rooms	Restaurant	Close to Beach	Swimming Pool	Air-Conditioning
Chios: *Stélla Tsakíri* (Dr)(Dr) Plateía Pirgos, Volissós, 82103. *0274 21421.* FAX *0274 21521.* A cluster of traditional stone houses, meticulously renovated by an Athenian sculptor. They all have terraces, full kitchens, and original features.	9				
Chios: *Kýma* (Dr)(Dr)(Dr) Evgeníou Chandrí 1, Chíos town, 82100. *0271 44500.* FAX *0271 44600.* A friendly, efficient, family-run hotel, overlooking the beach. It was originally built as a waterside villa for a Greek shipping magnate.	60		■		■

Hotel	Rooms				
LESVOS: *Vaterá Beach* (Dr)(Dr)(Dr) Vaterá beach, 81300. *0252 61212.* FAX *0252 61164.* A modern and friendly, family-run establishment, overlooking a sandy beach. All rooms have spacious balconies commanding wonderful views of the Aegean and the mountains. *Nov–Apr.*	24	●	■		■
LESVOS: *Clára Hotel and Bungalows* (Dr)(Dr)(Dr)(Dr) Avláki district, Pétra, 81109. *0253 41532-3.* FAX *0253 41535.* A pastel-painted, well-landscaped, hillside complex, looking north to Pétra and Mólyvos. All rooms have balconies and postmodern, minimalist decor. There are also tennis courts. *Oct–Mar.*	41	●	■	●	
LESVOS: *Olive Press* (Dr)(Dr)(Dr)(Dr) Behind Mólyvos beach, 81108. *0253 71205.* FAX *0253 71647.* A charming and atmospheric hotel, converted from an old olive press. The rooms are arranged around an inner courtyard and are all spacious. There are also 12 self-contained studios with kitchens. *Oct 15; Nov–Mar.*	45	●	■		■
LESVOS: *Laureate* (Dr)(Dr)(Dr)(Dr)(Dr) Vareiá beach, 81100. *0251 43111.* FAX *0251 41629.* This luxurious hotel is housed in a restored villa with private rooms, studios, and flats. It is set in a beautiful garden with avenues of bay trees and wonderful giant pines.	8	●	■	●	
LIMNOS: *Villa Afrodíti* (Dr)(Dr)(Dr) Behind Platí beach, Platí, 81400. *0254 23489.* FAX *0254 25031.* One of the cleanest hotels on the island and always busy. The attached restaurant is popular and facilities are good. *Oct–Apr.*	12	●	■	●	
LIMNOS: *Aktí Myrína* (Dr)(Dr)(Dr)(Dr)(Dr) 2 km (1 mile) N of Myrína, 81400. *0254 22681.* FAX *0254 22352.* A luxury hotel comprising stone cottages with gardens, set on terraces overlooking a private beach. The hotel is equipped with tennis courts, a fitness center, and water sports facilities. *Oct–Apr.*	125	●	■	●	■
SAMOS: *Olympia Beach* (Dr)(Dr)(Dr) On the beach, Kokkári, 83100. *0273 92353.* FAX *0273 92457.* This quiet, family-run hotel enjoys a seafront setting with good views. A traditional-style building with timber and marble interior. All rooms have balconies. Close to all amenities. *Nov–Mar.*	12	●	■		
SAMOS: *Fytó Bungalows* (Dr)(Dr)(Dr)(Dr) 800 m (2,600 ft) W of Pythagóreio, 83103. *0273 61314.* FAX *0273 62045.* A modern and comfortable hotel with a delightful garden and shaded terrace. Ideally placed for exploring the local beaches and the archaeological sites of Sámos. *Nov–Apr.*	75	●	■	●	■
SAMOS: *Sámaina Bay Hotel* (Dr)(Dr)(Dr)(Dr) Karlóvassi beach, 83200. *0273 34004-7.* FAX *0273 34008.* A comfortable hotel, not in an ideal location but well-run and long-established. Some rooms have a sea view, and the hotel has good facilities including a sauna and large lounge area. *Nov–Apr.*	75	●	■	●	■
SAMOTHRAKI: *Xenía* (Dr)(Dr)(Dr) Paleópolis, 3 km (2 miles) N of Chóra, 68002. *0551 41166.* FAX *0551 41230.* Originally built to house the American archaeological teams in the 1950s, this basic one-story hotel is magnificently set among oaks, between the Sanctuary of the Great Gods and the sea. *Oct–May.*	6	●	■		
THASOS: *Alkyón* (Dr)(Dr) Waterfront, Thásos town, 64004. *0593 22148.* This highly recommended, small hotel is run by a team of botanical and culinary experts. Botanical walking tours are offered. *Nov–Apr.*	11	●	■		
THASOS: *Alexándra Beach Hotel* (Dr)(Dr)(Dr)(Dr) Potós beach, 64004. *0593 52391-8.* FAX *0593 51185.* Perched on a headland above a 2 km (1 mile) beach, this hotel comprises a large complex with all amenities. Tennis courts, fitness center, and water sports gear hire are all rentable. *Nov–Apr.*	125	●	■	●	
THASOS: *Miramáre* (Dr)(Dr)(Dr)(Dr) Skála Potamiás, 64004. *0593 61040.* FAX *0593 61043.* A modern hotel situated in a leafy ravine at the southern end of the spectacular Chryssí Ammoudiá beach. *May–Sep.*	30	●	■	●	

For key to symbols see back flap

Price categories are for a standard double room for one night in peak season, including tax, service charges, and breakfast:
Dr up to 8,000 Dr
DrDr 8–12,000 Dr
DrDrDr 12–16,000 Dr
DrDrDrDr 16–21,000 Dr
DrDrDrDrDr over 21,000 Dr.

Restaurant
Restaurant within the hotel sometimes reserved for residents only.

Close to Beach
Within walking distance of the beach.

Swimming Pool
Hotel swimming pools are usually quite small and outdoors unless otherwise stated.

Air-Conditioning
Hotel with air-conditioning in all the rooms.

The Dodecanese

Hotel	Price	Number of Rooms	Restaurant	Close to Beach	Swimming Pool	Air-Conditioning
Astypalaia: *Australía* Opposite kástro, Astypálaia town, 85900. *0243 61275.* A modern, open-plan hotel situated on the seafront overlooking the castle. Balconies have sea views, and there is a tree-shaded garden. Below the hotel is a restaurant offering fresh fish and meat grills. *Oct–Apr.*	Dr	15	●	■		
Chalki: *Argyrénia* Póntamos beach, Nimporió, 85110. *0241 45205.* Set in lovely gardens off the road to Póntamos beach, the Argyrénia consists of chalet-style rooms with terraces. There are no cooking facilities, but tavernas can be found nearby.	Dr	9		■		
Chalki: *Captain's House Pension* Off main square, Nimporió, 85110. *0241 45201.* A delightful pension in a Neo-Classical mansion, run by an ex-Greek naval officer. Breakfast is served on the shady terrace. *Dec–Feb.*	DrDr	4				■
Kalymnos: *Galíni* Main square, Vathý, 85200. *0243 31241.* Family-run pension overlooking the boatyard and Vathý bay. Rooms are simple but comfortable. Breakfast is served on the terrace.	Dr	14	●	■		
Kalymnos: *Panórama* Waterfront, Pothiá, 85200. *0243 23138.* This small hotel is set back from the bustling seafront. It is beautifully decorated and offers magnificent views of the sea. *Oct–Mar.*	Dr	13		■		
Kalymnos: *Olympic Hotel* Agios Nikolaos, 85200. *0243 28801.* FAX *0243 29314.* Recently renovated, this hotel is located right at the heart of the marina, close to all amenities, and only minutes from the beach.	DrDrDr	42		■		
Karpathos: *Ammopí Beach* Ammopí beach, 85700. *0245 22723.* Situated right on the beach, the rooms of this small hotel are basic, but all have balconies and are a good value for the money.	Dr	6		■		
Kasos: *Anagénnisis* Town center, Frý, 85855. *0245 41323.* FAX *0245 41036.* An inexpensive and comfortable American/Greek-run establishment. Expect to pay more for rooms enjoying sea views.	Dr	12		■		
Kastellorizo: *Mavrothalassítis* Waterfront, Kastellórizo town, 85111. *0241 49202.* FAX *0241 49202.* An inexpensive, restored mansion hotel, run by Australian-Greek brothers, with *en suite* facilities and cool bedrooms.	Dr	6		■		
Kastellorizo: *Megísti* Waterfront, Kastellórizo town, 85111. *0241 49272.* FAX *0241 49221.* A municipal hotel, overlooking the harbor. Probably the most comfortable accommodation in the town. *Nov–Mar.*	DrDrDr	17		■		
Kos: *Afendoúlis* Evripílou 1, Kos town, 85300. *0242 25321.* FAX *0242 25797.* A small family-run hotel with very friendly management, in a quiet spot close to the sea. There is a lovely jasmine-filled garden. *Oct–Mar.*	DrDr	17		■		
Kos: *Chará* Chálkonos 6, Kos town, 85300. *0242 22500.* A pleasant, small hotel in a tree-lined street located a short walk from the town beach. All rooms have balconies. *Oct–Apr.*	DrDr	16		■		

Hotel	Rooms				
KOS: *Karávia Beach* DrDrDrDrDr Karávia beach, 2 km (1 mile) N of Pylí, 85300. *0242 41291-4.* FAX *0242 41215.* A luxury holiday complex, where the emphasis is on organized entertainment, including boat trips to the nearby islands. ● *Nov–Apr.*	300	●	■	●	■
KOS: *Porto Bello Beach* DrDrDrDrDr Waterfront, 2 km (1 mile) W of Kardámaina, 85300. *0242 91217.* FAX *0242 91168.* Situated right on the beach, this resort hotel consists of white-washed bungalows. Sea views and a children's playground. ● *Nov–Mar.*	350	●	■	●	■
LEROS: *Kávos* Dr Waterfront, Pantéli, 85400. *0247 23247.* This excellent, inexpensive guesthouse overlooks the picture-postcard fishing harbor at Panteli. Some rooms have balconies. ● *Oct–May.*	10		■		
LEROS: *Archontikó Angélou* DrDr Waterfront, Alínda, 85300. *0247 22749.* FAX *0247 24403.* This hotel is housed in a traditional mansion built in 1895 during the Turkish occupation. It is set in its own lovely grounds. ● *Nov–Mar.*	17		■		
LEROS: *Voulaféndis Bungalows* DrDr Waterfront, Alínda, 85400. *0247 23515.* FAX *0247 24533.* This luxury studio development is built around a traditional mansion. There are good facilities and a piano bar. ● *Oct–Apr.*	16	●	■	●	
NISYROS: *Charítos* DrDr Behind waterfront, Mandráki, 85111. *0242 31322.* FAX *0242 31122.* Set back from Mandraki harbor, the Charítos is handy for the ferries. A friendly pension with spacious rooms and balconies with sea views.	11		■		
NISYROS: *Porfýris* DrDr Mandráki, 85111. *0242 31176.* FAX *0242 31376* A pleasant, reasonably priced hotel overlooking the public orchards. There are good views of the islet of Gyalí from the terrace. ● *Nov–Apr.*	15		■	●	
PATMOS: *Artemis* DrDrDr At entrance to Gríkos resort, 85500. *0247 31555.* FAX *0247 34016.* This resort hotel, comprising traditional island-style accommodation, enjoys sea views and good facilities, including an athletic center. ● *Nov–Mar.*	24		■		
PATMOS: *Astéri* DrDrDr Mérichas bay, Skála, 85500. *0247 32465.* FAX *0247 31347.* This family-run hotel is in a quiet spot, overlooking Mérichas bay. The owner keeps bees and serves honey for breakfast. ● *Nov–Mar.*	26		■		■
PATMOS: *Australis* DrDrDr 500 m (1,650 ft) above town, Skála, 85500. *0247 31576.* Located in a peaceful area, this family-run pension is set in beautiful gardens. Breakfast is served on the jasmine-scented terrace. ● *Nov–Mar.*	18		■		
PATMOS: *Golden Sun* DrDrDrDr Off Chóra–Gríkos road, 85500. *0247 32318.* FAX *0247 34019.* A smart hotel situated in a small fishing village overlooking the bay of Gríkos. The roof terrace commands fine sea views. ● *Nov–Mar.*	24	●	■		
RHODES: *Spartális* DrDr N Plastíra 2, Rhodes town, 85100. *0241 24371.* FAX *0241 20406.* A basic but friendly hotel, handily placed close to the harbor for ferries and boat trips. There is a lovely breakfast terrace. ● *Nov–Mar.*	79				
RHODES: *Nikolís* DrDrDrDr Ippodámou 61, Rhodes town, 85100. *0241 34561.* FAX *0241 32034.* Housed in an atmospheric medieval building in the heart of the old town, this hotel has rear rooms with terraces overlooking a garden.	10	●			■
RHODES: *Rhodos Imperial Grecotel* DrDrDrDrDr Leofóros Ialyssoú, Ixiá, 85101. *0241 75000.* FAX *0241 76690.* The town's most lavish five-star hotel, set in beautiful gardens by Ixiá beach, 4 km (3 miles) southwest of Rhodes town. ● *Nov–Feb.*	402	●	■	●	■
RHODES: *Rhodos Palace* DrDrDrDrDr Ialyssós bay, Ixiá, 85101. *0241 25222.* FAX *0241 25350.* A luxury hotel with apartments and bungalows in extensive grounds. Facilities include indoor and outdoor pools. ● *Nov–Feb.*	785	●	■	●	■

For key to symbols see back flap

Price categories are for a standard double room for one night in peak season, including tax, service charges, and breakfast:
(Dr) up to 8,000 Dr
(Dr)(Dr) 8–12,000 Dr
(Dr)(Dr)(Dr) 12–16,000 Dr
(Dr)(Dr)(Dr)(Dr) 16–21,000 Dr
(Dr)(Dr)(Dr)(Dr)(Dr) over 21,000 Dr.

RESTAURANT
Restaurant within the hotel sometimes reserved for residents only.

CLOSE TO BEACH
Within walking distance of the beach.

SWIMMING POOL
Hotel swimming pools are usually quite small and outdoors unless otherwise stated.

AIR-CONDITIONING
Hotel with air-conditioning in all the rooms.

Hotel	Number of Rooms	Restaurant	Close to Beach	Swimming Pool	Air-Conditioning
SYMI: *Chorió* (Dr)(Dr)(Dr) Chorió area, Sými town, 85600. 0241 71800. FAX 0241 71802. This modern, stylish hotel is situated opposite the village windmills and enjoys views over the town. All rooms have balconies. ● *Oct–Mar.*	17				
SYMI: *Alýki* (Dr)(Dr)(Dr)(Dr) Waterfront, Sými town, 85600. 0241 71665. FAX 0241 71655. This restored sea-captain's mansion has an elegant interior. It is set in picturesque surroundings, the rooms enjoying sea views. ● *Oct–Mar.*	15		■		●
SYMI: *Niréfs* (Dr)(Dr)(Dr)(Dr) Akti Georgíou, Sými town, 85600. 0241 72400. FAX 0241 72404. Housed in a beautifully restored municipal hotel, this traditional island-style hotel has a cosmopolitan feel and is the island's finest. ● *Oct–Apr.*	36	●	■		
TILOS: *Eiríni* (Dr)(Dr) Waterfront, Livádia, 85002. 0241 44293. FAX 0241 44238. A family-run hotel with plain and tasteful decor, set in beautiful, lush gardens with hibiscus plants and banana trees. ● *Nov–Mar.*	28		■		
TILOS: *Panórama Studios* (Dr)(Dr) Livádia bay, 85002. 0241 44365. FAX 0241 44365. Chic and stylish studios with a shared terrace, set in a peaceful spot on a hillside overlooking the bay of Livádia. The terrace has a vine-covered canopy, draped with bougainvillaea and geraniums. ● *Oct–Feb.*	6				■
THE CYCLADES					
AMORGOS: *Aegíali* (Dr)(Dr)(Dr)(Dr) On hillside above port, Aigíali, 84008. 0285 73393. FAX 0285 73394. This chic hotel complex with good facilities, including a taverna and large pool, offers lovely sea views from its veranda. ● *Nov–Mar.*	30	●	■	●	■
ANDROS: *Paradise* (Dr)(Dr)(Dr)(Dr)(Dr) 700 m (2,300 ft) from beach, Andros town, 84500. 0282 22187. FAX 0282 22340. This elegantly appointed hotel in a Neo-Classical mansion has a snack bar, and minibus service for transfers and tours. ● *Nov–Mar.*	41		■	●	
FOLEGANDROS: *Kástro* (Dr)(Dr) North end of Chóra, 84011. 0286 41230. FAX 0286 41230. Rooms look down sheer cliffs to the sea from this 500-year old traditional house. It is part of the ancient Kástro walls, with its pebble mosaic floors and barrel ceilings. Quaint and handy for the central squares. ● *Oct–Mar.*	12				
FOLEGANDROS: *Anemómylos Apartments* (Dr)(Dr)(Dr)(Dr)(Dr) Waterfront, Chóra, 84011. 0286 41309. FAX 0286 41407. A fully equipped complex built in traditional Cycladic style around a courtyard with balconies overhanging the sea. ● *mid-Oct–Apr.*	17				
IOS: *Diónysos* (Dr)(Dr)(Dr)(Dr) Mylopótas, 2 km (1 mile) SE of Ios town, 84001. 0286 91215. FAX 0286 91633. This luxury, traditional-style hotel is situated right on the beach. There are good facilities and a transfer service. ● *Nov–Apr.*	40	●	■	●	■
IOS: *Pétra Holiday Village* (Dr)(Dr)(Dr)(Dr) Ios bay, Ios town, 84001. 0286 91409. FAX 0286 91049. A group of traditional-style houses overlooking Ios bay. Tastefully decorated with whitewashed interiors and private terraces. ● *Oct–Apr.*	18		■		■
KEA: *Kéa Beach* (Dr)(Dr)(Dr)(Dr) Koundoúros bay, 5 km (3 miles) S of Písses, 84002. 0288 31230-3. FAX 0288 31234. A luxury bungalow complex built in traditional Cycladic style and offering all facilities from a nightclub to water sports. ● *Oct–Apr.*	48	●	■	●	

KYTHNOS: *Kýthnos* DrDr
Mérichas bay, 84006. 0281 32247. FAX 0281 32092.
A basic but friendly hotel, situated right on the waterfront. Rooms at the front have balconies overlooking the sea.

KYTHNOS: *Porto Klaras* DrDrDrDr
Loutrá beach, Loutrá, 84006. 0281 31276. FAX 0281 31355.
Very well-appointed new apartments near the beach and hot springs, with a wide range of accommodation from family suites to doubles with sea views and a pretty garden bar area. Dec–Apr.

MILOS: *Delfíni* DrDrDr
Behind the harbor, Adámantas, 84801. 0287 22001. FAX 0287 22688.
This small, friendly hotel, set back from the harbor at Adámantas, is run by a local sea captain. Quiet location with breakfast terrace. Nov–Mar.

MILOS: *Pópi's Windmill* DrDrDrDrDr
Off main square, Trypití, 84801. 0287 22286-7. FAX 0287 22396.
A stay at Pópi's Windmill will not be forgotten. This luxuriously converted windmill has lovely views toward Adámantas port.

MYKONOS: *Cavo Tagoo* DrDrDrDrDr
500 m (1,650 ft) N of port, Mýkonos town, 84100. 0289 23692. FAX 0289 24923.
One of the island's most stylish yet friendly hotels. Winner of the Aegean architectural award, it features a range of Cycladic maisonettes with lovely furnishings, overlooking the bay at Tagoo. Nov–Mar.

MYKONOS: *The Princess of Mýkonos* DrDrDrDrDr
Agios Stéfanos beach, 84600. 0289 23806. FAX 0289 23031.
Favorite of stars like Jane Fonda, this is another Cycladic-style hotel in traditional blue and white. It has all the luxury facilities, from gym to conference rooms and satellite TV. Nov–Mar.

NAXOS: *Grotta* DrDrDr
Aplomata area, behind port, Náxos town, 84300. 0285 22215. FAX 0285 22000.
Beautifully situated on a headland, this hotel enjoys good views of both the town and the sea. Rooms are clean; all have balconies.

NAXOS: *Nissaki Beach Hotel* DrDrDrDrDr
Agios Geórgios, Náxos town, 84300. 0285 25710. FAX 0285 23876.
Recently renovated in traditional Cycladic décor, this hotel is situated next to the beach. Some rooms have views of the sea, others the pool.

PAROS: *Dína* DrDr
On main through road, Paroikiá, 84400. 0284 21325.
A small and friendly establishment, centrally placed and beautifully kept, with spotless rooms and plain but attractive interiors. Nov–Apr.

PAROS: *Hotel Asterias* DrDrDrDr
Paroikiá, 84400. 0284 21797. FAX 0284 22172.
Built by the sea, most of the rooms here have recently been refurbished, and all have balconies. The bar is outside, offering breakfast, snacks and drinks overlooking the sea. The center of Paroikía is nearby. Oct–Apr.

PAROS: *Astir of Paros* DrDrDrDrDr
Kolympíthres, 11 km (7 miles) N of Paroikiá, 84400. 0284 51976. FAX 0284 51985.
A deluxe resort hotel offering well-equipped rooms with balconies. Facilities include horseback riding and an art gallery. Nov–Mar.

SANTORINI: *Ermís* DrDrDr
Kamári beach, 84700. 0286 31664. FAX 0286 32240.
Set among beautiful gardens, this friendly, family-run hotel offers well-appointed rooms, not far from the town center. Nov–May.

SANTORINI: *Fanári Villas* DrDrDrDrDr
Ammoúdi bay, 84700. 0286 71008. FAX 0286 71235.
These are traditional *skaftá* cave houses that have been given the luxury touch. There is a bar and steps to Ammoúdi bay below. Dec–Mar.

SANTORINI: *Kavalári* DrDrDrDrDr
Near bus station, Firá, 84700. 0286 22455. FAX 0286 22603.
Formerly a sea captain's home, this unusual hotel is terraced into the rock face. It has spectacular views over the caldera and is a great spot from which to enjoy the sunset. Nov–Mar.

Hotel					
Kýthnos	15		■		
Porto Klaras	24		■		
Delfíni	23		■		
Pópi's Windmill	2		■		
Cavo Tagoo	72	●	■	●	■
The Princess of Mýkonos	38	●	■	●	■
Grotta	40		■		
Nissaki Beach Hotel	40	●	■	■	●
Dína	8				
Hotel Asterias	36		■		
Astir of Paros	57	●	■	■	●
Ermís	36		■	●	
Fanári Villas	13	●	■	●	
Kavalári	18	●	■		■

Price categories are for a standard double room for one night in peak season, including tax, service charges, and breakfast:
Dr up to 8,000 Dr
DrDr 8–12,000 Dr
DrDrDr 12–16,000 Dr
DrDrDrDr 16–21,000 Dr
DrDrDrDrDr over 21,000 Dr.

RESTAURANT
Restaurant within the hotel sometimes reserved for residents only.

CLOSE TO BEACH
Within walking distance of the beach.

SWIMMING POOL
Hotel swimming pools are usually quite small and outdoors unless otherwise stated.

AIR-CONDITIONING
Hotel with air-conditioning in all the rooms.

Hotel	Number of Rooms	Restaurant	Close to Beach	Swimming Pool	Air-Conditioning
SANTORINI: *Palace* DrDrDrDrDr 500 m (1,640 ft) from main square, Firá, 84700. *0286 22771.* FAX *0286 23705.* Fine views of the Aegean and the caldera can be enjoyed from this stylish hotel with spacious rooms and good facilities. *Nov–Mar.*	106	●	■	●	■
SERIFOS: *Aretí* DrDr Waterfront, Livádi, 84005. *0281 51479.* FAX *0281 51547.* A convenient place to stay for the ferry, this family-run hotel and cake shop has comfortable rooms with terraces and a peaceful tiered garden overlooking the sea. *Nov–Apr.*	13		■		
SIFNOS: *Artemón* DrDrDrDr Agiou Konstandinou, Artemónas, 84003. *0284 31303.* FAX *0284 32385.* Situated in Artemónas, 1.5 km (1 mile) from the capital Apollonía, the Artemón is a chic and tasteful hotel within walking distance of quiet beaches. There is a terrace with sea views. *Nov–Mar.*	23	●	■		
SIFNOS: *Aléxandros* DrDrDrDrDr Waterfront, Platís Gialós, 84003. *0284 71333.* FAX *0284 71303.* Situated on the hillside above the beach, this pleasant hotel has a restaurant, terraces, and a pool overlooking Gialós beach. *Oct–Mar.*	26		■	●	
SIKINOS: *Flóra* Dr Overlooking the harbor, Aloprónia, 84010. *0286 51214.* Excellent, modestly priced, Cycladic-style development on the hillside above the port. There are eight self-contained chalet-style rooms built around courtyards with wonderful sea views.	8				
SYROS: *Villa Neféli* DrDrDr Párou 21, Ermoúpoli, 84100. *0281 87076.* Housed in a Neo-classical building with a marble exterior, this hotel offers clean, basic accommodations. There is a lovely roof garden.	7		■		■
SYROS: *Omiros* DrDrDrDr Omírou 43, Ermoúpoli, 84100. *0281 84910.* FAX *0281 86266.* The former home of the renowned sculptor, Vitális, this 150-year old Neo-Classical mansion has been tastefully converted. It has a spacious roof terrace overlooking the port.	13				
TINOS: *Aeolos Bay Hotel* DrDrDr Agios Fokas beach, 84200. *0283 23339.* FAX *0283 23086.* A short walk out of town, overlooking the beach, this smart, comfortable hotel has pool and friendly resident parrot. Well-appointed and set in pleasant gardens with a breakfast terrace. *Nov–Mar.*	69	●	■	●	

CRETE

Hotel	Number of Rooms	Restaurant	Close to Beach	Swimming Pool	Air-Conditioning
AGIA PELAGIA: *Alexander House* DrDrDrDrDr On waterfront. *081 811303.* FAX *081 811381.* Situated in Agía Pelagía, 20 km (12 miles) west of Irákleio, this is a very pleasant, tasteful hotel arranged around a courtyard and swimming pool, a minute's walk from the beach. *Nov–Mar.*	83	●	■	●	■
AGIA PELAGIA: *Kapsís Beach Hotel and Bungalows* DrDrDrDrDr On waterfront, 100m (330 ft) before the village. *081 811112.* FAX *081 811076.* One of the best luxury hotels on the island in the upscale resort of Agía Pelagía, 20 km (12 miles) west of Irákleio. Superbly situated on a landscaped promontory, surrounded by sandy beaches. *Nov–Apr.*	680	●	■	●	■
AGIOS NIKOLAOS: *Istron Bay* DrDrDrDrDr 13 km (8 miles) E of Agios Nikoláos. *0841 61303.* FAX *0841 61383.* This delightfully secluded resort hotel overlooks a spectacular cove and has the luxury of its own sandy beach. Friendly atmosphere.	118	●	■	●	■

AGIOS NIKOLAOS: *Mínos Beach* DrDrDrDrDr Aktí Ilía Sotírou, 72100. *0841 22345.* FAX *0841 22548.* This exclusive resort hotel, with whitewashed bungalows, is set in handsomely landscaped gardens on the Gulf of Mirampéllo. The hotel has its own private beach. ● *Nov–Mar.*	130	●	■	●	■
CHANIA: *Terésa* DrDr Angélou 8, 73100. *0821 92798.* Renovated Venetian house with fabulous views of the harbor from its roof terrace and some of the rooms. Excellent value for the money.	8				
CHANIA: *Amforá* DrDrDrDr Párodos Theotokópoulou 20, 73131. *0821 93224.* FAX *0821 93226.* Beautifully restored 13th-century Venetian mansion with tastefully appointed rooms and a charming roof terrace overlooking the harbor.	20	●	■		
CHANIA: *Vílla Androméda* DrDrDrDrDr Eleftheríou Venizélou 150, 73133. *0821 28300.* FAX *0821 28303.* This elegantly restored Neo-Classical mansion was built in 1870 and was once home to the German consulate. The hotel comprises eight luxuriously decorated suites. ● *Nov 20–Jan 20.*	8		■	●	■
CHERSONISOS: *Creta Maris* DrDrDrDrDr Waterfront, 800m (2,640 ft) W of Chersónisos, 70014. *0897 22115.* FAX *0897 22130.* A luxury hotel consisting of individual bungalows close to Chersónisos. There is an outdoor theater and open-air cinema. ● *Dec–Jan.*	13	●	■	●	■
CHERSONISOS: *Silva Maris* DrDrDrDrDr Chersónisos beach, 70014. *0897 22850.* FAX *0897 21404.* Built in the sytle of an Aegean village, the hotel is situated on the east side of Chersónisos. Rooms have balconies with sea views. ● *Nov–Feb.*	13	●	■	●	■
ELOUNTA: *Eloúnta Beach Hotel* DrDrDrDrDr 2 km (1 mile) N of Elounta, 72053. *0841 41412.* FAX *0841 41373.* The Eloúnta, Crete's grande dame of resort hotels, offers every amenity imaginable from Jacuzzis, Turkish baths, and saunas, to scuba diving, jet-skiing and parasailing. ● *Nov–Mar.*	280	●	■	●	■
ELOUNTA: *Eloúnta Mare* DrDrDrDrDr 2 km (1 mile) N of Elounta, 72053. *0841 41102.* FAX *0841 41307.* A resort hotel on the Gulf of Mirampéllo comprising a central building and 47 traditional whitewashed bungalows, each with its own pool and garden. Private beach and full range of amenities. ● *Nov–Mar.*	96	●	■	●	■
IERAPETRA: *Astron* DrDrDr Michaíl Kóthri 56, 72200. *0842 25114.* FAX *0842 25917.* Comfortable, new hotel on the outskirts of Ierápetra. Balconied rooms with sea views and a sandy beach just 20 m (65 ft) away.	70	●	■		■
IRAKLEIO: *Lató* DrDrDrDr Epimenídou 15, 71202. *081 228103.* FAX *081 240350.* Pleasant hotel with superb views over the Venetian harbor and in a good central location below the Archaeological Museum.	50	●			■
IRAKLEIO: *Atlantís* DrDrDrDrDr Ygeías 2, 71202. *081 229103.* FAX *081 226265.* Tucked away on a quiet street this large, modern hotel enjoys panoramic views over the ferry port and city of Irákleio.	160	●			■
IRAKLEIO: *Galaxy* DrDrDrDrDr Dimokratías 67, 71306. *081 238812.* FAX *081 211211.* This attractive, modern hotel is set around a central court and swimming pool. The rooms are tastefully decorated.	144	●		●	■
KASTELLI KISAMOU: *Kíssamos* Dr Iróon Polytechníou, 73400. *0822 22086.* FAX *0822 22475.* A basic but very friendly, well-run hotel in the center of town. The only lodgings in town with heating and water throughout winter.	30				
LOUTRO: *The Blue House* Dr Waterfront, 73011. *0825 91127.* A traditional whitewashed house with blue shutters in one of Crete's most magical spots. Each room has its own balcony overlooking the tiny harbor. A 15-minute ferry ride from Sfakiá. ● *Nov–Mar.*	15	●	■		

For key to symbols see back flap

Price categories are for a standard double room for one night in peak season, including tax, service charges, and breakfast:
(Dr) up to 8,000 Dr
(Dr)(Dr) 8–12,000 Dr
(Dr)(Dr)(Dr) 12–16,000 Dr
(Dr)(Dr)(Dr)(Dr) 16–21,000 Dr
(Dr)(Dr)(Dr)(Dr)(Dr) over 21,000 Dr.

Restaurant
Restaurant within the hotel sometimes reserved for residents only.

Close to Beach
Within walking distance of the beach.

Swimming Pool
Hotel swimming pools are usually quite small and outdoors unless otherwise stated.

Air-Conditioning
Hotel with air-conditioning in all the rooms.

Hotel	Number of Rooms	Restaurant	Close to Beach	Swimming Pool	Air-Conditioning
Matala: *Oríon* (Dr)(Dr) 1 km (0.5 miles) S of Mátala, 70200. ☎ *0892 42129.* FAX *0892 42129.* A stylish, reasonably priced hotel in a wonderfully secluded position just outside Mátala on the south coast of Crete. Large swimming pool and several outstanding beaches within easy striking distance. ● *Nov–Mar.*	46		■	●	
Palaiochora: *Réa* (Dr)(Dr) Antoníou Peráki, 73001. ☎ *0823 41307.* FAX *0823 41605.* A friendly, family-run hotel with a shady, flower-decked terrace. There is a sandy beach only five minutes' walk away. ● *Nov–Mar.*	14	●	■		
Plakias: *Plakiás Bay* (Dr)(Dr)(Dr) Plakiás bay, 74060. ☎ *0832 31215.* FAX *0832 31951.* A small, whitewashed hotel bedecked with flowers and enjoying a superb position overlooking Plakiás bay. ● *Nov–Mar.*	28	●	■		
Rethymno: *Liberty* (Dr)(Dr)(Dr) Corner of Moátsou & Preveláki, 74100. ☎ *0831 55851.* FAX *0831 55850.* A comfortable hotel with a central location near the Municipal Gardens and close to the waterfront. ● *20 Dec–mid-Jan.*	35				■
Rethymno: *Fortétsa* (Dr)(Dr)(Dr)(Dr) Melisinoú 16, 74100. ☎ *0831 55551.* FAX *0831 54073.* One of the nicest hotels in Réthymno, on a quiet backstreet just behind the Fortétsa, one minute's walk from the seafront. ● *Dec–Feb.*	54	●	■	●	
Rethymno: *Grecotel Creta Palace* (Dr)(Dr)(Dr)(Dr)(Dr) On the beach, Misiría, 74100. ☎ *0831 55181.* FAX *0831 54085.* Resort hotel with its own beach in Misiría, 4 km (2 miles) east of Réthymno. Full range of facilities including a fitness club. ● *Nov–Mar.*	162	●	■	●	■
Siteia: *Archontikó* (Dr) Kondiláki 16, 72300. ☎ *0843 28172.* This hotel is housed in an elegant, old building with high ceilings and a tiny garden. There is a friendly, relaxed atmosphere. ● *Nov–Feb.*	9				
Spili: *Green* (Dr) Off main square, 74100. ☎ *0832 22225.* Situated in the mountain town of Spíli, 20 km (12 miles) south of Réthymno, this hotel is recognized by a forest of geraniums. ● *Nov–Mar.*	13				■
Zaros: *Idi Hotel* (Dr)(Dr) North of Zarós, at the foot of Mount Ida, 70002. ☎ *0894 31301.* FAX *0894 31511.* A delightful hotel with an almost alpine setting just outside Zarós, 38 km (24 miles) south of Irákleío. Zarós is famous for its spring waters.	59	●		●	
ATHENS					
Areos: *Park* (Dr)(Dr)(Dr)(Dr)(Dr) Leofóros Alexándras 10, 10682. ☎ *01 883 2712.* FAX *01 823 8420.* Situated opposite the relaxing Areos Park, this hotel has spacious rooms. There is also a good rooftop bar and a 24-hour coffee shop.	146	●		●	■
Exarcheia: *Exarcheíon* (Dr)(Dr) Themistokléous 55, 10683. ☎ *01 380 1256.* FAX *01 380 3296.* This hotel is close to the late-night action of Plateía Exarcheíon. The rooms are basic, and there is a good sidewalk café.	54				
Exarcheia: *Museum* (Dr)(Dr) Mpoumpoulínas 16, 10682. ☎ *01 380 5611.* FAX *01 380 0507.* The modern façade of this building hides a genteel interior. Situated opposite the National Archaeological Museum, it is frequented by academics. The rooms are clean and quiet.	58				

Hotel	Price	Rooms				
ILISIA: *Hilton* Leofóros Vasilíssis Sofías 46, 11528. *01 725 0201.* FAX *01 725 3110.* Athens' best-known modern hotel. All the rooms have large balconies, providing stunning views across the city.	DrDrDrDrDr	453	●		●	■
KOLONAKI: *Athenian Inn* Cháritos 22, 10675. *01 723 9552.* FAX *01 724 2268.* This hotel offers clean, basic rooms and friendly management. Situated in the heart of Kolonáki, among a choice of shops, restaurants, and cafés.	DrDrDrDrDr	25				■
KOLONAKI: *St George Lykavittós* Kleoménous 2, 10675. *01 729 0711.* FAX *01 729 0439.* Situated beneath Lykavittós Hill, this small, luxury hotel offers large rooms with a good views. The rooftop restaurant is excellent.	DrDrDrDrDr	167	●		●	■
KOUKAKI: *Marble House* Zínni Anastasíou 35, 11741. *01 923 4058.* At the end of a quiet cul de sac, this is a firm favorite among mid-range pensions for its cleanliness and helpful management. Most rooms are *en suite* and many have vine-covered balconies.	DrDr	16				
MAKRYGIANNI: *Athens Gate* Leofóros A Syngroú 10, 11742. *01 923 8302.* FAX *01 923 7493.* This centrally located, modern hotel offers comfortable rooms and a roof-top garden with views of the Acropolis and Hadrian's Arch.	DrDrDrDrDr	100	●			■
MAKRIGIANNI: *Divani Palace Acropolis* Parthenónos 19–25, 11742. *01 922 2945.* FAX *01 921 4993.* Beautifully upgraded to deluxe standard, this hotel is just a short stroll from the Acropolis. An original section of the Themistoklean Long Walls is on view in the hotel lobby.	DrDrDrDrDr	251	●		●	■
MAKRYGIANNI: *Iródeion* Rovértou Gkálli 4, 11742. *01 923 6832.* FAX *01 923 5851.* This hotel has large modern rooms, a patio shaded by pistachio trees and a roof terrace with views of the Acropolis.	DrDrDrDrDr	90	●			■
MAKRYGIANNI: *Royal Olympic* Athanasíou Diákou 28–32, 11743. *01 922 6411.* FAX *01 923 3317.* The Royal Olympic has wonderful large rooms, all with superb views of the Temple of Olympian Zeus. Good grill restaurant.	DrDrDrDrDr	304	●		●	■
METAXOURGEIO: *Stanley* Odysséos 1, Plateía Kairaskáki, 10437. *01 524 1611.* FAX *01 524 4611.* The Stanley hotel has large fully equipped rooms with balconies. Facilities include a rooftop garden and pool, a restaurant and busy bar.	DrDrDrDrDr	400	●		●	■
MONASTIRAKI: *Témpoi* Aiólou 29, 10551. *01 321 3175.* FAX *01 325 4179.* Overlooking the flower market and Agía Eiríni church, this hotel is ideal for those who want to explore Athinás market's food and stalls.	DrDr	24				
MONASTIRAKI: *Attalos* Athinás 29, 19554. *01 321 2801.* FAX *01 324 3124.* Ideally situated for shopping, near Monastiráki and Athinás, the Attalos offers adequate rooms, some with balconies. The hotel also has a roof garden with good views of the Acropolis.	DrDrDrDrDr	80				■
NEOS KOSMOS: *Christína* Petmezá 15, 11743. *01 921 5353.* FAX *01 921 5569.* This is a fairly standard businessman's hotel just a short walk from the Acropolis. The rooms are clean and homey.	DrDrDrDr	93	●			■
NEOS KOSMOS: *Athenaeum Inter-Continental* Leofóros Andrea Syngroú 89–93, 11745. *01 920 6000.* FAX *01 924 3000.* Decorated throughout by modern Greek artists, this luxurious hotel offers a choice of fine restaurants, bars, and shops. Facilities also include a fully equipped gymnasium.	DrDrDrDrDr	520	●		●	■
NEOS KOSMOS: *Ledra Marriot* Leofóros Andrea Syngroú 115, 11745. *01 934 7711.* FAX *01 935 8603.* As well as all the amenities expected from a luxury hotel, the Marriot's rooms are large and spacious, and the hotel boasts superb restaurants, particularly the trendy Polynesian Kona Kai.	DrDrDrDrDr	259	●		●	■

For key to symbols see back flap

Price categories are for a standard double room for one night in peak season, including tax, service charges, and breakfast:
(Dr) up to 8,000 Dr
(Dr)(Dr) 8–12,000 Dr
(Dr)(Dr)(Dr) 12–16,000 Dr
(Dr)(Dr)(Dr)(Dr) 16–21,000 Dr
(Dr)(Dr)(Dr)(Dr)(Dr) over 21,000 Dr.

Restaurant
Restaurant within the hotel sometimes reserved for residents only.

Close to Beach
Within walking distance of the beach.

Swimming Pool
Hotel swimming pools are usually quite small and outdoors unless otherwise stated.

Air-Conditioning
Hotel with air-conditioning in all the rooms.

	Number of Rooms	Restaurant	Close to Beach	Swimming Pool	Air-Conditioning
Omonoia: *La Mirage* (Dr)(Dr)(Dr) Maríchas Kotopoúli 3, 10431. *01 523 4755.* FAX *01 523 3992.* A favorite for those who want to be close to the 24-hour hustle and bustle of Plateía Omonoías. All rooms are double-glazed.	*208*	●			■
Omonoia: *Dorian Inn* (Dr)(Dr)(Dr)(Dr)(Dr) Peiraiós 15–19, 10552. *01 523 9782.* FAX *01 522 6196.* Situated in the heart of the city center, the roof garden of this chic hotel offers spectacular views over Athens and the Acropolis.	*146*	●		●	■
Omonoia: *King Minos* (Dr)(Dr)(Dr)(Dr)(Dr) Peiraiós 1, 10552. *01 523 1111-8.* FAX *01 523 1361.* The hotel's large and comfortable public lounge areas, including the restaurant and the bar, are good places in which to unwind. All the rooms in the hotel are quiet.	*194*	●			■
Omonoia: *Titánia* (Dr)(Dr)(Dr)(Dr)(Dr) Panepistimíou 52, 10678. *01 330 0111.* FAX *01 330 0700.* The entrance to this well-appointed hotel is through a shopping arcade close to Plateía Omonoías. Rooms are well equipped and the rooftop terrace bar and ground-floor café are always busy.	*396*	●			■
Plaka: *John's Place* (Dr) Patróou 5, 10557. *01 322 9719.* One of the better bargain backpacking hotels. The rooms are small but very clean, and bathrooms are shared.	*15*				
Plaka: *Koúros* (Dr) Kódrou 11, 10557. *01 322 7431.* Situated in the heart of Pláka, this cheap and cheerful small pension is housed in a converted Neo-Classical mansion house. Rooms are basic but clean and all have balconies.	*10*				
Plaka: *Faídra* (Dr)(Dr) Chairofóntos 16, 10558. *01 323 8461.* The hotel's location next to the Lysikrates monument more than makes up for the slightly tacky quality of its rooms and public areas.	*27*				
Plaka: *Acropolis House Pension* (Dr)(Dr)(Dr) Kódrou 6–8, 10557. *01 322 2344.* FAX *01 323 3143.* Housed in a converted 19th-century building, the rooms in this pension are large and airy. All rooms have private balconies.	*19*				■
Plaka: *Adonis* (Dr)(Dr)(Dr) Kódrou 3, 10557. *01 324 9737.* FAX *01 323 1602.* The Adónis is a modern, resonably priced hotel offering decent, basic accommodation and panoramic views across Athens from its roof garden. All the rooms have balconies.	*26*				
Plaka: *Adrian* (Dr)(Dr)(Dr) Adrianoú 74, 10556. *01 322 1553.* FAX *01 325 0461.* Situated in central Pláka, this hotel has simple, comfortable rooms as well as a quiet terrace to escape the bustle of the city.	*22*				■
Plaka: *Aphrodite* (Dr)(Dr)(Dr) Apóllonos 21, 10557. *01 323 4357.* FAX *01 322 5244.* This hotel is well located and offers clean, good-value rooms, some of which enjoy wonderful views of the Acropolis.	*84*	●			■
Plaka: *Ermís* (Dr)(Dr)(Dr) Apóllonos 19, 10557. *01 323 5514.* FAX *01 323 2073.* Despite a rather drab lobby, the rooms of this hotel are large, some having balconies overlooking a playground.	*45*				■

Hotel	Price	Rooms				
PLAKA: *Neféli* Angelikís Chatzimicháli 2, 10558. *01 322 8044.* A modern hotel, hidden away in a peaceful backwater in Pláka. The rooms are clean and of a good, basic standard.	DrDrDr	18				■
PLAKA: *Byron* Výronos 19, 10558. *01 323 0327.* FAX *01 322 0276.* Situated on the southern fringe of Pláka, this small and somewhat basic hotel is close to the Acropolis. Some rooms have balconies.	DrDrDrDr	20				
PLAKA: *Myrtó* Níkis 40, 10558. *01 322 7237.* Close to the central areas of Plateía Syntágmatos and Pláka, this small hotel is ideal for short stays and is popular with young couples.	DrDrDrDr	12				■
PLAKA: *Omiros* Apóllonos 15, 10557. *01 323 5486.* FAX *01 322 8059.* A lovely roof garden distinguishes this otherwise basic hotel, which is located in a quiet area of Pláka.	DrDrDrDr	37				■
PLAKA: *Electra Palace* Navárchou Nikodímou 18, 10559. *01 324 1401.* FAX *01 324 1875.* A popular hotel with a roof garden and swimming pool, the Electra Palace has good views and rooms with balconies.	DrDrDrDrDr	106	●		●	■
STATHMOS LARISSIS: *Novotel Athens* Michaíl Vóda 4–6, 10439. *01 825 0422.* FAX *01 883 7816.* Run by the French group, Novotel, this smart, centrally located hotel has modern, well-equipped rooms and a stunning rooftop garden and swimming pool.	DrDrDrDrDr	195	●		●	■
STREFI HILL: *Oríon* Anexartisías 5 & E Mpenáki 105, 11473. *01 382 7362.* FAX *01 380 5193.* Besides Stréfi Hill, just above the bustling Exárcheia area, this quiet hotel is popular with students looking for short-term accommodations.	DrDr	38				
SYNTAGMA: *Aretoúsa* Mitropóleos 6–8 & Níkis 12, 10563. *01 322 9431.* FAX *01 322 9439.* Decent value characterizes this centrally located hotel. The rooms are modern, and there is a roof garden as well as a lively bar.	DrDrDrDr	87	●			■
SYNTAGMA: *Astor* Karageórgi Servías 16, 10562. *01 335 1000.* FAX *01 325 5115.* The popular all-year-round rooftop restaurant of this hotel boasts stunning views over Athens. The double rooms from the sixth floor upward share this impressive view of the city.	DrDrDrDr	130	●			■
SYNTAGMA: *Amalía* Leofóros Vasilíssis Amalías 10, 10557. *01 335 1000.* FAX *01 323 8792.* Although the rooms are fairly small, all the bathrooms are marble. The hotel is centrally located and has good views of both the Parliament building and the National Gardens.	DrDrDrDrDr	98	●			■
SYNTAGMA: *Electra* Ermoú 5, 10557. *01 322 3223.* FAX *01 322 0310.* This centrally located hotel is ideally situated for shopping expeditions to Monastiráki. All the rooms are clean and pleasant.	DrDrDrDrDr	110	●			■
SYNTAGMA: *Esperia Palace* Stadíou 22, 10564. *01 323 8001.* FAX *01 323 8100.* A stylish city hotel with marble lobbies and tastefully decorated rooms. Its restaurant and bar are popular with Athenians.	DrDrDrDrDr	184	●			■
SYNTAGMA: *Grande Bretagne* Plateía Syntágmatos, 10563. *01 323 0251.* FAX *01 322 8034.* This luxurious hotel was built in 1852 and is the landmark of Plateía Syntágmatos, the most desirable hotel location in Athens. The lobby and rooms are beautiful and the service is excellent.	DrDrDrDrDr	450	●			■
SYNTAGMA: *NJV Meridien* Vasiléos Georgíou, 10564. *01 325 5301.* FAX *01 323 5856.* This grand hotel offers luxurious blue and white rooms, all of which are sound-proofed. There are good facilities and its Explorers' Lounge and Marco Polo restaurant are always busy.	DrDrDrDrDr	177	●			■

For key to symbols see back flap

Where to Eat

To dine out in Greece is to experience the democratic tradition at work. Rich and poor, young and old, all enjoy their favorite local restaurant, taverna, or café. Greeks consider the best places to be where the food is fresh, plentiful, and well-cooked, not necessarily where the setting or cuisine is the fanciest. Visitors, too, have come to appreciate the simplicity and health of the traditional Greek kitchen – olive oil, yogurt, vegetables, a little meat and some wine, always shared with friends. The traditional three-hour lunch and siesta is still the daily rhythm of the islands, and only in the main tourist areas will you find the Western European routine of a substantial breakfast, a larger and briefer lunch (1pm–2:30pm), and an earlier dinner (7:30–11pm). Greeks prefer a quick breakfast coffee, heavy lunch, and an evening *mezédes* selection, before a long, late dinner that can stretch well into the night.

Tsikoudiá, a strong spirit from Crete

Types of Restaurant

Often difficult to find in more developed tourist resorts, the *estiatórion*, or traditional Greek restaurant is one of Europe's most enjoyable places to eat. Friendly, noisy, and sometimes in lovely surroundings, *estiatória* are reliable purveyors of local recipes and wines, particularly if they have been owned by the same family for decades. Foreigners unfamiliar with Greek dishes may be invited into the kitchen to choose their fare. In Greece, the entire family dines together and takes plenty of time over the meal, especially at the weekends.

Many traditional restaurants specialize in either a regional cuisine, a method of cooking, or a certain type of food. In islands such as Crete, where a small minority of Greeks from Asia Minor have settled, you may find food to be spicier than the Greek norm, with lots of red peppers and such dishes as *giogurtlú* (kebabs drenched in yoghurt and served on pitta bread).

The menu *(see pp316–17)* in a traditional restaurant tends to be short, comprising at most a dozen *mezédes* (appetizers), eight main dishes, four or five vegetable dishes and salads, plus a dessert of fresh or cooked fruit, and a selection of local and national wines.

Restaurants vary from very expensive in the main island towns to the magnificently inexpensive. The cheapest of the traditional restaurants are known as a *mageirió*, though they are becoming increasingly rare. Here there is little choice in either wine or dishes, all of which will be *mageireftá* (ready-cooked), but the food is home-made and tasty and the barrel wine is at the very least drinkable and is often good if it comes from the owner's village. Many hotels have restaurants open to nonresidents. The large island hotels generally offer more expensive, international cuisine. Some will also offer a Greek menu, which tends to be a more elaborate presentation of traditional dishes. Smaller country hotels, however, occasionally have excellent kitchens, and serve good local wines; it is worth checking on any close by.

Windmill restaurant *(see p324)*, Skíathos town

Patmian House restaurant *(see p327)* on Pátmos

In the last few years a new breed of young Greek chefs has emerged in "*kultúra*" restaurants, developing a style of cooking that encompasses the country's magnificent raw materials, flavors, and colors. These dishes are served with exciting new Greek wines.

Tavernas

One of the great pleasures for the traveler in Greece is the tradition of the taverna, a place to eat and drink, even if you simply snack on some *mezédes* (Greeks rarely drink without eating). Traditional tavernas open mid-evening and stay open late; occasionally they are also open for lunch. Menus are short and

Outside diners at a taverna in Plakiás, Crete

seasonal – perhaps six or eight *mezédes* and four main courses consisting of casseroles and dishes cooked *tis óras* (to order), along with the usual accompaniments of vegetables, salads, fruit, and wine.

Like traditional restaurants, some tavernas specialize in the foods and wines of the owner's home region, some in a particular cooking style and others in certain foods.

A *psarotavérna* is the place to find good fish dishes. In small fishing villages you may find the rickety tables of a *psarotavérna* literally on the beach. Close to the lapping waves the owner may serve fish such as red mullet, bass, and octopus that he himself caught that morning. However, be wary of the large fish restaurants found in tourist areas, as they are usually over-priced and may serve frozen or imported fish.

Accordian player in a taverna on Sými

For delicious grills try a *psistariá*, a taverna that specializes in spit-roasts and charbroiling *(sta kárvouna)*. In the countryside, you may find lamb, kid, pork, chicken, game, offal, lambs' heads, and even testicles charbroiled, and whole lamb is roasted on the spit. At the harborside, fish and shellfish are grilled and served with fresh lemon juice and olive oil. Family-run country tavernas and cafés will invariably provide simple meals, such as omelettes and salads, at any time of day, but many of these places close quite early in the evening. After your meal in the taverna, follow the Greeks and enjoy a visit to the local *zacharoplasteío (see p314)* for a range of sweets and pastries.

Cafes and Bars

Cafes, known as *kafeneía*, are the pulse of Greek life, and even the tiniest hamlet has a place to drink coffee and wine. Equally important is its function as the center of communication – mail is collected here, telephone calls made, and newspapers read, dissected, and discussed.

All *kafeneía* serve Greek coffee, sometimes *frappé* (instant coffee served cold, in a tall glass), soft drinks, beer, ouzo, and local wine. Most also serve some kind of snack to order. All open early in the morning and remain open until late at night. As the social hub of their communities, country *kafeneía*, as well as many in island towns, open seven days a week.

A *galaktopoleío*, or "milk shop," has a seating area where you can enjoy fine yogurt and honey. A *kapileío* (wine shop with a café-bar attached) is the place to try local wines from the cask, and you may find a few bottled wines as well. The owner is invariably from a wine village or family, and will often cook some simple regional specialties to accompany the wine.

In a *mezedopoleío*, or *mezés* shop, the owner will not only serve the local wine and the *mezédes* that go with it, but also ouzo and the infamous spirit raki, both distilled from the remnants of the grape harvest. Their accompanying *mezédes* are less salty than those served with wine.

No holiday in Greece is complete without a visit to an *ouzerí*. You can order a dozen or more little plates of savory meats, fish, and vegetables and try the many varieties of ouzo, served in small jugs, with a glass of water to wash the ouzo down. It is a noisy and fun place to eat and drink.

Artemónas restaurant *(see p330)* on the island of Sífnos

A waterside restaurant at Skála Sykaminiás, Lésvos

Fast Food and Snacks

Visitors can be forgiven for thinking Greeks never stop eating, for there seem to be snack bars on every street and vendors selling sweets, nuts, rolls, seasonal corn, and chestnuts at every turn.

Although American-style fast food outlets dominate tourist centers, traditional Greek eateries provide intriguing alternatives. Try the food of the extremely cheap *souvlatzídiko*, which offers a mostly takeout service of *souvláki* – chunks of meat, fish, or vegetables, grilled or roasted on a skewer – with fresh bread. Another option is the *ovelistírio*, which serves *gýros* – meat from a revolving spit in a pita bread pocket. The food is sold "*sto chéri*" (in the hand, or to takeout).

Many bakeries sell savory pies and an array of flavorful bread rolls, and in busy areas you will always be able to find a café serving substantial snacks and salads.

If you have a sweet tooth you will love the *zacharoplasteío* (literally, "shop of the sugar sculptor"). The baker prepares traditional sweet breads, tiny sweet pastries and a whole variety of fragrant honey cakes.

Breakfast

For Greeks, this is the least important meal of the day. In traditional homes and *kafeneía* a small cup of Greek coffee accompanies *paximádia* (slices of bread rusks) or *koulourákia* (firm, sesame-covered, or slightly sweet rolls in rings or s-shapes) or pound cakes, filled with traditional homemade jam.

Elsewhere, and in many tourist cafés, this has been replaced by a large cup of brewed coffee and French-style croissants or delicious brioche-style rolls. During summer, some *kafeneía* will still serve fresh figs, thick yogurt, pungent honey, and slightly sweet currant bread, as well as a variety of American and continental breakfasts to cater to visitors' tastes.

Baklavás, a sweet cake of wheat, honey and nuts

Reservations

Although island restaurants generally have a casual atmosphere, they can be very popular; if it is possible to make a reservation, it is probably best to do so. Also, it is local practice to visit the restaurant or taverna earlier in the day to check on the dishes to be served. The proprietor will then take your order and reserve any special dish that you request.

Wine

The grape varieties that abound in Greece today produce wines that are quite distinct from those of western Europe. However, restaurateurs are only now learning to look after bottled wines. If the wine list contains the better wines, such as Ktima Merkoúri, Seméli, or Strofiliá, the proprietor probably knows how to look after them, and it will be safe to order a more expensive bottle. For a little less, good-value bottles include the nationally known Cambás and Boutári wines.

Wine from Límnos

Traditional restaurants and tavernas may stock only carafe wine, which is served straight from the barrel and is always inexpensive. Carafe wines are often of the region, and the Greek rosé in particular is noted for having an unusual but pleasing flavor.

How to Pay

Greece is very much a cash society. If you need to pay by credit card, check first that the restaurant takes your credit card – many proprietors do not accept the whole range. *Kafeneía* almost never take credit cards, and café-bars very rarely do, although many will be happy to take travelers' checks. Country restaurants, tavernas, *kafeneía* and bars will accept only cash.

The restaurant listings in this guide on pages 322–33 indicate whether or not credit cards are accepted at each establishment.

Kástro's bar *(see p329)* in the town of Mýkonos

Bright lights of Ouzerí to Kamáki *(see p324)* on Alónissos

Service and Tipping

Greeks take plenty of time when they eat out and expect a high level of attention. This means a great deal of running around on the part of the waiter, but in return they receive generous tips – as much as 20 percent if the service is exceptional, though more often a tip is between 10 and 15 percent. Prices in traditional establishments do include service, but the waiters still expect a tip so always have coins ready to hand. Tap water is offered free with a meal.

Western-style restaurants and tourist tavernas sometimes add a service charge to the bill; their prices can be considerably higher because of additional trimmings, such as air-conditioning and phones.

Basket of local bread from Rhodes

Dress Code

The Greeks dress quite formally when dining out. Visitors should wear whatever is comfortable, but skimpy tops and shorts and active sportswear are usually acceptable only near the beach – though most tourist establishments rarely turn away business. Some hotel restaurants have policies requesting formal dress; in the listings we indicate which restaurants fall into this category.

In summer, if you dine outside, take a jacket or sweater for later in the evening.

Children

Children become restaurant and taverna habitués at a very early age in Greece – it is an essential part of their education. Consequently, children are welcome everywhere in Greece except the bars. In formal restaurants children are expected to be well behaved, but in summer, when the Greeks enjoy long hours eating outside, it is perfectly acceptable for the children to play and enjoy themselves too. Special facilities such as high chairs are unknown in all but the most considerate hotel dining rooms, but generally, casual restaurants and tavernas are perfect for dining with children of any age.

Smoking

Smoking is commonplace in Greece, and with the exception of the most expensive dining rooms, you will have difficulty finding a no-smoking area. However, most restaurants are airy, and for at least half the year it is possible to dine outside in the open air.

Wheelchair Access

In country areas, where room is plentiful, there are few problems for wheelchair users. But in crowded tourist restaurants access is often restricted. The streets themselves can have uneven pavements on the islands, and many restaurants have narrow doorways and possibly steps. There are several organizations for assisting disabled vacationers, and those listed on page 337 provide specific information for visitors traveling to the Greek islands.

Vegetarian Food

Greek cuisine provides plenty of choice for vegetarians. Greeks enjoy a variety of dishes for each course, so it is generally easy to order just vegetable dishes for both first and main courses in any traditional restaurants, tavernas, or *kafeneía*. Greek vegetable dishes are substantial, inexpensive, and very satisfying. Usually they are prepared in imaginative ways to complement or enhance their flavor.

Vegans may have a little more difficulty but, as Greek cooking relies very little on dairy products, it is possible to follow a vegan diet on any of the Greek islands.

Picnics

The best time to picnic in Greece is in spring, when the countryside is at its most beautiful and temperatures are not too hot. Traditional seasonal foods such as Lenten olive oil breads, sweet Easter breads, pies filled with wild greens, fresh cheese, and young retsina wine make perfect picnic fare. In summer, peaches and figs, yogurt, hard cheese, tomatoes, bread, and olives are the ideal beach snacks.

People drinking coffee at the Liston in Corfu town

The Classic Greek Menu

The traditional first course is a selection of *mezédes*, or snacks; these can also be eaten in *ouzerís* or bars, throughout the day. Meat or fish dishes follow next, usually served with a salad. The wine list tends to be simple, and coffee and cakes are generally consumed after the meal in a nearby pastry shop. In rural areas traditional dishes can be chosen straight from the kitchen.

Taramosaláta *is a purée of salted mullet roe and breadcrumbs or potato. Traditionally a dish for Lent, it is now on every taverna menu.*

Mezédes are both a first course and a snack with wine or other drinks.

Souvlákia *are tiny chunks of pork, flavored with lemon, herbs, and olive oil, grilled on skewers. Here they are served with* **tzatzíki**, *a refreshing mixture of creamy yogurt, cucumber, garlic, and mint.*

Melitzanosaláta and revythosaláta *are both purées.* Melitzanosaláta, *left, is grilled eggplant and herbs; and* revythosaláta, *right, is chickpeas, coriander, and garlic.*

Olives

Fish are at their best around the coast and on the islands.

Melitzánes imám baïldí *are eggplants filled with a ragoût of onions, tomatoes, and herbs.* **Dolmádes** *(bottom) are parcels of grape leaves tightly stuffed with currants, pine nuts, and rice.*

Fried squid

ΜΕΖΕΣ
Mezés

Ελιές
Eliés

Ταραμοσαλάτα
Taramosaláta

Τζατζίκι
Tzatzíki

Σουβλάκια
Souvlákia

Ρεβυθοσαλάτα
Revythosaláta

Μελιτζανοσαλάτα
Melitzanosaláta

Ντολμάδες
Ntolmádes

Μελιτζάνες ιμάμ μπαϊλντί
Melitzánes imám baïldí

Χωριάτικη σαλάτα
Choriátiki saláta

ΨΑΡΙΑ
Psária

Πλακί
Plakí

Σχάρας
Scháras

Τηγανιτά καλαμάρια
Tiganitá kalamária

Choriátiki saláta, *Greek salad, combines tomatoes, cucumbers, onions, herbs, peppers, and feta cheese.*

Scháras *means "from the grill." This summer dish of grilled swordfish is served with a salad of bitter greens.*

Psária plakí *is a whole fish baked in an open dish with carrots, leeks, and potatoes in a tomato, fennel, and olive oil sauce.*

Bread in Greece

Bread is considered by Greeks to be the staff of life and is served at every meal. Village bakers vary the bread each day with flavorings of currants, herbs, wild greens, or cheese. The many Orthodox festivals are celebrated with special breads.

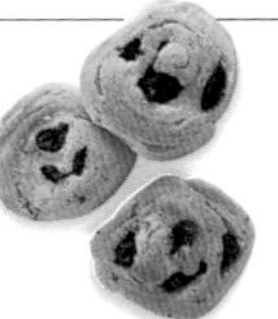

Olive rolls with herbs

Pita bread, unleavened

Paximádia **(twice-baked bread)**

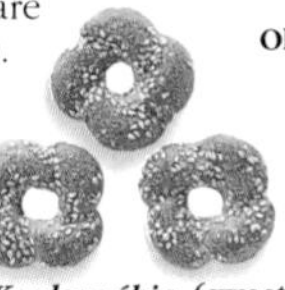

Koulourákia **(sweet or plain rolls)**

Tsouréki **(festival bread loaf)**

ΚΡΕΑΣ
Kréas

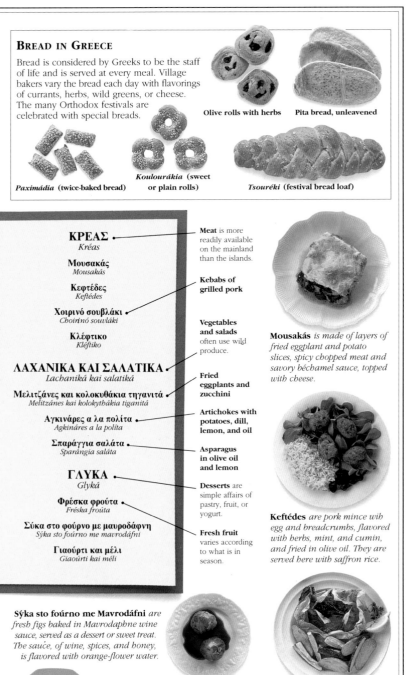

Μουσακάς
Mousakás

Κεφτέδες
Keftédes

Χοιρινό σουβλάκι
Choirinó souvláki

Κλέφτικο
Kléftiko

ΛΑΧΑΝΙΚΑ ΚΑΙ ΣΑΛΑΤΙΚΑ
Lachanikά kai salatikά

Μελιτζάνες και κολοκυθάκια τηγανιτά
Melitzánes kai kolokythákia tiganitá

Αγκινάρες α λα πολίτα
Agkináres a la políta

Σπαράγγια σαλάτα
Sparángia saláta

ΓΛΥΚΑ
Glyká

Φρέσκα φρούτα
Fréska froúta

Σύκα στο φούρνο με μαυροδάφνη
Sýka sto foúrno me mavrodáfni

Γιαούρτι και μέλι
Giaoúrti kai méli

Meat is more readily available on the mainland than the islands.

Kebabs of grilled pork

Vegetables and salads often use wild produce.

Fried eggplants and zucchini

Artichokes with potatoes, dill, lemon, and oil

Asparagus in olive oil and lemon

Desserts are simple affairs of pastry, fruit, or yogurt.

Fresh fruit varies according to what is in season.

Mousakás *is made of layers of fried eggplant and potato slices, spicy chopped meat and savory béchamel sauce, topped with cheese.*

Keftédes *are pork mince wih egg and breadcrumbs, flavored with herbs, mint, and cumin, and fried in olive oil. They are served here with saffron rice.*

Sýka sto foúrno me Mavrodáfni *are fresh figs baked in Mavrodaphne wine sauce, served as a dessert or sweet treat. The sauce, of wine, spices, and honey, is flavored with orange-flower water.*

Kléftiko *is usually goat meat wrapped in parchment paper and cooked so that the juices and flavors are sealed in.*

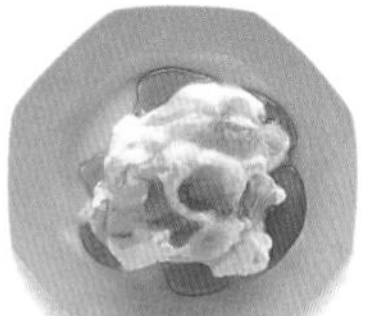

Giaoúrti kai méli *(yogurt with honey) is the most wonderful snack in Greece, served in specialty "milk shops," to be eaten there or taken home.*

Eating Fish on the Islands

GREEK COOKS HAVE ENJOYED a wealth of fish and seafood since ancient times. The warm and sheltered waters of the Aegean are the migratory path for tuna and swordfish and a feeding ground for tasty anchovies and the ubiquitous sardine. Coves and caves around the hundreds of rocky islands shelter highly prized red mullet, dentex, and parrot fish, and the long shoreline is home to a variety of shellfish and crustaceans. There is nothing better than eating simply prepared fish or seafood, fresh from the sea, in a harborside taverna with the Aegean shimmering in the brilliant sunshine. Fish can be grilled, pan-fried, or baked, and are served complete with their heads: to Greeks this is the tastiest part, and it helps to identify their variety.

Keeping fish fresh at the Lésvos port of Skála Sykaminiás

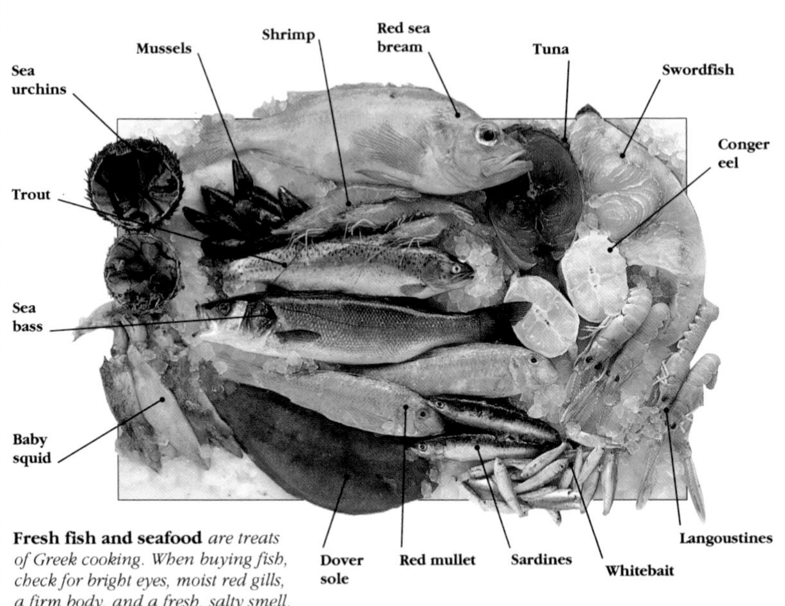

Fresh fish and seafood *are treats of Greek cooking. When buying fish, check for bright eyes, moist red gills, a firm body, and a fresh, salty smell.*

Tsirosaláta *is a typical year-round* mezés. *Thin strips of smoked fish, baked beet, and fresh herbs are served with olive oil and lemon juice.*

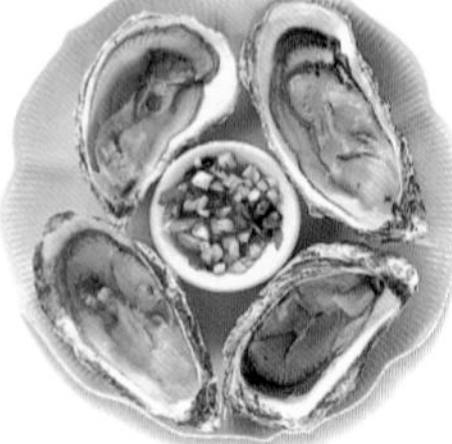

Streídia, *or oysters, were first "farmed" by the ancient Greeks. They are served with shallot, red wine vinegar, and parsley sauce.*

Achinoí *are sea-urchin roes. Gathered at full moon, when the roes are fattest,* achinoí *are a late-night specialty of many Cretan fish tavernas.*

Psarósoupa, *or fish soup, is served as a first course. Mussels, shellfish, shrimp, scorpion fish, sea bass, and other fish are cooked in a leek and herb broth.*

Astakós *is a rare and expensive treat. The lobsters, gathered by sponge divers, are served with olive oil and lemon juice.*

Tónnos psitós *is pan-grilled tuna steak with a medley of carrots, leeks, potatoes, and dill. It is served during the spring and autumn tuna migrations.*

Marídes *are tiny whitebait dipped in flour and fried in olive oil. A first or main course, they are served with a Kos lettuce, dill, and spring onions.*

Barboúnia, *or red mullet, has been the most esteemed fish in Greece since antiquity. It is usually fried whole.*

Bourthéto *are the small fish of the catch baked in a thick tomato sauce spiced with cayenne pepper.*

Garídes giouvétsi *is a modern dish of large shrimp baked in a tomato, olive oil, and parsley sauce and topped with feta cheese.*

Kávouras *is a late summer dish of simply boiled crab served with sharp, juicy, Ionian green olives and an olive oil and lemon juice sauce.*

Chtapódi, *a Greek favorite, is small pieces of barbecued octopus or squid served in red wine vinegar and olive oil.*

Sardélles *are sardines wrapped in grape leaves and grilled. The leaves are then discarded and the fish served with lemon and fresh dill.*

Lavráki *is a whole sea bass baked in olive oil, red wine vinegar, and fresh rosemary. The head is considered the source of the fish's flavor, which then filters through to the rest of the body. Sharp salad greens are the perfect complement to this delicate, sweet fish.*

What to Eat on the Islands

Bunch of grapes

Each group of islands has a distinct culinary identity reflecting geographical location and history. Many Ionian dishes are pasta-based, a legacy of the era of Venetian occupation. Those of the rocky and dramatic Cyclades are intensely flavored. The cooks of the Dodecanese and Northeast Aegean benefit from the rich harvest of the surrounding sea. Crete is unique in its long Turkish occupation and taste for highly spiced dishes. Some beautiful kitchen utensils and unusual ingredients from Minoan times have been excavated by archaeologists on Crete.

Customers at a banana stall by the edge of the road near Vái, Crete

Saláta limniótiki *is an Aegean* mezés *of new potatoes, dill, and capers.*

Agkináres a la políta *are artichoke hearts in olive oil and lemon juice.*

Fáva *is a purée of yellow Santoríni lentils, capers, and oil.*

Prása me sousámi *is baked leeks with sesame seeds.*

Mpriám *is a casserole of late-summer vegetables topped with a crust of breadcrumbs and cheese.*

Pastítsio, *a speciality of Corfu, is a pie with layers of pasta, a meat and tomato filling, and béchamel sauce, topped with cheese.*

Sofríto, *a specialty of Corfu, is a stew of meat, olive oil, wine vinegar, and tomatoes, flavored with fresh garlic.*

Glyká *are fruits preserved in heavy syrup. Here, pistachio nuts, morello cherries, and oranges are served with sweet bread.*

Cheeses

Greece produces several types of sheep's, cow's and goat's cheeses. Each is manufactured according to local traditions.

Féta in olive oil

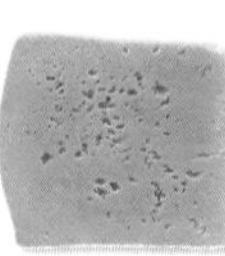

Kefalotýri

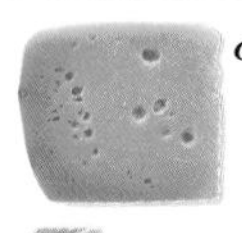

Graviéra

Féta

Kaséri

CRETE

Cretan cooking has a number of dishes unique to the island. The use of pork, a legacy of antiquity, is more popular here than anywhere else in Greece.

Chórta *are wild greens, here boiled, and served with olive oil and vinegar or lemon juice.*

Choirinó kritikó, *the classic dish of inland Crete villages, is thick pork cutlets baked until tender.*

Saligkária, *or snails, are a* mezés *served with the local spirit* tsigouthiá.

Saláta kritikí, *a watercress salad, here mixed with féta cheese and oranges, is served in spring as a* mezés *or with grilled meats.*

Arnáki psitó *is a grilled lamb cutlet flavored with lemon, olive oil, oregano, and sea salt, served with peppers.*

Stifádo, *here made of squid, is a casserole baked with herbs, tomatoes, olive oil, and vinegar. It can also be made with meat.*

Loukoumádes *are a snack of small deep-fried doughnuts soaked in honey-syrup and sprinkled with cinnamon.*

DRINKS IN GREECE

The three distinct areas of wine production in the islands are Ionian, Crete, and Aegean. Greek specialties include retsina, (wine flavored with pine resin), the spirit ouzo, and dessert wines from the north Aegean. Small cups of Greek coffee are drunk for breakfast.

Strong Greek coffee

Retsina, made by Kourtaki

Bottle of the spirit ouzo

Gentilini, a white wine from Crete

Red wine from Crete

Bougátsa *is a pastry of sweet custard or savoury cheese dusted with cinnamon and sugar.*

Sýka me tyrí *is a summer* mezés, *dessert or snack, of fresh figs with* mizýthra *cheese, which is made from féta whey.*

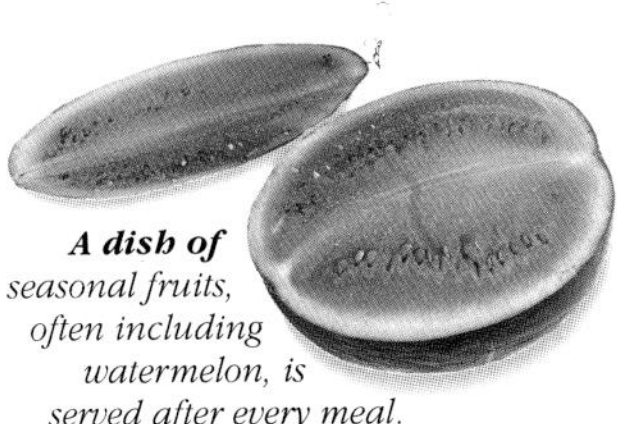

A dish of *seasonal fruits, often including watermelon, is served after every meal.*

Choosing a Restaurant

THE RESTAURANTS in this guide have been selected across a wide range of price categories for their good value, traditional food and interesting location. This chart lists the restaurants by area, starting with the Ionian Islands, and highlights some of the factors which may influence your choice. For more details on the restaurants, see pages 312–315.

THE IONIAN ISLANDS

Restaurant	Price	Air-Conditioning	Outdoor Tables	Live Entertainment	Local Wines
CORFU: *Nikólas* Seafront, Gimári. *0663 91136.* In Gimári, 2 km (1 mile) west of Kalámi, this taverna is delightfully situated on a quiet beach. Traditional Greek cuisine such as moussakas, grilled meats, and fresh fish are offered here. ● *Nov–Mar.*	Dr		■	●	■
CORFU: *Chez George* Palaiokastrítsa beach. *0663 41233.* This well-situated taverna offers good, reliable food. The restaurant specializes in seafood, from lobster and swordfish to mullet. ● *Nov–Feb.*	DrDr		■		■
CORFU: *Rex* Kapodistríou 66, Corfu town. *0661 39649.* Housed in a mid 19th-century town house, the Rex is a truly traditional Greek restaurant serving genuine Greek and Corfiot food. Specialties include swordfish *mpourdétto*, a spicy fish stew with peppers and potatoes.	DrDr	●	■		■
CORFU: *Tría Adélfia* Harborfront, Kassiópi. *0663 81211.* Despite the increasing tourist trade, this restaurant manages to retain its Greek atmosphere. The menu includes standard Greek fare such as moussaka and salads, while its fish is genuinely fresh, caught daily by the owner. ● *Nov–Mar.*	DrDr		■	●	■
ITHACA: *Fatoúro* Main square, Stavrós. *0674 31385.* Situated in a pleasant hill village, this simple taverna serves good, homemade, traditional dishes. There is no menu since the owner cooks what is fresh, including good vegetable stews and herb-covered salads. ● *lunch; Nov.*	Dr		■		■
ITHACA: *Trechantíri* Behind Plateía Doureíou Ippou, Vathý. *0674 33066.* A well-established family taverna in the market area where a husband-and-wife team provide good examples of traditional dishes such as moussaka or roast lamb, accompanied by generous salads and retsina. ● *lunch; Dec–Jan.*	Dr	●	■		■
KEFALLONIA: *Patsoúras* Ioánnou Metaxá, Argostóli. *0671 22779.* This small, family-run restaurant, also known as Perivoláki, has a pleasant garden, serves authentic island dishes such as *krasáto* (pork in wine) and the ubiquitous Kefalloniá meat pie. ● *Nov; Easter day, Christmas day.*	Dr	●	■		■
KEFALLONIA: *Anonymous* Antóni Trítsi 146, Argostóli. *0671 22403.* Three or four daily specials are always offered at this welcoming taverna. Dishes often include fresh fish and other typical Greek specialties. ● *Nov–Feb.*	DrDr		■		■
KEFALLONIA: *Dásos* Harborfront, Fiskárdo. *0674 41276.* This restaurant serves fresh fish as well as a good example of the island specialty, Kefalloniá meat pie *(kreatópita)*. This consists of beef chunks with a pastry topping, served with rice and tomato sauce. ● *Oct–Mar.*	DrDr		■		■
LEFKADA: *Káto Vrýsi* Dórpfeld, Lefkáda town. *0645 22722.* This traditional taverna provides classic Greek dishes such as moussaka,, chicken, salads, and the popular pasta dish, *pastítsio.* ● *Oct–Mar.*	Dr		■		■
LEFKADA: *Kávos* Haborfront, Nydrí. *0645 92520.* This stylish but casual taverna caters mainly to tourists and offers a wider range of salads, grilled fish, and meat than other local restaurants. ● *Nov–Feb.*	DrDr		■	●	■

Average prices for a three-course meal for one, including a half-bottle of house wine, tax, and service:
Dr up to 3,000 Dr
Dr Dr 3–5,000 Dr
Dr Dr Dr 5–8,000 Dr
Dr Dr Dr Dr 8–11,000 Dr
Dr Dr Dr Dr Dr over 11,000 Dr.

AIR-CONDITIONING
Restaurant with air-conditioning.

OUTDOOR TABLES
Tables for eating outdoors, often with a good view.

LIVE ENTERTAINMENT
Dancing or live music performances on various days of the week.

LOCAL WINES
A specialized selection of local Greek wines.

Restaurant	Price	Air-Conditioning	Outdoor Tables	Live Entertainment	Local Wines
PAXOS: *Táka Táka* Gáïos, 50m (165 ft) from the main square (look for signs). *0662 32329.* This delightful vine-covered garden restaurant is a long-standing favorite with the locals. The menu specializes in grilled meat and fish dishes. ● *Sep–June.*	Dr Dr		■		■
ZAKYNTHOS: *I Mantaléna* Seafront, 1 km (0.5 miles) E of Alykés. *0695 83487.* A superb family-run restaurant that serves a welcoming drink, water from its own well, wine from the family vines, and wonderful home-cooked dishes – the stuffed vine leaves, which are particularly delicious. ● *main public hols; Oct–Apr.*	Dr		■		■
THE ARGO SARONIC ISLANDS					
AIGINA: *Avra* Kazantzákis 2, Aígina town. *0297 24493.* A stone exterior and wooden furniture give this fish taverna a rustic feel. Beautifully situated by the sea, it offers specialties such as cuttlefish in wine.	Dr Dr		■		■
AIGINA: *Kóstas* Close to Agía Marína beach, Agía Marína. *0297 32424.* Greek specialties including rabbit *stifádo* (casserole) are cooked by the chef, who is also the owner. There is a garden with mulberry trees. ● *Nov–Mar.*	Dr Dr		■		■
AGKISTRI: *Therís* Megalochóri beach, Mílos. *0297 91400.* Sea views, a garden, and good home cooking make this a pleasant place to dine. Traditional dishes include lamb *kléftiko* and *stifádo.*	Dr Dr	●	■		■
KYTHIRA: *Sotíris* Main square, Avlémonas. *0735 33922.* This fish taverna is deservedly popular with the islanders, serving the catch of the day. Seafood is accompanied by the house white wine. ● *Oct–Apr: Mon–Fri.*	Dr Dr		■	●	■
KYTHIRA: *Taverna Magos* Harborfront, Kapsáli, 1.5km (1 mile) E of Chóra. *0735 31407.* This traditional taverna, situated in the heart of the picturesque harbor, overlooks the sea and offers fresh seafood and vegetable dishes. ● *Nov–Feb.*	Dr Dr		■		■
POROS: *Poúnta* Metropoléos, Póros town. *0298 26078.* Set in a peaceful location, the chef of this restaurant is considered the best in town. Housed in a traditional stone building with wooden interior, the menu offers Greek and European dishes.	Dr Dr	●	■		
SPETSES: *O Pánas* Ligonéri beach, 4 km (2.5 miles) W of Spétses town. *0298 73030.* A genuine *ouzerí* run by a Greek-American woman and her husband. Vegetarian *mezédes*, grilled meat, and seafood are available. ● *Oct–Apr: Mon–Thu.*	Dr		■	●	■
SPETSES: *Exedra* Palio Limáni, Valtíza harbor, Spétses town. *0298 73497.* Situated on the waterfront, this traditional Greek taverna offers good local dishes, such as shrimps *saganaki* and fish *á la spetsiota.* ● *Nov–Dec.*	Dr Dr		■		■
YDRA: *Kondylénia's* On coast road towards Kamíni, 1 km (0.5 miles) W of Ydra town. *0298 53520.* A lunchtime favorite for its stunning sea views of the Peloponnese, this taverna has interesting recipes such spinach, squid, and shrimp casserole. ● *Nov–Jan.*	Dr Dr		■		■
YDRA: *Xerí Eliá* Off main square, Ydra town. *0298 52886.* A wonderful old taverna with traditional stone walls and wooden ceiling. Lamb *kapamá*, fresh fish, and *mpaklavás* can be enjoyed in a large garden.	Dr Dr Dr	●	■	●	■

Average prices for a three-course meal for one, including a half-bottle of house wine, tax, and service:
- Dr up to 3,000 Dr
- DrDr 3–5,000 Dr
- DrDrDr 5–8,000 Dr
- DrDrDrDr 8–11,000 Dr
- DrDrDrDrDr over 11,000 Dr.

Air-Conditioning
Restaurant with air-conditioning.

Outdoor Tables
Tables for eating outdoors, often with a good view.

Live Entertainment
Dancing or live music performances on various days of the week.

Local Wines
A specialized selection of local Greek wines.

The Sporades and Evvoia

Restaurant	Price	Air-Conditioning	Outdoor Tables	Live Entertainment	Local Wines
Alonnisos: *To Kamáki* Ikion Dolópon, Patitíri. ☎ *0424 65245.* All variety of seafood *mezédes*, such as baked mussels, stuffed squid, and red mullet, are served at this popular *ouzerí.* ● *Mon lunch; Nov–Mar.*	DrDr		■		
Evvoia: *To Pyrofáni* Next to Agía Triáda, Límni. ☎ *0227 31640.* Freshly caught fish, lobster, and crayfish are available at this fish taverna. Try the *garídes saganáki* (baked shrimp), a particularly good house specialty.	Dr		■	●	■
Evvoia: *Gkoúveris* Leofóros Mpoudoúri 20, Chalkída. ☎ *0221 25769.* Sole, sea bream, and mackerel are grilled outside at this waterfront taverna. Dishes such as salads and boiled vegetables are also offered. ● *Easter day, Jan 1.*	DrDr	●	■		■
Evvoia: *Kávo d'Oro* Párodos Sachtoúri, Kárystos. ☎ *0224 22326.* This established taverna serves good home cooking. The olive oil-based vegetable and meat stews, *tolmades*, and eggplant are all worth trying. ● *Oct–Dec.*	DrDr		■		■
Evvoia: *Lalari* Harborfront, Kými. ☎ *0222 22624.* A seafront setting and friendly service characterize this excellent taverna. Local grilled shrimp, octopus, and baby red mullet are offered. ● *Sun dinner; Nov–Apr.*	DrDr		■	●	■
Skiathos: *I Mouriá* Behind the National Bank, Skiáthos town. ☎ *0427 23069.* This old stone town house produces some of the best food on the island. Favorites here are rich rabbit *stifádo*, fried squid, and boiled wild greens, all accompanied by carafes of pungent retsina. ● *Apr–Oct: lunch.*	Dr		■		■
Skiathos: *Troúllos* Troúllos beach, Troúllos. ☎ *0427 49255.* Tables almost spill out onto the sandy beach at this well-established taverna. Swordfish *souvláki* and whitebait are always good here. ● *mid-Oct–mid-Apr.*	Dr		■		
Skiathos: *Ta Psarádika* Next to fish market, Skiáthos town. ☎ *0427 23412.* This taverna is popular with locals, who come for warming tripe (*patsás*) soup in the winter, and a variety of delicious fish and *mezédes* in the summer.	DrDr		■		■
Skiathos: *Windmill* Kotróni Hill, Skiáthos town. ☎ *0427 21223.* Housed in an old windmill with wonderful views over the harbor and town, this restaurant offers mainly international cuisine. ● *lunch; Oct–Apr.*	DrDrDr		■		
Skopelos: *Mólos* On the waterfront, Skópelos town. ☎ *0424 22551.* This simple restaurant, overlooking the water, offers all the standard Greek fare. All dishes are made from high-quality fresh produce. ● *Nov–Dec.*	DrDr	●	■		
Skyros: *Asterias* Off main square, Skýros town. ☎ *0222 91380.* Traditional Greek cuisine as well as lobster with spaghetti, the local specialty, can be enjoyed at this quiet, family-run restaurant. ● *Oct–May.*	DrDr		■		
Skyros: *Christína* Near Hotel Neféli, Skýros town. ☎ *0222 91778.* This Australian-owned restaurant is pleasantly situated in a garden courtyard. Traditonal Greek and Middle Eastern cuisine is offered as well as a good selection of desserts. ● *lunch; Oct–May: Mon–Thu; Jun–Sep: Sun.*	DrDr		■		

The Northeast Aegean Islands

Chios: *O Dólomas* Dr
Near Morning Star Hotel, Kondári, 2 km (1 mile) N of Karfás. *0271 21040.*
Despite the tacky decor and often perfunctory service, the *mezédes* are excellent. Meals can be enjoyed in a pleasant, tree-shaded garden. *lunch; Mon; Oct.*

Chios: *O Moriás sta Mestá* Dr
Main square, Mestá. *0271 76400.*
Tasty rural specialties are offered at this grill house, including pickled *krítamo* (samphire). The local raisin wine is heavy and sherrylike.

Chios: *Apolafsi* DrDr
Agía Ermioni, 7km (4 miles) S of Chíos town. *0271 31359.*
Located right on the seafront, this recently refurbished taverna offers a range of seafood and *mezédes*. Enjoy your meal at a table by the water's edge. *Nov–Mar.*

Fournoi: *Níkos's* DrDr
Waterfront, Port town. *0275 51253.*
Also known as the Reméntzo, this is the spot for succulent *skathári* (black bream) or *astakós* (the local lobster variant). Customers pick their own fish, which is then grilled. *Nov–Apr.*

Lesvos: *Bennett's* Dr
Seafront, Skála Eresoú. *0253 53624.*
A British-run "international" restaurant with vegetarian options. Lasagne, garlic mushrooms, and apple crumble are typical, well-executed offerings. *Nov–Apr.*

Lesvos: *I Sykaminiá* Dr
Habourfront, Skála Sykaminiás. *0253 55319.*
The longest-running of three eateries in the area, the taverna functions as the locals' *kafeneío* in winter. Specialties include local sardines, anchovies, squid, and stuffed squash flowers. You can sit out under the mulberry tree.

Lesvos: *To Ammoudéli* Dr
On Plomári–Melínta road. *0252 31333.*
With terrace seating overlooking the sea, this inexpensive and cheerful establishment features seafood (the octopus is a specialty) and grilled meat. There is also a limited choice of *mezédes* and locally produced ouzo. *Aug, Nov 15–Apr.*

Lesvos: *Captain's Table* DrDr
Harborfront, Mólyvos. *0253 71241.*
Live music and family ownership ensure this restaurant has a lively, welcoming atmosphere. Fresh fish and a wide choice of *mezédes* are on offer. *Oct–Apr.*

Lesvos: *Vafeiós* DrDr
On road to Kaminiá, Vafeiós, 5 km (3 miles) SE of Mólyvos. *0253 71752.*
An extensive menu of local dishes, reasonable prices, and a lovely terrace setting make this a firm favorite with both islanders and tourists from nearby Mólyvos. The cuisine is rich, so come with an appetite. *Nov–Mar.*

Limnos: *Nasos Kotsinadelis Taverna* Dr
Tsimántria, 1.5km (1 mile) E of Kontiás. *0254 51277.*
This restaurant is housed in an old, traditional-style building, situated in the spacious and verdant village square, providing ample seating outside. The menu ranges from grilled meats such as *kokoretsi*, to grilled octopus.

Limnos: *O Plátanos* Dr
Central market area, Myrína. *0254 22070.*
Situated on an atmospheric little square hemmed in by old houses and the century-old plane tree, this restaurant offers traditional oven-cooked food such as *pastítsio* (macaroni pie) and vegetable casseroles.

Samos: *Oi Psarádes* Dr
Waterfront, Kondakaiíka village, 5 km (3 miles) E of Karlóvasi. *0273 32489.*
Abundant fish dishes, accompanied by a limited selection of *mezédes* and salads, are served on a terrace overlooking the sea. The taverna is at its best in May, just before the net-fishing season closes. *Nov–Mar.*

Samos: *The Blue Chairs* Dr
Main square, Vourliótes. *0273 35263.*
Dating from the 18th century, this is the oldest building in the square and, although recently refurbished, still retains its original features. The very helpful owner welcomes you to sample the range of *keftedes* offered on the menu.

For key to symbols see back flap

Average prices for a three-course meal for one, including a half-bottle of house wine, tax, and service:
Dr up to 3,000 Dr
DrDr 3–5,000 Dr
DrDrDr 5–8,000 Dr
DrDrDrDr 8–11,000 Dr
DrDrDrDrDr over 11,000 Dr.

Air-Conditioning
Restaurant with air-conditioning.

Outdoor Tables
Tables for eating outdoors, often with a good view.

Live Entertainment
Dancing or live music performances on various days of the week.

Local Wines
A specialized selection of local Greek wines.

Samos: *To Kýma* DrDr
Karlóvasi shore road. *0273 34017.*
Opened in 1984, this *ouzerí,* operating out of a small white house, offers consistent quality in its food. Generous seafood medleys and some of the best sunset views on the island found here. *Nov–Feb: lunch.*

Samothraki: *Orízontas* Dr
Kamariótissa port. *0551 41793.*
The best taverna in the ferry port by quite a margin. Quick-served oven food and bulk wine ensure that Orízontas is always busy. *Nov–Feb.*

Samothraki: *I Plateía* DrDr
Main square, Chóra. *0551 41224.*
Of the two excellent tavernas on Chóra's main square, this has sea views and a more daring menu than most establishments. Items such as stuffed squid complement old standards like *mýdia saganáki* (mussels with cheese). *Oct–May.*

Thasos: *O Gláros* Dr
Alykí bay. *0593 53047.*
This is the oldest and arguably the best value of several tavernas in this area. Fish, meat grills, and salads can be enjoyed on a vine-shaded terrace with views across Alykí bay. *Oct–May.*

Thasos: *O Plátanos* Dr
Main square, Sotíros. *0593 71234.*
Perched between the old church and the fountain, O Plátanos is run by a welcoming family. Excellent home-style grilled meat and casseroles are available, as well as homemade *tsípouro* (an ouzo-like drink). *Nov–mid-May.*

Thasos: *Kleoníki* DrDr
Near bus terminus, Theológos village. *0593 31000.*
Also known as Taverna Iatroú, this grill house specializes in locally raised suckling pig, goat, skewered lamb, and *kokorétsi* (offal kebab).

The Dodecanese

Astypalaia: *Kalámia* Dr
Livádi beach. *0243 61468.*
Situated right on the beach, this traditional taverna has a front and back garden in which to enjoy typical Greek cuisine and fresh seafood. *Oct–May.*

Chalki: *Pontamos* Dr
Póntamos beach, Nimporió. *0241 45295.*
Cool off under the shady carob tree at this atmospheric taverna perched above the sands. A bustling lunchtime favorite offering a good selection of Greek dishes and snacks. *Oct–Apr.*

Kalymnos: *Iliovasílema* Dr
Next to Plaza Hotel, Masouri beach. *0243 47683.*
Run by the local butcher, the furniture here may be garish, but the meat is wonderful. Excellent rabbit *stifádo* and roasts, as well as vegetarian dishes, are on the menu. The friendly atmosphere makes it a popular family choice. *Nov–Apr.*

Kalymnos: *Xefterís* DrDr
Next to Moní Christós, Pothiá. *0241 45340.*
Considered by the locals to be the town's best taverna, Xefterís has been run by the same family for more than 85 years. Tucked away in an alley, the menu features fresh fish, roast lamb, and vegetable dishes.

Karpathos: *Kalí Kardiá* Dr
On road to Vróntis beach, Kárpathos town. *0245 22256.*
This friendly Greek/American, family-run taverna is situated at the water's edge and offers a good selection of oven dishes as well as fresh fish. *Oct–Mar.*

Restaurant	Air-Conditioning	Outdoor Tables	Live Entertainment	Local Wines
Samos: To Kýma		■		■
Samothraki: Orízontas	●	■		■
Samothraki: I Plateía		■	●	■
Thasos: O Gláros		■		
Thasos: O Plátanos		■	●	■
Thasos: Kleoníki		■		■
Astypalaia: Kalámia		■		■
Chalki: Pontamos		■		
Kalymnos: Iliovasílema		■		
Kalymnos: Xefterís		■		■
Karpathos: Kalí Kardiá		■	●	■

KASOS: *Emporeiós* DrDr

Emporeió harbor, 1 km (0.5 miles) from Frý. *0245 41586.*

In a quiet setting with a pleasant garden, this traditional fish taverna always serves fresh seafood and barbecued meats at reasonable prices. *Sep–Jun.*

KASTÉLLORIZO: *Ta Platánia* Dr

Plateía Choráfia, Kastellórizo town. *0241 49206.*

Above the harbor, this restaurant specializes in food such as *revythokeftédes* (chickpea fritters) and oven-cooked dishes. Enjoy the free *halvá.* *Oct–May.*

KOS: *Frangolis* DrDr

Plateía Arístonis, Kakó Prinári, Kos town. *0242 28761.*

Deemed to be one of the island's best traditional tavernas, the Frangolis has an authenic Greek menu – rare in Kos town. Barbecued meat and oven dishes can be enjoyed in the tree-shaded garden.

KOS: *Olympiáda* DrDr

Kleopátras 2, Kos town. *0242 23031.*

Away from the bustle, this traditional taverna serves all the standard oven fare. A good value and very Greek with a cheerful service. *Easter period, Dec 25, Jan.*

KOS: *O Plátanos* DrDrDr

Plateía Plátanos, Kos town. *0242 28991.*

Named after Hippokrates' plane tree, this café overlooks the ancient agora. Classical music and cakes are enjoyed under a shady canopy. *Nov–Apr.*

LEROS: *Garbo's* DrDr

Harborfront, Agía Marína. *0247 24767.*

This stylish restaurant is always buzzing and has a large international menu including a good steak and kidney pie. *lunch; Oct.*

LEROS: *María* DrDr

On the waterfront, Pantéli. *0247 22967.*

An atmospheric and authentic fish taverna, the María serves a wide range of fresh fish from tiny crisp whitebait to *kalamári* (squid). *Oct–May.*

LIPSI: *Kalypsó* Dr

Kalypsó Hotel, on the waterfront, Lipsí town. *0247 41242.*

Attached to the hotel, this vine-covered restaurant, also known as Mr. Maungo's after the characterful proprietor, serves all the usual Greek favorites. Look out for delicious grilled octopus and *revythokeftédes* (chickpea fritters).

NISYROS: *Hellenis* Dr

Hotel Hellenis, Páloi beach. *0242 31453.*

Linked to the hotel of the same name, this traditional taverna specializes in local fare such as *revythokeftédes* (chickpea fritters) and skewered lamb.

NISYROS: *Nísyros* Dr

On main road, Mandráki. *0242 31460.*

With tables spilling across a narrow alley under a vine-clad canopy, the Nísyros is popular for lunch or dinner with all the usual Greek favorites. *mid-Oct–Mar.*

PATMOS: *Arion Café* DrDr

On the waterfront, Skála. *0247 31595.*

This sidewalk café is a popular meeting place. It has a Neo-Classical façade and cavernous music bar inside. Serves coffees, cocktails, and snacks. *Oct–Mar.*

PATMOS: *Alóni* DrDr

On Chóra–Grígos road. *0247 31007.*

Locals and tourists alike enjoy an evening at this open-air restaurant known for its live Greek music and excellent dance program. Expect to pay more for your meal, usually roasted meats and Greek dips, to cover the entertainment.

PATMOS: *Patmian House* DrDrDr

Off Plateía Dimarchíou, Chóra. *0247 31180.*

Tucked away in a quaint alleyway, this American-run restaurant is housed in a lovely old sea captain's mansion. Fine international cuisine is served in elegant surroundings, perfect for a romantic dinner. *Oct–May.*

RHODES: *Alatopípero* DrDr

Michaíl Petrídi 76, Rhodes town. *0241 65494.*

Choose what you fancy from a selection of trays laden with hot and cold *mezédes* at this excellent *mezedopoleío.* There is a wide range of vegeterian dishes including hot eggplant with feta cheese and seasoning. *lunch; Jan–Feb: Mon evening.*

For key to symbols see back flap

Average prices for a three-course meal for one, including a half-bottle of house wine, tax, and service:
Dr up to 3,000 Dr
Dr Dr 3–5,000 Dr
Dr Dr Dr 5–8,000 Dr
Dr Dr Dr Dr 8–11,000 Dr
Dr Dr Dr Dr Dr over 11,000 Dr.

Air-Conditioning
Restaurant with air-conditioning.

Outdoor Tables
Tables for eating outdoors, often with a good view.

Live Entertainment
Dancing or live music performances on various days of the week.

Local Wines
A specialized selection of local Greek wines.

Rhodes: *O Chrístos* — Dr Dr
Klaude Pepper 165, Zéfyros district, Rhodes town. ☎ *0241 31680.*
Beyond the commercial harbor, this traditional taverna is a good find. Off the tourist track, it serves Greek cuisine at reasonable prices. ● *Sun evening.* 💳

Rhodes: *Sandy Beach* — Dr Dr
Next to Sun Beach Hotel, Ialyssós bay, 5 km (3 miles) N of ancient site. ☎ *0241 94600.*
Situated right on the beach, this lunchtime favorite excels at Greek classics such as *kopanistí* (a purée of cracked olives, strong cheese, and paprika) and *skordaliá* (potato and garlic purée). There is also a range of ouzos. ● *Nov–Mar.* 💳

Rhodes: *Paliá Istoriá* — Dr Dr Dr
Mitropóleos 108, Ammos district, Rhodes town. ☎ *0241 32421.*
This award-winning eatery offers Greek and Mediterranean dishes with a twist. The imaginative and healthy creations range from beet with walnuts to lobster spaghetti. Dine beneath the shady pergola. Reservations advisable. ● *lunch.* 💳

Symi: *O Meraklís* — Dr
Next to Agios Ioánnis, Gialós area, Sými town. ☎ *0241 71003.*
Tucked away behind the bank, this traditional taverna is the closest you will get to good home cooking. Excellent vegetable dishes, fresh fish, and all the usual Greek favorites are available. Reasonable prices and friendly service. 💳

Symi: *Tólis* — Dr Dr
Pédi bay. ☎ *0241 71601.*
Situated right at the water's edge, this friendly, family-run taverna is a popular lunchtime haunt offering a small but appetizing menu including fresh fish of the day and local vegetable dishes. ● *Jul 27, Nov–Apr.*

Telendos: *Theíos Géorgios* — Dr Dr
Waterfront, Télendos harbor. ☎ *0243 47502.*
This reasonably priced, harborside taverna offers a wide range of appetizers, excellent fresh seafood, home-cooked dishes, and salads. Good views of nearby Kálymnos can be enjoyed from the tables along the waterfront. ● *Nov–mid-Apr.* 💳

Tilos: *Eirína* — Dr
Waterfront, Livádia. ☎ *0241 44206.*
With tables at the water's edge, this traditional taverna serves up good Greek fare. Vegetable dishes such as *fasoláda* (bean soup) and *gígantes* (favas) are especially good. Everything has a home-cooked touch. ● *Nov–Apr.*

The Cyclades

Amorgos: *Ambrosia* — Dr Dr
On Aigíali–Tholária road. ☎ *0285 73107.*
Traditional Greek cuisine and panoramic views of the sea are offered at this popular restaurant. Fresh fish and lobster are always available. 💳

Amorgos: *Vitzéntsos* — Dr Dr Dr
Harborfront, Katápola. ☎ *0285 71518.*
This popular but pricey harborside taverna serves island specialties such as kid and potato casserole. Fresh fish is also available daily. ● *mid-Oct–mid-Mar.*

Andros: *Archipélagos* — Dr
Seafront, Andros town. ☎ *0282 24430.*
Situated on the beach, this modern taverna is decorated in a traditional Greek style with a stone exterior. Standard Greek dishes and fresh fish are offered.

Andros: *Syróco* — Dr Dr
Behind main square, Mpatsí. ☎ *0282 41023.*
Housed in a 100-year-old building with a wooden interior, this restaurant offers traditional Greek cuisine as well as European food such as pizza and spaghetti. Service is good and there are nice sea views. ● *lunch.*

Restaurant	Air-Conditioning	Outdoor Tables	Live Entertainment	Local Wines
Rhodes: O Chrístos		●		●
Rhodes: Sandy Beach		●		●
Rhodes: Paliá Istoriá		●		●
Symi: O Meraklís	●	●		●
Symi: Tólis		●	●	●
Telendos: Theíos Géorgios		●	●	●
Tilos: Eirína		●		
Amorgos: Ambrosia	●	●	●	●
Amorgos: Vitzéntsos		●		
Andros: Archipélagos		●		●
Andros: Syróco		●		●

IOS: *Mpármpa-Manólis* (Dr)
Páno Foúrno, Ios town. ☎ *0286 91767.*
Situated in "The Village," this traditional *ouzerí* offers a wide range of *mezédes*, accompanied by a selection of ouzo or wines. ● *Christmas period.*

IOS: *Pithári* (Dr)
Plateía Evangelismoú, Ios town. ☎ *0286 91379.*
This friendly taverna is one of the island's best. Excellent traditional Greek cuisine is available along with barrel wines. ● *Oct 20–Apr 20.*

KYTHNOS: *To Kantoúni* (Dr)
Mérichas bay. ☎ *0281 32220.*
Perched at the water's edge with a wonderful view across the bay, this simple eatery specializes in grills and *sfougáta* (fried cheese balls). ● *lunch; Nov.*

KYTHNOS: *To Louloúdi* (Dr)
Panagía Kanála, Kanála. ☎ *0281 32362.*
This authentic taverna on the grounds of the church has a wide terrace overlooking the sea. Home cooking from goat stew to liver or local vegetables is offered. There is also good house retsina. ● *Oct–Apr.*

MILOS: *Varco* (Dr)
Harbor, Adámantas. ☎ *0287 22660.*
The inexpensive Varco is a waterfront taverna offering tasty, traditional Greek dishes and a good barrel wine. Fresh fish is also available. ● *lunch; Dec–Mar.*

MILOS: *Trapatsélli's* (Dr)(Dr)
Adámantas shore road. ☎ *0287 22010.*
Probably the islands's best-known fish restaurant, situated at the water's edge. There is an excellent and varied menu featuring unusual dishes such as cuttlefish *stifádo* and *spetsofái* (pepper and sausage stew). ● *Nov–May.*

MYKONOS: *Antoníni's* (Dr)(Dr)
Plateía Mantó, Mýkonos town. ☎ *0289 22319.*
For many this is the island's best eating place serving authentic Greek dishes at palatable prices. Enjoy the excellent *mezédes* followed by *stámnas*, a delicious veal casserole. ● *Nov–May.*

MYKONOS: *Kástro* (Dr)(Dr)(Dr)
Kástro area, Little Venice, Mýkonos town. ☎ *0289 23072.*
This legendary gay bar, overlooking the Kástro district, is a relaxing place to sip strawberry daiquiris and listen to classical music. ● *lunch; mid-Oct–Apr.*

MYKONOS: *Chez Katrin* (Dr)(Dr)(Dr)(Dr)
Nikíou, Mýkonos town. ☎ *0289 22169.*
Commonly known as Bobby's and beloved by the locals, this is one of the island's oldest international restaurants, known for its French cuisine and delicious chocolate mousse. Reservations advisable. ● *Nov–Apr.*

NAXOS: *Manólis* (Dr)
Old town center, Náxos town. ☎ *0285 25168.*
Traditional Greek cuisine can be enjoyed at this garden taverna in the heart of the old town. Dishes offered include *melitzánes* (fried eggplant), *skordaliá* (potato and garlic purée), and other well-known favorites. ● *Nov–Mar.*

NAXOS: *Oneiro* (Dr)(Dr)(Dr)
Parapórti area, Náxos town. ☎ *0285 23846.*
Fine views from the roof garden, romantic candlelit tables, and an international menu make the Oneiro a good choice. ● *lunch; Nov–Apr.*

PAROS: *Páros* (Dr)(Dr)
Off Agorá, Paroikiá. ☎ *0284 21319.*
Traditional Greek cuisine and Páros specialties such as cheese pies can be enjoyed at this family-run restaurant situated on the seafront. ● *mid-Oct–Mar.*

PAROS: *Tamarísko* (Dr)(Dr)
Off Agorá, Paroikiá. ☎ *0284 24689.*
Considered the best restaurant on the island, the international cuisine is a bargain and served in a peaceful, secluded garden. ● *lunch; Sep–Jul: Mon; Jan–Feb.*

SANTORINI: *Camille Stefaní* (Dr)(Dr)
Kamári beach. ☎ *0286 31716.*
This elegant restaurant is situated by the beach and offers French-influenced cuisine. The restaurant also has its own wine label. ● *Nov–Apr: Fri–Sun lunch.*

For key to symbols see back flap

Average prices for a three-course meal for one, including a half-bottle of house wine, tax, and service:
Dr up to 3,000 Dr
DrDr 3–5,000 Dr
DrDrDr 5–8,000 Dr
DrDrDrDr 8–11,000 Dr
DrDrDrDrDr over 11,000 Dr.

Air-Conditioning
Restaurant with air-conditioning.

Outdoor Tables
Tables for eating outdoors, often with a good view.

Live Entertainment
Dancing or live music performances on various days of the week.

Local Wines
A specialized selection of local Greek wines.

Restaurant	Price	Air-Conditioning	Outdoor Tables	Live Entertainment	Local Wines
Santorini: *Nikólas* Above central square, Firá. ☎ *0286 24550.* Long-established, traditional taverna in the heart of Firá with authentic Greek menu, fresh fish, and wines from the barrel. ● *Dec.*	DrDrDr				■
Serifos: *Tákis* On the waterfront, Livádi. ☎ *0281 51159.* Occupying a good location, right on the seafront, Tákis has a large menu including fish dishes and salads. There is also an extensive wine list. ● *Nov–Mar.*	DrDrDr		■		
Sifnos: *Artemónas* Agíou Kostandínou 3, Artemónas. ☎ *0284 31303.* Situated in the peaceful garden of the Artemónas hotel, this restaurant offers good homemade dishes. All vegetables are home grown. ● *Oct–May.*	DrDr		■		
Sifnos: *Liotrívi Maganas* Next to bus station, Artemónas. ☎ *0284 31246.* One of the best-known tavernas in the Cyclades, Liotrívi is famous for its local specialties. Greeks line up for the *revýthia* (chickpea stew), a Sifniot Sunday special. There is a lively traditional atmosphere with good barrel wines. ● *Dec.*	DrDr	●	■	●	■
Sikinos: *Kástro* Off main square, Síkinos town. ☎ *0286 51026.* This buzzing taverna in the Kástro area is popular with locals and visitors alike. There is excellent home cooking and sometimes spontaneous dancing.	DrDr		■		
Syros: *Lilís'* Piátsa, Ano Sýros area, Ermoúpoli. ☎ *0281 88087.* Famous for its stunning views of the bay and wide range of imaginative Greek *nouvelle cuisine* style dishes. There is live music on weekends. ● *Nov–Mar: lunch.*	Dr	●	■	●	■
Syros: *I Folia* Athanasíou Diákou 1, Ermoúpoli. In the Vrondádo district, this is rated one of the finest tavernas in the Cyclades. Basic and unpretentious, it specializes in classic dishes like casseroled pigeon and rabbit and cauliflower *keftédes* (meatballs).	DrDr	●	■		■
Syros: *To Iliovasílema* Kíni beach, Kíni. ☎ *0281 71211.* Named after the marvelous sunset, this popular beach-side taverna has a wide menu and is run by a famous family of Syriot musicians and singers. ● *Nov–Mar.*	DrDr		■	●	■
Tinos: *Palaiá Palláda* Pallháda area, behind the port, Tínos town. ☎ *0283 23516.* Situated in the Pallháda area, this restaurant offers traditional Greek taverna cuisine as well as fresh fish, meat grills, and a barrel wine. ● *Jan 1–20.*	Dr		■		
Tinos: *Taverna O Kípos* Tríon Ierárchon, Tínos town. ☎ *0283 22830.* This traditional Greek taverna offers good local food, including beef *stifado*, and a range of local cheeses. Enjoy your meal outside in the pretty garden.	Dr		■	●	■
CRETE					
Agia Roumeli: *To Farángi* Main square. ☎ *0825 91225.* Specialties at this family-run taverna include stuffed cabbage leaves, peppers, and vine leaves. Try the *sfakianés pítes*, pies with honey. ● *Nov 15–Mar.*	Dr		■	●	■
Agios Nikolaos: *Itanos* Kýprou 1. ☎ *0841 25340.* This popular taverna, situated off Plateía Venizélou, serves traditional Cretan cuisine such as charcoal-grilled goat meat. Sidewalk seating is available.	Dr		■		■

AGIOS NIKOLAOS: *I Tráta* (Dr)(Dr)
Pagkílou 17. *0841 22028.*
A fish taverna and grill house, the I Tráta offers fresh fish and meat grills as well as most traditional Greek dishes and Italian food such as pizza.

CHANIA: *To Dóloma* (Dr)
Kapsokalývon 5. *0821 51196.*
Lunchtime is the best time to eat at this modern restaurant with fast service and quality Greek cuisine. Especially good are the stuffed tomatoes.

CHANIA: *Akrogiáli* (Dr)(Dr)
Akti Papanikolí 19, Néa Chóra area. *0821 73110.*
The busiest and trendiest fish restaurant in Néa Chóra, 18 km (11 miles) from Chaniá, the Akrogiáli always offers a wide selection of fish and good service. Try the barbecued cuttlefish. ● *Nov–Apr: Mon–Sat lunch; Easter day & Dec 25: eve.*

CHANIA: *The Well of the Turk* (Dr)(Dr)
Kaliníkou Zarpáki. *0821 54547.*
This cozy restaurant, with candlelit tables and eastern music, is set in a stone built cellar. Spicy, original-tasting food is offered, including eggplant meatballs and stuffed *kalamári* (squid). ● *Sunday lunch; mid-Nov–mid-May: lunch.*

CHANIA: *Thólos* (Dr)(Dr)
Agíon Déka, Old town. *0821 46725.*
Housed in a 14th-century building, this open-air restaurant has tables on three levels. All food is carefully prepared and made from the best local produce. The restaurant also offers an extensive wine list. ● *Nov–Apr.*

CHANIA: *O Anemos* (Dr)(Dr)(Dr)
Sourmelí 40–42, Aktí Tompázi. *0821 58330.*
This chic restaurant, situated on the waterfront and below the city's old Venetian wall, specializes in seafood dishes and offers interesting choices such as squid cooked in ouzo. Fish is always fresh, and meat grills are also available.

CHORAFAKIA: *Eiríni* (Dr)
At entrance to village. *0821 39470.*
Situated in Chorafákia, 8 km (5 miles) north of Chaniá, this bustling taverna offers simple home cooking. Especially good are the *agkináres me koukiá* (artichokes with broad beans), and the oven-cooked goat or lamb in lemon sauce.

IRAKLEIO: *I Erganos* (Dr)
G Georgiádou 6. *081 285629.*
Traditional Cretan cuisine is offered at this family-run restaurant situated in an old house with four rooms. Specials such as *sygoúri* (meat soup) make this a winter rather than a summer choice. ● *lunch.*

IRAKLEIO: *Loukoulos* (Dr)(Dr)
Odos Korai 5. *081 224435.*
Classic architecture and luxurious décor make this an elegant restaurant. Listen to classical music on the terrace whilst sampling the mediterranean cuisine.

IRAKLEIO: *O Kyriákos* (Dr)(Dr)
Leofóros Dimokratías 53. *081 222464.*
Traditional Cretan food can be enjoyed at this old restaurant with a wooden interior. Customers select their dishes in the kitchen and see how they are prepared. ● *Wed evening; mid-Jun–Jul 10.*

KOUNOUPIDIANA: *O Mítsos:* (Dr)
Main square. *0821 64331*
Situated in Kounoupidianá, 4 km (2 miles) northeast of Chaniá, this old, family-run grill house offers the best grilled chickens in the Chaniá area. The service is quick, the food simple, and the atmosphere friendly. ● *Mon–Fri: lunch; Dec.*

KOUTSOURAS: *Archipélagos* (Dr)
Seafront, 18 km (11 miles) E of Ierápetra. *0843 51026.*
Situated in Koútsouras, this atmospheric restaurant is run by a young couple. Specialties here are *pítes* (stuffed pastry rolls filled with cheese, tomatoes, peppers, and spices). ● *lunch; Nov–Feb.*

KOUTSOURAS: *Kalliontzís* (Dr)
On the seafront, at entrance to village. *0843 51244.*
Situated in Koútsouras, 18 km (11 miles) east of Ierápetra, the Kalliontzís offers excellent home cooking and a warm, friendly atmosphere. The tables outside are under the shade of tamarisk trees. ● *Nov–Mar.*

For key to symbols see back flap

Average prices for a three-course meal for one, including a half-bottle of house wine, tax, and service:
Dr up to 3,000 Dr
Dr Dr 3–5,000 Dr
Dr Dr Dr 5–8,000 Dr
Dr Dr Dr Dr 8–11,000 Dr
Dr Dr Dr Dr Dr over 11,000 Dr.

AIR-CONDITIONING
Restaurant with air-conditioning.

OUTDOOR TABLES
Tables for eating outdoors, often with a good view.

LIVE ENTERTAINMENT
Dancing or live music performances on various days of the week.

LOCAL WINES
A specialized selection of local Greek wines.

RETHYMNO: *O Goúnos* — Dr
Koronaíaou 6. ☎ *0831 28816.*
Traditional Greek dishes such as rabbit *stifádo* and goat soup are offered at this taverna, a 150-year old building. There is traditional dance in summer.

RETHYMNO: *Mourayio Maria* — Dr Dr
Nearchou 45. ☎ *0831 26475.*
Situated in the old Venetian part of the harbor, this traditional restaurant is housed in a building which dates from the 16th century. Established for twenty-five years, the specialty is seafood, and in particular lobster. ● *Nov–Mar.* 💳

RETHYMNO: *Tavérna tou Kómpou* — Dr Dr
On Réthymno–Chaniá road. ☎ *0831 29725.*
Cretan specialties such as *apátzia* (smoked pork sausages) and *glykádia* (goat meat) can be enjoyed at this traditional taverna with cozy alcoves and a fireplace. Meats are charcoal grilled and there is a tree-filled garden. ● *lunch; Nov–Apr: Mon.*

SFAKIA: *Lyvikón* — Dr
Seafront. ☎ *0825 91211.*
Part of the Livikón hotel, this family-run restaurant, overlooking the sea, offers copious amounts of basic Greek food at reasonable prices. Dishes include fresh fish and *sfakianés pítes* (pies with honey). ● *Nov–Mar.* 💳

SITEIA: *Zormpás* — Dr Dr
Harborfront. ☎ *0843 22689.*
Eat *mezédes*, drink coffee, or have a full meal at this old fashioned Greek taverna. Dishes such as moussaka and *fasólia* (green beans) are on the menu. 💳

SOUDA: *O Mantás* — Dr Dr
Ellis 12. ☎ *0821 89413.*
Decorated in a traditional and simple Greek style, this famous fish taverna serves excellent fish. The service is good and the food a bargain. ● *Aug 20–Sep 10, Easter period, Dec 25, 26.*

ZAKROS: *Káto Zákros Bay* — Dr Dr
Seafront, close to Zákros archaeological site. ☎ *0843 93375.*
Guests are well looked after in this family-run taverna. Traditional dishes such as moussaka are available, and fish is freshly barbecued. The food is always well prepared and all vegetables, fruits, and meats are home grown. ● *Oct–Apr.*

ATHENS

ACROPOLIS: *Strofí* — Dr Dr
Rovértou Gkálli 25, 11742. ☎ *01 921 4130.*
The rooftop views of the Acropolis attract a constant stream of diners. The menu features all the mainstays of a Greek taverna including fried zucchini, octopus, and roast lamb. ● *lunch; Sun.* 💳

EXARCHEIA: *Kostogiánnis* — Dr Dr
Zaími 37, 10682. ☎ *01 821 2496.*
The entrance to this restaurant, within easy reach of the National Archaeological Museum, is past an enticing buffet display of shellfish and marinated fish platters. ● *lunch; Sun; Aug.*

EXARCHEIA: *Oasis* — Dr Dr
Valtetsíou 44, 10681. ☎ *01 330 1369.*
Set in a beautiful garden, this taverna offers wonderful dishes such as baked mackerel and melt-in-the-mouth roast suckling pig.

KOLONAKI: *Filíppou* — Dr Dr
Xenokrátous 19, 10675. ☎ *01 721 6390.*
This Kolonáki favorite offers all the standard taverna fare. Roast chicken with lemon potatoes and *dolmádes* are particularly good. ● *Sun; Aug 15.*

Restaurant	Air-Conditioning	Outdoor Tables	Live Entertainment	Local Wines
Rethymno: O Goúnos	●		●	■
Rethymno: Mourayio Maria	●	■	●	■
Rethymno: Tavérna tou Kómpou		■		■
Sfakia: Lyvikón		■		■
Siteia: Zormpás		■		■
Souda: O Mantás	●	■		■
Zakros: Káto Zákros Bay		■	●	■
Acropolis: Strofí	●	■		■
Exarcheia: Kostogiánnis	●	■		■
Exarcheia: Oasis	●	■		■
Kolonaki: Filíppou		■		■

KOLONAKI: *To Kafeneío* DrDr
Loukianoú 26, 10675. *01 722 9056.*
Excellent *mezédes* are served at this upscale Kolonáki *mezedopoleío*. Also featured are some of the better new-generation Greek wines. *Sun; Aug.*

KOLONAKI: *Dódeka Apostóloi* DrDrDrDr
Kanári 17, 10671. *01 361 9358.*
Typical *mezédes* are served in the downstairs wine bar at lunchtimes, and in the evenings international cuisine is offered upstairs. *Sun; May–Sep: lunch.*

LYKAVITTOS HILL: *Al Convento* DrDrDr
Anapíron Polémou 4–6, 11521. *01 723 9163.*
One of the city's better Italian restaurants, the food includes old favorites such as spaghetti *al vongole* and *carbonara* as well as *carpaccio*, arugula, and parmesan. *lunch; Sun.*

MONASTIRAKI: *Cafe Avissynía* DrDr
Plateía Avissynías, 10555. *01 321 7047.*
Tables are always packed for the accordionist and singer who perform every weekend. During the week, when the café is quieter, is a better time to sample the unusual Macedonian dishes. *Aug.*

MONASTIRAKI: *Oinodíki* DrDrDr
Plateía Avissynías, 10555. *01 321 5465.*
This tiny wine bar offers one of the best wine lists in the city and a limited selection of *mezédes* to complement the wines. *Jul–Aug.*

MONASTIRAKI: *Koutí* DrDrDrDr
Adrianoú 23, 10555. *01 321 2836.*
Set in a well-restored 19th-century house overlooking the ancient Agora, this restaurant serves fresh Mediterranean food. *Mon evening; Aug.*

OMONOIA: *Athinaikón* DrDr
Themistokléous 2, 10678. *01 383 8485.*
This old establishment serves a wide range of well-executed and delicious fish and meat *mezédes*. Meals are accompanied by carafes of ouzo and wine. *Sun; Aug.*

PLAKA: *O Dámigos* DrDr
Kydathinaíon 41, 10558. *01 322 5084.*
This basement taverna specializes in salt cod and garlic sauce, chunky french fries, and salad. The chilled retsina is excellent. *lunch; Jun–Sep.*

PLAKA: *Tsekoúras* DrDr
Corner of Tripódon & Epichármou 2, 10558. *01 323 3710.*
Distinguished by its indoor fig tree, this inexpensive and cheerful taverna serves delicious fava beans, stewed snails, salads, and grills. *lunch; Aug.*

PLAKA: *Dáfni* DrDrDrDr
Lysikrátous 4, 10557. *01 322 7971.*
Garish frescoes adorn the walls of this converted Neo-Classical mansion. Stick to the simple dishes, such as swordfish or *keftédes* (pork or beef meatballs). *lunch; Nov–Apr: Sun.*

SYNTAGMA: *Ideal* DrDr
Panepistimíou 46, 10678. *01 330 3000.*
Since 1922, this much-loved institution has been serving excellent Greek and international cuisine. Specials include milk-fed veal with eggplant, stuffed zucchini, and *agkináres a la políta* (artichokes in lemon juice). *Sun.*

SYNTAGMA: *Strofiliá* DrDr
Plateía Karítsi 6, 10561. *01 323 4803.*
Named after the owner's excellent wine made in Attica, this bar offers a wide range of wines by the glass and a few interesting *mezédes*. *Jun–mid-Sep.*

THISEIO: *Iródeion* DrDr
Apostólou Pávlou 29, 11851. *01 346 1585*
Unusual *mezédes* such as fried chicken breast and stuffed *kalámari* are served at this traditional *mezedopoleío*. A warm atmosphere and Acropolis views.

THISEIO: *Pil Poul* DrDrDrDrDr
Corner of Apostólou Pávlou & Poulopoúlou, 11851. *01 342 3665.*
Fashionable Mediterranean cooking and views of the Acropolis draw the crowds to this busy and expensive restaurant. *Sun.*

Survival Guide

Practical Information

Greece's appeal is both cultural and hedonistic. Its physical beauty, hot climate, and warm seas, together with the easy-going outlook of its people, are all conducive to a relaxed vacation. It does pay, however, to know something about the nuts and bolts of Greek life to avoid unnecessary frustrations – when to visit, what to bring, how to get around, and what to do if things go wrong. Greece is no longer the cheap vacation destination it once was, though public transit, vehicle rental, eating out, and hotel accommodations are still relatively inexpensive compared with most other European countries. Tourist information is available through the many EOT offices *(see p338)*, which offer plenty of advice on the practical aspects of your stay.

Soldier in ceremonial dress

When to Visit

Tourist season in the Greek islands – from late June to early September – is the hottest *(see p47)* and most expensive time to visit, as well as being very crowded. December to March are the coldest and wettest months everywhere, with reduced public transportation, and many hotels and restaurants closed throughout the winter.

Spring (from late April to May) is one of the loveliest times to visit the islands – the weather is sunny but not yet debilitatingly hot, there are relatively few tourists around, and the countryside is ablaze with brightly colored wild flowers against a backdrop of fresh, verdant vegetation.

What to Bring

Most of life's comforts are available in Greece, but a few items that are advisable to take include: a good map of the area in which you intend to stay *(see p360)*; an AC adaptor for your electrical gadgetry *(see p339)*; sunglasses and a sun hat, mosquito repellent, any medical supplies you might need, and a high factor suntan lotion.

Apart from swimwear, light clothing is all you need for most of the year, although a sweater or light jacket for the evening is also recommended, and is essential either side of tourist season, in May and October. During winter and spring, rainwear should be taken, as well as warm clothes.

Many religious buildings have dress codes (usually signposted) that should be adhered to *(see p339)*.

ΕΛΕΓΧΟΣ ΔΙΑΒΑΤΗΡΙΩΝ
PASSPORT CONTROL

Passport control sign at Athens airport

Visa Requirements

Visitors from EU countries, the US, Canada, Australia, and New Zealand need only a valid passport for entry to Greece (no visa is required) and can stay for a period of up to 90 days. For longer stays a resident's permit must be obtained from the **Aliens' Bureau** in Athens or the local police in remoter areas.

Non-EU citizens planning to work or study in Greece should contact their local Greek consulate a few months in advance about visa requirements and work permits.

Visitors on the beach in high summer

Customs

Visitors entering Greece from within the EU are no longer subject to any customs controls or other formalities. Limits for duty-paid goods have been similarly relaxed in recent years, though anything valuable should be recorded in your passport upon entry if it is to be reexported. Visitors coming from non-EU countries may be subject to the occasional spot check on arrival in Greece.

The unauthorized export of antiquities and archaeological artifacts from Greece is treated as a serious offense, and penalties range from hefty fines to prison sentences.

Any prescription drugs that are brought into the country should be accompanied by a copy of the prescription for the purposes of the customs authorities *(see p340)*.

Restrictions on the import and export of money are covered on page 343.

EU and non-EU visitors may bring in and export the following quantities of duty-free goods: 200 cigarettes or 100 cigarillos or 50 cigars or 250 grams of tobacco (18 years or over); 1 liter spirits and 2 liters wine or liqueurs (18 years or over); 50 grams of perfume and 250 ml eau de toilette.

◁ **A fisherman prepares nets on Sykaminiá harbor, Lésvos**

A family arriving at Athens airport

Traveling with Children

Children are much loved by the Greeks and welcomed just about everywhere. Baby-sitting facilities are provided by most hotels on request, but check before you book in *(see p295)*.

Discounts of up to 50 percent are offered on most forms of public transportation for children aged 10 and under, but in some cases it is 8 and under.

Swimming in the sea is generally safe for kids, but keep a close eye on them as lifeguards are rare in Greece. Also be aware of the hazards of overexposure to the sun and dehydration.

Women Travelers

Greece is a very safe country and local communities are generally welcoming. Foreign women traveling alone are usually treated with respect, especially if dressed modestly *(see p339)*. However, like elsewhere, hitchhiking alone in Greece carries potential risks and is not advisable.

Student and Youth Travelers

Within Greece itself, no discounts are offered on ferry, bus, or train travel, except to students actually studying in Greece. However, there are plenty of deals to be had getting to Greece, especially during low season. There are scores of agencies for student and youth travel, including **STA Travel**, which has 120 offices worldwide. IYHF (International Youth Hostel Federation) membership cards are rarely asked for in Greek hostels, but to be on the safe side it is worth joining before setting off. Most state-run museums and archaeological sites are free to EU students with a valid International Student Identity Card (ISIC); non-EU students with an ISIC card are usually entitled to a 50 percent reduction. There are no youth concessions available for these entrance fees, but occasional discounts are possible with a "Go 25" card, which can be obtained from any STA office by travelers who are under 26.

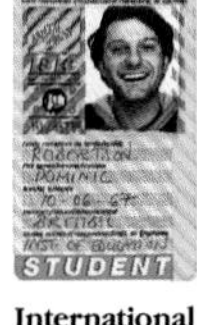

International student identity card

Facilities for the Disabled

There are few facilities in Greece for assisting the disabled, so careful planning is essential – sights that have wheelchair access are indicated at the beginning of each entry in this guide. **The Society for the Advancement of Travel for the Handicapped (SATH)**, publishes a quarterly magazine, *ACCESS to Travel*, which focuses on destinations, accommodations, and information useful to people with disabilities.

A sign directing access for wheelchairs at Athens airport

Directory

Greek Tourist Offices

Athens
Amerikis 2, 10564 Athens
01 322 3111.

Australia
51 Pitt St, Sydney, NSW 2000.
(2) 241 1663.

Canada
1300 Bay St, Toronto, Ontario M5R 3K8.
(416) 968-2220.

United Kingdom and Republic of Ireland
4 Conduit St, London W1R 0DJ.
0171-734 5997.

USA
Olympic Tower, 645 Fifth Ave, New York, NY 10022.
(212) 421-5777.

Useful Addresses

Aliens' Bureau
Leofóros Alexándras 173, Athens.
01 770 5711.

Hosteling International – American Youth Hostels
733 15th St., NW Washington, DC 20005.
(202) 783-6161.

Council on International Educational Exchange (CIEE)
205 East 42nd St., New York, NY 10017.
(212) 822-2600.

International Student and Youth Travel Service
2nd Floor, Níkis 11, 10557 Athens.
01 323 3767.

Society for the Advancement of Travel for the Handicapped (SATH)
347 Fifth Ave., Suite 610, New York, NY 10016
(212) 447-7284.

STA Travel
10 Downing St., New York, NY 10014.
(212) 627-3111.

Vacation Essentials

The EOT's Greek tourism emblem

For a carefree vacation on the Greek islands, it is best to adopt the philosophy *sigá, sigá* (slowly, slowly). Within this principle is the ritual of the afternoon siesta, a practice that should be taken seriously, particularly during the hottest months when it is almost a physiological necessity. Almost everything closes for a few hours after lunch, reopening later in the day when the air cools and the islands come to life again. The shops reopen their doors, the restaurants start filling up, and, at seafront locales, practically everyone partakes in the *vólta*, or evening stroll – a delightful Greek institution.

Tourist Information

Tourist information is available in many towns and villages on the islands, either in the form of government-run **EOT** offices (Ellinikós Organismós Tourismoú, or National Tourist Organization of Greece), municipally run tourist offices, the local tourist police *(see p340)*, or privately owned travel agencies. The EOT publishes an array of tourist literature, including maps, brochures, and leaflets on transportation and accommodation – be aware though that not all of their information is up-to-date and reliable. The addresses and phone numbers of the EOT and municipal tourist offices, as well as the tourist police, are listed throughout this guide.

Greek Time

Greece is always 2 hours ahead of Britain (GMT), 1 hour ahead of European countries on Central European Time (such as France), 7 hours ahead of New York, 10 hours ahead of Los Angeles, and 8 hours behind Sydney.

As Greece is now part of the EU, it follows the rule that all EU countries must put their clocks forward to summertime, and back again to wintertime on the same days, in order to avoid any confusion when traveling between countries. This should lessen the chance of missing a ferry or flight due to confusion over the time!

EOT office in the center of Athens

Opening Hours

Opening hours tend to be vague in Greece, varying from day to day, season to season, and place to place. It is therefore advisable to use the times given in this book as rough guidelines only and to check with local information centers for accurate times.

State-run museums and archaeological sites generally open from around 8:30am to 2:45pm (the major ones stay open as late as 8 or 9pm in the summer months). Mondays and main public holidays *(see p46)* are the usual closing days. Locally run and private museums may be closed on additional public holidays and on local festival days. Monasteries and convents are open during daylight hours, but will close for a few hours in the afternoon.

Opening times for shops are covered on page 346, pharmacies on page 341, banks on page 342, post offices on page 345, and OTE (telephone) offices on page 344.

Most stores and offices are closed on public holidays and local festival days, with the exception of some shops within tourist resorts. Major local festivals are included in the Visitors' Checklists in each main town entry in this guide.

Admission Charges

Most state-run museums and archaeological sites charge between 500 Dr and 2,000 Dr entrance fee. Reductions are available, however, ranging from around 25 percent for EU citizens aged 60 years and over (use your passport as proof of age) to 50 percent for non-EU students armed with an international student identity card (ISIC) *(see p337)*.

Though most museums and sites are closed on public holidays, the ones that do remain open are free of charge.

Events

The English-language papers *Athens News* has a What's On column, gazetting events all over the city and also those of special interest to children. Unfortunately, the two English-language listings magazines *Athenscope* and *The Athenian* have now folded, leaving only the Greek-language *Athinorama* to be deciphered. A list of Greek festivals and cultural events is given on pages 42–6, but it is also worth asking your nearest tourist office about events that are happening locally. Other forms of entertainment include the outdoor cinema in summer, which is very popular with the Greeks; most films are in English with Greek subtitles. There are also bars, discos, and nightclubs in the resorts,

A *períptero*, or kiosk, with a wide array of papers and periodicals

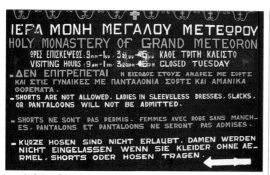

A typical sign about dress codes at a monastery

as well as tavernas and *kafeneía* (coffee shops), which are found in every town and village, and often form the center of social life.

Religion

Greece is almost entirely Greek Orthodox. The symbols and rituals of the religion are deeply rooted in Greek culture and are visible everywhere. Saint's days are celebrated throughout Greece *(see p46)*, sometimes on a local scale and sometimes across the entire country.

The largest religious minorities are the Muslims of Rhodes and Kos and the Catholics of Sýros and Tínos, though they constitute less than 1 percent of the island populations. Most other places for worship are situated in Athens.

A Greek priest

Etiquette

Like anywhere else, common courtesy and respect is appreciated in Greece, so try speaking a few words of the language, even if your vocabulary extends only as far as the basics *(see pp396–400)*.

Though formal attire is rarely needed, modest clothing (trousers for men and skirts for women) is *de rigueur* for visits to churches and monasteries.

Topless sunbathing is generally tolerated, but nude bathing is officially restricted to a few designated beaches.

In restaurants, the service charge is always included in the check, but tips are still appreciated – the custom is to leave between 10 and 15 percent. Public toilet attendants should also be tipped. Taxi drivers do not expect a tip, but they are not averse to them either; likewise hotel porters and chambermaids.

Photography

Photographic film is readily available in Greece, though it is often quite expensive in tourist areas and close to the major sights.

Taking photographs inside churches and monasteries is officially forbidden; within museums photography is usually permitted, but flashes and tripods are often not. In most cases where a stills camera is allowed, a video camera will also be fine, but you may have to pay an extra fee. At sites, museums, or religious buildings it is best to gain permission before using a camera, as rules do vary.

Electrical Appliances

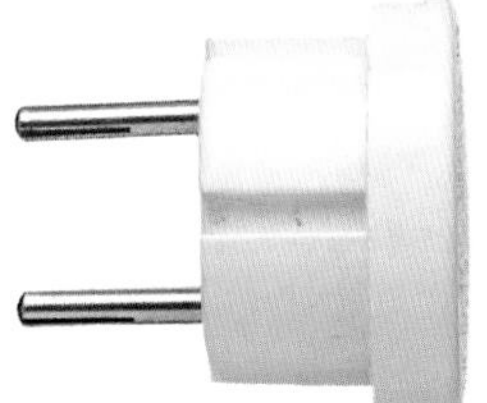

Two-pin adaptor, for use with all British appliances when in Greece

Greece, like other European countries, runs on 220 volts/50 Hz AC. Plugs have two round pins, or three round pins for appliances that need to be earthed. The adaptors required for British electrical appliances are difficult to find in Greece, so bring one with you. Similarly transformers are needed for North American equipment.

Conversion Chart

Greece uses the metric system, with two small exceptions: sea distances are expressed in nautical miles and land is measured in *strémmata*, the equivalent of about one-quarter acre).

US Standard to Metric
1 inch = 2.54 centimeters
1 foot = 30 centimeters
1 mile = 1.6 kilometers
1 ounce = 28 grams
1 pound = 454 grams
1 US quart = 0.947 liter
1 US gallon = 3.6 liters

Metric to US Standard
1 millimeter = 0.04 inch
1 centimeter = 0.4 inch
1 meter = 3 feet 3 inches
1 kilometer = 0.64 miles
1 gram = 0.04 ounce
1 kilogram = 2.2 pounds
1 liter = 1.1 US quarts

Directory

Embassies in Greece

Australia
Dimitríou Soútsou 37,
11521 Athens.
01 644 7303.

Canada
Gennadíou 4, 11521 Athens.
01 727 3400.

Republic of Ireland
Vassiléos Konstantínou 7,
10674 Athens.
01 723 2771.

New Zealand
Xenías 24, 11528 Athens.
01 771 0112.

United Kingdom
Ploutárchou 1,
10675 Athens.
01 723 6211.

United States
Vasilíssis Sofías 91,
10160 Athens.
01 721 2951.

Personal Health and Security

Fire service emblem

GREECE IS ONE of the safest European countries to visit, with a time-honored tradition of honesty that still survives despite the onslaught of mass tourism. But, as when traveling anywhere else, it is still advisable to take out a comprehensive travel insurance policy. One place where danger is ever-present, however, is on the road. Driving is a volatile matter in Greece, which now has the highest accident rate in Europe. Considerable caution is recommended, for drivers and pedestrians.

Personal Security

THE CRIME RATE in Greece is very low compared with other European countries. Nevertheless, a few precautions are worth taking, like keeping cars and hotel rooms locked, watching your handbag in public, and not keeping all your documents together in one place. If you do have anything stolen, contact the police or tourist police.

Police

GREECE'S POLICE are split into three forces: the regular police, the port police, and the tourist police. The tourist police are the most useful for vacationers, combining normal police duties with tourist advice. Should you suffer a theft, lose your passport, or have cause to complain about shops, restaurants, tour guides, or taxi drivers, your case should first be made to them. As every tourist police office claims to have at least one English speaker, they can act as interpreters if the case needs to involve the local police. Their offices also offer maps, brochures, and advice on finding accommodations.

Legal Assistance for Tourists

EUROPEAN CONSUMERS' associations together with the European Commission have created a program, known as **EKPIZO**, to inform tourists of their rights. Its aim is specifically to help vacationers who experience problems

A policeman giving directions to vacationers

with hotels, campsites, travel agencies, and so forth. They will furnish tourists with the relevant information and, if necessary, arrange legal advice from lawyers in English, French, or German. Contact the Crete office for their telephone numbers on the other islands.

Medical Treatment and Insurance

BRITISH and other EU citizens are entitled to free medical care in Greece on presentation of an E111 form (available from most UK post offices), and emergency treatment in public hospitals is free to all foreign nationals. Be aware, however, that public health facilities are limited on the islands and private clinics are expensive. Visitors are strongly advised to take out comprehensive travel insurance (available from travel agents and insurance brokers) covering both private medical treatment and loss or theft of personal possessions. Be sure, too, to read the small print: not all policies, for instance, will cover you for activities of a "dangerous" nature, such as motorcycling and trekking; not all policies will pay for doctors' or hospital fees direct, and only some will cover you for ambulances and emergency flights home. Paying for your flight with a credit card such as VISA or American Express will also provide limited travel insurance, including reimbursement of your air fare if the agent happens to go bankrupt.

Health Precautions

IT COSTS LITTLE or nothing to take a few sensible precautions when traveling abroad, and certain measures are essential if vacationing in the extreme heat of high summer. The most obvious thing to avoid is overexposure to the sun, particularly for the fair-skinned: wear a hat and good-quality sunglasses, as well as a high-factor suncreen. If you do burn, aloe gel is soothing. Heat stroke is a real hazard for which medical attention should be sought immediately, while heat exhaustion and dehydration (made worse by alcohol consumption) are also serious.

Be sure to drink plenty of water, even if you don't feel thirsty, and if in any doubt invest in a package of electrolyte tablets (a mixture of potassium salts and glucose) available at any Greek pharmacy, to avoid

Port policeman's uniform **City policeman's uniform**

An ambulance with the emergency number emblazoned on its side

Fire engine

Police car

dehydration and replace lost minerals. Always go prepared with an adequate supply of any medication you may need while away, as well as a copy of the prescription with the generic name of the drug – this is useful not only in case you run out, but also for the purposes of customs when you enter the country. Also be aware that codeine, available elsewhere in Europe, is illegal in Greece.

Tap water in Greece is generally safe to drink, but in remote communities it is a good precaution to check with the locals. Bottled spring water is for sale throughout the islands.

However tempting the sea may look, swimming immediately after a meal is not recommended since stomach cramps out at sea can cause problems.

Underwater hazards to be aware of are weaver fish, jellyfish, and sea urchins. The latter are not uncommon and are extremely unpleasant if stepped on. If you do step on one, the spine will need to be extracted using olive oil and a sterilized needle. Jellyfish stings can be relieved by vinegar, baking soda, or by various remedies sold at Greek pharmacies. Though a rare occurrence, the sand-dwelling weaver fish has a powerful sting, its poison causing extreme pain. The immediate treatment is to immerse the affected area in very hot water to dilute the venom's strength.

No inoculations are required for visitors to Greece, though tetanus and typhoid boosters may be recommended by your doctor.

Pharmacies

Greek pharmacists are highly qualified and can not only advise on minor ailments, but also dispense medication not usually available over the counter back home. Their premises, *farmakeía,* are identified by a red or green cross on a white background. Pharmacies are open from 8:30am to 2pm, but are usually closed in the afternoon and on Saturday mornings. However, in larger towns there is often a rotation system to maintain a service from 7:30am to 2pm and from 5:30 to 10pm. Details are posted in pharmacy windows, both in Greek and English.

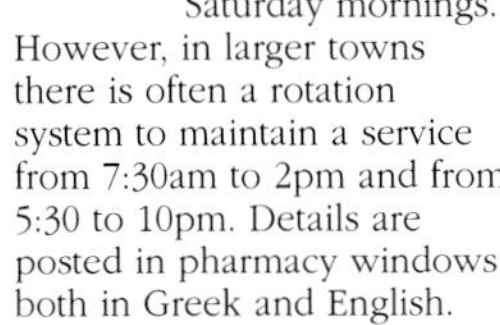

Pharmacy sign

Emergency Services

In case of emergencies the appropriate services to call are listed in the directory below. For accidents or other medical emergencies, a 24-hour ambulance service only operates within Athens. Outside Athens, in rural towns, and on the islands, ambulances are rarely on 24-hour call. But, if necessary, patients can be transferred from island ESY (Greek National Health Service) hospitals or surgeries to a main ESY hospital in Athens by ambulance and ferry, or helicopter.

A complete list of ESY hospitals, private hospitals, and clinics is available from the tourist police.

Directory

Nationwide Emergency Numbers

Police
100.

Ambulance
166.

Fire
199.

Road assistance
174.

Coastguard patrol
108.

Athens Emergency Numbers

Tourist police
171.

Doctors
105 (2pm–7am).

Pharmacies
For information on 24-hour pharmacies:
107 (central Athens).
102 (suburbs).

Poison treatment center
01 779 3777.

EKPIZO Bureau

Crete branch
Milatou 1 and Agiou Titou, Irákleio, Crete
081 240 666.

Banking and Local Currency

Eurocheque logo

CHANGING MONEY is straightforward on the Greek islands and does not pose any special problems. If there is no bank where you are staying, there will probably be a post office, and even in the smallest towns and resorts you can expect to find a car rental firm or travel agency that will oblige by changing cash and travelers' checks – albeit with a sizeable commission. The larger towns and tourist centers all have the usual banking facilities, including an increasing number of cash machines (ATMs).

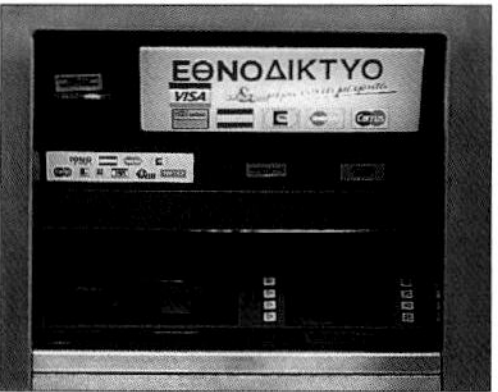

National Bank of Greece ATM

Banking Hours

ALL BANKS ARE OPEN from 8am to 2pm Monday to Thursday, and from 8am to 1:30pm on Friday. In the larger towns and tourist resorts there is usually at least one bank that reopens its exchange desk for a few hours in the evening and on Saturday mornings during the summer season.

Cash machines, though seldom found outside the major towns and resorts, are in operation 24 hours a day. All banks are closed on public holidays *(see p46)* and may also be closed on any local festival days.

Banks and Exchange Facilities

THERE ARE BANKS in all major towns and resorts, as well as exchange facilities at post offices (which tend to charge lower commissions and are found in the more remote areas of Greece), travel agents, hotels, tourist offices and car rental agencies. Always take your passport with you when cashing travelers' checks, and check exchange rates and commission charges beforehand, as they vary greatly. In major towns and tourist areas you may find a foreign exchange machine for changing money at any time of day or night. These operate in several languages, as do the ATMs.

Foreign exchange machine

Cards, Checks, and Eurocheques

VISA, MASTERCARD (Access), American Express, and Diners Club are the most widely accepted credit cards in Greece. They are the most convenient way to pay for plane tickets, international ferry journeys, car rental, some hotels, and larger purchases. Cheaper tavernas, shops, and hotels as a rule do not accept credit cards.

Bank of Greece logo

You can get a cash advance on a foreign credit card at some banks, though the minimum amount is 15,000 Dr, and you will need to take your passport with you as proof of identity. A credit card can be used for drawing local currency at cash machines. At a bank or ATM, a 1.5 percent processing charge is usually levied for Visa, but none for other cards.

Cirrus and Plus debit card systems operate in Greece. Cash can be obtained using the Cirrus system at National Bank of Greece ATMs and the Plus system at Commercial Bank ATMs.

Travelers' checks are the safest way to carry large sums of money. They are refundable if lost or stolen, though the process can be time-consuming. American Express and Thomas Cook are the best known brands of travelers' checks in Greece. They usually incur two sets of commissions: one when you buy them (1–1.5 percent) and another when you cash them. Rates for the latter vary considerably, so shop around before changing your money.

Travelers' checks can be cashed at most post offices *(see p345)* – an important consideration if you are traveling to a rural area or remote island.

Eurocheques, available only to holders of a European bank account in the form of a checkbook, are honored at banks and post offices throughout Greece, as well as many hotels, shops, and travel agencies. There is no commission charged when cashing Eurocheques, though there is an annual fee of about $12 for holding a European account and a fee of about two percent for each check used. All fees are debited directly from the account.

Visitors changing money at a foreign exchange bureau

Currency

The Greek unit of currency is the drachma (Dr), and denominations in widest circulation are notes of 100, 500, 1,000, 5,000, and 10,000 Dr, and coins of 5, 10, 20, 50, 100, and 200 Dr. No more than 100,000 drachmas in cash may be brought into Greece, and up to 40,000 Dr taken out. There is no limit on foreign currency and travelers' checks being imported, but anything over the value of 250,000 Dr in cash should be declared on entry, in case it needs to be re-exported. Large amounts of foreign currency, such as 6,000,000 drachmas, must be transferred through a bank.

Directory

To report a lost or stolen credit card, ask for the US operator and request the following collect numbers from Greece:

Mastercard
303-278-8000.

American Express
910-668-5110.

Diners Club
00 44 1252 513500.

Visa
410-581-9994.

To report lost or stolen travelers' checks, ask for the US operator and request the following collect from Greece:

American Express
801-964-6665.

Call these numbers directly from Greece:

Thomas Cook/ Mastercard
00 800 4128366.

Thomas Cook/Visa
00 800 44 128455.

Coins
These are the coins in widest circulation throughout Greece. They are shown at their actual size.

100 Dr

50 Dr

20 Dr

10 Dr

5 Dr

Bank Notes
The most commonly used bills are in denominations of 100 to 10,000 drachmas. The bills are all of equal size, but each denomination is a different color and carries a portrait of a historical or mythological figure.

10,000 drachmas

5,000 drachmas

1,000 drachmas

500 drachmas

100 drachmas

Communications

Post office logo

The Greek national telephone company is the OTE (Organismós Tilepikoinonión Elládos). Telecommunications have improved dramatically in recent years, and now there are direct lines to all major countries. These are often better than local lines, but the rates are among the highest in Europe. Greek mail is reasonably reliable and efficient, especially from the larger towns and resorts; faxes are also easy to send and receive. The Greeks are avid newspaper readers, and in addition to a vast array of Greek publications, there are also a few good English-language papers and magazines.

Telephones and Faxes

Public telephones can be found in many locales – hotel foyers, telephone booths, street kiosks, or the local OTE office. Long-distance calls are best made in a telephone booth using a phonecard – available at any kiosk in denominations of 100, 500 and 1,000 units. Alternatively, they can be made at a metered phone in an OTE office, where you can also make collect calls. OTE offices are open daily from 7am to 10pm or midnight in the larger towns; or until around 3pm in smaller communities. Charges are variable, but in general local calls are cheap, out-of-town domestic calls are surprisingly expensive, and long-distance calls are extortionate. You can call the operator first for specific rates, as well as information about peak and cheap times, which vary depending on the country you are phoning.

Ship-to-shore and shore-to-ship calls can be made through INMARSAT; for information on this service call the marine operator from Greece at 158.

Faxes can be sent from OTE offices, some post offices, and most car rental and travel agencies, though expect to pay a heavy surcharge wherever you go. The easiest way to receive a fax is to become friendly with your nearest car rental or travel agency – both will usually oblige and keep faxes aside for you – otherwise the OTE office is the place to go.

A public phone

Radio and TV

With three state-owned radio channels and a plethora of local stations, the airwaves are positively jammed in Greece, and reception is not always dependable. There are many Greek music stations to listen to, as well as classical music stations such as ER-3, one of the three state-run channels, which can be heard on 95.6 FM. Daily news summaries are broadcast in English, French, and German, and with a shortwave radio you will be able to pick up the BBC World Service in most parts of Greece. Its frequency varies, but in Athens it can be heard on 107.1 FM.

There is another 24-hour English-language station, Superstar, which is on 93.4 FM.

Greek TV is broadcast by two state-run, and several privately run, channels, plus a host of cable and satellite stations from across Europe. Most stations are a mix of foreign soap operas, game shows, sports, and films; foreign language films, which are frequently shown, tend to be subtitled rather than dubbed.

ET1, one of the two state-run channels, transmits news summaries in English each day at 6pm, while satellite stations CNN and Euronews televise news in English round the clock. Guides for television programs are published in all the English-language papers and magazines.

Using a Phonecard Telephone in Greece

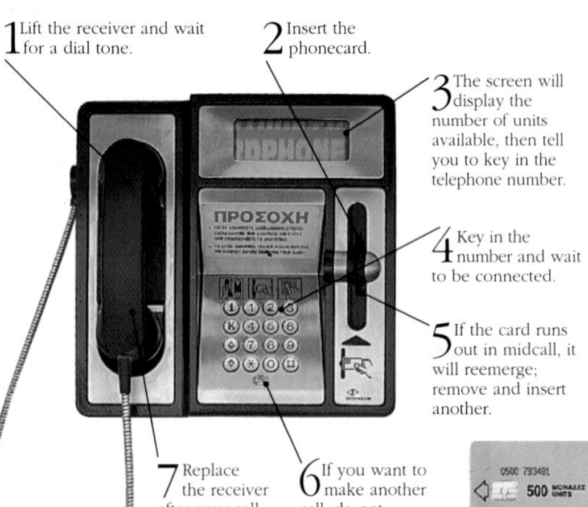

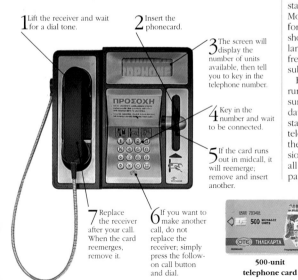

1 Lift the receiver and wait for a dial tone.

2 Insert the phonecard.

3 The screen will display the number of units available, then tell you to key in the telephone number.

4 Key in the number and wait to be connected.

5 If the card runs out in midcall, it will reemerge; remove and insert another.

6 If you want to make another call, do not replace the receiver; simply press the follow-on call button and dial.

7 Replace the receiver after your call. When the card reemerges, remove it.

500-unit telephone card

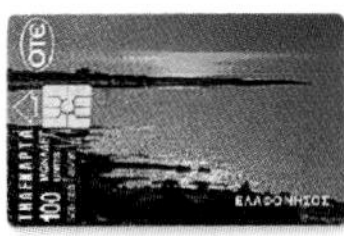

100-unit telephone card

Red mailbox for express mail

Yellow mailbox for all other mail

Newspapers and Magazines

The trusty corner *períptera* (kiosks), bookstores in larger towns, and tourist shops in the resorts often sell day-old newspapers and magazines, such as *USA Today* and the *Wall Street Journal*, but the mark-up is substantial. Much cheaper, and also widely available is the English-language paper published in Athens, *Athens News*, which is printed every day except Monday. In addition to this, the *Odyssey*, a bi-monthly, glossy magazine, is available in most of the resorts as well as the capital. These two publications are excellent sources of information on local entertainment, festivals, and cultural goings-on, while also providing coverage of domestic and international news. The most popular Greek-language newspapers are *Eleftherotypía, Eléftheros Týpos*, and *Kathemeriní*.

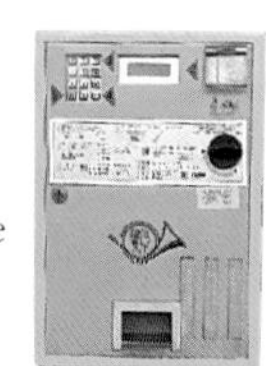
Stamp machine

Post

Greek post offices *(tachydromeía)* are generally open from 7:30am to 2pm Monday to Friday. Some main branches in the larger towns stay open as late as 8pm (main branches occasionally open for a few hours on the weekend as well).

All post offices are closed on public holidays *(see p46)*. Those with an "Exchange" sign will change money in addition to the usual services.

Mailboxes are usually bright yellow; those with two slots are marked *esoterikó*, meaning domestic, and *exoterikó*, meaning overseas. Bright red mailboxes are reserved for express mail, for both domestic and overseas destinations. Express is a little more expensive, but cuts delivery time by a few days.

Stamps *(grammatósima)* can be bought over the counter at post offices and also at *períptera*; the latter usually charge a ten percent commission.

Airmail letters from the Greek islands to most European countries take between three and six days, and anywhere from five days to a

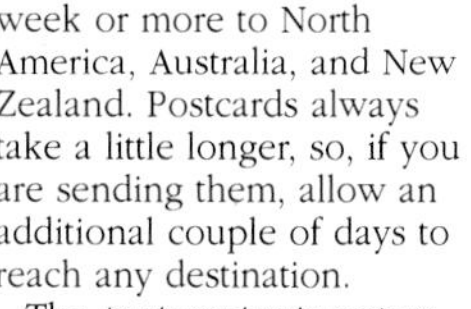
week or more to North America, Australia, and New Zealand. Postcards always take a little longer, so, if you are sending them, allow an additional couple of days to reach any destination.

The *poste restante* system – whereby mail can be sent to, and picked up from, a post office – is widely used in Greece. Mail should be clearly marked "Poste Restante," with the recipient's last name underlined. A passport, or other proof of identity, is needed when collecting the mail, which is kept for a maximum of 30 days before being returned.

If you are sending a parcel from Greece to a non-EU country, do not seal it before going to the post office. The contents will need to be inspected by security before it is sent, and if the package is sealed they will unwrap it.

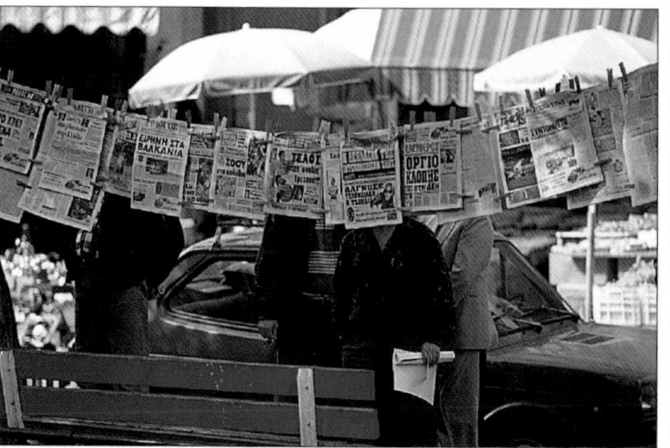
Athenians reading newspapers on a clothes line at a street kiosk

Directory

Domestic Calls

☎ *151 (domestic operator).*

☎ *131 (directory assistance for local calls anywhere in Greece).*

☎ *132 (directory assistance for non-local calls within Greece).*

International Calls

☎ *161 (international operator and directory assistance).*

☎ *162 (international directory assistance if calling from Athens).*

International Calls from Greece

Dial 00, the country code (a list is given below), the local area code (minus the initial 0) and then the number itself.

Australia *61.*
Ireland *353.*
New Zealand *64.*
UK *44.*
USA & Canada *1.*

International Calls to Greece from Abroad

Dial the international access code (a list is given below), 30 (country code), the area code minus initial 0 and then the number itself.

Australia *0011.*
Ireland *016.*
UK & New Zealand *00.*
USA & Canada *011.*

Shopping in Greece

Honey from Evvoia

SHOPPING IN THE GREEK ISLANDS can be an entertaining pastime, especially when you buy directly from the producer. This is often the case in the smaller villages, where crafts are a major source of income. Embroiderers and lace makers can be seen sitting outside their houses, and potters can be found in their workshops. Apart from these industries, and the food and drink produced locally, most other goods are imported to the islands and carry a heavy markup.

Olive-wood bowls and other souvenirs from Corfu Old Town

VAT and Tax Free Shopping

ALMOST ALWAYS included in the price, FPA *(Fóros Prostitheménis Axías)* – the equivalent of sales tax – is about 18 percent in Greece.

Visitors from outside the EU staying less than three months may claim this money back on purchases over 40,000 Dr. A "Tax-Free Check" form must be completed in the store, a copy of which is then given to the customs authorities on departure. You may be asked to show your receipt or goods as proof of purchase.

Opening Hours

ALLOWING FOR PLENTY of exceptions, shops and boutiques are generally open on Monday, Wednesday, and Saturday from 9am to 2:30pm, and on Tuesday, Thursday, and Friday from 9am to 2pm and 5pm to 8pm. Supermarkets, found in all but the smallest communities, are often family-run and open long hours, typically Monday to Saturday from 8 or 9am to 8 or 9pm. Sunday shopping is possible in most tourist resorts. The corner *períptero* (street kiosk), found in nearly every town, is open from around 7am to 11pm or midnight, selling everything from aspirin to ice cream.

Basket of herbs and spices from a market stall in Irákleio, Crete

Markets

MOST TOWNS in the Greek islands have their weekly street market *(laïki agorá)*, a colorful jumble of the freshest and best fruit and vegetables, herbs, fish, meat, and poultry – often juxtaposed with a miscellany of shoes and underwear, fabrics, household items, and sundry electronic equipment.

AB *(Alpha Vita)* Supermarket logo

In larger towns, the street markets are in a different neighborhood each day, usually opening early and packing up by about 1:30pm, in time for the afternoon siesta. Prices are generally lower than in the supermarkets, and a certain amount of bargaining is also acceptable, at least for nonperishable items.

Food and Drink

CULINARY DELIGHTS to look out for in the shops and markets of the Greek islands include honey, pistachios, olives, and a variety of herbs, and spices. Good cheeses include the salty feta, and the sweet *manoúri* from Crete; for something sugary, try the numerous pastries and cookies of the *zacharoplasteío* (the cake and candy shop).

Greece is also well known for several of its wines and spirits. These include brandy, ouzo (an anise-flavored spirit), retsina (a resinated wine) and, from Crete, the firewater raki.

Size Chart

Women's dresses, coats and skirts								
Greek		44	46	48	50	52	54	(size)
GB/Australian		10	12	14	16	18	20	(size)
US		8	10	12	14	16	18	(size)
Men's suits, shirts and jumpers								
Greek	44	46	48	50	52	54	56	(size)
GB/US	34	36	38	40	42	44	46	(inches)
Australian	87	92	97	102	107	112	117	(cm)
Women's shoes								
Greek		36	37	38	39	40	41	(size)
GB		3	4	5	6	7	8	(size)
US/Australian		5	6	7	8	9	10	(size)
Men's shoes								
Greek		40	41	42	43	44	45	(size)
GB/Australian		7	7 ½	8	9	10	11	(size)
US		7 ½	8	8 ½	9 ½	10 ½	11 ½	(size)

What to Buy in Greece

TRADITIONAL handicrafts, though not particularly inexpensive, do offer the most genuinely Greek souvenirs. These cover a range of items from finely wrought gold reproductions of ancient pendants to rustic pots, wooden spoons, and handmade sandals. Leatherwork is particularly noted on the island of Crete, where the town of Chaniá *(see p248)* hosts a huge leather market. Among the islands renowned for their ceramics are Crete, Lésvos, and Sífnos. Many villages throughout the Greek islands produce brightly colored embroidery *(kéndyma)* and wall-hangings, which are often hung out for sale. You may also see thick *flokáti* rugs. They are handwoven from sheep or goat's wool, but are more often produced in the mountainous regions of mainland Greece than on the islands themselves. In the smaller island communities, crafts are often cottage industries, which earn the entire family a large chunk of its annual income during the summer. There is usually room for some bartering when buying from the villagers.

Rug from Anógeia, Crete

Gold jewelry *is sold mainly in larger towns. Modern designs are found in jewelers such as Lalaounis, and reproductions of ancient designs in museum gift shops.*

Icons *are generally sold in shops and monasteries. They range from very small portraits to substantial pictures. Some of the most beautiful, and expensive, use only age-old traditional techniques and materials.*

Ornate utensils*, such as these wooden spoons, are found in traditional craft shops. As here, they are often hand-carved into the shapes of figures and produced from the rich-textured wood of the native olive tree.*

Kombolói, *or worry beads, are a traditional sight in Greece; the beads are counted as a way to relax. They are sold in souvenir shops and jewelers.*

Kitchenware *is found in most markets and in specialist shops. This copper coffee pot* (mpríki) *is used for making Greek coffee.*

Leather goods *are sold throughout Greece. The bags, backpacks, and sandals make useful and bargain souvenirs.*

Ornamental ceramics *come in many shapes and finishes. Traditional earthenware, often simple, functional, and unglazed, is frequently for sale on the outskirts of Athens and the larger towns of the islands.*

Special Interest Vacations and Outdoor Activities

Moped in Rhodes

If you feel you want more of a focus to your vacation in the Greek islands, there are many organized tours and courses available that cater to special interests. You can visit ancient archaeological sites with a learned academic as your guide, you can improve your writing skills, paint the Greek landscape, or develop your spirituality. All kinds of walking tours, as well as botanical and bird-watching expeditions, are available in the islands. Information on sailing and water sports and advice on choosing the perfect beach are covered on pages 350–51.

Visitors at the ancient theater at Delos *(see pp214–15)*

Archaeological Tours

For those interested in Greece's glorious ancient past, a tour to some of the famous archaeological sites, accompanied by qualified archaeologists, can make for a fascinating and memorable vacation. In addition to visiting ruins, many tours take in Venetian fortresses, Byzantine churches, caves, archaeological museums, and monasteries along the way. **Pharos** organizes tours with Minoan, Roman, and medieval interests. The island of Crete is one of their main destinations, taking in sites at Réthymno *(see pp254–5)* as well as the Minoan palace at Knosós *(see pp268–71)*.

Writing and Painting

With its vivid landscape and renowned quality of light, the Greek islands are an inspirational destination for artistic endeavor. Courses in creative writing, and drawing and painting, are available at all levels. The **Skyros Center** *(see p112)*, on the island of the same name, offers two locations – one in the main town and another in the remote village of Atsítsa – for a variety of self-development and therapeutic vacations, including themes directed toward writing and painting. **Pharos** also offers various creative vacations on Kýthira, Léros, Corfu, and Crete.

Tourists visiting caves near Psychró, in Crete

Nature Vacations

The Greek islands are rich in natural beauty, and you need not be a fanatical botanist or ornithologist to enjoy the stunning wild flowers and variety of birdlife. Spring is the best time to explore the countryside, when the colorful flowers are in bloom. It is also a good time to see the influx of migrating birds that rest and feed in Greece on their journeys between Africa and Europe.

Several tour operaters offer packages that take advantage of these factors. The **Hellenic Ornithological Society** in Athens specializes in tours concentrating on the wetlands and streams that attract migrating birds, and takes in the shrub-covered hillsides, which are rich in orchids during the spring. **F-Zein Ltd.**, also in Athens, and **Pharos Travel and Tourism, Inc.** in New York offer personalized tours that center around bird-watching and botany. More information on the wildlife of Crete and specialty tour operators is given on pages 242–3. Most packages also incorporate visits to nearby historical and archaeological sites into the tours.

A chameleon, found mainly on Crete

Walking

The hills of Greece are a walker's paradise, particularly between March and June, when the countryside is verdant, the sun is not too hot, and wildflowers abound. Many of the islands provide fine locations and scenery in which to walk. **Trekking Hellas** arranges walking tours in the White Mountains of Crete, and on Andros and Tínos in the Cyclades. **Athenogenes** also organizes tours in Crete, as well as Ikaría, and Sámos. **Metro Tours** and **F-Zein, Ltd.** can organize tours through the mountainous interior of Crete,

Walkers climbing Mount Ida in central Crete

or walking tours in Crete, Ithaca, Chíos, and Sámos. **The Greek National Tourist Organization** can help you arrange trips directed toward painting and wildlife.

For the independent trekker, guides such as *Trekking in Greece* (Lonely Planet) and *The Mountains of Greece: A Walker's Guide* (Cicerone Press) are invaluable sources of information.

Spas

Greece is well endowed with natural hot springs – a result of volcanic activity – and several islands have developed these as spas, offering such treatments as hydrotherapy, physiotherapy, and hydromassage. The main centers are listed on the EOT's (Greek Tourist Office's) information sheet *Spas in Greece*, and include Kos and Nísyros in the Dodecanese, Ikaría, Lésvos, and Límnos in the Northeast Aegean group, Zákynthos in the Ionian, and Kýthnos in the Cyclades.

Cruises and Boat Trips

Greece's unique combination of natural beauty and fascinating history makes a cruising vacation both relaxing and stimulating. Greek cruises run between April and October, and there is a variety of options available, ranging from a full luxury cruise to short boat trips. Operators such as **Hellenic Holidays** and **Royal Olympic Cruises** offer all-inclusive holidays on large luxury liners, with guest speakers versed in a range of subjects from archaeology to marine biology. Such cruises tend to incorporate the Greek islands into extensive routes from Italy to the Middle East, or to the Black Sea.

At the other end of the spectrum, there are many boat trips from tourist centers to nearby islands and places of interest. Organized locally, these are best booked there and then.

Boat trip sign in Corfu

Daytrip boats in Mandráki Harbor, Rhodes

Directory

Athenogenes
18 Plateía Kolonakíou,
10673 Athens.
011 30 1 361 4829.

F-Zein Ltd.
132 Syngrou Ave.,
Athens.
011 30 1 92 16285.
FAX 011 30 1 922 9995.

Guaranteed Travel
83 South Street,
Morristown,
NJ 07960.
973-540-1770.
FAX 973-540-8602.

Hellenic Holidays
1501 Broadway,
Suite 1512,
New York, NY 10036.
(212) 944-8388.
FAX (212) 944-2450.

Hellenic Ornithological Society
Emmanouíl Mpenáki 53,
10681 Athens.
011 30 1 381 1271.

Hellenic Professional and Bareboat Yacht Owners' Association
Office A8, Marína Zéas,
18536 Piraeus.
01 452 6335.

Hellenic Water-ski Federation
Leofóros Possidónos,
16777 Athens.
01 894 7413.

Hellenic Yachting Federation
Possidónos 55,
Piraeus.
01 930 4825.

Metro Tours
484 Lowell St.,
Peabody,
MA 01960.
(800) 221-2810.

Pharos Travel and Tourism, Inc.
230 W. 31st St.
New York, NY 10001.
(800) 999-5511.
FAX (212) 736-3921.

Royal Olympic Cruises
Aktí Miaoúli 87,
18538 Piraeus.
011 30 1 429 1000.

Smithsonian Institution
1000 Jefferson Dr. SW,
Washington, DC 20560.

Trekking Hellas
Filellínon 7,
10557 Athens.
011 30 1 323 4548.

Beaches and Water Sports

Blue flag indicating a clean beach

WITH THOUSANDS OF ISLANDS, crystal clear seas, and beaches of every kind, it is not surprising that so many water lovers are attracted to Greece. Although people swim most of the year round, the main season for water sports is from late May to early November. All kinds of water sports can be enjoyed, especially in the larger and more developed resorts, and rental fees are still quite reasonable compared with other Mediterranean destinations. But if you prefer a more restful vacation, you can always choose from the many beautiful and tranquil beaches to be found on the islands.

Tour company flags flying on Golden Beach, Páros

Beaches

BEACHES VARY GREATLY in the Greek islands, offering everything from shingle and volcanic rock to gravel and fine sand. The Cyclades and Ionian islands are where the sandy beaches tend to be, and of these the best are usually on the south of the islands. Crete's beaches are also mostly sandy, but not exclusively. The northeast Aegean and the Sporades are a mixture of sandy and pebbly beaches, and this is also true of the Dodecanese. Some islets, such as Chálki and Kastellórizo, have few or no beaches at all. But, in compensation, they often have exceptionally clear seas, which can be good for snorkeling.

Swimmers diving off the boards at a pool by the beach on Rhodes

Any beach with a Blue Flag (awarded annually by the Hellenic Society for the Protection of Nature, in conjunction with the European Union) is guaranteed to have its water tested every 15 days for cleanliness and purity, as well as meeting over a dozen other environmental criteria. These beaches tend to be among the best, and the safest for children, though they can be very crowded. Also worth trying out are beaches recommended in the headings for each entry in this guide. Occasionally the main beach near the port of an island is run by the EOT (Greek Tourist Office). There will be a charge for its use, but it will be kept clean and often have the added benefit of showers.

Topless bathing is widespread, although nude bathing is still officially forbidden, except on a few designated beaches; it is never allowed within sight of a church.

The Greek seas are generally safe and delightful to swim in, although lifeguards are almost nonexistent in Greece. Every year there are at least a few casualties, especially on windy days when the sea is rough and there are underwater currents. Sharks and stingrays are rare around beaches, but more common are sea urchins and jellyfish. Both can be painful, but are not particularly dangerous.

Water Sports

WITH SO MUCH coastline, facilities catering to water sports are numerous. Windsurfing has become very popular, and waters recommended for this include those around Corfu, Lefkáda, and Zákynthos in the Ionian islands, Lésvos and Sámos in the northeast Aegean, Kos in the Dodecanese, Náxos in the Cyclades, and the coast around Crete. The **Hellenic Water-ski Federation** can offer the best advice. For a little more money you could take up water-skiing or jet-skiing; and at the larger resorts parasailing is also available. If you need instruction, you will find that many of the places that rent equipment also provide training.

Vacationers learning the skills of windsurfing in coastal waters

Rental center for water sports equipment, Rhodes

Scuba and Snorkeling

The amazingly clear waters of the Mediterranean and Aegean reveal a world of submarine life and archaeological remains. Snorkeling *(see pp20–21)* can be enjoyed almost anywhere along the coasts, though scuba diving is severely restricted. Designated areas for diving are around Crete, Rhodes, Kálymnos, and Mýkonos, and also around most of the Ionian islands. A complete list of places where it is permissible to dive with oxygen equipment can be obtained from the EOT, or by mail from the **Department of Underwater Archaeology** in Athens. Wherever you go snorkeling or diving, it is strictly forbidden to remove any antiquities you see, or even to photograph them.

Sailing Vacations

Sailing vacations can be booked through yacht charter companies in Greece or abroad. The season runs from April to the end of October or early November, and itineraries are flexible. Charters fall into four main categories. Bareboat charter is without a skipper or crew and is available to those with previous sailing experience (contact the **Hellenic Professional and Bareboat Yacht Owners' Association**). Crewed charters range from the modest services of a skipper, assistant, or cook to a yacht with a full crew. Sailing within a flotilla, typically in a group of around 6 to 12 yachts, provides the opportunity of independent sailing with the support of a lead boat, contactable by radio.

Learning the techniques of sailing

Most travel agencies offer sailing vacations in a flotilla. They also offer the popular "combined vacation." This type of vacation mixes cruiser sailing with the added interest of coastal pursuits such as shore-based dinghy sailing and windsurfing.

Sailing aboard a yacht in the Greek seas

Directory

Useful Organizations

Department of Underwater Archaeology
Kallispéri 30,
11742 Athens.
Tel *01 924 7249.*

Greek Yacht Brokers' and Consultants' Association
PO Box 30393,
17455 Athens.
Tel *01 985 0122.*

Hellenic Professional and Bareboat Yacht Owners' Association
Office A8,
Marína Zéas,
18536 Piraeus.
Tel *01 452 6335.*

Hellenic Water-ski Federation
Leofóros Possidónos,
16777 Athens.
Tel *01 894 7413.*

Hellenic Yachting Federation
Possidónos 55,
Piraeus.
Tel *01 930 4825.*

Yacht Charter Companies

Hellenic Holidays
1501 Broadway,
Suite 1512,
NY, NY 10036.
Tel *212-944-8388.*
FAX *212-944-8388.*

Metro Tours
484 Lowell St.,
Peabody, MA 01960.
Tel *800-221-2810.*
FAX *508-535-8830.*

Thalassa Charter and Yacht Brokers
Grypári 72,
Kallithéa,
Athens.
Tel *01 956 6866.*

Ulysses Tours Inc.
645 Fifth Ave.,
NY, NY 10022.
Tel *212-371-7646.*

Travel Information

Reliable hot, sunny weather makes Greece an extremely popular destination for vactioners. During the warmer months (May to October), countless charter flights bring millions to the Greek islands, though it is also possible to reach Greece by car, rail, or bus, and continue to the islands by ferry. While many of the larger islands are accessible by plane, the ferry network reaches even the remotest islands. This is matched by the bus service, which has frequent services on all major routes and local buses to the tiniest communities. Traveling around by car or motorcycle offers the most flexibility on larger islands, allowing the traveler to reach places that are inaccessible by public transportation, but the roads in remoter parts can be rough and potentially dangerous *(see p360)*. If, however, you do not wish to rent a car, taxis can provide another inexpensive option, and on many islands taxi-boats sail around the coasts, offering pick-up and drop-off points along the way.

Olympic Airways passenger airplane

Getting to Greece by Air

The main airlines operating direct scheduled flights from the US to Athens and Thessaloníki are **Olympic Airways** (the Greek national airline), **Delta**, and **TWA**. One advantage of using Olympic Airways is that, if flying to Athens, you land at the West Terminal *(see p354)*, which means there is no need to change terminals for a connecting domestic flight.

From Europe, there are around 20 international airports in Greece that can be reached directly. Direct daily flights from London are offered by Olympic, **British Airways**, and **Virgin Airways**. Only Crete, Rhodes, and Corfu among the islands, and Athens and Thessaloníki on the mainland, handle both charter and scheduled flights. The other international airports can only be reached directly by charter flights. From outside Europe, all scheduled flights to Greece arrive in Athens, and only a few airlines offer direct flights – most will require changing planes, and often airlines, at a connecting European city.

From Australia, Olympic Airways operates flights out of Sydney, Brisbane, and Melbourne. These generally necessitate a stopover in Southeast Asia or Europe, but there are two direct flights a week from Australia, leaving from Melbourne and Sydney. Flights from New Zealand are also via Melbourne or Sydney. Other carriers with services from Australasian cities to Athens include **Qantas**, **Singapore Airlines**, **KLM**, and **Gulf Air**.

Travelers with duty-free goods

International passengers arriving at Athens' East Terminal

Check-in desk at Athens airport's West Terminal

A new airport at Spárta, 25 km (15 miles) east of Athens is under construction, scheduled to be completed by 2004.

Charters and Package Deals

Charter flights to Greece are nearly all from within Europe and mostly operate between May and October. Tickets are sold by travel agencies either as part of an all-inclusive package tour or as a flight-only deal.

Although they tend to be the cheapest flights available, charters do carry certain restrictions: departure dates cannot be changed once booked and there are usually minimum and maximum limits to one's stay (typically between three days and a month). Another consideration if you plan to visit Turkey from Greece is that charter passengers can go only for a day trip; if you stay any longer you will forfeit the return portion of your air ticket.

Booking agency in Athens

Flight Times

Flying to Athens from New York takes about 10 hours, although a nondirect flight can take more than 12. From Los Angeles the journey's duration totals from 17 to 19 hours, depending on the European connection. The flight from London or Amsterdam is around 3.5 hours; from Paris and Berlin about 3 hours (it's a little quicker fom Berlin). From Madrid it takes just over 4 hours, from Rome a little under 2 hours, and from Sydney or Melbourne, via Bangkok it is a 19-hour flight.

Air Fares

Fares to Greece are generally at their highest from June to September, but how much you pay will depend more on the type of ticket you decide to purchase. Charters are usually the cheapest option during peak season, although discounted scheduled flights are also common and worth considering for longer visits or during the low season, when there are few charters available. Reasonable savings can also be made by booking an APEX (Advance Purchase Excursion) ticket well in advance but, like charters, these are subject to minimum and maximum limits to one's stay and other restrictions. Travelers on a budget will often be able to find bargain flights through travel agents advertising in the Sunday newspapers, and inexpensive last-minute deals are also advertised on the Internet. Whoever you book through, be sure that the company is a fully bonded and licensed member of ASTA (American Society of Travel Agents) or an equivalent authority – this will guarantee that you can get home should the company go bankrupt during your stay; it also should guarantee that you receive compensation. Note that domestic flights in Greece are subject to an airport tax, which is explained on page 354.

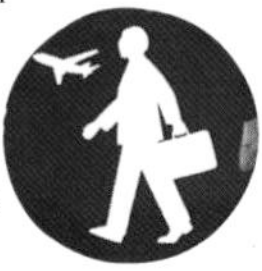

Departure gates symbol

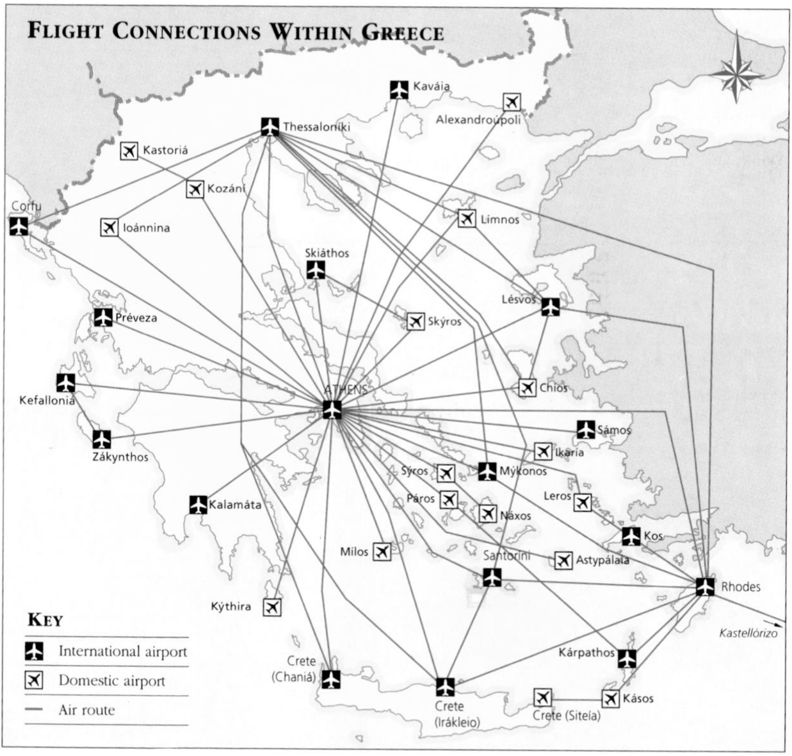

Flight Connections Within Greece

Kaváia
Alexandroúpoli
Thessaloníki
Kastoriá
Kozáni
Corfu
Ioánnina
Límnos
Skiáthos
Lésvos
Préveza
Skýros
Chios
Kefallonia
ATHENS
Sámos
Zákynthos
Ikaria
Sýros
Mýkonos
Leros
Kalamáta
Páros
Náxos
Kos
Milos
Santorini
Astypálaia
Rhodes
Kýthira
Kastellórizo
Kárpathos
Crete (Chaniá)
Crete (Irákleio)
Crete (Siteía)
Kásos

Key

- International airport
- Domestic airport
- Air route

5mm = 200km
1mm = 200m

Flight Connections in Greece

Olympic logo

ATHENS AIRPORT is the most important for the whole country. It has two main terminals (East and West) and an additional terminal for charter flights. As well as having the largest number of international flights, Athens also has the most connecting services to the islands. Nearly all of these depart from the West terminal, so unless you arrive in Greece on an Olympic flight you will need to change terminals. Thessaloníki also handles scheduled flights, but only from within Europe. Greece's other international airports are served by charters only, mostly from within Europe.

Interior of the West (Olympic) terminal at Athens airport

Domestic Flights

GREECE'S DOMESTIC airline network is extensive. **Olympic Airways** and its affiliate, **Olympic Aviation**, operate most internal flights, though there are also a number of private companies, such as **Air Greece**, **Aegean Aviation**, and **Interjet**, providing services between Athens and some of the major island destinations. Fares for domestic flights are at least double the equivalent bus journey or deck-class ferry trip. Tickets and timetables for Olympic flights can be obtained from any Olympic Airways office in Greece or abroad, as well as from most major travel agencies. Reservations are essential in tourist season.

Olympic Airways operates direct flights from Athens to over two dozen islands, and from Thessaloníki there are direct Olympic flights to nine of the islands *(see p353)*.

Athens Airport Main Terminals

The East terminal is the main one for international flights. Domestic and all Olympic Airways flights leave from the West terminal. The two are connected by bus.

Key

- Public access
- Check-in
- Passengers only
- Customs
- Passport control
- Baggage reclaim
- No access
- Boarding pass control

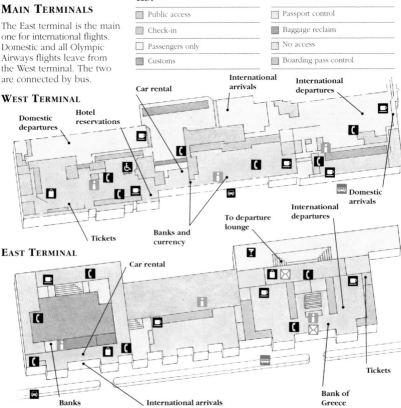

West Terminal

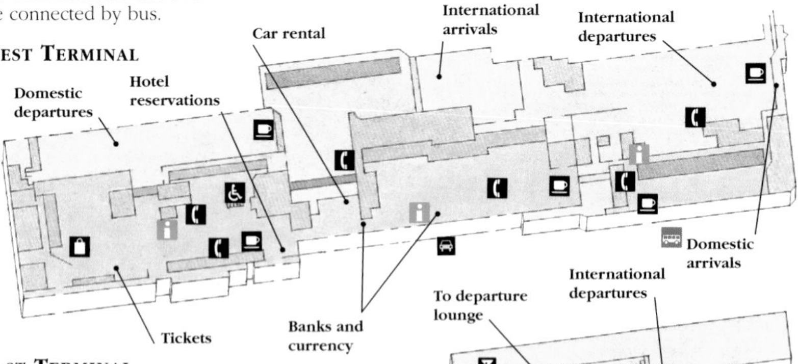

Domestic departures
Hotel reservations
Car rental
International arrivals
International departures
Domestic arrivals
Tickets
Banks and currency

East Terminal

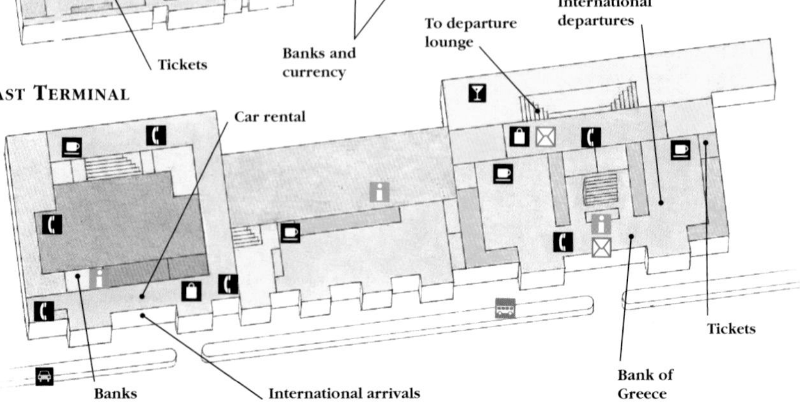

Car rental
To departure lounge
International departures
Tickets
Bank of Greece
Banks
International arrivals

There are a number of inter-island services available during the summer, and about a dozen of these flights operate throughout the year.

A small airport departure tax is charged on domestic flights between 62 and 466 air miles. For "international" flights (that is, those over 466 miles) the tax is doubled.

Transportation from Athens Airport

From Athens airport the most convenient way of getting to the city center is by taxi. There are stands outside the terminal buildings, and fares are cheap – less than in any other European city. The journey time may vary greatly, depending on traffic congestion; when the roads are fairly clear, it takes about 30 minutes.

Alternatively, the express bus 091 *(see p291)* runs from the West (Olympic Airways), East and Charter terminals to Plateía Syntágmatos in central Athens. Buses depart every half hour from 5am to midnight and continue hourly throughout the night.

A second express bus (19) runs from the airport terminals to Plateía Karaïskáki at the port of Piraeus. Departures are about every 50 minutes between 5am and midnight, with four departures between midnight and 5am.

Olympic Aviation island hopper airplane

Directory

Athens Airport

Athens West Terminal
Flight information:
01 936 3363.

Athens East Terminal
Flight information:
01 969 4111.

Olympic Airways

Arrivals and Departures
01 936 3363.
144.

Athens Office
Syngroú 96,
11741 Athens.
01 966 6666.

Crete Office
Plateía Eleftheriás, Irákleio.
0812 29191.

Rhodes Office
0241 24555.

Thessaloníki Office
Kountouriótou 3,
Thessaloníki.
031 230240.

Other Airlines

Air Canada
Othonos 10,
10557 Athens.
01 322 3206.

Air France
Karageórgi Servias 4,
10562 Athens.
01 960 1100.

British Airways
Vouliagménis & Themistokleous 1,
16674 Athens.
01 890 6633-34.
(Call this number for details of Qantas Airline services).
Thessaloníki:
0314 75300.

Delta Airlines
Othonos 4,
10557 Athens.
01 331 1673.

Gulf Air
Níkis 30,
10557 Athens.
01 322 9544.

KLM
Vouliagménis 41,
16675 Athens.
01 960 5000.

Singapore Airlines
Xenofóntos 9,
10557 Athens.
01 323 9111.

TWA
Xenofóntos 8,
10557 Athens.
01 325 4714.

Virgin Airways
Tziréon 8–10,
11742 Athens.
01 924 9100

Private Airlines (for Domestic Travel)

Aegean Aviation
East Terminal,
Athens Airport,
16603 Athens.
01 995 0325.

Air Greece
Filellínon 22,
10557 Athens.
01 324 4457.

Interjet
Syngroú 350,
17680 Athens.
01 930 2151.

KAL Aviation
Vasiléos Konstantínou 26,
11635 Athens.
01 729 2846.

Olympic Aviation
01 936 3565
(or via Olympic Airways).

Travel Agencies in Athens

American Express Travel Services
Ermoú 2,
10563 Athens.
01 324 4975.

Ginis Vacances
3rd floor,
Ermoú 23–25,
10563 Athens.
01 325 0401.

Hellenic Holidays
Lékka 3–5, Syntágma,
10563 Athens.
01 323 7800.

International Student and Youth Travel Service
1st floor, Níkis 11,
10557 Athens.
01 323 3767.

Manos Travel
Panepistimíou 39,
10564 Athens.
01 325 0711.

Olympic Airways Offices Abroad

Australia
37–49 Pitt Street,
Suite 303, Level 3,
Underwood House,
Royal Exchange,
Sydney, NSW 2001.
(2) 251 2044.

Canada
80 Bloor Street,
Suite 503, Toronto,
Ontario M5S F2V1.
(416) 964-7137.

UK
11 Conduit Street,
London W1R OLP.
0171-409 2400.
0171-409 3400
(ticket office).

United States
645 Fifth Avenue,
New York, NY 10022.
(212) 735-0200.

Traveling by Sea

GREECE HAS ALWAYS been a nation of seafarers, and with its hundreds of islands and thousands of miles of coastline, the sea has played an important part in the history of the country and continues to do so today. It is now a major source of revenue for Greece, with millions of vacationers choosing the idyllic Greek islands for their break. The network of ferries is a lifeline for the islanders, and for the tourist an enjoyable and relaxing way of island-hopping or reaching a single destination.

Traveling to Greece by Sea

THERE ARE REGULAR year-round ferry crossings from the Italian ports of Ancona, Bari, and Brindisi to the Greek ports of Igoumenítsa in Epirus and Pátra in the Peloponnese. During the summer, there are additional sailings from Venice and Trieste. Journey times and fares vary considerably, depending on the time of year, point of embarkation, ferry company, and type of ticket. There are also reductions possible for students, travelers under 26, and railcard holders.

Other year-round ferry services include the route from Haifa in Israel, via Cyprus, to Rhodes and Piraeus (with a stop-off at Crete in summer). From Turkey's Aegean coast ferries operate year round between Kusadasi and Sámos, and Çeşme and Chíos, with additional summer sailings between Bodrum and Kos, Marmaris and Rhodes, and Ayvalık and Lésvos.

If you are transporting your car into Greece by ferry, you will require a vehicle registration document and, in summer, will need to reserve ahead. Addresses and numbers of agents for advance bookings are given on page 359.

Car ferry leaving from Mandráki harbor, on Nísyros

Greek Ferry Service

THE GREEK FERRY service is good, though notoriously flexible with regard to schedules and departure times. From the smaller ports, your only concern will be getting a ferry that departs on the day, and for the destination, that you want. It pays to check the timetable on arrival as some services are more frequent and direct than others.

Matters get more complicated from the larger ports, such as Piraeus, the port of Athens. This is Greece's busiest port and has many routes emanating from its harbor. The hub of activity is at Plateía Karaïskáki, where the majority of ticket agents reside, as well as the port police. A number of competing companies run the ferry services, each with its own agents handling bookings and inquiries. This makes the task of finding out when ferries sail, and from which dock, a more challenging one. The ferries are approximately grouped by destination, but when the port is busy, ferries dock wherever space permits. So, finding your ferry usually involves studying each agency's information board or asking the port police *(limenarcheío)*.

In this guide, we show the direct ferry routes in tourist season on the individual island maps, pictorial maps for each island group, and the back endpaper for the countrywide network; tourist season is from June to August. In the off season, expect all services to be significantly reduced and some routes to be suspended altogether. The routes on these maps should be taken as guidelines only – check local sources for the latest information before you travel.

While not 100 percent accurate, the Greek tourist office's weekly schedules can serve as a useful guideline to departure times, or, alternatively ask at a local travel agency. Some of the English-language papers also print summer ferry schedules. Hydrofoils, catamarans, caïques, and taxi boats supplement the ferry services; for information on these see pages 358–9.

Motorcyclists waiting for a ferry at the port of Piraeus

Ferry Tickets

TICKETS FOR ALL ferry journeys can be purchased from the shipping line office, any authorized travel agency, on the dockside, or on the

Ferry sailing toward the harbor at Zákynthos

ferry itself. All fares except first class are set by the Ministry of Transport, so a journey should cost the same amount regardless of which shipping line you choose. As with international ferries, advance booking is essential for a car in tourist season. For motorcycles and cars a supplement is also payable. Cars can cost as much as three or four times the passenger fare.

Children under two travel free, those aged from two to nine pay half fare, and once over the age of ten, children must pay the full adult fare.

On major routes, ferries have essentially three classes, ranging from deck class to deluxe – the latter costing almost as much as flying.

First class usually entitles you to a two-bunk exterior cabin with bathroom facilities. A second class ticket costs around 25 percent less and gives you a three- or four-bunk cabin with washing facilities, such as a sink. Second class cabins are usually within the interior of the vessel. A deck class ticket gives you access to most of the boat, including a lounge with reclining seats. But during the summer, on a warm, starry night, the deck is often the best place to be.

Ferry Company Funnels

The funnels of each company's fleet are bold and brightly colored, and serve as beacons for travelers searching the harbor for their ferry. As each company is unlikely to have more than two or three boats in dock at a time – even in the busiest port, Piraeus – targeting the funnel is often the easiest way to find your ferry.

Minoan Lines

DANE Lines

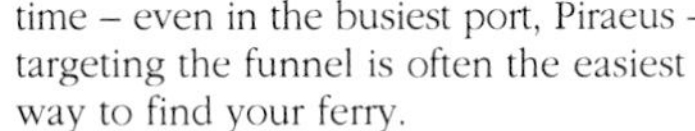

ANEK Lines

GA Ferries

Ventouris Sea Lines

NEL Lines

Piraeus Port Map

Piraeus is the largest and busiest port in Greece. This map shows the layout of the main harbor, and gives an indication of which dock you are likely to need for various destinations.

Key to Departure Points

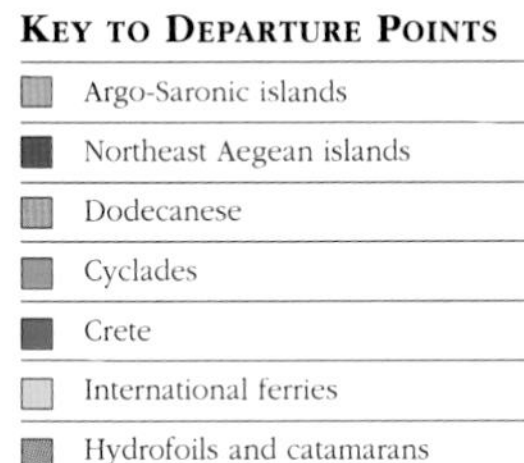

For key to symbols see back flap

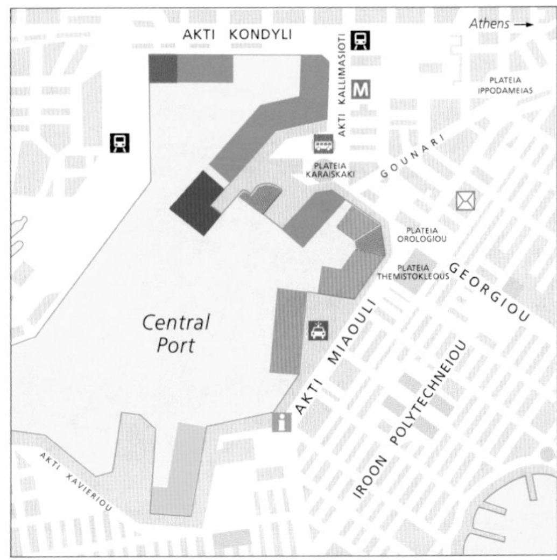

Hydrofoil, known as a "Flying Dolphin"

Hydrofoils and Catamarans

Some of the islands can be reached by Greece's 60 or so hydrofoils. The main operators are **Flying Dolphin** (run by the Ceres ferry company) and **Dodecanese Hydrofoils**, although all hydrofoils are known locally as "Flying Dolphins." They are twice as fast as a ferry but, as a consequence, are double the price.

Catamaran

The major drawback of hydrofoils is that most vessels function only in the summer months and are often cancelled if weather conditions are poor. In fact, on seas that are anything other than calm, hydrofoils are quite slow and can prove a bad idea for those prone to seasickness.

Hydrofoils can accommodate about 140 passengers but have no room for cars or motorcycles. Advance booking is essential, and it is a good idea to book as early as possible during tourist season. Tickets are bought from an agent or on the dock, but rarely on board the vessel itself. Routes are around the mainland and Peloponnese coasts and to island groups close to the mainland – the Argo-Saronic group, Evvoia and the Sporades, and to several islands within the Cyclades. There are also routes between Rhodes, in the Dodecanese, and Sámos, at the southern end of the Northeast Aegean.

Catamarans are a more recent innovation in Greece, offering an airline-type service in terms of seating, bar facilities, and on-board television. They are also better designed for handicapped passengers. There are services around the Ionian islands, and about half a dozen catamarans operating in the Aegean, mostly between the mainland port of Rafína and the islands of Andros, Tínos and Mýkonos. Costs are on a par with hydrofoils, and tickets should be bought from a travel agency a few days prior to sailing. If seats are available, they can be purchased on board.

Catamaran departure sign

Tourist Excursions

Many vacation resorts have small excursion boats that take groups of tourists to out-of-the-way beaches and caves, or on day-cruises and picnics. Routes and times are dictated by local conditions.

Passengers on a departing ferry

Up-to-date information and booking arrangements are available on arrival in the islands at any local travel agency or information center.

An excursion caïque on the Dodecanese island of Sými

Local Inter-Island Ferries

In addition to the large ferries that cover the main routes, there are smaller ferries making inter-island crossings in the summer. Local ferries, regardless of size, are subject to government price controls, but boats chartered by tourist agencies can charge what they like, and often prove expensive. These boats do, however, provide direct connections, which shortcut circuitous routes via mainland ports.

Taxi boat traveling around the coast of Spétses

Taxi Boats

Taxi boats (or caïques) are even more ad hoc, sailing along coastlines and making short trips between adjacent islands. They are usually available during tourist season and, as the smallest vessels, are most prone to cancellation in adverse sea conditions. They tend to be more expensive than ferries, given the short distances involved, but often provide a route where few or no others are available.

Routes and itineraries are at the discretion of the boat owners, and the only place to determine if one is going your way is at the dock.

Directory

US Agents

Hellenic Holidays
1501 Broadway, Ste 1512, New York, NY 10036.
(212) 944-8388.

Metro Tours
484 Lowell St, Peabody, MA 01960.
(800) 221-2810.

Useful Piraeus Telephone Numbers

01 422 6000-5 (Port police).
143 (timetable).

Hydrofoil and Catamaran Services

Flying Dolphin
Aktí Miaoúli 69, Piraeus.
01 428 0001.

Dodecanese Hydrofoils
Mandráki Harbor, Rhodes.
0241 24000.

Goútos Lines
Konítsis 43, Vrilíssia, Athens 15235.
01 613 5422.

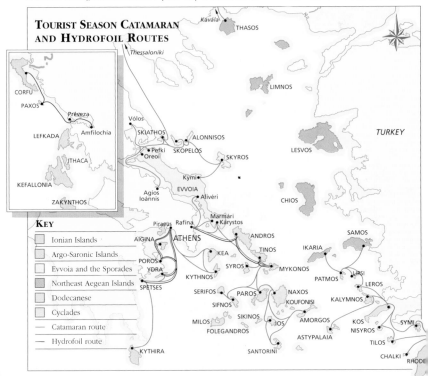

Tourist Season Catamaran and Hydrofoil Routes

Key

- Ionian Islands
- Argo-Saronic Islands
- Evvoia and the Sporades
- Northeast Aegean Islands
- Dodecanese
- Cyclades
- Catamaran route
- Hydrofoil route

Traveling by Road and Rail

THERE HAS BEEN much upgrading of the roads on the islands but, particularly in remote areas, they can still be rough, and in some cases suitable only for four-wheel drive vehicles. Cars and motorcycles are easily rented though, and the extensive bus network is complemented by many taxis. Maps from local travel agents are less than reliable, however, and visitors are advised to bring their own: GeoCenter and Freytag & Berndt are both good.

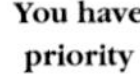

You have priority

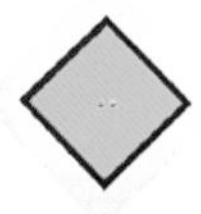

You have right of way

Do not use car horn

Wild animals crossing

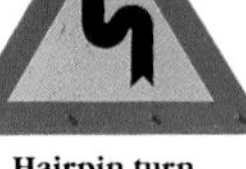

Hairpin turn ahead

Traffic circle ahead

TRAVELING TO GREECE BY CAR

THE MOST DIRECT overland route to Greece from the UK, via the former Yugoslavia, is currently not recommended to motorists. The alternative route is through France, Switzerland, and Italy, and from there to Greece by ferry. Motoring organizations, such as **ELPA** (the Automobile and Touring Club of Greece), offer advice on routes and regulations. You need a full, valid driver's licence, and insurance cover (at least third party insurance is compulsory).

RULES OF THE ROAD

DRIVING IS ON the right in Greece and, with the exception of some rural back-roads, road signs conform to European norms. The speed limit on national highways is 120 km/h (75 mph) for cars; on country roads it is 90 km/h (55 mph) and in towns 50 km/h (30 mph). Seat belts are required by law, and children under ten are not allowed in the front seat.

CAR RENTAL

SCORES OF CAR RENTAL agencies in all main resorts offer a range of vehicles from small cars to minibuses. International companies such as **Avis** and **Budget** tend to be considerably more expensive than their local counterparts, though the latter are generally as reliable. Liability is the minimum insurance required by law, but personal accident insurance is strongly recommended. A full licence that has been held for at least one year is needed, and the minimum age requirement ranges from 21 to 25 years.

MOTORCYCLE, MOPED, AND BICYCLE RENTAL

MOTORCYCLES AND MOPEDS are readily available for rent on the islands. The latter are ideal for short distances on flattish terrain, but for anything mountainous a motorcycle is a must. Make sure that the vehicle is in good condition before you set out and that the price includes adequate insurance coverage; also check that your own travel insurance covers motorcycle accidents, as many do not.

Dual-language road sign

The speed limit on national highways is 70 km/h (45 mph) for bikes up to 100 cc, and 90 km/h (55 mph) for larger bikes; helmets are compulsory.

Bicycles can also be rented in some resorts, though the steep mountainous terrain and hot sun can be deterrents to even the toughest enthusiast. Bicycles can, however, be transported free on most Greek ferries and buses.

GAS STATIONS

GAS STATIONS are plentiful in towns, though less so in rural areas – always set out with a full tank to be on the safe side. Fuel is sold by the liter, and there are usually three or four grades available: super (95 octane), unleaded, super unleaded, and diesel, which is confusingly called *petrélaio*. Filling stations set their own working hours, but generally they are open seven days a week from 7 or 8am to between 7 and 9pm.

Sign for a gas station

Rack of bikes for rent, at the beach in Kos town

Passengers aboard a taxi truck on the island of Lipsí

Taxis

Taxis provide a very reasonably priced way of getting around on the islands. All taxis are metered, but for longer trips a price can usually be negotiated *per diem*, or per trip. Drivers are generally amenable to dropping you off and picking you up a few hours later. Most rural villages have at least one taxi, and the best place to arrange for one is at the local *kafeneío* (café). Taxi trucks often take several passengers, each paying for their part of the trip.

Traveling by Bus and Coach

International buses connect Greece with the rest of Europe, though fares are not as cheap as charter flights during the vacation season.

Greece's domestic bus system is operated by **KTEL** (Koinó Tameío Eispráxeon Leoforeíon), a syndicate of privately run companies that provides almost every community with services of some sort. In remote rural villages the bus might stop once or twice a day, usually at the local taverna or *kafeneío*, while services between the larger centers are frequent and efficient. You can also usually rely on there being a bus service between the port and main town of any island, if the latter is situated inland.

On many of the larger islands travel agents offer a wide range of excursions on air-conditioned buses, accompanied by qualified guides. These include trips to major archaeological and historical sites, other towns and resorts, popular beaches, areas for established walks, such as the Samariá Gorge in Crete, and organized events, such as an evening out in a "typical Greek taverna."

Front view of a local bus on the island of Nísyros

Traveling by Train

Traveling to Greece by train from London takes over three days. The journey is via France, Switzerland, and Italy, crossing by ferry to Corfu and the mainland port of Pátra.

Within Greece, the network is run by the **OSE** (Organismós Sidirodrómon Elládos). The system is restricted to the mainland, but there are useful routes out of Athens to Pátra, Vólos (for ferries to Skiáthos and Skópelos), and up the Attic coast to Evvoia.

The distinctive front end of an express train

Directory

Motoring Organizations

ELPA (Ellinikí Léschi Periigíseon kai Aftokinítou)
Ground Floor, Athens Tower, Mesogeíon 2–4, 11527 Athens.
01 342 4390.
104 (road assistance).

Car Rental Agencies

Avis
Leofóros Amalías 46–48, 10558 Athens.
01 322 4951.

Budget
Syngroú 8, 11742 Athens.
01 921 4771.

Hertz
Leofóros Vouliagménis 576A, 16451 Argyroúpolis.
01 994 2850.

Buses

Eurolines
52 Grosvenor Gardens, Victoria, London SW1, England.
0171-730 8235.

Bus terminals in Athens
Terminal A: Kifisoú 100
01 513 2834.
Terminal B: Liosíou 260
01 832 9585.

Trains

Rail Europe (InterRail)
French Rail House, 10 Leake St, London SE1 7NN, England.
0990 848848.

OSE (information & reservations)
Sína 6, Athens.
01 362 4402.

Train stations in Athens
Lárissis station
01 823 7741.
Peloponnísou station
01 513 1601.

145 domestic departures from Athens.
147 international departures from Athens.

General Index

Page numbers in **bold** type refer to main entries.

A

B

H

I

Q

R

T

Acknowledgments

DORLING KINDERSLEY would like to thank the following people whose contributions and assistance have made the preparation of this book possible.

MAIN CONTRIBUTORS

MARC DUBIN is an American expatriate who divides his time between London and Sámos. Since 1978 he has traveled in every province of Greece. He has written or contributed to numerous guides to Greece, covering such diverse topics as trekking and contemporary Greek music.

STEPHANIE FERGUSON, a freelance journalist and travel writer, has hopped around almost 50 Greek islands. She became bewitched by Greece after a holiday 20 years ago and since then has contributed to eight guide books and written travel features on Greece for several national publications.

MIKE GERRARD is a travel writer and broadcaster who has written several guides to various parts of Greece, which he has been visiting annually since 1964.

ANDY HARRIS is a travel and food journalist based in Athens. He is the author of *A Taste of the Aegean.*

TANYA TSIKAS is a Canadian writer and travel guide editor. Married to a Greek, she has spent time in Crete and currently lives in Oxford.

ADDITIONAL ILLUSTRATIONS

Richard Bonson, Louise Boulton, Gary Cross, Kevin Goold, Roger Hutchins, Claire Littlejohn.

DESIGN AND EDITORIAL ASSISTANCE

Hilary Bird, Elspeth Collier, Catherine Day, Jim Evoy, Emily Green, Emily Hatchwell, Leanne Hogbin, Kim Inglis, Lorien Kite, Felicity Laughton, Andreas Michael, Ella Milroy, Lisa Minsky, Robert Mitchell, Jennifer Mussett, Tamsin Pender, Jake Reimann, Simon Ryder, Rita Selvaggio, Claire Stewart, Claire Tennant-Scull, Amanda Tomeh, Andy Wilkinson.

DORLING KINDERSLEY would also like to thank the following for their assistance: The Greek Wine Bureau, Odysea.

DK PUBLISHING would like to thank Alexis Theodorcopoulos, Frederick Jones, Christopher Barford, and Phoebe Todd-Naylor for moral support.

ADDITIONAL RESEARCH

Anna Antoniou, Anastasia Caramanis, Magda Dimouti, Shirley Durant, Panos Gotsi, Zoi Groummouti, Peter Millett, Tasos Schizas, Garifalia Tsiola.

ARTWORK REFERENCE

Ideal Photo S.A., The Image Bank, Melissa Publishing House, Tony Stone Worldwide.

ADDITIONAL PHOTOGRAPHY

Jane Burton, Frank Greenaway, Derek Hall, Dave King, Neil Lucas, National History Museum, Stephen Oliver, Roger Philips, Kim Sayer, Clive Steeter, Harry Taylor, Kim Taylor, Mathew Ward, Jerry Young.

PHOTOGRAPHY PERMISSIONS

DORLING KINDERSLEY would like to thank the following for their assistance and kind permission to photograph at their establishments:

Nelly Dimoglou Folk Dance Theatre, Rhodes; Museum of Greek Folk Art, Athens; Karpathos Museum; Markos Vamrakaris Museum, Syros; Kymi Folk Museum, Evvoia; Stavros Kois's House, Syros. Also all other cathedrals, churches, museums, hotels, restaurants, shops, galleries, and sights too numerous to thank individually.

PICTURE CREDITS

t = top; tl = top left; tlc = top left center; tc = top center; trc = top right center; tr = top right; cla = center left above; ca = center above; cra = center right above; cl = center left; c = center; cr = center right; clb = center right below; cb = center below; crb = center right below; bl = bottom left; b = bottom; bc = bottom center; bcl = bottom center left; br = bottom right; d = detail.

Works of art have been reproduced with the permission of the following copyright holders: © ADAGP, Paris and DACS, London 1997 *The Kiss* Constantin Brancusi 207br. The work of art *Three Standing Figures,* Henry Moore (1947) 207bl is reproduced by permission of the Henry Moore Foundation.

The publisher would like to thank the following individuals, companies and picture libraries for permission to reproduce their photographs:

AISA ARCHIVO ICONGRAFICO, Barcelona: Museo Archeologique, Bari 55tr; Museo Archeologique, Florence 52tl; AKG, London: 186b, 284t; Antiquario Palatino 51bl; British Museum 285b; Erich Lessing Akademie der Bildenden Künste, Vienna 52c; Musée du Louvre 51tl; Naples Archaeological Museum 141b; National Archeological Museum, Athens 24–5(d), 25t; Staatliche Kunstsammlungen, Albertinum, Dresden 29crb, Liebighaus, Frankfurt/Main 31c; Staatliche Antikensammlungen und Glyptotek, München 50b; Mykonos Museum 53t; ANCIENT ART AND ARCHITECTURE: 27ca, 28t, 32t, 32ca, 33cl, 35t, 54cb, 54b(d), 95b; ANTIKENMUSEUM BASEL UND SAMMLUNG LUDWIG: 58–9; APERION: John Hios 43c; ARGYROPOULOS PHOTO PRESS: 43t, 45cr, 46t, 46cb.

BENAKI MUSEUM: 23b, 34ca, 37t, 37c, 39ca, 287b; PAUL BERNARD: 31t; BIBLIOTHEQUE NATIONAL, Paris: Caoursin folio 175 4c(d), 36–7(d), Caoursin folio 33 185bl, Caoursin folio 79 185br; BODLEIAN LIBRARY, Oxford: MS Canon Misc 378 170v 32cb; BRIDGEMAN ART LIBRARY, London: Birmingham City Museums and Art Galleries *Pheidias Completing the Parthenon Frieze,* Sir Lawrence Alma-Tadema 56t; Bibliothèque Nationale, Paris *The Author Guillaume Caoursin, Vice Chancellor of the Order of St John of Jerusalem Dedicating his Book to Pierre d'Aubusson, Grand Master of the Order of St John of Jerusalem who is Seated Surrounded by High Dignitaries of the Order* (1483), illustrated by the Master of Cardinal of Bourbon Lat 6067 f 3v 22(d); British Museum, London *Cup, Tondo, with Scene of Huntsmen Returning Home* 27cb, *Greek Vase Showing Diver About to Enter the Sea in Search of Sponges* (c.500 BC) 165br; Fitzwilliam Museum, University of Cambridge *Figurine of Demosthenes,* Enoch Wood of Burslem (c.1790) (lead glazed earthenware) 55tl, *Attic Red-figured Pelike: Pigs, Swineherd and Odysseus,* Pig Painter (470–60BC) 83bl; Freud Museum, London *Figure of Artemis from Myrina,* Greek, Hellenistic Period (2nd century BC) 214tl; Giraudon/Louvre Paris *Alexander the Great, Portrait Head* (3rd century BC) Greek (marble) 30tr; House of Masks, Delos *Mosaic of Dionysus riding a Leopard* (c.AD 180) 33t; Kunsthistorisches Museum, Vienna *Elizabeth of Bavaria, Wife of Emperor Franz Joseph I of Austria,* Franz Xavier Winterhalter 79c(d); Lauros-Giraudon/Louvre, Paris *Rhodes Winged Victory of Samothrace* (early 2nd century BC) 128c; Louvre, Paris *Double Bust of Aristophanes and Sophocles* (15th century) 54t; National Archaeological Museum, Athens *Bronze Satue of Poseidon* (c.460–450 BC) photo Bernard Cox 50c; Private Collection *Two-tiered Icon of the Virgin and Child and Two Saints,* Cretan School (15th century) 36cl; Victoria and Albert Museum, London *Corfu,* Edward Lear 77b; © THE BRITISH MUSEUM: 24clb, 25cb, 26tl, 28cb, 29clb, 51tr(d), 51br, 53c(d), 58tl, 59tl, 59tr, 135cra.

CAMERA PRESS, London: ANAG 41tl, 41bl; Christopher Simon Sykes 73t; Wim Swaan 215t; TANYA COLBOURNE: 350t; BRUCE COLEMAN LTD.: Philip van de Berg 243cl; Luiz Claudio Marigo 87t; Natalio Feneck 111ca; Gordon Langsbury 243bl; Andrew J Purcell 20ca; Kim Taylor 111bl; World Wildlife Fund for Nature 111t; Konrad Wothe 243br.

C M DIXON PHOTO RESOURCES: 25ca; Glyptotek, Munich 30tr; MARC DUBIN: 18t, 19bla, 19bra, 44tl, 170t, 195t, 195b, 219b, 229c, 231b, 248b.

ECOLE FRANÇAISE D'ATHENES: 214tr; ECOLE NATIONALE SUPERIEURE DES BEAUX ARTS, Paris: *Delphes Restauration du Sanctuaire Envoi,* Tournaire (1894) 28–9; EKDOTIKI ATHINON: 3, 24crb, 160b, 183b(d), 184bl(d); ELIA: 105b; JANICE ENGLISH: 188t, 189t, 189b, 190c, 190b; ET ARCHIVE: National Archaeology Museum, Naples 30ca; MARY EVANS PICTURE LIBRARY: 83cr, 83bc, 83br, 129b, 152b.

FERENS ART GALLERY: Hull City Museums and Art Galleries and Archives *Electra at the Tomb of Agamennon* (1869), Lord Frederick Leighton 53b.
GIRAUDON, Paris: Chateau Ecouen *Retour d'Ulysse* Ecole Siennoise 83cl; Louvre Paris 58c, *Scène de Massacres de Scio,* Eugene Delacroix 38ca(d), 143b(d); Musée Nationale Gustave Moreau

Hesiode et Les Muses, Gustave Moreau 54ca; Musée d'Art Catalan, Barcelona 285cb; NICHOLAS P GOULANDRIS FOUNDATION MUSEUM OF CYCLADIC AND ANCIENT GREEK ART: 207tl, 207tc, 207tr, 207cl, 207cr,280b,287t; RONALD GRANT ARCHIVE: *Zorba the Greek,* 20th Century Fox 272b.

ROBERT HARDING PICTURE LIBRARY: David Beatty 42br; Tony Gervis 42ca, 42bl; Photri 354t; Adam Woolfitt 44c; HELIO PHOTO: 94ca; HELLENIC POST SERVICE: 41cla; HELLENIC WAR MUSEUM, Athens: 247t; HISTORICAL MUSEUM OF CRETE, Irákleio: *Landscape of the Gods-Trodden Mount Sinai,* El Greco 264tr; MICHAEL HOLFORD: British Museum 30cb, 50t; HULTON GETTY COLLECTION: 39cb(d); Central Press Photo 40clb(d).

IDEAL PHOTO SA: T Dassios 297c; A Pappas 231t; C Vergas 43clb, 43br, 44tr, 79b, 113b, 157t; IMAGES COLOUR LIBRARY: 90t, 266bl; IMPACT PHOTOS: Jeremy Nicholl 348b; Caroline Penn 43bl.

CAROL KANE: 194br; GULIA KLIMI: 45t; KOSTOS KONTOS: 24cr, 40cra, 40cla, 43crb, 46ca, 159b, 160c, 184br, 341t, 351c,355t.

FRANK LANE PICTURES: Eric and David Hoskings 242bl; ILIAS LALAOUNIS: 347cla.

MAGNUM PHOTOS LTD.: Constantine Manos 42t; MANSELL COLLECTION: 50–1.

NATIONAL GALLERY OF VICTORIA, Melbourne: *Greek by the Inscriptions Painter Challidian* Felton Bequest (1956) 52b; NATIONAL HISTORICAL MUSEUM: 36t, 38t, 38–9(d), 39t, 40b; NATURAL IMAGE: Bob Gibbons 243tl; Peter Wilson 250tl; NATURE PHOTOGRAPHERS: Brinsley Burbridge 243tr; Robin Bush 243cr; Michael J Hammett 20tr; Paul Sterry 111br, 243tc; ANTONIS NICOLOPOULOS: 350c, 351b.

OLYMPIC AIRWAYS: 352t; ORONOZ ARCHIVO FOTOGRAFICO: Biblioteca National Madrid *Invasions Bulgares Historia Matriksiscronica FIIIV* 34cb(d); Charlottenberg, Berlin 52tr; El Escorial, Madrid *Battle of Lepanto,* Cambiaso Luca 36cr(d); Museo Julia 51c(d); Musée du Louvre 58b; Museo Vaticano 55b, 59bl; OXFORD SCIENTIFIC FILMS: Paul Kay 21tr.

ROMYLOS PARISIS: City of Athens Museum 38cb; PICTOR INTERNATIONAL: 44b; PICTURES: 42crb, 350br; PLANET EARTH PICTURES: Wendy Dennis 242c; Jim Greenfield 21cb; Ken Lucas 111cb; Marty Snyderman 21tl; PRIVATE COLLECTION: 277c; POPPERFOTO: 40crb, 41cra, 41br.

REX FEATURES: Sipa Press/C Brown 41tr.

SCALA, Florence: Gallerie degli Uffizi 26cb; Museo Archeologico, Firenze 27t; Museo Mandralisca Cefalu 28ca; Museo Nationale Tarquinia 59br; Museo de Villa Giulia 26–7, 58tr; SPECTRUM COLOUR LIBRARY: 250tl; MARIA STEFOSSI: 16bl.

TAP SERVICE ARCHAEOLOGICAL RECEIPTS FUND HELLENIC REPUBLIC MINISTRY OF CULTURE: A Epharat of Antiquities 41cb, 56br, 284cb, 284b,285t,285ca; Acropolis Museum 286tl, 286tr; Andros Archaeological Museum 204cl; Agios Nikolaos Archaeological Museum 274c; B Epharat of Antiquities 62bl, 94t,94cb, 94b, 95t, 95c; Chalkida Archaeological Museum 116c; Chania Archaeological Museum 249c; Corfu Archaeological Museum 65t, 75c; Eretreia Archaeological Museum 5t, 115b, 117c; 5th Epharat of Byzantine Antiquities 35c; 14th Epharat of Byzantine Antiquities 133t, 136t, 140b; 4th Epharat of Byzantine Antiquities 14c, 161tr, 161c, 161b, 195c; IH Epharat of Antiquities 124t, 125t, 125b; IΘ Epharat of Antiquities 128b, 129ca, 129cb; Ikia Varelitzidenas 121c; Irakleio Archaeological Museum 262bl, 266t, 266ca, 266cb, 267t, 267c, 268br; K Epharat of Antiquities 131b; KA Epharat of Antiquities 63t, 152t, 152c, 214b, 215ca, 215bl, 215br, 223c, 226cl, 236cb, 237c, 348ca; KB Epharat of Antiquities 167b, 168t, 168c, 176t, 182tl, 182tr, 182c, 182b, 183t, 183c, 192t, 192cr; KΓ Epharat of Antiquities 245t, 259c, 260c, 260b, 261 all, 262t, 262c, 262br, 263 all, 268t, 268c, 268bl, 269tl, 269tr, 269b, 270t, 270c, 270b, 271b, 271t; KΔ Epharat of Antiquities 273c; Kos Archaeological Museum 168b; Milos Archaeological Museum 232t; Mykonos Archaeological Museum 210tr; National Archeological Museum, Athens 24t, 26tr,237b, 282c; Naxos Archaeological Museum 226t; Nea Moni Archaeological Museum 63ca; Numismatic Museum of Athens 271c; Rhodes Archaeological Museum 180cb; Vathy Archaeological Museum, Samos 150cr; 2nd Epharat of Byzantine

Antiquities 209c, 217t, 220t, 223b, 247c; 7th Epharat of Byzantine Antiquities 105t; 6th Epharat of Byzantine Antiquities 85c; Thessaloniki Archaeological Museum 29t; Thira Archaeological Museum 234tl; 3rd Epharat of Byzantine Antiquities 140b, 148tl, 149c, 151b; 13th Epharat of Byzantine Antiquities 146–7 all, 257cra, 273b, 275t; Tinos Archaeological Museum 208t; Γ Epharat of Antiquities 283b; TERIADE MUSEUM: *Dafnis and Chloe,* Marc Chagall ©ADAGP, Paris and DACS, London 1997; TRAVEL INK: Nigel Bowen-Morris 238–9; TRAVEL LIBRARY: Faltaits Museum 112tr; YANNIS TSAROUCHIS FOUNDATION: Private Collection *Barber Shop in Marousi,* Yannis Tsarouchis (1947) 40tr.

WERNER FORMAN ARCHIVE: Thessaloniki Archaeological Musem 34t; LORRAINE WILSON: 62br; PETER WILSON: 16c, 57bl, 63b, 284ca; BRIAN WOODYATT:14b.

Jacket: all special photography except NICHOLAS P GOULANDRIS FOUNDATION MUSEUM OF CYCLADIC AND ANCIENT GREEK ART: front cla; TAP SERVICE ARCHAEOLOGICAL RECEIPTS FUND HELLENIC REPUBLIC MINISTRY OF CULTURE: ΚΓ Epharat of Antiquities front cra, back tl; Irakleio Archaeological museum spine b.

Phrase Book

There is no universally accepted system for representing the modern Greek language in the Roman alphabet. The system of transliteration adopted in this guide is the one used by the Greek Government. Though not yet fully applied throughout Greece, most of the street and place names have been transliterated according to this system. For Classical names this guide uses the k, os, on, and f spelling, in keeping with the modern system of transliteration. In a few cases, such as Socrates and Philoppapus, the more familiar Latin form has been used. Classical names are left unaccented. Where a well-known English form of a name exists, such as Athens or Cofu, this has been used. Variations in transliteration are given in the index.

Guidelines for Pronunciation

The accent over Greek and transliterated words indicates the stressed syllable. In this guide the accent is not written over capital letters nor over monosyllables, except for question words and the conjunction ή (meaning "or"). In the right-hand "Pronunciation" column below, the syllable to stress is given in bold type.

On the following pages, the English is given in the left-hand column with the Greek and its transliteration in the middle column. The right-hand column provides a literal system of pronounciation and indicates the stressed syllable in bold.

The Greek Alphabet

Α α	A a	**a**rm
Β β	V v	**v**ote
Γ γ	G g	**y**ear (when followed by e and i sounds) **n**o (when followed by ξ or γ)
Δ δ	D d	**th**at
Ε ε	E e	**e**gg
Ζ ζ	Z z	**z**oo
Η η	I i	k**ee**p
Θ θ	Th th	**th**ink
Ι ι	I i	k**ee**p
Κ κ	K k	**k**id
Λ λ	L l	**l**and
Μ μ	M m	**m**an
Ν ν	N n	**n**o
Ξ ξ	X x	ta**x**i
Ο ο	O o	f**o**x
Π π	P p	**p**ort
Ρ ρ	R r	**r**oom
Σ σ	S s	**s**orry (**z**ero when followed by μ)
ς	s	(used at end of word)
Τ τ	T t	**t**ea
Υ υ	Y y	k**ee**p
Φ φ	F f	**f**ish
Χ χ	Ch ch	lo**ch** in most cases, but **h**e when followed by a, e, or i sounds
Ψ ψ	Ps ps	ma**ps**
Ω ω	O o	f**o**x

Combinations of Letters

In Greek there are two-letter vowels that are pronounced as one sound:

Αι αι	Ai ai	**e**gg
Ει ει	Ei ei	k**ee**p
Οι οι	Oi oi	k**ee**p
Ου ου	Ou ou	l**u**te

There are also some two-letter consonants that are pronounced as one sound:

Μπ μπ	Mp mp	**b**ut, sometimes nu**mb**er in the middle of a word
Ντ ντ	Nt nt	**d**esk, sometimes u**nd**er in the middle of a word
Γκ γκ	Gk gk	**g**o, sometimes bi**ng**o in the middle of a word
Γξ γξ	nx	a**nx**iety
Τζ τζ	Tz tz	ha**nds**
Τσ τσ	Ts ts	**it's**
Γγ γγ	Gg gg	bi**ng**o

In an Emergency

Help!	Βοήθεια! Voítheia	vo-**ee**-theea
Stop!	Σταματήστε! Stamatíste	sta-ma-**tee**-steh
Call a doctor!	Φωνάξτε ένα γιατρό Fonáxte éna giatró	fo-**nak**-steh **e**-na ya-tr**o**
Call an ambulance/ the police/the fire department!	Καλέστε το ασθενοφόρο/την αστυνομία/την πυροσβεστική Kaléste to asthenofóro/tin astynomía/tin pyrosvestikí	ka-**le**-steh to as-the-no-**fo**-ro/teen a-sti-no-**mia**/teen pee-ro-zve-stee-**kee**
Where is the nearest telephone/hospital/ pharmacy?	Πού είναι το πλησιέστερο τήλεφωνο/νοσοκομείο/φαρμακείο; Poú eínai to plisiéstero tiléfono/ nosokomeío/farmakeío?	po**o** **ee**-ne to plee-see-**e**-ste-ro tee-**le**-pho-no/no-so-ko-m**ee**-o/far-ma-k**ee**-o

Communication Essentials

Yes	Ναι Nai	neh
No	Οχι Ochi	**o**-chee
Please	Παρακαλώ Parakaló	pa-ra-ka-l**o**
Thank you	Ευχαριστώ Efcharistó	ef-cha-ree-st**o**
You are welcome	Παρακαλώ Parakaló	pa-ra-ka-l**o**
OK/alright	Εντάξει Entáxei	en-**dak**-zee
Excuse me	Με συγχωρείτε Me synchoreíte	me seen-cho-r**ee**-teh
Hello	Γειά σας Geiá sas	yeea sas
Goodbye	Αντίο Antío	an-d**ee**-o
Good morning	Καλημέρα Kaliméra	ka-lee-**me**-ra
Good night	Καληνύχτα Kalinýchta	ka-lee-n**eech**-ta
Morning	Πρωί Proí	pro-**ee**
Afternoon	Απόγευμα Apógevma	a-**po**-yev-ma
Evening	Βράδυ Vrádi	v**rath**-i
This morning	Σήμερα το πρωί Símera to proí	s**ee**-me-ra to pro-**ee**
Yesterday	Χθές Chthés	chthes
Today	Σήμερα Símera	s**ee**-me-ra
Tomorrow	Αύριο Avrio	**av**-ree-o
Here	Εδώ Edó	ed-**o**
There	Εκεί Ekeí	e-k**ee**
What?	Τί; Tí?	t**ee**
Why?	Γιατί; Giatí?	ya-t**ee**
Where?	Πού; Poú?	p**oo**
How?	Πώς; Pós?	p**os**
Wait!	Περίμενε! Perímene!	pe-r**ee**-me-neh

Useful Phrases

How are you?	Τί κάνεις; Tí káneis?	**tee ka**-nees
Very well, thank you	Πολύ καλά, ευχαριστώ Poly kalá, efcharistó	po-lee ka-**la**, ef-cha-ree-**sto**
How do you do?	Πώς είστε; Pós eíste?	**pos ees**-te
Pleased to meet you	Χαίρω πολύ Chaíro polý	che-ro po-**lee**
What is your name?	Πώς λέγεστε; Pós légeste?	**pos le**-ye-ste
Where is/are...?	Πού είναι; Poú eínai?	**poo ee**-ne
How far is it to...?	Πόσο απέχει...; Póso apéchei...?	**po**-so a-**pe**-chee
How do I get to?	Πώς μπορώ να πάω...; Pós mporó na páo...?	**pos** bo-**ro**-na **pa**-o
Do you speak English?	Μιλάτε Αγγλικά; Miláte Angliká?	mee-**la**-te an-glee-**ka**
I understand	Καταλαβαίνω Katalavaíno	ka-ta-la-**ve**-no
I don't understand	Δεν καταλαβαίνω Den katalavaíno	then ka-ta-la-**ve**-no
Could you speak slowly?	Μιλάτε λίγο πιο αργά παρακαλώ; Miláte lígo pio argá parakaló?	mee-**la**-te **lee**-go pyo ar-**ga** pa-ra-ka-**lo**
I'm sorry	Με συγχωρείτε Me synchoreíte	me seen-cho-**ree** teh
Does anyone have a key?	Εχει κανένας κλειδί; Echei kanénas kleidí?	**e**-chee ka-**ne**-nas klee-**dee**

Useful Words

big	Μεγάλο Megálo	me-**ga**-lo
small	Μικρό Mikró	mi-**kro**
hot	Ζεστό Zestó	zes-**to**
cold	Κρύο Krýo	**kree**-o
good	Καλό Kaló	ka-**lo**
bad	Κακό Kakó	ka-**ko**
enough	Αρκετά Arketá	ar-ke-**ta**
well	Καλά Kalá	ka-**la**
open	Ανοιχτά Anoichtá	a-neech-**ta**
closed	Κλειστά Kleistá	klee-**sta**
left	Αριστερά Aristerá	a-ree-ste-**ra**
right	Δεξιά Dexiá	dek-see-**a**
straight ahead	Ευθεία Eftheía	ef-**thee**-a
between	Ανάμεσα / Μεταξύ Anámesa / Metaxý	a-**na**-me-sa/me-tak-**see**
on the corner of...	Στη γωνία του... Sti gonía tou...	stee go-**nee**-a too
near	Κοντά Kontá	kon-**da**
far	Μακριά Makriá	ma-kree-**a**
up	Επάνω Epáno	e-**pa**-no
down	Κάτω Káto	**ka**-to
early	Νωρίς Norís	no-**rees**
late	Αργά Argá	ar-**ga**
entrance	Η είσοδος I eísodos	ee **ee**-so-thos
exit	Η έξοδος I éxodos	ee **e**-kso-dos
toilet	Οι τουαλέτες /WC Oi toualétes / WC	ee too-a-**le**-tes
occupied/engaged	Κατειλημμένη Kateilimméni	ka-tee-lee-**me**-nee
unoccupied/vacant	Ελεύθερη Eléftheri	e-**lef**-the-ree
free/no charge	Δωρεάν Doreán	tho-re-**an**
in/out	Μέσα /Εξω Mésa/ Exo	**me**-sa/**ek**-so

Making a Telephone Call

Where is the nearest public telephone ?	Πού βρίσκεται ο πλησιέστερος τηλεφωνικός θάλαμος; Poú vrísketai o plisiésteros tilefonikós thálamos?	po**o** vr**ees**-ke-teh o plee-see-**e**-ste-ros tee-le-fo-ni-**kos** th**a**-la-mos
I would like to place a long-distance call	Θα ήθελα να κάνω ένα υπεραστικό τηλεφώνημα Tha íthela na káno éna yperastikó tilefónima	tha **ee**-the-la na **ka**-no **e**-na ee-pe-ra-sti-**ko** tee-le-**fo**-nee-ma
I would like to call collect	Θα ήθελα να χρεώσω το τηλεφώνημα στον παραλήπτη Tha íthela na chreóso to tilefónima ston paralípti	tha **ee**-the-la na chre-**o**-so to tee-le-**fo**-nee-ma ston pa-ra-lep-tee
I will try again later	Θα ξανατηλεφωνήσω αργότερα Tha xanatilefoníso argótera	tha ksa-na-tee-le-fo-**ni**-so ar-**go**-te-ra
Can I leave a message?	Μπορείτε να του αφήσετε ένα μήνυμα; Mporeíte na tou afísete éna mínyma?	bo-ree-**te** na too a-f**ee**-se-teh **e**-na mee-nee-ma
Could you speak up a little please?	Μιλάτε δυνατότερα, παρακαλώ; Miláte dynatótera, parakaló	mee-**la**-teh dee-na-**to**-te-ra, pa-ra-ka-**lo**
Local call	Τοπικό τηλεφώνημα Topikó tilefónima	to-pi-**ko** tee-le-**fo**-nee-ma
Hold on	Περιμένετε Periménete	pe-ri-**me**-ne-teh
OTE telephone office	Ο ΟΤΕ / Το τηλεφωνείο O OTE / To tilefoneío	o O-**TE** / To tee-le-fo-**nee**-o
Phone booth/kiosk	Ο τηλεφωνικός θάλαμος O tilefonikós thálamos	o tee-le-fo-ni-**kos** th**a**-la-mos
Phone card	Η τηλεκάρτα I tilekárta	ee tee-le-**kar**-ta

Shopping

How much does this cost?	Πόσο κάνει; Póso kánei?	**po**-so **ka**-nee
I would like...	Θα ήθελα... Tha íthela...	tha **ee**-the-la...
Do you have...?	Εχετε...; Echete...?	**e**-che-teh
I am just looking	Απλώς κοιτάω Aplós koitáo	a-**plos** kee-**ta**-o
Do you take credit cards/travelers' checks?	Δέχεστε πιστωτικές κάρτες/travelers' checks; Décheste pistotikés kártes/travelers' checks?	**the**-ches-teh pee-sto-tee-**kes** **kar**-tes/ travelers' checks
What time do you open/close?	Ποτέ ανοίγετε/ κλείνετε; Póte anoígete/ kleínete?	**po**-teh a-**nee**-ye-teh/ **klee**-ne-teh
Can you ship this overseas?	Μπορείτε να το στείλετε στο εξωτερικό; Mporeíte na to steílete sto exoterikó?	bo-**ree**-teh na to **stee**-le-teh sto e-xo-te-ree **ko**
This one	Αυτό εδώ Aftó edó	af-**to** e-**do**
That one	Εκείνο Ekeíno	e-**kee**-no

expensive	Ακριβό Akrivó	a-kree-**vo**
cheap	Φθηνό Fthino	fthee-**no**
size	Το μέγεθος To mégethos	to **me**-ge-thos
white	Λευκό Lefkó	lef-**ko**
black	Μαύρο Mávro	**mav**-ro
red	Κόκκινο Kókkino	**ko**-kee-no
yellow	Κίτρινο Kítrino	**kee**-tree-no
green	Πράσινο Prásino	**pra**-see-no
blue	Μπλε Mple	bl**eh**

Types of Store

antique shop	Μαγαζί με αντίκες Magazí me antíkes	ma-ga-z**ee** me an-d**ee**-kes
bakery	Ο φούρνος O foúrnos	o f**oor**-nos
bank	Η τράπεζα I trápeza	ee **tra**-pe-za
bazaar	Το παζάρι To pazári	to pa-**za**-ree
bookstore	Το βιβλιοπωλείο To vivliopoleío	to vee-vlee-o-po-l**ee**-o
butcher	Το κρεωπολείο To kreopoleío	to kre-o-po-l**ee**-o
cake shop	Το ζαχαροπλαστείο To zacharoplasteío	to za-cha-ro-pla-st**ee**-o
cheese shop	Μαγαζί με αλλαντικά Magazí me allantiká	ma-ga-z**ee** me a-lan-dee-**ka**
department store	Πολυκάταστημα Polykatástima	Po-lee-ka-**ta**-stee-ma
fish market	Το ιχθυοπωλείο/ ψαράδικο To ichthyopoleío/ psarádiko	to eech-thee-o-po-l**ee**-o /psa-rá-dee-ko
greengrocer	Το μανάβικο To manáviko	to ma-**na**-vee-ko
hairdresser	Το κομμωτήριο To kommotírio	to ko-mo-t**ee**-ree-o
kiosk	Το περίπτερο To períptero	to pe-r**ee**p-te-ro
leather shop	Μαγαζί με δερμάτινα είδη Magazí me dermátina eídi	ma-ga-z**ee** me ther-**ma**-tee-na **ee**-thee
street market	Η λαϊκή αγορά I laïkí agorá	ee la-**ee**-**kee** a-go-**ra**
newsstand	Ο εφημεριδοπώλης O efimeridopólis	O e-fee-me-ree-tho-**po**-lees
pharmacy	Το φαρμακείο To farmakeío	to **far**-ma-k**ee**-o
post office	Το ταχυδρομείο To tachydromeío	to ta-chee-thro-m**ee**-o
shoe store	Κατάστημα υποδημάτων Katástima ypodimáton	ka-**ta**-stee-ma ee-po-dee-**ma**-ton
souvenir shop	Μαγαζί με "souvenir" Magazí me "souvenir"	ma-ga-z**ee** meh "souvenir"
supermarket	Σουπερμάρκετ/ Υπεραγορά "Supermarket"/ Yperagorá	"Supermarket" / ee-per-a-go-**ra**
tobacconist	Είδη καπνις Eídi kapnis	**E**e-thee kap-nees
travel agent	Το ταξειδιωτικό γραφείο To taxeidiotikó grafeío	to tak-see-thy-o-tee-**ko** gra-f**ee**-o

Sightseeing

tourist information	Ο ΕΟΤ O EOT	o E-OT
tourist police	Η τουριστική αστυνομία I touristikí astynomía	ee too-rees-tee-**kee** a-stee-no-m**ee**-a
archaeological	αρχαιολογικός archaiologikós	ar-che-o-lo-yee-**kos**
art gallery	Η γκαλερί I gkalerí	ee ga-le-r**ee**
beach	Η παραλία I paralía	ee pa-ra-l**ee**-a
Byzantine	βυζαντινός vyzantinós	vee-zan-dee-**nos**
castle	Το κάστρο To kástro	to **ka**-stro
cathedral	Η μητρόπολη I mitrópoli	ee mee-**tro**-po-lee
cave	Το σπήλαιο To spílaio	to sp**ee**-le-o
church	Η εκκλησία I ekklisía	ee e-klee-s**ee**-a
folk art	λαϊκή τέχνη laïkí téchni	la-ee-k**ee** **te**ch-nee
fountain	Το συντριβάνι To syntriváni	to seen-dree-**va**-nee
hill	Ο λόφος O lófos	o **lo**-fos
historical	ιστορικός istorikós	ee-sto-ree-**kos**
island	Το νησί To nisí	to nee-s**ee**
lake	Η λίμνη I límni	ee l**ee**m-nee
library	Η βιβλιοθήκη I vivliothíki	ee veev-lee-o-th**ee**-kee
mansion	Η έπαυλις I épavlis	ee **e**-pav-lees
monastery	Μονή moní	mo-n**i**
mountain	Το βουνό To vounó	to voo-**no**
municipal	δημοτικός dimotikós	thee-mo-tee-**kos**
museum	Το μουσείο To mouseío	to moo-s**ee**-o
national	εθνικός ethnikós	eth-nee-**kos**
park	Το πάρκο To párko	to **par**-ko
garden	Ο κήπος O kípos	o k**ee**-pos
gorge	Το φαράγγι To farángi	to fa-**ran**-gee
grave of…	Ο τάφος του… O táfos tou…	o **ta**-fos too
river	Το ποτάμι To potámi	to po-**ta**-mee
road	Ο δρόμος O drómos	o thr**o**-mos
saint	άγιος/άγιοι/αγία/ αγίες ágios/ágioi/agía/agíes	**a**-yee-os/**a**-yee-ee/a-yee-**a**/a-yee-es
spring	Η πηγή I pigí	ee pee-y**ee**
square	Η πλατεία I plateía	ee pla-t**ee**-a
stadium	Το στάδιο To stádio	to st**a**-thee-o
statue	Το άγαλμα To ágalma	to **a**-gal-ma
theater	Το θέατρο To théatro	to th**e**-a-tro
town hall	Το δημαρχείο To dimarcheío	To thee-mar-ch**ee**-o
closed on public holidays	κλειστό τις αργίες kleistó tis argíes	klee-sto tees arye**e**-es

Transportation

When does the… leave?	Πότε φεύγει το…; Póte févgei to…?	**po**-teh **fev**-yee to…
Where is the bus stop?	Πού είναι η στάση του λεωφορείου; Poú eínai i stási tou leoforeíou?	po**o** **ee**-neh ee **sta**-see too le-o-fo-**re**-oo
Is there a bus to…?	Υπάρχει λεωφορείο για…; Ypárchei leoforeío gia…?	ee-**par**-chee le-o-fo-**ree**-o yia…
ticket office	Εκδοτήρια εισητηρίων Ekdotíria eisitiríon	Ek-tho-te**e**-reea ee-see-tee-**ree**-on
round-trip ticket	Εισητήριο με επιστροφή Eisitírio me epistrofí	ee-see-tee-**ree**-o meh e-pee-stro-**fee**
one-way ticket	Απλό εισητήριο Apló eisitírio	a-**plo** ee-see-t**ee**-reeo

bus station	Ο σταθμός λεωφορείων O stathmós leoforeíon	o stath-**mos** leo-fo-**ree**-on
bus ticket	Εισητήριο λεωφορειου Eisitírio leoforeíou	ee-see-tee-ree-o leo-fo-ree-oo
trolleybus	Το τρόλλευ To trólley	to **tro**-le-ee
port	Το λιμάνι To limáni	to lee-**ma**-nee
train/metro	Το τρένο To tréno	to **tre**-no
railroad station	σιδηροδρομικός σταθμός sidirodromikós stathmós	see-thee-ro-thro-mee-**kos** stath-**mos**
moped	Το μοτοποδήλατο / το μηχανάκι To motopodílato / To michanáki	to mo-to-po-**thee**-la-to/to mee-cha-**na**-kee
bicycle	Το ποδήλατο To podílato	to po-**thee**-la-to
taxi	Το ταξί To taxí	to tak-**see**
airport	Το αεροδρόμιο To aerodrómio	to a-e-ro-**thro**-mee-o
ferry	Το φερυμπότ To ferympot	to fe-ree-**bot**
hydrofoil	Το δελφίνι / Το υδροπτέρυγο To delfíni / To ydroptérygo	to del-**fee**-nee / To ee-throp-**te**-ree-go
catamaran	Το καταμαράν To katamarán	to catama**ran**
for rent	Ενοικιάζονται Enoikiázontai	e-nee-ky**a**-zon-deh

Staying in a Hotel

Do you have a vacant room?	Εχετε δωμάτια; Echete domátia?	**e**-che-teh tho-**ma**-tee-a
double room with double bed	Δίκλινο με διπλό κρεββάτι Díklino me dipló krevváti	**thee**-klee-no meh thee-**plo** kre-**va**-tee
room with twin beds	Δίκλινο με μονά κρεββάτια Díklino me moná krevvátia	**thee**-klee-no meh mo-**na** kre-**vat**-ya
single room	Μονόκλινο Monóklino	mo-**no**-klee-no
room with a bath	Δωμάτιο με μπάνιο Domátio me mpánio	tho-**ma**-tee-o meh **ban**-yo
shower	Το ντους To douz	To dooz
porter	Ο πορτιέρης O portiéris	o por-ty**e**-rees
key	Το κλειδί To kleidí	to klee-**dee**
I have a reservation	Εχω κάνει κράτηση Echo kánei krátisi	**e**-cho **ka**-nee **kra**-tee-see
room with a sea view/balcony	Δωμάτιο με θέα στή θάλασσα/μπαλκόνι Domátio me théa sti thálassa/mpalkóni	tho-**ma**-tee-o meh **the**-a stee **tha**-la-sa/bal- **ko**-nee
Does the price include breakfast?	Το πρωινό συμπεριλαμβάνεται στην τιμή; To proïnó symperi-lamvánetai stin timí?	to pro-ee-**no** seem-be-ree-lam-**va**-ne-**teh** steen tee-**mee**

Eating Out

Do you have a table?	Εχετε τραπέζι; Echete trapézi?	**e**-che-te tra-**pe**-zee
I want to reserve a table	Θέλω να κρατήσω ένα τραπέζι Thélo na kratíso éna trapézi	**the**-lo na kra-**tee**-so **e**-na tra-**pe**-zee
The check, please	Τον λογαριασμό, παρακαλώ Ton logariazmó parakaló	ton lo-gar-yas-**mo** pa-ra-ka-**lo**
I am a vegetarian	Είμαι χορτοφάγος Eímai chortofágos	**ee**-meh chor-to-**fa**-gos
What is fresh today?	Τί φρέσκο έχετε σήμερα; Tí frésko échete símera?	**tee** **fres**-ko **e**-che-teh **see**-me-ra?
waiter/waitress	Κύριε / Γκαρσόν / Κυρία (female) Kýrie/Garson"/Kyría	K**ee**-ree-eh/Gar-**son**/Kee-ree-**a**
menu	Ο κατάλογος O katálogos	o ka-**ta**-lo-gos
cover charge	Το κουβέρ To "couvert"	to koo-**ver**
wine list	Ο κατάλογος με τα οινοπνευματώδη O katálogos me ta oinopnevmatódi	o ka-**ta**-lo-gos meh ta ee-no-pnev-ma-**to**-thee
glass	Το ποτήρι To potíri	to po-**tee**-ree
bottle	Το μπουκάλι To mpoukáli	to bou-**ka**-lee
knife	Το μαχαίρι To machaíri	to ma-**che**-ree
fork	Το πηρούνι To piroúni	to pee-**roo**-nee
spoon	Το κουτάλι To koutáli	to koo-**ta**-lee
breakfast	Το πρωινό To proïnó	to pro-**ee**-**no**
lunch	Το μεσημεριανό To mesimerianó	to me-see-mer-ya-**no**
dinner	Το δείπνο To deípno	to **theep**-no
main course	Το κυρίως γεύμα To kyríos gévma	to kee-**ree**-os **yev**-ma
starter/first course	Τα ορεκτικά Ta orektiká	ta o-rek-tee-**ka**
dessert	Το γλυκό To glykó	to ylee-**ko**
dish of the day	Το πιάτο της ημέρας To piáto tis iméras	to **pya**-to tees ee-**me**-ras
bar	Το μπαρ To "bar"	To bar
taverna	Η ταβέρνα I tavérna	ee ta-**ver**-na
café	Το καφενείο To kafeneío	to ka-fe-**nee**-o
fish taverna	Η ψαροταβέρνα I psarotavérna	ee psa-ro-ta-**ver**-na
grill house	Η ψησταριά I psistariá	ee psee-sta-**rya**
wine shop	Το οινοπωλείο To oinopoleío	to ee-no-po-**lee**-o
dairy shop	Το γαλακτοπωλείο To galaktopoleío	to ga-lak-to-po-**lee**-o
restaurant	Το εστιατόριο To estiatório	to e-stee-a-**to**-ree-o
ouzeri	Το ουζερί To ouzerí	to oo-ze-**ree**
meze shop	Το μεζεδοπωλείο To mezedopoleío	To me-ze-do-po-**lee**-o
take-out kebabs	Το σουβλατζίδικο To souvlatzídiko	To soo-vlat-**zee**-dee-ko
rare	Ελάχιστα ψημένο Eláchista psiméno	e-**lach**-ees-ta psee-**me**-no
medium	Μέτρια ψημένο Métria psiméno	**met**-ree-a psee-**me**-no
well done	Καλοψημένο Kalopsiméno	ka-lo-psee-**me**-no

Basic Food and Drink

coffee	Ο καφές O Kafés	o ka-**fes**
with milk	με γάλα me gála	me **ga**-la
black coffee	σκέτος skétos	**ske**-tos
without sugar	χωρίς ζάχαρη chorís záchari	cho-**rees** **za**-cha-ree
medium sweet	μέτριος métrios	**me**-tree-os
very sweet	γλυκύς glykýs	glee-**kees**
tea	τσάι tsái	**tsa**-ee
hot chocolate	ζεστή σοκολάτα zestí sokoláta	ze-**stee** so-ko-**la**-ta
wine	κρασί krasí	kra-**see**
red	κόκκινο kókkino	**ko**-kee-no
white	λευκό lefkó	lef-**ko**
rosé	ροζέ rozé	ro-**ze**

raki	Το ρακί To rakí	to ra-**kee**
ouzo	Το ούζο To oúzo	to **oo**-zo
retsina	Η ρεστίνα I retsína	ee ret-**see**-na
water	Το νερό To neró	to ne-**ro**
octopus	Το χταπόδι To chtapódi	to chta-**po**-dee
fish	Το ψάρι To psári	to **psa**-ree
cheese	Το τυρί To tyrí	to tee-**ree**
halloumi	Το χαλούμι To chaloúmi	to cha-**loo**-mee
feta	Η φέτα I féta	ee **fe**-ta
bread	Το ψωμί To psomí	to pso-**mee**
bean soup	Η φασολάδα I fasoláda	ee fa-so-**la**-da
hummus	Το χούμους To houmous	to **choo**-moos
halva	Ο χαλβάς O chalvás	o chal-**vas**
meat kebabs	Ο γύρος O gýros	o **yee**-ros
Turkish delight	Το λουκούμι To loukoúmi	to loo-**koo**-mee
baklava	Ο μπακλαβάς O mpaklavás	o bak-la-**vas**
klephtiko	Το κλέφτικο To kléftiko	to **klef**-tee-ko

Numbers

1	ένα éna	**e**-na
2	δύο dýo	**thee**-o
3	τρία tría	**tree**-a
4	τέσσερα téssera	**te**-se-ra
5	πέντε pénte	**pen**-deh
6	έξι éxi	**ek**-si
7	επτά eptá	ep-**ta**
8	οχτώ ochtó	och-**to**
9	εννέα ennéa	e-**ne**-a
10	δέκα déka	**the**-ka
11	έντεκα énteka	**en**-de-ka
12	δώδεκα dódeka	**tho**-the-ka
13	δεκατρία dekatría	the-ka-**tree**-a
14	δεκατέσσερα dekatéssera	the-ka-**tes**-se-ra
15	δεκαπέντε dekapénte	the-ka-**pen**-de
16	δεκαέξι dekaéxi	the-ka-**ek**-si
17	δεκαεπτά dekaeptá	the-ka-ep-**ta**
18	δεκαοχτώ dekaochtó	the-ka-och-**to**
19	δεκαεννέα dekaennéa	the-ka-e-**ne**-a
20	είκοσι eíkosi	**ee**-ko-see
21	εικοσιένα eikosiéna	ee-ko-see-**e**-na
30	τριάντα triánta	tree-**an**-da
40	σαράντα saráranta	sa-**ran**-da
50	πενήντα penínta	pe-**neen**-da
60	εξήντα exínta	ek-**seen**-da
70	εβδομήντα evdomínta	ev-tho-**meen**-da
80	ογδόντα ogdónta	og-**thon**-da
90	εννενήντα ennenínta	e-ne-**neen**-da
100	εκατό ekató	e-ka-**to**
200	διακόσια diakósia	thya-**kos**-ya
1,000	χίλια chília	**cheel**-ya
2,000	δύο χιλιάδες d´yo chiliádes	**thee**-o cheel-**ya**-thes
1,000,000	ένα εκατομμύριο éna ekatomm´yrio	**e**-na e-ka-to-mee-**ree**-o

Time, Days, and Dates

one minute	ένα λεπτό éna leptó	**e**-na lep-**to**
one hour	μία ώρα mía óra	**mee**-a **o**-ra
half an hour	μισή ώρα misí óra	mee-**see** **o**-ra
quarter of an hour	ένα τέταρτο éna tétarto	**e**-na **te**-tar-to
half past one	μία και μισή mía kai misí	**mee**-a keh mee-**see**
quarter past one	μία και τέταρτο mía kai tétarto	**mee**-a keh **te**-tar-to
ten past one	μία και δέκα mía kai déka	**mee**-a keh **the**-ka
quarter to two	δύο παρά τέταρτο d´yo pará tétarto	**thee**-o pa-**ra** **te**-tar-to
ten to two	δύο παρά δέκα d´yo pará déka	**thee**-o pa-**ra** **the**-ka
a day	μία μέρα mía méra	**mee**-a **me**-ra
a week	μία εβδομάδα mía evdomáda	**mee**-a ev-tho-**ma**-tha
a month	ένας μήνας énas mínas	**e**-nas **mee**-nas
a year	ένας χρόνος énas chrónos	**e**-nas **chro**-nos
Monday	Δευτέρα Deftéra	thef-**te**-ra
Tuesday	Τρίτη Tríti	**tree**-tee
Wednesday	Τετάρτη Tetárti	te-**tar**-tee
Thursday	Πέμπτη Pémpti	**pemp**-tee
Friday	Παρασκευή Paraskeví	pa-ras-ke-**vee**
Saturday	Σαββάτο Savváto	sa-**va**-to
Sunday	Κυριακή Kyriakí	keer-ee-a-**kee**
January	Ιανουάριος Ianouários	ee-a-noo-**a**-ree-os
February	Φεβρουάριος Fevrouários	fev-roo-**a**-ree-os
March	Μάρτιος Mártios	**mar**-tee-os
April	Απρίλιος Aprílios	a-**pree**-lee-os
May	Μάιος Máios	**ma**-ee-os
June	Ιούνιος Ioúnios	ee-**oo**-nee-os
July	Ιούλιος Ioúlios	ee-**oo**-lee-os
August	Αύγουστος Avgoustos	**av**-goo-stos
September	Σεπτέμβριος Septémvrios	sep-**tem**-vree-os
October	Οκτώβριος Októvrios	ok-**to**-vree-os
November	Νοέμβριος Noémvrios	no-**em**-vree-os
December	Δεκέμβριος Dekémvrios	the-**kem**-vree-os

TITLES PUBLISHED TO DATE

THE GUIDES THAT SHOW YOU WHAT OTHERS ONLY TELL YOU

COUNTRY GUIDES

AUSTRALIA • FRANCE • GREAT BRITAIN • GREECE: ATHENS & THE MAINLAND • THE GREEK ISLANDS IRELAND • ITALY • MEXICO • PORTUGAL SOUTH AFRICA • SPAIN • THAILAND

REGIONAL GUIDES

BARCELONA & CATALONIA • CALIFORNIA FLORENCE & TUSCANY • FLORIDA • HAWAII LOIRE VALLEY • NAPLES WITH POMPEII & THE AMALFI COAST • PROVENCE & THE COTE D'AZUR SARDINIA • SCOTLAND • SEVILLE & ANDALUSIA VENICE & THE VENETO

CITY GUIDES

AMSTERDAM • BUDAPEST • DUBLIN • ISTANBUL LISBON • LONDON • MADRID • MOSCOW NEW YORK • PARIS • PRAGUE • ROME SAN FRANCISCO • ST PETERSBURG SYDNEY • VIENNA • WARSAW

TRAVEL MAPS (TRAVEL PLANNERS)

GREAT BRITAIN & IRELAND • ITALY • SPAIN

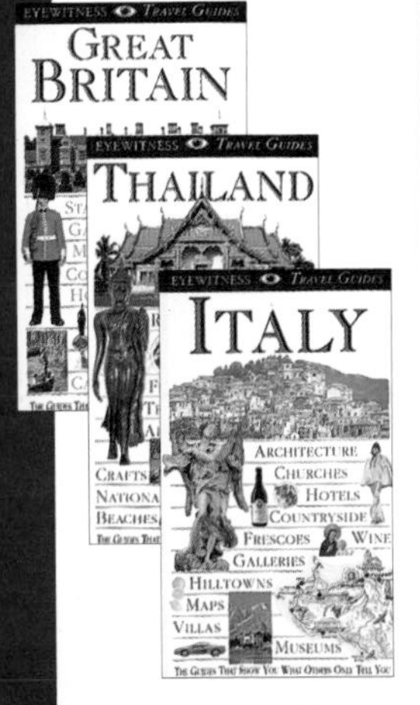

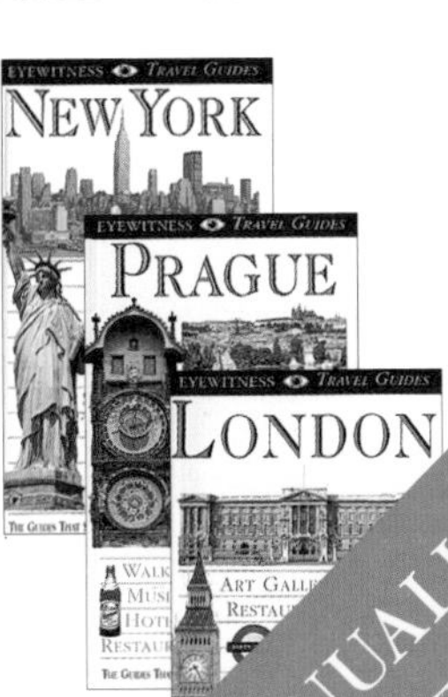

CONTINUALLY UPDATED

Main Ferry Routes around the Greek Islands

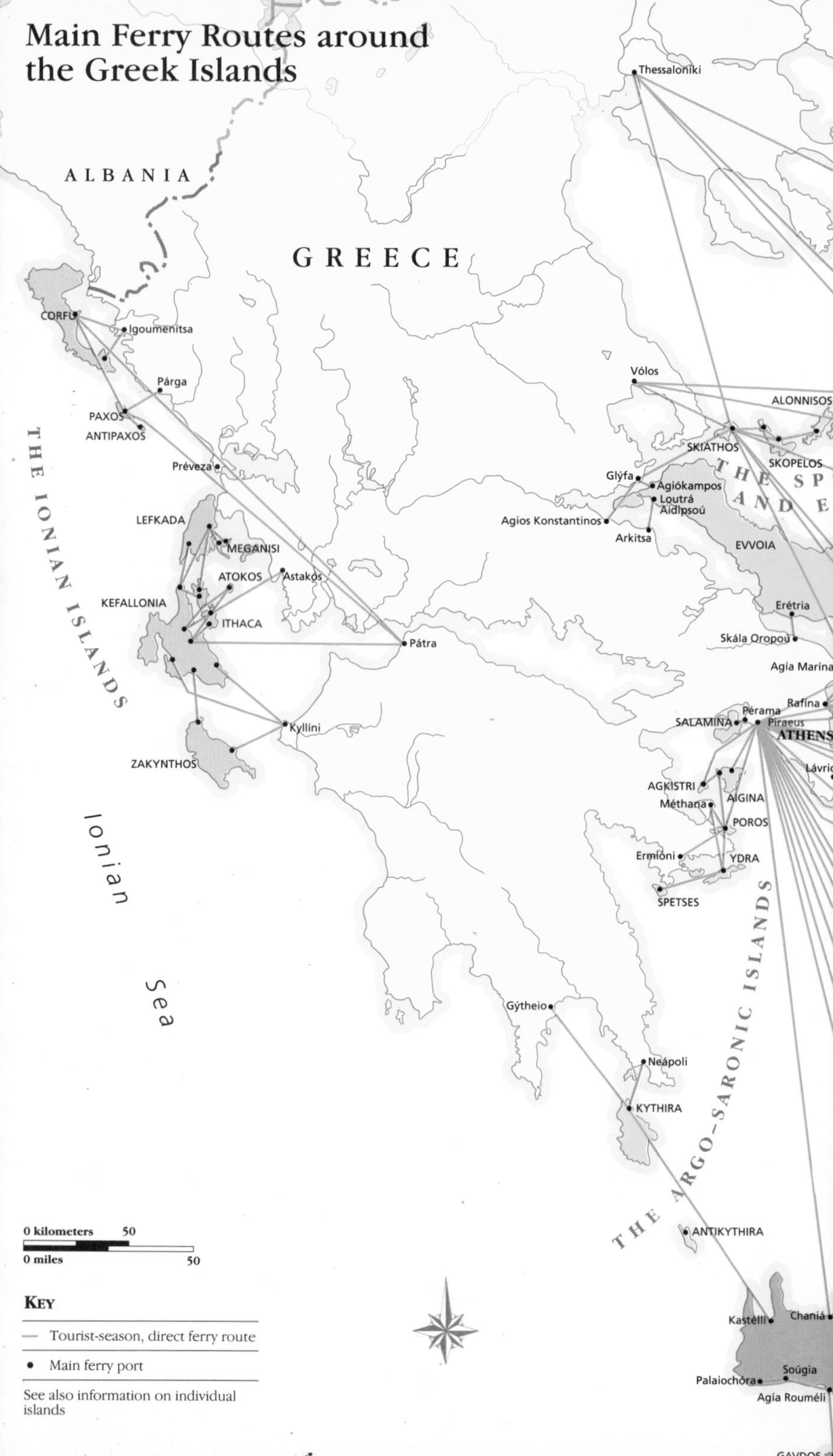

ALBANIA
GREECE
Thessaloníki
CORFU
Igoumenítsa
Párga
PAXOS
ANTIPAXOS
Préveza
LEFKADA
MEGANISI
ATOKOS
Astakós
KEFALLONIA
ITHACA
Pátra
Kyllíni
ZAKYNTHOS
THE IONIAN ISLANDS
Ionian
Sea
Vólos
ALONNISOS
SKIATHOS
SKOPELOS
Glýfa
Agiókampos
Loutrá Aidipsoú
Agios Konstantinos
Arkitsa
EVVOIA
Erétria
Skála Oropoú
Agía Marína
Rafína
Pérama
SALAMINA
Piraeus
ATHENS
AGKISTRI
AIGINA
Méthana
POROS
Ermióni
YDRA
SPETSES
THE ARGO-SARONIC ISLANDS
Gýtheio
Neápoli
KYTHIRA
ANTIKYTHIRA
Kastélli
Chaniá
Palaiochóra
Soúgia
Agía Rouméli
GAVDOS
0 kilometers 50
0 miles 50
KEY
Tourist-season, direct ferry route
Main ferry port
See also information on individual islands